THE ENIGMA OF
JAPANESE POWER

THE ENIGMA OF JAPANESE POWER

People and Politics in a Stateless Nation

Karel van Wolferen

Alfred A. Knopf   New York   1989

THIS IS A BORZOI BOOK
PUBLISHED BY ALFRED A. KNOPF, INC.

Library of Congress Cataloging-in-Publication Data
Wolferen, Karel van.
The enigma of Japanese power.
Bibliography: p.
Includes index.
1. Political culture—Japan.
2. Japan—Politics and government—1945 –   .
3. Japan—Economic policy—1945 –   .
I. Title.
JQ1681.w65   1989   306'.0951   88-45771
ISBN 0-394-57796-5

Manufactured in the United States of America
Published April 11, 1989
Second Printing, June 1989

To Leo Labedz
for his intellectual courage and integrity

Contents

Acknowledgments ix

1 The Japan Problem *1*
Confusing fictions *5*
The neglected role of power *17*

2 The Elusive State *25*
Power out of focus *26*
The System *43*

3 An Inescapable Embrace *50*
The absence of political competition *50*
The System at work in rural Japan *60*
Controlling the workers *65*
Encapsulated outsiders *72*

4 Servants of the System *82*
The subservient education system *82*
The house-broken press *93*
Accommodated mobsters *100*

5 The Administrators *109*
Preserving the System *109*
Structural corruption *127*
LDP battles, bureaucrats and political tribesmen *139*

6 The Submissive Middle Class *159*
The 'salaryman' model *159*
Familist ideology *163*
Submission and order *169*
Producers of salaryman culture *175*

7 Nurses of the People *181*
Forces of benevolence *181*
The unprotected *194*

8   Keeping the Law under Control   *202*
Laws above and beneath power-holders   *203*
Coping with the legal threat to the System   *212*
The prosecutor as judge   *220*

9   The Management of Reality   *227*
Political uses of contradiction   *227*
Much maligned logic   *236*

10   Power in the Guise of Culture   *245*
The ideology of Japaneseness   *245*
Orthodoxies as condition for Japanese order   *254*
The Japanese sense of uniqueness and superiority   *263*

11   The System as Religion   *273*
Expedient religions   *274*
Buddhists, Christians, Marxists and fanatics   *277*
The danger of secularisation   *290*

12   The Right to Rule   *295*
The legitimacy problem   *296*

13   Ritual and Intimidation   *314*
A less than perfect harmony   *315*
Order through ritual   *326*
Order through intimidation   *340*

14   A Century of Consolidating Control   *347*
The fundamental continuity   *348*
Consolidation   *362*

15   The Japanese Phoenix   *375*
The economics of national security   *375*
Legacy of a mobilised nation   *384*
Making Japan invincible   *395*

16   In the World But Not of It   *408*
The absence of political choice   *408*
An uncomfortable dependence   *415*
Victimised and alone   *426*

Notes   *434*

Glossary of Japanese Words   *477*

Index   *479*

Acknowledgments

I am grateful to a large number of people who have directly and indirectly helped me to write this book. Some must remain unmentioned, such as the hundreds whom I have interviewed over some two decades concerning a great variety of Japanese subjects.

Among those who were more closely involved with the book, three friends stand out. Without the assistance of Yoshino Okubo, who scoured libraries and prepared Japanese language material, it would have been a different book. William Wetherall and Ivan Hall supplied running comments and many invaluable editorial suggestions while going through various drafts of the manuscript. No less important was their unceasing moral support during times when I appeared to make little progress. I count myself extremely lucky to be their friend.

I am intellectually indebted to Chalmers Johnson for daring me to bring into explicit focus some aspects of my subject that I had theretofore thought of as having only marginal significance. Aside from this I thank him for his friendship and unrelenting encouragement over many years. Equal thanks to Sheila Johnson for her patient perusal of the early drafts of most of the chapters, and her innumerable editorial suggestions.

Thanks to Milos Sovak for his many helpful suggestions and enthusiasm. Jan van Rij, Edward Seidensticker, Ishida Takeshi, Gordon Berger, Stanislav Andreski, Harvey Stockwin, Robert Cutts and Eric Klestadt read parts of the manuscript and I want to thank them for their ideas and welcome criticism. Ian Buruma belongs in this list also, and is among those at the top of the list of people whose conversation over the years has stimulated my mind. I want to thank Professor Mikuriya Takashi for his help and Professor Ito Daiichi for his comments. I owe Clyde Prestowitz and Sheldon Garon for sending me the galley proofs of their important books.

There are those people whose sometimes off-hand remarks germinate in one's mind to become major ideas. I have met several over the years in Japan, but I want to mention two friends, Murray Sayle and Claus Regge, and thank them for giving me, probably without realising it, the initial ideas for several of the observations in this book.

A special thank-you is due to George De Vos who, more than twenty years ago, first urged me to write about Japan. This book is probably very different from what he had in mind then, but he gave me a lot of confidence.

I am grateful to Frits Bolkestein and Wim Kortekaas for their faith in my project, their help and friendship. The staff of the Foreign Correspondents' Club library in Tokyo was, as always, efficient and helpful.

Michael Grey put together the word-processing equipment on which this book was written; he made it run faster and came out to my mountain cabin to make emergency repairs. I could not, incidentally, have finished it in the available time without the superior XyWrite program.

It is hardly possible to thank William Miller enough for being a superb agent as well as a good friend, and for giving his unwavering support before I could begin and in times of crisis.

Wout Woltz and Jan Sampiemon, editors of *NRC Handelsblad*, are the best employers one could wish for. They not only help maintain this newspaper as one of the greatest in the world, providing me over the years with a maximum opportunity for comprehensive analyses, but also accommodated me with fraternal tolerance when my leave of absence grew longer and longer.

Last but not least, my warm thanks go out to Fusae Wako for faithfully maintaining the main logistical channel between Tokyo and Morigane in the foothills of Northern Ibaragi, during the eighteen months of isolation that it took to write this book, and for her loyal support for a long time before that.

It goes without saying that none of those mentioned are responsible for the conclusions or possible errors in this book.

With the listing of Japanese names I have followed the convention of family name first.

Morigane, Ibaragi, October 1988

THE ENIGMA OF
JAPANESE POWER

1

The Japan Problem

Japan perplexes the world. It has become a major world power, yet it does not behave the way most of the world expects a world power to behave; sometimes it even gives the impression of not wanting to belong to the world at all. At the same time, Japan's formidable economic presence has made it a source of apprehension both to the Western countries and to some of its Asian neighbours. The relationship between Japan on the one side and the United States and Europe on the other is in serious trouble. In the late 1980s the West is beginning to harbour doubts about Japan as a responsible partner in politics and trade. In Japan it has become common for officials and prominent commentators to suggest that their country has fallen victim to widespread international ill-will, and they are apt to dismiss unfavourable analyses as 'Japan-bashing'.

For almost two decades Westerners have been advised to have patience with Japan. It was argued that the Japanese understood the necessity of adjustments and were speeding up their efforts at 'internationalisation'. A sustained publicity campaign reiterating this goal, with the appropriate slogans popping up in innumerable speeches and countless newspaper and magazine articles, seemed to confirm this. But in the late 1980s an awareness is gradually taking hold in the West that the long-promised changes are not forthcoming, and that the explanations on which expectations of change have been based may have been wrong all along. In the meantime, increased criticism and demands, the first retaliatory measures and other forms of pressure from frustrated trading partners, particularly the United States, have changed the disposition of officials and commentators on the Japanese side. Their replies are becoming retorts. Their friendly counselling of patience has begun to change into a more belligerent message: the USA should put its own house in order, and Europe should stop being lazy and recognise its 'advanced nation disease' for what it is. Both sides have expressed a firm resolve to avoid an economic war, but around 1987 some people on both sides began to realise that they were in the middle of one.

The riddle that Japan poses for much of the world does not begin and end with its economic conflicts. But they are the most eye-catching, since they involve, it seems, practically all the countries with which Japan deals. For most observers the Japan Problem, as the conflicts have collectively become known, is summed up in Japan's annual record-breaking trade surpluses: $44 billion in 1984, $56 billion in 1985, $93 billion in 1986; until the near doubling of the exchange rate of the Japanese yen against the dollar caused a lower surplus of some $76 billion in 1987.

But the essence of the Japan Problem lies beyond such figures. Not only does Japan export more than it imports, but its exports, in combination with its inhospitality to foreign products, undermine Western industries. The term 'adversarial trade' was coined by Peter Drucker to distinguish the Japanese method from competitive trade, in which a country imports manufactures of the same kind as it exports. West Germany's trade surpluses are also very large, but West Germany practises competitive trade, as does the USA.[1] With sectors such as consumer electronics and semiconductors – the bases for more specialised industries – being taken over almost completely by Japanese firms, Westerners have begun to fear they may suffer a gradual 'de-industrialisation'. Once it has obtained the required technology, Japanese industry appears capable, with a concerted effort, of outcompeting and taking over from the original inventors and developers in any field.

Having hitherto focused almost exclusively on the trade surpluses, in 1988 the West was slowly coming to suspect that other astonishing developments might form part of an overall pattern of Japanese pursuits, a significant national endeavour, which is hardly understood at all. Months after the New York and London stock-market crash of October 1987 – which hardly seemed to affect Tokyo's stock market at all – prices of Japanese stocks reached new, and by Western standards astonishing, heights when measured against corporate earnings. Land prices in many areas of Tokyo doubled, tripled or even quadrupled within the space of one year. And from around 1986 Japanese firms, often spending significantly more than warranted by market value, suddenly began to invest very heavily in foreign real estate and to buy foreign banks and corporations.[2] Somewhat belatedly it began to dawn on a few anxious US and European observers that Japan, far from 'beating the West at its own game', might not be playing the Western 'game' at all; and that for the West, conversely, to emulate Japan would bring the world trading system to a screeching halt and lead eventually to the collapse of the non-communist international economic order.

Europe and the United States are, to say the least, disturbed by this entity in the Pacific Ocean that appears to be single-mindedly pursuing some obscure aim of its own. One can understand the Japanese wanting to make money, but their conquest of ever greater foreign market shares does not translate into noticeably more rewarding or more comfortable lives. Urban housing is cramped, confined and extraordinarily costly. The cost of living, measured against average income, is exorbitantly high. Only about one-third of Japanese homes are connected with sewers. Commuter trains are extremely overcrowded. The road system is ridiculously inadequate. These and other deficiencies in the infrastructure of daily living leave average Japanese city dwellers with a lower standard of comfort than that enjoyed by their counterparts in less wealthy European countries, and they proclaim the need for a shift in attention among Japanese policy-makers.

The flourishing of trade and industry has not been accompanied by any robust flourishing of the arts of the kind that history has often shown comes in times of great economic achievement. One can hardly say that much emanates from Japan today that enhances the less materialist aspects of life in the way of great music, great literature or even impressive architecture.

A number of thoughtful Japanese have concluded that something is amiss. A nationalistic Japanese anthropologist who finds dealing with foreigners 'a demanding and troublesome task' nevertheless laments the fact that his country is like a black hole in space, receiving culture but not transmitting any.[3] A respected intellect and former vice-minister diagnoses his compatriots as suffering from a 'Peter Pan Syndrome . . . retreating into an infantile dream world . . . Japanese businessmen and politicians continue to play Peter Pan, asking each other what the world can do for them'.[4]

The question of what drives the Japanese people has thus become something of an international conundrum. For what ultimate purpose do they deprive themselves of comfort and risk the enmity of the world?

It is usually explained that the Japanese are driven by collective concerns. And indeed, Japan appears to demonstrate the possibility of life organised in a genuinely communalist manner. As far as outsiders can tell, most Japanese accept with equanimity the daily demands that they subordinate their individual desires and interests to those of the community. This striking communalism is, however, the result of political arrangements consciously inserted into society by a ruling élite over three centuries ago, and the Japanese are today given little or no choice in accepting arrangements that are still essentially political. Under these arrangements, a Japanese individual must accept as inevitable that his intellectual and psychological growth is restrained by the will of the collectivity. To sugar the pill, this supposedly collective will is presented by most of his superiors as benevolent, devoid of power and wholly determined by a unique culture.

But this explanation does not answer the question of where this political force comes from. The power that systematically suppresses individualism in Japan does not emanate from a harsh central regime. Japan differs as much from the collectivist communist states in Eastern Europe and Asia as it does from the free-market states of the West.

Much of the bafflement over Japan is due to a relative lack of interest on the part of Western intellectuals and people of affairs. Certainly, Japan is visited by many Westerners and receives mention in their sweeping global assessments. But to a large extent it is still treated as a curiosity and is not clearly visualised as a functioning element in those global assessments. One-sided ignorance is particularly striking in the case of the United States, considering that its relationship with Japan is beyond question among the strategically most important in the world. The continual frustration of the US expectations with regard to Japanese policies, or their absence, indicates that Washington's understanding of its foremost Asian ally – despite all the talk of a 'Pacific era' – is woefully inadequate. In fact, the view of Japanese political processes and preoccupations apparent between the lines of public statements and articles written by US officials directly concerned with the relationship is often so faulty as to appal observers such as myself who believe that nobody in the non-communist world is served by a serious deterioration in the US–Japan relationship.

The uncommon manner in which power is exercised in Japan and the workings of the Japanese institutions responsible for the country's non-dictatorial collectivism and national motivation have received scant attention from Westerners in general. Japan is often lumped together with Europe and the United States in discussions of the political shift towards a supposed 'post-industrial', 'technetronic' or 'post-capitalist' society, while the question of how Japan is actually ruled remains neglected.

It is curious that this should be so. Japan was the first non-Western country in modern times to play a major international role. It defeated Russia shortly after the turn of the century, became the only country ever to attack the United States, has since produced the second largest and, in terms of per capita income, most prosperous economy, has wiped out or is threatening with extinction a number of its trading partners' industries and is on its way to gaining important financial leverage over the world economy. Moreover, two other non-Western countries, South Korea and Taiwan, have become significant industrial presences by following the Japanese, instead of the Western, example of industrialisation.

Inattention to the question of how power is exercised in Japan and how this determines trends in its international relationships is becoming dangerous. Japan has been much praised since the 1960s, but it has also been much vilified, and from the perspective of Tokyo in 1988 the antipathy appears to have overtaken the praise. Contacts between Japan and other countries are likely to increase, with (if experience is any guide) a further proliferation of problems and still more criticism.

This will probably be accompanied by Western measures that Japanese will interpret as hostile. Such measures may well reawaken irrational xenophobic sentiments in Japan and strengthen the old suspicion that, in essence, the world does not want to make room for it. The resulting strengthened nationalism, of which the first signs are already appearing, could mean the beginning of political instability in Japan and unpredictable, probably undesirable, developments for everyone. Under such circumstances, a better understanding of the nature and uses of power in Japan is no luxury.

Confusing fictions

The factor most corrosive, in the long run, of international trust is perhaps the confusion that exists on many levels of communication between Japan and its supposed allies and friends – the apparent impossibility, even, of reaching a point at which both sides can agree to disagree. The communication gap, dating from the early 1970s, that separates Japan from the West as well as from some of its neighbours appears to be widening all the time. Several commonly cherished fictions cloud the perception of outsiders and complicate communication, two of them being central to their seeming inability to come to grips with Japan.

The fiction of responsible central government

First, there is the fiction that Japan is a sovereign state like any other, a state with central organs of government that can both recognise what is good for the country and bear ultimate responsibility for national decision-making. This is an illusion that is very difficult to dispel. Diplomacy takes a government's ability to make responsible decisions for granted; it would be extremely difficult for foreign governments to proceed without the assumption of a Japanese government that can cope with the external world, as other governments do, simply by changing its policies.

Nevertheless, unless the relative lack of governmental responsibility in Japan, the fundamental cause of mutual frustration, is recognised, relations with Japan are bound to deteriorate further. Statecraft in Japan is quite different from in Europe, the Americas and most of contemporary Asia. For centuries it has entailed a balance between semi-autonomous groups that share in power. Today, the most powerful groups include certain ministry officials, some political cliques and clusters of bureaucrat–businessmen. There are many lesser ones, such as the agricultural co-operatives, the police, the press and the gangsters. All are components of what we may call the System in order to distinguish it, for reasons to be discussed later, from the state. No one is ultimately in charge. These semi-autonomous components, each endowed with discretionary powers that undermine the authority of the state, are not represented by any central body that rules the roost.

It is important to distinguish this situation from others where governments are besieged by special interest groups, or are unable to make up their minds because of inter-departmental disputes. We are dealing not with lobbies but with a structural phenomenon unaccounted for in the categories of accepted political theory. There is, to be sure, a hierarchy or, rather, a complex of overlapping hierarchies. But it has no peak; it is a truncated pyramid. There is no supreme institution with ultimate policy-making jurisdiction. Hence there is no place where, as Harry Truman would have said, the buck stops. In Japan, the buck keeps circulating.

If Japan seems to be in the world but not of it, this is because its prime minister and other power-holders are incapable of delivering on political promises they may make concerning commercial or other matters requiring important adjustments by one of the components of the System. The field of domestic power normally leaves no room for an accommodation to foreign wishes or demands. Such accommodation is made only with a great show of reluctance and very late in the day, when angry outsiders resort to coercion. Japan needs the world for its exports, to keep its economy running; but many Japanese in official positions appear to prefer their traditional isolation, wishing that the world with all its political complexities would leave their country alone.

The 'free-market' fiction

The second of the central fictions that have determined Western attitudes since shortly after the Second World War is that Japan belongs in that loose category known as 'capitalist, free-market' economies.

In spite of all that is written about it, defining the Japanese economy still causes trouble to foreigners and to Japanese alike. Japanese officials are usually indignant at any hint that their country is something different from the label they have put on it. On the other hand, Japanese economists have told me privately that a common mistake among Westerners writing on Japan is to exaggerate the function of the market. It horrifies Western academic economists, especially those of the conventional neo-classical persuasion, to hear it suggested that Japan does not in fact belong in the club of 'free-market' nations. For many of them, the idea that there can be a successful economy not based on the free play of market forces is tantamount to heresy. While Japanese officials have interests to protect, many Western economists have stuck their heads into the sand against this Japanese threat to a set of theories that claim to be universal.

Japan is obviously not a centrally controlled, Soviet-type economy. Does it, then, as a number of commentators have implied, belong to a category of its own? The rise of South Korea and Taiwan as industrial states, apparently driven by an extraordinary force similar to that of Japan, suggests not. Their experience invites a new look at the Japanese 'economic miracle' and shows that, even minus its cultural and psychological specifics, it can provide a model for certain other countries.

The Japanese, Korean and Taiwanese experiences show that a third category of political economy can exist, beside the Western and communist types. US political scientist Chalmers Johnson has isolated this category of industrial nations and labelled it 'capitalist developmental states' (CDSs).[5] The strength of the CDS lies in its partnership between bureaucrats and industrialists; it is a variant that traditional political and economic theory has overlooked.

An eloquent theoretical objection made by Friedrich von Hayek to government interference in the economy is that planners at the centre can never know enough about the many ramifications of social and economic life to make the right decisions.[6] According to this theory, centrally planned economies must always fail to prosper. Yet if this is true, how have Japan, South Korea and Taiwan, whose governments consider manufacturing and trade very much their business, managed to improve their national wealth and economic power?

The manner in which Japan, South Korea and Taiwan have found a way around the Hayekian obstacle is crucial to an understanding of their political economies. To begin with, their governments have never considered private enterprise antagonistic to their goals. Unlike the communist approach, which equates entrepreneurism with original sin, or the socialist approach of the European welfare state, where regulations obstruct the entrepreneur, the CDS encourages the private sector and treats it with great deference. The bureaucrats never attempt to gain full power over non-governmental corporations. They guide the economy, using businessmen as their antennae in doing so. They get to know what is happening far away from the centre by constant monitoring of the experiences of capitalists trying to find new ways of expanding their businesses.

The many mistakes these officials undoubtedly make are more than compensated for by the unifying force they bring to bear on industrial development. The economy prospers because areas of industry that show promise are stimulated by fiscal policies favouring investment. Industries considered of strategic importance are carefully nursed and protected against genuine foreign competition. Those that are in trouble are temporarily protected to give the firms concerned an opportunity to diversify, while those that appear to have reached a dead end are more easily abandoned by policies forcing reorganisation. In other words, this is a partnership sealed by a shared industrial policy and trade strategy. Market freedom is considered to be not a goal desirable in itself but one of several instruments for achieving the paramount aim of industrial expansion.

Japan pioneered the CDS model a century or so ago, during the Meiji period, when it transferred state industries into private hands (after state entrepreneurism had brought many governmental corporations to the verge of collapse).[7] It further experimented with it during the forced industrial development of Manchuria, from the early 1930s until 1945. In its post-war form this economic model, which has made Marxist–Leninist theory distinctly less appealing as an economic guide for politicians and intellectuals in the less developed nations of non-communist Asia, is structurally protectionist. It has to stay so if it wants to continue enjoying its proven benefits. The question remains as to whether the bureaucrat–businessman partnership will continue to pay off once industry has saturated the market at home and once overseas markets become inhospitable. Another question, raised with particular urgency by the case of

Japan, is whether international free trade as a system can survive so long as the countries without a trade strategy are locked in a struggle to accommodate these formidable capitalist developmental states.

Malleable realities

The question of whether or not Japan represents a largely uncharted economic and social–political category generates much controversy. Since 1945 Japan has been considered a Western ally and has been treated as a full member of the club of capitalist free-market nations – this despite recent doubts raised by trade conflicts. Clarifications from the Japanese side do not help settle the controversy. Very few scholars or commentators are given to serious theorising about the nature of their political economy. Officials, for understandable reasons, are the least interested in setting the record straight. Journalists and academics, moreover, wrongly apply Western social, political and economic concepts in discussing their society, with the result that the unsuspecting observer is nearly always misled as to how things actually work.

It is not at all difficult for Japanese commentators and official spokesmen to maintain such fictions, because it is socially acceptable in Japan for 'reality' to consist not so much of the results of objective observation as of an emotionally constructed picture in which things are portrayed the way they are supposed to be. How things are supposed to be tends to coincide, of course, with the immediate interests of one's group. For the past four centuries the Japanese people have been told to consider socio-political loyalty as the supreme virtue. The result, as one anthropologist has put it, is that truth is socially constituted.[8] Here we arrive at the first conceptual problem Japan has in store for the outside observer.

In the West 'reality' is not often thought of as something that can be managed, moulded or negotiated. It is not seen as depending on arbitrary ideas of how things *should* be. Indeed, Western philosophy – as well as Western horse sense – decrees that the general human capacity for self-deceit be countered by a constant watchfulness against illusions and delusions. If there is one single command that has reverberated throughout Western intellectual development ever since the Greeks, it is: 'Thou shalt not cherish contradictions'. This command is fundamental to logic, mathematics and the sciences.

Heirs to various Asian traditions of thought may be less uncomfortable with the idea of multiple and contradictory truth. Yet it is clear, if one observes the other Asian countries, that nowhere does one find as much 'management of reality' as in Japan. This has important political consequences. Japanese in positions of control show great agility in moving from one reality to another as they seek to explain 'facts' and motives to other Japanese or to foreigners. A rationally argued claim made by the other side may be countered by arguments belonging to an altogether different frame of reference – at which point the exchange reaches a dead end. Such manoeuvring is one of the ways in Japan by which the higher-ranking and the stronger claim their privileges.

In international exchanges these tactics sometimes exasperate logically reasoning Westerners, who conclude that arguing with Japanese is impossible. One must be prepared for the extremely skilful use of red herrings. Occasionally these are too crude to be diplomatically effective, as when new regulations threatening the export of European skis to Japan were defended with the argument that Japanese snow tends to be constituted differently from snow in the West. But a small library could be compiled of books and reports in which Western trading partners themselves repeat the sophistry with which Japanese officials wriggle themselves out of tight spots in international dealings.

In Japan the 'flexible' approach to reality goes far beyond the bounds within which other societies tolerate lame excuses and self-serving untruths. For instance, when a Western businessman or government representative appeals to a contract, a law or an international agreement, he may be told by his Japanese counterpart that Japanese society is guided not so much by cold rules as by warm human feelings responding to each situation as it occurs. Yet should the foreigner, at the next opportunity, appeal to this extra-legal tradition by, for example, urging bureaucratic intervention in a trade problem, he may well hear that such a thing is impossible in democratic Japan which, he should understand, is governed by laws. Both these arguments – that Japanese society is humanly flexible by not sticking to cold rules, and that it sticks to what the law says – are uttered with great conviction, and Japanese third parties are hardly ever inclined to point out the contradiction.

The crucial factor

The tolerance of contradiction is closely connected with a characteristic that, in the final analysis, is the most crucial factor determining Japan's socio-political reality, a factor bred into Japanese intellectual life over centuries of political suppression. It is the near absence of any idea that there can be truths, rules, principles or morals that always apply, no matter what the circumstances. Most Westerners as well as most Asians who have stayed for any length of time in Japan will be struck by this absence; and some Japanese thinkers also have seen it as the ultimate determinant of Japanese public behaviour.

Concepts of independent, universal truths or immutable religious beliefs, transcending the worldly reality of social dictates and the decrees of power-holders, have of course found their way into Japan, but they have never taken root in any surviving world-view. Political arrangements and social practices were originally sanctioned by Shinto, a religion of nature and ancestor-worship that tolerated contradiction and ambiguity. This indigenous Japanese religion (not to be confused with the 'state Shinto' that provided the ideological underpinnings of the Japanese empire from the late nineteenth century until 1945) never developed philosophical or moral doctrines. Even when such philosophical and moral teachings were imported from China, they did not displace domestic socio-political sanctions and assumptions. On the contrary, the Chinese ideas merely strengthened the existing this-worldly belief system that supported the power-holders of the day.

The notions transcending the here and now of socio-political expediency that are inherent in the original teachings of Confucianism and Buddhism have always been unwelcome to Japan's ruling élite. Christianity and, later, Marxism threatened to introduce transcendental concepts into the universe of Japanese thought, but both were either proscribed or forced to compromise their essential tenets. The accepted view that Japan has always displayed great religious tolerance applies only where new religions or belief-systems have not been deemed a threat to existing political arrangements.

To grasp the essence of a political culture that does not recognise the possibility of transcendental truths demands an unusual intellectual effort for Westerners, an effort that is rarely made even in serious assessments of Japan. The occidental intellectual and moral traditions are so deeply rooted in assumptions of the universal validity of certain beliefs that the possibility of a culture without such assumptions is hardly ever contemplated. Western child-rearing practice inculcates suppositions that implicitly confirm the existence of an ultimate logic controlling the universe independently of the desires and caprices of human beings. This outlook, constantly reaffirmed in later life, inclines Westerners to take it for granted that all advanced civilisations develop concepts of universal validity, and they are therefore not prompted to examine the effects of their absence.

True, the fact that Japanese have situational instead of general moral rules, and hold particularistic values rather than universalistic ones, is routinely noticed in writing on Japan. But this is often confused with the more superficial distinctions of current social science, and is not used consistently to provide clues to Japanese behaviour. Most authors, having dutifully mentioned that the Japanese continually adjust their beliefs to the situation they find themselves in, move on to other topics as though totally unaware of the momentousness of this observation.[9]

'Mutual understanding'

Where 'beliefs' are dependent on socio-political circumstances, and 'reality' is something that can be manipulated, it is fairly easy to maintain fictions. The international confusion of tongues brought about by such fictions is further complicated by the special meaning acquired by the word 'understanding' in the mouths of Japanese commentators and officials. The dire need for better 'mutual understanding' is frequently and enthusiastically endorsed. But *wakatte kudasai* means 'please understand' in the sense of 'please accept my explanation, regardless of whether it has any basis in fact'. It connotes acceptance or tolerance. 'Understanding' in this Japanese context is another word for agreeing. True 'understanding' of people or things implies accepting them the way they are, as long as you are not strong enough to change them. If you have strength, the other party will show 'understanding' by a certain degree of adaptation to your wishes. Thus in practice 'mutual understanding' implies that foreigners should accept the picture of Japan presented by its spokesmen. Foreigners who insist on protesting about Japanese trade methods despite the many Japanese explanations are seen as demonstrating a perennial lack of understanding. Japanese are often well aware of the political connotation of 'understanding' in their usage; as a newspaper editor warned, the time is gone 'when we were able to enjoy the often beautiful misunderstandings – and ignorance – of the foreigners'.[10]

'Buffers' and propagandists

Two important phenomena complicate the communication-gap aspect of the Japan Problem. One is Japan's use of 'buffers'. The second is its monumental propaganda effort.

By 'buffer' I refer to someone entrusted with the task of making contacts with foreigners as smooth as possible. He is a peculiarly Japanese institution and is readily recognisable in government offices as well as business corporations. Resident foreign diplomats and businessmen deal with Japan through an intermediary community of English-speaking and supposedly internationalised buffers who are expected to absorb the shocks that an unpredictable outside world might deliver to their institutions.

These buffers can be amazingly frank, can convey a genuine understanding of the foreigner's difficulties and often create an impression, if not of willingness to cater to his wishes, then at least of reasonableness with which the institutions they represent consider the foreigner's problems. Japan has a handful of super-buffers who spend much of their time travelling the globe, trouble-shooting and explaining the Japanese case at international conferences. Some of these, such as Okita Saburo and the late Ushiba Nobuhiko, were made ministers for external economic affairs, in which roles they only increased the confusion, because in spite of their title they had no mandate to decide anything and could therefore not really negotiate.

Sometimes still more influential ministers or leaders of economic federations, or the prime minister himself, play the buffer role when speaking with foreign trade envoys. Foreign negotiators who arrive home with the news that this time they have really talked with the proper authorities, who have impressed them with their readiness to take effective action, are deceiving themselves. People with such broad authority do not exist in Japan.

Overlapping with the buffer category is a class of informants, hierarchically ordered according to the positions they occupy in the business, political or bureaucratic worlds, who are constantly being interviewed by visiting dignitaries and journalists. The rest of the world learns about Japan via the accounts of a much smaller group than is generally appreciated. Visitors who have met a 'good source' in the shape of one of these informants are often under the impression that they have heard an interesting personal opinion. Most are unaware that these informants tend to regurgitate currently circulating platitudes, whether on some pressing issue of the day or on more general themes concerning the character and role of Japan, that convey an 'official reality' to which they routinely defer.

It often seems as if all Japanese spokesmen are hooked up to the same prompter with the same message recorded on a loop of tape. Although they may introduce some personal variation, the essence of the message is almost always the same and is predictable down to the finer details, if one is abreast of the current preoccupations of the press, or of the voluminous explanatory literature distributed by the ministries, economic federations and subsidised 'private' institutions.

To believe that these predictable assertions reflect personal opinions would be doing injustice to the intellectual capacities of Japan's more highly placed communicators. Their genuinely personal opinions are often very interesting, and can be at great variance with the public assertions. But to get to hear these opinions requires either a long period of acquaintanceship and large amounts of sake or, more rarely, a sudden realisation on their part that you are not going to believe the official line anyway.

The predictable assertions of the established informants may include criticism of certain points of government policy or of bureaucratic and business attitudes. But they practically always support the larger contentions of the System's major institutions, that Japan is a pluralist democracy with a free-market economy, that progress is being made in opening the market, that the growth of individualism must be stimulated, that most Japanese are beginning to see the need to become more cosmopolitan, that foreigners do not try hard enough to compete and that conflict with Japan arises mainly from foreign misunderstanding.

Taken together, the activities of Japan's buffers and informants constitute a propaganda effort that is not recognised for what it is, because it comes almost entirely in the guise of sincere efforts to 'explain' Japan to the world. The propaganda is all the more convincing because many informants believe these explanations.

A proliferation of apologists

Foreigners play an important role in the dissemination of opinion favourable to the System. A great deal of foreign criticism has been defused by the use of Japanese money. No country has ever spent as much on officially recorded lobbying expenses as the Japanese were spending in Washington in the mid- and late 1980s. The Japanese government and corporations hire the best lawyers and former US administration officials to defend their position. A large proportion of academic research by Western scholars who concentrate on Japan is funded by Japanese institutions. The idea that scholars and commentators can remain objective because no formal conditions are attached to what they receive is mostly an illusion when the money comes from Japan. Access to the necessary personal contacts and institutions is a great problem for businessmen and scholars working in Japan, who are therefore acutely aware that a genuinely critical stance may close many doors. A combination of money and the need for access, as well as political innocence, has bred large numbers of Japan specialists who are in varying degrees – however unwittingly – apologists for Japan.[11] Their public pronouncements and comments in the media regularly attest to this.

Defending Japan is the bread and butter of many real and supposed specialists, who hold forth at highly publicised seminars, panel discussions and conferences organised to improve 'mutual understanding'. Most representatives of the big foreign corporations in Japan, and also the foreign consultants, have had to become part of the Japanese System in order to function in it. They cannot risk alienating themselves from it by publicly coming out with critical analyses, and are therefore unreliable informants.

Japanese propaganda is also spread, consciously as well as inadvertently, by numerous newspaper and magazine articles mindful of the editorial convention of telling the imagined 'two sides' of a story. And it has had an impressive effect, as can be gathered from the fact that at the time of writing the US government and many US commentators continue to think that market forces can ultimately solve the bilateral problem with Japan, notwithstanding the systematic Japanese protectionism that has been staring them in the face for more than two decades.

The aura of 'inscrutability'

'Understanding' Japan has become a heavy export industry funded by several components of the System. Yet many Japanese, specifically those who must represent domestic interests internationally, are uncomfortable with the idea that they actually might be understood. The idea that there is a spiritual dimension to being Japanese, which by definition cannot be grasped by foreigners, is an important ingredient for Japanese self-esteem and therefore widely believed.

A top editor on one of Japan's five national dailies once told me that his paper, as well as its competitors, felt that they could print practically anything foreigners said, no matter how devastating their criticism might be, because editors and readers could always console themselves with their belief in the ultimate inability of foreigners to understand the more subtle aspects of what they were describing. Readers of critical foreign assessments may thus enjoy a superficial masochistic thrill without having to draw genuinely disturbing conclusions.

It is almost an article of faith among Japanese that their culture is unique, not in the way that all cultures are unique, but somehow uniquely unique, ultimately different from all others, the source of unique Japanese sensibilities and therefore safe from (if not off-limits to) intellectual probes by outsiders. Japanese are constantly persuaded of the specialness of their nation in their schools and corporations and through the media and speeches by functionaries, whenever an opportunity arises for comparisons with the outside world.

Western intellectual support for the idea of the utter strangeness of Japan, which is easily converted into the idea of uniqueness, goes back many centuries. When it was still 'on the other side of the world' Marco Polo turned Zippangu (as he called Japan) into something mysterious and paradisiacal, imagining roofs of solid gold on its emperor's palace. Jonathan Swift had Gulliver drop in on Japan after Luggnagg, as his final destination before returning home. The first Westerner to interpret Japan in modern times, Lafcadio Hearn, wrote just before the turn of the century of 'the immense difficulty of perceiving and comprehending what underlies the surface of Japanese life'.[12] Hearn thought that 'no work picturing Japan within and without, historically and socially, psychologically and ethically, can be written for at least another fifty years'. In 1946 Ruth Benedict published the admirable first attempt at an inclusive appraisal of 'the most alien enemy the United States had ever fought in an all-out struggle. In no war with a major foe had it been necessary to take into account such exceedingly different habits of thinking and acting.'[13]

The same things that led Lafcadio Hearn and Ruth Benedict to make such strong statements still lend vehemence to discussion of Japan today. Westerners still repeat Hearn's excited discovery of the topsy-turviness of it all. And Ruth Benedict's interpretation of Japan as a cohesive entity that can stand on its own, culturally cut off from the rest of the world and essentially different from it, has remained seductive to many serious observers. Physical isolation can no longer be blamed for this. In 1962 I was one of 202,181 foreigners entering the country, and in that year only 145,749 Japanese travelled abroad. Twenty-five years later some six and a half million Japanese went overseas, and over two million foreigners visited Japan. But despite this greatly increased international traffic, much of the earlier aura of remoteness has remained. Japan is still the object of romantic musings. For some Westerners who decry the decline of polite manners, industriousness and other such things in their own countries, it is something of a Utopia.

We are often warned, especially in academic literature, that we must resist treating Japan as too special a case. And it is a good thing, of course, to emphasise that the Japanese are human and to show that they share the essential human traits; the intellectual desire to incorporate Japan more fully into the world is in itself laudable. Yet in their zeal to carry out this mission, some Westerners go to unwarranted extremes in pointing to the similarities and ignore those habits and institutions which cannot be forced, no matter how hard and consistent the attempt, to fit Western patterns of experience.

When studying a people by comparing them to other peoples one faces the age-old choice of whether to emphasise 'sameness' or 'otherness'. In the case of Japan this has led to great discrepancies in the views held by informed commentators. No important human practices and attitudes found elsewhere in the world are entirely unknown to the Japanese. Conversely, in other countries one can recognise habits and institutions corresponding with those in Japan. But to describe the Japanese experience more often than not requires the addition of phrases such as 'much more so' or 'much less so'. There is a point at which differences in degree and in the combination of elements add up to a difference in kind, particularly in the context of socio-political organisation – dependent as that can be on the ambitions and caprices of small groups of power-holders.

At the crossroads

Countless newspaper articles, magazine features and scholarly assessments have asserted over the past quarter-century that Japan had reached a crossroads. Perhaps no other country is so regularly examined by journalists and scholars for signs of impending change: not just the routine kind of change that may be expected in any society, but something basic, a change in the way people see themselves and consequently a change in the attitude of the entire nation towards the world.

Implicit in most reports on the Japan-at-the-crossroads theme is the idea that Japan *must* change; the things setting Japan apart from the rest of the world are often seen as anomalous and temporary. In the 1960s it was widely believed that Japanese youth was going to change things once it had reached positions of influence. At the same time, demands by labour were going to bring about drastic changes in the socio-economic structure. In the 1970s it was thought that the many employees who went abroad for their corporations were going to 'internationalise' Japan upon their return, and that widespread hankering after better living conditions would redirect Japanese efforts through a change in priorities. Later it became fashionable to think that the 'internationalisation' of the Japanese financial market and other unstoppable economic developments would force Japan to come to terms with the outside world's expectations of greater Japanese concern and initiative on behalf of collective international interests. In 1987 there existed a pervasive notion that the pressure of a supposed public demand for change, combined with loss of bureaucratic control over businessmen, was beginning to transform the Japanese political economy into one more clearly driven by market forces.

Today, Japan is stuck at the same crossroads as twenty-five years ago:

one where the Japanese people are expected to choose a new approach to the world, helped along by supposed changes in their own society but always in a direction mapped out by Westerners. No country should be condemned to waiting at the same uncomfortable spot for so long. What the crossroads stories appear to reflect more than anything else is myopic Western preconceptions about the possible forms that institutions and the organisation of affairs in non-Western nations can take. The march in the direction that many Western observers thought inevitable is just not going to take place.

For a while in the late 1970s Japanese officials began to fight back by contending that, if there was going to be evolution anywhere, it would be in the West. A government-sponsored publication spelled this out, saying that Japanese forms of social and economic management would 'become universal in all advanced industrial societies' if those societies wished to follow a rational course of further industrial development.[14]

Around this time the idea caught on in Europe and the United States that a number of Japanese practices might profitably be adopted. This is understandable. The question of whether the West should not be moving towards a society similar to that of Japan today inevitably arises in the minds of visitors who learn that Japan has next to no violent crime, no industrially damaging labour conflicts and an economic system that seems to weather oil crises and the like better than anyone else's. But the 'learn from Japan' approach has glossed over some crucial differences between Japan and the West. The adoption of parts of the System is not likely to work without most of the rest of the Japanese package, and the costs of that package cannot be paid by the West. An evolution of Western practices in Japanese directions would entail the reproduction of conditions inconceivable as long as social and intellectual freedom are valued.

There is reason to emphasise Japanese differences precisely because the crossroads view persists. Many sober Western analysts continue to expect large-scale change. 'Japan Inc., to the extent it ever existed, is being further dismantled,' asserts a highly respected economic daily.[15] Japanese slogans about 'internationalisation' are taken at face value. The official Japanese line in the 1980s is that the various forms of governmental guidance carry much less weight with the private sector than in the past. But even though this contention is regularly accompanied with figures intended to show that current tariff regulations make Japan about the freest market in the world, Japan has not in fact transferred into the category of Western free-market economies. What is true on paper in Japan is often – and always more frequently than in the West – not true in practice. Tokyo's officials are extremely inventive in devising subtle controls and euphemistic labels to render them more palatable. Foreign governments and columnists, automatically assuming that Japan sees itself faced with new choices and a new sense of responsibility, continue to expect major developments. But barring some great upheaval unforesee-able at present, it is unlikely that Japanese institutions will come to mesh more smoothly with the outside world, because this would entail the break-up of the bureaucracy–business partnership that forms the heart of the System.

The crossroads view should be discarded for yet another reason. It creates frustrations when expected changes fail to materialise, and ultimately leads to further vilification of Japan.

Having abandoned the crossroads view, we are left with the Lafcadio Hearn–Ruth Benedict thesis of cultural singularity. But this approach fails, in itself, to relate Japan to any wider, universally understandable realm of human experience. It is also, on a more practical level, powerless to help foreign governments and businesses formulate a *modus vivendi* with Japan.

There is, however, a way out of the conceptual maze. The Japan problem appears less mysterious, and many of the puzzles are soluble, when instead of the common approach of looking for cultural explanations we ask questions concerning the way power is exercised in Japan.

The neglected role of power

There are four general approaches to the study of human affairs, emphasising, respectively, their social, cultural, economic or political aspects. Problems cannot of course be told what to do, and therefore will not stay on one side of the boundaries some scholars have drawn between one approach and another. Human affairs, moreover, can be subsumed under any one of these headings; each incorporates the other three to at least some extent, because social, cultural, economic and political life are, of course, interrelated; when we choose one of these labels, we choose an emphasis.

The favourite perspectives of both Japanese commentators and foreign scholars studying Japan have been, by and large, the cultural and social ones, often amalgamated into one.

The political origins of Japanese culture

Japanese politics is still largely portrayed (very enthusiastically so by Japan's official spokesmen) as obeying cultural dictates. Japanese authors who choose a non-Marxist vantage-point practically always take it for granted that their native world is a product of the predilections of past generations of the people as a whole. Most writing on Japanese politics and its history does not give the impression that there have been power-holders at every stage with the means to organise the lives of those they controlled. A major recent effort by three prominent scholars to arrive at a new, all-encompassing perspective of Japanese socio-political life is an elaborate attempt to reduce everything to cultural factors, as if power has never been exercised in Japan.[16] Such reductionism is all the more remarkable because, if there is one nation whose predominant social and cultural idiosyncrasies can be traced back to political decisions that can clearly be seen in isolation from other influences, it is Japan.

If I had to explain the essential characteristics of Holland, where I was brought up, I could trace political determinants in the development of its economic, religious and general social life, but I would not necessarily adopt a political emphasis. Holland shares the European heritage of Greek and Hebrew thought, Roman law and the powerful force of Christianity, as Japan shares in the continental Asian heritage of Confucianism, Buddhism and Taoism. But the Dutch patricians were not in a position to choose what suited them from among Christian tenets and Roman ideas of jurisprudence, to be incorporated into Dutch culture as they saw fit. Nor did the absolute monarchs of Europe often have the power to control their borders effectively against ideas they did not like.

Any European country offers a whole jumble of possible leads to original causes of whatever one wants to explain. The same is true of India, to take one other example. And where must one look for the beginnings of what is most essential in Chinese culture? To the state, or to the philosophy that justified it?

Such 'chicken and egg' questions are less applicable to Japan. Looking back over its history, it is clear that political arrangements have been a major factor in determining the development of Japanese culture. Japan's relative isolation meant that the élite, in its efforts to hang on to power, could readily control the inflow and the impact of foreign culture. Power-holders could also pick and choose, from among what the rest of the world had to offer, those techniques and attitudes best calculated to consolidate their own positions. Such relatively wide control over culture meant a near absolute control over potentially subversive thinking.

Political control over culture

It is generally acknowledged that Chinese ideas and methods have helped shape official Japanese culture to a greater extent than any other influence. Apart from the great legacy of the writing system and the techniques and styles of artistic production, these cultural imports primarily served political purposes. In the sixth century Japan's rulers adopted Buddhism, explaining that they did so for political reasons. The introduction of the Chinese model of state administration, shortly afterwards, was obviously also a political move.

Diplomatic channels to China were subsequently closed, and kept closed at the discretion of generations of Japanese rulers until 1401, when shogun Ashikaga Yoshimitsu established trade relations with the Ming court. In spite of the huge profits and many luxuries this brought Yoshimitsu, his successors again put a stop to the Chinese traffic. During the periods when court and shogun did not maintain official relations with China, Japan's southern provinces continued to trade, and some Chinese cultural influence must have continued to filter through, but it does not seem to have had a lasting effect on Japanese élite culture.

From the middle of the sixteenth century the Portuguese were allowed to bring their firearms, medicine, astronomy, clocks and, most significantly, their religion. But this hospitality was reversed not long after the turn of the century, when the shogun began to fear them as a political fifth column, realising the potential threat posed by a Lord beyond the clouds towards whom his underlings could redirect their sense of loyalty. The result of this political insight was a policy of almost hermetic seclusion, kept in force until the middle of the nineteenth century.

The new set of rulers that came in with the Meiji Restoration of 1868 promoted the import of practically anything their official missions to the United States and Europe considered useful for a new Japan. When this, inevitably, resulted in the spread of subversive ideas, they clamped down on them and began propagating an 'ancient' tradition, which they had themselves manufactured from bits and pieces of earlier political ideology, glorifying the emperor as head of the Japanese family state.

Until 1945 Japanese power-holders had a special police force with the task of eliminating 'dangerous thoughts'. Half a dozen officers of that police force became ministers of education, justice, labour, home affairs and welfare after the war.[17] And the essential character of Japanese nationalism in the 1980s is still determined by notions incorporated in the mythology fabricated by the Meiji oligarchy.

Fourteen centuries ago Japanese power-holders could rummage among what China had to offer and limit such outside cultural influences almost totally to institutions and beliefs that suited them. They again succeeded remarkably well with Western influences in the second half of the nineteenth century. In between, after centuries of civil strife, the power-holders suppressed those indigenous Buddhist sects that threatened to inject religious competition into the political realm, and selectively stimulated or arrested various social, economic and cultural trends depending on their importance to their own staying in power. The power-holders could even reverse the development of technology, as when they banned and forgot the firearms introduced by the Portuguese. They preferred not to run the risk of commoners acquiring the skills to rise up against them; firing a musket or rifle is a great deal simpler than swordsmanship, and sword-wielding opponents are more easily kept at bay before castle walls than gun-toting ones.

As we have seen, no intellectual leverage over the power of the political élite was possible, since the notion of a universal or transcendental truth was never permitted to embed itself in Japanese thought. The power-holders could control even this; indeed, no law ever restrained their power. It is thus no exaggeration to say that political arrangements have been crucial in determining the limits on Japanese religious life and thought.

A scholar of comparative political history has pointed out that, whereas in nineteenth-century Europe an 'intellectual mobilisation' – with lawyers, *philosophes*, freemasons, writers and journalists participating – could be distinguished from social and political action, in Japan no such a distinction could be made. The daimyo and samurai who took up 'Dutch studies' were equally engaged in intellectual activity, but 'they are distinguished from "intellectuals" in nineteenth-century Europe by the extraordinary singleness of political purpose with which they pursued these studies'.[18]

Power patterns have both directed and inhibited Japanese intellectual pursuits. Japanese ideas of justice and the place of law in society have been fashioned by rulers in terms of expediency, and have not influenced the attitudes and methods of those rulers in any critical way. Supposedly typical aspects of Japanese society and culture, such as group life, company loyalty and the love of harmony, the lack of individualism, the near absence of litigation, ultimately originate in political arrangements and are sustained for political purposes.

So long as Japan is considered primarily in social and cultural terms, one always runs up against a basic question: what is the origin of the great differences between the habits and institutions of the Japanese and those of other peoples? Part of the answer lies in Japan's historical isolation. But it is the political approach that can answer the question most satisfyingly, since it makes it possible to recognise the strong forces behind the shaping of Japanese society.

We have no difficulty in accepting that Soviet society, sixty years after the Bolshevik Revolution, has acquired characteristics it would not have had if it had known liberty, if it had been spared oppression by a ruling *nomenklatura* class and if it had no built-in impetus for people to lie for personal advantage. By comparison, Japan constitutes an altogether different, freer and more pleasant society. But the Japanese System has so far been as inescapable as the political system of the Soviet Union, and it has much deeper foundations.

Bias against the power perspective

Why, even so, does the cultural explanation of Japanese political life appear so much more attractive than the political perspective on Japanese culture? Perhaps because a superficial first look at the country would not urge one to look at it through political spectacles. There is no tyrant in sight; not even is there a clear centre of political power. The situation would not, on the face of it, suggest any particularly strong coercion over the individual. Even after a long stay in Japan one does not notice much coercion traceable to, say, a police force or some other government agency. Literature on Japan abounds, rather, in descriptions of a striving for harmony. Japanese power, in short, is highly diffuse; and, while this makes it particularly pervasive, it is not so immediately noticeable.

Yet I suspect that there is another, more important, reason for the success of the culturalist perspective among Westerners. Many people in democratically organised societies feel uncomfortable with the notion of power. Even the less threatening word 'politics' evokes distaste, associated as it often is with greed, lying and other things beneath our dignity. 'Power' is a dirtier word still, eliciting pleasurable emotions perhaps only in those who are themselves power-hungry.

The concept of 'power' has been eliminated from the vocabularies of a fair number of contemporary scholars studying human affairs. So unpleasant are its connotations for intellectuals, especially Americans, that they tend to deny or renounce it,[19] sometimes to the point of seriously suggesting that the concept be banished altogether.[20] One explanation for this might be that the idea of power clashes emotionally with the ideal of equal opportunity, which has gained the force of an ideology. Power in the sense of control by a small group of people over the majority, and power of the kind wielded by a master over a servant, are unpleasant possibilities. Thus intellectual constructs are created that sanitise power relations and view them as the perfectly rational result of collective decisions.

This is no place to linger over the foibles of contemporary political science, but a few observations may help to place this approach in perspective. Since the Second World War academics have offered us, by and large, a cellophane-wrapped, hygienic version of our socio-political world. In this version, the concept of power is sometimes replaced by that of an allegedly more neutral 'influence' in which the element of (potential) force is absent. Master–servant relationships are, if noticed at all, considered in exclusively economic terms, as something moreover that works for the good of everyone; while the idea of power 'red in tooth and claw' emerges only in reference to revolutionary situations.

This view, especially as purveyed by the adherents of 'pluralist theory', leads to the acceptance of any political arrangement as basically what it ought to be, though with room for improvement of certain details. Even where power is not eliminated from scholarly discourse, its sharp edges are removed. It is often treated as if it were a scarce commodity that can be allocated through forces akin to those of the market-place. This economic explanation of the political world denatures the idea of power. It cannot explain the very real bloody noses of, say, Japan's teachers fighting against the attempts of national educational administrators to regain control over 'moral thinking' in the schools. It cannot envision a country rushing headlong into disaster because of the disastrous way in which power is exercised.

The parcelling out of responsibilities and duties in the manner of the democratically organised Western communities – the basis for 'pluralist theory' – is possible only with some prior agreement on how to limit power, and on the guises in which it is allowed to affect ordinary citizens. This approach to power presupposes the existence of laws that are taken seriously. It also assumes that the ideal of pluralist representation is a reality, and uses this reality as a point of departure.

Japanese citizens do not in practice have recourse to the law; in fact, the idea of 'citizen' as distinct from 'subject' is hardly understood. Pluralist representation exists on paper, of course, but to believe that this informs Japanese practice is taking very much on faith.

If, between the lines of the following chapters, I give the impression that power in Japan is something to be wary of, this is intentional. Unlike power-holders in the countries that have provided the models for 'pluralist theory', Japanese power-holders systematically use power in ways and for ends over which the voter has ultimately no control whatsoever.

Exposing political motives

By recognising Japanese power where we should, we see things we would otherwise not be aware of. One is that the System as such is in better shape than at any other time in this century. We can see that the defeat in the Second World War and the occupation represent less of a watershed in Japanese political life than has generally been thought. The pre-war and wartime bureaucratic power system, minus its military components, has consolidated its power after the war, and is in the process of consolidating it even further.

The political perspective I propose also affords a fresh view of Japanese international business dealings. It has long been agreed that the priority of the large Japanese corporations is the expansion of market shares rather than medium-term profits. And it has often been noticed that, in order to achieve their strategic aims, they will forgo healthy profits for much longer periods than Western firms could possibly afford. Enlarging one's market share, like enlarging the territory one controls, depends on the desire for greater power, a political motive. Making maximum profits depends on a desire for money, an economic motive. The two approaches are of course related and mixed in both Western and Japanese corporations; but the results of the difference in emphasis are momentous. The bureaucratisation of Japanese business in the post-war period via increased bureaucratic controls and protection, as well as the replacement of entrepreneurs by ministry-friendly administrators, is directly related to the politically motivated drive for ever greater international market shares.

The history of Japan's drive in the 1970s to carve out niches of power in foreign markets without reciprocity is repeating itself in the late 1980s in the financial world. Japanese firms are buying many Western financial institutions. They are investing their massive profits (made by consolidating the conquest of international market shares for finished goods) not at home, where it would solve quite a few domestic and international problems, but abroad, where there are still opportunities to carve up market shares. The effect of the much publicised 'liberalisation' of financial and capital markets by the Ministry of Finance has been to foster the international emancipation of the Japanese banks, security houses and insurance firms, enabling them to compete better in the money markets of the world, and to give the trading companies a large new field for foreign investment.

These developments could be of considerable political significance, since the possibility of counteracting Japan's unilateral economic conquests will be greatly limited if Tokyo gains the kind of leverage over the world's financial markets that its current drive to expand market share appears to be heading for. There has been a consistent failure on the part of the West to foresee effects of this kind – a result of its apparent inability to envision the possibilities as the Japanese do.

The Japan Problem for the Japanese

As a nation, Japan is a problem for itself because the way Japanese power is exercised results in conflicts with, and isolation from, other countries. But Japan is also a problem for Japanese individuals. Discussions with many of them over the past quarter-century have convinced me that they are adversely affected by the way that power is exercised in their country. They are less free than they should be. Japanese are treated by their school system and their superiors in the way a landscape gardener treats a hedge; protruding bits of the personality are regularly snipped off. It is simply not possible for a political system to be unkind to the individual without this having grave consequences for the psychological development of its citizenry.

I believe that the Japanese are individuals, all 120 million of them. Not all may want to assert their individuality; most, having been so conditioned, do not. But I have met quite a few who want to be taken for distinct persons, rather than as indistinct members of a group. These independent thinkers are disturbed. In many cases they have withdrawn into the private world of their own mind. Japanese culture harbours a vast, unconnected and uncharted archipelago of such private worlds. Individualistic Japanese are generally non-political because they would constantly burn their fingers if they were to challenge the existing power arrangements. But they are Japanese despite their refusal to be conformist.

In recent decades it has become common, in referring to Japan, to dismiss the ideal of personal growth as a manifestation of Western ethnocentrism, and to surmise that Japanese have their own specifically Japanese way of individual differentiation. Yet there are criteria for personal growth that are not culture-bound. Just as it is in the bud to become a rose, and in the cub to become a tiger, the growing human being has the built-in purpose of becoming a mature, well-integrated individual.[21] My experience in other Asian countries and my acquaintance with well-integrated Japanese individuals have strengthened this belief.

Many serious commentators on Japan have studiously avoided statements that could be labelled as value judgements. However, my position is that it is an illusion to think that meaningful discourse on political matters can be kept free of judgements that are not ultimately connected with beliefs of some kind. Striving for objectivity goes hand in glove with a constant alertness to possible prejudices, but the very selection of subject-matter already betrays personal concerns, and these are not necessarily prejudices. Many things may be relative, but standards for a desirable way of organising life do exist, and choices should be made. The place of human beings in their society should not be left to chance.

Plato, who made the great discovery that self-knowledge depends on an understanding of the character and scope of political life, was fully aware of the corrupting potential of power. His magnificently rational and poetic mind first saw the need for liberation from myths, from tradition and from brute power as the fundamental justification for political action. I see no reason why this should apply only to Western societies.

The philosopher Leszek Kolakowski, born in Poland and forced to come to intellectual terms with communist society, has thought about this more than most of his colleagues born in the West, and is most to the point:

> the freedom of individuals has – we may presume – an anthropological foundation. This is admittedly a doctrine which cannot be proved or disproved in the normal sense of the word 'prove'. And yet our hope that freedom is not going to be ultimately destroyed by the joint pressure of totalitarianism and of general bureaucratisation of the world and indeed our very readiness to defend it depend crucially on our belief that the desire for freedom, for sovereign individual self-assertion in free choice, is not an accidental fancy of history, not a result of peculiar social conditions or a temporary by-product of specific economic life forms, of market mechanisms, but that it is rooted in the very quality of being human.[22]

Kolakowski knows that this is a philosophical issue which can never be conclusively settled by empirical investigation. But he is right in considering it an issue which 'we simply may not disregard or reject on the ground that [it is] insoluble according to the rules that govern scientific inquiry'. Once one has taken the philosophical position that freedom is desirable for the individual, one is entitled to employ the critical approach when scrutinising any political arrangements that severely hamper this freedom beyond the reasonable requirements for maintaining social order.

2

The Elusive State

Japanese life often seems like a play that has suffered a bad mix-up in its staging. The lines the actors speak do not fit the characters their costumes indicate they portray. Institutions, processes and behaviour related to the exercise of power suggest one thing at first sight but something quite different on closer acquaintance.

At the most basic level of political life Japan is of course no different from anywhere else. Some Japanese love power, and some achieve it. The vast majority, as everywhere, submit willingly to the exercise of power for fear of personal punishment or social chaos. The Japanese have laws, legislators, a parliament, political parties, labour unions, a prime minister, interest groups and stockholders. But one should not be misled by these familiar labels into hasty conclusions as to how power is exercised in Japan.

The Japanese prime minister is not expected to show much leadership; labour unions organise strikes to be held during lunch breaks; the legislature does not in fact legislate; stockholders never demand dividends; consumer interest groups advocate protectionism; laws are enforced only if they don't conflict too much with the interests of the powerful; and the ruling Liberal Democratic Party is, if anything, conservative and authoritarian, is not really a party and does not in fact rule.

Why not, one might ask, simply rename things? But that would be too simple. With Japanese socio-political institutions the familiar labels sometimes indicate familiar functions. At other times they stand in varying degrees, for something different. A major source of confusion is that Japanese journalists and most Japanese scholars have not cultivated the habit, common among their Western counterparts, of pointing out discrepancies. They tend to treat the institutions the way their labels dictate.

This does not mean that Japan, as many Japanese like to think, cannot be 'understood' by outsiders. It does mean, though, that patient effort is necessary in unravelling a peculiar kind of complexity, with little help and much hindrance from accepted Western political terminology. The reality of the Japanese political world has a way of slipping through one's fingers. In covering Japan for my newspaper, I feel the need at every turn to redefine the familiar terms, since they evoke images partially if not totally inappropriate to the Japanese reality. Indeed, a serious observer of the Japanese power structure will sometimes feel the urge to rewrite the whole political lexicon.

Power out of focus

Let us begin by examining the concept of the state. It is fashionable nowadays not to recognise the state as something different from government or nation. Yet the distinction, as will gradually become clear, is a necessary one, and is particularly illuminating in the Japanese context.

A nation is defined by a shared language and a sense of cultural separateness. Japan is clearly a nation. The state is not as easily described or measured, but its various definitions agree that it is the ultimate repository and arbiter of power within a country. Where in Japan, then, must one look to find the state? Formally, and in accordance with Japan's official status as a parliamentary democracy, sovereignty resides with the people and legislative power with the elected bodies of the two houses of the Diet. But this congregation of freely chosen representatives of the people, which the constitution calls the highest organ of state power, cannot truly be considered the final arbiter of what is permitted to go on in Japan. This should not in itself be startling; there are quite a few other countries where power does not reside in the institutions in which it is supposed to reside. In such cases, however, one expects to be able to point to an alternative institution, or a person or set of people, in *de facto* charge. In Japan there is no such clearly demarcated group of power-holders.

The only other institutions apart from the formal legislature that present themselves as plausible centres around which the state is organised are the bureaucracy and big business; but ultimate power rests in neither of these. One will find many obvious bosses, but no one boss among bosses, nor one single controlling group of them. Japan is highly centralised in the sense that its capital is the economic and cultural hub of the country. Tokyo, no less than Paris or London, is the city where 'everything happens'. Large companies must maintain important (if not main) offices there, if only to be close to ministry officials. The most important educational institutions are concentrated there. Local governments must wait on the central bureaucrats in order to plead for essential budget funds. Outside Tokyo there are hardly any important publishing or entertainment industries. Yet there is no political core to this geographical centre.

To grasp the reality of the state is not easy in any country, but in Japan it is like groping in the proverbial bucket of eels. The lines of command, the focus of responsibility, the ins and outs of decision-making, all remain maddeningly elusive.

Kings without power

Foreign observers must always remind themselves that, with Japanese political life, things are rarely what they seem.[1] This rule of thumb has been reiterated many times over the centuries by foreigners who visited Japan. Indeed, the very first non-legendary accounts of Japan already suggest that the real aim of Japan's supreme political institution had little connection with its ostensible function. Chinese chroniclers of the Kingdom of Wei, in the third century, noted with some amazement that, although the land of Wa (as they called Japan) was formally governed by a queen named Himiko, she was hidden in a well-guarded palace and communicated with the outside world via one man, leaving the business of ruling the country to her younger brother.[2]

World history abounds in priest-kings, god-kings and sorcerers or shamans with secular power, and Himiko, whose business was 'to know the will of the gods', might seem to be one of their number.[3] But the nominal chief of the Kingdom of Wa had no real clout. And the subsequent history of the emperors epitomises the Japanese proclivity to separate formal from factual power.

Once Japan's empresses and emperors were less vigorously appeasing the multitude of their ancestral gods, the minutiae of a mind-boggling ritual would still have allowed them no time for governing, even had they been permitted to do so. A few early emperors did, apparently, have political control, but this control was soon delegated, first to the crown prince and later to imperial advisers.

In the tenth and eleventh centuries Japan had a well-defined group of power-holders in the form of the Fujiwara, a cunning family that usurped such control over the country as was possible, legitimising its position by marrying its daughters to successive emperors. For roughly a century following the decline of the Fujiwara, the real power behind the throne lay with retired emperors. Finally, after a transitional period during which most power was held by another family, the Heike, *de facto* rule passed to the warrior dynasties that were to control Japan until the industrial era. In 1185 the general Minamoto no Yoritomo gained formal permission from the court to police all sixty-six provinces of Japan. Then, seven years later, he was granted the title of *seii tai shogun*, 'barbarian-subduing general-issimo' – an office that, after further consolidation, would remain the official focus of Japanese power until 1867.

The court as a political entity fell into neglect in the meantime. Some emperors were destitute. Ogimachi (1557–86), for instance, had to peddle his calligraphy and the palace furniture to make ends meet. The single exception to the imperial enfeeblement, and this for only three years, was Emperor Go-Daigo, who succeeded in challenging the military dictators and restoring the court's authority between 1333 and 1336. There were weak kings in the history of other countries too, before the emergence of constitutional monarchies changed the character of kingship. But in Japan it was the institution itself that was powerless.

The delegation of power in Japan did not stop at the office of shogun. A point was reached in the thirteenth century where there was, as the historian George Sansom remarks, 'the astonishing spectacle of a state at the head of which stands a titular Emperor whose vestigial functions are usurped by an abdicated Emperor, and whose real power is nominally delegated to an hereditary military dictator but actually wielded by an hereditary adviser of that dictator'.[4] The last reference is to the Hojo family, which controlled the shoguns as earlier powerful families had once controlled the emperors.

Such arrangements clearly suited the powerful men who throughout the centuries controlled their fellow Japanese. Not one of them ever made a serious attempt to grab the throne for himself. This is even more remarkable if one thinks of the marvellous model for usurpation provided by China, where successful rebellious generals were forever starting new dynasties.

The advantages of delegated power, however, seem always to have made up for the lack of visible glory. The Fujiwara family that established the norm for this kind of rule felt no urge, it seems, to destroy a system that provided its heirs with all the privileges of a ruler except the title. The tradition has, indeed, an obvious advantage for the holders of real power. One is considerably less vulnerable if someone else bears the title that should go with the might one possesses. If the source of real power is unclear, it will also be unclear how to attack it.

The rigged one-party system

Japan's Asian neighbours are completely familiar with this division between the form and substance of authority. Much of the formal power structure in Asia today is fictitious. The official trappings of the non-communist states were borrowed, introduced either by colonial administrations, as in India, Indonesia, the Philippines and Malaysia, or, as in Thailand and Japan, by local reformers who believed that Western forms would keep their countries free and give them respectability in the eyes of the West.

These Asian systems are partly, sometimes largely, a façade hiding an unseen power structure. Only by elucidating the older, indigenous forms of political behaviour can one make sense of the political processes. In the West, too, informal and extra-legal relationships may have considerable influence on the exercise of power. Yet in almost all Asian countries personal connections are vastly more important than the more recent, formally impartial institutions. The formal governmental processes in Asia should not, however, be dismissed as pointless pantomime. The official structures imported from the West have interacted with the older political habits and radically altered them. Japan is no exception here.

But since Japan has the most complete set of democratic trappings outside the West and is generally thought to belong in the same geopolitical category as the Western advanced industrial states, observers tend to be more easily misled about the political reality there than elsewhere in Asia. Japan is also less obviously ruled by an authoritarian hand than most of its neighbours. Its government does not lock up people in order to stay in power. For such reasons it has long been assumed that constitutionalism flourishes there.

Japan has all the institutions considered indispensable for a parliamentary democracy, and on the face of it there is nothing conspicuously out of the ordinary about them. In the heart of Tokyo stands a Diet building, site of meetings of a Lower House and an Upper House whose members would be incensed at any suggestion that they took their democratic tasks lightly. Every four years, or more frequently, the Japanese public has the opportunity to choose these representatives from a wide assortment of candidates.

The odd thing is that ever since 1955 this freedom has resulted in a one-party rule that has not been seriously challenged.[5] If one excludes the ten months in 1947–8 when conservatively inclined socialists participated in a confused coalition, one may say that ever since the end of the war the same relatively small group of politicians has played musical chairs with ministerial seats, making room only for its protégés, with no demonstrable public influence on important political decisions.

This group of politicians is now called the Liberal Democratic Party (LDP) – a total misnomer, as already seen, for a coalition of *habatsu*, political cliques. It has no party organisation to speak of amongst the grass roots, and no generally agreed upon mechanism to regulate succession to its leadership, nor does it stand for any identifiable political principles. It may have a membership of less than one and a half million one year, more than three million a year later and less than one and a half again the year after that.[6] It is thus scarcely a political party at all in the accepted Western sense.

Japan is rarely described as having a one-party system. Instead it is argued that the populace has so much faith in the politicians who have brought the nation economic success that it cannot get enough of them. Until recently this was the view held by the most influential foreign scholars writing on Japan. And this, understandably, is how the LDP explains its unchallenged position to the outside world; when a US president speaks to a Japanese prime minister of their shared commitment to pluralistic democracy, the latter is not going to contradict him.

But the truth is that the LDP has maintained itself in power by gerrymandering; by using money to assure itself of the roughly 48 per cent of the popular vote it requires; and by hammering home the message that only by electing LDP candidates will rural districts get infrastructural improvements. Under the circumstances that it has itself helped create, this message is accurate enough: local governments are highly dependent on a system of financial supports allocated by the central bureaucracy, a system not regulated by impartial rules. Politicians are needed to mediate with government officials, and LDP politicians have the best, if not the only, access to them.[7] In election campaigns most LDP politicians endlessly stress their ties with precisely those officials who can allocate the funds for a project desired by the constituency. The rigging of the system is further abetted by the supposedly non-partisan agricultural co-operatives, and by the innumerable construction companies and their sub-contractors whose facilities serve in effect as election offices.

The LDP's absolute majorities are further guaranteed by uneven representation whereby a single assiduously courted rural vote is worth three votes in the cities. Outside the big cities LDP candidates employ an exceedingly thorough style of pork-barrelling to get re-elected.

The LDP is thus first and foremost a vote-getting machine. Its electoral fortunes depend not on public identification with a political programme, but on arbitrary factors: on the turn-out at the polls (the higher in rural areas the better) and on care in the party's endorsement of candidates so as to avoid too much division of its vote in the multiple-member con-stituencies. As one of Japan's most prominent political scientists pointed out in 1960, when the LDP wins twice as many seats as the Japan Socialist Party (JSP) this does not mean that its ideas or welfare policies are valued twice as much, but that its money carries twice the weight of the mere opinions of the JSP.[8]

Parliament's Grecian chorus

The LDP can continue to rig the system because the 'opposition' is made up of parties that appear to believe that their proper permanent station in the scheme of things is outside the government. The second largest party, the JSP, makes it easy for the LDP to present itself as the only viable governing party. Its advocacy of unarmed neutrality and its long-standing anti-US stance seem almost designed to make the party unattrac-tive to the general voter. The other ideological party, the Japan Commu-nist Party (JCP), is in some ways slightly less unrealistically doctrinaire, and attracts a large number of sympathy votes from non-communists. None the less, its earlier history as an undisguised instrument of Moscow's foreign policy, together with post-war fears of anything labelled 'commu-nist', make it unacceptable even as a coalition partner to the other minority parties.

The small Democratic Socialist Party (DSP) and the Komeito Party sometimes behave as if they would like to participate in officially running the country, but even then only as coalition partners with the LDP. They have never seized opportunities to combine with the JSP that could conceivably have led to a non-LDP government.

The permanent political 'opposition' in Japan does not function in any fashion recognisable to voters in Western parliamentary democracies. It has been significant as a nuisance and as an obstacle to the kind of legislation that reminds liberal-minded Japanese of pre-war methods and controls. It can embarrass the LDP in one or more of the standing committees of the Diet by obstructionist activity drawing the attention of the newspapers. But it does not engage the LDP in significant debate on policies.

Inasmuch as the LDP would be castigated as dictatorial if it passed legislation in the absence of the 'opposition', boycotts of Dietary proceedings are an effective demonstration of symbolic anger. The minority parties resort to them in protest against the LDP's 'high-handedness', or to call attention to 'political ethics' (a polite reference to corruption on the part of LDP members), and occasionally to show disagreement with the national budget. In 1983 the minority parties caused a Diet stalemate that lasted a record twenty-eight days, and many other times they have paralysed legislative proceedings for one or two weeks. In the spring of 1987 a minority-party boycott helped solidify opposition among LDP supporters to a proposed sales tax, forcing the withdrawal of a tax-law revision bill. More commonly the LDP, under boycott pressure, agrees to a compromise over a symbolic issue with only a very minor effect, if any, on practical policy. With few exceptions Diet debates are performances that are democratically reassuring but with not the slightest influence on developments in the country's affairs.

The Japanese parliamentary opposition, in short, is like the chorus in a Greek tragedy. Its monotonous comments on the state of the nation and lamentations over the sins of the LDP are ritualistic and harmless.

Weak ministers

The LDP is habitually referred to as the 'ruling party', but this too is a misnomer. Little legislation emanates from it. In some instances policy initiatives are traceable to powerful LDP groups, but most of the time they are of marginal importance. The LDP hardly ever establishes new administrative priorities. The limits on its power are best seen in the political decisions it *fails* to make – decisions aimed, for instance, at lessening conflict with other countries or at improving the domestic infrastructure. Certain individuals and groups within it exercise power in a largely indirect manner, but not power of the kind that is generally considered relevant to the running of a state. What distinguishes LDP parliamentarians from other Japanese is personal privileges and the ability to relay to the bureaucrats requests for favours from lobbying supporters. In the late 1980s many Western observers had the impression that the LDP had become newly active in debating and sponsoring policies in the areas of industrial restructuring, opening the domestic market, financial liberalisation and educational reform. This notion, based on a plethora of committee reports and newspaper articles stressing the desirability of new policies, was largely inaccurate. In the national discussion the developments in these areas were highly exaggerated; and most were forced on

Japan by external circumstances, were kept to a minimum and were monitored by the bureaucrats rather than by the LDP.

Seated above a weak parliament, the Japanese prime minister, who is invariably president of the LDP, in theory has opportunities to exercise great power. But in fact his power does not permit him to do things that foreigners, including foreign governments, expect a prime minister to be able to do. If he focuses most of his energies on one goal and is given more than a couple of years in office, he may subtly effect a small shift in priorities among the administrators. His immediate power is for all practical purposes limited to dissolving the Lower House. If he tried to do much more, his rivals in the LDP, along with the 'opposition' parties, would almost surely combine to bring him down.

The power of the Japanese prime minister is less than that of any head of government in the West or Asia. Proof of this, if still needed, was provided by the recent experiences of Nakasone Yasuhiro. As prime minister, Nakasone never allowed any doubt about his ambition to rule. He also tried harder than any of his post-war predecessors to strengthen his office. In the end, though, he failed to bring about the policy adjustments he championed – except for the break-up of the company running the largest losses in the world, the Japan National Railways.

According to the constitution, executive power is vested in the cabinet. But most Japanese cabinet ministers do not run the departments whose portfolios they hold. They tend to have little or no influence within their ministries. The almost yearly cabinet reshuffles give them no time to absorb sufficient detail to outsmart their senior bureaucrats. A strong politician can make his mark on a policy area through a certain amount of leverage in senior personnel appointments, and by climbing the ranks of the corresponding policy group within the LDP. Some bureaucratic preserves, such as education, transport and construction, are less self-willed than others such as the trade and industry or finance ministries. But ministers who make significant decisions are so extraordinary that they fuel inter-departmental gossip and press comment for years afterwards.

If cabinet members were to insist on exercising the kind of power the formal rules give them, they would in nearly all cases run into insurmountable bureaucratic sabotage. Cabinet meetings are, with extremely rare exceptions, wholly ceremonial affairs, lasting between ten and fifteen minutes, for the sole purpose of endorsing the policy adjustments that the administrative vice-ministers (the top bureaucrats in each ministry) have agreed on the previous day at their own meeting. The cabinet does not discuss any new business of which the bureaucrats have no knowledge, as is common in European countries, or business that has not been worked out in all its details by the bureaucrats.

The importance of the politician's role admittedly varies somewhat, depending on the perceived urgency of new administrative programmes. In the 1950s, for example, a number of LDP parliamentarians, themselves mostly former bureaucrats, helped set the agenda for the various adjustments necessary in preparing for unlimited industrial expansion – which was taken for granted as the top national priority. In the early 1960s Prime Minister Ikeda Hayato overcame finance ministry resistance to an unimpeded application of 'high-growth' policies. Subsequently the politicians rarely interfered with this agenda and certainly never introduced new priorities. On the other hand, L DP Diet members have continued to influence the interventions of the education ministry throughout the past few decades. Again, in the late 1970s and the 1980s certain LDP politicians increased their power when the role of mediator in inter-ministry quarrelling over jurisdiction in new industrial fields such as telecommunications was thrust upon them. On the whole, though, while one must guard against underestimating the clout of the L DP, it is difficult to escape the conclusion that the power of officialdom is significantly greater where ruling the country is concerned.

The authoritarian bureaucracy

Is the power of the Japanese state, then, to be found in the bureaucracy? A fair number of experienced observers have reached this tempting conclusion.

In the everyday business of governing Japan, groups of officials, especially those of the ministries of finance, international trade and industry, construction, and post and telecommunications, wield a great deal of power, definitely more than they are theoretically authorised to exercise. They restrain, control and provide spurs for the economy. They make nearly all laws – which, if not everything, is quite something in terms of measurable power. These laws are almost always rubber-stamped by the Diet, and the bureaucrats typically proceed to use them as means to achieve their own cherished aims. Their informal powers, moreover, give them even greater control over the realms of social activity for which they are formally responsible. This informal power, because it is not exposed to debate about its merits, is very open-ended.

It might help solve the riddle of Japanese power, then, to consider Japan an 'authoritarian bureaucratic state'; but to try to pinpoint just who among the bureaucrats is in charge is to get lost again at once. Pressed to endorse decisions their respective ministries object to, the administrative vice-ministers will not give in to each other. Regular participants in the vice-ministerial meetings that precede the ceremonial cabinet meetings have told me that controversial issues always result in impasses, because there is simply no way to break a deadlock caused by a recalcitrant ministry.

Intense rivalry among officials has long prevented their achieving a general dominance over Japanese policy-making. By the same token, territorial jealousies among ministries and agencies, which frequently turn into well-publicised wars, obstruct the formulation of sorely needed unified national policies. Even apart from such internal rivalry, the jurisdiction of the bureaucracy as a whole is definitely curtailed, even though nobody seems to be able to point out exactly where its parameters lie.

The zaikai

We are left with one main group of participants in the Japanese power game, a group that is a favourite among theorists who postulate conspiracy in considering Japan's policies. It is the *zaikai*, the broad circle of top business functionaries, especially those who speak through the powerful business federations. Since Japan is known internationally almost exclusively through the products of its industry and the impact they have on other economies, foreigners are tempted to think that the captains of industry dominate its political decision-making. According to this interpretation both the LDP and the bureaucrats serve as proxies for the *zaikai*.

This picture is false. True, Japanese corporations operate in an extremely favourable political climate in so far as industrial expansion remains the national goal in the eyes of economic officials and the LDP, and most of the methods used to achieve this goal are accepted as a matter of course. But this has not turned the presidents and chairmen of industrial corporations into Japan's secret rulers.

Admittedly, the business federations, especially Keidanren, have extraordinary powers. Keidanren is a federation of leading industrial organisations such as the automobile manufacturers' association, the shipbuilders' association, the iron and steel federation, the petroleum association and the chemical industry association, together with trading companies, wholesale businesses, banks, insurance companies and securities companies. Second in importance, Nikkeiren (Japan Federation of Employers' Associations), has had the task of helping control the labour movement and keeping the lid on wage increases. The Keizai Doyukai (Committee for Economic Development) has provided a forum in which élite *zaikai* members can formulate a theoretical basis for business policies; it attracted attention in the mid-1950s with proposals for a Japanese-style 'reformed capitalism'. The fourth and oldest organisation, the Japan Chamber of Commerce and Industry (originally the Tokyo Chamber of Commerce, set up in 1878), monitors the world of the smaller corporations.

It would be a mistake to think of the founders and major leaders of the post-war federations as entrepreneurs, or as representing entrepreneurs. One of the reasons for the success of the bureaucrat–businessman partnership is that these organisations at the apex of the industrial hierarchy were, in their formative stages and long afterwards, led by bureaucrats who had been responsible for wartime economic mobilisation and by bureaucratised leaders of wartime cartels. These men provided the main impetus for the merger of the rival conservative parties to form the LDP in 1955.[9] They have also had a decisive influence over post-occupation education policies and the shaping of the school system.

In the late 1980s the *zaikaijin*, business elders, form a gerontocracy at the top of an ever more bureaucratised business world. As chairmen of the boards of their respective companies, they often continue to wield tremendous power, greater even than that of the presidents. The chairmanship leaves them with more time and opportunity to engage in committee work. They enhance the reputation of their firms, as they pontificate on what is desirable for society and add their contributions to the ubiquitous platitudes regarding Japan's tasks and future role in the world. But they have no ability to steer Japan towards new priorities more consonant with those tasks and the international role.

As a class, contemporary businessmen buy political power on a regular basis. Individual business sectors, even large individual corporations, maintain leverage over most LDP Diet members by footing the incredibly high cost of maintaining an intensive publicity presence in their constituencies. Some businesses buy specific political power from individual LDP members who play a pivotal role in stimulating or retarding bureaucratic decisions affecting them.

But such power is still rather limited, and informal bureaucratic control over business reaches very far. Even within the economic sphere, the *zaikai* is highly dependent on the ministries for protection of its existing industries against international competition on the domestic market, and for guidance and co-ordination as it moves in new industrial directions.

Thus each of the three bodies described above may display surprising power at times and unexpected weakness at others. No elegant equation showing precisely how they relate to each other in their shares of power is possible. The essential fact is that none of them can be perceived as forming the apex of the Japanese power hierarchy.

The unnecessary state

If there are no other groups that can compete for power with the three we have just been discussing, where then must one locate the Japanese state? Is it perhaps possible that, finally, in this unexpected place, we have a state which is actually at some stage of withering away?

Do the Japanese *need* a state? At least from the Middle Ages until the middle of the nineteenth century, the Japanese political élite apparently did not think so. But this had not always been the case. When the Yamato rulers of what is now central Japan consolidated their holdings in the middle of the seventh century, they attempted to bring other clan chieftains under control with measures designed to turn Japan into a centrally directed state after the Chinese model. But this 'state' did not last long and did not result in an enduring pattern of centralised power. The country was divided into administrative units, and officials were dispatched from the capital to serve fixed terms as governors. After a while, officials remained where they had been sent and passed their power on to their heirs. Once contact with China was broken, the need for a state seems to have vanished from the thoughts of Japanese power-holders. Even the powerful Fujiwara family, at a later stage, never consolidated undisputed control over the entire country.

Oda Nobunaga (1534–82), the first of the three 'unifiers' of Japan, might possibly be said to have wanted to establish a state. He tried to attain central rule by conquest, supplanting enemy lords with men he strictly controlled.[10] Significantly, in justifying this campaign of military 'pacification' he used the term *tenka* ('the realm') for an entity that was greater than the existing collection of warrior domains.[11] But his 'realm' was never consolidated.

His successor, Toyotomi Hideyoshi (1537–98), who by 1590 had nearly accomplished the unification of the country, probably came the closest to a paramount leader that Japan has ever had. But instead of eliminating the lords he had defeated, he allowed most of them to retain and rule their domains. He in fact helped bring about the feudal arrangements revolving around semi-autonomous lords called daimyo – that great political balancing act that kept the Tokugawa shoguns in power for over two and a half centuries.

The Tokugawa

Japan's biggest missed opportunity before recent times for the establishment of a state followed the decisive battle of Sekigahara in 1600, which ended some three centuries of intermittent civil war and set the stage for a new political arrangement. Securing the allegiance of all surviving warrior lords, Tokugawa Ieyasu took over the shogunate, and the long period of relative peace named after his family began – peace, but not political unity. No truly centralised government was ever attempted, since both shoguns and daimyo were preoccupied with safeguarding what they possessed for their heirs. Any unifying national ideal encroaching on the power of subordinate or rival lords would have been too risky.

The Tokugawa *bakufu* – as the shogunate was commonly known – controlled roughly only a quarter of Japanese territory. It did so directly as well as through five thousand or so *hatamoto* (retainer) families who, in return for annual stipends, served it as officers and clerks. Beyond this it could count on the loyalty of a small number of blood-related (*shimpan*) daimyo and 170 (on the average) *fudai* daimyo, who retained discretionary powers within their domains, and whose ranks supplied the *bakufu* ruling élite after the second Tokugawa generation. This left an average of 80 *tozama* or 'outside vassals' whom the shogun had to keep off-balance.

Some of the larger *tozama* domains were practically independent states, autonomous except for their relations with other domains. By means of check-points on the roads, an espionage network and strategically positioned fiefs of loyal daimyo, the shogunate made sure that these potentially troublesome domains remained isolated from each other. It was a coalition of several of these large 'outside' domains that was finally to overthrow

Tokugawa rule. When this happened, Japan had already evolved into a highly complex political entity, but not into one with unambiguous central leadership, and not into a state.

The intense sense of the inviolability of all things Japanese that is characteristic of the nation includes a strong sense of the inviolability of its territory. But as we have seen, for centuries the preservation of this territory required no sense of belonging to a state. This was probably related to the unusual circumstance that nobody bothered Japan, save for two attempts at invasion by the Mongols under Kublai Khan (in 1274 and 1281). As long as they were left alone, the Japanese, in stark contrast to the Chinese, seemed not to need the concept of the state.

They were not to be left alone for ever. In 1853 United States Commodore Matthew Perry arrived and, backed up by four ominously black warships, demanded provisions and refuelling facilities for US ships passing Japan as well as humane treatment for castaway sailors and the opening of ports for trade. The treaty he managed to conclude eight months later did not give the USA substantial concessions, and allowed Japanese officials to wriggle out of what the Americans thought they had promised. But it became the precedent for treaties with Britain, Russia and the Netherlands, and it spelled an end to Japan's official seclusion policy. At last Japan was forcibly confronted with the turbulent community of world powers, and thus the need for a foreign policy.

The pulling apart of the Meiji state

The Meiji oligarchy that took control in 1868, largely as a result of this foreign intervention, was obsessed with creating a strong state. Within three years of the overthrow of the Tokugawa shogunate it had abolished the feudal domains, explaining that 'to maintain equality with foreign nations, words must be made to mean in reality what they claim to signify, and the government of the country must center in a single authority'.[12] The warning was hardly superfluous, considering that some of the more powerful domains had been dealing with the foreign powers on their own and even initiating acts of war.

The first attempts at building a state appeared surprisingly successful, earning the admiration of the Western powers, especially when victory in the Russo–Japanese War of 1905 appeared to demonstrate Japan's naval prowess. But the system of central rule proved to be not sturdy enough to outlast its creators. Whereas the original oligarchy had been able to iron out differences of opinion and formulate unified policies, the next generation of leaders, with no such sense of fellowship, failed to form an effective oligarchy. The Naimusho,[13] the Army, the Navy, the Ministry of Foreign Affairs, the Ministry of Finance, the Privy Council and other vital institutions of the state were all led by men who identified with these institutions rather than with the centre of power they were expected to represent. They were often not even on speaking terms with each other.

Today, with the advantage of hindsight, one can see that the Meiji reformers, for all their achievements, were also responsible for the leadership problem Japan still faces. On close scrutiny, the state they established seems almost to have been designed not to outlast them. They personally were needed to keep it tied together, since the rules they made never clearly specified who should be in charge. Oligarchic rule was initially meant to be a temporary arrangement only, to be replaced by a well-co-ordinated system blending Japanese and Western institutions. But the understandable fear of diminishing their own power made modern Japan's political architects ignore the question of political accountability, which is essential for such co-ordination.

As time went on, the different organs of the state, mistaking parochial interests for that of the nation, began to develop a sense of autonomy resembling that of the abolished fiefs of the Tokugawa period. After the turn of the century there was much jockeying for power among the Privy Council, military chiefs, bureaucrats, politicians, influential businessmen and palace advisers. For the first two decades or so of the twentieth century the original oligarchs continued to be a cohesive force in the capacity of *genro*, 'elder statesmen' with enough clout to prevent serious ruptures. But by the time they had passed from the scene, Japan's leaders, each claiming a mandate from the emperor, were vigorously pulling the country in different directions.

The emperor had formal sovereignty but was not supposed to rule. The legislature was not designed to have genuine power but, through a mistake in its design, came to live an oppositional life of its own.[14] The cabinet outgrew its role as a kind of advisory body, but the constitution was silent on what it ought to do instead. After the First World War, the formal government was furnished by the political parties, which were paid for by big business. But these parties never gained much actual power in their competition with the other centres of power endorsed by the Meiji constitution.

The extent of potential dissension among these 'servants of the emperor' was illustrated by the 'Go-Stop Incident' involving the powerful Naimusho and the Army. In 1933 a private 2nd class twice crossed a road against the red of a 'go-stop' (traffic) sign in Osaka. The policeman in charge of the crossing took him in, but the soldier disclaimed any duty to obey police instructions, and a fight ensued. The dispute percolated up to ever higher levels. The chief of staff of the Fourth Division saw an opportunity to reprimand the police and uphold the Army's dignity. Army Minister Araki concurred and had the chief of the élite Kempeitai (military police) bring charges against the policeman for insulting, assaulting and bringing disgrace on a professional soldier.

On the police side, the issue travelled up via the desks of the regional police chief, the mayor of Osaka and the director of the bureau of police in the Naimusho, till finally it reached that of the minister of the interior himself. All agreed that apologising was out of the question, and that the soldier should be brought to trial. Since similar cases had occurred in Tokyo, Nagoya, Akita and Fukuyama, the Naimusho was resolved to challenge the arrogance of the Army. But the Army bureaucrats persisted in obstructing attempts to prosecute, till the conflict finally reached the ears of the emperor, who asked the Army Minister Araki about it. The latter thereupon instructed his vice-minister for political affairs to work things out with the chief of the bureau of police in the Naimusho, and a prefectural governor was brought in to mediate a compromise.[15]

The pre-war headless chicken

In the 1930s, as hopes for the development of a democracy on Western lines were dashed, power progressively slid into the hands of the military. Yet even while this happened, no one knew who was in charge of them either. The Army and the Navy each had its chiefs directly answerable to the emperor, and did not even consult with each other. Formulation of defence policy was greatly hampered by conflicting aims, conflicting strategic priorities and conflicting views concerning the hypothetical enemy. The services procured separately. A cadet from the naval academy could not even have discussed weaponry with a soldier, since the two used entirely different terms. Meanwhile, both Army and Navy were torn by internal strife. In the Army, for instance, the Imperial Way Faction (Kodo-ha) engaged in a bitter struggle with the Control Group (Tosei-ha). They were divided by the differing backgrounds of officers and the differing degrees to which they valued practical planning above reliance on the power of the Japanese spirit. To these were later added the Purification Group (Seigun-ha), and the Kokutai genri-ha, radical young officers who were responsible for the crucial 'February 26' rebellion in 1936.[16]

The dissipation of central political power that started at the beginning of this century and culminated in Japan's drifting beyond anyone's control in the 1930s gave fanatical middle-ranking Army officers the opportunity to 'hijack' the nation. In September 1931 elements of the Japanese Kwantung Army attacked the Chinese garrison in Mukden, thereby beginning the conquest of Manchuria. When this act of gross insubordination went uncensured by the government in Tokyo, the Army understood that it could have its way, and on its own initiative set up the puppet state of Manchukuo. The intimidating actions of fanatical officers that followed set Japan on the course that was to lead to Pearl Harbor and from there to Hiroshima.

Attacking a country with an industrial machine ten times the size of one's own must be considered suicidal behaviour, and it is very unlikely that a consolidated leadership would have allowed it. It can be argued, indeed, that the Japanese surprise attack which brought the United States into the Second World War was a direct consequence of the rivalry between the Army and the Navy. The Army, in setting Japan on the path to war, took it for granted that the Navy would take care of defence against US might, while the Navy, wishing to hold on to its power and its credibility as a patriotic body, refrained from directly expressing the belief, widespread among its ranks, that victory was impossible.[17]

The war itself did little to pull the political bodies of the country together. It undoubtedly strengthened the power of the bureaucrats, but this power was not concentrated in the hands of a single man or institution.

> The cabinet remained a federation of ministries and agencies, each scrupulously guarding its privileges and autonomy. The Prime Minister was never the chief executive; he was the chief co-ordinator whose task was to ensure a united cabinet policy. He could neither dictate to the other ministers nor change them at will; replacing a minister was a complicated task which required both pressure and persuasion.[18]

The Japanese at war never gave to any one person (or one government institution) powers remotely comparable to the power held by Hitler, Mussolini, Stalin, Churchill or Roosevelt. Even towards the end of the war the government never declared the martial law that would have given it the powers needed for an all-out defence of Japan. 'One reason for that was that none of the leading élites wanted the others to gain more power.'[19]

Post-war misunderstanding

In the wake of the disastrous adventure of the Pacific War, no new attempt to establish genuine central control was made. General Douglas Mac-Arthur and his political reformers arrived in 1945 to dismantle what they, along with practically everyone else, imagined to be the remnants of a solid dictatorship similar to those of Hitler and Mussolini. The idea that it could have been the absence of strong leadership which had brought Japan to attack the Western allies appears not to have occurred to anyone. As for the Japanese themselves, the domestic concerns that demanded their attention did not encourage them to repeat Meiji-style experiments with a centralised state.

Forced to make a priority of foreign policy, the men of Meiji had been preoccupied with the notion that a strong central ruling body was needed to deal with other states. But from 1945 until well into the 1970s Japan had little need to worry about whether or not it was a state, since it was hardly ever called upon to act as a political entity. Foreign-policy requirements were simply not felt. Japan's first important post-war prime minister, Yoshida Shigeru, made the notable political discovery that Japan need not exert itself for national security in the traditional sense, since the USA was ready to take care of it. It was subsequently realised that all other activities by which a state is externally known and recognised could similarly be carried out by US proxy.

Japan became totally dependent on the United States, not only for its defence but also, ultimately, for its diplomacy. In effect, the USA provided a diplomatic shield behind which Japan, with the help of neo-mercantilistic trade practices, built up its formidable post-war economic machine. The so-called omni-directional diplomacy, which, until Nakasone Yasuhiro became prime minister, Japan presented to the world as an idealistic innovation, was in fact an attempt to be all things to all men who bought Japan's products and sold it raw materials. Tokyo could maintain such a stance only to the extent that Washington would tolerate it. Thus Japan's extraordinary relationship with the USA entails significantly more than diplomatic help, mutual trade and promised military protection. It has allowed Japan to deal with countries on the basis of purely economic priorities, with scant regard to political consequences.

Today's truncated pyramid

At home, in the meantime, the relationships that count do not normally involve major problems, notwithstanding the great rivalries. The bureaucrats tinker with the economy, making adjustments to facilitate its further growth. The politicians and almost everyone else keep out of their way. Parliamentary representatives, largely chosen for their pork-barrelling skills, attend mainly to the business of getting re-elected. Since this depends largely on their ability to spread the national wealth politicians are perpetually indebted to the bureaucratic guardians of the budget. The industrialists continue to expand their foreign market shares, and enter new markets with the help of the bureaucrats. They are kept in line by their peers; and they pay the politicians. Nobody is boss, but everybody, in some way or other, has leverage over somebody else, which helps ensure an orderly state of affairs.

In addition to the bureaucrat–LDP–business triad, there are several other powerful, semi-autonomous bodies. The press is one of them; the gigantic dailies copy each other's approach, coming up with a well-nigh uniform stance on most issues of the day. Speaking mostly with one voice, they tend to have much influence on popular sentiment concerning domestic issues and on attitudes towards international relations.

Another influential body, the National Federation of Agricultural Co-operatives, presides over a multitude of local co-operatives, regional federations and special business organisations catering to the 8 per cent of Japan's workforce employed in farming. It maintains a symbiotic relationship with the Ministry of Agriculture. The ministry, in co-operation with the LDP, keeps the price of domestic rice at around five times the world price. In return, LDP candidates in many rural areas are given almost unconditional support.

There are other organisations over which the bureaucracy's control is rather limited. Gangster syndicates run huge protection rackets and are allowed considerable powers of intimidation in the entertainment districts that exist in nearly every locality. The police maintain an unacknow-ledged symbiotic relationship with the gangster syndicates in the interest of keeping crime under organised control. The police themselves form another semi-autonomous body with far-reaching discretionary powers. Japanese public prosecutors decide for themselves, often on relatively arbitrary grounds, when and when not to prosecute.

Power in Japan is thus diffused over a number of semi-self-contained, semi-mutually dependent bodies which are neither responsible to an electorate nor, ultimately, subservient to one another. While all these bodies share aspects of government, it is impossible to find one among them that gives the others their mandate. No one has final responsibility for national policy or can decide national questions in emergencies. Japan here differs from societies, such as that of the United States, where power is fragmented among numerous councils, agencies, boards, courts and the like. In the latter there still is a line of command; there are ways of getting through to a centre, of having that centre make and implement policies. Japan is different again from West European societies, even those with very strong interest groups that diminish the power of the centre. At European cabinet meetings, initiatives are taken and decisions are, ultimately, made. In Japan the various 'governing' bodies remain them-selves ungoverned.

Now you see it, now you don't

Which brings us back to the elusive Japanese state.

The public, of course, perceives a 'state' in the presence of the tax collector, the police and a vast body of regulations. But the Japanese state vanishes once one considers the question of accountability. It is interest-ing that the average Japanese does not consider the puppet state of Manchukuo to have been 'our colony'; it was the Army's colony, not Japan's. The Japanese tend not to see themselves as being symbolically part of a state whose responsibility they therefore share.

There is an apparent paradox here, for the enthusiasm with which ordinary Japanese greeted the conquests of imperial Japan, and the extent to which they identified with the national purpose, are well documented. However, they are not by their own lights fraudulent in disowning the Army, since they do not see it as having represented their state. It was just a group, one of many, which in retrospect caused a great deal of trouble.

The state means different things to different people, but it should at least show some 'existential consistency'. It should continue to be there from one moment to the next, and not suddenly trickle away like sand through one's fingers. Washington was perplexed when in May 1981, on the day following a visit to the US president, the then prime minister, Suzuki Zenko, told Japanese newspapers that he had not meant what everybody understood to be a clear statement about an 'alliance' with the United States in the joint communiqué he had just countersigned. The immediate foreign reaction in such a situation is to suspect disingenuous motives; it hardly occurred to anyone that Suzuki, the 'premier', might not represent a state. In the imbroglio that followed in Tokyo the foreign minister resigned. But his successor, Sonoda Sunao, hardly improved the situation when he stated that joint communiqués were not binding on their signatories.

The minimum to expect from the state is that it should behave as a unified body, at least to the extent of speaking with one voice. Where is the state if the Ministry of Foreign Affairs chastises a foreign corre-spondent, as happened with a colleague of mine, for the inaccuracy of a dispatch written on the basis of information obtained from the Ministry of Agriculture? Or if one ministry, as has happened fairly often, denies before diplomatic negotiators what another ministry has just conceded?

The frustration of many a foreign negotiator, meeting the umpteenth mediator sent his way, can be summed up in the single cry 'Take me to your leader'. Japan does not have one. It is pushed, or pulled, or kept afloat, but not actually led, by many power-holders in what I call the System.

The System

One could label the entire body politic, meaning all and everyone participating in some way in the power process, 'the state'. But this confuses, for the state would become something very nebulous indeed, and we would still have to postulate accountability, which in turn presupposes a centre. How, then, is one to label an entity which is not a state, but which does encompass the political life of a country? To me, the word 'system' seems to invite the least confusion. It denotes little more than the existence of a set of relationships, with reasonably predictable effects, between those engaged in socio-political pursuits. The term 'system' is also frequently used to suggest an arrangement of inescapable forces against which the individual is helpless without resort to violence. It hints at something beyond the range of the potentially corrective powers of democratic politics; it is something that cannot be reasoned with – although it may occasionally be duped. As it happens, the Japanese are rarely allowed to forget the existence of socio-political arrangements that are infinitely stronger than any kind of might the individual could ever bring to bear on them and have, at best, only a dim notion that ideally one should have recourse to democratic processes as a means of changing them. The term 'system' is thus very useful in speaking of political Japan, and I will give it the capital 'S' it deserves for denoting something, neither 'state' nor 'society', that nevertheless determines how Japanese life is lived and who obeys whom.

The public-private realm

Foreigners have often sensed in Japan something not generally covered by the notion of 'state'. 'Japan Inc.' is the term that has become popular in an attempt to grapple with the question. But the metaphor is misleading in that Japan has nothing comparable to a chairman of the board, a president or even a board of directors as a means of providing a unified view on which to base important decisions.

On the other hand, Japanese official spokesmen who do not like the notion of 'Japan Inc.' will sometimes point to Western Europe and contend that, since much more industry is nationalised in, for instance, Britain or France, it is in those countries rather than in Japan that government and business interests have truly amalgamated. Such spokesmen have succumbed to the temptation, lying in wait for all commentators on Japan, to compare apples with oranges.

Certainly, where the size of its bureaucracy is concerned, Japan is not impressive compared to the West, where the welfare state has created a notoriously swollen officialdom. There are only 4·4 Japanese public-sector employees per 100 inhabitants, which is one-third the figure for Great Britain and just over half that for both the USA and West Germany. But this is irrelevant in the context of the Japanese System. In the mixed economies of Western Europe, even in France, the private and public elements are still fairly well delineated. State interference can be administered in measurable doses, monitored and singled out for praise or protest if need be. By contrast, Japanese bureaucratic participation tends to resist analysis.

The mingling of the private and public domains in Japan is nevertheless not a mysterious process. Various practices facilitating bureaucratic participation can be singled out. Japanese government bureaux have extraordinary powers of awarding licences and other permissions for commercial pursuits, and of withholding advantages like subsidies, tax privileges or low-interest loans at their own discretion. Ministries can resort to 'administrative guidance' to force organisations in their realm of endeavour to adopt 'voluntary' measures. It is by such means that the Ministry of International Trade and Industry has moulded, joined and in other ways shaped industrial sectors to make them collectively fit for optimum performance on the foreign and domestic markets. The Ministry of Finance and the Bank of Japan also exercise powerful control, thanks to the once nearly exclusive dependence of Japanese corporations on bank loans for capital. Even though a majority of the large firms have by the 1980s made so much profit that they are awash in self-generated capital, the relationship between these bureaucratic and industrial bodies of Japan remains close to a degree without parallel in the Western world. By issuing binding instructions to the commercial banks, the Bank of Japan still maintains a very large voice in allocating the funds for all really big investments.

The bureaucrats also preside over a proliferation of public and semi-public corporations serving all manner of economic and political purposes – including, incidentally, the provision of post-retirement sinecures for the bureaucrats themselves. Deriving funds largely from Japan's postal savings system (the largest financial intitution in the non-communist world), the budget for these public policy companies is not subject to parliamentary approval and thus allows unnoticed spending in furtherance of specific bureaucratic goals.[20]

Some three hundred bureaucrats annually join the business world as directors or senior advisers of corporations they monitored during their government career. Since the retirement age is fifty-five, such bureaucrats will have another twenty years or so in which to help ensure 'smooth communications' between industry and the ministries or the central bank This crucial phenomenon is called *amakudari*, 'descent from heaven'. A personal acquaintance with government officials and a close familiarity with bureaucratic priorities are almost indispensable in reaching agreement to 'adjust' policy. Thus the *amakudari* bureaucrat surpasses any official channels in his effectiveness in maintaining the flow of information between bureaucracy and enterprises.

In the higher reaches of the System, bureaucrats, former bureaucrats in top business positions, former bureaucrats turned politician and the former bureaucrats or bureaucratised businessmen who head the business federations are as one, as they mingle and busily monitor the economy and maintain social control. One has only to replace the term 'bureaucrat' with 'administrator', and the traditional divisions of the industrialised state disappear almost altogether.

Most post-war business bosses are best characterised as administrators rather than as entrepreneurs. The most powerful one-third of LDP Diet membership consists mostly of former ministry officials, and their methods and attitudes are those of administrators. Japan's top administrators, in whichever formal category they are found, have also been selected by the same filter: the law departments of the former imperial universities, especially the University of Tokyo (more popularly, Todai) and, to a much lesser extent, the University of Kyoto.

A good deal of antagonism exists in the higher reaches of the System, but it rarely, if ever, pits the official organs of state against the industrial organisations. Groups of businessmen side with groups of bureaucrats against other groups in both domains. The rifts run diagonally through the truncated pyramid. Whereas the great rivalries and territorial wars among the different ministries are highly significant, true confrontations between bureaucrats and recalcitrant corporations are rarely heard of (and when they are, are talked about for years after). Only much lower down, among the newer firms and especially the vitally important sector of small subcontracting firms, can one find genuine entrepreneurs.

Harnessed capitalists

Between the small and medium-sized enterprises at the bottom of the industrial hierarchy and the ministerial–corporate top lies the highly disciplined array of firms that has made Japan famous in the post-war world. These 'private' corporations, in the Japanese version of 'capitalism', are only semi-autonomous. Most of the large firms belong – with varying degrees of closeness – to conglomerates, of which there are six colossal ones: Mitsui, Mitsubishi, Sumitomo, Fuyo, Sanwa and Dai-ichi Kangyo Bank.

These conglomerates, known as 'corporate groups' or *gurupu*, contain highly diversified industrial companies that are clustered around their own banks, together with real-estate agencies, insurance firms and the famous trading houses. The entire structure in each case is tied together by interlocking directorates. Between 60 and 70 per cent of all shares outstanding on the Japanese stock exchanges are held by Japanese corporations and financial institutions. They keep these shares within their conglomerate family, in a pattern of reciprocal shareholding. Because the shares are considered to be 'political' shares rather than investment, they are never sold. To keep over half of a company's shares in such cross-holding deals eliminates the possibility of take-overs by outsiders.

No one is in charge of a *gurupu*, and no one is ultimately responsible for it. The *shachokai*, or presidents' council, which meets regularly, is an institution for mutual control, in that the participating presidents of all the major firms in a corporate group attend not as stockholders of their own companies, but as representatives of the stock their company holds in all the other member companies.[21] One of the functions of these meetings is to discuss joint investments and the creation of new sister companies in new industries.

Another popular term for the corporate group is *keiretsu*, but this label was originally used for yet another type of conglomerate in which the members are even more closely related to one another. These are the hierarchically ordered systems of subsidiaries, suppliers, subcontractors and distributors associated with a particular major manufacturer. Each large member of a *gurupu* stands at the apex of a vertical *keiretsu* that may encompass several hundreds of companies. There are also newer and smaller corporate groups that have sprung up around post-war giants that did not belong to one of the six major conglomerates.

The precise organisation and degree of control over members varies from group to group, but the obligation to extend mutual aid and to keep as much business as possible within the group is taken for granted.

The *gurupu* have succeeded the *zaibatsu*, which before 1945 were organised around holding companies and were ordered to disband by the United States occupation authorities. The post-war groups are more effective because the occupation purge provided an opportunity for reorganisation in which much dead wood was eliminated.[22] More important, the substitution of the banks for the old holding companies established a network of financial pumps (their survival guaranteed by the central bank) without which the 'economic miracle' would have been considerably less impressive, or perhaps not have taken place at all. Rather than doing away with the controlled pre-war and wartime industrial system, the occupation actually reinvigorated it.

Japanese industry is even more tightly controlled than the foregoing suggests. Individual members of the corporate groups are also organised by industrial sector in overlapping, guild-like, but again strongly hierarchical structures. Obligatory conformity to unwritten rules limits their policy-making options. The industrial collectivities have nearly complete extra-legal powers to apply sanctions whenever individual members step out of line or do not seem to understand what the others consider good for them. Ultimate sanctions such as enforced bankruptcy are rare, since a slight signal of displeasure is generally heeded.

The awesome combination of intertwined hierarchies nourishes a myriad of subcontractor firms reaching right down to the small sweatshops, at which level one may still find whole families working a ten-hour day. It is at this sub-level of Japan's often discussed 'dual structure' that one is reminded of 'capitalism' in the sense that Westerners use the term. These small enterprises are still run by entrepreneurs who shoulder formidable risks. However, they are dependent on the market only to a limited extent. Their chief function is to provide what amounts to cheap labour for the firms higher up in the hierarchy. Collectively, they serve as a shock-absorbing cushion in periods of economic downturn and help to explain Japan's high bankruptcy rate, since they regularly go under in large numbers, only to reappear in different manufacturing roles.

Mutual restraints

It is impossible, from out of this huge system, to extricate anything that can really be called a state. The existence of a state is implied, of course, whenever Japan passes laws and adopts measures for foreign consumption – when, for instance, the bureaucrats lower tariffs on imports. In practice, though, that means almost nothing. The workings of the System inevitably negate effects that would be normal anywhere else in the industrialised world. The System overrules the state at every turn.

One must be careful at the same time not to see the System as monolithic. This is no oriental despotism in modern guise. The despot is nowhere in sight, nor is there any ever-vigilant Big Brother. Indeed, any component of the System that might aspire to such a role would promptly find the other components lining up against it. The preservation of its own power is the first priority of every System component. This is achieved by ceaseless restraint, mutual scrutiny and interference among the components, preventing any one of them from growing strong enough to dominate the rest. The Japanese know from bitter experience that things can go desperately wrong when, as happened in the 1930s, this balance is upset.

In their dealings with the outside world, the various components of the System strive in more or less the same direction towards the attainment of similar goals. It is this that creates the impression of a gigantic conspiracy at work. Yet domestically they work partly against each other and help to curb each other's power. The elementary flaw in the 'Japan Inc.' metaphor has always been that it evokes images of a smoke-filled boardroom where deals are made and conspiracies are hatched for economic conquest. Were this but true, things would be much easier for foreign governments, since one can at least negotiate with a board of directors.

Their unity of purpose in disseminating a particular world-view and propaganda encouraging the maintenance of existing power relations within the System, as well as defusing the discontent of trade partners, is greatly underrated by Japanese and foreigners alike. On the other hand, their ability in a crisis to sacrifice existing power relations for the sake of a unified policy programme is vastly overrated.

A paralysed superpower

For domestic purposes, this System without a core works reasonably well, even though areas of social malfunction tend to go on malfunctioning for lack of decisive action. Japan trundles along while officials, politicians and businessmen tinker endlessly with minor policy adjustments.

Post-war industrial reconstruction was an obvious priority that did not need to be determined by a strong political centre. In the course of reconstruction, the political assumption naturally emerged that unlimited industrial expansion was the priority for the nation. The bureaucracy took it upon itself to administer this policy to the detriment of other potential areas of concern, and no politician offered any opposition to the designs of the economic administrators. The *de facto* one-party system of Japan guaranteed that there would be no interference from messy parliamentary democratic processes. But it also meant that the politicians abdicated responsibilities that in Western democracies are crucial for major policy adjustments. Basically Japan is still acting in line with policies dating from the 1950s. Strong rivals, each claiming to carry out the 'imperial will', are no longer pulling Japan in different directions as they did in the earlier decades of this century. The problem today is that Japan is dragged too forcefully in one direction, for lack of a mechanism to set new priorities.

The political give-and-take among the System's components interferes with the nation's need to deal with the rest of the world. To take only one example, many if not most Japanese politicians have an unacknowledged stake in what is euphemistically known as *boeki masatsu*, or trade friction. They want to keep it from doing too much damage, and they ask the bureaucrats to take limited 'cosmetic' action. But if the issue disappeared, so would a lucrative source of income, since the sectors of the business community that most fear foreign competition in the home market are also the most generous with 'political donations'.

From an international perspective, the Japanese System in its present shape is an anachronism. It might have fitted a poor and isolated Japan, but it is unsuitable for Japan as an international partner. Its finely meshed all-Japanese components are glaringly deficient in providing the country with an effective means to establish a *modus vivendi* with a potentially very hostile world.

The System presents a variety of apparent paradoxes. It has no strong leadership, yet it creates the impression abroad of a purposeful giant bent on economic conquest of the world. It has no political centre, yet domestically it almost always succeeds in bringing antagonistic groups within its folds. The System is elusive. It eludes the grasp of Westerners who want to deal with it. The Japanese who participate in it cannot get a conceptual grip on it, much less change it. It exists without most of its participants being consciously aware of it; and it has no shape or form, let alone any justification, in law.

3

An Inescapable Embrace

The absence of anyone in charge amidst numerous political forces, each endowed with potentially state-undermining power and concerned with its own interests, does not result in social chaos. So marked, in fact, is the orderliness of life in Japan and the discipline of its people that one is led to suspect the existence of another very potent political force that fosters cohesion.

Japanese are brought up to accept that much of their lives will be managed for them. Their environment does not generally encourage them to 'play things by ear'. Often, activities intended for relaxation and enjoyment are pursued with a display of great discipline. From school parties to cherry-blossom viewing, collective undertakings are almost always preceded by such painstaking preparations, and proceed so predictably, that outsiders have had occasion to remark that all the fun has been organised out of them.

What is true for individual Japanese – that they act as if constantly aware of precisely how much elbow-room they are allotted – is generally true for Japanese organisations too. Sustained opposition to existing socio-political arrangements is rare. To be sure, Japanese institutions strive to increase their prominence, if only as the best guarantee against losing their position in the hierarchy. But except for a small number of very tiny and (significantly) very radical fringe groups, none of them evinces the slightest interest in disturbing the established order.

The absence of political competition

Japan has none of the institutions, such as religions or clan organisations, that in other Asian countries and in the West have supplied an alternative power base from which to challenge the established élite. Thus there is no age-old example of sustained opposition to the political order such as could inspire a labour movement or even such a simple phenomenon as consumer activism. There are interest groups, farmers' co-operatives and workers' unions, but nearly all of them have been absorbed by the System and harnessed to its aims.

Defusing traditional challenges

Japan's power-holders have had many centuries in which to refine their techniques for rendering harmless or absorbing potentially threatening organisations. Their experience here goes back at least to the time when Buddhism first became 'a mere prop to the existing social order and to the traditional value system'.[1] In most other political systems, religions have usually produced the strongest institutions competing for power with temporal rulers. To some extent at least, they have tended to free the individual from the grip of the power-holders.

Thus the Hindu kings, themselves members of the warrior caste, were obliged to keep a wary eye on the priestly caste of Brahmins. The *purohita* (a kind of prime minister) represented this spiritually superior caste, and even when his duties were mainly ceremonial he was expected to have a decisive influence over the opinions of the monarch. In contemporary India religious considerations are still a factor of major and seemingly increasing importance in political life. In Thailand the Buddhist religion is mentioned in the same breath with the monarchy as a basic source of national values. In the Philippines the initiatives of the Catholic bishops, invoking universal principles, were crucial to the ousting of President Marcos in 1986.[2] The governments of Indonesia and Malaysia cannot afford to risk the grave displeasure of their Islamic leaders, because these are backed in turn by the power of Muslim fundamentalism. Organised opposition to the South Korean government is largely rooted in the expanding Catholic and Protestant churches of that country. And modern political systems in which sovereignty resides with the people – the model Japan formally subscribes to – derive, of course, from a fundamental European assumption of the separation of church and state, which for centuries has supplied a theme of political commentary.[3]

In China, where religious competition with worldly authority was weak at best, the highly centralised administrative system faced another kind of challenge. The state consisted of a massive bureaucracy run by mandarins, with an emperor at its centre and radiating outward from the capital. But alongside that authority there existed an entirely different social organisa-tion: the family clans and the local gentry who represented the apex of the regional family power structure. The tension between these two systems was always a potential source of conflict.

In Japan the social and political hierarchies were congruent, not separate. Whereas in China it was the blood-tie that determined member-ship in the family – filial piety, the supreme injunction of Confucianist morality, overriding even political loyalty to emperor or state – the Japanese household, or *ie*, had a political significance. The underlying criterion for membership was a shared task; its members were not necessarily blood relations, and succession to the headship was often arranged through adoption. Significantly, the Tokugawa regime singled out the *ie* as the basic building block of its political system. It became, in effect, a corporation whose members lacked the right to own property and were obliged to submit to the formally recognised power exercised over them by its head. In such ways the traditional household, which in China could exist in opposition to the state, was in Japan absorbed by the body politic. We will examine this crucial development more closely in Chapter 6.

Neutralising citizen movements

Would-be opponents to the Japanese political status quo face barriers that, being both flexible and intangible, are all but impregnable. Power in Japan is so diffuse that it eludes confrontation. The individual components of the System manage by peaceful means to bring within their fold all major and most minor social elements that they come up against. Any antagonist, real or potential, is either rapidly rendered harmless and forgotten or, if its size or capacity to make noise precludes ignoring it, assimilated quite naturally as a functioning part of the System.

Take, for instance, the consumer movement. Middle-class Japanese housewives are a potentially important political presence. Finding themselves with increasing leisure, they have developed an enthusiasm for neighbourhood causes, and hardly a neighbourhood today is without its *fujinkai*, or women's group. The Japanese housewives' association, Shufuren, was one of the earliest pressure groups, established in 1948 mainly to counter post-war black marketeering. In the late 1960s and early 1970s it joined Chifuren (an umbrella organisation of a multitude of *fujinkai*) in spearheading consumer campaigns that gave the impression of a new kind of political activism. But after some minor successes, such as a regulation making it mandatory for manufacturers of canned fruit-juice to indicate the percentage of genuine fruit juice, and a lowering of prices on colour TV sets, its activism was effectively blunted.

The System – ubiquitous, intangible, enveloping, absorptive – had seen a threat and neutralised it. In 1975 top representatives of the business world produced a 250-page report for the ministries and businessmen concerned, in which they concluded that 'the citizens' movements should be highly valued as new sources of energy in the operation of the economic community, and should be considered, if possible, in the planning and drafting of policies', but 'in case the voltage of energy unleashed by the movements rises high and begins to flow recklessly, it should be curbed. The government authorities need to display a firm attitude in the face of action that will disturb the legal order.'[4]

The administrators have managed to reduce the 'voltage of energy' to a very low level indeed. Even though in the late 1980s the number of consumer groups is estimated at almost thirteen thousand, and though

Chifuren claims a combined membership of more than six million housewives, their existence is hardly ever noticed. This is remarkable, given the wealth of justifications for agitation afforded by the excessive mark-ups on most items (particularly food) and the prevalence of racketeering. Especially remarkable is the silence surrounding the fact that the spectacular rise in value of the Japanese currency (roughly double against the dollar in the period 1985–7) is reflected in the price of very few important consumer goods and no domestic products, while some prices have actually been raised in view of the allegedly 'uncertain situation'.

The officials who in the 1970s made a brief show of considering citizens' opinions in their administrative decisions no longer feel any urgent need to placate consumer groups. Some municipalities have given these a token 'voice in policy-making', thus defusing their combative spirit. The Consumers' Union of Japan, the umbrella organisation under the presidency of Takeuchi Naokazu, now fights *against* the removal of import restrictions on agricultural products, and *against* the adjustment of product standards to facilitate the import of foreign consumer goods. In other words, the most significant element in the consumer movement is zealously working to keep food prices high and to limit consumer choice to domestic produce.

No mysterious process of indirect promotion of consumer interests is at work here, but rather the power of the organisation's president. Takeuchi is a former top-ranking official of the Ministry of Agriculture, Forestry and Fisheries. Although he left his ministry in a disagreement over the use of pesticides, and cannot thus be called a genuine *amakudari*, it is inconceivable that he would work against the interests of his former colleagues in this most protectionist-minded segment of Japan's officialdom.

Pressure groups

A popular theory about how government policies develop holds that 'interest groups' or 'pressure groups' manage to 'capture', as it were, the segment of the public service whose co-operation they need. One Japanese group that, quite exceptionally, has done exactly this is the Japan Medical Association (JMA), which since the 1950s has won great prominence among Japan's pressure groups by functioning as such groups are expected to function outside Japan – only more so. Unlike most of its fellows, it has tended to confront the bureaucrats rather than accommodate them in exchange for favours.[5]

Led until 1982 by a forceful personality, Takemi Taro, it created an obedient rank and file while using aggressive methods such as lambasting the government in full-page newspaper advertisements in order to dominate decision-making concerning medical matters. It has had a major voice in banning oral contraceptives, thus preventing any decline in the lucrative abortion industry.[6] It has run its own candidates in national elections, and bankrolls a number of regular LDP candidates.

The JMA can stop the import of particular medical equipment, if this threatens to eliminate the need for lucrative cures; it can, on arbitrary grounds, prevent the use of medicines and methods of treatment; and it protects the widespread racketeering made possible by the health insurance system. Not only is the income of Japanese doctors from the health insurance scheme calculated partly by the quantity of medicine they prescribe, but they themselves have the right to sell this medicine in their offices. This has led to corrupt relations with the pharmaceutical industry, to an alarming degree of over-medication and to some very rich doctors.

Since the departure of Takemi Taro, the power of the JMA has declined, but it is one of the minor components of the System. Health and Welfare Ministry officials have become so used to bowing to the wishes of the association that the laws they draft still seem to have been formulated by the doctors themselves.[7] It is significant that the one major exception among Japanese pressure groups, functioning the way Westerners expect pressure groups to function, should do this in an extreme fashion. The practitioners of medicine have taken over the very area of government that ought to be controlling them in order to safeguard medicine as a public service.

Post-war society saw a mushrooming of pressure groups: of housewives, families of the war dead, veterans, wounded veterans, former landlords (who lost their property in post-war land reform), returnees from former colonies and brothel owners – to mention only the best known. They became a familiar subject of newspaper comment in the mid-1950s, especially after brothel owners formed the All-Japan Association for Prevention of Venereal Diseases in an attempt to block passage of the Anti-Prostitution Law (they failed, so that roughly half a million ladies of the night had to find new descriptions for their profession). A very successful pressure group, drawing press attention, was Chuseiren, later to become the main federation of small and medium-sized companies.[8]

These new actors on the political stage caused mixed feelings. In 1958 two veterans' groups succeeded in having the budget for war pensions increased by 30 billion yen, while the JMA managed to reserve an extra 21 billion yen.[9] Japanese political commentators and editorial opinion interpreted such things as undermining the democratic political process; the pressure groups were accused of lack of concern for the general welfare, and of selfishly pushing measures from which only they would benefit.[10] Ironically enough, at the very time in the 1960s when Japanese were seeing the pressure groups as undemocratic, Western observers were citing them as the best proof that 'democracy' was finally gaining a foothold in Japan. Even in the 1980s they are still seen as a force for greater pluralism.

A closer look reveals that it is a rather odd kind of pluralism they serve. With the exception of the doctors, the 'capturing' in Japan takes place largely in the wrong direction, with officials and the LDP making use of the groups in exchange for certain subsidies and a minimal degree of accommodation. When all groups that have close organisational ties with the administrators are eliminated, the category of genuine pressure groups is very small. It diminishes still further if one excludes those with semi-official ties to other major components of the System. Finally, one is left with a core of groups the majority of which have one leg in the camp of the openly anti-System activists and occasionally battle with riot police to demonstrate the fact that they will not be bought and cannot be incorporated in any way. The farmer–radical-activist coalition which continues to block expansion of the new Tokyo International Airport at Narita is a prime example.

Pollution activists

Among the post-war pressure groups that have stayed outside the System, the most successful – measured by the extent to which the System has had to accommodate them – are those that have fought on behalf of the victims of industrial poisoning. Even so, it took some ten years before pollution problems received serious consideration in Japan. Only when cats that had eaten mercury-laden fish began to have spasms and jump into the sea did the problems of Minamata (the municipality that was later to become a symbol of environmental pollution the world over) first attract some limited attention from the press. Several years more passed before the plight of the human victims became a national issue. They had been rapidly increasing in number, dying sometimes of sheer exhaustion as a result of the spasms caused by their injured nervous systems.

The corporation responsible for dumping mercury waste into the sea maintained that there was no connection, and hired gangsters to man-handle petitioning victims and their families.[11] The victims themselves, mainly from poor villages, were ostracised. The bringers of bad tidings – doctors who were studying the Minamata cases and similar mercury-poisoning cases in Niigata – were at first discredited. The Kumamoto University research team saw their findings suppressed and research money cut off. A campaign was waged against a certain Dr Hagino Noboru who was treating patients in Toyama prefecture for the so-called *itai-itai* ('ouch, ouch') disease, a mysterious affliction in which bones became so brittle, owing to cadmium that had been allowed to seep into rice paddies, that they fractured at many places. The suppression of evidence and the hiring of doctors to claim lack of scientific grounds for the complaints were repeated in other parts of Japan until riots, the storming of the factory responsible for the mercury waste in Minamata, a national press campaign and foreign publicity finally made such approaches untenable.

The first lawsuit on behalf of pollution victims, filed in 1967 by leftist lawyers, was quickly followed by three more. In the early 1970s, prodded by this legal action and popular discontent with the badly polluted air of the capital region, officialdom, together with some politicians and businessmen, concluded that some measures had become inevitable.

Strict industrial regulations were introduced; overnight, it became fashionable to decry industrial expansion achieved at the expense of the living environment. Courts of justice, too, though they took ten or more years to conclude trials, were beginning to award damages to victims. But experience in most cases showed the judiciary playing only a subsidiary role; the System had responded to pressure caused by an outcry greatly amplified by the press. Its response was evidence that it can be moved to right wrongs, provided the wrongs are sufficiently eye-catching and can awaken widespread public indignation.

In the late 1970s the anti-pollution campaign seemed to portend a new kind of opposition to the way Japan was being managed, and citizens' movements were thought to have created permanent changes by stimulating political awareness on the regional level. Opposition mayors were elected. But in the meantime oppositionist policy programmes were adopted by LDP-run municipalities. In LDP eyes, the opposition had been absorbed.[12] By the mid-1980s the activist groups were comparing themselves to 'wind-chimes in winter' – an allusion to the small bells hung outside windows in summer, whose tinkling, thought refreshing at the time, becomes irritatingly irrelevant in winter. The number of cities with opposition mayors declined from 136 in 1974 to 60 in 1988.[13] Hasty anti-pollution measures, an adjustment of election rhetoric by local LDP candidates and a reconfirmation of the LDP as the sole fount of plenty with regard to costly projects had brought to an effective halt grass-roots opposition to the status quo.

Pressure groups as election campaign staff

While the consumer and anti-pollution activists have gradually faded out of the political picture, other types of pressure group have remained politically important, not because of any changes in the political process achieved by their 'pressure', but for the work they do on behalf of LDP politicians.

Since the government party has almost no grass-roots organisation, candidates for parliamentary elections must rely on personal organisations of supporters, known as koenkai. In most cases the chances of an incumbent staying in parliament relate first and foremost to the membership and influence of the koenkai that he keeps going between elections. And almost from the moment that pressure groups made their appearance it was clear that they would, if properly treated, make ideal koenkai. Thus it comes about that pressure groups are right up front in Japanese political life, canvassing votes, collecting funds and performing all manner of odd jobs for individual LDP candidates.

For the LDP parliamentarian friendly connections with various ministerial bureaux are crucial in achieving such a relationship with a pressure group, since the politician must prove, by at least token measures, that he is doing something in return. In speaking to his constituents the incumbent rarely beats around the bush. Should they want a new airport, they are assured that he has the best entrée, or *paipu* (from the English word 'pipe'), to the Transport Ministry and the Finance Ministry; if wider roads are needed, or a new bridge, then he has more friends at the Ministry of Construction than any other candidates. In the multi-member constituency, the LDP politician compares his access to bureaucrats with that of his fellow LDP members; and everyone understands that the minority parties do not have a *paipu* into the ministries.

The party 'colleagues' against whom an LDP candidate fights in parliamentary elections almost always belong to different LDP *habatsu* (cliques). Thus it is important for *habatsu* leaders to cultivate good relations with national umbrella organisations controlling local pressure and petition groups. This is why the veterans' organisations, the association of war wounded and the organisation of the families of war dead continue to be a significant force pressuring the LDP to endorse and participate in controversial symbolic activities extolling the military past.[14] A politician whom I accompanied on his initial round of a hamlet recently added to his constituency made a special point of first seeking out the house of a man without legs – the local representative of the association of war wounded.

Bureaucratic extensions

Many pressure groups will start by going directly to the officials whose co-operation they need for their original purposes. Relatively weak regional industrial and trade associations have used the bureaucracy 'to help them strengthen their organisational foundations through government legislation legalising their status and providing for compulsory membership'.[15] Pressure groups, established to promote specific agricultural or other economic interests, will find open doors at the ministries that must deal with those interests. If a group appears large and potentially powerful enough, it will be actively courted by the officials. In return for having its wishes taken into account it provides detailed information about conditions, personalities and important events in its locality. It thus becomes part of the 'radar' whereby the bureaucrats effectively steer the System as a whole. Since the information moves in only one direction, towards Tokyo, the administrators gain firmer control over segments of Japanese life that have hitherto been less effectively incorporated in the System. And this increased control is often exercised through the pressure groups in question.

Regional pressure groups usually continue to exist after the original reason for their creation has been lost sight of. Often, their activities and purposes become diffuse and vague, significant primarily in providing a focus of loyalty for people who do not belong to large companies yet feel the need for social immersion. Once the interest groups attach themselves to politicians, as almost all do outside the large cities, their primary function is simply to organise election campaigns. At this point, the original movers may become disaffected, but they will lose their influence; nor will appeals to 'fundamental principles' be understood. Even though these original activists may want more than the group is getting out of the cosy relationship with officialdom, the rank and file 'consider it prudent or even inevitable to depend upon or adjust themselves to the existing mechanism', since disturbing the established reward-allocation mechanism implies ingratitude and can be risky.[16] Control of a pressure group caught up in the embrace of the System tends to pass to leaders who use it for their own purposes. The group nevertheless can continue to command far-reaching loyalty.[17] Loyalty becomes an end in itself; if there are hints of conflict in the group, the notion that solidarity should come first can easily be implanted by bureaucrats and politicians. It is often even possible for the representatives of the System to help bring about a change of leadership.

If the pressure groups, or the industrial and trade associations, are important enough they are likely to pass into the hands of former bureaucrats who are parachuted into top positions of the organisation. In such cases, the pressure groups often become stepping-stones to a political career for the former official.[18] The fact that many LDP Diet members were once bureaucrats should make it clear just how cosy negotiations among pressure-group executives, bureaucrats and politicians generally are.

The System undermines potential opposition, or buys acquiescence, at considerable cost to governmental flexibility. Ministries become intensely involved with the groups they must control, and show signs of identification with the groups' goals. That is why, for instance, the Agriculture Ministry remains an immovable obstacle to the liberalisation of food imports – something that other System components believe is necessary, and which would serve the entire System well as a hedge against foreign trade-related retaliation. Thus the impulse of the System to maintain itself by absorbing antagonistic and potentially hostile groups leads, ironically, to its own partial paralysis.

The pressure groups are, wherever possible, also used by government agencies in their disputes and power struggles with other government agencies and components of the System. At one point during a campaign to open segments of the market inhospitable to imports, the then prime minister Nakasone received thousands of telegrams and postcards urging him not to take any drastic steps. Since the wording of these entreaties was remarkably similar, it was understood that they all came from a limited number of agricultural associations and industrial interest groups. At a subsequent cabinet meeting Nakasone angrily reminded his ministers that it was hardly the proper task of their departments to ask industry to start a protest movement.

New pressure or petition groups are constantly being formed, and sometimes they become the means by which certain claims of the public are brought to bear on the System. Elastic as the System is, it accommodates these groups to some extent. But it will not allow an essential change in the status quo or genuine sustained opposition.

Creating your own 'opposition'

A well-tested ploy used by components of the System to defuse problems before they grow out of hand, or to expand control over an area which still eludes their grasp, is to establish their own 'opposition' group. The alternative unions created by management in the 1950s and 1960s to suck in members of the potentially threatening Marxist-inspired national unions are a celebrated example of this strategy. Similarly, the Nosei Suishin Kyogikai (discussion group for the promotion of agricultural policy), which played a pivotal role in co-ordinating rural pressure groups in the 1960s, was in fact the brain-child of Agriculture Ministry officials seeking to strengthen control over their parish and to increase their own bargaining power with the Finance Ministry in the budgeting season.[19]

The emergence of a new house-trained opposition group proved most helpful to the LDP when it suffered from criticism and voter disaffection because of bribery scandals and a temporary wave of press indignation. In 1976 six LDP members, led by the son of one of the LDP's great post-war bosses, Kono Yohei, left the party, ostensibly to set up an opposition party, the New Liberal Club. The NLC made occasional opposition-like noises and advocated clean politics, thus enabling some disgruntled voters to quieten their consciences yet still stick with the LDP. For in effect the NLC was an LDP *habatsu* outside the LDP, voting with the LDP on any issue that came along. This meant that the LDP did not have to worry about losing its formal parliamentary majority. After the elections of December 1983, when the LDP suffered a record loss of seats (although not of the popular vote), Prime Minister Nakasone asked the NLC to join the cabinet and gave it the portfolio of the Ministry of Home Affairs. Many Japanese and foreign journalists, forever on the look-out for momentous, trend-setting events, concluded that the long-awaited era of 'coalition government' had arrived.

It was not to be. Two and a half years later, when the LDP gained a record number of seats and seemed to have no further use for the NLC, the 'opposition' party was quietly disbanded, and its Diet members slipped back into the ranks of the LDP as smoothly as they had left it ten years before. As Japan's largest daily, the *Yomiuri Shimbun*, said in an editorial:

> The NLC absorbed the urban votes which the LDP lost as a result of the Lockheed scandal and developed new conservative votes. In a period of the near balance of power in the Diet between the LDP and

the opposition parties, the NLC supported the ruling party and thus contributed to political stability.[20]

The System at work in rural Japan

It is generally recognised that farmers in Japan, as in many industrially advanced countries, are politically pampered. Japanese agriculture is so heavily protected that rice is at least five times as expensive as in other rice-producing areas of the world. Indeed, the Japanese consumer pays exorbitant prices for most agricultural produce.

Yet again the situation is not as straightforward as it seems. The protection of Japanese agriculture does not necessarily benefit the rural population in general or even the small group of producers. Farm production is highly inefficient. And it is kept inefficient because the purposes of a giant organisation with virtual control over practically all agricultural endeavour are well served thereby. This organisation, which is generally referred to as the *nokyo*,[21] is an indispensable element in the System, one without which the present order could hardly have survived the post-war decades. The *nokyo* forestalls potential political action by the farmers. It helps guarantee the LDP's unchallenged parliamentary majority and, in turn, the undisturbed exercise of power by Japan's administrators.

The term *nokyo* is all but synonymous with 'Japanese agriculture'. It refers to the central federation of agricultural co-operatives, together with its subsidiary companies, sister organisations and specialised federations, as well as the local co-operative offices. Collectively, these organisations are usually viewed as a pressure group representing Japan's 6·3 million farmers.[22] But this is an excellent example of the misapplication of terminology that commonly obfuscates the role of Japanese institutions. It is not even that the element of potential opposition inherent in interest groups has been lost in the *nokyo*; it has never been present.

Even though it consists of non-profit organisations that draw government subsidies, the *nokyo* conglomeration is best compared to a *keiretsu* (the groups of corporations tied together by interlocking directorates and mutual shareholding, discussed in Chapter 2). The farmers form an almost completely captive market for this agricultural *keiretsu*, in that they have little choice except to avail themselves of its services, which range from marketing produce and supplying seed and fertiliser to banking, insurance and organising wedding ceremonies.

The *nokyo* may also be seen as a 'supplementary organ' to the agricultural bureaucracy.[23] Also, one of its major functions is to help elect LDP politicians – an activity that is clearly outside the bounds of its legal tasks, since as a federation of subsidised organisations the *nokyo* is supposedly non-partisan.

Controlling the villagers

To appreciate just how much the *nokyo* does for the System, one must take account of how limited the control of Japanese central governments over the countryside has traditionally been. For centuries the villages were virtually autonomous in regard to maintenance of internal order. For the majority of them, the 'joint control system' of the Tokugawa shogunate existed only on paper. There was much regional variation, but in many places the political patterns that developed through village self-rule formed a fairly effective shield against central administrative authority.

To break through this shield, the Meiji state established a variety of nation-wide organisations, but it never succeeded completely. Another channel through which Tokyo attempted to instil proper patriotic behaviour was the local landlords, who personally stood to gain by village compliance. Again, the powerful pre-war Naimusho could punish recalcitrant villages by depriving them of such necessities as repairs to their river banks after a typhoon.[24] Even so, village tradition continued in many places to spawn independent attitudes. Under such circumstances the agricultural co-operatives organised around the turn of the century were naturally seized upon by the government and the landlords as yet another channel through which to control the farming population. As late as 1924, however, less than half the farms had joined the local co-operatives, which were grouped in about two hundred federations. Rural recalcitrance was finally overcome when in 1943 all co-operatives were placed under central control and the prefectural federations dissolved. The Imperial Agricultural Association, or Nogyokai, was born as part of the effort to bind tightly together as many organisations as possible for the sake of the war effort; membership was no longer a matter of choice.

In contemporary Japan, the hold exerted by the Tokyo authorities on rural communities via their law-enforcement personnel has remained fairly tenuous. The policemen who serve two or three years in the hamlets and villages drink sake with the local inhabitants and are given seats of honour at communal events; they are great sources of information and advice for the villagers, but they remain outsiders. The construction industry provides another important instrument of control, but rural Japan is most effectively made to serve the System – and the LDP in particular – through the agricultural co-operatives that were in fact inherited from the wartime system.

The centralised Imperial Agricultural Association provided the infrastructure for the post-war *nokyo* system. Its offices, equipment and employees, and most of its roles, were simply taken over by the ostensibly new organisations set up with the encouragement of the United States occupation.[25] Since nearly all Japanese farmers are dependent on its services, the post-war system also inherited the total, or near-total, organisation rate.

The government's food control system, which contributes to extraordinary high prices for Japanese agricultural products, is inextricably inter-twined with *nokyo* interests. Equally important to the *nokyo* are the agricultural protectionist barriers that constitute a major bone of conten-tion with the US government. For this reason Japan's 'overprotected agriculture', and by implication the *nokyo* system, has been under attack since the late 1970s from the business world and the bureaucrats of the Ministry of International Trade and Industry, who hope to shift inter-national criticism away from themselves. Yet these rival sides within the System have stopped short of publicly analysing the true problem. It was pointed out by Japanese specialists as early as the 1960s that the *nokyo* could not be said to represent the farmers. The prefectural federations behave like subcontractors of the central *nokyo* institutions, and the promotion of the interests of the upper-level organisations sometimes causes considerable friction between them and the local *nokyo* 'chap-ters'.[26] The combined interests of the *nokyo* and the Ministry of Agri-culture form a greater obstacle to agricultural liberalisation than the farmers' interests.

A symbiotic conglomerate

By whole-heartedly embracing their role as 'subsidiaries' of the Ministry of Agriculture, the *nokyo* organisations have found a way to survive. The farmers themselves are by and large ambivalent towards the system they have been roped into, especially in view of the failure of government plans to modernise agriculture, for which *nokyo* practices are blamed.[27] Very few Japanese farmers can make ends meet by farming. More than four-fifths of all farming households have supplementary income from other work – usually with small factories, trucking companies or service establishments in the nearest town. In over 85 per cent of the households, earnings from this so-called part-time work are greater than from farm produce. But because Zenkoku Nokyo Chuokai (better known as Zenchu), the general headquarters of the *nokyo* conglomeration, is very vociferous every year when officials are deliberating the artificially high price of rice, Japanese and foreigners alike receive the impression that Japanese farmers are very powerful and can make the government dance to their tune. In fact, the real power is the *nokyo*–Agriculture Ministry combination. No other ministry has a force of such guaranteed impact to back it up in dealing with the Ministry of Finance. Its budget proposals are sacred cows. And no other business enterprises have as much freedom from regulation as those guided and co-ordinated by Zenchu.

The government's payment for nearly the entire rice harvest goes straight to the Norin Chukin (Central Bank for Agriculture and Forestry), whence it 'circulates in all the sections of the *nokyo* organisation like blood, supplying nourishment to each segment'.[28] The Norin Chukin transfers the government's rice money, via the prefectural Shinyo Nokyo Rengokai (*nokyo* credit federation), to the savings accounts of the individual households that contributed to the sale. This automatic transfer means that the cost to the *nokyo* banking organisation is a fraction of that at ordinary commercial banks. The same money flows back and forth within the *nokyo* family of corporations, in the form of loans to the rural population through credit facilities, and as payment for all manner of services. The central *nokyo* bank reserves roughly half of the amount for outside investment. When a general meeting of *nokyo* members endorses a nation-wide campaign, headquarters may automatically deduct contributions from all savings accounts. This makes possible the copious propaganda for *nokyo* interests at home and abroad, not to mention ritualised petition activities directed, on a scale that no other group can match, at the Finance Ministry and the LDP.

The more than ten thousand local *nokyo* units in towns and villages all over the country buy farm products (other than rice) and market them through the *nokyo* trading companies on a higher level. On top of this they sell the rural population practically everything it needs for farming, and much else besides. The totality represents an almost perfect model of a captive market, given the savings accounts already in *nokyo* hands. The subsidiaries also provide health and welfare facilities, credit, storage and warehousing, guidance and instruction. One of their most interesting ventures is a 'mutual aid' business which has grown into the largest insurance operation in the world.

When the relevant laws were first drawn up, the US occupation initially insisted that the insurance activities of the *nokyo* be placed under the supervision of the Ministry of Finance. However, agriculture officials argued convincingly that the *nokyo* did not intend an actual insurance system, but a system based on the custom of Japanese farmers helping each other in times of disaster. Little did the finance bureaucrats and the insurance corporations suspect that by the beginning of the 1980s the assets of the *nokyo*'s 'mutual aid' business would reach more than 4·9 trillion yen – a great deal more than the total assets of the world's largest commercial life insurance company, Japan's Nihon Seimei, and five times the assets of Tokyo Marine Fire Insurance, the largest property insurance company in the country. Every grass-roots *nokyo* unit is an insurance outlet. Since this operation is classified, along with its other centrally organised businesses, as a species of non-profit organisation, the *nokyo* is allowed, unlike the 'commercial' companies, to sell both life insurance and property insurance. All in all, probably no other Japanese industrial conglomeration has been as spectacularly successful.

The rural voting machine

Come election time and the *nokyo*'s insurance salesmen, orange buyers and seed suppliers are transformed into enthusiastic campaign staff for the local LDP candidate – at least, in theory. Although the *nokyo* units derive their power from the assumption that they form an unbeatable voting machine, one which must remain tied to the LDP, their electoral effectiveness in fact varies greatly from place to place. On the whole the LDP's dependence on the farm vote is on the decline, but in the late 1980s there were still eleven out of forty-six prefectures with more than 30 per cent of their households classified as farmers, and nineteen prefectures with more than 20 per cent such households. When the General Agreement on Tariffs and Trade (GATT) ordered Japan to liberalise imports of twelve agricultural products in 1987, as many as 359 out of the 445 LDP Diet members signed a declaration opposing compliance with the ruling of that international body. Irritated local *nokyo* units have been known to work, very occasionally, for an opposition candidate. But even though farmers of a different political persuasion do, of course, belong to the *nokyo*, it is agreed that the organisation as such has no choice but to stick with the LDP.

This still leaves room for choice among LDP candidates competing with each other in the multiple-seat constituencies. If a regional *nokyo* sets its mind to serious electioneering, it can muster a tremendous force to oppose LDP headquarters' intentions, as a case in Miyazaki prefecture demonstrated. Angered by the choice of candidate made by party officials in Tokyo, the *nokyo* organisation decided to back an alternative LDP politician. During the election campaign between four and five thousand *nokyo* personnel and farmers assisted him every day. A rally at which the original candidate planned to draw two thousand voters was countered on the same day by a rally attended by ten thousand brought together by *nokyo* chartered buses. *Nokyo* teams campaigned in all the shops, and in the final stage wives and teen-aged children joined a campaign staff which had grown to sixty thousand workers.[29]

The *nokyo* of Miyazaki prefecture, which is known as a fairly active voting machine, normally supplies some three thousand campaign workers free of charge. Shortly before elections are announced, meetings of the area groups are organised. Specialist groups such as the pig-raisers or mandarin orange growers, organised under another *nokyo* sub-umbrella, will also meet around this time. The strict election law forbids open electioneering, so at such meetings a 'report' is presented telling who the *nokyo* has decided to support. To get around legal stipulations, the candidate himself holds 'study meetings' reporting on his initiatives in Tokyo. As election time approaches *nokyo* salesmen pay extra visits to the farmers. Though door-to-door soliciting of votes is strictly forbidden, even during the official campaign season, it is easy to find a pretext – a new kind of insurance, a *nokyo* publication – for referring obliquely to the chosen candidate. Each house is visited at least twice during the campaign. The *nokyo* unit's office telephones members and urges them to come to meetings which they know to be election rallies and to which the *nokyo* also arranges transportation. Out of a sense of indebtedness to local *nokyo* officials, farmers rarely refuse to attend.

For more straightforward campaigning, the *nokyo* village units function not as *nokyo* sub-units but as branches of the Miyazaki Farmers' Federation. Unlike the *nokyo*, this federation is not politically restricted, but it conveniently happens that the chief of the one organisation is simultaneously the chief of the other, and that the offices of both occupy the same space.

Staff members of *nokyo* units are free to recommend anybody they choose, until the time when the organisation decides who to recommend. After that, they must stick to speaking on behalf of the chosen candidate. A staff member who complains about this task (because of personal support for the JSP, for instance) will be reprimanded by higher officials and risks demotion if he or she fails to follow the 'informal' *nokyo* guidelines.[30]

Controlling the workers

Japan's post-war economic system as we know it would not have been possible if a labour movement antagonistic to the purposes of the industrial conglomerates had been allowed to organise the workers. Contrary to widespread belief, this could conceivably have happened. The harmonious relationship between management and labour that is one of the most familiar aspects of modern Japan did not spring into being spontaneously. Quite a few unions had to be busted before 'harmony' was established. In fact, no other major element of Japanese society has been so forcibly adjusted to the System as the post-war labour movement.

In neutralising a genuine threat from labour in the 1950s, the System was aided by a quarter-century of administrative experience in coping with leftist activism; by the ideological rigidity of the 'left' itself; and by an early shift in the priorities of the US occupation.

Suppressing the pre-war labour movement

The first Japanese labour unions were organised around the turn of the century by intellectuals acquainted with European socialist thought. They were immediately legislated virtually out of existence.[31] But this did not forestall the bitter labour disputes that occurred after the Russo–Japanese War (1904–5), or the occurrence of considerable labour unrest in the 1920s.

The picture of a government relentlessly conspiring with big business to exploit the workers would not be altogether accurate. Indeed, the 'labour bureaucrats' (operating out of the Naimusho) actually initiated legislation to improve working conditions, for they were interested in minimising unrest engendered by exploitation, as well as in keeping the workforce healthy.[32] They even exerted themselves (unsuccessfully) on behalf of a trade union law. It appears that their somewhat protective attitude towards the workers was also intended to restrain the power of the *zaibatsu*.

Even so, the only union federation permitted to exist was Sodomei, which timorously steered away from any confrontation. At its pre-war peak, membership in the unions accounted for less than 8 per cent of the workforce.[33] Yet even this seemed bad enough to Japan's administrators, especially when the labour movement became more strongly inspired by Marxism. From the early 1930s onwards the fight against the unions, as hotbeds of 'dangerous thoughts' that would undermine the purposes of the nation, was relentless. By then the effort to suppress worker interests undoubtedly had the blessing of the government.

The legacy of the wartime enterprise union

The ultimate solution for ensuring administrative control over Japan's labour movement was discovered as a result of heightened wartime production pressures. In the 1920s some firms had begun to pretend that they were large substitute families for their workers. Understanding the advantages of this for social control, the Naimusho promoted on a national scale the company-as-family idea, which dovetailed nicely with ideas of Japan as a family state. Between 1938 and 1940 'councils' of workers and management were set up to spread enthusiasm for the war effort. They also ameliorated unhealthy conditions to some extent, and established minimum benefits for the workers.

By the end of 1938 local police and companies had organised more than nineteen thousand of such councils – 'patriotic industrial associations' or Sangyo Hokokukai – with three million members.[34] By the end of 1940, some two-thirds of the industrial labour force belonged to 60,495 units under centralised leadership.[35] All enterprises were ordered to co-operate; the reluctant among them faced unbending Naimusho bureaucrats who could call upon the police (supervised by the same ministry) to enforce their scheme. The above-ground unions had melted into this organisation by about 1941, much as the political parties and youth organisations were to dissolve into the Imperial Rule Assistance Association.[36]

In retrospect, the success of the Sangyo Hokokukai movement deserves to be considered one of the milestones of Japanese economic history. The generally accepted culturalist explanation of worker attitudes holds that enterprise unions are a result of a 'natural' Japanese inclination to identify with the interests of one's superior. This interpretation overlooks the fact that Japan's post-war labour unions were formed (and have continued up to the present) as enterprise rather than trade unions largely because the wartime associations 'simply shed their old skins and continued their existence after the war ended'.[37] Under the influence of the Sangyo Hokokukai the understanding, already gradually emerging, that workers should not move to other enterprises had suddenly been turned into a command. And, although many circumstances were different in the post-war period, this understanding, rooted by now in years of enforced habits, remained: employees should be loyal to their firm, do their utmost to increase production and not change jobs in mid-career.

Crushing the mushrooms

The Sangyo Hokokukai reorganisation of labour was to a large extent inspired by the example of Nazi Germany and Mussolini's Italy. In fact, the movement's most direct inspiration was a proposal adopted by the Naimusho that was 'a thinly veiled version of the Nazi labor program'.[38] These pre-war European fascist ideas still survive in Japanese labour–management relations today, yet immediately after the war Japan saw the fastest spread in history of unionism of a predominantly Marxist hue. Thanks to the encouragement of General MacArthur's occupation staff, three million workers were unionised within one year, and ten years later there were six million members. Nor were all of these unions patriotic association chapters in a new guise. The occupation had freed communists and left-wing socialists from jail, so that in the immediate post-war years Japan had no dearth of serious labour organisers. Within a year of Japan's surrender the moderate pre-war Sodomei was resurrected. Around the same time communists, who had gained the upper hand in staging radical disputes, organised Sanbetsu Kaigi, which drew twice as many members (1·6 million).

From the end of October to the beginning of December 1945 workers on the *Yomiuri* newspaper took over their company in an attempt to manage it themselves. Other bitter labour disputes followed. They included a 195-day strike at the Toho film company in 1948, a 56-day strike by the Toshiba unions, power industry strikes in 1946 and 1952, a postal workers' strike in 1947, a 63-day strike by coal-miners and steel workers' strikes in 1954. The number of worker hours lost by strikes in those days was comparable to that in the USA and Europe. Most famous of all was the move to hold a general strike in February 1947. Fearing that such a strike might get out of control and exacerbate the dismal economic state of the country, General MacArthur prohibited it, whereupon the labour movement's euphoria evaporated.

Shortly afterwards new laws forbade government employees to strike at any time.[39] And a subsequent shift in attitudes on a variety of politically significant matters showed that United States priorities had changed, giving the signal to the pre-war labour bureaucrats (who had remained in office) that they could begin to rein in the union movement. In this, the 'Red Purge' of 1949 whereby communists and left-wing socialists were removed from official positions, together with the return of pre-war and wartime officials following their 'depurging' in 1950, helped supply the necessary climate and bureaucratic personnel.

From a concentrated campaign to 'democratise' Japan by purging it of its pre-war and wartime leadership, US aims had shifted, with the revolution in China and the Korean War, to building a bulwark in the Pacific against

Asian communism. Thus the early post-war communist-guided labour movement, which had been encouraged by the US occupation, was deliberately crushed in the 1950s with US consent.

Some companies brought in gangsters to break up strikes. Nikkeiren, the Japanese federation of employers' organisations, was formed by business bureaucrats formerly in the forefront of wartime industrial organisations, for the specific purpose of combating the labour movement. A preferred tactic of companies with troublesome unions was to establish a moderate rival union. Within a short time this alternative union would generally attract many more members than the activist union, since employees soon realised that not to co-operate would block their promotion prospects.

In large corporations one may still find remnants of the more radical unions. Generally, however, management is happy enough to let them survive, since they provide a wonderful means for the more frustrated employees to let off steam. Whenever these radical unions go into action – usually concerning the size of the semi-annual bonus – they notify the management between which hours of what day and on which floor of the office building they will demonstrate. With their megaphones and chorused slogans, their red head-bands and their rhythmically raised clenched fists, these demonstrators look formidable enough; but I have never failed to sense order beneath the surface fury.

Radical communist unions have dug themselves in in some foreign companies. Foreign banks and airlines in particular are occasionally racked by their intransigent tactics, which have helped give some foreign businessmen operating in Japan an exaggerated impression of the strength of the labour movement. In one well-known instance, a radical union kept a noisy and embarrassing case going for years concerning the dismissal of a temporary employee from the office of the delegation of the European Community. The System is served by this kind of action in at least two ways: the communist activists have territory they can call their own, without needing to bother Japanese big business; and the foreign companies and delegations are reminded of the fact that operating in Japan requires a readiness to accommodate.

Exploitation and rituals

An essential aspect of the post-war union system is that a large segment of low-cost labour is supplied by a pool of non-unionised 'temporary' workers, who are often in fact permanent but at a lower level of the economic hierarchy. Enterprise unions shut out workers formally classified as temporary, even though they may have worked for the firm for many years, for the very reason that they are not in the lifetime-employment category. According to one estimate, only about one-fifth of all Japanese workers enjoy the lifetime employment and other benefits that supposedly characterise Japanese labour relations.[40] In the smaller companies whose existence as low-cost sources of subcontracted work is a decisive factor in the competitiveness of many large firms, unions are very rare, and no attempt is made by the national federations to establish them. Lower-class workers are paid considerably less than union members, risk losing their jobs in periods of economic downturn and would obviously benefit most from worker protection. But unions are not welcome on this level, and the administrators have sufficient control to allow no other significant movement to flourish alongside the tame federations. The System would be seriously undermined if workers in the subcontracting sector were ever effectively organised.

Employers learned in the 1920s and 1930s that it was not difficult to make workers forget unionisation by threatening dismissal. Loyal employees were rewarded with permanent employment and wages based on seniority, such programmes often being carried out with encouragement from the government.[41] In a devastated post-war Japan, where the inevitable craving for security again became the main motivation of employees, this practice of skilful union-busting led them to settle for the tame corporate unions. At the same time, many of these unions were worried lest affiliating themselves to the central trade-union federations might embroil them in ideological warfare. Thus the administrators, fearful as they were of industry-wide unionism, enjoyed a constant advantage.

The unionisation rate has steadily declined, from 55·8 per cent in 1949 to 28·2 per cent in 1986. Except for seamen, teachers and groups of public workers whose nation-wide unions could not so easily be tamed, there are today only management-supported company unions, which more often than not actively participate in campaigns to maximise production, at the cost of worker comfort. The leaders of these company unions usually have a close working relationship with members of the management, and they themselves will often join management at a later stage, similarly commanding obedience from their underlings in the union. Thus there is no conflict between management and 'organised' workers. The enterprise unions do little more than guard the so-called lifetime-employment 'rights' of their members, and hold largely ritualistic negotiations concerning wage increases and the size of the semi-annual 'bonus', for which there are national standards.

The radical communist union federation, Sambetsu Kaigi, was dissolved in 1950, and initiative in the labour movement passed to Sohyo, which until 1987 remained the largest and most significant of Japan's central labour organisations. Sohyo relied largely on public-sector employees. When first formed it was moderate and earned the blessing of the US occupation by indicating that it would stay on the non-communist side of the cold war. But before long it became identified with the activist 'left', and actually helped set the tone of its rhetoric, which was later to include protest against the mutual security treaty between the USA and Japan, and against the US bases.

In 1954 a number of formerly socialist unions that had belonged to the earlier moderate Sodomei broke away from Sohyo and formed Domei. This organisation, whose membership came mainly from the private sector, supported the Democratic Socialist Party (DSP, a breakaway from the JSP), which has consistently supported the LDP in parliamentary voting.

Once radical union activities had been crushed, Sohyo settled down to inspire and guide a series of national actions that posed no threat to anybody. In 1956 it invented the *shunto*, 'spring offensive'. Every spring until the mid-1970s personnel of the (now privatised) Japan National Railways played the leading role in nation-wide go-slow activities or, at a later stage, full strikes. The change of tactic to full strikes was made in accordance with the wishes of the authorities after irate passengers, who had been trapped for hours in packed commuter trains, went on the rampage at several stations. The *shunto* came to constitute an annual ritual. Along with the maps showing the advance through the islands of the 'cherry-blossom front', the newspapers would print detailed tables showing which railway lines would be affected during the one or two weeks of the campaign, thus warning loyal company employees as to when bedding should be brought to their offices. The word *shunto* was even added to the list of terms officially considered suitable as 'season indicators' in Japanese poems (which are regularly composed by hundreds of thousands of amateurs).

Sohyo's rite of spring was not entirely unwelcome to management. Restless employees, even if they did not participate, could derive some vicarious satisfaction from such massive action. And, despite the preponderance of ritual, these annual actions were at least more substantial than the lunch-hour strikes organised by company unions, in that they helped establish the yearly standard of wage increases for the nation as a whole.

When in 1981 the railway unions held their last strikes worthy of the name, they had already lost leadership of the *shunto* to unions in the metal-processing sector. From the late 1970s onward, standards for wage increases were decided through negotiations between the Japan Council of the International Metalworkers' Federation and the eight largest companies in the most important metal-using industries: steel, shipbuilding, cars and electrical machinery. Workers in these industries, however, have shown little muscle, so that the *shunto* in the 1980s tends to come and go almost unnoticed. The labour movement, deprived of its teeth and claws in the 1950s, would seem finally to have lost its voice as well.

At first sight the situation for Japanese labour does not look bad at all. May Day parades are big annual events, and newspaper editorials talking of 'demands' or the 'strategy' of labour create the impression of a lively movement. Such things hide the fact that Japanese labour does not participate in national decision-making. Domestication of the unions has forestalled the destruction of particular industries at the hands of powerful union bosses, but it has also deprived members of the chance to participate in any kind of discussion on the future course of the economy.

This was made abundantly clear once again in the spring of 1986. Amidst strong calls from industry and the bureaucracy for more consumer spending as a way of increasing domestic demand, and despite Japan's promises to its trading partners that it would undertake a gradual shift from exports to domestic spending as the main spur of its economic growth, Japanese firms were investing abroad their large profits of the previous years. Wage increases, moreover, were even less than the already low increases of the previous several years. There was no public comment on this from any official union representative.

A union to end all unions

The late 1980s also saw momentous organisational changes, prompted by the privatisation of Nippon Telephone and Telegraph (NTT) and the privatisation and regionalisation of the national railways, whose personnel had always been the mainstay of Sohyo. For five years a new umbrella 'council', Zenmin Rokyo, had, under the leadership of the DSP-affiliated Domei and under the auspices of the large corporations, been working on a grand scheme to bring all unions together in one moderate national body. In November 1987 this led to the inauguration of the Japanese private-sector trade union confederation, Zenmin Roren, or Rengo for short, and the announcement that Sohyo would disband itself in 1990.[42]

Rengo is emphatically opposed to organisations affiliated to the Japan Communist Party. At a convention in February 1985 NTT's Zendentsu, one of its organisational nerve-centres and Japan's largest enterprise union, scrapped terms such as 'class', 'reaction' and 'fascism' from its vocabulary.[43] In June of the same year Zendentsu became the first Sohyo member to call for Sohyo's dissolution. The dominance of the traditionally very moderate Domei group in Rengo is more marked than sympathetic Sohyo elements and the smaller disbanded federations anticipated.[44] Many public-sector unions are softening their ritual militancy so as to be able to join the new federation.

As early as the spring of 1983 a group of leftist union leaders, academics and intellectuals formed a counter-organisation to preserve such cherished concepts as 'class struggle', and a small federation consisting mainly of the most leftist-inclined former Sohyo unions will probably remain to remind the country of the 'sell-out' of its former associates to 'monopoly capital-ism' and the 'right'.[45]

Rengo's organisers have presented Japan with a grand scheme for the unification of the socialist JSP with the DSP. But the possibility of a larger and stronger opposition party does not appear to worry the administrators in the least. LDP, bureaucrats and businessmen alike applauded the plans for Rengo and helped them along. Nor must it be forgotten that the DSP, the small political party supported by Domei, has, save for joining the occasional ritual opposition boycott, been virtually indistinguishable from the LDP in its stance in the Diet. Rengo, in fact, fits in very well with the expressed wish of LDP ideologues to expand the party's constituency to include the labour unions.[46] It could become a useful petition group supplying electoral favours in return for mediation by LDP politicians.

Rengo certainly suits management purposes better than the earlier national federations. Its first president – Tateyama Toshifumi, who also led the ground-breaking Zenmin Rokyo – is an executive member of the Japan Productivity Centre, an organisation of the bureaucracy and big business one of whose aims has long been to teach enterprise unions the virtues of management–labour co-operation. Tateyama is, moreover, associated with various LDP–bureaucrat–business advisory groups. Rengo's main aim, declared at the time of its birth, will not be to seek continual wage increases, but to promote better working conditions and the general welfare of its members and their families. It also declares that it is not in favour of strikes. It is expected that the majority of relatively underpaid workers in the small and medium-sized subcontractor sector will remain outside its sphere of interest.

This further domestication of the federated unions on a national level has been accompanied by a further domestication of many of the enterprise unions. The surviving red flags and red head-bands (worn during lunch-hour strikes) are being replaced by flags of different colours – especially green, symbolising 'nature'. Where many enterprise unions used to emphasise money in their negotiations, their programmes now increasingly call for self-fulfilment and family happiness.

Encapsulated outsiders

The System is well served by an established opposition. This institutionalised, impotent opposition absorbs potentially genuine opposition. We have already had a glimpse of this in Sohyo, which is associated with the Japan Socialist Party, but the central example is the JSP itself. Japan's biggest opposition party ceased to provide a credible alternative to the LDP in the middle of the 1950s and has played a steadily diminishing role as a political counterbalance in parliament. Its members have long preferred to spend their time quarrelling over Marxist doctrine, partly because of their heavy electoral dependence on the more dogmatic segment of Sohyo.

Tamed opposition

Japanese Marxism, pre-eminently theoretical, has provided a safe niche from which to criticise the status quo without having to reconcile theory with reality. The intellectuals who determine the priorities of the JSP lack first-hand knowledge of the kind of life led by 'the people' on whose behalf they are supposed to be fighting the injustices perpetrated by 'monopoly capitalism'. The relationship of the Japanese government with the United States has exercised the socialists more than abuses at home for which the government could be held responsible. Their distorted picture of political reality may be seen in their long-time recognition of the Great and Wise Leader Kim Il Sung as the only representative of Korea and their endless debate (still in 1987) over whether or not to 'recognise' the reality of South Korea.

A large and powerful left wing of the JSP has clung to ideological purity as an end in itself, thereby blinding the party to its own possibilities. Its increasingly radical course in the late 1950s caused the most important right-wing faction to break off and form the DSP in 1960. The left wing continued to obstruct attempts at structural reforms and ideological moderation in the 1970s, pushing out more prominent right-wing figures. More recently, the assumption of leadership in 1986 by Doi Takako (the first woman to head a Japanese political party) appeared to have introduced a degree of belated pragmatism needed more than ever following the demise of Sohyo, the party's traditional power base.

There is, of course, nothing in the official rules to prevent a real opposition from becoming strong enough to take over the government; and some have argued that had the JSP taken a less doctrinaire ideological position and proposed workable policies, this party could have become a genuine opposition party. There is some truth to this, but it begs the question of why the JSP became so irresponsibly impractical and unattractive as to deprive the voter of a credible alternative to the LDP. The answer to that seems simple: the collusion of industrialist-bureaucrats behind the merger of the 'conservatives' into the LDP, and the symbiotic relationship of the ruling party with the ruling élite that had served in the pre-war and wartime bureaucracy, indicated to the realists among the Japanese left that there was very little if any chance that alternative political forces would ever be *allowed* to take over.

It is a widely observed phenomenon that when parties are far removed from the possibility of participating in government, their leadership tends increasingly to rely on radicalised posturing. The 'expressive' aims tend to overrule the 'instrumental' ones in their political manoeuvres. The JSP is a textbook example of this tendency.

As early as 1960 one of Japan's foremost political historians concluded that the LDP and the JSP should not be seen as confronting each other over substantive issues, but rather as fighting different kinds of matches in separate rings.[47] Thus neither side can lose to the other, and the function of the JSP is not even to compete but to absorb negative elements that naturally gravitate towards it. Small interest groups that for some reason or other will not be accommodated into the main System thus have the opportunity to join a leftist mini-System that can give them, not subsidies, but publicity and moral support. A good recent example is the group of Koreans who refuse to be fingerprinted for alien registration purposes, along with sympathetic Japanese activists and fingerprint refusers of other nationalities.

Keeping the lid on 'former outcasts'

In one very special case the JSP, together with the communists, helps defuse what might otherwise be a permanent source of trouble: the 'former outcast' communities. Euphemistically called *burakumin* ('hamlet people'), the members of these communities, though indistinguishable physically from non-*burakumin* Japanese, are descendants of a combination of ritually 'unclean' people (butchers, leather-workers, gravediggers) and lower-class itinerants. In the past, their exclusion from society was so complete that maps did not even show their villages. As Japan modernised, the official regulations declaring them a special community with special tasks – and thus privileges – were scrapped. But discrimination could not be legislated out of existence and, since *burakumin* had lost their monopoly over their allotted trades, their economic deprivation increased. Today, many try to escape the stigma by moving out of the neighbourhoods, but lists of *burakumin* locations and the services of private detectives are routinely used by employers and families to determine whether a job applicant or marriage prospect comes from a former outcast community.

Burakumin communities are mainly concentrated in the Kansai area, around Osaka, Kyoto and Kobe, and in Shikoku. In many other parts of the country, people are not aware of the existence of this minority or the extent of the discrimination it experiences. It is not a subject that is easy to raise, even with better-informed Japanese.

In association with the JSP, the Burakumin Liberation League (BLL) has arrived at a *modus vivendi* with the System. The BLL has developed a method of self-assertion through 'denunciation' sessions with people and organisations that it decides are guilty of discrimination. Confessions and apologies are usually forthcoming, but they have little significance. The BLL does not use legal channels to combat discrimination, an attitude appreciated by the bureaucrats, who actually encourage ritualised protest. The administrators prefer ceremonial self-criticism (as well as spending on special facilities and grants) to the development of norms necessitating a policy of integration, which would deprive the System of much peace and quiet and cut down on an important pool of low-cost labour.[48] There are some three million *burakumin*, and their household income, even with over half the married women at work, is between half and two-thirds the national average. Much of this workforce is engaged in hard physical labour, and it sustains back and shoulder injuries at rates six times the national average.[49]

At odds with the BLL are the *burakumin* allied with the Japan Communist Party, which is in favour of making use of the courts and inveighs against the BLL's increased dependency on government hand-outs. But the JCP sees the former outcasts in narrow ideological terms as oppressed in the same way as other Japanese victims of 'monopoly capitalism'. Neither side, in competing for *burakumin* allegiance, shows interest in any serious campaign to promote their emancipation.

The stubborn few

There remain a few elements actively opposed to the System that are intransigent and unassimilable. The student movement, notable even in its heyday for the ritualism of its opposition, dwindled almost to vanishing point in the course of the 1970s, but not before giving birth to highly radicalised extremist groups such as the 'Red Army', the Chukaku-ha and Kakumaru-ha, kept in the public eye mainly through terrorist activities abroad and the revenge killings of each other's leaders.

New radical groups that appeared in the mid-1980s caused great concern among the authorities (and a considerable strengthening of the riot police) when they managed, with impunity, to launch a number of primitive home-made rockets that missed their targets. To this day, Narita Airport remains heavily protected by sunken fences, electronic detection devices and a large police contingent. All this demonstrates that Japanese society is not free from deep political conflicts. But aside from the radical fringe – and in the 1980s it was very marginal indeed – the System has been able to eliminate virtually all genuine political opposition.

What would have happened to the interest groups if they had fought the System instead of joining it? This is not a hypothetical question, since one major Japanese group has in fact resisted attempts to neutralise it: the Japan Teachers' Union, better known as Nikkyoso. Its experiences show that the administrators' determination to bring oppositionist groups under control can hardly be exaggerated.

After Japan's defeat in 1945 the vast majority of Japanese agreed that the war had brought great suffering to themselves and had therefore been a mistake. But the teachers could not easily, as did most of their com-patriots, shrug off further responsibility for that mistake by laying it at the feet of faceless 'militarists'. Ever since the closing decades of the last century, they had been the chief civilian channel for the spread of the nationalist ideology, and in the 1930s the authorities had relied on them for the propagation of beliefs and attitudes designed to make young Japanese *want* to sacrifice their lives for Japan's expanding empire. Even when teachers knew they were being asked to spread lies, their only choice had been to conform or face dismissal. Many felt guilty. Even today, the main slogan of their union, repeated at every congress and during every interview, is 'Never send our students to the battlefield again'.

Nikkyoso dates from 1947, when communist and socialist groups merged, establishing a mixed moderate–radical Marxist leadership which it has retained into the 1980s. Partly because of the Red Purge, the moderate Marxists gradually gained strength, and they have dominated the federation since the early 1960s. The Ministry of Education is its sworn enemy.

Relations between Nikkyoso and this ministry were bound to be problematic. Ideologically, the two could not be farther apart. The leftist Nikkyoso adamantly opposes anything that might suggest a hankering after pre-war days. The Ministry of Education, whose wartime ranks remained relatively intact, with 'depurged' officials rejoining it in 1950–1 along with former Naimusho officials, has never stopped believing in the need for 'right thinking' in the schools, for 'moral education' to inculcate such thinking and for formal obeisance to the unchanged pre-war symbols of flag and anthem. Since the ministry supervises the content of school textbooks, it has managed gradually to tone down the earlier unambiguous rejection of the old nationalism, and has sponsored a euphemistic treatment and partial rationalisation of Japan's imperialist past.

From the very beginning, the teachers were suspicious of the aims of the post-war Ministry of Education. The communist-dominated Zenkyo, which later became part of Nikkyoso, warned at its inaugural meeting on 1 December 1945 that government-affiliated unions were being organised to allow the Ministry of Education to evade responsibility for its wartime activities, and to suppress the free union movement.[50] Conversely, the main ideological evidence against Nikkyoso in the eyes of the Ministry of Education and its allies among the politicians was that it declared itself to represent 'educational labourers'. This was a loaded term in pre-war days, one that implicitly rejected the Confucianist view, exploited by the ultra-nationalists, of teaching as a 'divine mission'.[51] A leftist bias, moreover, is the last thing that the officials want in Japanese education. It must be emphasised that the opposition of the bureaucracy and LDP to Nikkyoso has never been inspired by a concern with the quality of education. In the LDP, improvements in and budgetary allotments for education as such have no priority, while 'programs intended to weaken . . . Nikkyoso are vigorously championed'.[52] A law passed in 1950, containing clauses designed to undermine the organisational foundation of Nikkyoso, marked the almost total severance of communication between teachers and the government and started a war that is still in full swing.

The teachers' war

Until the mid-1980s the tenacity of the highly ideological teachers' union in the face of frequent attempts by the Ministry of Education to subdue it was impressive. In March 1954 Nikkyoso carried out massive school boycotts and rallies in opposition to legislation prohibiting organisations that incite teachers to engage in political activity. The law was passed amid fist-fights in the Diet between LDP and JSP parliamentarians.[53] Two years later the government introduced regulations requiring local school-boards to be appointed rather than elected. The president and a former president of the University of Tokyo declared their objections to a bill that ran 'counter to what we have been advocating since the war'.[54] On 18 May half a million teachers walked out of their classrooms. On 1 June socialist Diet members fought hand to hand with LDP members on the Diet floor, and the next day the law was passed with five hundred policemen on guard in the chambers of the Lower House.

During the US occupation, education ministers had been non-political, non-bureaucratic figures with academic backgrounds. But almost immediately after the Americans left, the Ministry of Education was fortified with heavyweight former bureaucrats in order to help deal with the Nikkyoso challenge. In 1953 Odachi Shigeo, who had been mayor of Singapore during its notorious Japanese occupation, was made education minister. He came from the Naimusho – the only body of bureaucrats disbanded by the occupation authorities for its repressive activities before and during the war. With him he brought several purged officials and some former associates from the Naimusho. A number of officials of the Ministry of Education resigned in this period in protest against growing political influence over their department.[55]

Another former official of the dismantled Naimusho, Nadao Hirokichi, was education minister for an unprecedented four terms under four prime ministers from 1957. He was to gain an unusual reputation among ministry officials for toughness and strong-willed leadership,[56] and became Nikkyoso's most feared enemy because he was given the task of reversing the 'excesses' of occupation policy on education. A law for more stringent textbook controls was unacceptable to the Diet, being too reminiscent of pre-war censorship, but he achieved them in practice thanks to the Ministry of Education's version of 'administrative guidance'.

The biggest clashes, involving bloodshed in some localities, took place between 1957 and 1959 in the context of a protest against a government-sponsored efficiency rating system for grading teachers, which threatened to provide principals with a weapon against Nikkyoso members. The forms to be filled in for the rating asked vague and ambiguous questions, and the criteria adopted seemed highly arbitrary. The World Confederation of Organisations of the Teaching Profession, meeting in Washington in 1959, passed a resolution declaring the rating system to be harmful both to education and to the teachers themselves, and sent a telegram of protest to the Japanese government.[57]

This particular clash with the Ministry of Education cost Nikkyoso the withdrawal of an estimated 80,000 teachers, including 15,000 principals. More than 200 teachers were arrested, more than 400 dismissed or suspended, more than 1,000 demoted and more than 3,000 reprimanded, while more than 52,000 suffered a reduction in salary.[58] Nikkyoso's financial problems, which in the mid-1980s helped interested parties in the LDP and the Ministry of Education to drive a wedge into the organisation, date from this period.

The ideological disposition of Nikkyoso has made it easy for the System to portray it as out of touch with reality and disruptive of the national harmony. It is true that, besides opposing the reintroduction of moral education, Nikkyoso has also fought on the front line in an array of left-wing causes: opposition to Japan's so-called Self-Defence Forces, the mutual security treaty with the United States, US bases in Japan. But foreign scholars who have studied the subject conclude almost unanimously that the motive for supporting Nikkyoso among the majority of its rank-and-file membership has been concern for independent education rather than Marxist ideology.[59] The organisation, indeed, is sometimes referred to as *tanchozuru*, a white crane with a red head.[60] It is the activists within Nikkyoso who are usually considered the best teachers, 'the ones who are most energetic, who wish to improve the educational system, who are forward looking'.[61]

Whether Japanese education would have profited from a teachers' union with leaders who saw themselves primarily as teachers rather than as social activists committed to a bitter struggle is a moot question. What seems fairly certain is that if they had been just teachers they could not have opposed so strongly the reintroduction of control by Japan's administrators over moral instruction. This is borne out by the fate of other opposition groups that, by yielding to 'the embrace', have lost their ability to wage effective opposition.

The war between the LDP and the Ministry of Education on the one side and Nikkyoso on the other has torpedoed most attempts to introduce badly needed education reforms. It continues to smoulder, with the forces of the System gradually gaining ground, since the forces of the Japanese left as a whole are diminishing. Developments in 1987, with Nikkyoso's head and part of its membership cultivating friendly ties with central figures in the education-related groups of the System, suggest a gradual loss of resolve in the face of relentless pressure.

Nikkyoso is also a favourite target of the newer groups of rightists, who attack it with barrages of noise from their sound-trucks. Ever since rightists managed to abduct staff members of Nikkyoso headquarters as 'hostages', the entrance has been heavily guarded. Twice a day, rightist sound-trucks circle the building for ten to fifteen minutes, subjecting it to high-decibel harassment. Physical clashes have occurred regularly when rightists tried to prevent Nikkyoso from holding its annual conventions. In September 1968, 270 rightist groups mobilised 2,620 members to harass one such a meeting, and it has become increasingly difficult to find venues for them; many municipalities have withdrawn permission for the use of public halls on the grounds that the chaos resulting from the attentions of the rightists disturbs ordinary people. The police refuse to protect Nikkyoso from this rightist disruption.

Tortured political conscience

Why have the teachers alone persisted in their opposition to the System?

A possible explanation lies in the unusual background shared, at least until recently, by all Nikkyoso leaders. None of them attended either the University of Tokyo or any of the other élite universities that produce the administrators, and they were thus barred for ever from the world of decision-making. Yet at the same time they were intellectuals who felt special responsibilities towards the community. They had taught at elementary schools in villages and small towns during the Depression. They had been educated in teachers' training schools that were notorious for their strict ideological discipline, and they were subsequently made to participate in the spreading of a nationalist mythology they did not believe. All these circumstances are conducive to serious reflection on the meaning of one's job, and to rigid intellectual postures in later life.

But there is probably another, related reason. We have seen at the outset of this chapter how religion often provides a source of alternative power, countering and restricting the power of the rulers of the moment. The leadership of Nikkyoso, by faithfully adhering to the pseudo-religion of Marxism, drew upon such a source. Some of the earlier organisers of the movement spent years in prison because of their beliefs. Nor is it a coincidence that Nikkyoso came to provide ideological and intellectual guidance for Sohyo, for it had demonstrated an ability rare in Japan to manipulate universalist ideas as tools in gaining a measure of leverage over the established order.

Marxism has been, and to some extent still is, a powerful force in Japanese academia. Many of the very same professors who educated the ruling élite have adhered to a peculiar set of anti-capitalist theories, as unrealistic as they are rigid. The System has had no choice but to tolerate them, and we have already seen the safety-valve value of such token radicalism. It is when intellectual radicalism aspires to action that the System moves in to prevent the contagion from spreading. The experiences of Nikkyoso, on the receiving end of physical violence by rightist groups and the legislative and ideological onslaughts of LDP circles and the Ministry of Education, are no isolated manifestations of intolerance. Police, public prosecutors and judges systematically discriminate against people and groups whose activities are inspired by leftist ideology.[62] The System abhors ideological heterodoxy as a threat to its own existence.[63]

All this suggests, in fact, that the time may have come to revise some post-1960 assumptions regarding the Japanese left and Japanese radicalism; for many who flocked to leftist causes were at heart liberals. The tragedy is that, as prisoners of the rigid Marxist ideology of their groups, they lost their natural allies, the Americans – the very allies who had given them what post-war freedom and opportunities they had. The name Nikkyoso has for long evoked images of ideological intransigence, yet in its context it can also be seen in a different way. Along with some other tiny groups of citizens with interests to protect but without the inclination to help further the fortunes of the System, it has no access to basic administrative decisions. Without their firm ideological commitment Japanese leftist groups could not for long have fought off the encroachments of the System. In that sense, they are both victims and beneficiaries of their own doctrines.

This was, at least to some extent, probably foreseen by the US occupation authorities. One occupation official who certainly cannot be accused of doubting the wisdom of General MacArthur remembers that 'high [occupation] officials not only had considerable admiration for the leadership and organising skill of [communist leader] Nozaka [Sanzo], but an off-the-record conviction that his followers would fight hardest and most effectively to sustain the new democratic system'.[64]

Japanese 'pluralism'

Despite its intolerance towards those infected by leftist ideology, the System is not Big Brother. In fact, so much heed is paid to a whole variety of discontent and so much tolerance shown towards the obstruction of policy adjustments sponsored by officials and LDP circles, that some serious observers have concluded that the Japanese political system, however much it deviates from the Western parliamentary tradition, is a pluralist system after all.[65] Yet while this view is understandable as a defence against the Marxist-inspired perspective – firmly entrenched among Japanese intellectuals – of a ruling élite in the service of 'monopoly capitalism', there are good reasons to disagree with it. To stretch the idea of pluralism to encompass the Japanese political reality is to deprive it of its original meaning.

Political pluralism does not simply mean, as is sometimes supposed, the existence of many groups and government institutions limiting each other's elbow-room; if such were the case, Japan has been a veritable model of pluralism since before the turn of the century. Pluralism in national decision-making implies the ability of sizeable groups of the population to help choose, via their representatives, the nation's long-term goals. The Japanese people have had no say whatsoever in the choice of unlimited industrial expansion, at the cost of other desirables in life, as the long-term goal. Most Japanese may have been enthusiastic about it at first (in the same way they were once enthusiastic about the growth of the Japanese empire), but 'GNP-ism' ceased being an inspiration some time in the 1970s. The absence of pluralism in the true sense can be seen in the absence of political parties with the political imagination to work out new and more rewarding priorities, as well as in the absence of the opportunity for imaginative Japanese to create them. To say that the vast majority of Japanese are not interested in such political competition, because they have never known it, does not make the System a pluralistic democracy.

The term 'conservative coalition' that has been used to characterise the Japanese political system[66] is misleading, too, for similar reasons. A coalition presupposes a degree of political choice which the components of the System are not given.

In the late 1970s and 1980s some specialists concluded that Japan could profitably be labelled a 'corporatist state'. Corporatist theories see key organisations at the top of professional and interest hierarchies as competing for influence on policy-making. This is indeed true for Japanese policy adjustments – in other words, administrative decisions. But that still leaves the more crucial initiatives that lead to policy *changes*, initiatives that compete with existing policies. The Netherlands, Sweden and Austria have been held up as good examples of states whose operations can be clarified by corporatist theory. And the political system of these countries is so very different from that of Japan – in such essentials as the choices that citizens are offered and the recourse they are given if they believe administrative decisions to be wrong – that to call Japan a corporatist state is to render corporatist theory almost meaningless.

The essential characteristic of the Japanese System that is thrown into relief by both the pluralist and corporatist theories (the two most popular perspectives in contemporary political science) is, in the end, the lack of political instruments to change overall Japanese policy. The Japanese political system should impress us for what it does *not* try to accomplish in areas where action appears sorely needed and where, in other states, governmental co-ordination would be taken for granted.

4

Servants of the System

The System's embrace is truly inescapable; it extends to institutions – typically, labour movements, parts of the educational world and the press – that in other non-dictatorial societies frequently exist in more or less permanent tension, if not open hostility, with the forces of the established socio-political order. We have already taken a look at Japan's 'house-trained' labour unions. Its schools and its newspapers are no less crucial to the System's survival. And the extraordinary scope of the embrace is emphasised still further by its inclusion of one entity that in other countries is generally considered beyond the pale: the criminal element.

It may seem perverse to lump schoolchildren, journalists and gangsters together. But Japanese schools, newspapers and organised crime have in common that they are each highly politicised as servants of the System. The System abhors genuine opposition too much to leave any important social institution alone. Institutions strong enough occasionally to intimidate the main groups of administrators will be incorporated as minor components, participating at a lower level, of the power hierarchy. The press and, in a peculiar fashion, the criminal syndicates are examples of this. A relatively weak institution may be completely subjected to the System's overall purposes, as has happened to Japanese schools.

The subservient education system

It is ironic, but hardly surprising, that the teachers' union – Nikkyoso, the most belligerent anti-System institution – should owe its existence to the very institution that in a most crucial way nurtures the System and promotes cohesion among its disparate and rival components.

Nikkyoso has blocked the introduction of forms of moral education that would serve the System in a more explicit manner. Though Japanese education is thus considered sorely deficient by an important segment of the administrative class, it still imparts an ideology, seldom recognised as such, favourable to the System.[1] Much more significant, however, is the almost total subordination of education to the maintaining of a hierarchy of supposed merit. The schools operate as a sorting mechanism and recruiting agent for placement in the various overlapping hierarchies. This function, dominant in what are considered Japan's best schools at every level, is stressed to the near exclusion of everything else, and much to the detriment of the intellectual development of the nation's youth.

Anti-intellectual schools

Japan's education system has gained a reputation overseas as one of the best, if not *the* best, in the world. This reputation rests partly on the high (often highest) scores Japanese schoolchildren attain in international mathematics tests, and on the presumed connection with Japan's economic successes. It is backed up by remarks of specialists impressed by the discipline in Japanese schools, the commitment of mothers and the ability of pupils to absorb masses of facts.

That Japanese pupils do well in international written tests is not surprising. To take just such tests is what Japanese pupils are trained for from elementary school to high school. However, if the tests were to evaluate, say, the ability to draw conclusions, to abstract from facts, to connect abstractions, to organise one's thoughts in an essay, to express oneself in another language or just the ability to ask questions, they would reveal where the Japanese education system is deficient.

The aims of Japanese schools could hardly be further removed from the original sense of the English word 'education': to bring forth and develop the powers of the mind, rather than merely imparting factual information. Far from sharpening the reasoning ability of its charges, the Japanese education system, on the whole, is hostile to such a purpose. Spontaneous reasoning, along with spontaneous behaviour, is systematically suppressed in practically all schools; there is no patience with originality. Pupils are not taught to think logically, or to ask the right questions – indeed to ask any questions at all. Instead, the emphasis is on rote memorisation. Japanese students who 'have done well' carry vast masses of facts around with them in their heads; if they have been able to connect these facts and work them into a coherent view of life, they have had to do so entirely on their own. The overriding purpose of the Japanese education system was summed up by an authority on the subject as 'shaping generations of disciplined workers for a techno-meritocratic system that requires highly socialised individuals capable of performing reliably in a rigorous, hierarchical, and finely tuned organisational environment'.[2]

By deciding who will end up at what level and in which segment of which hierarchy within the System, Japanese education performs a function that can be found in most, if not all, other countries; but it fulfils this function in a more relentlessly rigid fashion than anywhere in the West and perhaps most of the communist world as well. It shapes élites who, dispersed throughout the System, will give it cohesion, in somewhat the same way as the old-boy networks of the English public schools and universities, but in a much magnified and multiplied form.

Path to the pinnacles

The selection begins at a very early stage, but to see why it should do so we must start at the other end, where the universities supply their annual batches of graduates to the larger corporations and the bureaucracy.

Japanese higher education forms a hierarchy, with Todai (the University of Tokyo) – more specifically, its law department – at its apex. Todai's graduates have the best chance of gaining admission to the Ministry of Finance, the best jumping board for a try at the prime ministership or another career in the LDP. It also provides the business conglomerates with many of its future top managers. The University of Kyoto and other former imperial universities, on almost the same level as Todai, produce a smaller part of the élite. Yet it is not easy to convey just how much the Todai label is venerated. For a century past, its law department has 'ordained' almost all Japan's top administrators; a diploma from this school is practically a ticket into the ruling class.

Students of French government may think they recognise this phenomenon, and point out the role of the *grandes écoles*. But the variety among the latter is considerably greater, and it matters very much what subjects a student has studied there, and how hard.

One rung down the hierarchy, but still highly respectable and difficult to get into, come Waseda and Keio, two private universities in Tokyo. Waseda's reputation rests on graduates who became politicians and journalists, while Keio has always given access to the higher reaches of the business world. Farther down again one finds the medium-ranking universities such as Chuo, Meiji, Sophia (run by Jesuits) and Rikkyo. And beneath these is a plethora of smaller provincial and private universities and colleges, women's junior colleges and specialised training institutions for subjects like art and music, the last-named forming a small hierarchy of their own.

The quality of university education has never been the criterion for reaching the heights of Japan's administrative apparatus. Once it became clear, in the final decades of the last century, that political decision-making would become the privilege of a class selected by examination rather than by heredity or some other non-meritocratic criterion, debate centred not on the quality or even the content of what was being taught but on which examinations, given by what authority, would provide the filter.[3] What students today actually absorb from the law course at Todai, which gains them access to the peaks of the administrative hierarchies, is unimpressive when compared with what students must know to graduate from many European and the better American universities.

The quality of instruction in the lowest-ranking schools is not necessarily less than in the élite schools. The universities in the middle reaches and above would not lose their rank and reputation no matter how much they were to deteriorate. For though the bureaucracy and the large firms give entrance exams that are theoretically open to everyone, in fact they hire according to a quota system, taking in a more or less established portion of graduates from each of the various universities. The educational hierarchy corresponds with the economic–bureaucratic one. A middle-ranking firm would not dream of trying to take on a Todai graduate; and by the same token a graduate from, say, Chuo University rarely climbs to the highest levels of business and never of government.

Japanese are acutely aware of which schools the people they deal with have attended. A non-Japanese acquaintance of mine was once asked by his girlfriend not to meet her for a few months, because her sister was under investigation for an arranged marriage and the candidate to become her husband had graduated from Todai. Nothing, including a relationship of one member of the family with a foreigner, could be allowed to stand in the way of such a prize catch.

What students do during their four years as undergraduates is of little account, unless they do it in the faculties of medicine, engineering or the physical sciences – which mostly lead to careers outside the business–bureaucratic 'élite course'. Law, economics and commerce – with a nearly exclusive emphasis on what writers on the administrative aspects of these fields have said – are the favoured subjects for gaining entry to the higher levels of the System. In four years of teaching at Waseda University, I found that students in the highest-ranking politics and economics department had little to do. They read a few, often obscure, books on their subject, of which they generally remembered precious little. I was instructed that students should normally be given passing grades so long as they had regularly attended classes.

Graduation is virtually automatic. Students who can demonstrate that they have worked harder than most have better chances of being admitted to the bureaucracy and top business firms. But graduates who have spent four years doing nothing at name schools can always find employment at a higher level than more capable graduates with lower-ranking diplomas. For most students the university means pure relaxation, a brief fling at life before entering the regimented world of business organisations.

Cramming for a career

Many Japanese think that the 'rest' students get at the 'better' universities is well deserved, because getting into them is an extremely nerve-racking process. Though money and parental connections sometimes play a role, especially in entering medical and dental schools, in the vast majority of cases the ambitious youth must try to outscore ten, twenty or more rivals in entrance examinations. The least complicated way of accomplishing this is to get into a high school with a reputation for producing a large crop of successful candidates. Japanese high schools are, in fact, ranked by this criterion. Three out of the 5,453 high schools in the country supply about 10 per cent of the successful candidates for Tokyo University.[4]

This means that at high schools considered better than average – and the evaluation of schools in such terms is almost a national pastime – pupils spend most of their time training to pass exams. The name schools have the best idea of what will be asked in the (exclusively written) exams. And since the professors who compose these exams are often quite arbitrary in their view of the correct answers, the object of these schools is not so much to teach a subject as to turn out experts who can read the minds of those professors.

Where English teaching is concerned, for example, high-school pupils learn to pass exams consisting only of multiple-choice questions, put together by professors who themselves are uncomfortable with the real language. The tests often contain ambiguities or downright grammatical errors. After ten years studying English, which along with mathematics and Japanese is one of the three major examination subjects for all the universities, students are, with rare exceptions, unable to communicate in this language.

Mathematics and physics are better suited to written exams, and consequently much attention at school is devoted to passing maths tests. Where history or social studies are concerned, the examinations seem, as one expert puts it, 'like nothing more than a giant trivia contest compiled by scholars instead of popular culture freaks'.[5]

The critical importance of entrance examinations has brought a lucrative subsidiary industry into being in the form of special schools offering private tuition after normal school hours. Called *juku*, they too are ranked on the basis of how many of their students have passed which examinations. Many students who fail the tests for the highly reputed universities will try again, sometimes three or four years in a row. In the meantime, they attend *juku* where they review the examinations of past years, or crammer schools (*yobiko*), which have sprung up just to accommodate them. The learning at these schools has become highly esoteric: published question papers from earlier examinations are reviewed, dissected and commented upon, much as a classical scholar would treat a newly discovered ancient Chinese text. Some professional crammers even develop probability theories for their clients, not unlike the 'theorists' who peddle a systemic approach to gambling at Las Vegas.

To be admitted to a highly reputed high school it is almost mandatory to have attended a highly reputed middle school. Most pupils whose parents have decided to go for high stakes in the System sit for the entrance examinations of two, three or even four different schools. To get into one of the most promising middle schools, it helps to have passed through the right primary school. Thus the latter's reputation in turn depends on the proportion of its pupils delivered to high-ranking middle and high schools. There are books on the market with the special drills for children preparing for elementary school entrance exams. But often the selection begins even earlier.

From the cradle to the ministries

A relatively smooth ride upward from elementary school to university is provided by certain expensive private institutions that consist of universities with their own 'attached' high, middle and elementary schools and sometimes even kindergartens. Once one is on such a track, the exams at each level are largely perfunctory. This has come to be known as the 'escalator' system, and the best way to get on an escalator is to attend a kindergarten leading to higher-level schools. As a consequence there are famous and extraordinarily expensive kindergartens that actually give entrance examinations of their own. Keio, Gakushuin, Seijo Gakuen and Aoyama Gakuin are among well-known private universities at the top of escalators that start at kindergarten level. According to eyewitnesses, kindergarten exams typically test ability to recognise letters in the Japanese syllabaries, skills with building blocks and the like. At a crucial point in one routine test attended by one of my informants, the toddler was given a wrapped sweet; all eyes were on him to see whether he neatly folded the wrapper or threw it on the floor.

But still we are not at the beginning. Some mothers arrange private tuition for their three-year-olds so that they may stand a better chance of passing the kindergarten exam. Entry into one of the famous kindergartens of Tokyo usually requires training at a *juku* for infants. Parents have been known to move to Tokyo for the sole purpose of getting their child into the right kindergarten. One maternity hospital has even advertised that delivery could be arranged as part of a package deal, guaranteeing that the baby would qualify for the right kindergarten.

Girls aiming for a position in the bureaucracy may compete with boys in this system. But for most girls with ambitious parents there is a parallel hierarchy of private women's colleges in which placing is important, not only for mothers who wish to make 'good marriages' for their daughters, but also for company recruiters who seek high-class brides for their employees. A blue-collar ladder of high schools supplying high-quality factory workers to manufacturing industries also exists.

'Examination hell'

The education system is one of the most criticised elements of the System. A former vice-minister of the Ministry of International Trade and Industry (MITI) contends that 'our present educational system only seems to be able to turn out inferior versions of robots'.[6] One of Japan's most versatile essayists thinks it turns out trained seals.[7] The public at large habitually decries the *shiken jigoku*, literally 'examination hell', and the social type it has brought into being, the *kyoiku mama*, or 'education mother', who deprives her children of a normal childhood while pushing them up the educational ladder. The *kyoiku mama* is driven by powerful motives. To a great extent the mother is held responsible for the performance of her child, whose successes or failures in examinations have a great effect on her status in the neighbourhood.[8] The family feels that it has invested a great deal in the youthful scholar, and sometimes behaves as if a life were at stake in the period leading up to the exams. Failure in an exam can be psychologically devastating, and not only to the candidate. The often superhuman effort exacted from the child and the tensions affecting the whole family in connection with *shiken jigoku* provide much of the drama of middle-class family life in Japan.

Children who want to demonstrate their earnestness are expected to give up hobbies, sports and a social life in order to devote themselves totally to the approaching exam, often for two years in advance. Preparation entails cramming till very late at night after school and *juku* hours. One *juku* holds cramming classes for twelve-year-olds from 9 p.m. on Saturday to 6 a.m. on Sunday. Some children are made to undergo physical endurance training reminiscent of the army-camp approach. Fourteen-year-olds who are still at their desks at 1 a.m. are not unusual. That they absorb next to nothing after a couple of hours of cramming is immaterial; they show the world that they are in earnest and have the required endurance.

Such a selection system can continue to function only as long as the children put up with it, and their disciplined behaviour cannot be understood without considering their relationship with their mothers. In a typical Japanese upbringing, ideas of proper conduct are instilled into the child less by reference to a universal scheme of how the world works than by manipulation of the child's emotions. He or she learns to recognise good or bad behaviour generally by its effect on the mother's disposition. One result of this is that the *kyoiku mama* is able to instil in her child very strong feelings of guilt, which she uses as a spur.[9]

Stories about suicides in connection with examination worry or failure receive much publicity and create the impression that *shiken jigoku* is a major cause of death among school-age children. It is not, but aberrations in personality development and difficulties in parent–child relations are undoubtedly aggravated by chronic exam anxiety.

Even though practically every Japanese will agree that the exam system is cruel and ought to be abolished, most people realise that nothing will ever be done to change this method of selection. On the whole, it suits the System admirably. Even if the masses of facts pumped into their heads are largely useless, even if (as with English) the students have picked up bad habits difficult to unlearn, the people selected to reach the top will be very tenacious and have extremely good memories. Officialdom and the business world value persistence, dedication and memory much more highly than inventiveness.

These observations are not new. One of the first foreign teachers in Japan, the American missionary William Griffis, wrote of Japanese teachers in 1874 that their 'chief duty was to stuff and cram the minds of . . . pupils. To expand or develop the mental powers of a boy, to enlarge his mental visions, to teach him to think for himself, would have been doing precisely what it was the teacher's business to prevent.'[10]

The school system fosters a high degree of consistency in family background among members of the administrator class. Although the ladder of success is in theory accessible to all, poor families cannot afford the expensive private schools and can rarely provide the environment needed to prepare for the famous government establishments. The meticulously pre-sorted 'members' of Japanese corporations will maintain contact with former classmates who may be of value to the company through their positions in other parts of the System. The importance of non-contractual and extra-legal ties in Japanese corporate and bureaucratic life has given this finely woven network the function of a nervous system. It enables important information to reach relevant segments dispersed over the entire System literally within minutes. It helps to soften friction among system components. Within the business conglomerates, communication is heightened by informal groupings often derived from the schools that top employees have attended.

The creativity problem

An education system geared almost entirely to the production of experts in taking multiple-choice tests does not select original thinkers. Moreover, since intellectual curiosity can become a threat to convention it is actively discouraged, rendering the Japanese learning environment extremely inhospitable to creative thought. Some segments of the business world and the bureaucracy have in recent years been voicing concern over the generally acknowledged low level of creativity in Japan. When a Japanese resident of the United States won the Nobel prize for medicine in 1987, many press comments pointed out that he would never have won it without the stimulation of decades of study and laboratory work abroad. Scientists at Japanese universities are hampered by an extremely rigid academic hierarchy that keeps talented researchers in subservient positions, and by excessive regulations decreed by education bureaucrats.

For three post-war decades the creativity problem did not worry anyone much, since many basic inventions were in the public domain and technology could be bought cheaply. But as Japanese industry begins to reach into areas in which no one else is ahead, and as foreign patents threaten to become less simple to obtain than in the past, the need for Japanese inventors increases. This concern is reflected in the regular reports that MITI devotes to the creativity problem, as well as in the so-called fifth-generation computer project, whose unusually young researchers are being encouraged to behave more like relaxed Westerners, in the hope that creativity will follow.

In the summer of 1985 an *ad hoc* council for educational reform, established by then prime minister Nakasone and consisting of academics, intellectuals and businessmen, issued a preliminary report which could only be read as a rebuke to the entire educational system. The council characterised the products of Japanese education as stereotypes without clear individuality, unable to think properly and form their own judgements. It also spoke of barriers to creativity. In short, it summed up much of the discontent that has been voiced by the liberal segment of the intelligentsia for years. Yet in its suggestions as to remedies the report showed the imprint of the council's less liberal-minded members – the representatives of the Ministry of Education and the educational reform lobby in the LDP. (This led the private Women's Council for Education to release its own report, accusing Nakasone's club of ignoring the real wishes of parents.) In further reports issued in 1986 and 1987 the council back-pedalled still further, showing signs of hedging on the need to produce individual thinkers.

Producing the 'quality labour force'

The economic overlords may complain about the creativity problem, but they must take considerable responsibility for the style of present-day schooling. In the early 1960s representatives of the business federations suggested measures for a partial reshaping of national education to turn schools into 'places for training a disciplined, high quality labour force' in the interest of optimal economic development.[11] Two years later the education committee of Nikkeiren (the Federation of Employers' Organisations) came up with more specific advice concerning the role of middle schools.[12] Following this, other large business institutions also presented their advice, and proposals were incorporated in an outline prepared by the government's central education committee.[13] Translated into concrete plans by subsequent committees, these proposals were reflected in the gradual curriculum changes made by the Ministry of Education in the 1970s.

The result of these changes, according to statistics compiled from teacher estimates, has been that 30 per cent of elementary schoolchildren, 50 per cent of middle-school pupils and 70 per cent of high-school pupils cannot keep up with the learning pace. Adjustments on behalf of slow learners are not possible in the government schools – which roughly nine out of ten pupils attend – since their entire curriculum, as well as the speed at which it is to be covered, is prescribed by the Ministry of Education.

As part of the same set of plans suggested by the business world, education authorities have begun to divide all pupils into five rankings, based on performance, in order to determine which higher-level schools they could be 'promoted' to. The pressure on pupils further increased in the mid-1980s with the introduction of the related *hensachi* system, whereby pupils take regular mock-tests, sometimes every month, to monitor their chances of achieving the levels allowing them to sit for the exams of choice schools.

Nearly all pupils will pass to higher grades and graduate, as this is normally automatic in Japan. But most of the large body of pupils who lack the outstanding memories favoured by the education system are, by the time they are twelve years old, fully aware that they will have to spend the rest of their lives on the middle or lower rungs of the social ladder. Nikkyoso, the teachers' union, believes that the sense of hopelessness this engenders is the direct cause of the increased unruliness and delinquency among middle- and high-school pupils. Aggravating the problem of keeping order is the huge size of the normal class – 40 to 50 pupils – which makes personal contact with the teacher nearly impossible. On the other hand, the new ranking system has given teachers much power to control pupils indirectly.[14]

Discipline begetting violence

In the first half of the 1980s the Japanese public was constantly reminded of the shortcomings of the educational system in connection with violence at schools. For several months in 1983 newspapers were full of stories of teachers being attacked by their pupils. Some teachers were ambushed by vengeful students after their graduation. Others had school lunches or scissors thrown in their faces. The stories that reached the ears of the police and the press most probably represented only the tip of the iceberg, since Japanese schools are extremely worried about their reputations, and irregularities are largely kept secret. Then, in 1985, a much more serious problem surfaced in the form of *ijime*, the bullying and organised teasing that takes place on a large scale in Japanese schools. Reports were devoted to it by the National Police Agency and Ministry of Justice, followed by the Ministry of Education, which for the first time in its existence decided to investigate violence in 40,000 elementary and secondary schools. A national Nikkyoso conference discovered that about half its membership thought that keeping order sometimes required corporal punishment. A group of lawyers found that at a majority of the 985 schools they investigated pupils were beaten or kicked by teachers nearly every day. This form of disciplining was seen as closely connected with *ijime*.

Setting the tone, the *Asahi Shimbun* carried an editorial that gave examples. A middle-school teacher visited the home of a girl who had been caught smoking and suggested she commit hara-kiri with a kitchen knife, then kicked her head when she prostrated herself on the floor to apologise. The newspaper concluded that, since studies reveal many more incidents than are reported in the press, corporal punishment in schools must be assumed to be an everyday matter.[15] Investigating authorities discovered that teachers often take the lead in group punishment of those they consider misfits, and often consent to ostracism of a pupil who violates unwritten rules. Although conformism is highly appreciated in Japanese society, press commentators concluded that *ijime* as a means of promoting it could not be tolerated. Liberal-minded members of the aforementioned committee for education reforms went so far as to suggest, in conversations with press representatives, that the problem reflects a disorder of Japanese society in general – thus revealing an awareness of the seldom acknowledged fact that mild (and sometimes not so mild) forms of intimidation help maintain the hierarchy of power within that society.[16] In fact, the teacher abetting the bully is almost paradigmatic of how the System works.

The mass production of rules

The bullying problem provided the press with sensational copy and opportunities for indignant editorials; but its significance went far beyond this. It is a symbolic issue, with profound moral implications, between two camps struggling for control of the methods whereby upcoming new generations of Japanese adapt to the System.

To some extent, every such problem serves the purpose of the disciplinarian Ministry of Education and a group of education-minded LDP politicians, both of which want to create a climate of opinion favourable to the reintroduction of pre-war practices. They are opposed by activist teachers and groups of concerned intellectuals and parents. The administrators believe that the main problem with the education system has been its lack of proper 'moral' instruction ever since the US occupation purged it of nationalistic teachings. Official opinion, as voiced by former prime minister Nakasone, sees the source of the problem in individual homes and a general lack of discipline.

The Japanese federation of bar associations, Nichibenren, has concluded that the real trouble, on the contrary, is too much discipline. The increasing unruliness at public middle schools and high schools, which Nikkyoso attributes to the inability of pupils to maintain the pace and to the recently introduced ranking system, has caused many schools to react by tightening the rules. School regulations have proliferated considerably since the end of the 1970s and in many cases have become absurdly restrictive.

The lawyers' federation has compiled a report concluding that serious violation of the human rights of children is widespread.[17] A majority of the schools investigated prescribed to the smallest detail how pupils must sit, stand and walk, and to what height and at which angle they should raise their hands. The route to be travelled from school to home is often laid down as well. Some schools have rules forbidding classmates to talk with each other in the street. The order in which school lunches are to be eaten is sometimes prescribed. School rules apply even at home and during vacations: it is generally forbidden to go out after six at night; it is decreed at which time the pupil must rise, even on Sundays. Only selected books may be read. The schools, and not the parents, decide which TV programmes may be watched. Some schools demand that permission be asked even for vacation trips with the family.

That all pupils at the spartan schools must wear their school uniform at all times goes without saying, but hairstyles must be identical as well. The girl with naturally curly hair or hair that is not deep black is well advised at the beginning of the school year to bring a note from her mother verifying this, since heavy punishments await girls who perm or dye their hair.

It is clear that many of these rules were designed on the principle that more rules mean fewer disciplinary problems. This was, at least partly, a miscalculation. The lawyers and Nikkyoso see a direct connection between meaningless rules and pupils who resort to violence against their teachers and each other.[18] The increased discipline and its appeal to society's assumed need for 'productive' members are throwbacks to the Meiji period, when there was a similar reaction to liberal ideas concerning the right to a general humanistic education.[19]

The new retrogressive trend appears unstoppable as the power of Nikkyoso diminishes. The lawyers register the excesses but are not equipped to fight them. The Japanese press sounds occasional alarms, but adopts no consistent stance and hardly bothers with searching analysis. The same editors who seem to disagree with the approach of the educational bureaucrats also appear to endorse the official attribution of unruliness to a lack of discipline in the home. Their position on the right of the administrators to lay down educational priorities and patterns of discipline is, at best, ambivalent in a way that typifies the Japanese press.

The house-broken press

The Japanese press is more independent than the education system, and at first sight appears to play an adversarial role in the System. Yet its almost consistent 'anti-establishment' attitude is quite superficial. The newspapers never really 'take on' the System. They will occasionally rage at some of its elements, but are rarely consistent for more than a few weeks. And the rage is often to the benefit of competing elements. Most important, they make no attempt to analyse the System, to provide a critical frame of reference enabling readers to ask questions concerning the System's essential nature and the direction in which it is taking them.

In this respect contemporary journalists seem less courageous than some of their predecessors working for the first newspapers or in the 1920s. The revolutionary changes of 1868 brought with them the idea of the press as an aid to the nation's leaders. Many early journalists were samurai who had been bypassed in the selection for government appointments. In the 1870s these pioneers carried on lively debates about the new tasks of the oligarchy and about the relative desirability of Japan's choices in political development – discussion that was possible at this stage because 'even though concepts of journalistic freedom had not yet matured, neither had the government's more stringent methods of controlling the press'.[20] The concepts and methods developed simultaneously, and by the middle of the decade the papers were employing 'prison editors' willing to serve the gaol terms provided for in the Press Ordinance of 1875.[21]

The tradition of self-censorship

As the nineteenth century entered its closing decades, the power-holders did not need to resort to much force to gain the co-operation of the newspapers. Journalists were to play an important role in spreading the new myth of a divine emperor and the nationalist ideology of a 'family state'.[22] In the first three decades of the twentieth century, control of the press was accomplished largely through a self-censorship encouraged by the very inconsistency and capriciousness of official censorship. It was often not clear what would be censored, since official instructions were vague, abstract and ambiguous.

Many important events – the rice riots, the attacks on Korean residents following the great Kanto earthquake of 1923 – were given little or no attention. Mention of the establishment and development of the Communist Party was strictly taboo. Even apart from such obviously politically important subjects, unpleasant facts in general were ignored either out of 'patriotism' or as a result of pressure from above. Laws and special codes were only a minor means in this suppression; a favourite method of government officials was personal warnings that went unrecorded.[23] This is still a preferred device of the Japanese bureaucracy in general: elusive control for which no one can be held responsible.

Freedom of the press was increasingly curtailed from 1920 onward. But contrary to the common view among today's Japanese intellectuals, that resulted less from growing 'militarism' than from a combination of bureaucratic control and media 'self-control'.

Self-censorship continues to be a conspicuous characteristic of the Japanese press. Newspapers, agencies and broadcasting companies gather their news from government and business via *kisha* (reporter) clubs, which came into their own in the war years, when censorship was official. The *kisha* club represents the institutionalised symbiosis between journalists and the System's organisations they report on.[24] They help the journalist, since he or she need never worry about missing a vital development, and they provide the power-holders with their main means of co-ordinating media self-censorship. There are about four hundred *kisha* clubs, attached to all the ministries and government agencies, the Bank of Japan, the LDP, the police, industrial associations – everything and everybody, in short, that help make Japan go round. They cater to roughly twelve thousand journalists representing more than 160 media organisations. To gather genuine news from important organisations without going through the *kisha* clubs is difficult and sometimes virtually impossible. Formal press conferences in Japan are stage-managed to a ludicrous degree.

The prime minister is followed every day by three people from each of the major newspapers, who stick with him wherever he goes and pick up whatever he says. When Nakasone was prime minister, *kisha* club members were forbidden to follow him only during his weekly meditation at a Zen temple. A favourite journalistic method is to arrive at a politician's doorstep very late at night. Long hours of waiting may then be rewarded with an invitation to come in and talk with an LDP heavyweight *en famille* and clad in pyjamas. The inner circle of most loyal reporters, who are allowed to confer informally with a politician, will not risk their status by publicising major discoveries or revelations; both sides understand that much information gathered this way will never see print. *Kisha* club members may also receive presents from the person they are expected to cover.

Most Japanese journalists spend the entire day with fellow *kisha* club members, and generally have little contact with informants outside this environment. Their club makes collective decisions on what its members may or may not report, occasionally even on the tone of their reports. Such rules can be strict. According to a Japanese colleague of mine, a reporter from one of the major newspapers was banned from his *kisha* club for six months because his paper had carried a story which they had all agreed not to print. The fact that a colleague from another desk had been responsible, having picked up the information from an alternative source, was not considered a mitigating circumstance. The *kisha* clubs are fairly exclusive, and many of them are closed to foreign journalists, notwithstanding a decade or more of negotiations by successive chairmen of the Foreign Press In Japan.

It hardly needs to be pointed out that the *kisha* club system makes for very cosy relations between the newspapers and the people whose activities and aims they are expected to scrutinise. There is hardly any incentive for individual journalists to investigate anything by themselves, and no reward at all for presenting a case in a manner that contradicts the conclusions of their colleagues. But, typically, when a political or industrial scandal breaks and is reported by all media, Japan is treated to a veritable avalanche of information on it, since many of the journalists were aware of the details all along. As one veteran foreign journalist observes:

> When a big scandal breaks the public is suddenly immersed in a torrent of revelations that gush forth from the newspapers, magazines, and broadcasting stations day after day, week after week, until the scandal itself seems to be the whole political process, unique and unrelated to anything else in the past. For that reason scandal after scandal erupts and subsides, yet no political lessons are learned and no real reform is achieved.[25]

While editors and journalists routinely emphasise 'the public's right to know', and sometimes ceremoniously take the government to task for depriving the public of that right, they themselves often help to keep secret the details of how the administrators actually run Japan. Most journalists who have specialised in a particular field are fully aware how far practice diverges from the official 'reality'. It is amazing, however, to what extent they confuse the two in fields they do not personally cover. Few have faced up to the reality of a System which operates fundamentally at variance with the conventions and rules of parliamentary democracy. Those who have fall back on the worn-out cliché of 'monopoly capitalism' to describe it.

The effect of self-induced editorial ignorance can be rather eerie. Newspapers, for instance, may lament a parliamentary boycott by the minority parties on the grounds that it prevents Japan's elected representatives from discussing momentous events happening in the world – blithely ignoring the fact that foreign policy issues, even those affecting the national interest in a direct manner, are never debated in the Diet. Concerning a major embezzlement case, a *Yomiuri Shimbun* editorial stated that stockholders and the union should have monitored the goings-on in the company in question; yet such bodies have never had anything remotely resembling that kind of role in a Japanese company. Similar examples can be found practically every day.

A well-tuned single-voice choir

The major source of the power of the Japanese press is its monolithic nature. In the first morning edition of the five major national dailies (whose combined morning and evening editions have a circulation of 39 million copies) the choice of news and the tenor of editorial comment may vary somewhat. But by the last morning edition – read in the large cities – there is a homogeneous approach to all but certain routine controversies (such as that on defence spending) in which newspaper attitudes are sometimes recognisably different. Editors furiously read each other's early editions, and keep adjusting their own. The rare scoop is normally saved for the last morning edition, sold in the cities, because if it appeared earlier no one would know that it was a scoop. Lead articles in the days following important events tend to be non-committal, vague and ambivalent, and are generally indistinguishable from each other. Most of what these papers print is a predictable product of desk editors, compiled from 'feeds' supplied by a number of reporters and influenced by extraneous political factors. The result is almost never challenged, again with the exception of the routine controversies. All Japanese read approximately the same things every day and have their opinions formed by what is in effect a single source.

This unified voice of the press is often critical and sounds like the lamentations of the smaller parties in the Diet. Rapping the authorities over the knuckles is considered proper every once in a while, but is little more than a ritual. Some components of the System use this predictable behaviour of the press to get back at, or gain leverage over, rival components. In fact, the press plays an important part in the continuing balancing act with which some groups of power-holders prevent others from becoming too strong.

Political controversies on a limited number of recurrent themes induce a practically unanimous press reaction as immediate and predictable as the salivating of Pavlov's dogs at the sound of the bell. Even when there is a break in unanimity, the pattern is very predictable. For instance, the *Asahi Shimbun*, which has the most prestige, is inclined to frown on anything Japan's 'rightist' forces are supposed to stand for, including pleas for a greater Japanese share in the burden of its own military security. It was similarly suspicious of Nakasone's efforts to increase political leverage over the bureaucracy. The *Asahi's* editorial line is influenced by columnists and editorial advisers who tend to be anti-USA and were in some cases weaned on an old-fashioned Japanese version of Marxism.

The most important press development in recent years has been the *Yomiuri Shimbun's* break with the conventional anti-US, anti-defence stance. The *Yomiuri*, the largest newspaper, distributes nine million copies a day. The *Mainichi Shimbun* still tends to follow the *Asahi* line on these matters, as all the others used to do. The *Sankei Shimbun*, the smallest of the four non-economic national dailies, has a right-leaning reputation. This reputation appeared to be confirmed by its refusal to go along with an agreement the Japanese media made with the Chinese government, in return for permission to station correspondents in Peking, to write only positive reports about China under Mao Tse-tung. The defection of the *Yomiuri Shimbun*, the anti-left stance of the *Sankei* and the staider interpretations of the *Nihon Keizai Shimbun*, the largest financial and economic paper, have helped much in breaking post-war taboos on the discussion of military matters. At the same time, less attention than before is given to the voices of leftist groups.

The press as social sanction

Japanese journalists are sometimes conscious of their own daunting dilemma in a society that does not reward those who point out its contradictions. The press is ideally situated to note and comment when the power-holders fail to adhere to the official rules, yet is severely hampered in doing so by its own journalists and editors, who fear rending the fabric of reality as presented by the System. What is a Japanese journalist to do with the wealth of information he has concerning actual practices in the System? Should he consistently point out the institution-alised breaches of major rules, his own small part of the real (as distinct from the ideal) world might well come crashing down and crush him. The perennial problem is how to know where to draw the line on honest reporting. The ability to sense the appropriateness of self-censorship is commonly referred to as the 'adult mentality' of journalists.[26]

An uncomfortable sense of not living up to professed standards of journalism, which are certainly part of the training of journalists, is nevertheless fairly common. The problem is complicated by the press's self-imposed but socially accepted (and expected) function in preserving the social order and guarding public morality. There are outlets for the resulting frustration. As in many other instances of apparently insoluble conflict in Japanese society, the tendency is to find a temporary solution in ritualised behaviour. Thus the newspapers, mindful of the traditional precept 'Punish one to warn one hundred', wage periodic campaigns in which a great deal of indignant energy is released.

About every other year the newspapers 'discover' a teacher who has had the temerity to sell examination questions to ambitious parents. Officials of the International Telephone and Telegraph Corporation were once caught smuggling small consumer items into the country, and the press lambasted them until the company contritely promised to lower the (exorbitant) international telephone rates. The top executive of a famous department store was dragged through the mire after it was found that Persian antiquities sold in the store were manufactured in Yokohama. Another example was the press treatment of the owner of Hotel New Japan, after the hotel went up in flames and was found to have lacked some of the mandatory safety facilities. 'Developments' in such selected cases are kept on the front pages for weeks and sometimes months on end, while the people held responsible are thrown in the gutter and kicked in unison by indignant editors, often before any arrests have been made.

Other department-store or hotel bosses, or executives of whatever organisation may be chosen next, are definitely frightened and fore-warned. Society is served this way by having the ubiquitous racketeering reined in a bit. In a country where laws exist for the administrative purposes of the bureaucracy rather than the protection of citizens, the press plays a critical sanctioning role. It can do this because Japanese strongly fear the consequences of having their reputations blemished. This concern with preserving their good name substitutes to a large extent for legal sanctions in keeping organisations and people in line.

The 'mondai' phenomenon

The Japanese press serves the System in that the journalists indirectly help indoctrinate the public to accept it as inevitable. Sometimes, though, their corrective function is directed at some malfunctioning aspect of the System itself. From time to time, the Japanese nation throws itself on a particular subject with a real vengeance as the media hit it day after day. A subject that attracts such intense negative attention is known as a *mondai*, which in various contexts means 'problem', 'issue' or 'question'.

The *mondai* of school bullying described above set a record by lasting more than a year. Most press-generated *mondai* are on the front pages for a couple of months at the most, but during this time it is very predictable what the conversations in bars, coffee shops and elsewhere will be about. At the least, they create a sense of togetherness and concord. Alternative opinions about the *mondai* of the month, other than those the media make current, would be almost as surprising to one's Japanese conversation partners as disagreeing with their routine comments on the state of the weather.

The most monumental of *mondai* in recent decades was the *kogai mondai*, focusing on industrial pollution of air, land and water. The national press went on a concerted campaign of publishing scary stories that lasted for roughly half a year. This finally caused people to stop eating fish almost entirely, and severely threatened the market for sea-food. Possibly to prevent that from getting out of hand, the *kogai mondai* was wiped off the front pages by a barrage of news stories and articles concerning the possibility of a large earthquake destroying much of the capital, in which the emergency preparations of the government were questioned. The near monolithic voice of the press may sometimes cause massive over-reactions to events that occasionally seem to come close to the edge of mass hysteria.

Restraining a racket

The press sometimes turns on abuses to which the officials have shut their eyes. The *sarakin*, 'salary-loan' companies, provide a good example. These gangster-connected usurers maintain normal business relations with banks, insurance firms and other financial institutions, and often work out of respectable offices.

The reason for their existence is the very underdeveloped state of Japanese consumer credit. Japanese have for decades brought their savings (on the average a little under one-fifth of their income) to the commercial banks and the postal savings system, whence the money has flowed exclusively in the direction of big industry. Banks have not been equipped to judge the creditworthiness of potential borrowers, and untied loans to private individuals were for long almost unheard of. In the late 1970s and early 1980s, when other circumstances had increased the demand for consumer credit, the *sarakin* entered the picture, enticing office workers into taking out short-term loans without the need for collateral. The catch lay in interest rates at around 40 to 70 per cent or even higher. A large number of inexperienced borrowers sank ever deeper into debt, a process heartily encouraged by the loan sharks.

In 1984 the press began to record family murders and suicides brought about by this state of affairs. There were horror stories of gangsters coming to front doors demanding to be paid, destroying the name of the debtor among his neighbours in the process; of letters sent to the debtor's children at school; and of despairing housewives becoming prostitutes under the guidance of the *sarakin*.

The laws regulating this business were contradictory, and decisions in a number of extreme cases that underwent the process of legal conciliation were not encouraging. With no institution or group to represent the victims, the press found itself the only watchdog, and did in fact bring about a certain alleviation of the problem, stimulating new (though inadequate) legislation and bureaucratic guidance that created a category of less usurious *sarakin*.

The process that led to the legislation clearly illustrates how, under the System, the interests of the consumer are the last to be considered. Jurisdictional disputes among ministries, and moves by LDP politicians to protect the usurers in exchange for 'political funds', blocked five bills and delayed legislation for six years.[27] The law that was eventually enacted legitimated the *sarakin* and established a ceiling of 73 per cent on interest rates, to be lowered to 40 per cent at a date when the 'economic conditions' of the *sarakin* permitted – all this while there was a competing law on the books limiting interest rates to 20 per cent! The parties best served by the new law are the bigger *sarakin* and the Ministry of Finance. The latter had been most upset over the unorganised condition of this newest sector in an otherwise well-controlled financial world; now, the new law calls for registration of *sarakin* businesses, which means the ministry has established channels for compulsory information in one direction and administrative guidance in the other.

Insufficient legal protection of the public has helped the development of many rackets in Japan. The *sarakin* are only one example; others include the *juku* crammer schools, doctors who overprescribe medicine and the *koenkai* that help elect LDP politicians. Racketeering is also rife in Japan's real-estate business and stockmarkets. None of these is the target of serious reform attempts, and it is left to the press to react to such excesses as actually threaten to disturb the social order.

Accommodated mobsters

The most startling example of how the System uses groups of presumed outsiders for its own ends is seen in the relationship between the police and the criminal gangs. Japan has a flourishing and rather romanticised underworld of roughly a hundred thousand gangsters called *yakuza*. Unlike American mafiosi, modern mainstream *yakuza* have remained clearly separated from the respectable business world; a major portion of their profits derive from illegal activities. Nor do they seek to hide what they are, being eminently recognisable in their dark blue double-breasted suits, white ties and dark sunglasses.

The police estimate that *yakuza* income from illegal activities alone reaches some 1·5 trillion yen a year. Independent experts consider this a colossal underestimate; it overlooks what may be an equally large sum earned in the sex industry operating on both sides of the law. According to a lawyer working for the largest criminal syndicate, the Yamaguchi-gumi, the same estimate also overlooks important profits from debt collecting, 'settlement' of bankruptcy cases and other rackets.[28] Either way, gangsters are in a lucrative business; together with dentists, they are just about the only Japanese clients for large American automobiles, which are heavily overpriced by Japanese dealers.

The ultimate symbiosis

In a traditional service that goes back centuries, the gangsters, who exert control over themselves within crime syndicates, help the police keep non-syndicate crime under control. The Tokugawa shogunate officials in charge of public order showed themselves masters of pragmatic government by reasoning that, since crime can never be entirely eliminated, organised crime should be used to help keep the unorganised kind to a minimum. Crime in those days centred on the Tokaido, the famous road between Kyoto and Edo (later Tokyo), which was used by people of high rank as well as by highwaymen and other rabble. The simple solution of the shogunal officials was to give responsibility for keeping order on the road to the bands of shady elements that organised the inevitable gambling and prostitution.

The *yakuza* are celebrated in the cinema and tolerated in the social landscape. Just like the cowboy operating on the fringes of the law, the cinema *yakuza* often champions the victims of injustice. Unlike the cowboy, however, he is never portrayed as an individualist and loner. The belief is still common among ordinary Japanese that the *yakuza* preserve venerated customs and virtues that in mainstream society have yielded to modernity, which means, for the most part, intensive group solidarity and simplistic demonstrations of absolute loyalty towards a master. *Yakuza* films like samurai films romanticise the traditional manliness of an imagined warrior past. In fact, 'the samurai heroes are in some ways less traditional, less essentially Japanese than the yakuza'.[29] Outside the cinema, real-life *yakuza*, especially the older ones, tend to believe that they are indeed guardians of tradition; the 'pure' Japanese behaviour on the screen actually rubs off on to the organized criminals, who love these films.

The record of a police interview illustrates this: 'I am obliged to obey the words of my boss at any cost. If he said that a crow is white, I would say it is white. If I had to wear white clothes [be killed in gang warfare] or wear blue clothes [go to prison] as a result of that, I would accept it.' Pseudo-blood-ties are created through ceremonies in which the newly united sip sake from the same bowl. A lawyer specialising in defending *yakuza* says that, whereas he first viewed their use of kinship terminology as nonsensical sentimentalism, he began to realise how persuasive it is for the *yakuza* themselves. 'Neither logic nor money can control a self-willed gangster. But by brandishing the supreme and irrational principle of the "father-hood" of the boss, the organization can make members submit to anything.'[30]

Yakuza are accustomed to protection from people in high places. Both before and after the war they were used by the corporations to help break strikes. Large and famous firms with impeccable reputations are not above using them for intimidation purposes – in the rare case, for instance, of litigation against them. It is an open secret that gangsters sometimes do the dirty work for politicians. Prime Minister Sato Eisaku had a *yakuza* 'bodyguard' on call, and a number of other politicians used to take the precaution of having gangsters attend political rallies. Considering how much can be accomplished in Japan by intimidation, it should be no surprise that some LDP politicians still consider good relations with highly placed *yakuza* to be useful. It has not been considered sensational when a cabinet minister attended a gangster wedding, or sent flowers. Former prime minister and *éminence grise* Kishi Nobusuke was vice-chairman of a committee organising a *yakuza* funeral in 1963.[31] In 1974 he sent a congratulatory telegram to Taoka Mitsuru, son of the Yamaguchi-gumi boss, on the occasion of his wedding.[32]

The world of the *yakuza* borders on and partially blends with that of the rightists, who portray themselves as the only true patriots. The extreme right encompasses more than eight hundred groups with well over one hundred thousand members, one-fifth of whom are highly active. The activists remind Japan of their existence primarily by making a noise, zigzagging through traffic with their sound-trucks blaring martial music, and by a few bombing attempts directed at the teachers' union. But in 1987 a reporter of the *Asahi Shimbun* was murdered by a gunman thought to belong to a mysterious extreme rightist organisation called Sekihotai. Since then this outfit has also threatened to kill former prime minister Nakasone Yasuhiro, besides issuing further 'warnings' directed at the newspaper.

Apart from the extremist fringe, there exists an extensive network of sympathisers with rightist causes that reaches into the media, the universities and the LDP. The two best-known rightists of recent times, privately wealthy power-brokers who pulled wires for many a top politician, reached their positions partly through gangster connections. They are Kodama Yoshio, who attracted much attention through his involvement in the Lockheed bribery scandal until his death in 1984, and Sasakawa Ryoichi, who still attracts attention through his philanthropic activities. In 1982 Sasakawa, lobbying hard for the Nobel peace prize, established the US–Japan Foundation, to promote cultural exchanges with the USA, and he is the largest private donor to the United Nations. In 1978 he received from the Japanese government the First Order of the Sacred Treasure and in 1987 the First Order of Merit with the Grand Cordon of the Rising Sun.

Both *yakuza* and rightist recruit among the juvenile delinquent element, especially the notorious *bosozoku*, or motor-cycle gangs. Between 30 and 40 per cent of newcomers to the Yamaguchi-gumi are *bosozoku* members.[33]

Throughout this century police and corporations have used gangsters to counterbalance Marxist influence. At the time of the 1960 struggle in connection with the extension of the security treaty with the USA, a struggle that pitted radical leftist student protesters and leftist unions against the government, Kodama Yoshio mediated between the LDP and Tokyo gang bosses in organising an army of over 30,000 *yakuza* and rightists to help the police preserve order during the scheduled visit of President Eisenhower.[34] The gangs had prepared leaflets, armbands, transport facilities and logistical support before the visit was finally cancelled because of the unrest. The *yakuza* around this time were brimming with confidence, and their number reached a peak of nearly 200,000 in 1964.

In the mid-1960s, when they appeared to be becoming too powerful, the police cracked down on some gangs, and in some parts of the country they have occasionally assisted citizen groups attempting to keep *yakuza* out of their neighbourhoods. But no serious attempt to break the gangs has ever been made. It is not corruption that is at the bottom of this, but the fact that Japan's low crime statistics would probably rise if the police had to cope unaided with a chaos of criminals operating individually or in small groups. As one student of the Japanese police concludes: the 'relationship is mutually beneficial: police and gangsters each find it advantageous to maintain rapport and to enhance it with a façade of cordiality. This nucleus of goodwill and understanding seems to remain even when the police must severely crack down on a gang after a major incident.'[35]

Police specialists regularly visit gangster headquarters to find out whether any members have been ostracised and, if so, proceed to pick them up. Both parties are served by this, since it means that there will be no lone-wolf criminals roaming the streets plotting revenge. The large syndicates openly maintain offices – adorned with gang emblems – in the cities.

Police and gang bosses have occasionally held summit conferences aimed at delimiting territory and tacitly confirming informal standing agreements. Deals are continually being made, especially in connection with firearms investigations. The police will ask the *yakuza* to part with illegal guns in exchange for turning a blind eye to, say, a case of stimulant drug smuggling. Gangs have been known to buy guns simply so that they can comply with such requests.[36]

Self-proclaimed Robin Hoods

Japanese gangsters seem convinced that they fulfil a socially important function. Leaders can be interviewed about *yakuza* activities, and will argue fairly convincingly that without their organisation antisocial youth would have nowhere to go and be a great nuisance. This echoes the contention of the greatest modern *yakuza* of them all, the late Taoka Kazuo, that he made sure that the drop-outs of society did not run wild.[37] Although they do not advertise the fact, the gangs are indeed among the few Japanese organisations that welcome members of the minority *burakumin* and Korean communities, which face considerable discrimination. This is one reason why so many gangs originated in the Kansai area, around Kyoto, Osaka and Kobe, where such communities are concentrated.

In his memoirs Taoka claimed that his gang had protected the Kobe police headquarters against attacks by a Korean gang that he helped eliminate. During a one-hour television programme devoted to the Yamaguchi-gumi and broadcast in August 1984 by NHK (comparable in function and prestige to Britain's BBC), executives of the mob were given the opportunity to explain their alleged great services to society to an audience of 25 million viewers.

An 'in-house' magazine published by the Yamaguchi-gumi gives some idea of how Japan's mobsters like to see themselves.[38] Inside the front cover is a reminder of the goal to which the syndicate has dedicated itself: the development of 'our country and our society according to the *kyodo* spirit', which means that members must (1) preserve harmony in order to strengthen the group; (2) love and respect people outside the group and remember what is owed to them; (3) always be courteous and always be aware of senior–junior relationships; (4) learn from the experience of seniors and work for self-improvement; and (5) show restraint in contacts with the outside world.

This is followed by poetry on nature and life. An essay by Taoka Kazuo explains how the big boss became a member of the All-Japan Anti-Drug Movement because drug trafficking is no good and members of the syndicate should not become involved in it. Another executive of the syndicate relates how the socially oppressed gathered in outlaw bands during the Tokugawa period to share each other's warmth and understanding. An executive assistant follows this with suggestions as to how to make the Yamaguchi-gumi more respected by people on the outside, explaining that it is not just simply a criminal gang. The magazine continues with a eulogy for a dead gangster written by his daughter. A readers' column gives a member from a sub-gang the opportunity to delve into the past and explain how his gang helped the city authorities of Kobe deal with outrageous behaviour by Koreans and Chinese shortly after the war. There are warnings against expanding one's territory too rapidly, the point being stressed that establishing local gang branches is not quite the same as the expansion of a commercial franchise network. There are complaints about injustices in Japanese society and advice by bosses of sub-gangs on how to further internal harmony. Another look at history portrays the police as powerless in the face of street robberies, rape, murder, kidnapping and the like until the author's gang came to the rescue. After a lesson on law, and a poem by a mobster to console the spirit of his dead boss, the magazine ends with personal information on individual gang members about to be released from jail and when and where the welcoming ceremonies will be held. There is information on the funerals and weddings of members, and last of all a list of addresses where every member who is in prison can be reached.

Most Japanese have difficulty differentiating between Robin Hood-type folklore and the rather unappetising reality. Even apart from the extortion rackets that victimise food and entertainment establishments in many districts, the *yakuza* can drive away the clientele of any shop simply by moving in next door with an operation of their own.

The unwritten rules of the System hold that gangsters may run protection rackets, prostitution and related illegal businesses, but that they are forbidden to carry guns and deal in narcotics. The police are also extremely wary of efforts to combine federations into a nation-wide syndicate, since this undermines the police's divide-and-rule advantage. An iron rule is that *yakuza* must make sure no innocent bystanders get hurt in their battles. It is clear that the special relationship with the police can last only so long as society is not being undermined by drug addiction and there is no flow of innocent blood. There have been numerous instances where gangs have voluntarily offered up for prosecution members who broke these rules. But arrest and incarceration carry the significant advantage of promotion in the *yakuza* hierarchy.

Corporate fixers and land-sharks

One case where the System has waged a feeble campaign against one of its own extra-legal components involves the *sokaiya* ('general meeting fixer'), a businessman type of extortionist gangster who emerged in the 1970s. He is less popular than the tattooed heroes of the cinema. His victims are the large and respected corporations.

The emergence of these extortionists was possible because of the wide and permanent gap between the formal reality and the substantial reality in the business world. Since Japanese firms officially have shareholders, shareholder meetings are necessary so as not to disturb this formal reality. In actual reality, the joint stock companies have never had any intention of giving shareholders outside the directorates of their own corporate groups a voice of any kind whatsoever. The *sokaiya*'s purpose was to ensure that this situation could be maintained.

It all began when gangsters were called in to beat up victims of industrial poisoning who, by buying shares and demanding to be heard at shareholders' meetings, had found a means of penetrating the armour of indifference of the polluting corporations. This drew the attention of other *yakuza* to the vulnerability of other Japanese businesses, and within a decade an extremely well-organised extortion system, against which no large firm was safe, had come into being. In 1982 there were roughly 6,300 *sokaiya* – one-fifth of them operating on their own, a quarter allied to the large crime syndicates and the rest belonging to newly specialised extortionist gangs.

By the late 1970s the *sokaiya* had developed a refined style, pretending to run 'research institutes' and publishing periodicals on economic subjects. Many large firms created a specialised staff for '*sokaiya* affairs' and almost always ended by paying up. If they failed to pay enough, elderly presidents were, for the first time in their lives, grilled for hours on end at their annual stockholders' meetings. If adequately paid, however, the gangsters would enforce the unwritten rule of 'no questions' at these ritual meetings. A 1982 amendment to the commercial code made *sokaiya* practices illegal in theory, but this was no consolation for the majority of victims. The directorates which co-operated with the police continued to suffer ordeals in their meetings. By then the *sokaiya* had become a necessary evil in many corporate eyes. They protected companies that were hiding scandals. Quite apart from that, how could directors break their relations with 'friendly' *sokaiya* and expect to be protected against 'hostile' ones? Thus ever more subtle tactics were devised to keep the institution going. Some *sokaiya* receive money for the anniversaries of their 'consultation bureaux' or to mark the establishment of new offices or new publications. Others sell 'membership cards' at incredible rates for 'administrative consultation'. Though much reviled, this parasitic phenomenon is not without benefit to the System. The *sokaiya* refrain from exploiting the more vulnerable segments of society, and the corporations try to reduce the amount of 'dirt' that the *sokaiya* dig up by keeping their practices more honest.

The gangster who meets the representatives of large firms, and publishes something he pretends is an economic magazine, is more sophisticated than in the days when he wore a double-breasted blue suit, white tie and sunglasses. Similar signs of increasing 'respectability' can be discerned in some other segments of the *yakuza* world as they slowly move into new businesses, such as the above-mentioned *sarakin*, that are not necessarily illegal.

In the late 1980s yet another new breed of gangster, the *jiageya* ('land-turners' or 'land-sharks'), has put in an appearance. Like the *sokaiya* and *sarakin* before them, they are the result of economic developments conducive to racketeering. During 1986–7 extraordinary increases in land prices that were already the highest in the world, the result of an insatiable demand for real estate among corporations awash with cash, accelerated the concentration of wealth in still fewer hands. Sometimes, though, the grand plans of the real-estate investors are thwarted by individuals who refuse to sell their plots or to move out of apartments earmarked for demolition. The *jiageya* are used here, first to 'persuade' such reluctant tenants and owners to change their minds, then, if simple words do not work, to intimidate them with noise, prank calls and dump-trucks crashing through walls. Several cases of arson have been traced to *jiageya*. An example of the lukewarm press reaction this kind of thing elicits is the *Yomiuri Shimbun* editorial that said that 'the [real-estate] industry in its entirety is urged to strongly reflect upon its business practices in order to regain public trust, the key to successful business'.[39]

The great succession war

In the 1980s the relationship between police and *yakuza* became somewhat uncomfortable. Weapon smuggling increased considerably, while in some prefectures mobsters were mowing each other down, as if, as an inspector of the national police said in dismay, 'they thought they were making a film'. The police have also grown unhappy with the internationalisation of the *yakuza*.[40] The increased use of meta-amphetamines (stimulant drugs) smuggled by the *yakuza* has undermined their general reputation still further.[41] On top of all this, leadership problems in the Yamaguchi-gumi following the death of Taoka led to an all-out gang war in the mid-1980s, which only gradually died down before peace was ceremonially restored in February 1987.

The details of the affair throw light on much more than the internal business of the *yakuza* themselves. The real trouble began in July 1984 when, after three years of power struggle, the widow of the great boss handed a dagger to Takenaka Masahisa, ceremonially sealing his succession to the leadership of the biggest gang. But a rival, an advocate of more moderate policies, had by then founded an alternative Yamaguchi-gumi, which became known as the Ichiwakai.

Although a majority had joined the breakaway syndicate, the Yamaguchi-gumi regained most of its forces a month later, and a period of bloody encounters began during which it became clear that the rebel *yakuza* would lose. The emblem of the Yamaguchi-gumi had proven too strong a symbol to be ignored. Furthermore, 'not everyone', as the police put it, 'has gangster qualifications', and the hasty recruiting with which the Ichiwakai tried to stop its decline merely accelerated it.

The emergency 'solution' resorted to by the Ichiwakai syndicate was to assassinate the new Yamaguchi-gumi boss, Takenaka, together with his two highest lieutenants. As viewers all over Japan watched on no less than three television channels, 1,500 gangsters in black accompanied Takenaka's coffin, borne on the shoulders of eight bosses of subordinate gangs, with 400 riot police in attendance; and the nation understood that a turbulent period in the world of the *yakuza* had begun. Even so, half a year and 174 armed clashes, 16 dead and 47 wounded later, the *yakuza* showed themselves sufficiently public spirited to agree to an armistice so as not to damage the reputation of Kobe, situated in the hottest war zone, since the city was about to host an international sporting event, the Universiad.

On a small scale and in the exaggerating context of traditional *yakuza* group rituals, what happened between the Yamaguchi-gumi and the Ichiwakai is what happens between components and dissidents at the lower levels of the System. In this case, the absence of an *éminence grise* in the gangster world who could have effected a compromise solution acceptable to the warring parties – a service that *éminences grises* are constantly expected to perform in the System – led to the use of naked force.resulting in bloodshed. But the power dynamics it entailed, with the larger body gradually absorbing the sources of strength of the smaller one and eventually rendering it ineffectual, are illustrative of those of the System at large.

5

The Administrators

Japan has a clearly discernible ruling class. Its members – mainly bureaucrats, top businessmen and one section of the LDP – are all basically administrators; there is no room among them for the aspiring statesman. It is not, strictly speaking, a hereditary class. It is fairly open, though less so today than during the first decade after the Second World War. Sons of administrators have a great advantage in the process of joining it; and it is exclusively a male preserve; either way, most boys, regardless of birth, know their chances by the time they reach their teens.

Ruling élites everywhere seek to perpetuate themselves. They are distinguished from each other by size and exclusiveness; by the degree of internal unity; and by attitudes towards the mass of the governed. Entry into Japan's relatively large administrator class is strictly via a very narrow ladder up the school hierarchy. It is riven with internal conflict, yet to the rest of society it presents an amazingly united front. And since its survival depends on that of the System, its highest shared goal is to preserve the System.

Preserving the System

The essential condition for the survival of the Japanese System is continued protection of the administrator class by keeping the criteria for membership, and the rules governing transactions among the administrators themselves, informal. The System is what it is by virtue of informal relations that have no basis in the constitution, in any other laws or in any *formal* rules of the ministries, the LDP, the corporations or any other of the administrator institutions.

Informal human networks

'Connections' are crucial to life in Japan at all levels of society. Success depends almost entirely on who one knows. *Kone* (a Japanised abbreviation of the English word 'connections') often provide the key to admission to desirable schools, and to finding good jobs. If one wants the best medical treatment, a special introduction to busy doctors is almost indispensable. Most Japanese are thoroughly indebted in this sense to numerous other Japanese, and others in turn are indebted to them; one of the main characteristics of Japanese life is an unremitting trade in favours.

In the upper levels of society, the *kone* multiply to form whole networks of special relationships. These may derive from one-time favours, school ties or shared experiences, or may involve intricate mutual back-scratching deals. They are referred to as *jinmyaku* – *jin* meaning 'personal' and *myaku* a 'vein' such as is found in mineral deposits, so that *jinmyaku* means a vein, or web, of personal connections running through the fabric of society. *Jinmyaku* are much more widespread, and of incomparably greater importance, than old-boy networks in the West.

Among top bureaucrats, politicians and businessmen, marriage facilitates the building up of informal contacts with the élite. LDP politicians reinforce their positions by marrying the daughters of older, influential politicians, then match their own sons and daughters with the children of prosperous and influential businessmen. The resulting networks are known as *keibatsu* (family groupings through marriage). There are matchmakers who specialise in consolidating administrator ties. One is a group of women graduates from Gakushuin, the former peer school.[1] Another is a club of Diet members' wives, established by the wife of Prime Minister Ikeda, who constantly exchange information on candidates for arranged marriages. The Takanawa-kai, a group consisting of some one thousand women graduates from famous universities as well as élite officials from MITI, the Ministry of Finance and the Foreign Ministry, meets some six times a year at parties and has produced hundreds of highly placed couples.[2] Probably the most exclusive group of all, the Karuizawa-kai, established in 1942, attracted widespread attention when one of its members, Shoda Michiko, married the crown prince. It brings representatives of Japan's most eminent industrialist and political families together, as well as those connected with the *keibatsu* of the imperial family. The sons and daughters of members meet at private parties given at the summer retreats of the rich in Karuizawa.[3] There are also private individuals whose full-time personal hobby is to find marriage partners for top politicians and bureaucrats, and who work closely with the secretariats of the élite ministries.

Without informal contacts the top administrators cannot fulfil what they are expected to accomplish. The actual power of a highly placed Japanese depends on his *jinmyaku*. A bureaucrat without a good *jinmyaku* cannot climb to great heights. A minister without an elaborate *jinmyaku* is worthless to his ministry and his clique within the LDP. The power of Japan's top politicians is derived from a large complex of intermeshing *jinmyaku* forged with favours, money, marriage ties and political acumen. At the middle social levels, building a *jinmyaku* requires time, energy, charm, flattery and a liver strong enough to cope with large volumes of alcohol. The value of an employee to his company is largely determined by his *jinmyaku*. The effective pursuit of corporate aims depends to a great extent on who the managers can get hold of on the telephone to fix what needs to be fixed. For these lesser administrators, a good *jinmyaku* means a good income, many people in one's debt and security after one's retirement.

Breeding the top administrators

Graduating from the University of Tokyo (Todai), especially its law department, means being automatically hooked up to a huge network of connections that is easily activated at any time. It is not the academic qualities of the Todai law department that make it the undisputed summit of the Japanese education system, but the fact that traditionally its graduates have entered the highest administrative ranks, which means that new graduates can readily plug into the established alumni network.

Of all the section chiefs and bureaucrats of higher rank in the Ministry of Finance, 88·6 per cent are from Todai. For the Foreign Ministry the figure is 76 per cent, for the National Land Agency 73·5 per cent and for the Ministry of Transportation 68·5 per cent.[4] Between 80 and 90 per cent of the annual twenty to thirty recruits to the Ministry of Finance are from the Todai law department.[5] Nearly all post-war Japanese prime ministers who exercised any influence at all have been graduates of Todai – with the conspicuous exceptions of Tanaka Kakuei and Takeshita Noboru.[6] In most post-war cabinets the crucial portfolios have been held by Todai graduates. Even in the cabinet of Tanaka Kakuei, seven ministers had passed through its law department. Over a quarter of all parliamentarians and more than one-third of all LDP members are Todai graduates. In the mid-1970s the number of Todai graduate executives exceeded the number of non-Todai executives in 43 of the 50 top business firms.[7] In 1985 the presidents of 401 out of the 1,454 largest firms were Todai graduates, with another 140 and 72 from the virtually equivalent Kyoto and Hitotsubashi universities.[8]

When it became clear in the prime ministerial contest of 1972 that Tanaka Kakuei would be the main rival to Fukuda Takeo, a prominent Todai graduate who had reached the apex of the Finance Ministry, the then *éminence grise* of the business world, Ishizaka Taizo, strongly objected. 'We cannot', he declared, 'give the position to a man who is an ignorant labourer.' Even though Tanaka was one of the most successful self-made businessmen in Japanese history, Ishizaka – as Keidanren chief, ostensibly representing a world of entrepreneurs – felt not the remotest affinity with him. Ishizaka himself had graduated from the Todai law department and had been a Communications Ministry bureaucrat before climbing to the presidency of Japan's first insurance firm. His case is typical. Inayama Yoshihiro, the weightiest influence in Keidanren in the 1980s (until a year before his death in 1987), Nagano Shigeo, whose name was practically synonymous with Japan's Chamber of Commerce and Industry from the late 1960s on, and Uemura Kogoro, a pivotal figure in Keidanren before becoming its president in 1968, were all Tokyo University graduates and government bureaucrats in an earlier phase of their careers. The cream of Japan's industrialists and almost all bank presidents have reached the top via the Todai route.

The world of the Todai law department graduates (to which one should add graduates of the law department of the University of Kyoto) is highly exclusive. Outsiders, even those from tributary 'élite courses', often feel that they never truly 'belong' to the ministry they serve. Hatano Akira, justice minister in one of the Nakasone cabinets but a graduate of the humble night-school of Nihon University, was pointedly ostracised by Justice Ministry and procuracy bureaucrats – and made no secret of hating them in return. Naito Yosaburo was one of the few non-Todai graduates to reach the post of vice-minister (in the Education Ministry). Earlier in his career, finding himself up for promotion from section chief to bureau chief, he urgently pleaded with his superior to pass him over, for fear of the jealousies it would create among his senior colleagues, all graduates from Todai law department.[9]

Con-artists and other swindlers in Japan habitually pass themselves off as Todai graduates. And real ones are extremely valuable on the *omiai* (arranged marriage) market. It should also be said that many prominent anti-establishment figures and vocal critics of the political system – of whom Maruyama Masao is the most famous example – are also graduates of the Todai law department. Although they can hardly be grouped with the administrators, their Todai backgrounds help them greatly by, as one Japanese student of the phenomenon puts it, allowing them to work in a 'safety zone'.[10]

Shielded administrators

The System protects the administrator class. As a whole the élite is insulated from the vagaries of ideologically inspired politics. Individually, its members enjoy a significantly greater protection from the consequences of their actions than do ordinary Japanese.

How far such protection can go was illustrated by the case of the Sanko Steamship Company, most of which was owned by Komoto Toshio – leader of an LDP *habatsu* (clique), several times a minister and at one point a leading prime ministerial candidate. In the summer of 1985 Sanko, in seeking judicial protection, presented Japan with its biggest post-war bankruptcy case. The company maintained the largest tanker fleet in the world (264 ships with a capacity of 21 million tons at the time of its demise), 110 offices in Japan and abroad and several daughter companies. Its bankruptcy resulted from an irresponsibly speculative policy of expansion over many years whereby it went on ordering more ships in the midst of heavy debts and long-term difficulties that cried out for major adjustments. Without the shield of Komoto's position it could never have done this. Large Japanese companies are almost bankruptcy-proof because of the extent to which their 'main banks' will continue to supply them with credit. Komoto's company had long passed the stage where it could have been rescued. Yet it was only after the two subsidiary banks learned that the prime minister (Nakasone) and finance minister (Takeshita) would not help their fellow *habatsu* boss that they prevailed on Sanko's main bank to limit the inevitable heavy losses they would all suffer.

Some administrators are better protected than others. The bureaucrats are without doubt the most shielded category of all. Article 15 of the constitution, which gives the people the right to choose and dismiss civil servants, could not be further removed from reality. To all intents and purposes, Japan's bureaucrats are situated above their own formal administrative laws. They are also usually let off the hook in money scandals involving politicians.

The extent of the protection they enjoy can be surmised from the circumstances surrounding the sale of equipment to the Soviet Union by a Toshiba subsidiary in violation of COCOM (the international organisation that supervises certain types of Western trade with communist countries) rules – an incident of great significance to the US–Japan relationship because it linked the trade problem with defence concerns in the minds of many American law-makers. The administrators responded to agitation over this issue with the ritual resignation of the president of Toshiba and highly publicised personnel changes. Yet no one pointed a finger at the MITI bureaucrats, who had refused assistance from the Foreign Ministry and the Self-Defence Agency in monitoring violations of the Japanese COCOM law, and who could not possibly have been unaware that companies such as Toshiba were not taking the law seriously.

LDP parliamentarians who are former bureaucrats are another fairly safe category. Without a bureaucratic background, they tend to be more vulnerable; though political position undoubtedly makes a great difference here.

The case of the Sanko Steamship Company, together with three or four other post-war bankruptcies involving large firms, demonstrates that not all large Japanese corporations are perfectly secure. Although Japan's top businessmen and business federation leaders are well protected, their protection is less automatic than it is for the bureaucrats and politicians. Businessmen, of course, are 'administrators' only at the top of their category, which gradually shades off into the category of the genuine entrepreneur.

The mutual-aid rule

An essential factor in Japanese politics is the never-ending strife among the administrators, especially those in government agencies and LDP cliques. This strife limits domestic policy and determines the national attitude towards the world. But it is not strife between a public and a private realm. Now and then an issue may occur on which one or more of the four business federations makes a point of opposing the stance of a segment of the bureaucracy, but government officials almost always get on better with the companies they watch over than with their colleagues in other ministries. And politicians by and large enjoy a symbiotic relationship with both bureaucrats and businessmen.

The predictable patterns of mobility within the administrator class reflect these relations. Career bureaucrats constantly move from bureau to bureau within their ministry but never to another ministry, unless it be on temporary loan for some special purpose or to a new government agency that several ministries are trying to control. The standard leap is from the bureaucracy into business or the LDP; the reverse is unheard of. A situation like that in the United States, with a continuous traffic of political appointees and outside experts into and out of ministries, would be abhorrent to Japanese bureaucrats, who find the cabinet ministers sent to them by the LDP bothersome enough.

As reward for a quarter-century of patiently fulfilling their duties, career bureaucrats may expect a second career as LDP Diet members, as executive of a government or semi-governmental corporation, or, most commonly, as executive of a large firm or bank. Their delayed rewards as *amakudari* ('descent from heaven') bureaucrats usually include at least a doubling of income and sometimes much influence and handsome fringe benefits.

Businessmen too may run for an LDP seat, but they do so less often than bureaucrats. Although neither businessmen nor LDP politicians can join the civil service, leaders of the business world do head bureaucratic committees and can be put in charge of long-term policy projects.

The most important unwritten rule among the administrators is that each category must help keep the others in business. They do so in ways that are nowhere formally specified; indeed, some of the ways in which they lend each other assistance are distinctly against the letter or the spirit of the formal rules. The bureaucrats keep the LDP in business by buying off the public with subsidies and public works. The LDP parliamentarians keep the bureaucrats in business by not rocking the boat and not making the slightest attempt to change the policies of industrial expansion that emerged in the immediate post-war period. The LDP and the bureaucrats keep the businessmen in business by protecting their businesses against foreign competition and underwriting their expansionist programmes.

Staying in power by building Japan

Few sectors illustrate the relations among the three main categories of administrators as clearly as that of construction. It is also worth taking a close look at the Ministry of Construction and the businesses it controls, because the construction industry has become essential to the preservation

of the System. Together with the agricultural business conglomerate, the
nokyo, described in Chapter 3, it helps guarantee the LDP its domination
of the Diet.

The Ministry of Construction does not rank as high in prestige as the
Finance Ministry, the Foreign Ministry or MITI, but it receives a larger
share (fluctuating between 8 and 14 per cent) of the general accounts
budget, and roughly a quarter of the so-called second budget, which is
more than any of the other ministries. The 'second budget' – the Fiscal
Investment and Loan Plan funded by the postal savings system – is roughly
two-thirds the size of the formal budget, and is administered by officialdom
at its discretion. The Construction Ministry has the authority to issue
licences to the entire industry. It directly maintains 232 construction,
maintenance and research offices and 655 smaller area offices. In 1986
more than half a million public works projects were carried out, the
majority of them under the direct or indirect supervision of the ministry. It
also has 162 extra-departmental institutions under its wing, including
public corporations that absorb some of its *amakudari* officials.

Construction investment accounts for between 15 and 16 per cent of
Japan's GNP every year, and the industry provides jobs for some 5.3
million workers. Construction Ministry officials must thus be counted
among Japan's most powerful bureaucrats. Their power dates from the time
when the Korean War energised the government's construction policy,
and accumulated profits from that war led to an urban building boom and
massive electric power projects.

The powerful role of the ministry in the distribution of the national
wealth is witnessed nearly every day of the year by the large number of
petitioners visiting its offices. The offices of bureau chiefs and the vice-
minister draw such large crowds that since the early 1960s signs on the
doors instruct petitioners to return in the afternoons, enabling the highest
officials to do their administrative work in the mornings. Among them are
many representatives of local government, interested for example in the
ministry's authority to designate the classification of roads. It can elevate a
municipal or prefectural road to the rank of national road, whereupon it
will be maintained by the government, freeing money that the local
government can spend for other purposes.

The horror of interventionist ministers

Since the minister of construction is in an ideal position to attract
'political funds' for himself and his associates, the portfolio is one of the
most sought after among powerful LDP members. For the purposes of
jinmyaku-building the post of construction minister is considered to be of
equal value to that of prime minister or secretary-general of the LDP.
Prime ministers always try to make sure that the position goes to a member
of their own *habatsu*. It is a sign of very great strength within the
government party if a *habatsu* leader who is not prime minister can get one

of his followers appointed construction minister. Tanaka Kakuei is the most famous example of such a leader.

Construction Ministry officials, like other Japanese bureaucrats, are ambivalent about 'strong' ministers. On the one hand, they want their department to be nominally headed by an LDP politician powerful enough to help them get a larger share of the national budget. On the other, they are afraid of political intervention in staff assignments. The normal relationship between Japanese bureaucrats and their ministers is clearly demonstrated by one case that was considered the height of abnormality – that survives, indeed, in Japanese bureaucratic memory as a true reign of terror. Kono Ichiro, minister between 1962 and 1964, notoriously ignored all the unwritten rules of personnel administration, just as he had done before at the Agriculture Ministry. He imported three officials from the National Police Agency and gave them top positions, including that of director of the minister's secretariat, which is the second highest bureaucratic position after that of administrative vice-minister.[11] His chief sin here was to undermine the still fragile bureaucratic identity of the Construction Ministry, since the latter had been fashioned out of remnants of the disbanded Naimusho, whose central core had been the police force.[12]

The unwritten rules were designed to alleviate tensions caused by the ubiquitous bureaucratic sectionalism. Most Japanese ministries and government agencies suffer from being divided into factions that sometimes quarrel to the point of mutual paralysis. In the Construction Ministry the latent conflict, which goes back to the time when the construction bureaucrats occupied a low-ranking position in the engineering bureau of the pre-war Naimusho, is between technical career officials (gikan) and administrative career officials (jimukan). To preserve a balance between the power of the jimukan and gikan groups, the ministry is wisely organised so that the roughly 10,000 employees of the first group and the roughly 13,000 belonging to the second cannot trespass on each other's territory. Representatives of the two groups take turns in occupying the top position of administrative vice-minister (in no other ministry are technical bureaucrats promoted to that level). The directorships of the regional bureaux go to the gikan, but the vitally important secretariat of the ministry is dominated by the jimukan. The chiefs of the road bureau and the river bureau are always gikan. The city bureau and economic affairs bureau are always headed by jimukan, while the headship of the housing bureau is passed back and forth between the two groups. A division of labour is strictly observed in each bureau, with a gikan supporting a jimukan boss, or vice versa.[13]

By disregarding bureaucratic sensitivities Kono's appointments wrought havoc in the ministry. Although it has been headed by other uncommonly strong ministers (compared with the ministries that have more prestige), none of them has dared to intervene in bureaucratic routine. Kono had graduated not from Todai but from Waseda, and had been a newspaper reporter before he entered politics in the early 1930s. Another major politician who had no bureaucratic background, and had not even attended university, was Tanaka Kakuei. Using methods very different from the brute force approach of Kono, Tanaka showed how politicians can control Japanese bureaucrats. He never went against the grain of bureaucratic expectations; he gave the construction bureaucrats increased confidence, and increased discretionary powers. They loved him while he was construction minister, when he was prime minister and long after that as he continued to dominate the ministry. And they love him to this day.

Electioneering and rigged tenders

Retired Construction Ministry officials generally do well in elections. This is very gratifying to the ministry, because strong representation in the LDP is necessary to prevent rival interests from hindering the passage of bills beneficial to the construction sector. With every ministry, the more ex-officials it has among the ranks of the LDP, the more readily its budget proposals and draft bills are accepted.

The strength of construction bureaucrats in elections was discovered during the Upper House elections of 1959, when a former vice-minister for only six months, Yoneda Masafumi, gained a record number of votes in the national constituency. A very close second to this record was marked by Kajima Morinosuke, chairman of Kajima Corporation, one of the major construction companies.[14]

It is common in Japanese election campaigns to hear all candidates listing the roads, bridges and tunnels they helped to have built. But the main strength of construction-related candidates derives from local organisations under the control of the Construction Ministry. The regional construction bureaux are potential co-ordinators of election campaigns in nearly every locality. They unabashedly support former construction officials running for office; sometimes the current minister of construction himself joins openly in the campaigns.[15] The Construction Ministry also has a strong though unofficial voice in the appointment of heads of prefectural engineering departments, which likewise translates into considerable electoral power.[16] And there is close co-operation between the river bureau of the ministry and the flood-prevention unions that exist in most of Japan's numerous inhabited valleys.[17]

The construction companies themselves form enthusiastic and hard-working pivots for the *koenkai*, the support associations that build and maintain vote-getting networks. The president of some large construction firm or other is likely to figure prominently in the campaign machine of an LDP candidate, whether or not the latter is specifically identified with the construction world as such. The companies typically lend secretaries and cars to the candidate, so that he can give continued evidence of his existence during the years between elections.

The truly symbiotic relationship between LDP politicians and the construction business is built on a system of rigged tenders. Reduced to its essentials, the system works as follows: for a construction firm to be allowed to bid on a public works project, it must first bribe a powerful politician. It will then meet with all the other nominated contractors for a negotiating session, called *dango*, at which it is decided which of them will get the job. The session is presided over by a local boss, called *dangoya*; if the locality has no *dangoya*, a major contractor will mediate.[18] The *dango* system ensures that all participating contractors will get to work on a government project at one time or another.[19] For large-scale public projects the politician may receive more than one billion yen from a single firm.[20]

While the formal authorisation of contractors is governed by law, the bureaucrats are not in a position to refuse inclusion of specific firms recommended by LDP members. The *dango* that contractors conduct among themselves behind the façade of public bidding does not formally concern the government officials. The contractor appointed through the *dango* process decides his price in accordance with inside information from the officials, and his 'competitors' set their bids above it.[21] The committee that officially makes the choice is controlled by a few influential men, and its deliberations are largely perfunctory.[22] In 1982 the Ministry of Construction, in response to public criticism of the *dango* system, gave 'administrative guidance' to the effect that the number of contractors participating in tenders for public work projects be doubled from ten to twenty. But a year later this instruction was retracted under severe pressure from the group of LDP members most intimately connected with the construction industry.[23]

The ministry itself is not averse to rigged bidding either. A firm that accepts an *amakudari* bureaucrat from the construction ministry is guaranteed at least one large construction project. A tacit agreement exists among the 'competing' firms to respect political decisions from the ministry in such a context. For example, if one of the companies participating in 'competitive' bidding to build a dam intends to provide a retiring Construction Ministry official with his second, lucrative career, this particular company is promised that it will win the contract. If it takes ten years to construct the dam, the company can survive for ten years by accepting a single *amakudari*.[24] There is no outcry against these practices by opposition politicians, since a fair number of them are also trying to gain electoral advantage through the construction industry.

One of the most powerful LDP politicians of the late 1980s, Kanemaru Shin, played a major role in preserving and strengthening the *dango* system against measures planned by the Fair Trade Commission.[25] Kanemaru, a pivotal figure amidst LDP members representing the construction industry, is expected to profit enormously from major public works projects such as the planned bridge across Tokyo Bay.[26] It is unlikely that Takeshita Noboru could have become prime minister without Kanemaru's help.

Since the 1970s marriage ties with the progeny of bosses in the construction industry have been much sought after among LDP politicians. Former prime minister Nakasone's daughter is married to the son of the president of the giant Kajima Corporation.[27] Takeshita is also extremely well ensconced in construction business circles. His eldest daughter married Kanemaru's eldest son. His half-brother, who is also his secretary, is married to the daughter of the president of a medium-sized construction company (Fukudagumi). His third daughter married the second son of the former president of Takenaka Komuten, one of Japan's better-known construction firms.[28] He is also directly supported by eighteen construction companies.[29] Shortly after he became prime minister, almost all the requests for projects from Takeshita's own prefecture, Shimane, were included in the first draft of the 1988 budget. Prefectural authorities are accustomed to expending much energy every year in petitioning to have initially ignored projects 'restored' in subsequent budget drafts prepared by the Ministry of Finance, but this time the governor of Shimane found himself expressing his appreciation for what he termed the (bureaucrats') 'congratulatory gift' to the newly appointed prime minister. The local government of Ehime prefecture, which elected to the Diet the construction minister in Takeshita's first cabinet, was similarly happy to discover that its proposals for public works projects had been accepted in the first budget draft.[30]

Sociable builders

It is said that aspiring bureaucrats with brains and a good family background try to get into the Ministry of Finance, while those with brains only go to the Ministry of Construction. Nearly all the latter can eventually become directors of corporations, with no fear of being stopped by competitors with better family connections. All it takes is a tough liver to cope with their 'evening duties', construction bureaucrats being among the most lavishly entertained of all administrators.[31]

The National Tax Agency lists the construction industry as the second most 'sociable' industry, second only to the more amorphous category of wholesalers; in 1985 it spent 635·82 billion yen on entertainment.[32] Construction officials may also expect invitations from mayors, local government leaders and members of parliament. Construction civil servants, followed by those of MITI, are the most frequently seen bureaucrats in Tokyo's most exclusive and outrageously expensive class of restaurant. Sometimes, the ministry itself picks up the bill. In 1977 it attracted some attention for having spent 8·23 million yen dining and wining auditors checking accounts at eight regional construction bureaux.

The Construction Ministry is often referred to as the 'godfather' of some 350 contractors. Its officials serve them by including them among the nominees for a tender, by giving them vital information in advance, by refraining from 'exaggerated' inspections[33] and by using their influence in the private-sector market. Although public projects pay less than private construction contracts, they have been much in demand since the slow-down in corporate investment following the oil crisis. Furthermore, 40 per cent of the contracted amount for public works is paid in advance, which means large funds for short-term investment, because much of the work is done by subcontractors who accept delayed payment of up to a year.

The regional construction bureaux are notorious for involvement in bribery cases – and those that come to light are certainly but a fraction of the whole. Only rarely do accusations touch the ministry. In 1973 a vice-director of the river bureau was arrested and made to resign, whereupon he was given a lucrative advisory position; the ministry had sacrificed one official to prevent the damage from spreading.[34] A saying goes within the ministry that 'accepting cash or women may be fatal', the implication being that other kinds of present and entertainment fall within acceptable bounds. One perfectly safe type of bribery is the giving of senbetsu – cash as a parting present to retiring staff. Since even minor officials such as employees in a local office of a regional construction bureau may receive more than a million yen, higher officials probably receive rather staggering sums.[35]

It is clear that construction firms without ample funds to spend on politicians and bureaucrats, and without a jinmyaku to maximise the effect of the money, cannot survive. Signs of the pork-barrel operations that keep the LDP in power – and also keep millions of regular construction personnel, day-labourers, part-time farmers and farmers' wives employed – can be seen all over the Japanese countryside. Huge concrete waterways hold what were once small creeks by the rice-fields; even the worst cloudbursts barely manage to cover their bottoms with water, and they are sometimes so overgrown that they are hardly recognisable as canals at all. Municipalities of small houses and shops lining half a kilometre of road are sometimes equipped with an administrative office and assembly hall complex of modern opera-house proportions. Concrete skeletons tell of projects that were never finished; a costly tunnel exists to take one single curve out of a road. The Japanese countryside is never finished; there is always room at the high end of a remote valley for one more small dam to hold back some rain-soaked earth. In the face of such vested interests, local opposition politicians in prefectural and municipal governments cannot afford, whatever their ideological views, not to co-operate with representatives of the System.[36]

Ups and downs for the guardians of the 'economic miracle'

Not all Japanese bureaucrats are as easy-going with respect to the businesses they supervise, or as vulnerable to LDP pressure, as those of the Ministry of Construction. The Agriculture Ministry belongs in the same league as the latter, but the other two economic ministries, Finance and MITI, are considered more 'responsible' and enjoy greater prestige.

Standing at the apex of Japanese officialdom, the Ministry of Finance (MOF) is unofficially in charge of protecting the System against the excesses that the informal relationships of a myriad *jinmyaku* could inflict upon Japan.[37] If the officials of some other ministry seem too subservient to the interest groups they subsidise, or too easily swayed by politicians, they will be brought up short when they come to negotiate their share of the national budget with MOF officials. To be treated favourably where special requests or new projects are concerned, a ministry must have a good general reputation with the MOF, and a basic requirement for this is that it keep its figures straight.[38]

Another of the major functions of the MOF is to regulate the flow of funds from banks into the business sector. Since the war Japanese corporations have had little choice but to rely for capital on bank borrowings rather than on equity raised in public markets.[39] The banks have been practically the only source of finance for industry. They hold large portions of the shares of companies within their corporate grouping. Working closely with each other, and with the very limited number of institutional investors – a group restricted almost entirely to insurance companies and trust banks – the hierarchically ordered banks have a tremendous steering power. Directing them in turn are the Bank of Japan and MOF bureaucrats. The central bank must give approval to the so-called city banks (attached to the *keiretsu* conglomerates) for their lending strategy. Each quarter, the banks submit plans and receive 'window guidance' in return. In the 1980s, with the days of scarce capital over, popular wisdom and the officials themselves maintain that 'window guidance' is only perfunctory; but foreign bankers in Tokyo and other specialist observers consider it still to be a powerful means of control. The central bank has not succeeded in its attempts to gain independence from the MOF, which therefore has the ultimate say over 'window guidance'. Its direct control is formidable as well. A knowledgeable observer compares the function of the MOF's banking bureau

> to that of a franchiser. The banks, for their part, serve as franchisees. At the fortress-like MOF building in Kasumigaseki, 40-year-old *kacho* [section chiefs] in shirt-sleeves lay down the law to groups of blue-suited bankers, visiting in groups of five at a time. For decades these rituals were – and still are – the core of financial government. Little that matters is written down and codified. The regulations belong to an oral tradition, as interpreted by the *kacho*. The system endures, because the central motivation is to protect the banks' profit.[40]

The unformalised nature of this process so vital to the Japanese economy is clear. As the author further notes, 'regulation' does not have the meaning attached to it in the West. There are no referees; the 'officials are in effect player-managers who urge along their teams of bankers'.[41]

MOF bureaucrats generally receive privileged treatment from their colleagues in other segments of officialdom. And the general picture of them among the public comes closest to the ideal of the disinterested, hard-working, self-sacrificing civil servant whose only thought is for the public good. Hard-working most of them certainly are. A common joke has it that the children of budget bureau bureaucrats are all born during the same few months in the winter, since for most of the year they hardly ever see their wives. In recent decades the divorce rate among them has been uncommonly high, probably reflecting the fact that the élite expectations of their upper-class brides no longer include husbandless households.[42]

Although it cannot afford to appear to be anything but a model of public service, the training of this élite-of-élites and the environment in which it operates make it no less ruthlessly ambitious than officialdom in other ministries, and probably more so. Its members take it for granted that the LDP will endorse them for national elections in larger numbers than officials from other ministries. They also expect to receive the highest *amakudari* positions that the business hierarchy can offer, often ending up with well-paid top managerial posts in government corporations, banks, insurance companies or securities houses, as well as conglomerate firms.

The higher one's rank in the bureaucracy, the better the *amakudari* post. Former administrative vice-ministers are the most likely candidates for the governorship of the central bank, the Export Bank or the Japan Development Bank, or for the presidency of a public corporation. Whatever a bureaucrat's final destination, though, he can reach it only via the proper *jinmyaku*, which means that throughout his career he must cultivate patron–client ties with businessmen and politicians.

The golden age of the MOF bureaucrats extended from the United States occupation era to the mid-1960s. This was the period when, operating in tandem with MITI bureaucrats, they more or less ran Japan. They monopolised monetary and budget policies. They were at the same time secretive and extremely well informed, to the extent of earning the epithet 'Japan's CIA'. And since no one else understood enough about what they were doing, or for that matter about the financial resources they could draw upon, their instructions went nearly unchallenged.

This period of glory drew to a close as subsidies for co-opted interest groups began to tie the hands of MOF bureaucrats. For several years attempts were made to remove this major hindrance, the most eye-catching of them being the 'break fiscal rigidification' movement of 1967–8. The budget bureau of the ministry first sounded the alarm over a loss of flexibility in budget decisions due to obligatory increases in fixed expenses. Rice growers and many other parties receiving government benefits had become so accustomed to annual increases in their income that, together with salaries and other rising costs for which the government was directly responsible, they absorbed too much of the increases in revenue, leaving very little or nothing to be appropriated at the ministry's discretion.[43]

In a fine demonstration of how powerful certain individual bureaucrats can be, the director of the budget bureau, Murakami Kotaro, in the autumn of 1967 launched a major propaganda campaign involving the press, other ministries and major figures in the LDP. The impression he tried to create was that a crisis loomed, necessitating a rescue operation by his bureau in the form of dramatic changes in budgetary policy. In spite of much support from LDP heavyweights and other administrative circles (including a parallel plan by Miyazawa Kiichi, then head of the Economic Planning Agency), the movement had little effect on the next budget and died a quiet death. The campaign backfired because the budget bureau claimed that the period of high economic growth was over even while the economy continued to grow at the usual high rates. An added problem, typical of a ministry sometimes described as 'all bureaux but no ministry', was the embarrassing failure of any of the other bureaux to lift a finger in support of the budget bureau.[44]

Whether the bureaucrats were aware of it or not, the 'break fiscal rigidification' movement and subsequent less intensive campaigns were, in fact, efforts to establish the budget bureau of the MOF as the strongest political body in Japan. They were a reaction to what it perceived as a gradual encroachment by strong LDP politicians (especially Tanaka Kakuei) on its prerogatives. If they had succeeded, they would have given the finance bureaucrats freedom to introduce new sets of national priorities. As things are, Japanese budgets do not reflect any national priorities that are newly established or consciously reconfirmed; there is no central political body that can direct significant shifts in existing priorities.[45]

The cake of national resources is sliced in an almost totally predetermined fashion, dictated by the need to ensure political peace through regular spending on behalf of LDP clients and interest groups attached to the bureaucracy. This rigidity of customary practice within the System means that deficit spending is a continuous nightmare for the finance bureaucrats. They are known, almost to a man, as 'fiscal conservatives'; and they are 'conservative' for good reason. Once a trend is set in motion in Japan, it is very difficult to stop, let alone reverse. The informal relationships that keep the political economy going are such that the major participants could not be convinced they must forgo the benefits of current practice. No overriding rules for restricting excesses are recognised, and appeals to the national interest do not work. Yet since the late 1960s deficit spending has been a significant means whereby the bureaucrats help steer the economy. It created large government debts and, until the late 1980s, considerable fear of the treasury becoming trapped in ever deepening dependence on government bonds.[46] For the MOF, the government bond problem has meant no-growth budgets (except for a few items) and a gradual decline of its leverage over other ministries.[47]

Only with the discovery in the late 1980s of new 'money-game' techniques for raising income, and with the privatisation of Nippon

Telegraph and Telephone (whose stocks reached such an astronomical price-earnings ratio that it became the most expensive company in the world) were the MOF bureaucrats relieved of their worries. While Japan's banks, security houses and insurance companies – all operating to a large extent under the wings of the ministry – were growing (at least on paper) at near exponential rates, and becoming a dominating force on the international capital and financial markets, the cream of the élite administrators appeared to be entering a new glory period.

Every Japanese ministry usually has one principal enemy among the other ministries. For the Ministry of Construction it is the Ministry of Transport, which has territorial claims over the roads and wants a share of the petrol tax. For the Ministry of Finance, it is the Ministry of Post and Telecommunications, which runs the postal savings system, the largest financial institution in the non-communist world. Since 1976 the proportion of postal savings has exceeded that of savings accounts at commercial banks. The MPT has also gained clout through its authority to set slightly higher interest rates for the postal savings system, as well as its willingness to close its eyes to tax evasion making use of multiple savings accounts under false names. It is also protected by a strong group within the LDP that partly depends on electoral help from postmasters in the post offices to be found in almost every hamlet of Japan.[48]

A major reason for the hostility of the MOF towards the MPT, however, is the rivalry over choice *amakudari* positions in institutions making use of postal savings funds. The chief of MOF's secretariat has to secure more than twenty high-level positions for retiring officials every year. In order to safeguard its *amakudari* programme the ministry has helped establish new institutions such as housing loan companies, and has succeeded in supplying presidents to some of them.[49] A beneficial by-product of the competition for *amakudari* positions is that it provides a strong incentive for bureaucrats to keep their ministries small.

A ministry that has suffered even more spectacularly in its bureaucratic battles with the Ministry of Post and Telecommunications is the Ministry of International Trade and Industry. The struggle between the two ministries in the first half of the 1980s over the relatively new sector of telecommunications technology and industry was serious, and involved mediation by several LDP politicians before an inter-ministerial memorandum finally effected an armistice. Even before this, MITI's powers had been on the wane. As Chalmers Johnson, the chronicler of this well-known institution, has put it: 'In a certain sense, MITI is a classic example of a bureaucracy that has pursued suicidally successful policies. . . . The ministry is a little like a poverty agency that has actually succeeded in eliminating poverty.'[50]

With the end of super-high economic growth and the consolidation of the industrial apparatus, MITI has had to revaluate its tasks. It has thrown itself eagerly into new projects for the development of high technology and the information industry. But partly through the claims of rival

bureaucrats in these new sectors, it cannot command the nearly unconditional obedience it was once used to.

It is MITI that has been most closely identified with Japan's post-war
'economic miracle'. For many decades it was a victor in power struggles
with those who stood in its way, notably the Fair Trade Commission
(FTC), the official watchdog of the Anti-Monopoly Law. As the first
major work on the informal relationships among the administrators
summed it up:

> The Ministry has the powerful backing not only of industry but also
> of trade associations and the four big-business organisations that are,
> in effect, its constituency. Consequently the Ministry functions as a
> promoter and protector of industry more than as a regulator and has
> consistently pursued the policy of aiding and supporting business and
> industry in the face of opposition from the Fair Trade Commission.[51]

The FTC is about the only official Japanese institution that has tried to
hold out, for some of the time at least, against the System's informal
practices and relationships that undermine the formal rules. Although it
fails practically every time, it helps preserve the illusion that the formal
rules are taken seriously. Very occasionally, though, the FTC gets the
better of the economic bureaucrats. In one famous case in 1974, the
Petroleum Association and executives from twelve oil firms were charged
with having fixed prices during the oil crisis of the previous year. They
claimed in defence that they had merely followed the instructions of
MITI. But this cut no ice with the Tokyo High Court, and the case was
closed ten years later with fines and suspended prison sentences for the
executives.

The relationship between MITI and the large corporations, like that
between the MOF and the banks, tends to be highly informal and
personal. The effectiveness of the Japanese bureaucracy is not judged by
impersonal standards. What counts is how much a ministry has 'protected
well-performing firms' or 'adjusted the benefits among various members of
the business world', rather than what the overall effect has been on the
economy or society.[52] Also, when giving instructions to business, officials
at the director-general level can officially use their *hanko* (seals), but
verbal or informal written communication from directors is equally
effective. Business connects with the ministry mainly through the bureau
directors. The latter can call the chairmen of business associations to give
them orders. Consultation preceding the guidelines also takes place at the
director level. If MITI guidelines are not followed, business leaders must
expect retribution. The basis of MITI's power over industry lies in its
ability to withhold licences and legal permissions whenever companies
balk at its wishes. Informal guidelines concerning one area of business are
often heeded because of an implied threat to withhold co-operation
in another area that the firm may want to venture into. Corporations also

toe the line because they know that MITI, which commands a vast information-gathering network, may publicise some piece of wrongdoing from their past, undermining their prestige.

The leverage that businessmen in their turn can apply, in relation to MITI bureaucrats, is effected through the politicians. Many of the more than two hundred Diet members' associations have relationships of mutual support with corporations. Consequently, the LDP is fairly vulnerable to business pressure, and it is customary for directors-general at MITI to respond to pressure from the LDP.

Although the more hidebound directors regard precedent as very important in the ministry's affairs, MITI offers relatively wide scope for originality and for taking risks. Considerations of the ultimate purpose of a policy have been known to overrule custom and precedent. The entire organisation must sometimes be 'defended' by recourse to daring measures. And if a risky course of action is successful, the director responsible basks in glory and will be promoted. 'Mental flexibility' – or rather the potential to adjust, chameleon-like, to changing conditions – is highly appreciated among MITI officials, which is one reason why those with a reputation as 'economists', meaning that they stick to positions based exclusively on economic theory, tend to rise no higher than bureau director.[53]

Fairly early in their careers, Japanese bureaucrats are rewarded with a sense of truly exercising power, and with the respect of others. Informants among MITI officials confirm, even so, that in the long run their main aim, as with all bureaucrats, is to cultivate job opportunities for themselves in the world of private business.

Ministry diplomats

Most cabinet ministers leave no legacy of initiatives in the ministry or government agency they have officially headed. Their major task is to defend their ministry against potentially antagonistic interest groups in the System. Some activist ministers, though, especially those who aspire to the prime ministership, are much more than figureheads. MITI and the MOF are less easily controlled by such ministers than, say, the ministries of Construction, Transport, Health and Welfare or Education. But a strong and politically astute minister holding the economically vital MITI or finance portfolios will take care to cultivate close relations with high officials and promising younger ones, and create loyalty debts by speeding up their careers through indirect manipulation.

This art of high-stakes *jinmyaku*-building was practised to great effect by such prime ministers as Ikeda Hayato, Sato Eisaku, Fukuda Takeo and, above all, Tanaka Kakuei. Takeshita Noboru has been doing it, and future candidates for the prime ministership such as Miyazawa Kiichi and Watanabe Michio have also excelled at it.

That this can have a major effect on MITI was demonstrated in June 1984 with the appointment of Konaga Keiichi as administrative vice-minister – *de facto* head of the ministry. The entire Japanese bureaucracy held its breath and marvelled at this development; for the 53-year-old Konaga was the first person to reach this top position who had not graduated from Todai. When, thirty-one years previously, he had joined MITI in a 'class' of thirty-eight entrants, there were only four others who had not been to Todai; still more extraordinary was that he came from Okayama University, which hardly anyone had heard of.

How could an official with such credentials ever have climbed to a top administrator position? The answer is not hard to find. When Tanaka Kakuei became MITI minister, he was given Konaga as a secretary, and Konaga remained in the post when Tanaka became prime minister. Thanks to this connection, and to his own undoubtedly superior skills, Konaga gained the reputation of having a unique system of channels to powerful politicians. It was these connections that enabled him to help bring about the armistice with the Ministry of Post and Telecommunications, and his colleagues hoped that he could use them to help revive the once proverbial dynamism of the ministry. At the vice-ministerial meetings held every Monday and Thursday to confirm the policy decisions to be automatically adopted by the cabinet the following day, the diplomacy of an official such as Konaga can be of crucial importance to a Japanese ministry.

Structural corruption

Control and interdependence among the administrators are generally discussed in terms of three issues: control over and the protection of business by the strong economic ministries; the power-play between the bureaucracy and LDP politicians; and business support for the LDP. We have still to examine the third issue and the vitally important question of political funding, but before doing this it is worth looking at the career of a single politician who managed to build within the System an empire the likes of which modern Japan had never seen.

His name, Tanaka Kakuei, has already cropped up in various connections. A survey of his career is helpful here since the empire that he built within the world of the administrators was the very epitome of the interlocking networks of unofficial relations and unwritten criteria for political behaviour that make the System what it is. He was the greatest *jinmyaku*-builder of them all, and his story proves that the man who attains complete mastery of that skill can all but take over the country.

'Shadow shogun'

Few episodes tell more about Tanaka's power than the way the prime minister and nearly all the other important LDP figures rushed to his bedside when, one day in 1983, he was reported to be having breathing difficulties. When in 1985 he suffered the stroke that marked the beginning of his political decline, even Miyazawa Kiichi, long identified with the anti-Tanaka forces, hurried to the hospital; he knew that, at that time, Tanaka's endorsement was still a prerequisite for becoming prime minister.

Tanaka began his career as a worker on road-building sites. After elementary school, he enrolled in a night-school course in civil engineering for which he could pay only after finding a job with a contractor in Tokyo. His father, a petty horse-dealer, was addicted to gambling, and his mother had to labour to prevent the family from going bankrupt. Such a childhood fits the popular Japanese stereotype of the son whose mother, through her suffering, urges him on to ever more formidable accomplishments.

At the age of nineteen Tanaka opened his own small office for building designs. His great chance came when he married a divorcee whose family owned a construction company, which he was allowed to reorganise in 1943. He accepted a risky war contract for relocating a piston-ring factory to Korea, and managed to preserve a small fortune in hard currency about which no one asked any questions after the defeat. With that financial springboard, he obtained a seat in the Lower House in 1947. In the record time of ten years he was made postal minister, and five years later became the youngest minister of finance Japan has ever had. Then, in 1972, this self-made man without formal schooling made history by becoming prime minister.

At this point Tanaka was venerated as a national hero, a living symbol of Japan's vigorous post-war economy, social mobility and democracy. When, two months after taking over as prime minister, he returned from Peking with diplomatic accords to his credit, press and public spoke of a 'Tanaka boom', confident that Japan would show the world what it could do, under the leadership of this 'computerised bulldozer'.

Some eleven years later Tanaka was to be the focus of an almost hysterical revulsion of feeling following his refusal to show remorse after the first verdict in the famous Lockheed bribery case had found him guilty as charged. The press portrayed him as a villain whose conduct was unbecoming in a Japanese and who therefore deserved to be ejected from society. His bad luck had, actually, begun in 1973. Around the time when he and bureaucrats loyal to him launched a grandiose plan for 'remodelling the archipelago' (basically a scheme for preparing the countryside for a vast expansion of industrial capacity), the first significant doubts began to surface about the effects of the overheated, run-wild economy on Japan's quality of life. The Hosannas that had grown to a massive chorus when he followed Nixon to Peking became increasingly muted as inflation and economic uncertainty mounted. These were largely a result of miscalculations by the bureaucrats dating from before Tanaka's days, but by 1974 many Japanese found the cause of what was wrong in Japan in Tanaka's 'money politics', a concept that had just been invented by the newspapers. Cartoons showed Tanaka with a safe on his back, or with banknotes coming out of his ears, nose and mouth – a walking symbol of an economic miracle that had gone slightly sour.

Tanaka was forced to resign as prime minister towards the end of 1974, because a couple of muck-raking articles in a respectable magazine had exposed some of his shady financial dealings. But open season was declared on him only after the Lockheed scandal broke in the spring of 1976. In the summer of that year he was indicted on charges of bribery and of having violated the foreign exchange and foreign trade control laws. He was jailed for a few days, during which time – most damaging of all – the newspapers dropped the honorific *san* (Mr) when referring to him by name.

It was from that period, after quitting the LDP (but not his Diet seat) in symbolic atonement, that Tanaka began seeking in deadly earnest to expand his powers. He expanded his clique, which fluctuated between 80 and 90 members when he was prime minister, to reach a peak of 122 members. In addition to building a *habatsu* larger than the major opposition party, he strengthened it with an interlocking network of *jinmyaku* covering the bureaucracy and the business world, and created many 'hidden Tanaka followers' in the rest of the LDP.[54] The entire apparatus became known as the Tanaka *gundan*, or 'army corps'. It enabled Tanaka to keep his old ally Ohira Masayoshi in power as prime minister, to select the next prime minister, Suzuki Zenko, and also Suzuki's successor, Nakasone Yasuhiro. All this he did while not even a member of the 'ruling party' – the ultimate instance of the type of power that is unacknowledged yet all-pervasive.

On 27 February 1985 Tanaka was struck down by a brain infarction, the probable result of an exhausting daily schedule and a history of breathing difficulties. Also responsible, in the view of his political intimates, was Tanaka's barely contained fury with Takeshita Noboru, then a third- or fourth-ranking subcommander of the 'corps', for setting up a 'study group' of forty Tanaka *habatsu* members in an obvious bid for the prime ministership, which he attained in October 1987.

For a while political attention in Japan had narrowed to a degree beyond belief. Ever since the 1960s the LDP, thanks to its monopoly of power, had been the exclusive subject of sustained media interest, while in the late 1970s and early 1980s the focus had been further restricted to the machinations within the Tanaka *gundan*. Finally, in the spring of 1985 curiosity was concentrated on Tanaka's sick-bed, which could not be approached by anyone except his immediate family and his faithful secretary, Hayasaka Shigeo. Two armies of photographers, one on the roof of a building opposite Tanaka's hospital, the other balancing on top of step-ladders outside the wall of Tanaka's palatial residence, were not even sure in which of the two places his bed was located.

In the meantime, top administrators found themselves suddenly uncertain about whom to turn to for orders. Tanaka's incapacity created difficulties concerning appointments to top positions in the national railways and NTT, the telephone and telegraph corporation that through privatisation had just become Japan's largest private enterprise. Negotiations relating to public works in many prefectures were stalled. Prime Minister Nakasone and his cabinet were suddenly very unsure about their chances of survival.

Many years earlier, Tanaka had discovered what is one of the central themes of this book: the emptiness at the heart of the System. Like the middle-echelon officers of the pre-war Kwantung Army, he found that this void made it relatively easy, once he had developed the right technique, to force rival power-holders into line behind him. He proceeded to set up an informal shogunate within the shell of a parliamentary democracy that was not working the way it was supposed to. Perhaps he would never have been allowed to take over the System completely, but he came as close to it as any other Japanese individual in modern times.

Tanaka's power derived from many factors that reinforced each other, but his two major strengths were that he could spur the bureaucracy into action, and that he could virtually guarantee re-election for the members of his *habatsu*.

To the extent that Japanese voters judge their Diet representatives by their ability to extract commitments from the central bureaucrats for roads, bridges, hospitals, railways and schools, Tanaka was undoubtedly the best representative they could have wished for. Niigata, Tanaka's prefecture, was once one of the poorest and most neglected areas along the relatively isolated Japan Sea coast. Today it is covered with paved roads, abounds in bridges and has tunnels that lead to hamlets of only a few dozen inhabitants. Two super expressways run through it, and a 'bullet train' stops at gigantic concrete stations serving what are little more than villages in the rice fields. There is probably no other place on earth where the pork-barrel has been so openly put on display as in Niigata. The inhabitants of the rest of Japan have reason to be jealous, for in the mid-1980s per capita funding, paid by national taxes, was 60 per cent more than the national average, and even in the late 1980s it received more public works money than any of the other forty-six prefectures.

Tanaka conquered the bastion of the Todai-ordained bureaucrats through a display of personal charm, a great interest in bureaucratic preoccupation and, most important, a phenomenal memory for legal stipulations and loopholes and for information culled from countless conversations with the best experts in officialdom. He knew where the bureaucratic skeletons were buried. He knew, as no other politician before or since, which section of which ministry was formally responsible for what kind of decisions. I have interviewed high-ranking officials who, long after his reputation had been tarnished, would fondly recall how Tanaka remembered small details of advice they had given him *en passant* eight or more years previously. His energy and knowledge earned him lasting admiration and respect from practically all bureaucrats with whom he came in contact.[55]

His talents were recognised by the former bureaucrats who ran the LDP. After Kishi and Ikeda had rewarded him with, respectively, a lucrative ministerial position (Posts) and the most important cabinet portfolio (Finance), Prime Minister Sato put him in charge of the finances of his own clique and made him secretary-general of the LDP and MITI minister.

Early in his political career Tanaka had organised the farmers and seasonal workers of Niigata. Exploited for generations, they had emerged after the war as leftist activists, but now they clung eagerly to this reliable politician who was achieving such miraculous and immediately noticeable results in the conservative stronghold of Tokyo.

Among the koenkai, the associations of vote-gatherers, Tanaka's Etsuzankai was to earn a unique fame, and has provided a model for many others. With 92,000 members in Niigata alone, it maintained a grand network of branches that, among many other activities, kept careful track of when funerals and weddings took place. Until 1975 newly wed couples and people over eighty celebrating their birthday received felicitations personally signed by Tanaka. After this method was banned, they received telegrams. At every funeral ceremony burned a thick candle adorned with Tanaka's name in brush-style calligraphy. The Etsuzankai arranged many marriages and has helped at least ten thousand people find jobs. Family relations of those benefited feel lifelong obligations towards Tanaka. In Tokyo, Tanaka held court, receiving from dozens to hundreds of petitioners every morning. All these functions – arranging marriages, finding jobs, organising weekend trips for senior citizens, helping visitors, settling local disputes – are part of the daily routine of most LDP politicians today. But it was Tanaka who perfected the method of performing them on a massive scale.

Tanaka's most original contribution to the political history of Japan was his discovery that the techniques of effective local vote-gathering were applicable at the national level. He showed interest in the problems of village heads, municipal officials, school directors, local politicians and anyone with prestige, anywhere in the country. His formidable memory enabled him, at the very least, to speak reassuringly to people over the phone, even if he could not come up immediately with the necessary funds or bureaucratic intervention. By so doing he made admirers of large numbers of local bosses throughout Japan, who saw him as their representative in Tokyo. They did not even have to support him 100 per cent; Tanaka would genially negotiate over the phone for 'half support' from those with conflicting loyalties or others who, for the sake of their reputation, hesitated to identify themselves with him too closely.

The Tanaka machine offered the best hope of election to new LDP candidates in the multiple-member constituencies, thus enabling Tanaka to recruit the most talented former bureaucrats. This was the 'carrot'; there was also a 'stick'. When Tanaka wanted to bring a hostile LDP member into line, he could generally do so by threatening to support a rival candidate – who would thus have the better chance of winning – in the constituency of the obstructionist. Thanks to his highly placed police contacts Tanaka also had access to much information useful in keeping his opponents under control, by subtle blackmail if need be.

The gigantic group of politicians that Tanaka gathered around him by means of favouritism on a national scale had, and still has, the reputation of containing the best administrative talent to be found in Japan. Tanaka himself likened it to a large general hospital where every politician who saw his position threatened could find help. In the rank and file of his *gundan* there were specialists in every conceivable political problem; his 'infirmary' was even hospitable to politicians who did not belong to his group or even to the LDP.

The mother's milk of politics

In the wake of the 1974 elections and the Lockheed scandal, the newspapers became obsessed with *kinken seiji*, money politics, and *seiji rinri*, political ethics. They had discovered that 'what Tanaka's discerning eye saw above all was that money was indeed the mother's milk of politics and that whoever controlled the largest amounts, controlled the system'.[56]

Money politics was universally decried. No one could defend it publicly, or explain in the press that without it there would be no LDP. The immediate 'remedy' was a tightening of the Political Fund Control Law, thus indicating that the relationship between the LDP and business remained an area where all was not as it should be. The term 'political ethics' as used by editorial writers and politicians of all stripes came to mean, simply, the ejection of Tanaka from the Diet. It became a weapon in the continuing fights among LDP *habatsu*, and a rhetorical device of ceremonial opposition. If Tanaka could only be forced to resign as a representative of the people, the Japanese political world could begin to clean itself up: such was the drift of numerous editorials until 1985.

The regulated money-flow from business to LDP underlines the officially approved partnership of the two. Leaders of the *zaikai* – the cream of Japan's financial, industrial and trade organisations – played a major part in the process that led to the birth of the LDP in November 1955, and it was only natural that they should keep it alive by providing the necessary funds. Organised political funding already had a long history, and the two major pre-war parties – both thoroughly co-opted by the bureaucracy – were each paid by one of the two largest business conglomerates: Minseito by Mitsubishi, and Seiyukai by Mitsui.

Until the merger of the Liberal Party and the Democratic Party in 1955, the political bosses received most of their money personally from individual businessmen, and those friendly with the most generous tended to climb highest. But this led to scandals, which undermined popular trust in the early post-war political system. The *zaikai* was extremely worried about possible political gains by the left, and in January 1955, at the height of their campaign to neutralise this threat, the four major business federations established the Economic Reconstruction Round Table to arrange a better funding system. The organisation was headed by the then vice-president of Keidanren, Uemura Kogoro, who had played a pivotal role in linking up military and civilian economic planners before the war, and was one of the top bureaucrats in charge of wartime economic planning. Its purpose was to channel money directly to the parties' headquarters, thereby obviating the factionalism and unseemly individual scrambles and helping to unify the 'conservatives'.[57] Its successor, the People's Association (Kokumin Kyokai), established in 1961 and re-named People's Political Association in 1974 (a cosmetic change brought on by the 'money politics' scandal), supplied some nine-tenths of the LDP's official income in the late 1960s and 1970s.

Every year, at a New Year's meeting with business representatives, the three top LDP executives formally request 'donations', mentioning a 'target'. In 1985 this was 10 billion yen. Which sector will donate how much is decided later by discussion among industries themselves. Between New Year's Day and the beginning of the new fiscal year on 1 April the director of the LDP's treasury bureau must visit several hundred industrial federations and large enterprises to encourage the flow of donations.[58] Ministry of Home Affairs figures show that each time an LDP politician reaches a recognised higher position, the donations he receives from businesses rise by between 55 and 100 per cent. In 1985 Nakasone Yasuhiro received five times as much as in the year before he became prime minister.

A new method of increasing permissible funding from corporations is for associates of an LDP politician to organise 'encouragement' parties and charge between 20,000 and one million yen for tickets. Companies are sometimes forced to buy a number of these tickets through their industrial association. The hotels at which the parties are held may also sell tickets to business associates and other members of the *keiretsu* to which they belong. Such tickets do not violate the law, and the supervising Ministry of Home Affairs considers them 'payment for refreshments'. In two months of partying in Tokyo and Osaka in 1984 LDP member Tamaki Kazuo netted a profit of 445 million yen ($2·6 million at the then exchange rate) on the refreshments he served, in addition to the officially declared 1,229 million yen ($7·2 million) from formal donations in his constituency.

Ministries chip in, too. As one career official complained to a newspaper reporter:

Many times I have bought tickets for the parties of prominent members of a Diet committee related to my work. The expense was covered by our ministry's budget. Besides that we also have to pay from our own pocket for tickets of politicians with whom we must cultivate connections. I personally go to about 15–20 parties in a year, which is a financial burden for me.[59]

Particularly in the case of the LDP, registered income is only a small part of the picture. There are many indirect ways of collecting money from the business world. One is through the stock market. Insider trading is very common in Japan, and a politician may buy stock that will subsequently shoot upwards in value through a variety of manipulations. (Insider trading is in theory, of course, not allowed. But between 1948 and 1987 only one case resulted in prosecution. Japanese corporations and brokers are not subject to the kind of regulatory supervision to which Western stock exchanges are submitted. If they were, the *keiretsu* structure would be endangered, and large securities houses would be out of business.) The money that LDP politicians collect in their own prefectures need only be registered with the local authorities, and no one keeps track of this. More significantly, all important LDP members have secret and very lucrative arrangements with corporations and banks, and there are 'tunnel organisations' channelling money to individual *habatsu*.

This unregulated flow of money from business to politicians is an old tradition. An early foreign commentator on Japanese politics marvelled at the immense fortunes made by Meiji-period party politicians through bribes. Once Diet politicians discovered the power they had unwittingly been given in the right – the only significant one they had – to force the government to make do with the previous year's budget, they were systematically bribed by the bureaucracy as well.[60] They needed it, for the custom of buying votes appears to be as old as electioneering in Japan.[61]

Contemporary LDP politicians can be very open about their 'secret' income. Accompanying them on routine trips through their constituencies, I have actually seen them accept tens of millions of yen in a brown paper bag. Registered income is only a fraction of what LDP politicians need to maintain their staffs and *koenkai* in normal years, to buy votes indirectly in election years, to buy the support of rival *habatsu* as they climb to the party presidency and sometimes to bribe 'opposition' parliamentarians as part of their intricate political manoeuvres.

It is impossible to calculate a reliable average, but I estimate that in a year without elections in the mid-1980s it cost about 400 million yen (some $3 million by the 1987 exchange rate) to maintain a presence in a constituency.

And these are just basic expenses. Komoto, owner of the once heavily protected Sanko Steamship Company, attracted wide attention with a dramatic attempt to buy the prime ministership. Following introduction of a new party rule providing for a primary among grass-root LDP members as a way of ranking candidates for the party presidency, the figure of 1·4 million party members in 1979 suddenly swelled by another 1·7 million. When it subsequently became clear that the primary would not after all be held, the party 'lost' practically all of these, and the count was back to 1·4 million in August 1980. Komoto himself had paid the membership fees of a majority of them.

Tanaka's election to the party presidency allegedly cost between three and five billion yen. The re-election of Nakasone as LDP president in 1984 cost his *habatsu* more than one billion yen, and another billion was kept in reserve to cope with unexpected problems.[62]

The pay-off

The benefits that the business community buys with the money spent on LDP politicians are fairly clear-cut. In 1984 the most generous with (registered) donations, accounting for about a third of what businesses officially spent on the LDP, were the commercial banks. No wonder that the highly touted liberalisaton of the financial sector helped only Japanese institutions. The traditionally high contributions from the protected steel and machinery sectors were followed, in third place, by the telecommunications industry, 11 per cent of the total. This was a year in which the United States had been pressing hard for the opening of the telecommunications market.

One specialist has found that

the commission charged by the Tanaka machine to get the bureaucracy to act – for example, to get a building contract out of the Ministry of Construction or to slow down the implementation of some market opening scheme from the Ministry of Posts and Telecommunications – was three percent of the value of the project.[63]

LDP members who mediate on behalf of city or prefectural governments for public projects paid for by the central government routinely receive 2 per cent of its value.[64]

One could cite endless other examples. Doctor and dentist associations gave more than a billion yen in registered donations in 1984. They give much every year in return for continued tax privileges and government toleration of the racketeering made possible by the health insurance system. In the early 1980s companies running supermarkets splurged on tickets to fund-raising parties, having belatedly realised that bureaucratic regulations unfavourable to them could have been modified if they had cultivated the right LDP members.[65] During a debate at LDP headquarters in 1984 as to whether office automation equipment should be taxed, a large group of LDP members flocked to the meeting room and loudly proclaimed their opposition within earshot of industry representatives in the corridors. As Kato Mutsuki, chairman of the LDP research commission on the tax system, has said, it is easy to tell who is close to what industry.[66] He himself has the most intimate *jinmyaku* ties with the Ministry of Transport, and is extremely friendly with the Japan Federation for the Promotion of Car Mechanics (the latter protects the interests of some 78,000 garages with 570,000 repairmen, a good portion of whose income is derived from the mandatory biennial tests that cost all car owners roughly 200,000 yen a time). He was in the front line of the fight against proposed reform of this system, which is generally considered to be a colossal racket.[67] Again, life insurance salesmen have been actively promoting LDP candidates prior to elections, and by no coincidence the LDP in 1984 proposed, despite opposition from the Ministry of Finance, certain income tax exemptions desired by the insurance companies.

Business sectors, especially those whose markets are expanding or shrinking or otherwise stand to benefit from government interference, tend to rank politicians according to their knowledge of the problems of the industry in question, the degree of their willingness to co-operate and past services rendered. The politician may expect financial support in accordance with that ranking.

Scandals

Few post-war Japanese prime ministers have not been tainted at some point in their career by scandal or the suspicion of corruption owing to their symbiotic relationships with businessmen. Yoshida Shigeru milked the coal companies in connection with a law for the reconstruction of key industries.[68] Kishi Nobusuke was a political merchant, suspected of having made a fortune in connection with reparations, aid loans and concession hunting in Taiwan, Vietnam, the Philippines, Indonesia and South Korea.[69] The shadowy fixer Kodama Yoshio was one of Hatoyama Ichiro's major financial supporters after the war. Ashida Hitoshi and Fukuda Takeo were indicted in connection with the Showa Denko scandal that caused a big stir in 1948. Ikeda Hayato and Sato Eisaku were involved in the shipbuilding scandal of 1954. A series of scandals that came to light in the 1960s, and were dubbed 'the black mist' by the press, appeared at one point or another to involve practically everyone who was anyone in the LDP.[70]

Even though these and other scandals have caused intermittent outcries, corruption in Japan is in a sense legitimised by its systematic perpetration. It is so highly organised, and has become so much a part of the extra-legal ways of the Japanese System on so many levels, that most citizens and foreign residents do not recognise it for what it is, but accept it as 'part of the system'. The press calls it 'structural corruption', implicitly acknowledging that it is a necessary aspect of the System in its present condition.

If everyone in Japan accepts the situation, why was such a fuss made over Tanaka's money deals that he had to resign as prime minister? And why the continuing hullabaloo over Lockheed? The fact that the Lockheed scandal was first exposed in the United States undoubtedly made it more difficult to sweep it under the carpet. Even so, why was Tanaka incessantly pilloried after 1976? Three years after his arrest, it was revealed that another aircraft manufacturer, McDonnell Douglas, had paid as much as Tanaka received from Lockheed (500 million yen) to the director-general of the Self-Defence Agency. Yet the spark of scandal was swiftly extinguished, and practically no one remembers it now. Why Tanaka?

Everyone knew that it had cost a great deal of money to climb to his position, to strengthen his *habatsu*, to do what he did for the people of Niigata and to get the bureaucracy to act on schemes he believed beneficial to Japan. The money must have come from somewhere; no Japanese politician gets by on his own money alone. This had been illustrated by *habatsu* leader Fujiyama Aiichiro, a famous businessman and former foreign minister who almost bankrupted himself trying in vain to become prime minister.[71] Ikeda Hayato, in advising the members of his *habatsu*, had made no bones about where political funds ought to come from – not from one's own pocket or from one's own business; others should take care of a politician's expenses.[72]

Punishment for the threatening outsider

Tanaka's difference lay in the fact that he made a large proportion of his political funds through his own business deals. At one point it seemed as if there was hardly any other business in Niigata apart from the construction business. Tanaka speculated in real estate without risk because of his inside information concerning government projects. He owned a number of dummy companies that did nothing but buy and sell land.

Tanaka once explained to his secretary, Hayasaka Shigeo, that he could not have followed the example of his fellow politicians because he did not have their background. No Todai in his past linked him to the rest of the System.[73] Unlike Ikeda, Fukuda Takeo and Ohira Masayoshi, he had not served in the Ministry of Finance, thereby establishing strong financial ties to banks, insurance firms and basic industries such as steel. Unlike Miki Takeo, he had not married into a fortune made by chemical fertilisers, or been supported by utility companies.

Here perhaps is part of the explanation for the collective condemnation of Tanaka. He was relatively independent. The business components of the System did not, ultimately, have a grip on him. They can veto the choice, or retention, of a prime minister only so long as he is not privately very wealthy. Tanaka remained, in the end, an outsider. This was made poignantly clear after the Lockheed verdict in 1983, when he refused to make the smallest gesture that could be interpreted as a sign of contrition. Many even of his sympathisers agreed with his enemies that this was going too far, and that he was behaving in an 'un-Japanese' manner. Ritual penance was what everyone expected, and if he had gone further and resigned his Diet seat to 'let the people speak' in the forthcoming election, a resounding victory would have given him maximum political elbow-room. He was, however, furious and chose to defy the élite of the nation.

Yet the main reason for the anti-Tanaka clamour probably lies in that essential aspect of the System that we have been considering in this chapter: its informality. In some ways Tanaka was too honest. He had gained his power by exploiting the unofficial opportunities inherent in the political system more skilfully than anyone had done before him. Then he tried to make explicit what had been only implicit; he tried to systematise the System. What Tanaka did became too obvious. In the 1974 Upper House election campaign, waged when he was prime minister, there was no attempt to hide the many attempts at vote buying or the pressure on corporations to order their employees to vote for LDP candidates. Moreover, the structural corruption that every administrator knew existed, but could pretend to be ignorant of, began to be practised in such an open manner that there was no longer any way to deny it.

With this was combined another disturbing development. The unschooled political genius who had broken all barriers to move into the centre of a world dominated by Todai-ordained administrators had, through brilliant craftsmanship at both the grass-roots and Tokyo levels, become seemingly invincible. The balance among cliques within the LDP had been upset by the supremacy of Tanaka's *gundan*. For concerned Japanese this was terrifying. In many eyes, the essence of Japanese 'democracy' lies in preserving a balance among the components of the System, and within the LDP subsystem.

Tanaka's dominating presence provoked a chronic reaction that, among administrators, sometimes reached frenzied proportions. A great irony of the saga was the behaviour of the newspaper editors. They tried to be exorcists instead of analysts; one of the most interesting developments in post-war Japanese politics prompted moral indignation rather than rational thought. Even though Tanaka's greatest power, the power that enabled him to choose Japan's prime ministers, dated from *after* his downfall as prime minister and *after* his arrest in the Lockheed case, during the same nine years that his power kept growing the press predicted at regular intervals, and nearly unanimously, his imminent demise. The predictions were partly intended as self-fulfilling prophecies. In its role as guardian of the nation's morals, the press tried, by reporting his waning powers, to make Tanaka go away. This would probably have worked with a smaller man, but Japan's editors consistently underrated Tanaka. And because he simply thumbed his nose at them, their voices became ever more strident and hysterical. They stopped only when it became clear that the 'shadow shogun', partly paralysed and suffering from a speech impedi-ment, was finally losing control over one of the greatest *jinmyaku* systems Japan had ever seen.

LDP battles, bureaucrats and political tribesmen

A major problem of Japanese politics is that the LDP has not been able to develop a generally accepted method for choosing its president. For a while this was solved by prime ministers who picked their own successors with the encouragement and blessings of the business world. Thus Kishi handed the job to Ikeda, who in turn passed it on to Sato. But when Sato was forced to retire in 1972 he did not appoint anyone, starting a power struggle that was to provide the main substance of political news and discussion for a dozen years.

'Habatsu' politics

Political commentary in Japanese newspapers concentrates almost solely on what clique leaders are doing to keep or gain leverage over each other. When in the spring of 1987 Takeshita Noboru finally declared his intention of running for the LDP presidency, thereby splitting the Tanaka *gundan*, he touched off half a year of media speculation concerning Nakasone Yasuhiro's successor. Yet not once did editorial comment take up the question of who among the four contenders might make the best prime minister. Japanese political comment is for the most part narrowly focused on the perennial guessing-game as to who is doing what to whom in Byzantine manoeuvrings. References to policy find no place in it; there are no policy differences to refer to.

Sophisticated theories that see LDP cliques as *de facto* political parties vying with each other for influences in political decision-making are wrong. *Habatsu* compete with each other for the prime ministership and for unmediated access to the bureaucracy in order to deliver on pork-barrel promises. No idea or principle concerning how power ought to be exercised enters into it.[74] *Habatsu* politics does not correspond to any form of pluralism. It is a power game, entirely bereft of meaningful political discussion, and one over which the voters exercise no influence at all.

The number of *habatsu* fluctuates because of splits and mergers; during the 1970s and 1980s there have been from five to seven important ones at any one time. They take their names from their leaders, who are the prime candidates for the presidency of the LDP and thus the prime ministership. The *habatsu* are a source of never-ending friction, and sometimes of such severe tension that the LDP appears on the verge of disintegration. Cabinet posts are apportioned in accordance with the size of each *habatsu*, and if one of them is seen as receiving a single portfolio too many, this prompts immediate debate over the 'sensitive' or 'very delicate' situation. The *habatsu* help regulate the distribution of political spoils, and perform an essential function in the disbursement of funds. Because the multi-member constituencies encourage competition among LDP candidates themselves, highly placed *habatsu* members are expected to campaign on behalf of their fellow members and against LDP candidates belonging to other *habatsu*. Local LDP offices, where they exist at all, are meaningless and may even be regarded with hostility in these internecine contests.

Alliances between *habatsu* are needed to produce prime ministers, and successful ones are generally referred to as the 'mainstream' of a government's support. The rival, 'anti-mainstream' *habatsu* are still rewarded with cabinet posts, but they are also watched carefully for moves that could spell the beginning of a campaign to undermine the incumbent. In recent years, defections and new link-ups between segments of rival *habatsu* in overlapping 'study groups' have made it increasingly difficult to distinguish between 'mainstream' and 'anti-mainstream'.

The great Kaku–Fuku war

Since 1985 the manoeuvrings of the *habatsu*, the configuration of their alliances and the probabilities of succession to the prime ministership – the very substance, that is, of Japanese politics – have become less predictable. This is because Tanaka no longer makes the important choices. Even before Tanaka gained the power to do this in the late 1970s, the struggle within the LDP stuck to fairly predictable patterns, for one major conflict dominating everything else had, in fact, become institutionalised. This lengthy episode in post-war Japanese politics is commonly referred to as the Kaku–Fuku war – Kaku from the first character of Tanaka's given name, and Fuku from the first character of Fukuda's family name.

The conflict came into the open in 1972 when Tanaka bought the presidency of the LDP, and ended with Fukuda's nearly total defeat in the late 1970s. As we have already noted in several contexts, LDP politicians function mainly as brokers who, standing between the guardians of the budget and local interests, regulate the distribution of Japan's plenty. After the death of Kono Ichiro in the waning days of the Sato government, only two politicians – Fukuda and Tanaka – had the *jinmyaku*, the claim of accumulated indebtedness on entire ministerial bureaux, the talent and the stamina to be boss among these brokers. The two giants had much in common. Both began the day by meeting large numbers of petitioners at their homes. Both were exceptions among cabinet ministers in that they had maintained their power over the bureaucrats in a succession of different cabinet positions. Both had been responsible for important promotions within the ministries and had thus created a coterie of personally loyal bureaucrats. But their differences, rooted in schooling and social background, were much more important. When Sato Eisaku withdrew as prime mininster, each knew that he could not tolerate the other in the top position. Their rivalry was sharpened by more than the lure of the office as such; as became clear in the following years, it was a fight over a right to manage Japanese politics extending far beyond the office of prime minister.

While Tanaka was prime minister, Fukuda, though defeated, had not as yet relinquished any real power. Made finance minister by Tanaka in order to get the budget back into manageable shape after what one scholar has called 'the largest pork-barrel in the history of Japanese public finance',[75] he continued to exert extraordinary influence in the same position under Prime Minister Miki Takeo. At this point Fukuda had probably gained an ascendancy over Tanaka that he might have maintained had Tanaka not been pushed underground. He played a major role in stirring up the scandal over Tanaka's 'money politics'. But when this forced Tanaka to step down, he still had to contend with Ohira Masayoshi, also a former Ministry of Finance bureaucrat and an old ally of Tanaka from previous *habatsu* fights. A party elder, Shiina Etsusaburo, was asked to find a way out of the impasse caused by the roughly equal strength of Fukuda and Ohira, and he found a solution in the elevation of a boss of a much smaller and weaker *habatsu*, Miki Takeo. The latter's reputation as an unusually 'clean' politician was an advantage for the LDP that year.

With Miki as compromise prime minister, it seemed, at least to some, that pork-barrel methods would decline. Miki himself had an active dislike for what Japanese politics entailed in practice, and apparently wanted to introduce genuine parliamentary proceedings into Japan. Although this ambition was unlikely to be achieved, if only for Miki's lack of a strong power base, the enthusiasm with which talk of 'clean politics' was greeted by the press created the illusion that the nation was getting ready to dump the system of power brokerage.

If the illusion ever took hold at all, it was shattered by Fukuda's famous handshake with Ohira, which paved the way for Miki's ejection from office at the end of 1976, and for Fukuda's rise to the prime ministership. Ohira took over from Fukuda, as they had agreed. But Fukuda did not step aside gracefully. And the most dramatic climax, perhaps, of LDP history occurred in the forty-day battle of 1979, when both he and Ohira presented themselves as candidates for prime minister in the Diet. Tanaka made sure that Ohira won, but Fukuda and Miki betrayed the Ohira government in 1980 by keeping their *habatsu* members out of the Diet during voting on a routine no-confidence motion tabled by the opposition. This is widely believed to have caused the heart attack that Ohira died from ten days before the national elections. His death produced a sympathy vote and large gains for the LDP that added to Tanaka's power, leaving him free to pick Suzuki Zenko as the next prime minister.

In retrospect it seems that the question of which LDP *habatsu* would have the greatest power behind the scenes was settled in 1978. Neither Ohira nor Suzuki showed ambition to rule as master of the brokers, so that relations between the bureaucrats and special interest groups were tended mainly by Tanaka's *gundan*. This had still not changed in the late 1980s, for even though Tanaka himself was incapacitated and out of the picture, his disloyal ex-retainer, Takeshita Noboru, was prime minister and formally in charge of the *gundan*, with his relative through marriage

Kanemaru Shin, veteran sub-boss of Tanaka's 'machine', as the power behind the LDP throne.

Bureaucrats in the LDP

The Kaku–Fuku war reflected to some extent an older struggle between bureaucrats-turned-politicians and grass-roots politicians. Tanaka's was the second attempt by a grass-roots politician to wrest control over the party from the smaller but dominating group of former bureaucrats, for Kono Ichiro had also tried it, unsuccessfully, in the first decade of the LDP's existence. While the political division between the two groups was much clearer in earlier days than it is now, the distinction none the less continues to be made, and Diet members are sometimes classified as *tojinha*, grass-roots politicians, or *kanryoha*, former bureaucrats. Members of the latter group resent the label since they wish to make it quite clear that they were, after all, elected by the people.[76]

In the 1950s and 1960s there was a clear division of labour between *tojinha* and *kanryoha* members of the LDP. The role of the former was mainly restricted to getting re-elected and keeping the number of LDP members in parliament up to strength. The former bureaucrats, as befitted genuine administrators, used their knowledge of legal stipulations and their *jinmyaku* with former colleagues and the *zaikai* to promote the policies that helped create Japan's economic success.[77] Following the deaths of Ono Bamboku and Kono Ichiro in 1964 and 1965, there were no longer any strong party politicians who could challenge the bureaucrats-turned-politicians, until Tanaka, ensconced in the *habatsu* of former bureaucrat Sato Eisaku (and making himself indispensable to the latter with his money-making skills), rose above all the others.

There is no insurmountable class division between the former bureaucrats and the rest of the LDP. The two groups mingle in the *habatsu*. Their differences did not trouble Tanaka's alliance with Ohira's *habatsu*, which is particularly known for its strong *kanryoha* character. A symbiotic relationship has evolved between the two groups, with the former bureaucrats teaching the grass-roots politicians the techniques of tackling the bureaucracy, and the latter initiating the former into the art of electioneering. Former bureaucrats are no longer promoted to ministerial positions as quickly as Kishi, Ikeda and Sato were, which means that one source of irritation for the grass-roots politicians has disappeared.

Nevertheless, the smaller *kanryoha* group is without doubt the more important segment of the LDP. It is still easier for former bureaucrats to collect funds from the business world, whereas the grass-roots politician may risk ending up in the orbit of shady right-wing organisations or rich but dubious individuals. There are only a handful of notably strong and capable *tojinha* politicians, among them former finance minister Watanabe Michio. Tanaka himself carefully cultivated and used the bureaucrats, and it is significant that the younger and increasingly powerful Watanabe is grooming ex-bureaucrats to be his main followers in the LDP. In the Lower House elections of 1986 a strikingly large number of former career officials, twenty-five in all, tried to get themselves an LDP seat for the first time. A sign of how valuable they are still considered as a means of strengthening a *habatsu* is that in these elections – the last before a change of prime minister – all four rivals hoping to succeed Nakasone, together with Watanabe Michio, were seeking to recruit them into their own ranks.[78] Another proof that former bureaucrats still enjoy a privileged position in the LDP was the fact that they were given most of the top slots for the national constituency in the Upper House elections of 1986.[79]

The former bureaucrats in the LDP are expected to represent the interests of their former ministry to some extent at least, because if they did not their *jinmyaku* with their former colleagues would fade and they would become less useful to the LDP. And, while Japanese scholars and journalists have been disagreeing as to whether the politicians or the bureaucrats hold the most power, relations between the two groups range in fact from the mutually supportive to the truly symbiotic. The antagonism that Kono Ichiro created as agriculture and construction minister by dismissing and appointing officials left and right was exceptional. More representative of the norm is something Ohira Masayoshi wrote around the time of the LDP's formation: 'a minister must consider himself only a temporary visitor to his government office and must try as hard as he can not to be disliked by his officials'.

Minister and ministry

No easy assumptions should be made about the relationship between minister and ministry. The ex-bureaucrat minister who has come from a different ministry is often easier to work with than a minister returning to his old stamping ground. And *tojinha* ministers may speak up more fervently on behalf of the bureaucrats they supposedly lead than their *kanryoha* colleagues would, since in almost all cases they must make a greater effort to cultivate bureaucratic support for the furtherance of private political goals.

Where the power to influence highly placed LDP colleagues, whether inside or outside the cabinet, is concerned, the grass-roots politician has the advantage. The difference is clearly illustrated by former bureaucrat Miyazawa Kiichi and arch-politician Kanemaru Shin. The former has held most of the important cabinet posts, yet has some difficulty in making even subordinate leaders in his own *habatsu* see things his way, whereas Kanemaru is considered the best manipulator of Diet members to be found in the LDP. On the other hand, Gotoda Masaharu, a former bureaucrat (head of the National Police Agency), has been an exception. Both Tanaka and Nakasone used him as their right-hand man in dealing with the bureaucrats, while at the same time he has great powers of political manipulation. And while Takeshita did not want to run the risk of being upstaged by Gotoda and thus excluded him from his cabinet, he, Gotoda and Kanemaru Shin conferred three weeks after the formation of the Takeshita government to arrange for monthly meetings among them.[80] If there was a centre of gravity to the LDP in 1988, it was formed by this trio.

Different *habatsu* have varying reputations among bureaucrats. The members of Abe Shintaro's *habatsu*, formerly Fukuda's clique, are said to be very demanding, whereas the bureaucrats generally feel comfortable and relaxed with a minister from among Tanaka's people.[81] Ambitious LDP members try to establish a power base in influential ministries such as Finance, Construction, Transport or Agriculture. The very powerful will have their *habatsu* 'colonise' a ministry. A good example of this is the dominance the Tanaka *gundan* has gained over the Ministry of Post and Telecommunications where, ever since the late 1970s, the younger members of the group have unfailingly been rewarded with the parliamentary vice-ministership. For anyone entering the new telecommunications field it is considered a prerequisite that he should establish friendly relations with members of the Tanaka *gundan* – or the Takeshita *habatsu*, as it has come to be known since 1987.

On their side, the bureaucrats have many resources and well-developed techniques for coping with politicians. They are highly adept at making subtle adjustments in response to the changing pattern of *habatsu* alliances. As they say: 'Bureaucrats must move their antennae like those of an insect in the direction from which power emanates'.

What bureaucrats might do to upset a hypothetical *non*-LDP government must remain in the realm of speculation, but there is the example of Fukuda Takeo, who, when chief of the budget bureau of the Ministry of Finance, played a key role in undermining the Katayama cabinet. (Formed in May 1947 as the first and only socialist Japanese government, it lasted only nine months.) Fukuda could not find the money Katayama wanted for a sensitive programme, even though he came up with the needed funds for the next, conservative, prime minister, Ashida.[82]

On a day-to-day level, ministries use a number of routine mechanisms to keep their minister in good spirits and to prevent him from prying too much into their affairs. A special 'secretary', one of the brighter middle-echelon officials, is assigned to gauge the direction of the minister's thinking and inclinations. Together with the chief of the ministry's secretariat (the second highest career position), he must sometimes make a show of taking the minister's side against entrenched opposition among his fellow officials.

Bureaucrats will not openly criticise, let alone openly defy, political leaders. Politicians can afford to talk down to bureaucrats, and to berate them in public. They will sometimes do so to demonstrate their own superiority, but such superiority is mostly illusory. Although the Diet is immune from criticism by the bureaucrats (whose widely shared views about the ignorance and incompetence of politicians never, by tacit agreement, appear in print), its members are kept informed only to the extent deemed necessary by the bureaucrats.

Yet there is an incentive for bureaucrats to make themselves popular among LDP politicians, in that to do so improves the chances for a positive evaluation of their administrative skills. The minister has a major weapon at his disposal in his power to dismiss top officials who get in his way. If he uses this power, however, he may permanently damage his chances of future benefit from his stint at the ministry. Personnel management is one of the bureaucratic sanctuaries where no minister can tread with impunity. If he interferes too explicitly he cannot build a *jinmyaku*.[83] His influence in this area must be exercised through hints, preferably directed at former administrative vice-ministers. At MITI, to take one example, the group of former vice-ministers has most influence in determining the highest appointments in the ministry. In over 90 per cent of all cases, the MITI minister will go along with the appointment of vice-minister made by the outgoing vice-minister.

Even if a minister uses all his remaining powers, it will not enable him in practice to redirect Japanese policy in any noticeable manner. A minister may have influence over a ministry in the sense that he can promote or fire officials, and exert leverage in the allocation of resources to benefit his supporters and constituency. But this is different from wielding strong political power over a bureaucracy. Except when it is part of a long-standing campaign to assert control over education, for example, a minister's 'policy-making' is generally too limited to deserve the name at all.

The political division of labour

The bureaucrats also take the initiative in policy adjustments that are likely to run into hindrance from interest groups or provoke noisy opposition in the Diet. The main instruments for taking such an initiative are the numerous deliberation councils, or *shingikai*, in which well-known scholars, journalists and businessmen and noted representatives of the interest groups concerned are asked to take part. Participation in these councils is considered an honour, and much is made of an allegedly evolving 'consensus': opinions that are generally manipulated to echo those of the bureaucrats in question, who also participate. The *shingikai* often helps the bureaucracy to scatter and neutralise potential opposition to a plan.

The law-making process is usually over by the time a bill is submitted to the Diet. In nearly all cases, the people's elected representatives merely rubber-stamp what the bureaucrats put under their noses. The actual haggling over bills, if there is any, takes place within LDP ranks, and its outcome is determined by differences between ministries and negotiations with the business world and other major petition groups. Once a bill is submitted to the Diet, the LDP makes every effort to get it adopted; it is difficult to get it amended on the floor of the Diet, since that would imply a loss of face for the ministry concerned.

In the Diet, LDP members tend to be lost without the help of the bureaucrats. In most parliamentary systems, political discussion is waged between members of parliament. In Japan this is extremely rare; to the extent that 'discussion' does take place, it consists of tricky questions asked by opposition members and answered, basically, by expert officials. Well-prepared bureau chiefs and bureau directors accompany their minister when he attends hearings of the Diet committees, and 'supplement' his non-committal explanations with their own stereotyped answers.[84] In most cases the minister lacks a general grasp of the administrative area of which he is formally in charge.[85] Guiding LDP Diet members through material related to government policy tends to occupy an important part of a top-ranking bureaucrat's schedule. In MITI, directors spend roughly half, and directors-general about one-third, of their time with politicians.

The worst that can befall a Diet member is to be thought 'indifferent' or insufficiently 'sincere' by his constituency. To avoid this happening, the average LDP member must spend an extraordinary amount of his time going around his district, demonstrating his concern. He also must show that he really does have access, which he calls a *paipu* ('pipe'), to people in high places in Tokyo. When elections are in the offing, he will bring thousands of people from several villages to a central place – a gymnasium or public hall – where a senior member of his *habatsu*, preferably a minister, will make his appearance as living proof of this 'pipe'.

Once he becomes a minister, the LDP politician is expected to pay very special attention to the client groups his ministry has gathered under its wing. To demonstrate 'sincerity' in their eyes, he will also have to indulge in much ritual behaviour, often including a visit to the office of his colleague in the Ministry of Finance in the period when the final budget adjustments are made. In fact these final touches are always settled on a lower level among the bureaucrats, but in typical cases the minister will emerge from the office of the Minister of Finance making a show of how hard he negotiated. On one such occasion, after a minister had exclaimed 'I got it!', he was asked by a reporter what it was that he had actually got, whereupon the minister replied: 'You will have to ask the vice-minister about that – all I had to do for him was pay my respects to the finance minister.'[86]

The prime minister

The Japanese prime minister has less real power than any head of government in the Western world, or in most countries of Asia. He also has considerably less power than he is implicitly credited with by most casual foreign observers. In the autumn of 1964, when Sato Eisaku was prime minister, a movement was launched to strengthen the office of prime minister and thereby central political control over the bureaucracy.

Based on ideas inherited from the previous Ikeda cabinet, a cabinet assistant (*naikaku hosakan*) system was to be established, manned by special secretaries advising the prime minister. The plan failed because of strong opposition from both the LDP and the bureaucracy. Politicians did not want it because they feared it would come between them and the ministries, endangering a major source of political funds; the civil servants were against it because the new institution might have endangered some of their established prerogatives.

In the end, the prime ministers themselves saw the danger of ending up with even less control if they were surrounded by a permanent group of their own cabinet assistants. Normally, the existing temporary assistants, drawn from officialdom to give advice on special current issues, double as spies, enabling their ministry to take counter-measures if prime ministerial thinking threatens to result in action affecting them. With an arrangement of permanent cabinet assistants, the prime minister would need yet another instrument of control to check on them.[87]

Yet while the prime minister cannot establish new national priorities or enforce important measures he believes are vital to Japan's international position, one prime minister can still make a big difference from the next. Tanaka is, of course, the example that immediately comes to mind, though his importance in Japanese political history derives mainly from what he accomplished after he ceased to be prime minister. But that a prime minister can make a difference could not have been more dramatically illustrated than by the last two prime ministers chosen by Tanaka, Suzuki Zenko and Nakasone Yasuhiro.

The epitome of leaderlessness

Suzuki Zenko had polished the Japanese skills of side-stepping decisions to an extent unprecedented among post-war Japanese prime ministers. In the years when Tanaka was prime minister, a then invisible Suzuki had helped keep order within the ranks of the LDP, thus giving Tanaka a reason for picking him as prime minister. Keeping party order requires hypersensitivity to changing power patterns among and within the *habatsu*, together with subtle mediating skills. Japan's political commentators soon agreed that Suzuki indeed excelled in these skills, but that he correspondingly lacked any human urge to make decisions, so that his political passivity broke all records within memory.

His elevation to prime minister was totally unexpected, because few people had ever noticed him before. What was apparent soon enough, however, was that he had no understanding whatsoever of economic or diplomatic affairs. Suzuki's paramount interest was never to incur anyone's wrath, and the way to ensure this was to do absolutely nothing. One example among many was the diplomatic crisis that developed with South Korea and China over the rewriting of colonial and wartime history in Japanese middle-school textbooks. At the peak of the crisis, he weighed in with his official solution: that the Ministry of Education and the Ministry of Foreign Affairs should settle the problem between them, even though the former had all along been staunchly refusing to make the symbolic gestures called for by the latter.

The bureaucrats despised Suzuki. His ministers ignored him to an extent previously unkown in post-war Japan. Insiders leaked the information that he was not treated with the usual deference at the short cabinet meetings, and that only on his first foreign trip was he accorded the small signs of respect that a prime minister normally receives. Again, although Japanese cabinets usually try to preserve at least a semblance of unity towards the outside world, Komoto Toshio, the director-general of the Economic Planning Agency (with the rank of minister), acted independently to place economic stimulus measures on the government's programme, evoking denials from the Ministry of Finance that this was part of the government's policy.

None of this is exaggeration. One of the nicknames that Suzuki earned as prime minister was 'tape-recorder' because for meetings that could not be avoided the bureaucrats had to train him to recite the answers by heart. The bureaucrats began to shield him carefully from visiting foreign dignitaries and editors, but a press conference with European journalists before Suzuki's visit to Europe, made for the announced purpose of lessening misunderstanding, could not be avoided. Some three weeks beforehand I received a call from the Foreign Ministry asking me whether I wanted to ask a question and what that question would be. I then received instructions to ask my question, 'so as not to cause confusion', immediately after the question of another specified journalist had been answered. Before the press conference I twice received revised instructions as to my place among the seven chosen questioners. On the big day, Suzuki sat back and, with eyes half closed, recited the answers he had memorised, which sometimes sounded odd since some correspondents, perversely, had rephrased their questions.

But the highlight of the 'press conference' came at the end when, using the most courteous language, a German journalist asked Suzuki amid quiet applause whether he was aware of the fact that everything had been prearranged to look spontaneous, but that some fifty European newspaper and television reporters had come in the belief that each had an equal chance to ask questions; did not Suzuki think that this was unfortunate, given the official reason for his European trip? The question was interpreted impeccably, yet Suzuki merely recited the answer to the question my colleague had originally submitted to the Foreign Ministry.[88]

That Suzuki was an international liability for Japan became clear when he denied a statement included in a joint communiqué signed together with President Reagan.[89] At the subsequent annual summit meeting in 1981, the US president was visibly uninterested in discussing anything with him. The preparations for the next summit in 1982 gave Japanese bureaucrats more than the normal headaches, for a pre-summit meeting between the US president and the Japanese prime minister had become an established opportunity to reduce the possibility of unpleasant surprises, and President Reagan had pointedly not found time to meet Suzuki. By then a yardstick for Japanese success at the summits was the degree to which other heads of government ignored Suzuki, and Japanese newspapers were stating uninhibitedly that Suzuki was not intellectually equipped to think seriously about matters that would come up for discussion.

In one sense Suzuki was the ideal Japanese prime minister, judged by standards often presented as ideally Japanese. He was self-effacing and believed above all in 'consensus'. But the press was nearly unanimous in suggesting that over-consistent adherence to such ideals would not do, and that Suzuki was simply not doing his basic duty.

Behind-the-scenes rescue

It occasionally happens that a powerful behind-the-scenes figure averts an impending crisis. In 1982 the serious deterioration in relations between the US president and the Japanese prime minister was halted when Kishi Nobusuke subtly blocked the re-election of Suzuki Zenko. In the early summer of that year Tanaka Kakuei had several times visited this elderly bureaucrat-politician at his country retreat. They had been considered natural enemies; Kishi was the political patron of Fukuda, Tanaka's main adversary, while Kishi's son-in-law, Abe Shintaro, was the anointed heir to Fukuda's *habatsu*. But descriptions of the Kishi–Tanaka meetings given by their aides to a few journalists gave the impression that the two powers behind the LDP behaved like gods on Mount Olympus, benignly looking down on the political scurrying going on below. The upshot of whatever agreement they made was that Kishi sent a message to Suzuki explaining that he would not necessarily back his candidacy for a second term. Suzuki immediately announced that he would not be available for re-election, surprising most of the Japanese political world with what was wrongly dubbed the only decision he ever made.

The motives for Kishi's move have never been disclosed, but they are not difficult to guess. He had long been considered a 'friend of the United States', and certainly understood the 'special relationship' between the two countries. Imprisoned as a class 'A' war criminal, he was never put on trial, and re-entered politics with the USA's blessing. He was particularly identified with the effort to revise the US–Japan Security Treaty, and helped promote close strategic relations with the United States in other ways too. He must have been acutely aware of the disastrous effect Suzuki was having on these relations.

The *habatsu* leader whom Tanaka and Kishi chose to become prime minister in November 1982 was Nakasone Yasuhiro. He was asked to repair the damage done to the US–Japan relationship; and from his very first statements, made even before he took office, he showed great

enthusiasm for doing just that. Shortly afterwards Kishi, uncharacteristi-
cally, publicly praised Nakasone's diplomacy. He also made sure that his
son-in-law Abe Shintaro continued to support the Nakasone government
in times of *habatsu* strife, against the wishes of Abe's political boss, Fukuda
Takeo.

The man who wanted to govern

As early as the 1970s political commentators had been speculating that
Nakasone Yasuhiro would be a possible exception in a line of relatively
featureless prime ministers. He did not disappoint them. But he had also
long been considered rather unsuitable for the prime ministership for
precisely the same reasons as made him colourful: his emphatic ideas,
quotable pronouncements and nationalistic preoccupations. He had
drawn an uncommon degree of attention as director-general (with the
rank of minister) of the Self-Defence Agency, which he attempted to
shake up without much lasting effect. Long before this, in January 1951,
he had had the audacity, as a new Diet member, to present General
Douglas MacArthur with a 'manifesto' summing up 'what the Japanese
think', which earned him an early reputation among Americans as a
radical nationalist. In this document he expressed concern that Japan's
continued subservience to the United States would threaten Japanese
sovereignty. He was also one of the few LDP members who openly argued
for constitutional change.

From the moment he became prime minister, Nakasone left no doubt
that he had every intention of ruling. Any uncertainty about this was
dispelled at the very beginning of 1983, when he confronted the Ministry
of Foreign Affairs with a *fait-accompli* decision to travel to South Korea,
whose relations with Japan were surrounded by controversy. His leadership ambitions were equally clear in his choice of cabinet ministers.
Hitherto, such choices had been determined by the *habatsu* power balance
and only very rarely by the ability of the candidates themselves. All
Nakasone cabinets were distinguished by an uncommonly high number of
'strong' ministers, and by the retention of key ministers through several of
the traditionally frequent reshuffles. In 1985 Nakasone confessed to his
former classmates at a school reunion that he wanted to be a president-type
prime minister who could carry out strong policies the way Mrs Thatcher
did. And on 25 July 1986, shortly after forming his third cabinet, he held
separate meetings with eleven ministers, instructing them to overcome
resistance from bureaucrats in dealing with important pending issues. At
the first meeting of this new cabinet the preceding Tuesday, he had said
that ministers must not become the spokesmen of their departments but
should have an overall understanding of national issues. He often chose to
answer questions in parliament himself instead of leaving it to his ministers
and their bureaucrats; and he drew attention with his (by Japanese
standards) clear and straightforward answers.

A resolute manner and firm commitments tend to cause shudders among the administrators. Important decisions on every level are generally made only if accompanied by a display of collective agreement, or if implement- able without anyone noticing. A third option very commonly resorted to, especially in international dealings, is to avoid decisions in the hope that the reasons for them will disappear by themselves – a hope often fulfilled in practice. Against this background, Nakasone's decisiveness shocked many and made him unpopular among his fellow LDP members.

The Japanese press reacted negatively to his first cabinet and united in dubbing it a 'Tanakasone government' because of the large proportion of representatives of the Tanaka *gundan* in it. But the editors overlooked how relatively purposeful this first Nakasone cabinet was, and entirely missed the fact that it had created new possibilities in Japanese policy develop- ment; for this relationship in Japanese politics brought together its most talented power-broker and the first prime minister in recent memory who actually wished to rule.

While Tanaka continued catering to his pork-barrel empire, Nakasone addressed himself to issues ranging, for once, beyond those immediately connected with economic growth, the pork-barrel or the need to hang on to the top post. He referred to a backlog of 'unsettled post-war business', by which he meant inhibitions and taboos inherited from the post-war occupation period. In line with this, he evinced great personal concern with various questions connected in some way or other with Japan's sovereignty, such as education and international responsibility. He invited questions in the Diet on defence matters, which, touching as they do on national pride, form a potential political platform. He could afford to do so because his tenure was guaranteed as long as Tanaka was in charge and the two did not fall out with each other. Tanaka's machine not only dominated the LDP, but was also the best means for an enterprising prime minister to cope with the bureaucracy.

The major help in dealing with the bureaucracy in successive Nakasone governments came from Gotoda Masaharu, Nakasone's chief cabinet secretary (an important co-ordinating function with the rank of minister). The appointment was considered Nakasone's most spectacular choice, as the post had hitherto been reserved for a member of the prime minister's own *habatsu*. Gotoda had been discovered by Tanaka and was considered one of the most capable politicians in the *gundan*, a man sometimes referred to as Tanaka's 'brain'. Tanaka had often used him to penetrate phalanxes of recalcitrant bureaucrats when he was in a hurry to get things done. He had been director-general of the National Police Agency, and he knew how to use the power he derived from his very special *jinmyaku*. He became Nakasone's right-hand man, and the key figure in his cabinets. And when Nakasone created a new government agency (the Management and Co-ordination Agency) to facilitate quick responses to emergencies, he appointed Gotoda as its first director-general.

When, for the first time in twelve years, a Japanese prime minister was given the chance to stay in his position for more than two years, the significance was international. Nakasone had said that he would help Japan play a world role in keeping with its economic power, and he made important symbolic gestures towards that end. He presented Japan unambiguously as an active member of the Western alliance, and he introduced a style of direct personal diplomacy in dealing with the US president.

President Reagan was pleasantly surprised, when Nakasone first visited him, to find himself face to face with a leader who appeared to see the Soviet Union through the same glasses as he did. He asked the Japanese prime minister to call him 'Ron', whereupon Nakasone offered an abbreviation of his first name in return. The fact that even close male friends in Japan seldom call each other by their given names made the symbolism all the more significant in Japan. The 'Ron–Yasu' relationship muted, for a couple of years, the strident voices from Washington taking the Japanese to task for various sins in connection with trade and defence. The relationship was skilfully used on the Japanese side. It swept some important problems under the carpet, and strengthened the illusion in the USA that Japan had finally found itself a leader.

Nakasone's popularity as measured by Japanese public opinion polls broke all records. Tanaka alone was rewarded with similarly high figures, when his government was one year old, but his popularity subsequently sank to a record low. The support figures for the Nakasone government remained high; contrary to what has often been alleged, the Japanese public appreciated a prime minister who gave clear answers and made a strong impression at home and abroad.

These public feelings contrasted starkly with the aversion a majority of LDP parliamentarians felt for Nakasone. He was said to be lacking in personal warmth because of his rational approach to problems and his relative impatience to achieve political goals. With Tanaka incapacitated from 1985 onward, Nakasone's leadership seemed in jeopardy as he was confronted with renewed *habatsu* wrangling. The record LDP victory in the 1986 elections earned him an extra year as prime minister, but popular support is the last thing that keeps a Japanese prime minister in power, and Nakasone had to select Takeshita as his successor in the autumn of 1987.

Deliberation councils as political lubricant

Nakasone's strenuous efforts to govern and initiate policy did not, in the end, produce substantial changes in policy or programme. But the changes he wrought in style, symbolism and atmospherics were important enough in themselves. His major achievement was a breakthrough in relations with South Korea – thereby fulfilling the American wish that Japan should be more considerate of its Asian ally. Perhaps equally important was that he gave Japan stature at the annual summit conferences, and earned the respect of his counterparts when he had to chair one himself in 1986. The national railways were privatised during his tenure, and he challenged a number of 'taboos' connected with Japan's wartime past.

But the bureaucrats and special interest groups in the LDP, jealous guardians of their own territory, showed no intention of solving the problems that were thrown into their laps, even after agreeing that they were urgent. Nakasone found himself encapsulated by these semi-autonomous forces. He had no say over the Agriculture Ministry or, for that matter, the Ministry of Finance.

One interesting innovation in the exercise of power by a Japanese prime minister was introduced when Nakasone found a new use for the deliberation council, or *shingikai*. As we have seen, the *shingikai* is commonly used by bureaucrats to help defuse or avoid opposition to their plans. Special *shingikai* are also established by or for prime ministers in order to present high-minded schemes, long on abstract ideals and short on concrete proposals, which they can pass off as policy. But where his predecessors commanded their *shingikai* to contemplate edifying but vague subjects such as 'the life cycle' (Miki), 'the development of society' (Sato), 'discussion for the future' (Fukuda) or 'garden cities' (Ohira), Nakasone used his in an attempt to break through taboos and bureaucratic obstacles and to prepare legislation. He established *shingikai* that reported directly to him, and he hand-picked their chairmen and key members; nor did he leave it to their imagination how he expected to be 'advised'.

Before becoming prime minister Nakasone had been closely associated with the Ad Hoc Committee on Administrative Reforms, a type of *shingikai* in which top businessmen, academics and retired bureaucrats studied ways of reducing the size and burdens of government. Three of its assignments so far completed are: the break-up of the Japan National Railways, the creation of the Management and Co-ordination Agency (by combining the Administrative Management Agency with some elements from the Prime Minister's Office) and the ostensible privatisation of Nippon Telephone and Telegraph. Nakasone himself compared the changes aimed at by the administrative reform committee and his other *shingikai* to the changes Japan underwent following the Meiji Restoration, or immediately after the Second World War. He exaggerated, of course; during his tenure there was no sense of acute crisis such as might have encouraged the cumbersome System to embark on a project of self-renewal. In the end, Nakasone's innovations in overcoming bureaucratic obstacles had little more than a marginal effect.

It became fashionable to decry Nakasone's use of *shingikai* as undemocratic. Decisions, it was said, were taken even before the groups conferred; moreover, several of their top members had been at school or in the Imperial Navy with Nakasone, or had been in the Naimusho, in which Nakasone served briefly as police inspector. All this was true, but it merely corresponded to the accepted way in which the bureaucracy had always used the *shingikai* and to the equally accepted way of using one's *jinmyaku*. The remarkable aspect of Nakasone's aproach was that he manned his advisory groups with an unusually high proportion of specialists lacking a bureaucratic background. This had the effect of making the bureaucrats, after some hesitation, begin to realise that they would to some extent have to accommodate these 'amateur' groups with information and co-operation, if only to safeguard the interests of their ministries and bureaux.

New LDP tribes

There were other causes for the slight alteration that came about in the relationship between the LDP and the bureaucrats. The gradual shifting of the Japanese economy into less frenetic growth; increasing budget deficits and the resulting increased friction between segments of the bureaucracy; the failure of the 'break fiscal rigidification' movement; and territorial struggles between ministries involving the new industrial sectors: all these had their effect.

Nakasone's talk of changes comparable to those of the Meiji period was not mere political rhetoric, and his experiments with *shingikai* were more than a passing indulgence. In fact, he was continuing a campaign begun by Tanaka Kakuei to increase the leverage of LDP politicians over the bureaucrats. To understand this better it is necessary here to introduce, in its theory and its widely diverging practice, one last formal institution of the administrators.

The most important institutional interface between LDP politicians and the bureaucracy is the Seichokai, or Policy Affairs Research Council (PARC). It consists of seventeen divisions that cover roughly the same administrative territory as the ministries. The politician who becomes chief of some of these divisions gains access to a magnificent *jinmyaku* incorporating both industrialists and bureaucrats. After an average one and a half years as division chief, he automatically becomes a member of the *zoku* ('tribe' or 'family' within the LDP) that concerns itself specifically with the sector in question, monitoring developments and influencing it through support for legislative proposals by the bureaucrats. Former ministers and parliamentary vice-ministers also often become members of the *zoku* relating to the ministry they served.

The Seichokai divisions do not normally make decisions. They provide a point of interaction between bureaucracy and LDP that is hidden from scrutiny and, as far as can be gathered, totally informal. In co-operation with the small group of officials concerned and powerful *zaikai* representatives, the politicians can bring pressure or subtle blackmail to bear, against which background legal stipulations are almost totally irrelevant. In cases of structural changes in a particular sector, or of the emergence of a new branch of industry, the *zoku* politicians carry considerable weight. But in the final analysis their involvement is mostly parasitic. Through its contacts with trade and industrial associations and federations, PARC helps organise obligatory 'voluntary donations' and the inevitable 'help' in elections. A phone call by the chairman of a division requesting the corresponding business circles to provide funds often elicits an instant response.[90]

The politicians wielding power via the divisions of PARC began their climb to recent prominence in the second half of the 1960s, when bureaucrats of the corresponding ministries with client interest groups joined them in confronting the guardians of the budget.[91] The latter eventually were obliged to satisfy the politicians with real instead of ritual explanations.[92] But the biggest factor in the growth of *zoku* power was Tanaka's initiatives.[93] The *gundan* has exploited the gradual structural shift in the relationship between bureaucrats and politicians better than any normal *habatsu* could. It dominates many *zoku*, including such newly important ones as that of post and telecommunications. Because they remain interested in a particular policy area for relatively long periods, *zoku* members are generally much better informed than LDP politicians used to be. This fact alone has given them a new type of leverage over the bureaucrats.

The ranking of a politician within the LDP and thus his access to and position within a *zoku* depends, first of all, on the number of times he has been re-elected. Appointments to cabinet posts in the late 1980s generally require some six or even seven successful elections. One election can make one a junior member of a Diet committee or PARC division. A two-term Diet member can become vice-chairman of a division or executive member of a Diet committee. For a parliamentary vice-ministership, which is a very lucrative post because of the contacts one can make in the business world, three terms are needed. A fourth- or fifth-term Diet member can become a committee or division chairman. But the latter post is not the most important. To join the small inner circle of *zoku* bosses the LDP member must almost always have served first in an executive position in a division, returning there after holding the cabinet post of its corresponding ministry.[94]

The French comparison

We have seen in Chapter 3 that whereas the Japanese System may superficially qualify as a 'pluralist' or 'corporatist' political system, it differs from the countries most often mentioned as models of these systems in ways so basic that one doubts how much such labels actually explain. Japan has also been referred to fairly frequently as an 'administrative state'. This poses the question of how the System compares with a good example of a Western 'administrative state' such as France.

There are many similarities. French bureaucracy, dating from the absolutist state of the seventeenth century and strengthened by Napoleon as a mechanism for national policy-making, has long been one of the most powerful in the world. It is permanent and highly centralised, and no one in power can ignore its entrenched opinions on many issues. As in Japan, the central bureaucracy has jurisdiction over local government, most education, public works, the courts, the police and other areas that in most other Western countries are either under the control of independent local authorities or in private hands.

Like Japan, France has institutionalised the élite-forming process to a high degree. Another striking resemblance is the phenomenon of *pantouflage*, meaning the continual shift of civil servants into the private sector. Again, many French bureaucrats move into politics.[95] They maintain important informal relations with each other across the division between the private and public realms (which are less clearly separated than in the Anglo-Saxon world or West Germany). It would seem at first sight that France has come closest to developing a class of administrators akin to that of Japan,[96] a class, moreover, that in the post-war period has been similarly preoccupied with creating optimum conditions for economic expansion.

But a closer look shows revealing differences. The higher-ranking French civil servants have had a relatively wide-ranging education at one or the other of some five *grandes écoles*. Good memories may be valued, but so are a liberal education, intellectual prowess and an extreme articulateness. The top bureaucrats have generally entered one of the five major *grands corps d'état* (Inspection of Finance, the Diplomatic Corps, the Court of Accounts, the Council of State, and the Bridges and Roads) before being placed in various ministries. They are much more mobile than Japanese bureaucrats, and can be temporarily detached to occupy leading positions in other government agencies, state enterprises, banks or the private sector. The general view of the élite-school-and-*corps* background is that it enables the individual to grasp rapidly the essentials of any kind of situation, so that he or she is fitted to almost any type of executive position.[97] In Japan, top bureaucrats are moved from section to section to increase their versatility, but they remain in their first ministry and must identify with it to an extent that is detrimental to the functioning of officialdom as a whole.

In the same context, *pantouflage* is not quite the same as *amakudari*. With the exception of newly created government corporations or agencies, the Japanese companies and banks opening their doors to an *amakudari* bureaucrat expect him to ensure smooth relations with the ministry he has retired from, but not to perform the kind of decision-making and leadership role expected of a French bureaucrat entering the private sector.

Another vital difference is the presence of that other strong French tradition: political thought that is made articulate and represented by a non-bureaucratic élite. As one French specialist sums it up:

> Covered by a protective law and enjoying tremendous job security and enormous prestige owing both to their élite backgrounds and their technical competence, the senior civil servants form a distinct professional group, whose views on almost every point are at odds

with the views of that other important group of professionals, the politicians. Thus two different concepts of the profession of state-craft are in constant danger of clashing with each other.[98]

Members of the *grands corps* are indispensable in helping draft and control legislation. But the French minister is generally a considerably more significant figure than his Japanese counterpart.[99] On the other hand, the French bureaucracy cannot take its role as much for granted as can the Japanese bureaucracy. It has undergone political vicissitudes depending on the degree of political confusion created by party politics and the relative strengths or weaknesses of French presidents, and it faced heavy attacks as an élite institution before the First World War, in the 1930s, after the Second World War and in 1968.

The crucial difference, of course, is that the French bureaucracy serves a highly centralised state. For all its expertise, it requires directives from an identifiable government to function properly. The power of a De Gaulle or a Mitterrand is beyond comparison with that of any Japanese prime minister. The French administrators, in other words, have a means to shift national priorities.

'Plus ça change . . .'

In the late 1980s many Japanese political commentators and some scholars were claiming to detect major structural changes in the direction of more political guidance over Japanese policies – changes illustrated, they asserted, by the *zoku* phenomenon. The same argument was much used to counter criticism from Japan's trading partners, the implication being that the Japanese political economy would gradually become better capable of changing or adjusting priorities. To interpret the emergence of the *zoku* as a sign of essential changes in the relationship between bureaucrats and politicians, and thus as a harbinger of a change in the way Japan would be governed, was, however, more than a little premature.

The more things changed, the more, or so it appears, they stayed the same. Indeed, the old patterns were more pronounced in the late 1980s, because better organised. Many LDP politicians hoped to follow Tanaka's example and systematise what they were already doing. This may have resulted in spreading somewhat more of the national wealth, but the spreading is as haphazard as it was before. There is still no mechanism for ordering national priorities. The weaknesses of the budgeting system in the absence of such a mechanism have, if anything, become more marked.

Two essential and interrelated aims of the administrators – to retain control and to keep to a minimum the political influence of the common people – have not changed in any way. Since 1945 the Japanese people have become more politically sophisticated, but this sophistication is offset partly by the way in which they are bought off with subsidies and other regular income guaranteed by the LDP–bureaucratic combination, and partly by employment policies, to be discussed in Chapter 6.

Of course, certain shifts in power among the administrative bodies of politicians, *zaikai* and bureaucrats are constantly taking place. But they do not mean the development of essentially different relationships among these three major categories of administrator, or of essentially new motives. It would be wrong to conclude that higher civil servants are becoming the foot soldiers of LDP politicians. They have found a way to pretend that Diet members are in charge while in fact clinging to the principles and prerogatives of bureaucratic rule. The bureaucracy is still the *de facto* legislator for budgetary appropriations. LDP politicians belong to *zoku* primarily because of the financial and electoral advantages, not because they have suddenly realised that Japan ought to have new priorities and must shape new policies in accordance with them.

The only ultimate goal of the administrators is to preserve the System. Since 1945 this has been accomplished by nurturing a high-growth economy with the emphasis on industrial expansion at the cost of other desirables, and by social control. The participants in the System described in this chapter continue to show that, for all their mutual conflict, they excel in both these fields.

6

The Submissive Middle Class

The post-war aims of the Japanese System have been entrusted mainly to the economic organisations. The System is preoccupied with industrial and commercial pursuits, the expansion of which is felt as essential to its survival. Although one cannot locate a political centre, there does exist a hard core, as it were, of institutions – numerous, closely packed, inter-connected – that are tightly harnessed to these pursuits.

The administrators who stand at the apex of the interconnected hierarchies of manufacturing firms, banks and trading companies are concerned with something more than production or trade. Firms in the 'private' sector have in fact a double function. Politically, they are important for the hold they exert over the population by controlling the behaviour and thought of their employees to a degree far beyond anything that firms in the West aspire to or could get away with. It is the standard indoctrination that Japanese companies provide, and their success in forcing a life-style on their employees, that lends the System much of its solidity.

The 'salaryman' model

The human substance of the large hard core of the System is provided by the *sarariiman* ('salaryman'). He was originally named for the salary he received, as distinct from the wages of factory hands and other workers lower in the occupational hierarchy. But the term 'salaryman' connotes much more than 'office clerk' or 'white-collar worker'; it stands for a behavioural norm to aspire to. The salaryman has such predictable concerns and habits that it has become common in Japanese to speak of 'salaryman culture'. The production of books and magazines devoted primarily to acknowledged salaryman tastes (including comics as thick as telephone books) comprises one of Japan's biggest industries. The media carry the salaryman model of life to every corner of Japan.

Becoming a 'member'

The salaryman world is open to roughly one-third of the young Japanese males who have passed through the selection system described in Chapter 4.

Yet even after all the hurdles of the school system have been cleared, acceptance by a firm is often dependent on introductions from professors, further exams given by the firm and the result of detective work. Former elementary-school and high-school teachers, as well as neighbours, may be asked about the conduct of the recruit as a teenager. Many companies will want to verify that the recruit is not descended from the 'unclean' caste of *burakumin*, or to make sure that he is not a member of one of the so-called 'new religions', since this might cause loyalty problems.[1]

Acceptance is usually followed by an extended *rite de passage* which confirms and symbolises in a dramatic way that the young man is becoming a 'member' of the institution he has joined, and allows no doubt in his mind about his position relative to everyone else in the scheme of things.

Life in the 'adult world' usually begins with a ceremony during which, sometimes in the company of hundreds of his fellows, the recruit, in a fresh 'salaryman uniform' (sober grey or blue suit, with the company badge on the lapel), will for the first time hear the 'company philosophy' from the mouth of the president or a high executive. He will soon be able to recite this 'philosophy', and the shorter slogans that come with it, in his sleep.

During subsequent training, considerable attention will be paid to an often complicated corporate etiquette. Even the angle of a bow is specified: 15 degrees for colleagues of equal rank met in the corridors; 30 degrees, with both hands held rigidly down the seams of the trousers, for superiors and important visitors; 45 degrees, accompanied by polite and apologetic phrases, when something has gone wrong or when special courtesy is called for. Offering and accepting the ubiquitous business cards requires practice. The position one is to occupy with respect to superiors in reception rooms, automobiles or trains must be studied. One must walk slightly behind superiors in the corridors of the company, but enter a lift before a guest. A recruit talking with contemporaries in the corridors indicates that he has not quite understood the seriousness of it all. The outward impression the new salaryman makes is considered extraordinarily important.

At the same time, a remodelling of the recruit's mind is undertaken. Lengthy submersions in an ice-cold river clad in only a loincloth, a 24-hour march with soldiers and cleaning lavatories for an entire day with colleagues are some of the more extreme solutions which corporations have found for the problem of breaking in a new group of university graduates. Companies view their annual intake of new employees as a disciplinary problem, because it is only through discipline that the recruits will fully appreciate the special relationship they have entered into. They should not regard their company merely as a place to earn a living. If the salaryman cannot feel that he is merged with his firm, or cannot at least pretend to be totally bound up in it, he can hardly be considered a worthy and full-fledged member of society.

Some companies have arrangements with Zen temples for what comes down to endurance training. Roughly two thousand send their recruits to the barracks of the Self-Defence Forces. Most companies approach the problem of making new 'members' in a more relaxed fashion, but practically all have special training programmes which can last from two months to a year.

The recruit may be required to live in a company dormitory during this period, where he is made to rise before dawn, perform all manner of communal tasks, obey a curfew and be in bed with the lights out at ten. The larger firms that own recreation and meeting facilities in resort areas often isolate their recruits for a number of weeks for intensive practice in togetherness, mutual confessions and other exercises, some of which clearly constitute rites of purification and initiation. The ultimate purpose can be compared with that of the drill-sergeant in a military unit: to break down possible individual resistance to the aims of the whole organisation, and to inculcate a habit of obedience.

It is commonly assumed that university graduates today need this urgently. Thus Nikkeiren, the federation of employers' associations, organises an annual training programme for smaller firms, held in the facilities built for the Olympic Games. At the end of this programme recruits march around the stadium behind the emblem of their company. Nikkeiren spokesmen explain that urbanisation, affluence and the short-comings of the schools have made it more necessary than ever for young employees to undergo this kind of training.

Loyalty in bondage

Every year the newspapers print the results of an opinion poll in which new employees are asked whether they will attach more importance to their families or their firms. Each year there is a slight increase in the percentage favouring the family, which inspires another round of columns and articles on the changing ethics of the salarymen. In 1986 eight out of ten pollees stated that they would rate their private life above the demands of their company. But the experts at Nikkeiren do not take such expressions of independence very seriously. So far, it has been clear in practice that whenever the interests of the company and the family come into conflict, it is the family that will adjust as a matter of course. *Maihomu-shugi* or 'my-home-ism' – the tendency of young salarymen to rate highly the claims of wife and children – has not proved the threat that officials and the business élite thought it might become in the 1960s and early 1970s. The prefix *mai* ('my') still has a relatively negative connotation, whatever noun it is made to precede, because in the eyes of the industrial administrators it is associated with a loss of preoccupation with the workplace. But at the same time the competition among salaryman families to stock their small homes with the latest-model refrigerators, air-conditioners and stereo-sound colour television and a vast array of electrical labour-saving devices, and their tiny parking places with cars, was exactly what was needed to keep many of their firms running at full capacity.

Most companies give special consideration to the recently married salaryman. But following the birth of the first child, typically after some two years of marriage, the husband is expected to settle down to the serious business of devoting most of his energy, time and attention to his company.

Some sociologists and other commentators have argued that Japanese men prefer the company of fellow workers, and that they are uncomfortable when they have to go out with their wives and children. But one can argue that the salarymen have little choice, and that their discomfort stems from a lack of practice. A visit to rural areas, or the urban neighbourhoods where family workshops and blue-collar workers predominate, will confirm that most Japanese have no inherent difficulty with a social life centred on the family. The phenomenon of a middle class deprived to a large extent of men functioning as husbands and fathers is of relatively recent origin. 'If Japanese "naturally" – because of cultural preconditioning – were prepared to give up their egos to a large organisation, the organisation would not have to work so hard to instill loyalty and identification.'[2]

The salaryman is expected actively to demonstrate loyalty to his firm. There are various ways of doing this; he walked to work during railway strikes in the 1960s and 1970s; and he refrains from taking some or all of the holidays he is entitled to in the 1980s. His most common way to demonstrate loyalty is by working late hours or by spending time after office hours with colleagues and business associates – which means limiting the time spent with his family to the hours between eleven at night and seven in the morning.

This bond between company and employee can only be maintained, of course, so long as the employee has nowhere else to hire out his services. In most cases he hasn't. Although in the lower reaches of the business hierarchy – among the small subcontracting firms – a steady turnover of employees is fairly common, in the world of the salaryman to change one's job is for all practical purposes possible only in the first couple of years, if at all.

The 'psychological' explanation of this lack of mobility has been overworked. While salarymen are undoubtedly conditioned to believe that it is proper to remain with the same employer, the more important factor is that changing companies nearly always entails a set-back in income, prestige and future prospects. It is the policy of large companies – unless the transfer is a company arrangement to begin with – either not to accept white-collar employees from other companies, or to place them in a considerably lower position than the one they have come from.

This policy is clearly a political provision to help the salaryman maintain a keen sense of loyalty. The hesitant beginnings, in the 1980s, of a free labour market for specialists, particularly engineers and software developers, for whom the demand far outweighed the supply, prompted Keidanren, the Federation of Economic Organisations, to issue a report clarifying that this development should be considered an undesirable trend to be kept within bounds. The administrators in the business world make no secret of their wish that salarymen should remain wholly dependent on their firms, as children are dependent on their parents.

Familist ideology

For the administrator élite the salaryman's allegiance to his firm epitomises the ideal relationship between all Japanese and the System. It is most commonly expressed in the image of the corporation as a kind of family – an image that has made its way into numerous foreign assessments of Japanese economic life. It is widely believed that such familial relationships have evolved naturally out of a centuries-old tradition of psychosocial preferences. But in fact the company-as-family idea is a fairly modern innovation, even though the socio-political functions of the Japanese household and fictive kinship relationships inherited from the Tokugawa period helped prepare the way for it.

From a socio-economic as distinct from a political point of view, it was by no means inevitable that Japanese companies should become pseudo-families. Business firms in the Meiji period tended to be run by fairly individualistic entrepreneurs. The flagrant exploitation of workers and the resulting industrial unrest, not to mention the very conspicuous status differences, would hardly have made the family metaphor acceptable in those days, even to the most credulous observer.

Familistic organisation in industry did not, even so, spring out of nowhere. Fictive kinship relations have been common for centuries. Moreover, the Tokugawa shogunate gave the household, as we will see in a moment, a socio-political function that in some way prefigures that of the corporation. And there was an even more immediate model, a model that emerged in the context of the vigorous labour market created by rapidly expanding entrepreneurism in Meiji Japan. This market was originally formed by bands of workers controlled by bosses, who referred to each other as *oyakata* and *kokata* (literally, people who fill the role of 'parent' and 'child' respectively), and were bound together by quasi-familial ties in which loyalty and obedience were exchanged for supposed benevolence. Early labour unions were often, in fact, little other than these *oyakata–kokata* groups. They were to some extent comparable to the gangster organisations of today – indeed, around the turn of the century the two were sometimes related. The stevedores and coal-miners are good examples.

As the large corporations came to require more refined skills, and their fear of labour activism increased, entrepreneurs were prodded by their own requirements and the urgings of the government bureaucrats into recruiting and training workers with the purpose of forming regular bodies of permanent employees. Even so, it was decades before familistic ideas

began to catch on among the managers. When they did, many companies
were no longer led by independent-minded entrepreneurs. 'It was the first
generation of bureaucratic managers recruited straight from universities
who actually adopted the ideal of familism.'[3] Without these early administrators of the business world, the familistic rhetoric might never have
gained general acceptance. They had their counterparts in the
bureaucracy in the shape of fellow graduates of Todai's law department,
who were at that same time extolling an ideology of a 'family state' held
together by a benevolent emperor. Still, it was only in the second half of
the 1930s, when the war in China led the government to focus on
industrial programmes for increasing productivity, that the company-as-
family notion spread all over the country, with corresponding organisational adjustments. Some of the characteristics of Japan's famous 'lifetime
employment' system were first introduced in 1942 with the Ordinance on
Labour Management in Essential Industries.[4]

'Public' and 'private' realms

Wars always make it easier for bureaucrats to dictate to business managers.
In this case, Japanese bureaucrats were also helped by the lack of a
traditional distinction between the 'public' and the 'private' realm. Two or
three centuries ago, Japanese on all levels were kept under control
exclusively through personal ties, which were part of a complex of
paternalistic structures. The lowliest tiller of the land and his family knew
of no authority other than that of the land manager whose servants they
were. For the land manager and his family, authority was solely embodied
in a single figure above them: the vassal of the daimyo (baron). And the
latter, in turn, owed allegiance only to his daimyo.[5] As Tokugawa
economic life became more complex, self-regulating occupational classes
and functional groups developed. But even though the urban worker,
merchant or artisan was occasionally made aware that power also emanated from sources other than his own superior or guild, he would still have
had no sense of any impersonal political organisation, any possible
precursor of the state, that might judge his conduct objectively. 'Public'
affairs meant simply the sum of those things that occupied the attention of
his superior.

While over the centuries political integration increased and a national
culture evolved, there was no parallel development of the idea of
belonging to a state. Had such a notion established itself in Japanese
thinking, political attitudes would probably be quite different today.
Equipped with the concept of 'the state', one can imagine a boundary
drawn around authority. It enables the mind to create a map of separate
public and private realms – a prerequisite if one is to detect where and how
the first is unnecessarily encroaching upon the second. Without this
intellectual construct to help sort out one's thinking, the political order

and 'society' are congruent. And indeed, the Japanese intellectual tradition has consistently failed to distinguish between a political realm and 'society'.

In the ideal Japanese perspective – which survives in the negative connotation of 'my-home-ism' – the workplace, the multi-generational family as distinct from the nuclear family, the schools or the clubs are not considered part of a private realm. This means, of course, that the public realm can encroach all the way up to the threshold of the individual psyche. For many Japanese, family, friends and colleagues do not constitute a buffer giving protection or moral support in the face of government or company authorities; the political world lies immediately outside one's skin. Or, conversely, one might say that the whole world is a 'private' world, with ulcer-producing 'family' tensions and other problems soluble only through 'personal relations'.

The politicised household

It will be illuminating here to examine more closely a subject already touched on in Chapter 3: the Japanese *ie* or 'household', and how the Tokugawa version of it differed from its Chinese counterpart.[6] The Chinese comparison is profitable, for while the two countries share certain Confucianist notions regarding the family, the *ie* denotes a social unit that unlike its Chinese counterpart is determined less by blood-ties than by a shared economic role. The 'kinship' family may well, of course, overlap with the economic unit that the *ie* represents, but the distinction becomes abundantly clear if one considers Japanese and Chinese practices concerning succession through adoption. Where there was no male heir to become the new head of a family, the Chinese would adopt someone as close to the family blood-line as possible. In Japan the crucial question often was suitability for the succession; even a natural son might be bypassed if considered lacking in the necessary qualities.[7] A fairly common solution for households with unsuitable sons, or no sons at all, was to adopt a son-in-law, or even to adopt a young girl and then choose for her a suitable husband who could subsequently be adopted into the household. This tradition is not dead. A close friend of mine, a childless Buddhist priest,[8] spent ten years searching – in vain – for a young lady so that he could adopt her and arrange her marriage with a young priest, who would then inherit his small temple. In Japan, again, maids, farmhands and the like were considered participants in the *ie*, whereas family members no longer under the common roof were not. By contrast, Chinese generally continued to feel a deep sense of membership in the family even after generations of separation by, say, the Pacific Ocean.

The corporate character of the Japanese *ie* did not come about in the natural course of events, but developed as a result of regulations enforced by the Tokugawa shogunate as part of its elaborate system of social control. The household was, quite consciously, transformed into a political unit some three and a half centuries ago – first of all the samurai household, but later also the well-to-do village households and city households engaged in business. Individuals did not own property, the *ie* did. Individuals were registered as members of the *ie*, whose head was responsible for them. The head also had nearly unlimited legal power over the members of his household.

The significance of the *ie* as a political unit derived from its metaphysical attributes. It was not just a social convenience; it had been given – according to the ideology that evolved around it – existence and various other blessings by a continuous line of ancestors (real or fictitious), and would, given a proper succession, continue indefinitely into the future. The *ie* was like a ship launched by gods and never sold as scrap: home to an ever-changing crew whose sacred duty was to keep it afloat and on course.

For power-holders this was a marvellous basic unit to work with, and the Meiji oligarchy extended the legal *ie* organisation to all layers of the population. In the twentieth century the *ie* was legally obliged until 1945 to produced moral citizens.[9] The post-war civil code stripped the household and its head of their legal rights and duties, and dropped the formal concept of *ie* altogether. But it survives in organisational ideals.

In the Tokugawa and early Meiji periods, households engaged in business were *ie* by legal definition. When the managers began replacing the entrepreneurs in the early part of this century, they simply re-adopted the *ie* imagery, superimposing this originally political construct on their companies. Today many of the large firms have their 'ancestors' in the form of legendary founding presidents and their immediate successors, ancestors who frequently bequeathed a 'philosophy' or 'moral' code for the benefit of generations of employees. These are sometimes expounded in the glossy literature put out by Japanese companies, which often ask one to believe that commercial gain is the last thing on the mind of Japanese managers. Companies are portrayed as benefiting the people, if not the whole of humanity, and a fair number have, in fact, inserted in their promotional literature a line or two about their ideal of contributing to world peace. But above all, according to accepted theory, the company benefits and exists for its employees, whose 'sincere efforts' are expected in return for all that previous managers have done to bring it where it is.

Primacy of the workplace

It is instructive to look at the equation of family with workplace from yet another angle, in comparison with Western experience. Before the Industrial Revolution, the European family was the elementary unit of economic production, just as in China and Japan. But as industrialisation progressed, Westerners began to find employment outside the family, in impersonal workplaces: the work function became separated from the family unit. Japan, on the other hand, after a transition period followed by the consolidation of today's System, has ended up with a situation in which, one might say, the family function has become separated from the work unit. The *ie* of today are the work groups in the large corporations.

China has had a long history of tension between the clan system and representatives of the central government. Unsurprisingly, after 1949 there have been many reports of conflicts between devotion to the family and the demands of an artificially collectivist state. The Chinese communists, notably during the Great Leap Forward, tried to establish among their subjects the very attitude that the Japanese have for some time demonstrated without special prodding from a central government: the willingness to sacrifice personal and family interests for the sake of communal economic pursuits. The way things are fixed in the System gives the salaryman no other choice. And Japan's ruling élite is quite happy with the unwittingly ideological conclusion of sociologists that work units, and not families, are the basic building blocks of Japanese society.[10]

Songs and sacrifices

The salaryman's intensive involvement in his company makes necessary a reassuring symbolism, confirming that his time, energy and personal interests are being sacrificed for a worthy cause; the company must appear to be something more than an organisation established for the purpose of making a profit or providing its employees with a livelihood. It is generally presented as having intrinsic value. Sometimes a company Shinto shrine on the roof provides a vague but ever-present reminder of spiritual significance attached to the communal effort to continue the voyage of the company from past generations through the present into the future. One important symbol for the large modern company is its emblem, reminiscent of the family crests (comparable to the Western coat of arms) of the prominent *ie* of the past. Some firms – again like the old merchant *ie* – also have a 'constitution' consisting of pieties and prescribed duties. And each large company is expected to have its own *shafu*, a 'company spirit' derived from ideals set forth in catechism-like tracts. Whoever makes a tour of contemporary Japanese factories is likely to end up with stacks of booklets and pamphlets setting out the special wisdom and traditions of the firms, interspersed with platitudes concerning the general welfare.

The shared company culture is regularly reaffirmed by the communal singing of company songs. The employees of Hitachi Shipbuilding and Engineering sing:

> *Fresh light at dawn, Peace country Japan is born. . . . Let's build good ships, Our duty is important, We pray for Hitachi zosen which develops the nation's wealth. . . . We are full of vitality, Hitachi zosen . . . brings about people's happiness. . . . We are proud of harmony, Our ambition is to connect the countries of the world with ships, May (God) bless Hitachi zosen, May it develop day by day.*

The personnel of Victor Company of Japan Ltd see it thus:

> Geniuses in the world assemble here where music is played, Essence of culture, Pride of human technics, Victor, Victor, Our Victor, the Nation's welfare, Family harmony, We realise them both, We enjoy accomplishing our mission, Highest technology of the age, Pride of the world. . . . The flame which makes our products is in our sincerity, Essence of culture, Pride of human technics.

Workers at Obayashi-gumi, a construction company, sing:

> Let's make a rainbow bridge in the sky, If we build full of hope, songs of construction will echo, They will echo to tomorrow's sky, Obayashi-gumi is constructing the world, Let's sculpt dreams on the earth, New things will be created. The road starts from here and leads to a sparkling dawn, Obayashi-gumi is developing for the world.

Employees of the Toyota Motor Corporation confirm that they are full of

> Wishes for overflowing sunshine and green, We open the new age with guts and an eternally expanding human network . . . We keep growing tomorrow, with a unified mind and continuous effort, Our, Our, Our Toyota. . . . We form our history with a worldly dream, wisdom and rich technology, Bright future, with a unified mind and new strides, Our, Our, Our Toyota.

Songs from any other four companies would cover roughly the same ground. Expressions like 'brighter future' and 'harmony' are rarely absent. The songs often mention belonging to a large family, helping to build the nation and a great determination to achieve goals oftener than not only vaguely defined. Many songs refer to what others in the past have done to create the present, thus implying a duty to carry on the good work.

Although Japanese salarymen do not exactly begin the day with joint prayer, this is the impression given by the *choreikai*, the morning meetings held in an estimated 80 per cent of Japanese firms.[11] Employees are intensively and constantly involved in meetings, work discussion groups, 'quality control circles' and the like. All of this helps to shape a personality susceptible to manipulation. The passionate clinging to the symbols of the firm, the founder and the corporate ideology; the singing of the company song; the joint calisthenics: all are symbolic acts designed to reassure the employee of his membership in the company and of its nurturing powers. The symbols, though abstract, are immediate and familiar. The trite phrases, repeated like incantations, dull the critical faculties. All this consumes much of the salaryman's emotional energy, leaving little psychological reserve for personal attachments outside the company.

Submission and order

The loyalty of the Japanese to his firm has become almost proverbial as a result of much popular writing about Japanese economic achievements, and it is necessary here to place it in a clearer perspective. From the time they were again allowed to visit Japan, a little over a century ago, Western authors have been greatly impressed by the force of Japanese loyalty,[12] and still tend to the conclusion that it is the highest value in Japanese life. This assessment, though true, can be misleading unless one makes clear what Japanese loyalty really consists of.

Piety for superiors

To begin with, Japanese loyalty is directed solely at a group or person, not a belief or abstract idea. And since organisations that are potentially hostile to the System have been weeded out of society almost entirely, Japanese loyalty is most directly supportive of the established socio-political order.

Loyalty is frequently mentioned in the same breath as 'filial piety', as both values are central to the Chinese Confucianism that the Japanese aristocracy imported long ago to buttress its power. The influence of the injunction of filial piety must have been considerable. B. H. Chamberlain wrote shortly after the turn of the century: 'There are no greater favourites with the people of Japan than the "Four-and-Twenty Paragons of Filial Piety", whose quaint acts of virtue Chinese legend records.' One Paragon had a cruel stepmother, who loved fish. Despite her awful treatment of him, he lay down naked on a frozen lake, melted a hole with his body heat and caught two carp that came up for air. Another slept naked so that all the mosquitoes bit him and left his parents alone. My favourite, though, is the seventy-year-old Paragon who dressed in baby clothes and crawled on the floor, deluding his ninety-year-old parents into believing that they could not be so very old after all.[13]

The Meiji government not only propagated filial piety to strengthen politically significant family morality and to foster patriotism, but also decreed that filial piety and loyalty to the emperor were one and the same thing. An even greater political revision of the Chinese ethical system had taken place long before that. The Tokugawa rulers had turned the ethic upside-down by making loyalty to one's lord the highest command, rather than filial piety.

Having shoved the divinely pedigreed emperor aside, Japan's early rulers could not appeal to universally held principles in persuading lower lords to follow and obey them. This was a big problem, solved to some extent by maintaining a military hierarchy, which set standards for loyalty towards the government. The discipline and ethic of obedience that automatically prevail in all military organisations provided an ideal setting for development of the Japanese loyalty cult. In such a context, loyalty has nearly always meant obligatory blind obedience to one's master. In medieval Europe, a knight could forsake his lord in the name of God, and he had specified rights; the feudal system was based on reciprocal fidelity between leaders and retainers. The relationship between leader and retainer in Japan, by contrast, was 'characterised by obligations incumbent only on the follower, who had to be absolutely obedient to his leader's commands'.[14]

Today, the obedience of contemporary Japanese towards their superiors is generally no longer blind or totally unconditional, yet the element of choice is in most cases still lacking. When most employees of large corporations feel that they have had enough of their present boss, they have no option but to remain 'loyal' because, as we have seen, if they were to leave they would not find another job with a comparable income. Even today, loyalty to one's superiors overrules other established moral considerations. A national television audience was reminded of this in 1976 when a group of executives consistently, elaborately and rather obviously committed perjury to 'protect' their employers during parliamentary hearings in connection with the Lockheed bribery scandal. Systematic deceit in such cases where 'loyalty' is involved is to a large extent socially sanctioned and widely admired.

When it is carried to its culturally praised ultimate expression, celebrated in Kabuki plays and some contemporary films, the ethic of loyalty is morally unacceptable to Westerners, as for example when parents murder their own child in order to save the life of the child of their lord. Most important, however, it must be understood that the Japanese ethic of loyalty is, in essence, an ethic of submission.

Loyal subcontractors

Not only are employees forced to be 'loyal' to the Japanese firm, but its small subcontractors also have no choice but to accept less or delayed payment for their parts and semi-finished products in times when business is bad for the big ones.[15]

The salaryman world and its preoccupations may set the tone of contemporary Japanese life, yet it encompasses no more than roughly one-third of the working population. Businesses with between 100 and 1,000 workers provide some 16 per cent of jobs, and those with more than 1,000 another 15 per cent. Outside this world, the relative job security known as 'lifetime employment' (which generally ends between the ages of 55 and 58) does not apply. However, entrepreneurial ambitions provide a respected alternative to salaryman hopes and attitudes; the dream of having a company of one's own is still widespread, and is an important contributing reason in the survival of the so-called dual economy. Supporting the towering hierarchy of large conglomerates there exists a vast collection of medium-sized and small firms that can be squeezed when times are bad.

Almost half Japan's manufacturing workforce is engaged in factories with fewer than fifty workers. These are often no more than sweatshops in which husband and wife may work ten or more hours a day. As subcontractors these small companies – which make parts, or assemble finished products for distribution by the famous firms – provide cheap labour, and in times of economic downturn absorb much of the shock. When the yen doubled in value against the US dollar between 1985 and 1987 these small companies were asked to bear a large share of the loss in profits of companies eager to hang on to foreign market shares.[16]

Japan has a much larger proportion of such small enterprises than the highly industrialised Western countries. Only 0·2 per cent of all Japanese corporations employ more than 1,000 workers (though this percentage still represents more than 2,000 companies). Self-employed workers and family workers (mainly women) form 29 per cent of the Japanese labour force, compared with 8 per cent in Britain, 9 per cent in the US, 14 per cent in West Germany and 17 per cent in France.[17] The resilience of this vast segment of smaller firms in the face of economic vicissitudes is of vital importance to the formidable international competitiveness of the large Japanese firms. A large number of bankruptcies among small firms is balanced by a roughly equal number of openings; the same entrepreneurs launch into another line of business. In large areas of Tokyo and Osaka back streets rarely visited by outsiders, one hears the same incessant clickety-clack of small machines behind hundreds of wooden doors as one did ten or twenty years ago; but the clickety-clack produces entirely different things today.

The freedom of the small entrepreneurs is real in that they can give their own name to their companies and be their presidents. But it is unreal to the extent that almost two-thirds of all small manufacturers are financially dependent on one of the larger firms, which can dictate the conditions under which they work. On this level, too, much is made of the family metaphor. The 'parent firm' helps the subcontractor with supplies and technical assistance, including investments in machinery. It will not, under normal conditions, turn to cheaper subcontractors. But the 'child firm' must accept its role as shock-absorber in periods of economic downturn.

Here too the System is at work, and its embrace is also apparent in the numerous associations of small and medium-sized businesses, and the federations of these associations, that support LDP candidates at election time. With the LDP behind them, the bureaucrats help preserve the dual economy by not burdening small manufacturers with stringent regulations and, most significantly, through formal and informal tax privileges. MITI has an agency for small and medium-sized enterprises that, by co-ordinating an intricate support system of financing by local banks, helps maintain a hierarchy among the smaller businesses. The larger members in the community of small firms, which feel more beholden to the LDP, help control the smaller ones.

The class structure of employment

Besides controlling the thought and behaviour of the salaryman, the Japanese business world helps preserve order in the System in other ways too. Relationships within firms are strongly hierarchical, and so are the ties among firms – intensively so in the case of subcontractors. The firms do not employ a cross-section of the population, but narrowly selected groups that emerge at various levels from the schooling hierarchy. Thus the larger firms, themselves hierarchically ordered in conglomerate groupings and industrial associations, emphasise still further the hierarchic order of society by, as it were, 'grading' the population.

Prospective employees are not very interested in the kind of company they join, whether it deals in insurance or in chemicals. But they are extremely interested in its ranking, because this directly determines their own ranking in society. Nor does the salaryman recruit worry much about the prosperity of the company he joins. Whereas in the West and most other non-Japanese political economies economic factors such as profitability determine a company's success, in Japan success is measured more by political indicators: the company's size and market share and, related to these, its position in the hierarchy.

Another way in which Japanese firms help maintain the social order is by systematic discrimination against women. Women make up a very important part of the workforce. More than half of those who are married supplement the family income with full-time or part-time employment, often in subcontracting firms. But these working women furnish the System with a gigantic pool of relatively cheap labour through purposeful corporate policies, which have been explicitly excused by appeals to 'Japanese social customs and traditions' and are supported by the bureaucracy. From the age of eighteen or twenty, girls work in the service sector or in offices; then, in their mid-twenties, they marry and retire. Many return to the labour force in their mid-thirties, after bringing up a child or two. Most women in offices start their career with 10 per cent less pay than male colleagues hired in the same year, and this gap widens to about 30 per cent. When they return to work, they cannot claim seniority in the way that the men can under the 'lifetime employment' system, and are typically employed on a 'part-time' basis though they may work as many hours as their male colleagues at half the pay, and with few if any fringe benefits.

Keeping women in their proper place

In the wake of litigation by a few activist female employees in the 1970s, most large firms will not summarily dismiss young women when they reach 'retirement age' or marry.[18] But the pressure on them to leave 'voluntarily' is nearly always irresistible. Unless she works for a bank, insurance firm, government office, department store or foreign company – organisations that do offer careers to women – a female employee approaching the age of twenty-nine will have to find a husband or an alternative source of income.

Since the spring of 1985 Japan has had an Equal Employment Opportunity Law, which basically enjoins corporate Japan to 'attempt' to treat male and female employees equally. The law does not spell out the consequences of not making such an attempt, and the final wording – a result of years of bureaucratically guided *shingikai* discussion – is widely considered a victory for management. The law was the minimum Japan could come up with for the sake of its international image, and it was passed just in time for ratification of the UN's Convention on the Elimination of All Forms of Discrimination against Women.

The role of Japanese women in the economic process has become a problem that is only partially reflected by pressure from activist groups. The number of working married women in 1985 had doubled compared with twenty years before, the phenomenon of the 'honeymoon baby' has drastically decreased, and the gradual increase in the still very low divorce rate is largely due to the initiative of wives wishing to pursue a career. To help defuse strains and tensions, the administrators actively endorse the picture of their 'traditional' Japanese family purveyed by the mass media and establishment 'social critics'. From the vehement reactions in serious magazines to the emancipation activists who were bent on strengthening the equal employment law, one would conclude that the continuation of Japanese 'culture' was at issue.[19]

Although in reality Japanese tradition has never frowned on working women, and today the majority of working married women are obliged to help make ends meet in their families, the officially sponsored portrait of 'wholesome' family life invariably shows that the proper place for women is at home. In a country where stereotypes are treasured, emphasis on the established proper roles of women is especially noticeable. It extends to demurely polite deportment, a studied innocent cuteness, a 'gentle' voice one octave above the natural voice and always a nurturing, motherly disposition. The model woman in the world of the salarymen is a cross between Florence Nightingale and the minister of finance (as women are almost always totally responsible for household finances). Superior intelligence is a liability for girls and women, and must be disguised. Women are frequently subtly and sometimes not so subtly degraded in TV programmes and comic strips. Many bookstores have an SM section in which the most popular items are magazines and books with pictures of ladies tied up to look like rolled meat. In 1985 a director-general of the cultural affairs bureau of the Ministry of Education, Miura Shumon, caused a small stir when he wrote in a couple of magazine articles that rape, although not gentlemanly conduct, was not so bad if practised on modern young women whose moral standards had slipped anyhow.

The picture is not entirely negative. A great step in the legal liberation of Japanese women was taken under the auspices of the United States occupation when adultery as a criminal offence was scrapped from the law books. Under the old code, in keeping with Confucianist practice, only the wife could ever be guilty of this crime. Also, there seems to be no doubt that behind a majority of closed doors the Japanese wife is the more powerful member of the family, and that the salaryman shackled to his firm could use as much emancipation as his wife. But the expectations of proper behaviour are hammered home through a plethora of comic books and films and the numerous soap operas serialised by television stations. Soap operas in all countries that have them tend to support standard social mores, but the Japanese type is generally tougher on nonconformists. The enterprising and independent young woman who persists in going her own way beyond a certain point will meet with all manner of obstacles and calamities. With very few exceptions, happy endings conform to the unwritten rules about work, marriage, giving birth and taking care of elderly parents and in-laws, as marking the proper stages of a Japanese woman's life.

The unrepresented middle class

We have seen how rural Japanese are tied to the System, and how doctors, professors and small manufacturers are also a part of it. Relatively independent are the shop owner, the beauty-salon operator, the artist and some others. Even here, shopkeepers are often tied to dealer associations controlled by manufacturers, while in the other categories too associations proliferate and frequently make relatively heavy demands on their members to conform. Yet no category is as limited in its freedom as that of the salarymen.

It is through salaryman life and all its organisations that the System exerts its most effective economic sway over the Japanese population. The most glaring contrast in comparison with other industrialised countries is the absence of any counterbalancing power of labour, since there is almost no labour market for salarymen.

Most salarymen are urban consumers, and it is they who, through relatively high amounts of savings, subsequently channelled into the *keiretsu* for capital investments, have played a crucial role in sustaining the economic 'miracle'. It is they who in the late 1980s were still subsidising Japan's export industries by being systematically deprived of low-cost imports and by paying considerably higher prices than consumers in the Western industrialised countries for almost all daily necessities.

In most other countries the rise of the middle class upset and basically changed political relations. In Japan such a disturbing influence has been minimised. However important he may be to the survival of the System, the salaryman's interests are woefully under-represented. One reason why housing policy is neglected is that the LDP sees no electoral advantages in it.[20] We have seen in Chapter 3 how consumer movements initiated by salarymen's wives have been systematically encapsulated and undermined.

In Chapter 4 we saw how one type of racketeering, the *sarakin*, was reorganised under government auspices with an eye to the interests, not of the consumer, but of the larger *sarakin* firms, of the Ministry of Finance and of the politicians.

All efforts to organise the political potential of the salaryman, including a Salaryman Party, have failed. The claims made by the company on his total person leave him with insufficient time, energy and ideas to become a political force. The salarymen have been referred to as Japan's new middle class, but this white-collar class has never grown into a bourgeoisie that could be a threat to the traditional Japanese body politic.

Producers of salaryman culture

A mammoth industry sees to it that Japanese have their 'circuses' as well as their 'bread'. Japanese mass culture is tailor-made to sustain the orderly world of the salaryman. It stands out for the dearth of anything that might tax the political imagination. The days of the serious Japanese cinema, exploring social and political issues, are long gone. Since the 1960s the Japanese movie studios, which are very much part of the System, have churned out totally predictable fare made according to a small variety of rigid formulas. Toei studios have long had intimate connections with the Yamaguchi-gumi crime syndicate, and have made hundreds of films celebrating the traditional 'morals' of gangsters, as well as films on wartime and post-war history with a nationalistic slant. Twice or three times a year, perhaps, a more independent director will produce a quality product; but even when these satirise contemporary social practices, they lack implicit analysis of their origins. Japanese avant-garde theatre groups sometimes claim to make 'political statements', but their messages are abstract and imponderable.

The organisation of mass culture

A crucial factor in Japanese popular culture is its degree of commercial organisation. There is little room for the maverick. One example is film director Oshima Nagisa, one of the few Japanese artists to concern themselves seriously with socio-political questions such as the student movement of the 1950s and 1960s and the plight of Koreans living in Japan. He ended by being relegated to the margins of the Japanese movie industry, to the extent of having to finance his projects from foreign sources. Even the serious art world is highly organised, with rankings that determine income. Japanese painters, print-makers, musicians and stage performers are tied to systems that are much more hierarchical, forbidding and unbendable than in the West.

Control over Japanese mass culture is easily accomplished without open or direct governmental restraint. Japanese, talented or not, are unlikely to contribute to it unless either they are employed by a hierarchically ordered firm in the entertainment sector, or they are in some way tied in with the *jinmyaku* connections of executives in such firms. As is true of the education system, this industry abhors imagination that goes against the grain of socio-political expectations. The police are activated only by photographs and film scenes showing pubic hair. Everything else pertaining to mass culture can be controlled because the 'private' institutions that produce it are informally linked to a number of élite groups. They include film and television studios, as well as most of the gigantic newspaper and publishing firms. But the best example, probably, is afforded by the advertising world, and in particular Dentsu, the largest 'advertising agency' in the world.

The hidden media boss

Dentsu does more than any single corporation, anywhere in the world, to mould popular culture, both directly and through hordes of subcontractors. It also orchestrates major events such as expos and visits from the pope. It is highly active politically, about which more in a moment.

Dentsu is directly responsible for one-third of all advertising on Japanese TV, and virtually monopolises the scheduling of sponsors during prime-time hours, not to mention the control it exerts through its many subsidiaries and subcontracting firms. Some 120 film production companies and more than 400 subcontracting graphic arts studios are under its wing. Advertisers wishing to insert commercials in television programmes between 7 and 11 p.m. have almost no choice but to go via Dentsu, because it controls their selection and much of the programme material.

Programme makers jokingly refer to Dentsu as the 'editing bureau of Tsukiji' (the neighbourhood that houses its monumental head office).[21] It can play this role because in Japan volume of business tends to correspond directly to degree of political clout. Under such circumstances, it is a privilege to be treated with consideration by Dentsu, and advertisers tend to follow its instructions rather than the other way round. The same is even true for the commercial television channels, which have become highly dependent on Dentsu.

The result is that Dentsu's sway over the substance of Japanese TV culture is quite unlike any kind of social control through the mass media anywhere in the world. And this is of great political significance. Nowhere has the drug of TV been applied as successfully as in Japan, and nowhere else has the addiction taken such a hold, with sets in restaurants, shops, tour buses and even taxis. Very few, if any, countries can be proud of the overall quality of their television programmes, but the global cultural desert has areas of greater and lesser misery. Sometimes NHK (comparable to the BBC) – ironically enough, the station most directly linked with officialdom – will broadcast a serious programme in which reporters are allowed to raise genuine questions about social issues. For the rest, however, Japanese television ranges from pseudo-scholarly, sanitised and carefully uncontroversial 'serious' fare on NHK, through soap operas that on all channels almost caricature cherished Japanese mores, to utterly vacuous show programmes.

Quizzes and amateur song-fests are copied from foreign examples, but in Japan they reach an apotheosis of mindlessness. Popular 'stars' are mass-produced; with 'careers' rarely lasting more than two years, they are a caricature of the Western phenomenon of entertainers famous merely for their fame.[22]

There are no accepted standards for measuring such things inter-nationally. However, if television programmes in most West European countries and the USA are adjusted to viewers of an average mental age of eleven or twelve, those in Japan are attuned to an average age of eight or nine. Dentsu is the major instrument for determining the quality of Japan's daily entertainment, and it has managed to reduce nearly everything to the lowest common denominator. Though institutions producing mind-deadening entertainment exist in other countries too, we are dealing here with an organisation possessing almost unfailing power to keep others out and to restrain or arrest the development of popular culture of a higher quality.

The closed circuit of Dentsu power

Dentsu handles about a quarter of all advertising budgets in Japan; it places over one-fifth of the ads in the major newspapers and close to a third of those in the more important magazines. The other three-quarters is taken care of by some 3,000 smaller firms, the largest eight of these reaching combined sales about equal to those of Dentsu. By comparison, the largest advertising agency in the United States, Young & Rubicam, has a US market share of only 3·46 per cent (in 1986). Dentsu gets higher commissions than the smaller agencies, and can set conditions of pay-ment. New magazines may be asked to take advertisements free of charge for a trial period before they will be considered as an outlet; if they do not comply, Dentsu has enough influence to arrange a reduction in their existing advertising income.[23]

Dentsu has become unbeatable thanks to its *jinmyaku*. Its hiring policies have always aimed to maintain and expand its pool of sons and other close relatives from the top level of administrators and executives in the television and publishing world, as well as of special clients and pro-fessional backstage fixers. Its employee ranking system reflects the extent to which these recruits are believed to be able to foster informal relations with clients, government agencies, broadcasting companies and pub-lishers.[24] One Dentsu executive was quoted as characterising this as 'taking hostages' to maintain favourable relations with big sponsors.[25]

Conversely, Dentsu provides presidents and top-level executives for major newspapers, national and regional TV stations[26] and other firms connected with the mass media, as well as its own subsidiaries. One landing spot for Dentsu personnel is Video Research Company, the rating agency that assesses the popularity of TV programmes. Set up by Dentsu in 1962, two years after the US firm Nielsen introduced the TV programme rating system in Japan (the second largest TV market in the world), it can be called upon to rid TV of programmes that are unpopular with the administrators. For example, a programme called *Judgment* that concerned itself with controversial issues (the *burakumin*, school textbook censorship by the Education Ministry and problems regarding the tax system) was taken off the air, allegedly because of low viewing rates.[27]

Advertising agencies in other countries are intermediaries. In Japan, Dentsu itself often decides how companies must advertise and where. In the USA, the one other country where commercial television is a major industry, an independent rating agency determines how commercially successful the programmes are; in Japan this function remains in Dentsu's hands.

Dentsu is in a position to intimidate large firms, since it can make corporate scandals known and hush them up again. Moreover, companies hardly dare switch agencies because of rumours that Dentsu will report irregularities in their business to the authorities.[28]

Dentsu helps shelter big business from the scrutiny of consumers. A Dentsu executive once boasted in a speech that the *Yomiuri* newspaper, after having invited consumer activist Ralph Nader to Japan, heeded a warning from Dentsu by breaking up a planned two-page special report and toning down the fragments. Around the same time, the *Mainichi* newspaper, also under instructions from Dentsu, ran a 'moderate' story on the consumer movement.[29] Dentsu is able to apply enormous pressure on the media not to report, or to downplay, incidents that might harm the prestige of its clients. A famous case is Dentsu's controlling of news about the arsenic contamination of Morinaga Milk Industry's powdered milk in 1955. Another is the way Dentsu in 1964–5 censored news of deaths caused by cold medicine produced by Taisyo Pharmaceutical. As one reporter from the Kyodo news agency remembers: 'Whenever news of a death through that medicine reached us, companies such as Dentsu applied pressure on us not to report it at all, or not to mention the name of the pharmaceutical company. Sometimes they telephoned us; at other times an executive would visit us.'[30]

Weekly magazines exercise a certain amount of self-censorship over stories that might adversely affect large Dentsu clients. They may also expect pressure prior to publication, since the contents of an upcoming issue are usually known to Dentsu.[31] Dentsu is given additional leverage by a system whereby it buys a regular chunk of a magazine's advertisement space, guaranteeing the magazine a regular income and freeing it from the need to find advertisers on its own.[32] Its success in the censorship business derives not only from its financial leverage, but also from having once been merged with the monopolistic Domei Tsushinsha news agency that purveyed government propaganda between 1936 and 1945, and from its very close connections with Japan's two major news agencies, Kyodo Tsushin and Jiji Press, both of them likewise descendants of the wartime Domei Tsushinsha.[33] These links are reinforced by cross-shareholding.[34] Dentsu is kept informed of the news that Kyodo handles, and especially with local newspapers can instantaneously intercede on behalf of its clients.[35]

Relaying the administrators' voices

Another major function of this media institution is the bolstering of 'traditional values' with the aid of 'opinion polls', together with public-relations work for the bureaucrats and the LDP. It collects intelligence for the Prime Minister's Office and the LDP, and helps manufacture 'public opinion' through slanted polls. It is in charge of the more sophisticated aspects of LDP election campaigns. It handles propaganda concerning controversial issues such as the safety of nuclear power generation, and concerning projects of the various ministries. It co-ordinated political manoeuvres to unseat a string of oppositionist mayors and prefectural governors in the late 1970s, and has waged campaigns against politically significant local consumer and environmental movements.

Such work for the bureaucrats and the LDP is mainly done by Dentsu's 'ninth bureau', which has sections corresponding to the ministries of Construction, Transport, Agriculture, Post and Telecommunications, Education and Finance and the Prime Minister's Office. Officially privatised but in fact nearly unchanged public corporations such as NTT and Japan Railways are handled by this bureau as well. The ninth bureau absorbs over one-third of the PR budget of the prime minister's office and some 40 per cent of that of the other ministries.[36] Dentsu also has a near monopoly on disposal of the LDP's PR budget.

One reason why the LDP and Dentsu maintain such cordial relations is that Dentsu's oligopolistic power allows it to charge such high commissions from business clients that the LDP – always short of 'political funds' – need not pay much, nor be prompt in paying it. The ninth bureau was established shortly after the formation of the Tanaka Kakuei cabinet in 1972. A year later Dentsu published a memorable report, *Reflections on the PR of the LDP*, containing the often quoted assertion that, whereas the LDP already maintained fairly advantageous connections, via the reporter club system, with reporters of the daily press, TV and radio, its relations with important weekly magazines other than those published by the newspaper companies were not yet based sufficiently on 'fixed rules'.

The System's propagandists

Japan's second largest 'advertising agency', Hakuhodo (with roughly 40 per cent of Dentsu's volume of sales), is also well ensconced among the

administrators, especially those of the financial community. This is
understandable, for two successive presidents of the company and several
other executives have been *amakudari* bureaucrats from the Ministry of
Finance.[37]

But the most interesting of the smaller outfits making propaganda for
the administrators is the very active Tokyu Agency. Whereas Dentsu
normally receives orders through the bureaucrats, when Nakasone Yasuhiro was prime minister he would telephone Tokyu Agency directly to pass
on instructions. The link is close because Goto Noboru, the great boss of
the Tokyu Group and president until 1987 of the Japan Chamber of
Commerce, has Nakasone, a former classmate at Todai, at the apex of his
jinmyaku.[38]

One of Tokyu Agency's greatest assignments was the celebrations in
connection with the controversial National Foundation Day that
Nakasone promoted as part of his programme to clear away post-war
taboos. Even larger in scope was its co-ordination of a nation-wide
propaganda effort in connection with Nakasone's administrative reform
programme.[39] It formed a pressure group, enlisting housewives' associations for the purpose, and organised marches and demonstrations in front
of the Diet building. On one occasion in March 1983 it managed to
mobilise 15,000 'demonstrators'. Tokyu Agency lost money on these large
assignments, but the connections it solidified through them have made it
the fastest-growing 'advertising agency'.

The role of the major 'advertising agencies' as servants of the System
illustrates admirably the impossibility of drawing a line between the
private and public sectors in Japan. If the 'policy platforms' that successive
LDP governments are expected to come up with usually sound like
advertising copy, it is because the slogans that they substitute for political
ideas are manufactured in one or the other of the above-mentioned
agencies.

The questions usually asked to determine whether there is collusion
between business and government become irrelevant when applied to the
cases of Dentsu, Hakuhodo and Tokyu Agency. It is inconceivable that
they would stand idly by if politically engaged groups should ever try to
undermine the System on which they depend.

7

Nurses of the People

In its 'fighting spirit', its compulsory togetherness, its consciousness of rank within the company and more especially its proprietary treatment of the employee as a 'family' member, in a way that hinders his development as an independent individual, 'salaryman life' is clearly reminiscent of the military tradition. Indeed, most walks of Japanese life are highly regimented. It is ironic that the only country in the world whose constitution deprives it of the right to wage war, whose official spokesmen seriously suggest that it can teach the world to love peace and which formally decries the use of military power, whenever and wherever and no matter by whom it is resorted to, should so often remind one of a military organisation. The flocks of high-school pupils dressed in black uniforms cut like those of Prussia at the turn of the century are just the surface. The emphasis on collective exercise; the drills continued for their own sake far beyond the point where skill ceases to improve; the social approval given to *gambaru* (not giving up, sticking with something beyond reason); the sentimental emphasis on the 'purity' of single-minded youthful exertions; the spartan discipline in judo, karate, kendo and aikido training: all these represent a militarised approach to social order. The virtues of self-control and endurance that the Japanese are taught to hold in highest regard, along with loyalty, are among the most important that soldiers must cultivate.

This is not surprising, when one considers that Japan was ruled by soldiers during much of its history. For many centuries the military provided the chief model for proper conduct. The Tokugawa shogunate was a warrior regime maintaining something akin to martial law. In time, it evolved into a bureaucratic government with parallels to the Soviet Union after Stalin, complete with ideology and a privileged ruling class. But its ideals of social discipline remained those of the barracks and the battlefield.

Forces of benevolence

Outside the cities of Tokugawa Japan, life seems to have offered few consistent pleasures for the common people. Most of the house codes of the feudal domains were oppressive. Some daimyos ruled extremely harshly, and were hostile to outsiders, overseeing every act of their subjects and forbidding contact with people from other domains. None the less there existed a Confucianist-derived ideal of benevolence as befitting anyone with power over others. Although no superior was bound by it, widely praised historical examples of benevolent power-holders provided a certain incentive for daimyos and samurai to be lenient when they could afford to be. It was understood, too, that benevolent government favoured peasant productivity, the economic basis of the political system.[1]

After the Meiji Restoration, the posture of leniency was given a clear political purpose. Most major figures in the Meiji oligarchy accepted the necessity for occasional accommodation of the public's wishes. Even Yamagata Aritomo, the arch-opponent of the incipient political parties, who moulded much of the bureaucracy and the military, understood that merely to cripple the parties without compensation would not 'eliminate those factors which made the people susceptible to [their] siren voice'.[2] The Ministry of Education, Yamagata calculated, could handle social control, but not before local governments were reformed. Flexible and pragmatic in its policies, the Meiji directive élite was adept at easing repression when it suited its purpose in presenting the 'paternalistic' side of 'paternalistic authoritarianism'.[3]

This strategy worked. The most formidable oppositionist campaign – the Freedom and Popular Rights movement, which appealed to an imperial promise for the convocation of assemblies and open political discussion[4] – lost its momentum, and was destined thenceforth to survive only as a source of inspiration for equally ineffective political opposition movements in later decades. The Meiji oligarchy, and subsequent governments too, understood that whenever possible the power of propaganda should substitute for direct repression. The bureaucrats preferred not to carry out frontal attacks on organisations that were, or could become, sources of political challenge. Instead, they emasculated them, typically by presenting them with 'guidance' and official help. Thus the earlier part of the twentieth century saw the hurried organisation of societies for the betterment of discontented workers and other obviously disadvantaged groups. In the 1920s the Naimusho bureaucrats entrusted with labour policy promoted factory legislation and workers' health insurance that somewhat mitigated the effects of exploitation by business corporations.[5] Along with this 'benevolence', of course, went the suppression of 'dangerous thoughts', but even here, as we will see, there was much leniency.

Those who today may apply naked power in the name of the state, the police and public prosecutors (the most noticeable reminders, along with the tax collectors, that something like a state exists), have turned the habit of leniency into a kind of second nature. But a condition is attached:

the recipient must in turn acknowledge the goodness of the established social order; political heterodoxy elicits tough measures.

Nannies, monitors and missionaries

From the time of its formation in the 1870s it was understood that Japan's police force, unlike its sword-wielding samurai predecessors, could not merely scare the populace into submission. Kawaji Toshiyoshi, first chief of the Tokyo metropolitan police and architect of the modern Japanese police system, neatly summed it up by saying that the government should be seen as the parent, the people as the children and the policemen as the nurses of the children.[6]

This view of things was not as far-fetched as it may sound. Kawaji had seen the Parisian police force in action when he went to Europe in 1872 as a member of one of the many Meiji study missions, and he closely followed and expanded upon this French model. The Parisian police – in those days the most respected internationally – performed incidental functions ranging from the enforcement of health regulations to the licensing of prostitution and the supervision of a wide range of commercial activities.[7] The importance of the police role in public administration during the Meiji era can be seen from employment figures for 1880, when the total number of prefectural and city officials for the Tokyo metropolitan area was only 912, whereas the police bureau had a force of 4,400 men. Not until the second decade of this century did the figures begin to balance.[8] The Japanese police looked after health regulations and could issue licences and permits for a great variety of businesses. They monitored the publishing world, the theatres and political gatherings.

One of Kawaji's major recommendations was that the men responsible for this wide-ranging monitoring of society should be placed under a ministry of their own. The Naimusho, established in 1873, was to remain the most powerful institution of the administrators until finally, after the war, it was divided up into ministries of Welfare, Labour and Construction, a new Home Affairs Ministry to oversee local government and a National Police Agency. Even today, these organs of officialdom view their roles as partly inherited from those of their mighty predecessor.[9]

An important function of the police from the turn of the century was to monitor the potentially explosive new relationships between early entrepreneurs and the labourers they hired in factories and on building sites. The combined office and residence (*chuzaisho*) of the rural policemen was often established on factory land and supported by an entrepreneur. The latter sometimes even paid the salaries of these policemen, who thus became virtual factory guards, a deterrent against labour unrest.[10]

Until 1945 the Japanese police were also, of course, in charge of suppressing political heterodoxy. This was made easier by an extremely elaborate information-gathering network, with spies throughout the

civilian population. All Japanese were regularly checked within the
framework of a home visit programme. Police called on important families
and landowners once a year, people without property twice a year and
unemployed or suspicious citizens three times. Yet even while clamping
down severely on anything that might upset the established order, the
police understood that a tranquil Japan was best achieved through
leniency and accommodation. Even after the dreaded Tokko (Special
Higher Police – later known as the 'thought police') acquired great power
through the Peace Preservation Law of 1925, people with the 'wrong
thoughts' were not treated harshly once they had shown repentance.
Recantation of one's beliefs would result in dropped charges and,
frequently, in official assistance in finding a job for smooth reintegration
into the community.[11] The established process for this, actively encouraged by the Ministry of Justice and known as tenko (best translated as
'apostasy'), involved the suspect's 'conversion' to belief in the benevolence of the 'family state' under the emperor.

The friendly neighbourhood police state

The disbanding of the Naimusho by the occupation authorities after the
Second World War brought great changes in police behaviour. Today,
they are rarely overbearing towards individuals (as distinct from their
exhortations directed to the public in general through megaphones and
loudspeakers); they generally blend in with the area they patrol, and
cultivate a friendly and helpful demeanour.

Every neighbourhood in the cities has its koban, or police box –
introduced in 1888 on the advice of a captain in the Berlin metropolitan
police[12] – and the countryside is dotted with the chuzaisho where local
policemen live with their families. The koban is a source of information on
many matters, from unfindable addresses to treatment for a sick pet. All
people still receive twice-yearly home visits from the koban-based police,
who use these opportunities to collect gossip about the neighbourhood and
inquire after any 'unusual behaviour'. Many foreigners in Tokyo are
excluded from these rounds, but I, for example, received a visit from the
policeman of the chuzaisho in a nearby hamlet within a month of settling in
the countryside to work on this book.

Subtle social control is greatly facilitated by the ease with which the
police can trace the movements of most people by means of the domicile and
family registers (for Japanese) and the alien registers (for foreigners),
and the observations of attentive neighbours. The limited scope for the
Japanese to change their employment helps greatly in keeping society
under survey. In residential neighbourhoods, newcomers with obscure
backgrounds are scrutinised by trusted acquaintances of the police. If
anything untoward appears to be going on in a particular household, a
police officer may visit it sooner than the twice-a-year routine calls for. A
number of embezzlement cases have been discovered in this way, through

tips from neighbours who noticed refrigerators, TV sets, cars and the like being delivered to a home in quick succession.[13]

The police like to compile records of minor infractions, especially of people who are not well established in communities. This gives them an excuse to ask people to come for questioning at any time. A curious personal experience may illustrate this. I was once summoned to a police station for no reason I could think of. Waiting for me was a copy of an apology I had written four years previously for having been one day late in registering my re-entry into Japan at the office of the Tokyo ward in which I lived. Since the final date for registering had fallen on a public holiday, and since my written explanation and apology were contrite in the degree prescribed for such occasions, I had not expected to hear of it again. However, while the friendly police were taking the prints of all my fingers and of both full hands and asking dozens of seemingly irrelevant questions, it became clear that they wanted to see me for something entirely different – most probably it was a case involving an acquaintance, which happened to have been solved before my arrival at the station.[14]

The public is not undivided in its admiration of policemen. To some extent they are still feared. But, especially in the countryside, people bring them presents, offer them free meals and invite them to drinking parties. In the cities, the police can rely on a large number of enthusiastic informers: people who monitor the life of the streets while selling cigarettes from tiny window-shops, or respected members of the neighbourhood such as doctors or dentists, who may double as parole officers. There are in addition thousands of volunteer crime-prevention associations based on neighbourhood organisations and occupational groups, all linked by federations.

I once spent a Saturday afternoon with a small group of middle-aged housewives patrolling the streets of one of Tokyo's major entertainment districts. Their trained eyes would soon spot any teenagers from the suburbs, whom they would approach for questioning. The conversations usually ended with encouragement to return home on the next commuter train and avoid the temptations and traps awaiting innocent youth in the city. Encounters which in many Western countries would have resulted at least in foul language produced only bowed heads and muttered thanks for the advice given by the crime-prevention ladies.

The function of nursemaid to all citizens is still cherished by the contemporary police:

The police actually seem to play the role of a social worker or a clergyman in their approach. They investigate the suspect's personal background and try to determine why he went wrong. They convince the suspect that he is essentially a good person, but that he made a mistake. If they yell at him in the interrogation, their anger is not because they hate him, but because he is a good person who did wrong and will not admit it.[15]

One need not be a criminal to earn such nursing attention. One detects it in the admonishing tone of instructions suddenly emanating from the loudspeaker on a police box or cruising patrol car. In the apartment-block districts of some smaller cities the police may try to make people feel part of a community by wishing them good morning through a public address system at 7 a.m., and by providing music for calisthenics, uplifting talk and reminders to be careful about all manner of things.

Nagging and instructing nursemaids

The public, on its side, tends to obey police directions, however unnecessary and overbearing. Pedestrians will usually wait for quite superfluous traffic lights to change on narrow streets that could be crossed in a stride or two, or even where no vehicles can pass because of a blocked-off road.

A good example of tolerance of police interference can be witnessed every year during the cherry-blossom season in Tokyo's Ueno Park, which attracts a large number of partying groups, mainly office workers, who sit on mats beneath the blossom, picnicking, drinking, singing and clapping their hands in unison as is the custom at office parties. But the police have staked out large territories for themselves too, and use their megaphones liberally for exhortations and warnings. These go on until about 8.30 p.m. when, with the revelry in full swing, the police begin to shout that it is time to go home. Amazingly, within thirty minutes or less the park is nearly totally empty. Practically everyone obeys, even though the police are making arbitrary rules; in fact, the park is open twenty-four hours a day.

Another example of this combination of police meddling and almost blind obedience by the public occurs regularly on crowded major roads where snow has turned to slush. Lit-up signs along the road and cruising police cars command drivers to put on snow-chains, whereupon hundreds upon hundreds of people stop and fumble, often in the dark, to follow orders, only to ruin their chains and damage their tyres, not to mention the road, in the process.

The Japanese, especially in the cities, are constantly made to feel like subjects rather than citizens. They live in a cajoling and exhortative environment. They are continually warned about dangers, reminded of the proper way to do things, gently chided. Kawaji's nurses of the people have stayed on as permanent instructors. The loudspeakers on cruising police cars and on the bigger police boxes recall a worrisome mother; something is always *abunai*, dangerous. The hint of aggrievedness in the tone emphasises further the likeness to a Japanese mother; people walking the streets are made to feel like potentially naughty children.

In the railway stations that almost all commuting salarymen pass through every day, incessant announcements giving mostly superfluous information acquire the quality of an acoustical whip, spurring on commuters as though they might otherwise clog the passageways and platforms. Together with the ubiquitous admonishing of the police, this constitutes the daily manifestation of authority outside the workplace. The intrusion is only aural; no one is picked up by the collar, no flashlight is shone in the face. But one is reminded, ever so mildly, that authority is immanent in the world.

For drivers there are other, special reminders. In some prefectures one can still find nearly life-size concrete or plastic policemen clad in full, if weatherbeaten, regalia. In some areas these have been replaced by large pictures of policemen printed on vinyl sheets, or by highly stylised structures with fluorescent paint that in the beam of headlights suggest the white bandolier and red nightstick of traffic police.

The remorseful suspect

A specialist in cross-cultural comparisons of police methods has concluded that Japan is a paradise for the cops because Japanese society polices itself.[16] One might add that it is also a paradise, comparatively speaking, for those caught by the police, since few of them are actually punished. In the treatment of offenders the nursemaid function is clearly demonstrated. Occasionally the police will be strict, for the sake of setting an example; but generally, if people committing misdemeanours are sufficiently apologetic and promise to improve their behaviour, they have a very good chance of being let off the hook after a perfunctory lecture.[17]

Even where, with more serious offences, the police pursue the matter, the public prosecutor, or procurator as he is called in Japan, has nearly unlimited power to let the culprit go. The code of criminal procedure permits dropping a case in consideration of the suspect's character, age and circumstances, or the development of events *following* the offence. This allows the prosecutor to act as 'the interpreter of public morality in that he decides who shall be made an example of, who shall be given another chance, and what is most required by the public interest'.[18] In recent decades just under half of all cases of serious violations of the criminal code were dropped for reasons unrelated to lack of evidence. Older people and first offenders tend to be treated with great leniency. This is, of course, not unusual elsewhere, but the Japanese prosecutor has considerably greater discretion than his Western counterpart.

Even if suspects are indicted and convicted, they are often not given prison sentences. In 1986 only 3·2 per cent of all prosecution cases, including traffic violations, received such sentences, and 57·4 per cent of these were suspended.[19] Suspended prison sentences of two to three years for rapists are fairly common. As a result, this country of 120 million inhabitants has only about 50,000 people behind bars.[20] One reason is the low budget for penal facilities, the Ministry of Justice being notoriously weak in negotiating with the Ministry of Finance. But there is more to it than that. The enormous discretionary autonomy of the Japanese law-enforcement authorities enables them to shift emphasis from punishing the misdemeanour or crime to 'converting' the offender to the side of society.

In practically all instances the most important factor determining the choice made by the public prosecutor is the extent to which the suspect makes a display of remorse. Police and prosecutors love apologies. Not the simple one-time kind, which rarely suffice even in normal Japanese social intercourse. What is expected from suspects is a continuous stream of apology, the intensity and profusion of which must indicate the degree of their 'sincerity'. Some suspects may, in fact, go down on their knees. Thus the Japanese law-enforcement system does not apply punishment to fit the crime, but rather to fit the demeanour of the culprit after the crime. We must not mistake this for 'compassion'. Japanese bureaucratic orgnisations are not so disposed. The decision of what to do with suspects entails a symbolic determination as to whether they are still fit for society. And the overriding criterion for this is each suspect's thorough understanding of, and readiness to go through, the required redemption ritual. The unspoken rationale behind this is that co-operative citizens are preferable to costly prisoners whose imprisonment may teach them only to become worse criminals.

Confess!

Japanese can be apologetic in a general way. They sometimes give the impression of thinking that their mere presence is a nuisance to others. Generalised apologies demonstrate 'sincerity'. But the really solid apologies that the nurses of the people expect must be related directly to the misdemeanour or crime. Thus a major task for the police is to make a suspect confess. In this context the legal rights of the individual are as good as irrelevant. Police and prosecutors place a tremendous emphasis on admission of guilt, regardless of the constitutional guarantee that citizens are not obliged to testify against themselves. Confession is still considered the necessary first step for a return to normal society.

The hankering after confessions by Japan's law-enforcement officers has led to excesses that received considerable attention in the serious monthly magazines in 1983. A committee formed by the three bar associations in Tokyo uncovered a pattern of forced confessions and false convictions that was verified by a meeting of falsely accused people in May of that year and by the private testimony of legal specialists.[21] Thirty cases of officially acknowledged false confessions were investigated, leading to the conclusion that harassment without regard for a suspect's rights is common, and that de facto torture is occasionally practised in Japanese police detention cells.[22] The public was further made aware of the possibility of systematic injustice when, in July 1983, Menda Sakae, a convict who had spent thirty-one years waiting to be executed, was found not guilty by the Supreme Court after re-examination of his case, and when two more convicted murderers were found innocent and released shortly afterwards.

Even without much overt coercion, the police are at an advantage in extracting confessions. Only a small proportion of suspects are actually detained, but if the police choose they may keep a suspect in custody upon issue of a warrant, without access to counsel or bail, for a period that can be extended up to twenty-three days.[23] In order to permit this, legislation passed in the occupation period was rescinded.[24]

Another advantage for the police is that Japanese society heartily approves of apologies where a non-Japanese observer would see absolutely no need for them. Thus a Japanese will sometimes ask forgiveness for an imaginary transgression simply in order to appear 'sincere'. Being picked up by the police is, in any event, shameful, and there is comfort in converting an overwhelming sense of shame into an admission of guilt, since guilt can more easily be coped with; unlike shame, it can be expiated.[25] Cut off from everyone except their interrogators, and with no reminder given them that they have rights even in custody, suspects become psychologically malleable in the hands of the police. Many will confess to crimes they have not committed – an even more tempting course when they are told that it will result in the charges being dropped, whereas non-co-operation will land them in prison on even weightier charges.

If suspects do not co-operate and the police have decided that a confession is absolutely necessary, subtle forms of blackmail may be brought into play. Much can be expected of the threat that the suspect's family will become involved. In a fair number of recorded instances, relatively simple-minded suspects were told that their father and mother would also be arrested if they did not confess. To imagine the strength of this threat it is necessary to realise that the mere prospect that the family will be told of the police investigation has in itself a horrifying effect. A vague belief in collective guilt still survives from centuries of military government, so that even today the family of a criminal suspect may be ostracised by the community.

For those particularly reluctant to confess, there are early-morning-to-midnight interrogations for days on end. In total contravention of the intent of the post-war legal codes, nine out of ten detainees are brought back to one of 1,236 police detention centres after the police have passed their cases on to the prosecutors. A police law dating from 1908 allows these police jails to be used temporarily when there is insufficient space in the Ministry of Justice detention centres, of which today there are only 153, and the judiciary bureaucrats have been pressing for legislation that would fully endorse this practice.[26] Suspects who, in the view of the prosecutors, need not be investigated further are sent directly to the ministry's detention centre, which indicates that the use of the 'substitute prison' system is primarily for extracting confessions.[27]

The aforementioned 1983 investigation by Tokyo lawyers revealed that, in the police detention facilities used as substitute prisons, suspects are under 24-hour surveillance, either directly or via closed-circuit television. They are forced to sleep under glaring fluorescent lights and are not allowed to pull their blankets over their faces.[28] Many suspects are so shocked by these conditions that their bodily functions are impaired and they have great difficulty sleeping and eating. The food is minimal and of dismal quality. The investigators use the expression 'confession for a bowl of *domburi*', referring to the dish of meat or vegetables with rice that suspects may order (and pay for themselves) as a reward for confessing. In some cases suspects are forced to sit in one position on the concrete floor all day and are not allowed to move around, stand up or even lean against the wall.

In 21 of the 30 investigated cases the suspects became ill.[29] Some became too weak even to climb stairs. Here is an important weapon for the interrogators, since many suspects in such circumstances begin to fear that if they do not confess they will not be allowed home alive. They also tend to become disoriented and, without clocks and windows, lose their sense of time. In the tiny interrogation rooms, desks are sometimes used as instruments of torture by pushing them hard against the suspect's chest. In 25 of the 30 cases suspects were continuously shouted at by a number of policemen; 20 said that physical violence was used against them; 23 were forced to continue answering questions though half asleep from exhaustion; one suspect was questioned for 327 days.[30] In 23 of the investigated cases suspects 'confessed' in order to be delivered from the long interrogation sessions, during which mealtimes are ignored and no water is provided. Permission to use the toilet was given only on condition that they confess.

There is no reliable way of ascertaining whether such excesses are rare or not. The authorities are not interested in a formal investigation. What emerges very clearly from the accounts of the victims is the great deficiencies in the position and attitude of defence attorneys. In many cases their participation in the process is virtually irrelevant. Some clients were actually advised by their lawyers to grin and bear it. Criminal lawyers regularly complain that the police consistently obstruct the lawyer's visits that suspects are entitled to.[31] In a 1981 questionnaire sent to all Japan's attorneys by the human rights protection committee of the Japanese federation of bar associations, Nichibenren, the answers indicated that, contrary to popular belief, mistaken verdicts based on false confessions are not just a phenomenon of the chaotic immediate post-war years, but have been increasing.[32] Forced confessions, in the lawyers' estimate, were responsible for 60 per cent of all such verdicts.

Two things are clear. First, there are no institutional guarantees against a recurrence of the documented excesses. Second, regardless of the manner in which it is extracted from the suspect, the confession, in violation of constitutional guarantees, remains an important, if not the most important, aim of police and prosecutor methods.

Lest the impression be given that the nurses of the people are in fact a collection of ogres, I must emphasise that the behaviour of the police foot-soldiers in the local *koban* is, by and large, exemplary. Their general helpfulness, their willingness to listen while neighbourhood people unburden themselves and their friendly efforts to mediate in quarrels are all the more remarkable when one considers their fatiguing (18–20-hour) shifts. The hierarchical divide between the career officer and the ordinary policeman is exceptionally great, even for a Japanese institution.[33] And pressure from above makes itself felt via an efficiency rating system under which, in many parts of the country, the police in the street are expected to meet fixed quotas in turning up misdemeanours, motoring offences, and so on.[34]

Excommunication

In the standard relationship between police and suspect, confession followed by a profuse apology will open the sluices of the System's benevolence. Once suspects are 'won over', they are kindly treated. Foreign researchers have been struck by the jovial familiarity shown by police officers and co-operative suspects handcuffed to them or held by a rope tied around their waist.

Only from those sentenced to the ultimate penalty is the benevolence of society withdrawn. Much secrecy surrounds the death sentence, and it has provoked no debate of the kind seen in the West. A meeting held in 1981 by two hundred intellectuals, artists and entertainers failed in an attempt to launch a national anti-death-penalty campaign. The penalty is controversial only among a group of jurists who argue that its application is much too arbitrary. The Ministry of Justice does its utmost to keep everything connected with the death penalty out of the newspapers. An investigation team of Amnesty International was unable to ascertain whether any executions had taken place in the year prior to its visit. Very few Japanese have any idea about the number of convicts executed since the war; most guesses put it at a few dozen, whereas the actual figure, as of 1987, is 570. The family of the convict is in most cases notified only after the sentence has been carried out. It is left to the warden to decide whether or not to tell the condemned man when he will be taken to the gallows. Thus many prisoners on death row who are not in the process of appeal live in continual dread that the next morning may be their last.[35] Such prisoners are poorly fed and may not smoke. About the only people who show any regular concern for them are Christian missionaries.[36] Death row, in fact, is one of the few areas of Japanese society where these missionaries have made genuine converts.

Centuries of favours

The theory of the benevolence of law-enforcement officers accords with a view of power relations assiduously promoted by Japanese power-holders since at least the 1870s. Today, on a personal level, the Japanese are asked to believe that their superiors have the best in mind for them. On a communal level, the LDP and the bureaucrats are supposed to be guided by this same disposition. Everlasting gratitude of subjects towards their superiors has been, next to unconditional loyalty, the major command of Japanese socio-political life, and it is bound up with the officially sponsored faith in the ultimate beneficence and virtue of the existing political order.

Traditionally, benevolence in Japan was considered to be not a condition for rule, as it was in China, but something extra bestowed upon the people out of the goodness of their ruler's heart. Subordinates received privileges or goods because they had humane superiors, not because they had a right to anything. Whereas Chinese emperors were expected to be benevolent and maintain justice in order to keep the 'mandate of Heaven', their Japanese counterparts, as direct descendants of the sun goddess, were not in need of heavenly endorsement; they were themselves assumed to be in perpetual possession of benevolence. There is no clear evidence that this claim of totally unselfish benevolence was ever widely believed.

Japan's re-entry into the international world in the middle of the nineteenth century did not undermine this ideology. The oligarch most closely associated with the Meiji constitution, Ito Hirobumi, stated it clearly in his later years: 'It was not the people who forcibly wrested constitutional privilege from the Crown as in other countries, but the new regime was to be conferred upon them as a voluntary gift.'[37] The unfathomable benevolence of the emperor figured largely in the 'family state' and 'national essence' ideology (see Chapter 10) current from shortly before the turn of the century until 1945. Nitobe Inazo, one of the first explicators of Japan to the West, wrote that Japan had never had 'the despots of occidental history', and asserted – forgetting the murder of at least one emperor and many assassination attempts – that Japanese annals were 'never stained by such a blot as the death of Charles I, or Louis XVI'.[38] Unlike the subjects of other monarchs, Japanese are alleged to have loved their emperors by definition. A Japanese who in 1910 received his doctoral degree at the London School of Economics with a dissertation on Japanese political development explained the context of Japanese emperor-worship:

[It is] almost an impossibility for a sensible Japanese to denounce that which is associated with the pleasantest ideas of his native land, with the peace, tranquillity, happiness, and prosperity which his fathers enjoyed and he himself is still enjoying, and which he consciously recognises as the basis of the stability, dignity, unity and strength of the nation.[39]

Japanese Buddhist teachings supported the native and imported Confucianist concepts of the obligations towards one's lord in return for his beneficence, by placing them in a metaphysical context. As another of the earlier commentators on Japanese culture explained to a European audience:

the universe itself is the manifestation of kindness, or grace, or favour. The sun shines. The rain fertilises the fields. The flowers blossom. Everything is the manifestation of favour. We, human beings, are favoured with this great grace of the universe. We were born from parents. We are living in the land. We are cultivated by the teaching which was revealed by various sages and wise men. Americans wear silk garments which are made in Japan. The train, which was invented in England, is now used all over the world. We live in the house which was built by carpenters. We can buy anything without special labour owing to the manufacturers' and traders' labours. Is not, therefore, everything in the world indeed the expression of favour?[40]

This in itself admirable ethical sentiment was easily skewed to political uses.

In her classic study of fundamental Japanese motivations, the anthropologist Ruth Benedict spoke of the Japanese as 'debtors to the ages and the world'.[41] Until 1945 Japanese children were taught that they owed a debt of gratitude for everything that ancestors, teachers and superiors had ever done to make the world habitable. This load, which all Japanese still carry to some extent and which once justified the greatest personal sacrifices, is referred to as *on*. It differs from common social obligations, or *giri*, in that complete repayment of the debt is never possible. In the context of power relations, an *on* obligation justifies the permanent subordination of the receiver of a 'favour' to his benevolent superior.

While the System is no longer presented as a source of all blessings in life, as the pre-war 'family state' under the emperor was, Japanese are still implicitly expected to take its benevolence for granted. In actual practice, Japanese can be quite cynical about the supposed benevolence of those placed above them. A political representative whom voters have sent to the Diet in Tokyo is judged by whether or not he can deliver the bridge, road or other benefits he has promised the constituency. Villagers have for centuries fended for themselves as best they could, and in the process they have developed a strong sense of their right to certain customary amenities.[42] Eavesdropping on salarymen imbibing sake will confirm that one of their favourite pastimes is grumbling about their superiors. But this cynicism has not undermined the habit of profusely apologising and expressing gratitude towards supposed benefactors. And the benevolent motives of officialdom and the large companies are taken for granted by the leaders of those institutions themselves.

A safe society

The nurses of the people and the self-policing people themselves have managed to make their society, industrialised, urbanised and congested as it is, safer than at most other periods of Japanese history, and safer than most other countries are today. One need not worry about being mugged, let alone murdered, in the small alleys of Tokyo. People can walk most streets at night without fear. Japan has become the envy of the world for, next to its successful trade, its low crime statistics. Only 1·47 people per 100,000 of the population were murdered in 1984, as compared with 7·92 people in the United States, 3·24 in Britain and 4·51 in West Germany.[43] Burglaries and petty theft are fairly common, but the statistics for robberies with assault are even more lopsided when compared with the West: 1·82 cases per 100,000 population in Japan, 205·38 cases in the USA, 50·02 cases in the UK and 45·77 cases in West Germany.[44]

Besides the networks of police informants and crime-prevention squads of ordinary civilians, the symbiotic relationship between the Japanese police and organised crime must also be part of the explanation for this great discrepancy. The unavailability to ordinary people of hand-guns and strict control of their introduction into Japan help as well, as does the absence of a crime-producing drug problem. Heroin addiction is rare, and the measures taken against its distribution and use are merciless. No sympathy is shown for the suffering of the addict, no weaning with substitutes; if caught, drug users go 'cold turkey'. The use of stimulants like meta-amphetamine ('speed') by housewives, office employees and teen-agers is a problem, but has not led to a kleptomania epidemic. Marijuana is treated as a dangerous hard drug, and suspected users – mainly among those exposed to Western youth culture, especially in the entertainment world – may expect pre-dawn raids on their apartments. If caught they go to prison, and foreigners among them may be deported.

The unprotected

The System protects and caters reasonably well to the needs of a broad band of society running from the top almost to the bottom. It is no doubt vastly superior to those other major products of social engineering: the totalitarian systems of the twentieth century based on Nazism and Leninism.

The question remains of whether an arrangement that is good for most of the people gives adequate protection to minorities. And here one must conclude that the System is selective in its benevolence. The criminally arraigned, as we have already seen, are not well protected. Neither are ethnic minorities such as Koreans, or social minorities like the once officially outcast *burakumin*. These minorities face systematic and con-sistent discrimination in education and employment, not least by such supposedly exemplary institutions as the police and the public schools. Official family registers and private information-gathering agencies enable employers and parents of marriageable youth to eliminate members of minority groups from consideration. Law-enforcement officers, also, extend little benevolence to minorities, but treat them as separate, problematic communities.[45]

Involuntary nonconformists

A closer look at the treatment of the mentally ill shows Japanese society's adamant attitude towards even its involuntary nonconformists. In any country, of course, those who society decides are mad have a good chance of being locked up, the very worst cases perhaps against their will. But a constitutionalist political system is supposed to provide safeguards in the form of standards for judging who is or is not dangerous and guarantees for the safety and personal dignity of those placed in institutional custody.

In July 1985 the International Commission of Jurists severely criticised the way in which Japanese mental patients are treated, stating that it violates the Japanese constitution as well as the Covenant for Civil and Political Rights that Japan has ratified. The organisation discovered an extraordinarily high death rate among the incarcerated, and established that institutions are heavily overpopulated, that unnecessary violence is practised and that patients are exploited, poorly fed and forced to live under miserable conditions. It also concluded that many patients were locked up without good reason. The year before, the International League of Human Rights based in New York had claimed that an abnormally high number of mentally retarded are incarcerated in Japan. It also stated that normal Japanese practices in treating the mentally ill constitute a violation of human rights.

Some 340,000 people currently reside in Japanese mental institutions, 87 per cent of which are privately owned. Four-fifths of the population of these institutions are locked up without their own consent, as against only one-twentieth in Britain. Two-thirds of these are under lock and key, in the majority of cases without any means of communicating with the outside world. An estimated 200,000 inmates have been locked up for much longer periods than is justified. The Japanese law allows anyone responsible for a person who is thought to be mentally ill to have the final say whether or not to commit that person to a mental hospital, and allows the institution, in turn, to determine how long that person must remain.

Japanese with physical or mental handicaps have customarily been hidden from society by their relatives, because many consider such handicaps shameful. In recent years increasing numbers of the mentally retarded have been brought to institutions instead of being kept in back rooms. Medical personnel at a cross-section of those mental hospitals willing to co-operate in an investigation told researchers that roughly

70 per cent of all patients could be treated at home if discrimination were not a factor. Besides the genuinely mentally ill or retarded, there are numerous cases of parents being sent to a psychiatric institution owing to a combination of senility and the proverbial quarrels with daughters-in-law. Sometimes incarceration is also deemed a proper solution for dealing with uncontrollable youth.

Large profits can be made by crowded private psychiatric hospitals. The national health insurance system allows for much racketeering, and running costs, with only one doctor per 68 patients – as compared to one for 14·3 patients in ordinary hospitals – are small.

In 1984 nineteen suspicious deaths in one mental hospital drew the attention of the Japanese press to the issue, resulting in a number of revelations from different parts of Japan about forced incarceration, maltreatment and deaths. But the general secretary for the Japanese Fund for Mental Health and Human Rights, Totsuka Etsuro, sees little hope that the bureaucracy will take effective action. Changes in the law pending in 1987 were expected to have only cosmetic effects. The reaction of the Ministry of Health and Welfare to the allegations from Geneva and New York has been that Japan has its own culture, different in some ways from that of the West, and that Japan therefore has a right to treat its mentally retarded in its own way.

Enemies of the System

One type of nonconformist that the Japanese System has reacted against consistently and vehemently is the leftist. I have already traced the war between the Marxist-inspired teachers' union and the Ministry of Education, and referred to the cracked heads of many post-war labour organisers; but it is also no secret that police and prosecutors discriminate quite heavily against participants in any conflict thought to be ideologically motivated. 'Ideology, not income, structures the misuse of authority.'[46] Ordinary violent quarrels are generally handled good-humouredly by the police and subsequently forgotten. But fights involving blue-collar workers in their place of work are strictly pursued and generally prosecuted.[47] The Supreme Court supports law-enforcement officials in this bias, and decides against labour in most cases, sometimes reversing verdicts of the lower courts.[48]

Japanese who disagree with the way in which the System works and who translate their discontent into political action are considered subversive and looked upon as potential bomb-throwers. Radical students receive considerably harsher treatment from police and prosecutors than most other people brought before them. The reaction of the police to leftists is 'almost visceral'.[49] As an American scholar summarised: 'The police seem to be galvanised when discussing Communists or leftist labor unions, and they told me on numerous occasions that they consider them a threat to Japanese society and to the police establishment.'[50] Applicants for the police force who reveal leftist leanings are deemed unsuitable for police work and filtered out.[51] One author, who served for ten years with the police in Hyogo prefecture, describes the automatic retort of 'Aka!' ('red' or 'communist') that higher police officers are likely to use against anyone, not only on the outside but also within the police force, who questions police methods and priorities.[52]

It is also accepted as a part of Japanese reality that the police should assiduously clamp down on activist leftist groups while allowing the activist *rightist* groups to run wild. In the Ginza area of central Tokyo, one of the busiest places in the world, one will find, day after day, year after year, a sound-truck with flags and banners parked at a strategic spot. It belongs to the famous pre-war ultra-nationalist agitator Akao Bin (he used to call himself the 'Hitler of Japan'), who was shouting himself hoarse at the very same spot when I first passed it in 1962. In the name of free speech, he is allowed to blast the crowds with high-volume exhortations against leftist causes and world communism. The shoppers ignore this senile old rightist, but it is inconceivable that the police would permit a leftist activist an equal opportunity to harangue passers-by year after year with his beliefs.

Rightists are given much freedom to cruise through traffic with blaring sound-trucks and to make deafening speeches on busy street corners. They are in fact allowed to disturb and obstruct meetings sponsored by the Socialist Party, with the police turning a blind eye. And rightist threats, as we have seen, have made it difficult for the teachers' union to find venues for its conventions.

Compounding the anger of police and prosecutors when confronted with leftist activists is the latter's refusal to recant their beliefs. To the police, their crimes, if any, appear less important than their 'wrong attitudes'. The fact that they will not apologise renders them less than 'fully Japanese' in the eyes of the law-enforcement officials. Extremists who are incarcerated, sometimes only on charges of premeditation, preparation for criminal action or conspiracy, are treated much worse than ordinary prison inmates guilty of proven crimes. They are expected to buy improved treatment by forswearing their ideological commitment in a way reminiscent of the pre-war *tenko*, in which committed Marxists and intellectuals renounced their 'wrong thoughts' and acknowledged the virtues of the imperial order. The pressure today is only on certifiable extremists, but this does not alter the fact that demands for apostasy are in violation of the constitution.

The general lenience of the police and judiciary has, as can be imagined, created a multitude of grateful suspects and convicts in Japan. On the other hand, it is not difficult to imagine how easily politically engaged youth can become radicalised by their discriminatory attitudes, as providing 'evidence' that society can improve only through violent revolution. Activist students are basically faced with only two options: to stop being politically involved, or to join the ranks of the radicals and resort to extra-legal activities. Thus the power-holders have had a direct hand in the creation of Japan's extremists.

The System's strongest component

To avoid the kind of abuses of which *tenko* was a major feature, the United States occupation authorities disbanded the Naimusho and decentralised the police, making them answerable to prefectural public safety commissions. But it soon became clear that the latter arrangement had no future. In the 1950s influential bureaucrats from the disbanded ministry wormed themselves into key political and bureaucratic positions for social control. The alleged threat from the left seen in the labour movement helped expand their power. 'As politicians, they continued to behave like officials of the [Naimusho] in their defense of the existing order from the leftist threat. No issue concerned the ex-bureaucrats more in the first half of the 1950s than the recentralisation of the nation's police forces.'[53] In the forefront of this successful campaign was former Naimusho official Nadao Hirokichi, who appeared in Chapter 3 in his later role as Nikkyoso's most dreaded enemy. Top positions in the National Public Safety Commission, the National Police Agency and the interior, labour, welfare and education ministries were never in 'neutral' or 'moderate' hands long enough to give the leftist opposition a chance to influence social policy adjustments.

The Police Law of 1954 caused an uproar among intellectuals and the left, who (inappropriately) compared it with the Peace Preservation Law of 1925, in whose name the Naimusho had locked up a multitude of Japanese with 'dangerous thoughts'. The 1954 law was actually less than the social control bureaucrats had hoped for, but enough to undo many of what they considered the 'excesses' of occupation reforms. Already in place were special security regulations, first issued in Fukui prefecture in the aftermath of an earthquake in 1948 and later copied by Kobe, Osaka and Tokyo, regulating and limiting demonstrations. The Supreme Court, in three separate suits, has refused to declare these regulations unconstitutional and in 1960 declared that demonstrators were in essence 'rioters'. The maintenance of public order is the court's absolute priority, one that is reflected in strict judicial decisions against those who appear to threaten this order.[54] The court has twice insisted on retrials by the Tokyo high court after the latter passed not-guilty verdicts on defendants charged under the security regulations.[55]

The great '*ampo* struggle' of 1960, in which many leftist groups united in their opposition to Prime Minister Kishi's handling of the extension of the US–Japan security treaty, represented the high-water mark for the Japanese anti-establishment movement and provided the authorities with a moral pretext to expand the powers of the police. The most eye-catching aspect of this has been a display of power by the *kidotai*, or riot police. In their sense of a mission to safeguard the security of the nation, these heavily trained troops are the closest successors to the élite forces of the Imperial Army. The sense of belonging to a separate community, strong enough among the police in general,[56] tends to be particularly intense here, as is mutual devotion between commanders and men.

In the same organisational category with the *kidotai* are the security police who gather information on potential trouble-makers, including leftist unionists and members of the Communist Party. The security police insist that they do not use eavesdropping devices (forbidden by the constitution), but informed observers are convinced otherwise.[57] These suspicions were borne out when the news leaked out that in November 1986 workers of Nippon Telegraph and Telephone had found that the telephone of the chief of the international division of the Communist Party had been connected to a wire-tapping cable. The cable led to an apartment rented by the son of a policeman, whose contract with his landlord was countersigned by a former policeman of the public security division. There had been numerous earlier cases of JCP officials' telephones being tapped, but the party had never before collected enough evidence to satisfy the prosecutor. This case, too, was dropped when top career policemen apologised to the prosecutor's office and the prosecutor accepted that the policemen responsible for the tapping had only followed orders from superiors. Thus, though wire-tapping is unconstitutional, the higher levels of the police are allowed to get away with it.

In the 1970s and 1980s events involving Japan's international reputation – US presidential visits, visits by the Queen of England and the South Korean president and two summit conferences – have enabled the *kidotai* and security police greatly to expand their routine powers without public or news media resistance. Terrorism by Japanese extremists abroad and crude kitchen-made rockets fired off by untraceable extremists at home have further helped to create a climate of tolerance for strengthening the police. The *kidotai* on their side are past masters of tactical restraint, being especially careful not to turn opinion against them by making martyrs.

Successive state visits or summits have encouraged the police to break their own records of money spent on equipment, and to interfere further in the lives of ordinary citizens. The 1984 visit of President Chun Doo Hwan of South Korea prompted the police to stop cars on Tokyo's elevated expressways for 'practice searches' a month before the event; and foreign diplomats visiting the Foreign Ministry were stopped and questioned by guards. Even these security measures were outstripped by those surrounding the Tokyo summit of 1986. About 50,000 buildings and small apartments were investigated or searched. Some 900 leftist activists were arrested for no clear reason. Sewers were investigated and sealed every day. During the summit, much of central Tokyo within a 1·5- to 2-kilometre radius of summit and lodging sites was sealed off by a *cordon sanitaire* to all but a few summit-related vehicles and individuals with special passes. Thirty thousand policemen were mobilised to guard the summiteers, and all over the city cars were stopped for vehicle searches. The *kidotai* was able to try out the equivalent of $40 million worth of new equipment (in addition to which the cost of security measures as such reached an estimated $17 million).[58]

One of the most significant aspects of the nurses of the people is that they are governed by no one but themselves. This gives them an unusual place among the components of the system. Regional public safety commissions still exert theoretical control; but aside from the fact that these tend to be composed of old-fashioned conservatives with rightist ' histories,[59] the police force is in any case highly centralised. A quarter of a million policemen and their clerical assistants are controlled by a mere 450 career bureaucrats. The top level, as with all components of the mainstream of the System, has consisted ever since the 1880s of graduates of the University of Tokyo's law department. When these administrators think the situation calls for it, they will demonstrate their independence. For example, when Tagawa Seiichi, home affairs minister and chairman of the National Public Safety Commission, wanted to give a formal talk to police officers in the Kansai area following a 1984 scandal involving the police, the National Police Agency flatly rejected his request with the excuse that it would not accord with usual practice among the officials concerned.

Appointments to the crucial posts of head of the National Police Agency (NPA) and the Tokyo Metropolitan Police Department (MPD) are made by the outgoing chief of the NPA. The appointment of the MPD superintendent-general is subject to formal approval by the prime minister, but the NPA 'stands absolutely independent, formally, from all other bureaucracies and branches of government'.[60]

There is no check on the police apart from public opinion as supposedly reflected in the press, and the latter has had no effect in restraining the recent expansion of their power. The police maintain smooth relations with the press via the kisha clubs attached to major police bureaux. Reporters are well taken care of, with some press facilities paid for by the police, and they generally pass on news as it is interpreted and handed to them by police officers who exist for this purpose.[61]

Significantly, a newspaper like the *Asahi Shimbun*, which normally raises its editorial eyebrows at authoritarian practices, cannot rebuke the police for over-zealous efforts (such as the car searches 'for practice'), since to do so might make it look irresponsible in the face of an alleged extremist threat to the nation.

Before the war, the police had rivals for power in the form of other bureaux within their own Naimusho and the formidable Army and Navy. Today, they no longer face competition from any of the System's components. The Self-Defence Forces, Japan's euphemistically named military, are no competitor under current conditions. In fact, many 'civilian' staff members of the National Self-Defence Agency, which has the same status as a ministry, are former policemen.

Measured by what they can do in emergency situations, the police are the strongest component of the Japanese System. They have the means to pull off a successful *coup d'état*, should an ambitious clique ever gain control over them. In some ways, their effectiveness inspires confidence; in other ways, their ambivalence towards democratic principles and the concept of law gives reason for concern. Under normal conditions the police guarantee a safe System, but not a lawful one.

8

Keeping the Law under Control

Although the System may not be Big Brother, the Japanese are asked to accept that it loves them in return for social obedience. This means, among other things, not questioning – at least not continuously and systematically – the political system. They are asked to believe not that they themselves are citizens with rights, but that the administrators have big hearts. To put it simply: whereas power in the West is masked by the illusion of principle, in Japan it is masked by the illusion of benevolence. In the Western tradition, intellectual probing of the socio-political environment is allowed and sometimes encouraged; the Japanese tradition requires emotional trust.

Japanese are conditioned to accept as natural the unequal tie to a social superior, and many develop a psychological need for it. This is fully justified by Confucianist-derived theories, but in China a philosophical tradition tried to find a rational justification for inequality. Chinese Confucianism set out to resolve the basic conflict between the need (deduced from historical experience) for a hierarchical society and the need to mitigate the injustices inherent in such an unequal order. In India, too, the relations between the exercise of power and subjection to it posed an intellectual problem that was solved by religious sanction. In Japan the unequal relationship was made acceptable by appeal neither to religion nor to any rational theory of statecraft, but to a claim of inherent benevolence.

The starkest contrast is in the way the Japanese and Western intellectual traditions handle the fact of inequality and the need for obedience. To understand this crucial difference better, it is necessary to lay bare the intellectual underpinnings of the Japanese socio-political world, and there is no better place to start than with elementary religious and legal thought. Religion and law, in that they both concern ultimate beliefs, are almost always intimately connected during their early development. In respect of both, Japan and the Western nations stand at opposite extremes when viewed in the collective context of human civilisation. To place the two traditions side by side can thus be very instructive. In the West, as we shall see, power-holders became increasingly tied to codes over which they had lost control; whereas in Japan, at least until the end of the Tokugawa period, power-holders were portrayed as the ultimate embodiment of truth and virtue.

Laws above and beneath power-holders

On the European side, the idea of legitimate tension between individuals and their political rulers goes back at least to the time when Socrates was forced to take poison for 'corrupting' the youth of Athens by insisting on the superiority of individual human reason over society.

Socrates' most famous pupil, Plato, understood that the human impulse to seek power causes much evil. The noblest task of the city-state (the *polis*) was, in his view, guaranteeing justice to curb power in the raw.[1] This idea lingered on after the breakdown of the Roman Empire, when political life in Europe was no less chaotic or vicious than it was amidst the incessant civil wars of medieval Japan.

The ultimate reality

Even before Charlemagne, when brutal upstarts and usurpers ruled without much regard for life, there survived at least a dim notion of a reality beyond the thirst for power and the caprices of local overlords. The European monasteries of the early Middle Ages kept alive Mediterranean philosophical constructs implying the possibility of opposition to political arrangements, and provided a faint reminder of transcendental beliefs. The laws of the Roman Empire – which had kept order in Europe longer than any empire that was to follow – were a memory that remained.

In ancient Japan the Yamato chieftains turned power into a right, and thus obedience into a duty, by having it endorsed by *kami*, the Shinto spirits of their ancestors and spirits of nature – a basic method known in many parts of the world. During the fourth century, when they had conquered enough territory to warrant the term 'kingdom', they extended their power through a web of real and artificial kinship ties, and established a Shinto shrine to the ancestral deity of the sovereign family, where all their subjects could worship.[2] Henceforth the emperors bore the title 'one with the divine sanction to hold the world together'.[3] Ritual purification, significantly, was necessary for crimes and other things one wanted to conceal from the gods.[4] Thus Japanese law, like that of so many other cultures, was totally intertwined with the observances of an indigenous religion. Early Confucianism was added to this Shinto tradition from the fifth century onward; its precepts, sanctifying a strictly hierarchical social order, were blended with native practices as a justification for political organisation. As Japan became more familiar with this great secular source of morals, which reached it through Korea, it developed its own simple penal law.

When Buddhism arrived from Korea in the middle of the sixth century, the Japanese aristocracy seized upon its doctrines as an instrument to promote popular obedience. Shotoku Taishi, Japan's first 'law-giver', devoted pride of place to the new religion in his 'constitution'. This document inspired by Chinese models and still emphasised in elementary schools today as a landmark in Japanese history, consists of a collection of platitudes about good relations between rulers and subjects. It did not place any legal restraint on the acts of the ruler. Neither Confucianism nor Buddhism introduced any rules curbing the exercise of power in Japan.

In early Western discourse, the legitimation of morals and behaviour depended on paramount principles above and beyond immediate social reality. The abstractions to which medieval priests and Renaissance thinkers appealed were considered true precisely because they transcended worldly concerns. Thus there was a firm concept of permanent limitations to worldly power. By contrast, the Confucianist scholar and Buddhist monk in Japan, even when dealing with higher, abstract levels of reality, remained fully dependent on temporal rulers. Warriors and commoners were ordered to follow their teachings only in so far as these accorded with the political priorities of the day. Unlike Western kings and lords, Japanese power-holders could not be commanded to answer morally for their deeds. They were never judged by standards that they themselves had not established.

The officially sponsored spread of Buddhism entailed risks in that some of its doctrines enjoined the individual to follow the Way shown by an inner light rather than by external guidance. But at the same time it compensated for this individualistic streak by preaching the spirit of resignation. As one Japanese specialist has noted, Japanese Buddhism did not develop an independent ethic, 'and the vital ability of Buddhism to free people from community pressures and tradition was almost totally lost'.[5]

Shotoku Taishi and most of his successors were not bothered by the incompatibilities of Shintoism, Confucianism and Buddhism so long as these creeds served their political purposes. This was well illustrated by a religious feast, held about one and a half centuries after the introduction of Buddhism, at which five thousand Buddhist monks chanted sutras to celebrate the bestowal of a high civil rank on a Shinto god recently installed in a newly built Shinto shrine in the palace.[6] The amalgamation of the two religions was clearly an official policy designed to strengthen their joint endorsement of existing worldly rule. They have existed more or less amicably side by side throughout most of the ensuing centuries. Kami were enshrined near some Buddhist temples, becoming their (Shinto) guardian deities, and Shinto divinities appeared as Boddhisatvas as easily as Greek gods pop up in Roman mythology.

An indispensable requirement for the development of laws that curb the power of rulers, as distinct from laws used to control and curb the activities of the ruled, is the concept of legitimate opposition. And this notion of legitimate resistance to one's rulers is alien to the Japanese tradition.

The way superiors dealt with those below them was regularised to some degree by the ritsu-ryo legal system based on Japan's first legal codes: the

Taiho code formulated in AD 701 and its replacement, the Yoro code, written seventeen years later. Both were inspired by the legal writings of T'ang China.[7] *Ritsu* meant the chastisement of wrongdoers and was left virtually as the Chinese had written it, save for the scaling down of punishments (which came in a choice of five degrees: flogging, beating, forced labour, exile and death). *Ryo*, a body of administrative law, was amended to suit Japanese needs and enlarged by some new rules. Whenever practices contradicted *ryo* they were maintained under the label 'contemporary practice'.[8] This is an early example of the enduring Japanese habit of only partially assimilating foreign systems and papering over the discrepancies with euphemisms. Among many examples in contemporary Japan is the anti-monopoly law that, as part of the post-1945 'free-market' system, exists in fraternal harmony with all manner of cartels.[9]

By the time Japanese political power had fully passed into the hands of the *bushi*, the warrior class – as it most definitely had in what came to be known as the Kamakura period (1185–1333) – there existed no less than three systems of law. One applied to the imperial court; a second was for the proprietors of the landholdings (*shoen*) that were part of early Japanese feudalism; and the third was for the shogunate, the formal military government. Law, however, here meant whatever edicts the rulers cared to promulgate: edicts that were generally arbitrary and unrelated to any overall concept of justice. By the time the daimyo (the barons of later Japanese feudalism) emerged towards the end of the fifteenth century, what was and what was not lawful depended wholly on the locality, and many domains had no formal codes at all.

Separation of church and state in Europe

Power-holders are more ready to believe that they are subject to laws if they are aware of some superior or coexisting force that must be accommodated. This may take the form of either an anthropomorphic god, an abstract notion of Justice, or the State.

A major factor in the earlier phases of European legal thinking was the notion of a separation between church and state. At the end of the fifth century, Pope Gelasius I had redefined a variety of older ideas concerning the existence of two orders of human affairs, one governed by priestly authority and the other by secular rulers. The notion of the possibility of the state maintaining a justice transcending arbitrary feudal authority survived in Europe as part of the dim memory of the Roman Empire. At a later stage, the universities joined the monks in upholding an intellectual tradition embodying theories and moral precepts that were without question considered valid in an ultimate sense, applicable at any time to any person and in any circumstances. These theories and precepts were inextricably linked with the concept of law.

In 1159, a quarter-century before the establishment of the Japanese shogunate, the first major European work on political theory since Roman times explicitly stated the king's subjecthood to law and ultimately to God.[10] In *Policraticus*, or *The Statesman's Book*, John of Salisbury argued that 'inferiors should cleave and cohere to their superiors, and all the limbs should be in subjection to the head; but always and only on condition that religion is kept inviolate'.[11]

Salisbury contended that even the murder of sovereigns is warranted if their flouting of justice is too flagrant. This was theory; the many European rulers who were killed were in fact mainly victims of the greed for power of their enemies. In Japan, too, emperors ran some risk of being killed. A thirteenth-century history written by a highly placed Buddhist priest relates several murders and assassination attempts.[12] Imperial crown princes were usually brought up outside the parental palace because of the risk to their lives from scheming members of the court. But a *theoretical* justification for killing the descendant of the gods was totally inconceivable throughout Japanese history.

In thirteenth-century Europe one of the greatest medieval political theorists. St Thomas Aquinas, made clear that the state existed for the citizen, and his work constitutes one of the most powerful reminders to kings that they are subject to 'Christ's law'. Late-medieval European thought evolved the idea that the maintenance of justice was the first and principal task of the state. 'The Platonic idea of the Legal State proved to be a real and active power: a great energy that not only influenced the thoughts of men but became a powerful impulse of human actions.'[13]

Christian authority became a powerful legitimating force because worldly rulers craved its endorsement. Charlemagne was eager that people should believe he was crowned by God. Later, from the eleventh to the fourteenth centuries, the nobles of Rome and the Holy Roman emperors together with other European sovereigns had perhaps little reverence for the pope, and were never above using his blessings to further their own political ends, but they needed the church's endorsement and had to be careful not to be branded heretical. Political writing during these centuries was much concerned with the relative powers of church and state, and the tension between the two.[14]

It is true that intellectual constructs often have little correspondence with the reality they are supposed to reflect; and there are views of history that belittle the practical power of ideas, see principles as illusory and admit only the cynical manipulation of subject populations by vested interests. But this approach is blind to aspects of European history that demand attention in any comparison with Japanese history. Western theory has often been strongly reflected in political reality. Henry IV knelt in the snow outside the papal palace of Canossa in a show of humiliation that has been remembered ever since. Frederick II may have fought the papacy as if he were at war with any ordinary state, but even he could never publicly question the pope's authority.

Equality before a universal law

The popular participation in government practised by the Germanic tribes of northern Europe brought with it early notions of political equality that mingled with the systematic medieval theories of the rule of law. The Stoics, known in medieval Europe through the writings of Cicero, had argued that all human beings are fundamentally equal, and under their influence medieval scholars began to view the law as an entity even more universal than Plato had suggested.

The 'absolute' monarchs of Europe, in organising more sophisticated structures of national power, could not destroy this tradition. The Divine Right they claimed was still a sanction, one that made them accountable to God; the weight of religious and philosophical tradition meant in fact that no political power could be considered absolute any more. Power-holders submitted to the authority of principles, in the form of laws that were 'irrevocable and inviolable because they express the divine order itself, the will of the supreme lawgiver'.[15]

The idea that power must be subjected to moral ends eventually leads, in European history, to concepts of the sovereignty of the people.[16] By the time of the Renaissance and Reformation, when political and religious conflicts were nearly tearing the universities apart[17] and man no longer stood in the centre of a universe ruled by God, reinterpretations of Stoic philosophy had gained a hold over European thinkers, who no longer needed Christian dogma to support the concept of universal law and universal moral good. Hugo Grotius, the Dutch jurist and founder of international law, asserted that even the will of the Almighty cannot change the principles of morality or abrogate the fundamental rights guaranteed by natural laws.

Legal thinking in the contemporary world is ultimately based on this reasoning. It gave the state a legal basis through the concept of state contract. It led directly to the moral philosophies of Immanuel Kant, John Locke, Montesquieu and Spinoza, positing the existence of 'natural rights' as a rational basis for liberalism, and through these to contemporary ideas of international law, human rights and the idea of 'justice' in general.

Moving through Japanese history one finds, by contrast, only the strengthening of an ideology in which rulers figured as the embodiment of morality. The neo-Confucianist teachings current from the late seventeenth century onward offered, in essence, little more than an elaborate scholastic vindication of the innate ethical flawlessness of the military dictatorship. We will come back to this at length in Chapter 11.

A borrowed legal system

In the middle of the nineteenth century, around the time when Japan was forced to open its ports to foreigners, Japanese laws were basically a means of enforcing a strict and detailed, government-dictated code of social behaviour and relationships. Thus Japanese legal practices, including the torture that was extensively practised to extract the confessions that were mandatory for a guilty verdict, were a cause of much initial friction with Westerners. They were also the reason why the Euro-American powers insisted on extraterritoriality for their subjects in the treaties of 1858 and subsequent years.

The major incentive for the Meiji oligarchy to include a constitution and legal codes in its overloaded agenda for catching up with the West was the refusal of foreigners to submit themselves to Japanese jurisdiction in the treaty ports. An almost undisguised Western contempt for Japanese legal practices aggravated the sense of inferiority and weakness felt by the new leadership. Meiji officialdom therefore worked hard to convince the Western powers that modern law was being introduced. When in 1890 Foreign Minister Aoki Shuzo proposed new treaties abolishing extraterritoriality, he informed the West that his government had been working to create reliable judges for nearly six years, and declared that, by the time the treaties went into effect another six years later, no foreigner would have to worry about being judged by incompetents.[18]

The leaders of the Restoration had improvised a haphazard arrangement based on ideas from the archaic Yoro code, which though introduced exactly 1,150 years earlier had never been officially supplanted by the rules of the Tokugawa shogunate. To update Japanese legal practice, it was decided first of all that the French civil code and all the other Napoleonic codes should be translated. Mitsukuri Rinsho, a twenty-three-year-old official enamoured of Western ideas, was given this horrendous task a year after the oligarchy had taken over. A noted Japanese legal scholar compares him to an architect who had to begin by making his own bricks,[19] because he had to invent terms for concepts that were totally alien to Japanese thinking, without being able to consult either dictionary, legal commentary or foreign lawyer. It took this devoted man less than five years.

A French adviser to the government, Emile Gustave Boissonade de Fontarabie, drafted Japan's first modern criminal code, which was promulgated in 1880. His own sense of the urgency of this project is apparent in his protest against torture, the continued use of which was evident from screams audible in the compound in which he had been given an office. A rivalry subsequently developed between those who pleaded for the adoption of French law and those who believed English law to be more suitable; but in the end the Prussian model and German *Rechtstaat* principles proved more attractive than either to a government that had by then consolidated its position, and the influence of a German legal adviser, Hermann Roesler, eclipsed that of Boissonade. By 1898, when Japan promulgated its first complete civil code, German influence had clearly outweighed the earlier flirtations with the more liberal English and French laws.

The unprotected citizen

As should be very obvious at this point, nothing in their history encourages ordinary Japanese citizens to think that the law exists to protect them. Never adding up to a system based on rational, philosophical principles of justice, traditional Japanese law consisted of little more than lists of commands to be blindly obeyed by commoners. In practice the consequences of this were uneven. There seems to have been considerable room for leniency in the Heian period. But in the Muromachi period (1333–1568) a great deal of cruelty became common, and did not disappear until after the opening of the country. In the two and a half centuries of Tokugawa rule, the law was applied according to social status; townsmen and farmers could be cut down on the spot by a samurai if he found them rude or in other ways unmindful of their station in life – or, according to some sources, just to try out a new sword.

The Meiji reforms brought great relief, and many freedoms, by comparison with the days of the shogunate, even if the spirit of the imported letter of the law was largely missing. The promulgation of the Meiji constitution in 1889 was accompanied by fireworks, partying and panegyrics in the press. Yet neither this 'gift from the emperor' nor the other Western-inspired laws were to give the Japanese a sense of protection against arbitrary power. The constitution had been preceded in 1888 by debates on the 'rights' and 'duties' of the people. In the end, the people were finally given rights and freedom, but only on condition that they would never disturb the social order or violate laws that restricted those same rights and freedom.[20]

Once Japan's power-holders were confronted with some of the logical consequences of their own imports, they reacted swiftly to make sure that the population and its intellectuals would not harbour the 'wrong thoughts'. Yamagata Aritomo inveighed against reliance on the law in safeguarding society, supposing this to be a cause of many social problems. But at the same time Yamagata himself did not scruple to use the law freely 'as a bulwark against politics'[21] – meaning democratic, parliamentary, adversarial party politics. Law was rapidly being pressed into service as a major tool of the administrators.

After the turn of the century, the economist Kawakami Hajime, who introduced Marxist theory into Japan, summed up the overall result:

> individuals are not believed to exist for and of themselves as autonomous entities; only the state does. In Japan, state sovereignty is heaven-granted while individual rights are bestowed by the state. The state allows limited individual rights to the extent that they further the aims of the state. Thus, individual rights are always instruments of the state, not to be utilised for the aims of the individual. While in the West individual rights are thought to be

granted by heaven and thus inalienable . . . respect for individual rights and individual identity in the West is inconceivable for the Japanese, just as Japanese respect of state sovereignty and the state is inconceivable for Westerners.[22]

Yet some Japanese obstinately took their cue from Western legal thinking. In 1937, shortly after the outbreak of war with China, a scholar contended that justice is

> an objective spirit that transcends the reality of the state while providing the foundation for its existence. In other words, rather than a principle created by the state, justice is the fundamental principle that gives rise to the state. The state does not define justice; on the contrary, justice rules the state.[23]

The magazine issue in which these words appeared was immediately banned.

Other experiences of the first four and a half decades of this century – the hated Peace Preservation Laws of 1925 and 1928, the 'thought police', the partiality of judges, police and prosecutors – did nothing to familiarise the Japanese people with the idea of political rights. Such notions had to wait for the programme to 'democratise' Japan after its defeat in 1945. An important effort was then made to help ordinary citizens perceive their legal rights. But was it the great watershed in Japanese legal history that it is supposed to have been?

Post-war watershed?

There can be no doubt that much has changed because of the intervention of the United States occupation. Few Japanese today are afraid to speak their mind. And there exists a fairly common idea that the government has, at the very least, an *obligation* to show benevolence. Benevolence is no longer something voluntarily bestowed on the nation by the emperor.

Nevertheless, the general view of law remains similar to what it was before 1945. On the whole, Japanese still think of law as an instrument of constraint used by the government to impose its will. Japanese officials are free to pick and choose among laws, using them to further their own causes. When law and bureaucratic policy appear to conflict, officialdom adjusts the law to the policy by newly 'interpreting' it.[24] The wording of many laws has been left purposely vague to make such expediency easier. A Japanese scholar compares many laws passed in the Diet to contracts signed before being read.[25] LDP Diet members have a stake in legislation favouring their pork-barrel clients; they are not in the business of scrutinising bills to determine whether these contribute to, or detract from, social justice. An education minister remarked in 1958, in connection with a law relating to efficiency ratings of teachers: 'Anyone is free to interpret laws as they like, but as to this law, I want you to respect the view of the education minister.'[26] He was not joking.

The professors of the law department of the University of Tokyo, the nearly exclusive breeding-ground for top administrators, appear to view the law as essentially an aid to administration. They still blindly accept the centuries-old premiss that the government is automatically superior to the people, believing that 'by nature, the people cannot understand the political realm and therefore should not criticise the administration's policies'.[27] Conversely, laws are deemed legitimate by the populace only because they are administered by a class of people who have always had the right to do so, and not because they conform to any popular sense of justice. As it applies to the ordinary citizen, law is still 'synonymous with pain or penalty'.[28]

Of course, Japan formally subscribes to international concepts of justice. But Japanese political habits have prevented these from becoming a truly living force. Human rights, democratic freedom and a new idea, the 'right to peace', are made much of, but as ideas remain vague and undefined. None has instilled sufficient conviction or been accompanied by sufficient political will to nurture explicit theories applicable to concrete political programmes.

Champions of disadvantaged groups may bandy arguments about 'rights', but my experience of such campaigns suggests that any satisfaction they may obtain results from tactics of intimidation and other kinds of pressure, not from a general concept of justice. Traditional attitudes, reinforced by contemporary practice, obstruct the establishment of an unambiguous concept of 'rights'. The word *kenri* was introduced to convey this idea, and one of its two characters connotes impartiality. But a well-known Japanese legal scholar comments that 'at the present time almost everyone disregards the sense of impartiality that the word implies. For the average Japanese this word conjures up something related to egoism.'[29]

This absence of a sense of 'rights' has many striking consequences. One, often lamented by foreigners, is the lack of civic courage among Japanese. Another is the manifest obstacle it poses to genuine internationalism. In no way does Japanese education, or any other element in the System, teach people that it is proper to stick out their necks on behalf of some causes. This attitude is clearly reflected in the ethic of submission of the salaryman world; and in Chapter 10 we will see how it is further reinforced by a powerful ideology of 'Japaneseness'.

The distinctions I have hitherto made have often been explained in terms of a facile division between 'Western individualism' and an allegedly Asian readiness to sacrifice individual interests for the sake of the community. However, this is not a satisfactory perspective. With respect to legal awareness, a sense of political rights and civic courage, attitudes in Asian countries such as South Korea and the Philippines diverge very widely from those in Japan.

There was a short period in the early 1970s when four major court trials, started by leftist activist lawyers on behalf of pollution victims, suggested a development of revolutionary proportions.[30] The success of this litigation and the intensive publicity that accompanied it made a large number of ordinary Japanese realise for the first time the possibility of using the courts for the articulation of grievances. It suddenly seemed that any group or person, even those without close ties to strong elements within the System, had access to a forum from which to influence major social decisions.[31]

The officials concerned reacted with alacrity. Amidst an acute sense that the administrators were losing control of society in one area, and that the tendency might spread to other spheres, decisive action was taken to ensure that successful litigation on such a scale would be a one-time-only affair. Laws and administrative directives were quickly introduced to return initiative from the hands of the judges back to the bureaucrats. Leftist lawyers had talked the pollution victims into going to court, so a campaign against a leftist-influenced association of lawyers and judges was intensified. Judges, as we will see later, were put under indirect but effective pressure to restrain their enthusiasm for the rights of pollution victims. In the smaller trials that followed the litigants had clearly much less chance of success than did the victorious trail-blazers.

Coping with the legal threat to the System

If Western democracies relied as little on law as Japan does, they would be rocked by incessant civil commotion and probably witness a collapse of the authority structure. Conversely, if Japan were to use the law as it is used in the Western democracies, and as it is supposed to be used under the Japanese constitution, the present Japanese authority structure would collapse.

The constitution, a legacy of the occupation, could not be more democratic. It contains more explicit safeguards protecting the citizen than those of Western Europe and the USA. But it in no way reflects Japanese political priorities. The line it draws between law and administration, making the judiciary autonomous from the rest of government, goes against the practice of Japan's entire history. If the possibility of legal challenge to the power-holders had been realised, it would have brought an end to a period of at least fifteen centuries in which power-holders made sure that their subjects could not gain leverage over them by appealing to transcendental truths. But it was not to be.

A truly independent, non-politicised judiciary as provided for in the formal post-war rules, and a population gradually familiarised with the possibilities of litigation, would have checked consolidation of the post-war System as we know it. The consistent and non-partisan enforcement of anti-trust laws would have checked it. Adherence to the election laws would have checked it, as would consistent judicial investigation into the corrupt relationship between big business and the LDP, and the various other informal relations and practices that keep the System going. A populace sophisticated in the tactics of litigation could go to court over numerous extra-legal administrative measures that restrict many kinds of activity today. The practical possibility of entrepreneurs taking bureaucrats to court would have undermined many of the administrative aims of the System. And, in the most general terms, the System, driven as it is by a myriad *jinmyaku*, could not survive the political inspection made possible by consistent application of the legal process.

The System has so far been spared such embarrassment partly thanks to circumstances condoned if not fostered by the officials, but also through conscious and clear-cut bureaucratic design. Today, institutional arrangements, quite aside from popular attitudes inherited from more authoritarian eras, greatly discourage the Japanese from taking legal recourse. Indeed, close examination of current practices forces the conclusion that the law is purposely, and as much as possible, kept out of the System.

Minimising and moulding the judiciary and bar

The role of law in the System is most effectively minimised by keeping the number of lawyers and judges very small. Japan does not have enough legal professionals to support even a fraction of the litigation common to European countries, not to mention the United States.

Going to court to claim a right is therefore an option that a Japanese is never encouraged to consider. The number of civil suits per capita brought before the courts is roughly between one-twentieth and one-tenth of the figures for common-law countries.[32] Virtually all cases of civil conflict are settled by conciliation, either out of court or before a judicial verdict is reached. This custom goes back at least to the Tokugawa period, when the authorities forced people to settle their differences by conciliation. A settlement out of court is satisfactory for many contemporary Japanese, but those who would prefer the less arbitrary judgement of a court are still given hardly any choice.

The common explanation for the persistence of this method is that it is consonant with an ancient and deeply rooted cultural concern with maintaining harmony. Litigation, by creating winners and losers, works against this ideal. Even lawyers and judges who are highly critical of contemporary Japanese justice tend to be convinced by such culturalist interpretations of this extraordinary – for an advanced industrial society – phenomenon.[33]

Yet there are good reasons to reject the culturalist explanation and, instead, view current judicial practice as a political legacy from the days when the Japanese were forced to settle by conciliation. The System prefers conciliation, and makes sure that it remains the preferred alternative to litigation. Relationships among Japanese groups – as distinct from the internal relationships among their members – tend to be anything but harmonious, and it is not easy to see why an individual would worry about disturbing 'harmony' with another individual who does not belong to the same social circle or is not a neighbour.[34] In times when Japanese were given the opportunity to haul each other before a magistrate, as they were in the Kamakura period, they appear not to have been at all shy about it.[35] Similarly, after the introduction of the modern legal system in the Meiji period, Japanese culture does not appear to have been as great an obstacle to litigation as it is said to be today. Another fact pointing, rather, to a political preference on the part of the System is that, as has been generally noticed, Japanese conciliation procedures almost always give the advantage to the more powerful disputant – thus helping maintain the status quo. A multitude of legal appeals taken to their logical or just conclusion might well break the System apart.

The judiciary and bar are kept artificially minuscule by strict controls over entry into the legal profession. The Ministry of Justice is gatekeeper to the Legal Training and Research Institute (LTRI), through which all those aspiring to become judges, prosecutors or lawyers must pass. This institute offers two years of not particularly heavy training, and graduation is almost automatic for everyone who is considered politically sound. But the annual passing rate for entry into the school is extremely low, at roughly 2 per cent; 486 out of 23,855 candidates passed the entrance examination in 1985. In 1986 eighty of the successful candidates were taking the exam for the fifth time. The semi-official justification for this state of affairs is the small share of the national budget that goes to the judiciary.[36]

The widespread idea that the Japanese are reluctant to enter the legal profession is pure myth. As one specialist has pointed out, the number of Japanese, relative to the total population, who took the judicial examination in 1975 was slightly higher than the figure for Americans taking a bar examination. And since 74 per cent in the United States passed in that year, compared to 1·7 per cent in Japan, the desire to become a lawyer in Japan must actually be much stronger.[37]

The number of judges has not even doubled since 1890, whereas the population has more than trebled.[38] The demand for more judicial personnel obviously exists. Japanese courts are so overloaded with cases that even the simplest take between two and three years to resolve at the district court level. A bigger case may take ten years, if there are appeals. Final decisions that come a quarter-century after a plaintiff or defendant first faced a judge are not unusual.

Finding a lawyer is no simple matter either, and their scarcity makes them expensive. As of 1986 a mere 13,161 lawyers had been admitted to the bar.[39] This means that Japan has one lawyer per 9,294 people, as compared with one for 360 in the USA, 872 in Britain and 1,486 in West Germany.[40]

Even after court proceedings have started, the plaintiff is still under great pressure to switch to the conciliation procedure. The judge will almost always continue to plead for an out-of-court settlement on the grounds that it saves time and money. If plaintiffs insist on a clear decision from the court, they may be given to understand that because of their non-co-operation the case will most likely go against them. Judges themselves tend to believe that to choose to pursue a case through the legal process reflects an inferior moral attitude.[41] Under such circumstances, it is not difficult to understand why very few Japanese will resort to litigation and stick it out to the end. If a Japanese does decide to go to court, more often than not his distrust of the legal process grows. A survey by the Japanese federation of bar associations, Nichibenren, revealed that people with experience of litigation thought that judges 'do not know the reality of society' and that during the proceedings they were not given a sufficient chance to state their case.[42]

Given the awesome power of the System to deprive the Japanese citizen almost completely of the means to litigate, it should come as no surprise that action taken by the private individual against the government is virtually unthinkable. The Supreme Court refuses to use the powers of review given it by the post-war constitution as a means of safeguarding democracy.[43] In combination with the far-reaching formal powers of government agencies in pursuing broad social policy, this has had the effect of almost totally insulating bureaucratic activity from judicial review.[44] When activists persist in countering administrative decisions with lawsuits, the officials perceive this as a 'radical', almost violent action, hampering national policy-making.[45]

The bureaucrats have ample opportunity to mould the judiciary via the entrance exams and training at the government-run LTRI. Trainees are carefully watched. Those considered suitable to serve as prosecutors receive special training that is kept secret from fellow trainees destined to become lawyers and judges. They are invited to the homes of highly placed prosecutors, and automatically hooked up to the *jinmyaku* of the seniors.[46] One result is a tightly hierarchical procuracy that remains easily controllable from above.

Prospective judges are also carefully screened for their political predilections, and trainees who show sympathy with the liberal causes of the day are carefully weeded out. As for the lawyers, the LTRI does not create very self-confident ones. One authority has noted:

Japanese attorneys show no sentiment of independence worthy of their task before judges. The Japanese attorney lives in an environment where everyone thinks the government is good and where private initiative is disdained. Because of this he is obsessed by an inferiority complex when in court. Some attorneys address the judge with great deference, as if they were begging them to give judgment in their favour, and out of court they display an ill-founded mistrust of the judiciary.[47]

In fact, there appear to be good grounds for a certain degree of mistrust.

Dependent judges

Socially instilled acceptance of the world as it is makes the Japanese relatively pliable in the hands of the judicial authorities. The judges themselves seem almost equally malleable, and have allowed their authority to slip from their grasp. Post-war judges are in theory independent of administrative control, and may be judged only by their colleagues. But the dividing line between judiciary and administration, so carefully drawn by the occupation authorities, was carefully undrawn once the occupation ended. Since then, the bureaucracy has crept up on the judges. Their fear of bureaucratic opinion, in connection with tenure and promotions, looms almost as large now as it did before the war.

The pivot of bureaucratic control is an institution set up for an entirely different purpose: the General Secretariat of the Supreme Court. In the post-war arrangement, all courts were supposed to be autonomous. To guarantee this, judges were given power to decide on all matters pertaining to their own courts, and to help maintain this autonomy each court was provided with its own secretariat. The General Secretariat of the Supreme Court was itself meant to perform a similar task,[48] while judicial administration at the highest level was put in the hands of the Conference of the Justices of the Supreme Court. The authority of the latter body has, however, gradually become perfunctory, and effective power has been transferred to the General Secretariat.[49]

At the lower levels, judges have been encouraged to leave miscellaneous matters of court administration to the 'director' of the court, on the grounds that this would leave them free to concentrate completely on judicial proceedings.[50] In 1955 the Supreme Court revised the rules pertaining to lower courts in an effort to knit together the judicial administration of the entire country. As a result, the ultimate administrative authority of each court was entrusted to its 'director' and newly devised standing committees, controlled in turn by the General Secretariat of the Supreme Court. The latter body of bureaucrats now monitors the entire Japanese judiciary. The bureaucrats, rather than practising judges, control appointments, promotions, salaries and dismissals. The General Secretariat of the Supreme Court can monopolise all kinds of information and documents concerning the lower courts, and has steadily expanded its grip over the judiciary through its own regulations and selective staff appointments.[51] It also has virtually complete control over the Legal Research and Training Institute.

This important shift of power was accomplished without much difficulty. The judges of the highest tribunal have been a poor match for the bureaucrats. Two-thirds of the fifteen Supreme Court judges are not career judges but, mostly, *amakudari* bureaucrats from various ministries; they serve relatively short terms, and remain fairly ignorant of judicial administrative matters.[52] Many of the career judges educated under the old constitution returned to their benches after the war without changing their ideas.[53] On the other hand, most prominent members of the General Secretariat of the Supreme Court in the early post-occupation period were dyed-in-the-wool bureaucrats from the pre-war Ministry of Justice. They had fought against major structural changes in the immediate post-war years, but had been overruled by a combination of occupation authorities and democratically inclined judges from the pre-war Daishinin (Supreme Court).[54] For some years considerable friction persisted between the reformist and traditionalist groups, but in 1950, when anti-leftist hard-liner Tanaka Kotaro was installed as chief justice of the Supreme Court, the post-war judiciary was already taking on the shape it has today. By 1954 a person such as Ikeda Katsu, closely identified with pre-war 'thought control' measures and verdicts, could be appointed Supreme Court justice, a position he held for ten years. Ishida Kazuto, another pre-war jurist who had been important in prosecuting 'thought crimes' in the late 1930s and early 1940s, became chief justice in 1969.[55]

The General Secretariat of the Supreme Court represents the so-called 'élite course' of the judicial bureaucracy. A typical judicial bureaucrat begins as assistant judge in one of the six bureaux of the secretariat. Almost always, he will have graduated from the University of Tokyo or Kyoto; ideally he will have passed the entrance exam to the LTRI while still a student. Besides his *gakubatsu* (school clique), he will often have *keibatsu* ties,[56] formed through marriage to, for example, the daughter of a top official in the secretariat or the prosecutors' office. With such advantages the General Secretariat careerist is in a privileged position to reach the pinnacles of the Japanese judicial world.[57]

The officials of the pre-war Ministry of Justice have been gradually replaced by this élite, whose members tend to be appointed as administrative chiefs of district courts and directors of high courts. The career judges who account for one-third of the Supreme Court come from their ranks. In this manner the Japanese judiciary has gradually reverted to the pre-war system in which a privileged group of judicial bureaucrats held sway over practising judges. In response to criticism concerning that group's lack of court experience, adjustments have been made so that it no longer totally monopolises the higher positions. Even so, in appointments to the Supreme Court experience at the secretariat still far outweighs practical judging experience.[58]

The Supreme Court has gained a reputation for overturning decisions against the government made by lower courts. It has also reversed decisions restraining police control of leftist demonstrations, and decisions granting the right to strike to government employees such as railway and postal workers. Strict secrecy has not been able to hide the fact that the Supreme Court sometimes instructs lower courts as to the kind of decision it expects them to make, for example in the areas of labour and medicine. In 1987 it was revealed that in Decemer 1983 the Supreme Court had summoned judges involved in some forty flood-related suits in various parts of the country, and told them how it would decide in an upcoming verdict concerning government responsibility for river management.[59]

In ordinary criminal cases, the Supreme Court has demonstrated sensitivity to human rights ideals, but in cases involving the administration, or political controversy, it has a reputation for extreme passivity.[60]

Battle with Seihokyo

Japan's top judges have done nothing to stop the administrators transferring liberal-minded judges to unimportant areas, or discriminating against them where promotion and pay are concerned. The General Secretariat of the Supreme Court has conceded that it practises this kind of discrimination, but contends that the reasons for it cannot be revealed.[61] Its effects were very clearly revealed in a series of controversies involving the young lawyers' association, Seihokyo, established in 1954 by 107 scholars and 157 lawyers with the aim of protecting the constitution at a time when revision had become a political issue. (Constitutional revision is ardently desired by some segments of the ruling élite,[62] and opposed with equal ardour by groups unwilling to entrust the issue to anyone at the top.)

At one time, Seihokyo counted 230 judges among its membership,[63] and it played a role in drawing attention to the important environmental pollution cases discussed earlier. In 1969 the director of a local court in Hokkaido berated a judge of that court, believed to be a member of Seihokyo, for his handling of a lawsuit to test the constitutionality of the Self-Defence Forces. No administrator had ever interfered so openly with the supposedly independent judiciary, and his action was seen as a warning to members of the jurists' organisation. A second warning came in the form of failure to reappoint a district court judge, the first time this had happened to a judge not involved in any scandal.[64] Although the dismissal was in violation of constitutional guarantees, no explanation was given, and it is widely believed that it was meant to intimidate other judges who were members of Seihokyo. In 1971 the chief of the General Secretariat stated that 'a judge should not join a group with a political colour', and several more warnings were subsequently issued, each carefully avoiding direct reference to Seihokyo.[65]

In the late 1960s a number of magazines criticised allegedly 'biased verdicts' due to the influence of Seihokyo, but there was such similarity in the arguments that they were suspected of having a common source. The articles objected to the rate at which prosecutors were being denied requests for the detention of student activists on the basis of the extra-legal security regulations. One magazine called Seihokyo 'pro-communist' (a segment of its members can fairly be so described), and ran a series of articles on communist influence in the courts, which were distributed by the Supreme Court to courts all over the country.[66] These officially approved magazine articles, as well as informal remarks by conservative jurists, agreed in labelling Seihokyo a 'revolutionary' group. This prompted one specialist to marvel at the fact that, although Seihokyo membership included some of the best-known scholars at Todai, including the university president himself, plus half of all successful candidates in the national bar examination and even several Diet members, no revolution had yet broken out in Japan.[67]

By 1968, when the chairman of the National Public Safety Commission stated that the courts should be more co-operative with the police, cabinet members were also getting into the act. In March 1969 Justice Minister Saigo Kichinosuke commented at a cabinet meeting: 'We cannot touch the courts, but some kind of brake should be applied.'[68] This was the period when radical student activism, including the occupation of university buildings, was causing considerable anguish among the ruling élite.

Subsequently, assistant judges working in the General Secretariat (and thus well set on the 'élite course') were advised to give up their membership of Seihokyo. Ten assistant judges complied. Similar advice was given at district courts all over Japan. In April 1970 the director of the General Secretariat, Kishi Seiichi, warned against membership of Seihokyo, without mentioning it by name.[69] Rightist groups joined the campaign, requesting the Diet's impeachment commission to impeach judges who were Seihokyo members.

The procedure followed here in coping with an organisation seen as a threat to the aims of the administrators of Japan's court system was fairly typical. No official hearings were conducted. Mention of the organisation by name was generally avoided, and no explicit directives against membership were issued, since this would have contravened the principle of freedom of opinion too blatantly. But a 'climate of opinion' was created, with the help of a section of the media, in which it became extremely difficult to remain a member of Seihokyo without having a sense of acting improperly. Quite apart from this, membership of Seihokyo carries a risk of discrimination in salary, rate of salary increase and chances of promotion.

Scared judges

Before the war, the chief flaw in the court system's independence was that it was under the control of central administrators who could pressure recalcitrant judges in various ways, for example by demoting them to less desirable benches.[70] Today it is agreed by those concerned with developments in the Japanese judiciary that the impartiality of judges is undermined by worry about promotion and postings, which come up for review every three years. They are graded according to a secret marking system, introduced in the 1970s, that takes into account the number of cases they clear within a certain period; this includes cases dropped in favour of conciliation procedures.

Judges aware that the chief administrator of their court will rate their performance according to the speed with which they clear their docket are not inclined to take time absorbing the arguments of plaintiffs who may already have irritated them by rejecting their advice for a settlement out of court.[71] Nor will they have much patience with explanations extending outside the realm of their own social experience; most judges, for example, tend to be ignorant of gangster blackmailing techniques, while in cases involving industrial accidents they have been known to imply that plaintiffs knew the risks they were taking in deciding to work in a dangerous place. On-the-spot investigations are rarely resorted to, because these are known to be frowned upon by the administrators and thus detract from a judge's chances of promotion.[72]

A former high court judge asserts that the atmosphere at the courts is such that few judges, if they wish to stay in the good books of the bureaucrats, can afford to be guided solely by their conscience.[73] Bureaucratic standards are applied throughout the system. Judges who meet these standards have a good chance of being appointed to administrative jobs and subsequently rising in the hierarchy. Those who listen mainly to their conscience as they conduct trials are generally not promoted.[74]

Japan's legal system is, thus, highly politicised. At elections to the Lower House, Japanese voters are also given the unusual opportunity to indicate, if they wish, disapproval of recently appointed Supreme Court justices. To no one's surprise, not one of these has ever been voted out of office in this way, since most voters are unaware of whom or what they are endorsing. This questionable instance of 'direct democracy' is in Japan a purely ritualistic addition, one that encourages a totally misleading view of the workings of the System and the character of the judiciary.

The prosecutor as judge

In criminal cases, too, the courts do not offer the protection they are supposed to provide. The idyllic lenience of Japanese law enforcement described in the previous chapter has a shadow side darker than mere intolerance of leftist activism. The fate of Japanese suspects is, except in extremely rare cases, not decided at their 'trial' at all. The real trial consists of the investigation, plus the judgement of the character of the suspect, made by the prosecutors' office. And, in line with what we saw in the previous chapter about the great importance of showing remorse, the attitude of suspects towards the representatives of the System is often more important than their guilt.

As we have seen, prosecutors have virtually unlimited discretion in deciding whether or not to prosecute. They are of course unlikely to take a case to court if they believe that they have insufficient evidence to win it.

But whatever they decide, they are free to go by their own rules, or those of their superiors, regardless of the evidence in hand or their personal belief regarding the suspect's guilt.

Infallible guardians of the System

It is difficult to quarrel with a judicial system that keeps people out of prison as far as possible yet maintains a violent crime rate below that of other industrialised countries. This admirable achievement must be noted. Also, Japanese prosecutors try to be scrupulously fair within the interpretation of fairness prevalent in the judicial–bureaucratic community. Their sense of a duty to uphold the dignity of their office is beyond doubt.

The problem with the Japanese prosecutor is that, once he has decided to prosecute, he will not accept being shown in the wrong. As one Japanese specialist puts it: 'prosecutors want to be God'.[75] Losing a case is much worse for them than it is for their Western counterparts. Their own authority is at stake, and by extension that of the entire bureaucratic apparatus. They need not worry much. They have a 99·8 per cent chance of winning when they take a case to court.[76] Of 63,204 people receiving their first criminal trial in 1986, only 67 were acquitted.

To all intents and purposes, then, the prosecutor is judge. But as we have seen, to judge blindfold is an alien notion for the prosecutors, and they are quite ready to tip the scales of justice out of social considerations. For all their humanity and sense of proportion, the prosecutors remain human with human failings. They are also beholden to the System and, whether consciously or not, must therefore discriminate against the ideologically motivated. The incredibly high conviction rate is usually explained by Japan's judicial authorities as the result of police and prosecutors doing their homework extremely well. In fact, however, it amounts to official endorsement of the prosecutors' infallibility. That they may have human failings is not recognised, for this would undermine the theory of the benevolent social order they represent. The situation is thus no different from what it was before the war, when judges rendered a guilty verdict on practically every suspect placed before their bench by the prosecutors.[77] Functioning institutional guarantees that the prosecutors represent the public interest do not exist. A formal checking committee of ordinary citizens is controlled by the prosecutors' office, and its findings (as, for instance, in cases related to political scandals) can be ignored with impunity.[78]

The superior power of the Japanese procuracy dates from the 1920s, when it gained control over the judiciary to the extent that the judges could almost be considered its servants. In court sessions, the prosecutors sat with the judges on the dais. In the 1930s their office played a major role in upholding the 'national essence' ideology and combating those whom they thought endangered it, including politicians. Possibly the second most significant figure, after Yamagata Aritomo, in the history of twentieth-century Japanese social control was one of their number, Hiranuma Kiichiro. A fanatical believer in the moral superiority of the officials carrying out the 'imperial will', the man known as the 'dean' of the nationalistic right-wing,[79] Hiranuma fought the foreign heresies of Marxism, liberalism and democracy, and together with his clique dominated the Ministry of Justice until the end of the war. He served an unprecedented nine years as procurator-general and went on to become minister of justice, president of the Privy Council, and prime minister (for eight months in 1939), then home minister and class 'A' war criminal, before dying in prison in 1952.[80] Even after the war, the influence of his followers helped to prevent, despite constitutional reform, any genuine change of the judicial guard.

Hiranuma was the epitome of the Japanese politicised prosecutor. He would manipulate the parties he despised and convict the politicians of bribery, forcing them out of office while simultaneously using them to further his own political career. A post-war imitator of the manipulating Hiranuma was Baba Yoshitsugu, who manoeuvred a top leader of the LDP, Kono Ichiro, into his debt, giving him much political leverage in the years leading to his appointment as procurator-general.[81]

Today, the prosecutors are again in practice the strongest power within the justiciary bureaucracy. Their office is theoretically a subordinate institution within the Ministry of Justice, but positions above section chief in that ministry are monopolised by prosecutors and a few judges, while the vice-minister – the *de facto* head of the ministry – is always a public prosecutor,[82] and is also invariably subordinate to several superiors in the pecking order of the procuracy.

There is reason to suspect regular miscarriages of justice caused by the prosecutors' nearly unassailable position, since being openly contradicted in Japan entails a loss of face. As one prominent Japanese legal scholar has noted, the prosecutor's activities are not directed by the principle of *in dubio pro reo* ('when in doubt, favour the accused').[83] Prosecutors can rely on the fact that judges, also, do not want them to lose face; it is common for defence lawyers to view not only the prosecutor, but the judge as well, as their enemy in court. Judges, moreover, have an important reason for going along with the prosecutors in that their own stock will fall if their sentence is revised on appeal.[84]

In the extremely rare case of a not-guilty verdict, Japanese prosecutors forget all impulses to lenience and continue to appeal, fighting tenaciously to regain the 'dignity of the office'. The latter expression is common and has nothing to do with notions of the dignity of the law. Related to it is the expression 'dignity of fixed judgement' with which the prosecutors' office has long resisted retrials.[85]

Circumstantial evidence adduced in finding the accused guilty is frequently rather flimsy, and we have seen earlier how heavily the Japanese prosecutor's success depends on confessions. As one of the most perceptive political scientists writing on Japan has put it:

Japanese police, procurators, and judges think of the confession as the 'king of evidence' (*shoko no o*). It is the decisive element of proof sought by every procurator before he takes a case into court and the single most important item determining the reception his efforts are likely to receive from most Japanese judges when he gets there. Compared with having a good confession, circumstantial evidence is definitely secondary; and given this preference for confessions on the part of procurators and judges, it is small wonder that Japanese policemen are much more attuned to obtaining them than to building 'objective' cases.[86]

Until the occupation authorities tried to change Japanese practice, confessions – often extracted by tricks or what amounted to torture – were the basis of nearly all prosecution successes. Since the end of the occupation, convictions based on confessions have again predominated, accounting for 65 to 75 per cent of the total. As we saw in Chapter 7, this contravenes the constitution, which stipulates that no person shall be convicted or punished if the only proof against him is his own confession (article 38). Many accused, moreover, have already retracted confessions subsequently used as circumstantial evidence. The attitude of the judge is very important in this context. The rare judge will balk at the ways of the prosecutor. On 16 December 1987, for example, Tokyo district court judge Sorimachi Hiroshi found a suspect not guilty of burglary and attempted rape and openly criticised the relentless efforts of the prosecutors to extract a confession. My own interviews with judges and lawyers indicate that the fraction of one per cent of cases that the prosecutors lose are those in which the few liberal-minded judges have been reluctant to accept retracted confessions as evidence.

Virtuous knights in damaged armour

The prosecutor must personify the ethical perfection of the System, and it is often pointed out that, whereas in all other government bureaux and agencies one finds cases of corruption and serious misbehaviour, the public prosecutors lead exemplary lives. This image is maintained partly through the great secrecy with which all judiciary bureaucrats surround themselves. Because of this secrecy, scholars studying these officals and their most celebrated cases find it difficult to verify the simplest details. Judges and prosecutors censor each other's memoirs and case histories,[87] their overwhelming concern being with the 'dignity of the office'. There is only one big chink in their armour that they cannot hide: their treatment of politicians and bureaucrats involved in a scandal.

Individual prosecutors operate, in theory, on their own, but in practice they are expected, before taking action against influential officials, ministers, Diet members or local government leaders, to write preliminary reports for their superiors all the way up to the minister of justice, and to wait for their consent. This controversial *shobun seikun* (request for instructions as to steps to be taken) system of responsibility within the procuracy has led to the dismissal of many political corruption cases.[88] Even when such corruption cases are not dismissed, the politicians involved will usually be allowed to emerge unscathed, and bureaucrats-turned-politicians need not at all fear being publicly tainted.[89]

For seven years before the great Lockheed bribery scandal, the prosecutors had done nothing about the rampant structural corruption among politicians. The previous big case, the Nittsu bribery scandal of 1968, had demoralised the procuracy to a considerable extent, since most prosecutors in the special investigation department of the Tokyo district prosecutors' office were subsequently transferred to local areas.[90] The Lockheed case could be tackled whole-heartedly only when the then prime minister, Miki Takeo, showed that he would do nothing to protect Tanaka Kakuei.

Even though details of the scandal first came to light abroad, in the investigations of US senator Frank Church's subcommittee, the prosecutors saw Lockheed as a chance to regain some of the prestige lost among the convolutions of Japanese politics. But simultaneously there was a shared view among the prosecutors and certain prominent figures in the LDP that Tanaka Kakuei was also a 'danger to Japan's democracy' – meaning, as we saw in Chapter 5, that he was getting too powerful for the comfort of his rivals.

Since LDP politicians tend to be at each other's throat much of the time, the prosecutors are subject to subtly changing and often contradictory pressures. Sometimes powerful LDP groups fight back quite openly, as when a special committee to study the fairness of the judiciary was established in the policy affairs research council of the LDP under a chairman who himself had been involved in a major scandal.[91] This committee's main focus was judicial handling of the Lockheed scandal.

Prosecutors justify their highly selective approach to corruption in the political world in terms of the varying vociferousness of the mass media in specific cases. Thus public opinion desired the arrest of Tanaka, so the prosecutors took action to 'maintain the current establishment' and their own prestige. On the other hand, with the subsequent Douglas-Grumman bribery scandal the press response was not vehement enough to persuade them to go after the politicians involved.[92] 'Public opinion' as interpreted by the five major national dailies is thus of great weight for Japanese prosecutors. Conversely, when they are concerned about possible political obstruction in a case they have decided to pursue, they will leak the fact that they are investigating it, together with the minimal amount of information the newspapers need to unveil the impending scandal on their front pages.[93]

Many judges, too, are concerned about media response to their decisions, which is always assumed to represent 'public opinion'. Lawyers likewise tend to accept public opinion as an important sanctioning force that must be reflected in court decisions. Thus even Seihokyo and other critics of Japan's judicial system praise the tenacity with which the prosecution is pursuing Tanaka Kakuei's case. They overlook the political bias involved (a bias well illustrated by the statement of Okahara Masao, the former presiding judge of the Supreme Court, that Tanaka would not win his case in either the high court or the Supreme Court) and seem unaware that the methods employed to deal with the imagined threat of Tanaka to the System can also be used in dealing with the imagined threat of, say, the consumer movement. A case clearly designed to damage the reputation of the consumer movement did in fact occur in November 1971, when an executive of the Japan Consumers' Union who had claimed that a Honda car was defective was instead charged with making threats against the manufacturer.[94]

Alternative protection

The social sanctioning role played by the Japanese press must be seen in the perspective of the practical shortcomings of the Japanese legal system. 'Although other jurisdictions share some of the limitations of Japanese law, none share so comprehensive a failure to provide effective sanctions or remedies for violation of legal norms,' writes an American expert on the subject.[95] The power-holders cannot do much to enforce the law, aside from locking people up in criminal cases. The Japanese courts have no contempt powers. Attachment of property is a possible ultimate sanction, but there are many ways in which the guilty can avoid it.[96] Penalties for violating legislated regulations are hardly ever invoked if the violator is a corporation or other large mainstream organisation. As already pointed out, what keeps Japanese organisations and their masters from sinning too much is the damage to their reputations if they are unlucky enough to be selected as the 'one example to warn one hundred'.

At the end of 1986 it was announced that the Ministry of Justice would in the near future close 149 of the 575 summary courts.[97] The summary courts are a post-war introduction aimed at giving ordinary people easier access to judicial procedures. Besides misdemeanours such as traffic offences and petty theft, they accept civil suits in which the award is less than 900,000 yen.

In official eyes, closure of the courts is justified by the minimal use made of them. But villagers in the areas served by these courts are concerned that it will cause an influx of 'professional mediators' such as gangsters; where there is insufficient legal protection, people need powerful friends. And faced with a System that relies so much on arbitrary processes, the small fry need personal relations to defend themselves. This helps explain the role of the local 'boss', the Diet member, the gangster and other 'fixers' in Japanese society. It explains the overriding importance of one's *jinmyaku* – connections are crucial to safety as well as to success. It is also a reason why the Japanese cannot risk alienating themselves from their social environment by taking an individualistic stance.

Japanese know that their compatriots are fallible, including those who control their society and those who sit in judgement on them. As pointed out in Chapter 7, they tend to be rather cynical about claims of benevolence; sometimes when explaining to foreigners the traditional ideas on which the System and its legal processes are based, they will say that most 'typical' Japanese accept these as the best possible, thereby implicitly excluding themselves.

Menda Sakae, who spent 33 years in prison, 31 of them on death row, before a retrial declared him innocent, asked me in an interview whether I thought that justice existed in Japan, implying that he did not. Some may argue that the very fact that he was finally acquitted proves that he is wrong. But aside from the argument that justice delayed for thirty-three years is justice denied, it took a hard campaign by sympathisers outside the judiciary before his acquittal was obtained. In the late 1980s humanitarian activists were fighting on behalf of some two dozen similar cases, aware that such cases cannot be left to the Japanese legal process. In October 1987, after thirty-three years on death row and strong pressure from support groups, Akahori Masao, whose confession was extracted under torture, was granted a retrial, which in the Japanese context means that the judiciary had already decided that he was innocent. Yet the final verdict setting him free was not expected for another year. Milovan Djilas has said that the country that is most just is the country most aware of its injustices. By this yardstick the Japanese System does not score very high.

9

The Management of Reality

The discrepancy between theory and practice, between how people say they have organised their lives and the way they actually live, belongs to the human condition. Japan stands out amidst this ubiquitous experience, not only because the discrepancy there is sometimes so colossal, but also because it does not seem to bother people.

A degree of discrepancy between formal and substantial reality is universal, but the difference of degree between Japan and the West is great enough to constitute a difference in kind. Not only are things in Japan almost never what they seem: a gap between formal and substantial reality has been institutionalised, because it is essential to the way power is exercised in Japan. Reality is allowed to exist on different levels far more clearly separated than is suggested by the usual dichotomy of theory and practice, or form and substance. If it were otherwise, the System, dependent as it is on informal relations, would cease to exist.

Political uses of contradiction

The absence of any urge to reconcile reality with theory is an obvious advantage to administrators concerned with lessening political and social tension. Conflicts can be defused or solved by the agile shifting of frames of reference that is possible in Japanese-style debates. This also leaves the room for manoeuvring that Japanese bureaucrats and politicians need in justifying or camouflaging their activities. In so far as the gap between official reality and actuality is institutionalised – accepted as a matter of course, and used for all kinds of purpose – actual practices remain largely unexamined and therefore unthreatened.

Japan's formal legal structure provides the bureaucrats with a multitude of administrative laws that help justify their actions, while at the same time they are free to move outside this structure, unhampered by popular appeals to the law, with all manner of directives. The System is strong and pervasive because it is not vulnerable to potentially disruptive scrutiny. The institutionalised gap between formal and substantial reality offers the ideal means for those in superior positions to control the weak.

A monument to the gap between formal and substantial reality in modern Japan was the Meiji constitution. The civil rights listed in this document were meaningless in that other existing laws made their implementation impossible. It was one of the first of the great pseudo-constitutions that are found today primarily in the communist world. The current constitution, although not so blatantly at odds with actual practice as its predecessor, does not provide the guarantees it embodies in theory. A relic of the United States occupation period, it anticipated basic changes in Japanese communal attitudes of which many did not occur or were prevented by bureaucratic institutions that had been left in place.[1]

A formidable discrepancy between theory and practice characterises much of the politics of most contemporary states. But in a democracy there is usually a body of citizens who deplore the discrepancy between theory and practice in socio-political affairs, and a significant number of them try to do something about it – to act, say, on behalf of disadvantaged minorities. In so doing, they appeal to shared principles, and officials, politicians and neighbours alike understand them. In the Western democracies the symbols of democracy may mask authoritarian practices to some degree, but there are limits. One lies in the possibility of 'throwing the rascals out', another in appeal to the rule of law. Neither is possible in Japan. As the secretary-general of the Parliamentarians' League for Revision of the Constitution says: 'Europeans and Americans tend to feel uneasy when they see a big discrepancy between the law and the actual situation. So they are always encouraged to change their laws and constitutions to meet the new situation. But in Japan they are not urged to remove those discrepancies.'[2]

In Japan an unimplementable constitution is not widely felt to be a problem. On the contrary, it suits those who fear that any kind of revision might lead to the reintroduction of undesirable pre-war stipulations, and it suits the power-holders to have legal arrangements that are out of tune with reality, since this helps preserve the informal political arrangements supporting the System. Open criticism and public debate are of necessity addressed to the formal 'reality', and much political criticism consists of lip-service to ideals that almost no one takes seriously – which also leaves actual power relations safe and untouched.

Thus in theory the captains of industry adhere to classical free-market practices and do not welcome bureaucratic interference. Officially, again, the political preferences of the public are represented by the politicians it has elected to the Diet. According to this same official reality, there exist an anti-monopoly law and a Fair Trade Commission to prevent cartels, and a judiciary that guards democratic freedoms and individual rights. Labour unions ensure that worker grievances get a fair hearing, and numerous other institutional safeguards protect the 'democratic free-market system' from its enemies. The absence of any independent judiciary, any labour unions primarily representing the interests of workers and any effective safeguards against business–bureaucratic market-fixing conspiracies is obscured. Without the institutionalised divergence between formal and substantial reality, there would have been no post-war economic 'miracle'.

Mental paralysis in the face of contradiction – the failure, even, to perceive contradiction – allows the unhindered exercise of power by the privileged over the non-privileged. The mechanics of submission and domination in the typical Japanese setting are intimately bound up with the possibility of being unreasonable and seeming reasonable at the same time. This reaches its ultimate manifestation in the manner in which the Zen master frustrates his pupil by unintelligible answers, until the pupil ceases all intellectual defence and submits to the master's purely arbitrary authority.

A farce of competing realities

The management of 'truth' in Japan often involves a set of not just two but three or four layers of reality among which highly placed participants in the System wriggle towards their goals. A spectacular example of this is provided by a mock political battle that will also serve to illustrate further some of the crucial relationships in recent political history described in Chapter 5.

In October and November 1983 Japan went through a 'political crisis'. It began with the verdict of the Tokyo district court finding political boss Tanaka Kakuei guilty in connection with the Lockheed bribery scandal, and climaxed in a 47-day opposition boycott of parliament and a vote of no-confidence against Prime Minister Nakasone.

Tanaka appealed against the verdict and left it at that. The rules say nothing about resigning from parliament under such circumstances, but the opposition raised a hue and cry because Tanaka did not make this symbolic gesture. It demanded that an unprecedented motion for his dismissal be discussed, and when Nakasone rejected this the minority parties walked out, paralysing the Diet.

Tanaka, it should be remembered, was not a member of Nakasone's party. He had resigned from the LDP seven years previously, the top managers of the LDP having concluded that it would not look good to have an indicted bribery suspect in their ranks. To be corrupt is one thing; to be tapped on the shoulder by the public prosecutor is quite another. Yet, as we have seen, Tanaka had more control over the LDP than any of its real members had ever had, and had already selected three prime ministers. Nakasone, who owed his position to Tanaka, found himself in a quandary. Parliamentary boycotts undermine the prestige of Japanese prime ministers, since containing an unruly oppositon is one of the few ways in which they are allowed to show leadership. Moreover, Nakasone urgently needed to have a number of laws passed. But even aside from his sense of indebtedness to Tanaka, he wanted to remain prime minister and knew that his chances of doing so, even until the end of the year, would be close to nil if Tanaka decided to withdraw his support. Hence he could not bring an end to the parliamentary crisis by simply giving in to the opposition.

The tensely awaited solution finally came when the obstreperous minority parties agreed to a compromise. They would table a no-confidence motion against the prime minister – which is one way of letting people know that they too have power. Nakasone 'accepted' this opposi-tionist plan to introduce a no-confidence motion against himself, in exchange for the opposition promise not ritually to object to the pending bills. It did not matter that opposition Diet members were absent from the sessions during which the laws were put to a vote, since they were no longer officially boycotting. Their votes would not have made any difference anyway; what mattered was their having formally called off their boycott. Nor were there any rules prohibiting the LDP from voting while the boycott was on. But in this case the minority parties would have screamed about the 'dictatorship of the majority', which would have had an unfortunate effect on public opinion – or (another sub-layer of reality) what the press would tell its readers their opinion should be.

This brief trip through Japan's political wonderland shows, first of all, that the formal rules of parliamentary democracy have no relevance at all. If they had been followed there would have been no crisis; there could have been no conflict regarding Tanaka's remaining in the Diet, and the LDP majority could at any time have voted on as many bills as it pleased. But this was only the beginning of the farce of competing 'realities'.

The compromise between the opposition and Nakasone was the formal reality as portrayed by the media. Press commentators almost uniformly showed Nakasone as reluctantly agreeing to it. According to this version of reality, the elections that followed the no-confidence motion and the dissolution of the Lower House were not in line with the prime minister's original plans. This generally accepted interpretation, however, con-tradicted numerous bits of leaked information, carried earlier in the same newspapers but now apparently forgotten, that indicated preparations on a large scale for elections in connection with an early parliamentary dissolution.

The manipulators of the journalistic chorus had thus done Nakasone a great favour. His biggest problem had been how to create the impression in the public eye that he was distancing himself from Tanaka, without Tanaka getting the same idea. Furthermore, by giving in to the opposition he had demonstrated how 'democratic' he was. And on top of this he found himself blessed with the early elections that he had been planning all along. To sum up: beneath the outer political forms, there exists a semi-official reality of expected ritual behaviour. Beneath this again, there is the true reality of power relations. The reality of these is in turn further scrambled by reporters who love to 'expose' real (and supposedly unseen) motives. The press, in the process, unwittingly distorts these motives since it, too, often ends up being manipulated.

Reality as created by politicians

One of the most telling episodes of recent Japanese political history, one in which the press helped establish a formal reality created by LDP bosses, was the ousting of Miki Takeo from the prime ministership in late 1976. According to the official version, Miki quit to 'take responsibility' for the loss the LDP had suffered in the elections that had just ended. This sounded reasonable, since Japanese prime ministers are expected to take symbolic responsibility for failures they have had nothing to do with, just as they bask in the glory of achievements that are not theirs.

This time, however, there was nothing reasonable about it. True, the Lockheed scandal had that year damaged the LDP more severely than any other post-war scandal, but Miki's incumbency had helped more than anything else to control the damage. For much of the year, the Japanese press had urged the LDP to engage in public soul-searching concerning its 'ethics' and had applauded Miki ('Mr Clean') for taking this seriously. It was widely agreed that the LDP would have lost much more heavily in the elections had Miki not been at the helm during the preceding year.

The true reason why Miki had to resign was entirely different. Heavy guns had been trained on him within the LDP ever since Tanaka's arrest, which Miki had done nothing to avert. Shiina Etsusaburo, the kingmaker responsible for Miki's prime ministership, implicitly accused him of un-Japanese behaviour by saying that 'Miki has no inkling of others' feelings'. Terrified lest his 'reformist zeal' tempt him to further 'excesses', leading figures in the LDP established a 'council to achieve party solidarity' (*Kyoto-kyo*) to work for Miki's dismissal. Under its auspices, Ohira Masayoshi and Fukuda Takeo were prevailed upon to cease the rivalry that had been the only reason for choosing Miki as prime minister in the first place. They made a deal settling the order in which they would become prime minister, after which for Miki to hang on as prime minister would have meant an almost certain split in the LDP. Unwilling to take the responsibility, and missing the chance to reintroduce a two-party system, he pulled back after a formula for changing intra-party election rules had been accepted, thus allowing him to save face. After some nine months of cheering Miki on and encouraging him to clean up Japanese politics, the press played the major role in creating the reality in which Miki resigned to take responsibility for the electoral misfortune.

Media-sponsored reality

In the uniformity of its interpretations of events, the Japanese press has the power to manufacture expedient 'realities' that would suggest a comparison with the controlled press of the communist world if it were not that the latter is far less successful in convincing foreign observers.

The Japanese press is the major source of information and misinformation about Japan. It has more influence on the dispatches of Tokyo-based foreign correspondents than the local press has on correspondents in other major capitals. Only the specialist in one fairly narrow subject can afford to rely solely on non-journalistic sources; generalists must depend on the Japanese media for a great deal of information about a number of relatively inaccessible fields in which they cannot possibly have enough first-hand knowledge, no matter how good their language skill or how hard-working their assistants. The same applies to even the best-equipped embassies and foreign firms.

Foreign journalists, diplomats and businessmen tend to trust the information given in Japanese newspapers because of its very uniformity. There is nothing like an air of unanimity concerning political events, of conveying the 'voice of the people', for creating a convincing air of portraying reality. Basically, the outside world receives its picture of Japan through one filter and, because the Japanese press is not followed with the suspicious scrutiny it deserves, that picture is often very misleading.

Take, for example, the coverage of the elections of December 1983, following the no-confidence motion and the dissolution of the Lower House that ended the 'crisis' described above. In its editorial comment and much of its reporting, the Japanese press ascribed the LDP's loss of thirty-six seats to popular discontent with the way in which the government had handled 'political ethics'. Editorials in major newspapers throughout the rest of the world were perhaps less adamant on the subject, but most referred to a supposed 'Tanaka burden' which Nakasone was forced to shoulder, or uttered platitudes about public reaction to corruption in the ruling party. In fact, neither 'political ethics' nor Nakasone's policies affected voter support for the LDP in any significant way. There had been a 2 per cent drop in the share of the vote for the LDP, but this correlated with the extraordinarily low turn-out (always disadvantageous to the LDP) due to weather conditions. The irony left unexplained by the Japanese press was that those candidates associated with Tanaka's critics had fared much worse than those associated with Tanaka.

When the press refers unanimously to the Lower House elections as a 'stern verdict on Nakasone's reluctant stance to restore political ethics among his party members', it describes a reality that has been agreed upon. A few articles in serious monthly magazines make feeble attempts to place cause and effect in a logical relationship, but by the time they appear the reality is no longer open for discussion.

Nakasone would have been howled at if he had tried to explain, with concrete figures, that the conclusion of the media was wrong. The artificial reality had become too firmly established for that. The LDP, which must also formally subscribe to the press-endorsed reality, got back at the jubilant minority parties by presenting its umpteenth (phoney) plan for 'establishing political ethics'. Amidst all the management of reality, to feign contrition is the ideal way to give the voter an impression of 'sincerity'.

The press role in the management of reality may be to the disadvantage of certain groups of administrators, but it is always to the advantage of other groups: in the above episode, the many enemies of Tanaka and Nakasone within the LDP.

Deference to the artificial reality that props up the System is habitual among newspaper editors. During the closing months of 1987 the steep increase in land prices caused by speculating corporations, and the activities of the gangster-affiliated *jiageya* who intimidated tenants into leaving their homes and owners into selling their property, became an embarrassing problem. The government was taken to task, also in the press, for not doing anything about it. But in January 1988 the problem vanished from the pages of the newspapers to make room for reports on how the government was planning to move the capital, and in that process alleviate the land price problem. About every ten to fifteen years plans for moving a number of government offices and universities out of Tokyo (or for constructing a new capital at the foot of Mount Fuji) get an airing in the press, and again in 1988 not a soul in government had any intention of carrying them through. But the press, rather than pursue the original and very pressing problem of land prices, helped spread an illusion among the public that something was being done.

There are numerous other instances in which the media help the administrators give the illusion of guarding the public interest. Take their reaction when, in January 1988, the Osaka district public prosecutor's office decided that a 'political donation' was a bribe. The victim of its selective judgement was an Upper House member, Tashiro Fujiro, of the Komeito (a party with a 'clean image'), who was indicted on charges of having accepted ten million yen in return for official favours. To LDP heavyweights with connections in the construction business, ten million yen is a mere pittance. The Komeito member's sin was to have accepted the money in exchange for a recommendation to the Transport Ministry, on behalf of the national federation of private gravel- and stone-shippers' co-operatives, for a partial revision of certain measures that discriminated against members of the federation. It should be remembered here that such a federation cannot take any ministry to court; that to mediate in such cases is an accepted task of the Japanese politician; and that if no LDP member can be found to do this, a well-connected member of a minority party will do. Nevertheless, the opposition politician resigned his Upper House seat and, while fervently protesting his innocence and emphasising that the money had been a political contribution, also made a big show of apologising for not fulfilling his 'ethical responsibility'. Had he not done so, the newspapers would have unleashed the full force of their indignation upon him. The obvious question as to why exactly the public prosecutor suddenly saw fit to ruin the career of an opposition Diet member failed to stir journalistic instincts. Instead, the press carried the usual homilies about the need for self-reflection among politicians. Editorials explaining that such things cannot be tolerated in Japan deceive the public knowingly. Not only are they tolerated, but uncountable transactions of the same type, involving ten or a hundred times more money, form the substantial reality upon which, as we saw in Chapter 5, Japan's entire political system is based.

The degree of transparency in manipulating reality varies. When the news went around the world that Prime Minister Suzuki Zenko had taken the drastic step of forming a new cabinet 'in order better to deal with international trade problems', everyone with any experience saw at once that this was nonsense. Cabinet reshuffles are routine affairs, taking place about once a year for the purpose of rewarding LDP parliamentarians with the ministerial posts they crave. The new set of ministers chosen by Suzuki had no intention of tackling international issues in any different manner from their predecessors; in the unlikely event that any individual among them had any such intention, he could never have carried it out.

The frequent discussions within the LDP about the need to dissolve the *habatsu* (the cliques of which the party is a coalition) are another case in point. Because the *habatsu* are considered the cause of much political corruption, many plans have been announced to do away with them. In the late 1970s some cliques actually announced their dissolution, with the newspapers printing photographs of *habatsu* offices being vacated. But an experienced observer would know that to take the *habatsu* out of the LDP would be like taking the skeleton out of a living body.

In many areas, however, the management of reality has made accurate analysis difficult or impossible, with the result that much generally accepted history is unreliable. Even well-informed Japanese journalists (who are generally highly specialised) tend to suppress their privileged knowledge of events in favour of an officially agreed-upon reality. There are many political and diplomatic events, even within recent memory, of which the true facts will never become generally known, despite the fact that they are accessible to a number of Japanese observers outside the diplomatic and political circles that want to keep them hidden.

Socially sanctioned deceit

In a world of competing realities appearances are crucial. Politicians who have been tainted by involvement or suspicion of involvement in scandals use election campaigns to 'purify' their status, a process referred to as *misogi*, after the Shinto purification ceremony. They use the word in their speeches, and even if they have claimed that they are not guilty they still talk about a period of *misogi* being over. In Japan, one can take responsibility for having created a suspicion of involvement.

The phrase 'correct image' (*tadashii imeeji*) is customarily used in referring to various kinds of whitewash job. A frequently used expression, 'the adjustment of views', means reaching agreement as to the nature of whatever is at hand. It indicates that 'reality' is seen as negotiable. And much of the 'explaining' of the 'true situation' that Japanese representatives love doing at international conferences, in mainstream publications and in a multitude of glossy subsidised magazines must be seen in this context. The power-holders are extremely eager to make sure that everyone 'understands' what has been agreed on.

Fairly often, rival segments of the Japanese élite decide that they must, for practical reasons, agree on an arbitrary interpretation of a situation at hand, which then becomes the official reality to which all will defer. This negotiated reality – which must not be mistaken for consensus – is very important in the absence of unambiguous political leadership and clear lines of command. It helps prevent the freewheeling chaos one would expect as the result of such political weaknesses. The cohesion among the administrators derives partly from a shared, tacitly agreed upon and arbitrary view of reality. Their common educational background and interwoven personal relations give them similar or identical frames of reference, influenced only minimally by individual assessments of a situation and existing quite separately from personal views of the world.

In their daily lives, the Japanese are very helpful to one another in minimising embarrassment, and will often make quite clear that what they have just said may not refer to factual reality. All one has to do is catch the signal. Foreigners are expected to do this also, for sometimes the excuses or 'explanations' given in international dealings are simply too crude to be taken seriously. To make things even easier, the Japanese have a relevant terminology: *tatemae*, or the way things are presented, ostensible motives, formal truth, the façade, pretence, the way things are supposed to be (often wrongly translated by Japanese as 'principle'); and *honne*, or genuine motives, observed reality, the truth you know or sense.

This *honne–tatemae* dichotomy is constantly referred to, and it is usually considered an ethically neutral if not positive aspect of Japanese society. But it also provides a frame of reference in which many forms of deceit are socially sanctioned.[3] The Japanese can be honest about their fakery to a degree that Westerners could not possibly be. They are allowed to pretend honesty without fear of being chided for dishonesty. To put it in the words of an anthropologically trained observer: 'Truth and morality are . . . specific to the interaction at hand. . . . The Japanese tend to accept apparent contradictions as complementary facets of the same truth. They rarely insist on consistency and are inclined to refer to narrowly logical people as *rikutsuppoi*, that is, "reason-freaks".'[4]

Mistrust of foreigners

Because of their own institutionalised gap between true and surface motives, Japanese tend to be suspicious of the motives of foreigners and foreign countries. They are forever searching for a hidden *honne* behind any foreign analysis of Japanese circumstances or of bilateral relationships. The *tatemae–honne* dichotomy helps explain the assertion, often made before and during the Second World War, that Japan's true intentions in Asia were never understood, whereas the West's true motives were much more insidious than it let on.

Once, after I had written a newspaper story summing up misconceptions in both Japan and the Western world that were contributing to a widening conflict, a high Japanese official used the Kyodo news agency to publicise his belief that the article should be seen in the context of an alleged attempt by the European Community to discredit Japan. Similarly, an article of mine in a United States publication, analysing the effect of the absence of a coherent Japan policy in Washington and enumerating some of the characteristics of the System, prompted discreet queries about the possibility of my having conspired with certain US interests. My sin was that, after many years of friendly relations with Japan's officials, I had not helped them hold up the *tatemae* to the world. The *honne* is strictly private, to be discussed and joked about over cups of sake.

Much maligned logic

In any discussion of political and social circumstances, it is logic that provides both steady points of reference and consistency. Its rules are not made up on the spot, nor are they newly arrived at by monthly discussion. They are certainly not dictated by politicians. And they continue to exist when we are not looking at them. This may seem labouring the obvious, but in Japan one meets intelligent people who claim that 'logic' is something invented in the West to allow Westerners to win discussions. Indeed, the belief is widespread that the Japanese can as happily do without logic now as they supposedly have for centuries past. This is of course untrue. Japanese engineers and scientists are as familiar with logical thinking as their counterparts anywhere else, and some have received Nobel prizes for it.

Yet, at least where social and political affairs are concerned, the Japanese are not driven by an overwhelming urge to perceive paradoxes and solve contradictions. Neither the three major Japanese spiritual systems (Shintoism, Buddhism, Confucianism) nor scientific thought have given the Japanese tools of leverage over their environment. The achievements of Tokugawa-period mathematics were considerable, and extended by the end of the seventeenth century to the invention of calculus, but it occupied a place akin to that of chess; it was treated like a game that could not possibly have any bearing on the nature of the universe, or on Japanese society within it. Modern scientific theory has fared little better. Its 'reality' remains divorced from social reality. Abstract thought tends to be practised as an end in itself and is not allowed to determine the nature of human exchanges, while social inquiry remains an exercise for its own sake, utterly removed from any points of reference in experience.

The schools reinforce these attitudes. Comparing Japanese and Western education, one authority concludes that 'schooling in logic is as old as Western civilisation itself. By contrast, the Japanese tradition . . . has long emphasised memorisation and imitation. One approach helps the internalisation of a moral and intellectual frame of reference, the second aids adjustment to the environment.'[5]

Islands in an intellectual vacuum

Throughout the centuries, political arrangements have deprived the Japanese people of that intangible but very important cultural achievement: a free universe of discourse. I know Japanese who think very clearly and make intellectual discoveries, and there must have been many in history who obeyed the human urge towards philosophical speculation. But the crucial thing to remember is that each of them has had to create his own intellectual world. There was no grand intellectual tradition to hold all this speculation together, to serve as a framework of reference; no body of philosophical speculation that might be attacked or added to. Without a logically ordered hierarchy of abstractions, product of a long intellectual striving to grasp reality, the relevance, the weight, the proportion and the balance of competing evidence are only haphazardly perceived.

Japanese scholarly debates tend to exist in an intellectual vacuum as tiny, self-contained universes of discourse. The academics who wage them have, moreover, such a dislike of being contradicted that they tend to cloud their contentions to a degree making refutation nearly impossible. Intellectuals are rarely asked to prove or disprove their hypotheses, and consequently are themselves not very good at critical evaluation. Maruyama Masao has observed that Japanese intellectuals adopt new domestic or foreign ideas in rapid succession: 'New ideas of whatever origin win extremely quick victory over the intellectuals'; they make no conscious effort to test the new ideas against their established convictions.[6] Radicalised students illustrate this tendency very well. They undergo intellectual and spiritual processes that are comparable to conversion experiences in other parts of the world. But they tend to repeat such experiences, and in the end little of anything seems to stick. Lasting intellectual commitment is extremely rare; not only is it not rewarded, it often conflicts with socio-political demands from the immediate environment. Many Westerners have had worthwhile conversations with Japanese, only to discover later that the conclusions reached seemed to have been totally forgotten.

At Japanese high schools, conflicting Western and Japanese ideas are treated side by side, without any effort to help the student resolve the confusion. School textbooks on political and historical subjects never suggest that there are desirable and undesirable systems of government.

Passions are absent. Judgments are missing. Students are introduced
not to the uniqueness or vitality or clash of historical forces, only to a
recital of their labels. Totalitarianism, capitalism, communism, and
a host of other 'isms', including freedom and democracy (which are
both 'isms' in Japanese), are mentioned but not examined in
concrete detail.[7]

The impression is left that the 'isms' are interchangeable and that all can
claim our respect with equal validity.

The poverty of the Japanese intellectual tradition is reflected in that
unenthusiastic institution, the Japanese university. Perhaps the most
striking characteristic of Japanese students is their general apathy. It
should not surprise anyone. My own experience of teaching at, among
other places, Waseda University suggests that if students discover the
excitement of intellectual pursuits at all, they discover it on their own.
Inspiring teachers are rare. Just as at the high-school level, education in
the sense of fostering and expanding the powers of the mind is almost non-
existent. If some Japanese university professors function as intellectual
guides, they do so out of the goodness of their heart and not because it is
expected of them. Many of the more gifted students go through phases of
extreme nihilism.

Disconnected knowledge

An intellectual tradition that is ultimately independent of power arrangements, such as that of the West, not only permits some degree of
intellectual control over political matters, but also promotes coherence in
the face of new ideas. ' 'Tis all in pieces, all coherence gone,' lamented
John Donne when medieval theories of the working of the universe could
no longer withstand the heretical hypotheses of a Copernicus or a Galileo;
but he underestimated the force of the Greek tradition of logical thinking
without which he himself would never have been concerned about
coherence in the first place. Japanese intellectual life, continuously
confronted with a great deal of novelty, is heir to no such tradition.

Although an unambiguous order rules social relationships, individual
things and ideas coexist in a feast of incongruity that both baffles and
amuses the outsider. Visitors to Japan realise almost immediately that they
are among inveterate collectors of ideas, methods and gimmicks. I know
coffee shops and other buildings done in a mixture of seven or nine
different architectural styles. There are mandolin-playing clubs at universities. One more example among thousands of others: the Japanese have
yodelling societies that give concerts (to which the Swiss cultural attaché
is invited), with the yodellers lined up on the stage in Swiss costumes.
Ideas, too, are imported *en masse*. Bookstores are crammed with works
translated from English, German and French. The translations rather

often fail to convey the spirit and purpose of the originals, though something of their new ideas undoubtedly seeps through.

No other people in history, perhaps, has been required to absorb such a plethora of new ideas as the Japanese were in the second half of the nineteenth century, following the Meiji restoration. A multitude of magazines and study clubs saw to their dissemination throughout a nation being remade. But the ideas, which took members of the former warrior élite and the new class of educated commoners by storm, were generally divorced from the context in which they belonged. The intellectuals who introduced them often made their selection with a practical purpose in mind. The outside world had become a bazaar where one could pick and choose religion, moral standards, art and political systems to be used as tools for modernisation, for strengthening the country, for catching up with other states.

Japan's only philosopher of some international repute, Nishida Kitaro, remembered how in lectures at Tokyo Imperial University in 1914 his German-trained teacher, Dr Raphael Koeber, inveighed against the half-baked theories of Japanese intellectuals. As Koeber put it: 'These scholars import only the flowers which amaze people, without trying to transplant the roots. As a result we have people who are greatly admired for bringing the flowers, but we cannot find the plants that should be producing them.'[8]

The medley of translations from French, German and English, the tumult of opinion which the opened floodgates had let in, produced no widely persuasive approach to life based on a set of consistent ideas. The more serious thinkers, having once begun to question the validity of their traditional learning, tended to react so vehemently that they sometimes lost their intellectual bearings completely. A rare exception was the liberal scholar Yoshino Sakuzo (1878–1933), who achieved an integrated view of society and had independent, realistic ideas about the direction in which the Japanese political system ought to be developed.

It became a habit among Japanese intellectuals to argue interminably about minor points of categorisation. Questions such as whether the Sino–Japanese War was a 'nationalist' or an 'imperialist' war can still excite some of them. Before and again after the Second World War, the community of Japanese Marxists was torn by a controversy as to whether or not Japanese society was still a 'feudal' one – since, if it were, this would necessitate a quick run through the bourgeois stage before a socialist revolution could take place. This grand debate divided a considerable part of the academic world into a *koza* and a *rono* faction, the latter believing that capitalism had already created enough of a working class to prepare for the proletarian take-over.[9] Often, one Western idea would be seized on to criticise and counteract another, without any attempt to relate either of them to Japanese experience. For all practical purposes, most of the gorging on abstract Western learning that occurred from the Meiji period until the surging nationalism of the 1930s has left the Japanese heirs to a farrago of disjointed, ill-digested bits and pieces of knowledge.

Avoiding distinctions

Some post-war Japanese intellectuals such as political theorist Maruyama Masao and his followers seem to be bothered by the continued refusal to apply universal principles by which the political process and individual purposes can be judged; they refer to the lack of such principles as the cause of many shortcomings in Japanese life. More nationalistically inclined Japanese may, however, consider the 'flexibility' of Japanese thought a virtue. Prime Minister Nakasone appeared proud of it when, in an interview on national television in August 1984, he implied that it has given the Japanese a great advantage over Westerners. He used the occasion to explain that Japanese are polytheistic, since, as individuals, they can accept Buddhism simultaneously with Shinto and Christianity, which makes Japanese thinking more tolerant than that of 'monotheistic Westerners'. It clearly did not occur to him that simultaneous acceptance of beliefs that are ultimately incompatible is for all practical purposes the same as believing in none of them.

Such examples do not encourage an understanding among the public that one cannot have one's cake and eat it too. Edward Seidensticker remarks that

> student thought, when elucidation is requested . . . tends to show an eclecticism that really cancels it out as thought. One enquirer asked a selected group of students what ideologies they thought themselves under the influence of. She offered this choice: 'Marxism . . . non-Marxist socialism . . . liberalism . . . humanism . . . pragmatism . . . anarchism . . . nihilism . . . Existentialism . . . nationalism . . . idealism . . . hedonism . . . ideology-free . . . others.' About half of the 47 students who described themseves as activists were content with Marxism alone. Three opted for liberalism and one for humanism, and all the rest professed adherence to multiple and frequently conflicting ideologies. Two of the subjects checked ten different items, and one checked every item on the list except 'others'. Perhaps in other political cultures this would have an element of humour about it, but not in Japan. Nowhere do disparate ideologies rest more comfortably side by side than in the head of a Japanese, and the total effect, of course, is of a raging anti-intellectualism.[10]

The avoidance of the distinctions and dichotomies considered essential by the religious and philosophical traditions of Mesopotamia, Persia, India, the West and China has been praised by the Japanese as quintessentially Japanese. The refusal to distinguish good from bad, for instance, was idealised as far back as the eighteenth century by one of Japan's greatest classical scholars, Motoori Norinaga, who contrasted native Shinto with the foreign creeds: 'The way of the gods does not contain a single argument that annoyingly evaluates things in terms of good or evil, right and wrong like the Confucian and the Buddhist Ways. It is opulent, big-hearted and refined.'[11] This alleged absence of any fundamental duality in traditional Japanese thought is extolled even today. Contemporary theorists on the national character proudly proclaim that Japanese prefer to live with intellectual ambiguity.[12] The well-known populariser of Zen in the West, Suzuki Daisetz – who made a fortune with some forty books in English explaining truths 'that cannot be captured in writing' – never tired of pointing out the shortcomings of Western 'dualistic logic'. Actually, the historical function of Japanese Zen, which thrived among the warrior class, was to lower the resistance of the individual against the blind obedience expected of him, as can be gathered from the common Zen imagery of 'destroying' or 'extinguishing' the mind.[13]

Blunted Confucianism

The malleability, relativity and negotiability of truth in Japan; the claimed superfluity of logic; the absence of a strong intellectual tradition; the subservience to the administrators of law; and the acceptance, even celebration, of amorality: these are, of course, all causally intertwined. They reinforce what I have referred to as the crucial factor in the exercise of Japanese power: the absence of a tradition of appealing to transcendental truth or universal values.[14] All other extant civilisations have developed religions and systems of thought that acknowledge the existence of a truth transcending socio-political concerns. Neither Shintoism nor Buddhism has been of assistance here.

It is helpful in examining the mental backdrop to the Japanese political tradition to make a comparison with intellectual and spiritual life in China. The dominating force there was Confucianism, a surrogate religion with roots in social experience, and thus very suitable for Japanese power-holders. Confucianist ethics were based on a very sophisticated understanding of human character and the dynamics of society; metaphysics had no place in it. The Chinese concept of heaven (T'ien) is very different from the Western (originally Mesopotamian) concept of a universe that was created, and subsequently controlled, by a Divine Power. The Chinese Heaven was, of course, viewed as superior to anything on earth, but it was not seen as the creator of the universe and was not visualised in a concrete form.[15] Nor was it considered important as a source of social knowledge. The Confucianist code of behaviour could hardly be more this-worldly in its orientation. Significantly, though, the principles it developed were taken to be universally true and applicable under all circumstances.

This prepared the Chinese mind for conceiving of a moral order separate from the social order. Though not based on any belief in a supernatural being or supported by metaphysical speculation, it transcended temporal authority and immediate social concerns. In this respect Chinese Confucianism does, after all, resemble the transcendental traditions of Christianity, Judaism, Islam, Hinduism and Buddhism.

However much the Japanese emulated the Chinese in other things, and however much Japanese power-holders craved obedient subjects, they were not interested in trying to produce moral citizens by invoking paramount abstract principles. To follow the Chinese one step further and, by abstracting a morality from socially desirable behaviour, to develop the idea of individual conscience in potential opposition to social practices was totally inconceivable. The Chinese individual can draw upon a tradition that instructs him not to surrender his moral judgement to society. As Confucius himself is supposed to have said: 'The moral man must not be a cipher in but a cooperative member of society. Wherever the conventional practices seem to him immoral or harmful, he not only will refrain from conforming with them but will try to persuade others to change the convention.'[16]

Confucius rejected absolute loyalty to an overlord in favour of loyalty to principle, to the Way.[17] The result was 'a goodly company of martyrs, who have given their lives in defense of the Way'.[18] This tradition has given the Chinese, at the very least, the freedom to speculate on the legitimacy of rulers, particularly when comets, earthquakes, floods or pestilence allowed little doubt about the wrath of Heaven. The revolutions and usurpations of the throne that punctuate Chinese history were always justified by reference to the mandate of Heaven. Even for the great mass of people, the concept of a moral order transcending considerations of political or economic expediency provided something to which they could, at least in principle, appeal so as to free themselves from the total arbitrariness of power.

The place that the Chinese have given to abstract principles, the power they have granted ideology, could hardly be better illustrated than by the social convulsions – the Great Leap Forward and the Cultural Revolution – they have lived through in very recent decades, which were among the most terrible in the history of the world and were all justified by appeals to a supposed historical 'truth' situated above society.

Ideological chameleons

One reason why Japan entered the modern industrial world with relative ease compared with China and other Asian nations lay in the very lack of any strongly held precepts, based on transcendental beliefs, to block the changes of mentality that were required to cope with the material changes. There was neither intellectual nor moral opposition strong enough to halt the influence of the many new concepts the country needed in order to modernise.[19]

Unrestrained by any tradition enjoining 'truth to oneself', the Japanese may 'believe' one thing and do something entirely different. It was relatively easy for them formally to adopt Western political institutions and ideals, because the moral possibility was retained of using these alien concepts and beliefs as tools for new ends suitable to Japan's own needs.

The ability to make rapid mental adjustments to changed social conditions also makes amazing chameleon-like changes in behaviour possible when Japanese find themselves in entirely different circumstances from the ones they are used to. In her classic study of Japanese behaviour Ruth Benedict noted that the most dramatic difference between Western and Japanese soldiers was the extent to which, as prisoners of war, the latter co-operated with the Allies. 'They were better than model prisoners. Old Army hands and long-time extreme nationalists located ammunition dumps, carefully explained the disposition of Japanese forces, wrote our propaganda and flew with our bombing pilots to guide them to military targets.'[20]

A former Japanese inmate of the Siberian prisoner-of-war camps writes that the Germans, Italians, Koreans and Chinese in those camps did not display such 'miserable capitulation' to the Soviets as did his countrymen. He speaks of the gutlessness and spinelessness with which the Japanese prisoners waved red flags, declared Japan an enemy country and shouted *banzai* for Stalin. He compares it with the opportunism in the behaviour of Japanese intellectuals, who first acted as though they believed the myth that the Japanese emperor was a living god, subsequently chanted 'democracy' as they bowed before the United States occupation authorities and, 'when sensing a threat from the Soviet Union, began to sing its praises as the fortress of peace in the world'.[21]

In a very different setting, far removed from the cruelty, hardships and constant fear of the Siberian camps, Japanese company representatives could be seen waving Mao's Little Red Book and mouthing the appropriate slogans on visits to China during the Cultural Revolution. A shift in outward attitudes towards the Arabs, from disdainful indifference to sycophantic solicitude, immediately followed the oil crisis. Films which show Arab countries in a bad light are under no circumstances shown in Japan. One phone call from a Middle Eastern representative to the most respected general newspaper, the *Asahi Shimbun*, is sufficient to ensure the withdrawal of a cartoon he does not like.[22]

Maybe the best recent example of the ease with which Japanese intellectuals take on the political colouring of their environment is the relationship between most of the Japanese media and the Chinese government. All the major Japanese newspapers except one (the *Sankei Shimbun*) agreed that they would publish only positive stories about China, Mao Tse-tung and the Cultural Revolution, and that they would promote good bilateral relations. This was in exchange for a guarantee that their correspondents in Peking would not be evicted. They never told their readers about this, and for many years the Japanese public had no idea what was actually happening in this large neighbouring country.

*

To sum up what is most crucial in Japanese political culture: the Japanese have never been encouraged to think that the force of an idea could measure up to the physical forces of a government. The key to understanding Japanese power relations is that they are unregulated by transcendental concepts. The public has no intellectual means to a consistent judgement of the political aspects of life. The weaker, ideologically inspired political groups or individuals have no leverage of any kind over the status quo other than the little material pressure they are sometimes able to muster. In short, Japanese political practice is a matter of 'might is right' disguised by assurances and tokens of 'benevolence'.

10

Power in the Guise of Culture

The cohesiveness of the System, the way it succeeds in enmeshing the populace, encapsulating troublesome detractors and neutralising potentially threatening opposition groups, must puzzle anyone who has realised that Japan has no controlling centre. One would not think that a country without a political core could make all its citizens march to the beat of a single drummer. In fact, it does not. But why is it, then, that the many drummers whose sounds the Japanese march to all happen to ruffle and roll the same music?

Part of the answer lies in the active suppression of the personal inclinations of the Japanese, in nearly all social contexts and on all levels, through a programme of character-moulding that helps ensure predictable and disciplined behaviour. Even in leisure activities, the majority of the Japanese appear to be obeying a disembodied but powerful voice telling them where to go and what to do. Those responsible for regulating the traffic of humanity will usually find it quite neatly arranged. Few Japanese in controlling positions will ever be embarrassed by the unexpected.

The ideology of Japaneseness

For most Japanese who give these things thought, the co-ordinating and propelling forces of their social world emanate from 'Japanese culture'. Many will volunteer that they easily work with others, submerge their individuality, totally devote themselves to their companies and co-operate with authority because harmony and loyalty are their highest cultural values. In the same vein, they will explain that they do not upset each other with court cases because their culture frowns on litigation and other confrontational acts.

It is difficult to quarrel with these assertions, because on the surface they appear innocent enough. After all, culture in its broadest definition encompasses everything that has a normative effect on personal behaviour and is transmitted from generation to generation.[1] In every society, culture ensures coherence of communal action and agreement on communal aims. It has been defined as 'the totality of man's products',[2] and as such it includes ideology and power arrangements of all kinds.

But when 'culture' is used to explain Japan, statements such as 'we do this because it is our culture' (i.e. 'we do this because we do this') are not perceived as tautology but are believed to give a valid reason for accepting all manner of practices whose political nature has been lost sight of. Culture thus becomes an excuse for systematic exploitation, for legal abuses, for racketeering and for other forms of uncontrolled exercise of power. In the international realm, culture is made an excuse for not living up to agreements and responsibilities, and for not taking action in the face of pressure from trading partners. A wide variety of political aspects of Japanese life are never scrutinised, since they are justified from the outset as 'culturally determined'.

'Culture' as ideology

The self-consciousness with which Japanese culture is constantly referred to should alert one to its ideological function. 'Culture' is, in fact, working overtime to explain the motives of every Japanese under all circumstances. The implication at times is almost that Japanese individuals have no motives other than those implanted in them by their culture, as if they were all enslaved by some national, autonomous nervous system.

In the prevalent, officially sponsored view, Japanese sacrifice themselves and their family lives for their company, not because this enables their company to expand with minimum costs, but because they are culturally inclined to sacrifice themselves for the group. They submit themselves to conciliation in disputes because of their cultural dislike for courts and lawyers, not because the Justice Ministry limits the number of judges and lawyers to only a fraction of what is required for the functioning of a modern legal system. Army-camp conditions at company dormitories supposedly follow from the Japanese cultural tradition of keeping an eye on youngsters. Japanese interest groups allow themselves to be neutralised by the bureaucracy, not because the politicians exploit them or because, lacking any legal mechanism for redressing their grievances, they are highly dependent on bureaucratic goodwill, but because they are all imbued with the cultural norms of 'harmony'.

The culturist explanation is found everywhere one turns for enlightenment. It even has a powerful hold over a majority of the foreign scholars studying social, economic and political aspects of Japan. In its context the basic determinants of Japanese socio-political life are implicitly placed outside the boundaries of scrutiny and criticism that a political system deserves. And when 'culture' is brought into the discussion, it is expected that all contentious argument should cease, for we are then in the presence of an immutable given. Japanese culture is treated by Japanese spokesmen as if everything subsumed under it is automatically above reproach. The harmony espoused by enterprise labour unions, the loyalty towards employers that keeps husbands away from their families and the inter-meshing relationships of the distribution system that exclude foreigners from the market are sacrosanct cultural achievements. One is made to feel that there is absolutely no room for critical, unappreciative or otherwise negative comments. In the late 1980s such comments as these have a good chance, even, of being labelled 'Japan-bashing' by official spokesmen and the press.

Blinding the world

Japanese officials, commentators and businessmen routinely appeal to 'cultural' reasons for not doing what foreigners think they ought to be doing. The Japanese 'plead understanding for their side in trade disputes on cultural grounds, because of traditional social harmony, or the long history of isolation, or delicate domestic sensitivities . . . never because it would force local businesses into unwelcome competition with foreigners'.[3] Morita Akio of Sony Corporation contends that reciprocity in trade 'would mean changing laws to accept foreign systems that may not suit our culture'.[4]

'Cultural differences' are also a favourite explanation when a Japanese firm tries to wriggle out of a contract. A famous instance of this was the sugar negotiations with Canberra in the late 1970s, after world prices had declined. The Australians were accused of forcing the 'non-contractual' Japanese to abide by the rules of an alien culture.

Westerners, especially Americans, have been quite vulnerable to such arguments. For a period in the mid-1980s, when a common retort to United States criticism of the relatively closed Japanese market was that foreigners were trying to change Japanese culture, the accusation quietened some critics who worried that their demands were indeed, perhaps, a form of sacrilege. The 'cultural defence' ploy is effective because Westerners are often afraid of being thought ethnocentric, which in many eyes is but one step away from being racist.

Government officials demonstrate great conviction that all their actions and everything Japan is held responsible for internationally can be explained by Japanese culture and must therefore be excused. When foreign criticism mounts, the officials and the press, instead of analysing and refuting this criticism, tend to speak of the need to improve their efforts at explaining the Japanese side. Explaining Japan to the world has spawned a formidable sub-industry of writing and publishing. Government agencies and private institutions sponsored by the large business federations are actively involved in the international dissemination of propaganda. A broad and continuous stream of glossy publications – put out by various ministries, the Japan Keizai Koho Centre (attached to the Keidanren), and other semi-official and private bodies – tries to convince foreigners, in particular Japan's irate trading partners, of the cultural origin and therefore the immutable status of the Japanese practices that elicit criticism abroad. The explainers are helped by foreign apologists, many of them scholars or diplomats who accept the culturist argument.

Sometimes there are signs of a recognition that the nature of this effort is propagandistic. After I had written an article for the US publication *Foreign Affairs* on the absence of dominating free-market forces and central leadership in Japan, one Japanese consulate in the United States reported to the Foreign Ministry in Tokyo that my effort might well have wiped out 50 per cent of what had been achieved by Japanese money and energy in a recent public relations campaign.[5]

Enforcing submission through ideology

The extraordinary degree of regimentation and conformism among the ordinary Japanese is maintained by systematically instilled submissive attitudes. The moulding of character so as to foster loyalty through submission dominates Japanese methods of upbringing and is manifest in many areas of adult life. The programme derives its vigour from an ideology that is not generally recognised for what it is: an ideology disguised by the respectable vestments of 'cultural analysis'. Members of each succeeding generation are told that they should obey the dictates of the group because they are Japanese and therefore endowed with a peculiar quality of character that makes them want to be loyal to the group. Japanese thought processes, in contrast with those of the West, are said to be non-rational, non-logical, situational, emotional and socially dependent; and this is presented not as a deficiency, but as a sign of superiority. This culture of submission – the essence of what the Japanese generally refer to as 'typical Japanese culture' – constitutes a pervasive, powerful creed that feeds communal sentiment and supports and justifies political arrangements.

Not every system of ideas or beliefs is an ideology. An ideology, in fact, aims to make contemplative thought superfluous. It bans the adventure of ideas; it is a substitute for explanation. As such, it diminishes our knowledge and thus our perception of socio-political reality, which is why it can be used to disguise existing power relations and serve those in whose interest it is to obfuscate the true political situation as part of an unceasing campaign to make that situation endure.

The ideology of Japaneseness differs, of course, from ideologies that seek to harness political energies to the realisation of a utopian future. Its task, on the contrary, is to make the existing Japanese socio-political world completely acceptable and immune to any advocacy of drastic change. Unlike Western ideologies, it is not something that overrides the immediate demands of society, and so it is not something the individual can appeal to in order to justify thought or behaviour going against the grain of social expectations.

While vast numbers of books help keep the ideology of Japaneseness an active ideology, there is no one work that could be considered its Holy Writ nor, of course, any central institution guarding doctrinal purity. The interests served by Japanese ideology are not quickly identified because they are not represented by a single set of dominating power-holders. This is another reason why this ideology is generally not recognised for what it is, for the dissemination of ideologies is usually assumed to require, first of all, a fairly strong central leadership.

Ideological propaganda, however, need not come from a single, conspiratorial source. A constellation of forces, all merely intent on preserving their interests, is capable of presenting a cohesive, self-serving picture of the world. For all their rivalry and conflicting interests, Japanese groups, each controlling its own province at least partly by 'conspiratorial' methods, are harnessed together in the effort to make the System prevail. Thus they all endorse and help spread the same set of mutually re-inforcing presentations of socio-political reality.

While the System is a fount of propaganda, it does not necessarily follow that all who help purvey this propaganda know that they are propagandists. On the contrary, the seductiveness of Japanese ideology is partly due to the sincerity with which it is offered. And though it is interesting to speculate whether most Japanese power-holders are aware of the deception their propaganda causes, the answer to this question is irrelevant to the analysis of Japanese power relations, since the effect remains the same.

The ideological function of the culturist argument becomes abundantly clear if one traces the lineage of the ideas that form its main ingredients, for at one time they were part of an unambiguous ideology of Japanese superiority.

Four centuries of propaganda

Many of the arguments with which the exercise of extra-legal power is explained and justified today were first heard some four centuries ago. They brought together and modified various strands of older ethical and metaphysical theories so as to buttress the political settlement that followed several centuries of civil war. With the consolidation of Tokugawa power, Japanese schools of thought lost whatever political independence they may have had, and while their teachings on the meaning of life and on proper conduct were amalgamated into a single orthodoxy, the 'heresies' of some previously influential Buddhist sects and of the Christians were suppressed.

The schools of thought acceptable to the shogunate are probably better described as spiritual or intellectual 'movements' within the orthodoxy. A couple of them gradually developed their own heresies, and these helped undermine the credibility of Tokugawa rule in the early nineteenth century. Yet despite their variety they formed, for some two hundred years, the intellectual bedrock for a stagnant political system; and this is a fact of almost inestimable significance.

After an interlude caused by the upheaval accompanying the reopening of Japan to the West and the revolutionary changes brought about by the early Meiji leadership, relatively free political discourse once again had to make way for government-sponsored ideology. 'Traditional cultural values' were not just relied upon to continue as cultural values usually do, without any helping hand from ministers and bureaucrats; they were 'revived'. The formal state ideology constructed in the Meiji period, which served the ruling élite until 1945, consisted of fragments of the scholastic defence of Tokugawa warrior rule, to which was added an important emphasis on the unique superiority of the Japanese political culture.

After another pause, caused by the defeat in war against the United States, the efforts of the social engineers accompanying General Mac-Arthur and indigenous enthusiasm for a legally constituted parliamentary democracy, bits and pieces of the old ideology of uniqueness are being used to knit together the various aspects of the culturalist explanation and to justify political discipline in contemporary Japan. But before examining this contemporary phase further, we must take a closer look at the ideas that Tokugawa and Meiji Japanese were brought up to believe, since without some knowledge of this historical background the intellectual claims now being made by Japanese about their psychology and society will remain largely unintelligible.

Bushido and Zen

The overriding concern of the Tokugawa power-holders was the maintenance of an order totally devoid of any social mobility. All their subjects occupied a fixed place in the formally prescribed class layers, and although power relations among them changed in the natural course of events, there was no theoretical acknowledgement that such changes were possible. Against the background of the shogunate's supreme preoccupation, all injunctions to obedience and submission were welcomed as proper education, regardless of their origin.

The power-holders could draw upon a rich heritage from which to distil a grand ethic of submission. For roughly half a millennium prior to the Tokugawa consolidation, much of Japan had been an intermittent battle-field. This almost constant civil warring naturally encouraged a behavioural code whose main ingredient was blind obedience to fighting leaders. Before 1600 Japan's warrior governments had developed ethics that were later subsumed under the term *bushido*, 'the way of the warrior', ethics that also fostered a willingness to fight to the death, or to execute oneself at the behest of one's lord or the shogunate.[6]

Among the many Japanese versions of religious–philosophical imports from China, Zen Buddhism served particularly well as a further support for the ethic of submission. It is totally amoral and idealises an anti-intellectual approach to life, which supposedly leads to superior modes of perception. The Tokugawa power-holders may not have been aware of it, but the first major propagandist of what was to become Tokugawa ideology was a samurai and Zen monk called Suzuki Shosan (1579–1655).[7] Via a chain of temples and as a private adviser to lower samurai, he spread the notion that to use one's intellect to make judgements is the source of all evil and, more specifically, the source of political subversion.[8] His influence was felt at a level where the new government apparatus touched the lives of commoners. To say that Suzuki Shosan had no respect for the individual is to put it mildly. To him one's body is nothing but 'a bag of phlegm, tears, urine, and excrement' that, in any case, does not belong to oneself, but to the lord to whose generosity one owes one's life.[9] Whatever the body contains, the idea that it may include an individual self is nonsensical.[10]

The glorification of a 'death in life' attitude continued to influence the ideology of Japaneseness at least until 1945. Bushido precepts had been processed into an etiquette for non-fighting samurai, an etiquette summed up in the famous *Hagakure*, written in 1716, which says in its first paragraphs that 'the Way of the samurai is found in death'.[11] The work is both humdrum and extremist. Various stories and aphorisms in it have, through numerous intermediary writings for the common man, gained immortality as part of the ideology of Japaneseness in its more simplistic guises. In 1970 the nation was treated to a real-life demonstration of bushido practice when the author Mishima Yukio (whose earlier flirtations with the warrior etiquette had been taken with a grain of salt) disembowelled himself after exhorting troops of Japan's Self-Defence Forces to rise in rebellion and restore the emperor.

While explicit theories of the self as a worthless entity suitable only for total service to one's superior are no longer widely held, Zen- and bushido-inspired imagery still informs Japanese idealism. Films and television series on samurai and *yakuza* themes tend to take it rather seriously. Though the codes of behaviour in these dramatisations seem extreme to contemporary Japanese, the implicit message is still that audiences today can learn something from the dedication, loyalty and readiness for self-sacrifice evinced by romanticised figures from the past. *Chushingura*, the great epic celebrating the real-life eighteenth-century vendetta conducted by forty-seven retainers against a shogunate official who had humiliated their lord (through misinforming him on a point of etiquette), is brought back again and again on TV, on the stage, in the cinema and in countless comic books. This historical saga, with its many subplots in which wives and daughters are sold into prostitution and relatives are murdered to give the future victim a false sense of security, was most aptly described by Arthur Koestler as 'by all Western standards a tale of sheer dementedness'.[12]

The samurai and *yakuza*, and for that matter the heroic soldiers in films on the Pacific War who represent the same kind of extremist dedication, are thought to be 'real men' in popular Japanese imagery. The ideal male is taciturn and anti-intellectual. As one newspaper editorialised: 'The Japanese do not trust talkative and eloquent people . . . [but] tend to respect people who are poor at speaking. An increasing number of Japanese are beginning to think that the . . . saying "eloquence is an indication of insincerity" applies exactly to Prime Minister Nakasone.'[13]

All this because Nakasone had stated more clearly than his colleagues what he believed to be desirable policies for Japan.

The 'sincerity' of the pure Japanese spirit

Central to the cluster of notions that inspire the imagery of a Japanese spirit is the ideal of *makoto*, which is usually translated as 'sincerity'. But the criteria for this 'sincerity' are somewhat unusual. As in Western languages, it implies that the façade one presents to the world matches one's inner life. But having *makoto* compels one to force one's thinking and emotions into line with what is expected by the surrounding society, rather than to show one's natural feelings. Ideally it involves rearranging one's conscience to fit one's demeanour, by pressing the squirming inner self down to a greater depth. This inculcated attitude of accommodating oneself to the audience undoubtedly has, in everyday Japanese life, a pleasing and soothing effect on the human environment.

Makoto is in conflict with the Western concept of 'genuineness', however, and on a deeper level is a highly political notion. It often promotes socially decreed hypocrisy, because suppressing the self too much is uncomfortable. Its connection with the ideal of fatalistic acceptance of one's socio-political environment is obvious; to be considered *makoto*, individuals must erase their individuality as much as is needed to make them fit in with socio-political exigencies. This connotation of *makoto* indicates a pragmatic awareness of the fact that, throughout the centuries of strict social discipline, many, if not most, ordinary Japanese have not genuinely believed that sacrificing themselves for the sake of others constitutes the ultimate meaning of life. One had to pretend in order to survive, then as today. The famous *Hagakure*, for instance, makes the point that when the wise samurai discovers the meaninglessness of the demanding etiquette, he should guard against giving any hint of this realisation to youth.

The Japanese spirit – as manifested by submission, by *makoto*, by persistence, by sacrifice – is above all a 'pure' spirit. This tradition draws heavily on another of the intellectual movements of the Tokugawa period – Kokugaku, or 'national learning', which went back to ancient Japanese writings for intellectual sustenance. A few decades into the eighteenth century, the devotees of Kokugaku idealised an imaginary prehistoric epoch in which an emperor, freshly placed on the archipelago by the Sun Goddess, presided over a pure and innocent grand family of happy Japanese. These scholars were the first to introduce the modern notion of a Japanese uniqueness and superiority traceable to the original innocence and purity of the race. Unlike the Chinese, the early Japanese needed no laws because they were naturally good and considerate of each other. As the nativist Kamo Mabuchi (1697–1769) expressed it:

> In ancient time, when men's dispositions were straightforward, a complicated system of morals was unnecessary. It would naturally

happen that bad acts might occasionally be committed, but the straightforwardness of men's dispositions would prevent the evil from being concealed and growing in extent. So that in those days it was unnecessary to have a doctrine of right and wrong.[14]

Motoori Norinaga (1730–1801), the towering figure of the Kokugaku movement, also argued that Japan differed from China because it possessed moral excellence. The Chinese rulers had invented the idea of the mandate of Heaven to justify their perfidy and protect themselves against uprisings, whereas the Japanese were moral by nature and superior because they had no need to enunciate moral norms.[15] Although the Kokugaku movement was mainly concerned with linguistic and textual exegeses of domestic classical literature, it had a decisive impact on the political ideology of the subsequent Meiji period and on nationalistic thinking in the twentieth century.

This 'pure' Japan, unsullied by Chinese cultural influence, was referred to as Yamato, after the kingdom that had conquered and assimilated most Japanese kingdoms by the early centuries of the first millennium. The true Japanese were seen as possessing a *yamatogokoro*, a Yamato soul or spirit, with sensibilities superior to those of any other people. The later Kokugaku scholar Hirata Atsutane (1776–1843), whose xenophobic teachings became very influential once Japan had been forced to end its seclusion, preached that it was absolutely essential to purify one's *yamatogokoro*. 'A true Japanese heart and soul was the only valid foundation for discerning truth and error.'[16]

Spiritual training

In the 1970s and 1980s many corporations began to worry about a flagging spirit among their employees, and a number have encouraged them to undergo a discipline called *seishin* training. *Seishin* means 'spirit' or 'mind', but in this context it is closely associated with the idea of 'pure Japanese spirit', and having more of it is supposed to increase one's dedication, perseverance and ability to endure hardship.

Such training usually consists of exercises that lead via mental and physical exhaustion to a breakdown of any resistance to commands. Chanting continuously for a full day and night, kneeling with overseers hovering around ready to whack the less vigorous trainee on his back, will do the job. Marathon running is another favourite. But most of the companies concerned stick to simpler Zen-style meditation (which includes the occasional whack on the back), or military drills of the kind that salaryman recruits receive at the company's mountain retreat. Either way, the achievement of the successful *seishin* trainee is the ability to remain mentally calm while unconditionally submitting to authority.

There are good reasons for the salaryman to take such training seriously.

Evaluations of the personal qualities of company staff members for the purpose of promotion often tend to be made 'in terms of a framework provided by the seishin orientation'.[17] The higher up one goes in Japanese organisational life, the more attention is given to such considerations, 'particularly along those avenues to leadership positions commonly described as "the élite course" '.[18] Many large Japanese corporations contain an élite subculture very responsive to this special emphasis on 'spirit', with its overtones from the past, prodding the salarymen – and especially the more ambitious among them – to adhere to its standards and to spread them downward.

Orthodoxies as condition for Japanese order

To people who have been brought up in an environment of free intellectual discourse, the severe restrictions that an ideology imposes on the uses of the human mind are not readily apparent. There is a world of difference between adhering to an ideology that one has freely chosen from among a variety of philosophical speculations on the human condition, and having been indoctrinated with an ideology in a socio-political setting that is hostile to competing ideas and beliefs.

Throughout the past four centuries, the Japanese have lived constantly with orthodoxies. And dominating orthodoxies have been and continue to be necessary for the manner in which Japanese power is exercised. In the 1980s the situation is of course much more relaxed than it was in the pre-war days of direct 'thought control'. But we have seen – to take only two examples – that police, prosecutors and the judiciary do not take kindly to ideological heterodoxy, and that the Japanese press does not begin to question the unwritten tenets on which the System is based.

Without the persistent suppression of ideas that could have given birth – as they did in other societies – to a tradition of critical political theory, the Japanese System could not have continued to the present day. Left to take its own course, Japanese culture would have evolved transcendental values, as all major cultures have. But it did not, because political power has been consciously used to suppress ideas that would demand a transformation of the System into a state.

The suppression of dangerous Tokugawa thought

Until well into the nineteenth century it was virtually impossible for Japanese commoners or samurai to shape a comprehensive body of critical thought contradicting what the shogunate wanted them to believe. But even when Japan's isolation ensured that the ordinary public had no way of knowing how other populations were ruled, there was still enough foreign- and domestic-inspired doubt to give the warrior regime a problem in convincing lower lords and their more intelligent vassals, as well as a class of literati, that the governmental structure which it headed could not be improved upon. There had, after all, been the early Chinese model of statecraft, and during the centuries of civil war some indigenous Buddhist sects had enriched the arid intellectual scene with teachings that might perhaps have grown into a conceptual foundation for attacking the incumbent power-holders. Then there were the expelled Portuguese missionaries, whose legacy could have inspired budding political theorists with ideas about alternative ways to run a country. And the Dutch, even though carefully kept in political quarantine on an artificial island off Nagasaki, were living specimens from a society with very un-Japanese attributes.

As a new scholastic class took over the intellectual lead from the Buddhist priests of pre-Tokugawa days, and as learning was encouraged among the samurai to keep this subsidised leisure class from meddling in politics, circumstances ripened for a proliferation of potentially subversive ideas among the élite. The warrior regime did not formulate, or order the formulation of, any ideology to guard against subversion, but it made clear what could and could not be said, and it enforced these rules. So there was no heretical thought, and 'those whose speech and practice were different were driven underground'.[19]

Discussion of government affairs was simply forbidden. Criticism of anything involving power relations was treated as treason. Although, over its two-and-a-half-century existence, the Tokugawa regime showed alternating cycles of severity and laxity, it always retained a complete monopoly on moral standards, including those relating to such 'dangerous phenomena' as samurai mixing with commoners or talking about the events of the day. Its officials maintained an elaborate censorship system that scrutinised even trivial literature and pictures. 'Since anything "new" posed a danger to the class structure, the government was especially eager to suppress books and broadsides that mentioned new currents of thought or anything unusual.'[20] It was against such a background of suppression that a number of neo-Confucianist movements flourished.

Neo-Confucian orthodoxy

Neo-Confucianism, especially that of the Chu Hsi school, was able to become the mainstay of Tokugawa orthodoxy because it offered a perspective on the universe that would be the dream of any authoritarian bureaucratic regime. According to it, both the social and the natural order are in concord with unchanging principles of nature. Thus questions as to why those in charge are in charge, and why everyone beneath them should remain 'in their proper station', were simply banned from rational discourse.

As we have seen in Chapter 6, Japanese neo-Confucianism developed theories in which the priorities of Chinese Confucianism were turned upside-down by making loyalty to the ruler, instead of filial piety, the overriding moral command. Yoshikawa Koretaru summed it up: 'There can be desertion of one's parents for the Sovereign's sake, but there can be no reason to desert the Sovereign for a parent's sake.'[21] Later, the Meiji oligarchy was to create a myth of the emperor as the benevolent father of all Japanese. Yamazaki Ansai, a student of Yoshikawa Koretaru and a highly influential early Tokugawa thinker, held that rulers, whether virtuous or depraved, should be served with blind loyalty. In a combination of neo-Confucianism and Shinto, Yamazaki viewed existing political and social structures as metaphysically blessed. For him, political change could never be legitimate and was simply unthinkable.[22]

In the latter part of the Tokugawa period, the Hayashi family and their academy became official standard-bearers of the neo-Confucianist explications of the laws of nature and human society, which by then had been precisely fitted to power relations under the regime.[23] Yet intellectual life was not completely predictable. Occasionally the Tokugawa 'schoolmen' could exercise their minds by following some lively dispute among their colleagues. The major political thinker of the period, Ogyu Sorai (1666–1728), shook them up by taking the ideas of earlier advocates of a return to an older Confucianism, and constructing a coherent theory of the immutability of established political institutions throughout historical change. For Sorai, the ancient Chinese sage-kings had created these institutions as instruments of the Confucian Way; they provided a moral principle embodied in governmental structures and surviving any transformations these might undergo.[24]

Whereas Tokugawa thought was not immune to change and encompassed scholarly trends that were at odds with one another, the more it changed the more its political thrust remained the same. The participants in Tokugawa intellectual life upheld an orthodoxy not in the sense that they all said the same thing, but in what they did not say. Their debates never recognised the possibility of dissent on basic socio-political matters. Together, they excluded the possibility of heterodoxy. In their world-view the moral autonomy of the individual person did not exist; this was the core of the ideology. The regime, for its part, appreciated the necessity of a certain measure of doctrinal flexibility. From the mid-eighteenth century onward, the intellectual fashion within the government and in many of the domain schools advocated the adjustment of ideology to uphold authority against the background of changing history.[25]

The teachers of the Wang Yangming (Oyomei) school, which stressed reliance on intuition in determining what was morally sound, were similarly staunch in their support of the shogunate until almost the very end.[26] As for the Kokugaku movement, Mabuchi started from the premiss that the temporal order was sacred, since ultimately it was governed by the inviolable imperial institution. Motoori Norinaga further endorsed the Tokugawa political arrangement by portraying it as completely in accordance with the intentions of the Sun Goddess. Besides finding it outrageous ever to judge the character of the sovereign, he preached unconditional submission to those of higher rank.[27]

The proponents of formally tolerated Tokugawa thought all propagated the view that the order that had been imposed was immutable, being in tune with nature and in accordance with the will of a multitude of divinities. Even among themselves, they strove for more 'purity' and for greater 'loyalty', just as in the 1920s and until the end of the war Japan's super-patriots, disagreeing with the authorities and the rest of the population, tried to outdo each other in demonstrations of love for the emperor.

Evidence that the demands for total submission went against the grain with many individuals three centuries ago is seen in the popular culture of the day. Drama and fiction were obsessed with the conflict between *giri*, meaning duty as stipulated by the dictates of a strict society, and *ninjo*, meaning natural human feelings – especially, in this context, the feelings of those obliged to kill a relative or abandon a lover. The *giri–ninjo* dichotomy is still used today, and many Japanese believe that *ninjo* are uniquely Japanese human feelings that cannot be understood by foreigners. The theatre and literature of the Tokugawa period were suffused with imagery based on this theme. Present-day kabuki would be practically nothing without it, and movie and TV audiences, and comic-book readers, cannot get enough of it either. In history, *giri* always won out over *ninjo* in the end. But in the meantime, the dramatic treatment of the quandary provided the symbols needed to understand the human predicament.

In contemporary Japan the tradition of political theory is too weak to eliminate the lingering neo-Confucianist sense that the socio-political hierarchy conforms to a natural order. Very few Japanese question the superior power of the bureaucrats, which has no legal basis whatsoever. The political arrangements of the Tokugawa period were presented as perfect in that they conformed to 'the order found in the manifold natural phenomena of heaven and earth'.[28] Today, the Prime Minister's Office and other government departments are forever conducting surveys of social practices, attitudes and opinion, not in order to know what is going on but to translate their findings into a model of proper Japanese behaviour. Study groups attached to government offices publish reports delineating an ideal Japanese identity. The public is regularly reassured, in the form of an opinion report, that 90 per cent of it belongs to the middle class. Japanese women are told that they *want* to give up their work after they marry and stay at home until they have brought up at least one child.

The construction of a national identity

While the moral injunctions chaining people to their proper stations that permeated life in the Tokugawa period had religious qualities, the various ideological strands were not yet woven into a single grand faith that could be summed up concisely. Only after Japan had come out of its isolation were ideological fragments, old mythology and new patriotic sentiments mixed into an all-encompassing Japanese faith, in the name of which millions of Japanese were to give their lives and still more millions of other Asians to lose theirs. The Meiji oligarchy, in its attempt to mould a state commanding the allegiance of commoners as well as the members of the samurai caste it had just abolished, quite consciously created the new faith to serve political purposes.

Many writers have concluded that no other people in a major nation lived through more changes in a mere score of years than the Japanese of the early Meiji period. B. H. Chamberlain, an eyewitness of the times, begins his famous book *Things Japanese* with the observation that to have lived through those events 'makes a man feel preternaturally old; for here he is in modern times, with the air full of talk about bicycles and bacilli and "spheres of influence", and yet he can himself distinctly remember the Middle Ages'.[29] What began as a *coup d'état* grew into a momentous political transition. Both power-holders and government structures were new. Probably the single most revolutionary change was one that followed from the creation of national military forces: after centuries of being forbidden on pain of death to possess any kind of weapon, able-bodied men of non-samurai caste were trained to fight. For the first time Japanese commoners became, very tangibly, involved in the aims of the state.

Just when the general public was becoming a political factor, the importation of foreign theories made many Japanese aware that government was something that could be scrutinised. The examples of foreign government systems prompted urgent questions about the government at home. Curious Japanese minds had to be inoculated against the potentially subversive foreign ideas of individualism, liberalism and democracy. The exercise of power in Japan had to be explained and justified in ways never required before, and new methods of control had to be introduced.

This entailed, among other things, the articulation of a national identity. No foreign wars of the kind that periodically ravaged Europe had stimulated a 'natural' growth of any consciousness of shared national aims. Between 1600 and 1850 France had been at war for a total of 115 years, Britain for 125, Russia for 124, Spain for 160 and Austria for 129.[30] During the same period Japan had fired at only one United States ship that, defying a ban, approached its coast.[31] Compelling new nationalist beliefs that would simultaneously strengthen Japan against the pushy Western powers and justify the rule of the new oligarchy were obviously necessary.

The Men of Meiji had concluded that the source of Western power, which in their eyes appeared overwhelming, lay precisely in those universalistic and transcendental systems of thought and belief that Japan lacked: the Western legal systems, the US constitution and especially the Christian religion. The impression was widespread that the Western powers had purposely adopted Christianity because it was the best instrument with which to conquer the world. Shortly before the Meiji Restoration one scholar had already explained that Christianity was 'a trick that European rulers used to "make their peoples docile and easy to lead" '.[32]

From the very start of the Meiji period, religion became an official concern. The oligarchs left no doubt that they considered it very much their business. A major figure among them, Ito Hirobumi, concluded that, because Japanese religions were feeble, some substitute had to be found.[33] The links between the government and religion were the subject of a hot debate in the early 1870s, touched on by Nishi Amane, a major thinker of the so-called Meiji Enlightenment, in a series of magazine articles. He advocated tolerance, but warned that religion should not interfere with the interests of the state. He also strongly urged that the government should not rely on religion: 'How can any regime avoid destruction and ruin if . . . it relies on something the falseness of which it conceals?'[34] He criticised moves by the new rulers to establish a state religion. The government in the meantime created a Shinto Department, organised a national shrine system and sent out missionaries to co-opt Buddhist priests in undermining the influence of Buddhism. But this early movement to establish a state religion petered out because of the reluctance of the priests to endorse and propagandise the new nationalist faith, and because the whole effort made Japan look bad in Western eyes.[35]

The solution proposed by another Meiji Enlightenment luminary, Nakamura Masanao (famous as translator of John Stuart Mill's *On Liberty*), was that the emperor should set an example by being baptised a Christian.[36] Emperor Mutsuhito (posthumously called Meiji) did not take this advice, though eventually he was made to set another kind of example by adding milk and beef to his diet. It was believed that since these products came from a big and sturdy animal they would make the Japanese as big and sturdy as the Westerners who had been eating beef and drinking milk for centuries.[37]

While Christianity did not prove to be the answer, the Meiji oligarchy did make the emperor the key to a quasi-religious solution. Invoking an imagined Japanese antiquity for the formula they settled on, the new power-holders sought to legitimise themselves through a divine emperor of their own creation.

'National essence' and the imperial blessing

In their attempt to convince the Japanese citizen that the emperor was a unique blessing, the Meiji power-holders had a rich tradition to draw on. Japan's first interpretative history, the *Gukansho* (written by a politically involved Buddhist monk in 1219), reaffirmed that the essence of Japan lay in the uniqueness of its sacred imperial line. Whereas China selected its emperors, the single Japanese line had been created by the Sun Goddess, who had also bequeathed the specific arrangement whereby emperors ruled – in ways that were different but appropriate to the various stages of history.[38]

Roughly a century later when, confounding the *Gukansho*, there were two rival emperors, the most learned participant in the politics of this schism, Kitabatake Chikafusa, wrote a scholarly treatise in support of the emperor of his choice. In this famous work on the divine nature of the imperial line, much was made of the unique relationship between throne and people. To describe this phenomenon Chikafusa used the ancient, Chinese-derived term *kokutai*, which in the Japanese context is generally translated as 'national essence'. This concept eventually became the centrepiece of the Yamatoist ideology with which the Japanese were indoctrinated until 1945.

As we just saw, a number of seventeenth- and eighteenth-century thinkers also found proof of Japanese superiority in the sacredness of the unbroken imperial line. Yamaga Soko, an important seventeenth-century theorist of the imperial institution, held that Japan – and not China – was the real Middle Kingdom, and that Shinto had guided the development of Confucianism. His arguments were built around the notion of *kokutai*.

The concept of *kokutai* was popularised again in 1825 by Aizawa Seishisai, compiler of the *Shinron* or *New Theses*, whose contentions were to become a major ingredient in the artificial religion constructed by the Meiji oligarchy. Ironically, it was the power of the West that inspired Aizawa, who believed that Western rulers had achieved a better *kokutai* than the Tokugawa regime.[39]

The power-holders who helped determine the ideas of the Meiji intelligentsia seized enthusiastically on *kokutai*. In censorship instructions to the press issued in 1873, *kokutai* was already included as a subject that could not be criticised.[40]

It took about twenty years before the various strands of Yamatoist propaganda were woven together into a comprehensive mythology of the state. It was spread among the public by two powerful organs that had also been created by the oligarchy: the conscript military and the national education system.

From the 1880s onward, Japanese history books for use in schools did not begin with the Stone Age, but with the gods from which the emperor was a direct descendant. Hints of the kind of indoctrination that the nation was to undergo for half a century could be gleaned from the Imperial Rescript to Soldiers and Sailors of 1882. But the Imperial Rescript on Education, issued eight years later, was the first official statement to serve as a basis for deciding what was and what was not truly Japanese. It enjoined the cultivation, to the greater glory of the emperor, of loyalty and filial piety and twelve other virtues. These ideas were incorporated in all the textbooks used in *shushin* (moral training), the first lesson of the day in all the schools. Already in 1892 elementary-school pupils were memorising lines in which they promised to sacrifice their lives gladly for the emperor.[41] As the Japanese Ministry of Education summed it up for the rest of the world:

Descended in a direct line from the heavenly deities, the Emperor has stood unshaken in his high place through all generations [in a relation to his subjects] of father and child rather than of master and servant. The imperial family was the parental house; the subjects were as relatives and connections.[42]

Before the arrival of Western ideas, Shinto revivalists could talk about little else apart from the sacredness of the emperor without falling back on Confucianism. Even though they would have preferred a 'return' to the pure Japanese innocence that existed before native religion was besmirched by Chinese thought, Shintoism had produced no sacred texts, doctrines, moral codes or philosophical treatises, and had little more to offer than the idea of an unbroken line of emperors. The discourse revolving around *kokutai* ideology also inevitably had to borrow Confucianist concepts of the family, but it broadened these to encompass the new centrally governed Japan, and incorporated Prussian organismic theories that supported a strong state.

The lessons extolling the 'family state' were accompanied by warnings that the national spirit could be threatened by dangerous and un-Japanese thought. Eager Meiji-period students were exposed to a vast spectrum of Western ideas that included British liberalism, Rousseau's popular sovereignty, Anglo-American empiricism, utilitarianism and social Darwinism. Hegelian ideas of the state found Japanese interpreters, even before the introduction of Marxism and anarchism. But increasing suspicion was thrown on Western systems of moral or political thought providing a conceptual framework that could encompass all human experience.

By the beginning of this century Yamatoist mythology had sufficient consistency to serve as a substitute religion. Whereas in the 1880s it was possible to believe that all nations had a *kokutai* in some form or another, after the turn of the century it was a monopoly of Japan.[43] Initially, *kokutai* was rendered in English as 'national polity', but later it was more often than not described as a concept that could not be conveyed in any foreign language, because it was imbued with uniquely Japanese spiritual significance. As a Japanese historian said, summing up the political evolution of the Meiji period:

A change had taken place from . . . when the state had been observed, studied and criticised . . . by law, by myth, and by the revival of ancient ethics the State was to be revered; it had become something to be obeyed submissively. One no longer explained the State, one *believed* in it![44]

That many appeared to believe in it can be gathered from a dissertation with which George Etsujiro Uyehara received a doctorate degree at the

London School of Economics in 1910. The Japanese, Uyehara explained, had lived under one and the same government ever since the first (mythological) emperor Jimmu, and had always scrupulously maintained their ethnic unity.[45] For him, proof that Japan was one big family resided in the fact that the Japanese all behave in the same way and have the same feelings. A 'strong affection for the country stirs their whole nervous system'. The emperor system 'penetrates to their very flesh and bone'. From the emperor, 'everything emanates; in him everything subsists; there is nothing on the soil of Japan existent independent of him. He is the sole owner of the Empire, the author of law, justice, privilege, and honour, and the symbol of the unity of the Japanese nation.' It occurred to the LSE doctoral candidate that the emperor was not much in evidence in the governing of Japan, but this was no problem, since 'there is no need for the Sovereign of Japan to make any attempt to show his personal greatness'.

'Samuraisation' of the countryside

The 'family state' ideology, along with military values and a military approach to social organisation, was effectively spread throughout the country by the large new army of conscripts. This and the education system together brought about a rapid 'samuraisation' of the country: a dissemination, among the lower layers of the population, of the disciplinary ideals and extremist 'loyalty' code that had exemplified the education of samurai.

In the first decades of the twentieth century the Army gradually infiltrated the countryside. It insinuated itself into local councils, exploited the rural population's commitment to the small community and combined its own priorities with those decreed by natural village custom. In 1910 the Imperial Military Reserve Association was established. It was followed in 1915 by the Greater Japan Youth Association, promoted by the military élite, the Naimusho and the Ministry of Education. In 1926 military training centres for youth were set up by the military and education bureaucrats. Nationally organised women's defence organisations completed the effort. Through these four organisations, which in 1935 had an enrolment of between eleven and twelve million people,[46] the Army set up a gigantic apparatus for indoctrination. Thus by the onset of the war in China the organisers of the 'family state' had gained considerable control over what went into the hearts and minds of Japanese between the ages of 6 and 40: via the schools up to age 14, via the youth associations between 14 and 20 and via military service and the reservist associations from 20 onward.

Heritage of pre-war 'culture'

If a Japanese official or intellectual today were to start talking about the 'heavenly task', 'sovereign path' or 'moral way', most of his compatriots would think that he had gone out of his mind. Even though a minority believes that Japan did not unconditionally surrender in 1945 (because the imperial institution was left intact), the atomic bombs of August 1945 proved that the unique and divinely ordained *kokutai* could not ultimately save the nation in war. For the first time in history, foreign conquerors arrived to disprove the notion of superior valour based on ethnic unity and an unbroken line of emperors. On New Year's Day 1946 the Japanese were informed by their morning newspapers of an imperial proclamation assuring them that 'the ties between Us and Our people . . . are not predicated on the false conception that the Emperor is divine and that the Japanese are superior to other races and fated to rule the world'. But a booklet published by the Japanese cabinet in November 1946 to explain the new constitution could still state that *kokutai*, now interpreted as meaning 'the basic characteristics of the nation', was the foundation of Japan's existence, and that its substance was the adoration of the people for the emperor as the national uniting force.[47] The Japanese concept of the nation automatically implies that it will endure for ever. In this respect the concepts expressed in the idea of *kokutai* are still a basic factor in contemporary thought.

In trying to establish how much of Tokugawa and Meiji ideology survives in contemporary Japan, one is on shakier ground. One reason for this is that the Japanese are content with vague meanings, another the great ambivalence with which the Japanese approach their traditional ideals and the problem of their identity. On the one hand, many of the common terms of early twentieth-century propaganda seem absurdly anachronistic today. On the other, popular books on psychological and sociological themes still preach the political submission of the individual by 'analysing' this as the Japanese way; corporations claim to be large and benevolent families, and the belief in racial uniqueness and superiority is fairly widespread.

The ethics of submission and wartime mythology continually appear as a theme in popular entertainment.[48] Much pre-war propaganda has seeped through to present-day Japan. In the late 1980s this appears to have the potential to flood the nation with the old imagery as a result of a collective attack of self-pity and self-doubt brought on by, say, international sanctions against Japanese trade.

The Japanese sense of uniqueness and superiority

Japanese are continuously being reminded of the uniqueness of their culture and the specialness of their beliefs, customs and approach to life by their teachers, newspapers and TV programmes. These ideas are confirmed by numerous oblique references in government publications, and hammered home by a unique species of literature devoted to the subject. Called *nihonjinron* ('theorising on the Japanese'), this literature not only emphasises the notion that Japanese are incomparably different, but often claims that the Japanese state of being is preferable, because superior, to what the rest of the world has to offer.[49] Though sometimes embodied in very far-fetched hypotheses, nihonjinron nevertheless gives expression to widely held popular beliefs. Japanese readers may dismiss what they think are exaggerations yet still be confirmed in their core ideas about the uniqueness of their society. The theories marketed under the nihonjinron label may conflict with each other in their parts, but all reiterate common themes of contrast between Japanese and Western thinking and behaviour.

Warm, wet and illogical

On the whole, nihonjinron concedes that Japanese do not believe in universal values and are 'not logical'. It portrays such traits as assets that supposedly give Japanese closer contact with the here and now of concrete circumstances, and make them more loving towards other people. Western ways and manners are said to be 'dry' or 'hard', those of Japan are 'wet' and 'soft'. Unlike Westerners – and, for that matter, the Chinese – who are individual and unconnected like grains of sand, the Japanese, as a result of their 'wetness' and 'softness', stick together like glutinous rice. Similarly, Western reason is held to be 'cold', 'dry' and 'intolerant', while the Japanese approach is thought to be 'warm', 'wet' and therefore more humane. Nihonjinron theorists believe that Japanese are extremely sensitive to each other's needs and have a special gift for wordless communication. All emphasise the primacy of the group rather than the individual, and imply that Japanese prefer to submerge their own selves in the communal life.

Nakasone Yasuhiro, one of Japan's stronger post-war prime ministers, is a devout adherent of nihonjinron theories. He believes in a special Japanese compassion that derives from a 'monsoon culture' (in the summer Japan is very humid, warm and sticky). For him, Christian love must have derived from the same Asian monsoon culture that produced Buddhism. It could not have come out of the desert climate of the Middle East, which produced the Judaeo–Christian values of 'an eye for an eye, a tooth for a tooth'. In a 1986 speech Nakasone did not mince his words in talking of Japan's international mission to spread its monsoon-inspired compassion to the rest of the world.[50] He also implied that contracts are a product of the non-compassionate desert culture.

This type of 'analysis' comes straight from the nationalist philosopher of ethics Watsuji Tetsuro (1889–1960), who was a major apologist for Japan's conquests, believing them to be part of a destiny imposed upon the nation by the pressure of world history. His famous pre-war work Climate and Culture has inspired many a nihonjinron practitioner.[51] In addition to the 'monsoon' and 'desert' type cultures, Watsuji also postulated the existence of a 'meadow' type, found primarily in Europe. Most Westerners are a mixed product of meadow and desert, which means they are capable of gentle love as well as dry, abstract, contractual reasoning. Japan has, according to Watsuji, a very peculiar version of the monsoon culture, producing people 'full of emotional vitality and sensitivity'. All this allegedly fosters intimate, family-style relations among Japanese.[52]

Ordinary Japanese people have never been encouraged to take this kind of writing with a grain of salt.

Very little serious writing by Japanese on anything relating to their society is entirely free of *nihonjinron* influence. It is also amazing how much *nihonjinron* has crept into assessments by foreign authors. The possibility of coercion or indoctrination as formative factors of Japanese behaviour is not considered in the universe of *nihonjinron* imagery. And therein lies its propagandistic force. In the *nihonjinron* perspective, Japanese limit their actions, do not claim 'rights' and always obey those placed above them, not because they have no other choice, but because it comes naturally to them. Japanese are portrayed as if born with a special quality of brain that makes them want to suppress their individual selves.

It is striking how casually Japanese seem to accept that they are physically 'a race apart' from other peoples. I have heard officials explain to foreign businessmen that medicine manufactured by foreign firms must undergo special tests before being allowed into Japan because of the different construction of Japanese bodies.[53] The former chairman of the association of agricultural co-operatives, Zenchu, Iwamochi Shizuma, once explained before an audience of foreign correspondents that since 'everyone knows that Japanese intestines are about one metre longer than those of foreigners' we should all understand that American beef was not suitable for digestion by Japanese. Visiting Washington in December 1987, the chairman of the Liberal Democratic Party's agricultural policy research council, Hata Tsutomu, also spoke of longer Japanese digestive tracts that had difficulty in coping with red meat.[54]

The great 'scientific proof' of Japanese uniqueness was supposed to have arrived with the famous studies of Dr Tsunoda Tadanobu, who discovered that Japanese brains are essentially different from Western brains or, indeed, the brains of most other people in the world. According to this researcher, Japanese hear insect sounds, temple bells, humming and snoring with the left half of the brain, whereas Westerners do so with the right half.

Dr Tsunoda implies that Japanese reasoning is different from that of other people because they use their two brain halves differently. His testing methods are highly suspect. My impression, based on an account by one of his foreign guinea-pigs, is that auto-suggestion plays an important role. Yet his books sell well in Japan, and his views have been officially credited to the extent of being introduced abroad by the semi-governmental Japan Foundation.[55]

A popular sub-category of *nihonjinron* theories concerns the Japanese language, which is widely thought by Japanese to be particularly difficult to learn, not because of its insanely complicated writing system, but because it possesses a 'spirit' unlike any in other languages. This spirit, called *kotodama*, was an important mythological ingredient of the pre-war ideology of superior uniqueness. It is seen as manifest in *yamato kotoba*, the supposedly pure Japanese words which can express profound meanings beyond the semantic capabilities of the linguistic borrowings from China and the West.[56] The belief in the uniqueness of the Japanese language is important for *nihonjinron* practitioners in general, who like to furnish new evidence of Japanese uniqueness by contrasting the delicate nuances and connotations of Japanese words with their supposedly cruder Western counterparts.

Inspired by a survey on the Japanese way of thinking conducted by the Institute for Statistical Mathematics, affiliated to the Ministry of Education, Yamamoto Shichihei, a major *nihonjinron* author, has concluded that Japan's youth are returning to the values and social attitudes of the Tokugawa period. He characterises this Tokugawa-type Japanese as conforming to traditional discipline in a relaxed manner, accepting and enjoying it without strenuous or conscious effort. For him this is the best way to enjoy the present, because one need not try to be anything but one's natural self. And he claims that all this is possible because Japanese society functions on the basis of a quasi-blood-relation community.[57] In 1971, pretending to be a Jew who admired aspects of Japanese uniqueness, Yamamoto wrote and published the first and one of the biggest *nihonjinron* best-sellers.

The *nihonjinron* writings can be seen as essays defending the ideology of Japaneseness against the encroachment of Western concepts of individual worth, against the Western example of political self-assertion and against the threat that Western logical consistency poses for Japan's political culture. As such, *nihonjinron* is comparable to the nativist Kokugaku reaction to Chinese learning in the Tokugawa period. Both then and now the attempt to prove superiority is evident. The Kokugaku scholars portrayed the Japanese as superbly moral in comparison with the Chinese, who had not understood the morality of their own teachings. Under Motoori Norinaga's most famous disciple, Hirata Atsutane, Japanese traditions were extolled as having had a major influence on foreign countries. Even in countries far to the west of India, people believed that heaven, earth and humankind were created by a great God. 'Accordingly, Japan is the original ancestor of all countries, the main or root country of the world. The Emperor is the sole true Son of Heaven and sovereign of the world, destined to rule all within the four seas as lord and master.'[58] Today Japan is portrayed as teaching foreigners to 'love world peace'; and it is held up to the world as a model of strength achieved through harmony. Throughout *nihonjinron* there are echoes of Japanese wartime imagery about the loss of will in the West, contrasted with the strength and dynamism of a Japan made superior through collective hard work.

The Japanese government (encouraged by then prime minister Nakasone) has decided to sponsor an inter-university centre that will investigate the distinctiveness of Japanese culture in order to present its findings to a world that, so the explanation goes, is full of misunderstanding about Japan. Judging by the writings of some of the scholars associated with the project, an entirely new approach to the concept of civilisation will be attempted.[59]

The ulterior aim of the centre seems to be to lift assessments of Japan – its history, social customs and politics – out of the general international discourse. To its credit, the Japanese press – though not averse to presenting explanations based on the *nihonjinron* perspective – has demurred at government participation in the new institute in Kyoto. The *Asahi Shimbun*, for instance, remarked that foreign countries will not pay much attention to the pronouncements of a group of Japanese professors who follow the lead of their 1930s predecessors, and a *Yomiuri Shimbun* editorial reminded the authorities that the era has passed when the government can decide how an individual must live.

The myth of homogeneity

An essential tenet of *nihonjinron*, and a core concept of Japan's current political ideology, is the supposed homogeneity of the Japanese people. The old myth of racial purity and social homogeneity has come back in a new guise. Ignoring the great regional variety in customs, attitudes and concerns – as well as the almost 3 million *burakumin* (decendants of former outcasts), plus almost one million Japanese-born Koreans, the Okinawans, a small number of Ainu and hundreds of thousands of naturalised and native-born Japanese of recent Korean, Chinese and other foreign ancestry – the Japanese are asked to be proud of the fact that their country harbours no minorities and that they are all driven by the same group-centred ethics. Judged by the context in which it is constantly used, 'homogeneity' is a code word for uniqueness.

The Ministry of Foreign Affairs, in a 'blue book', a diplomatic report published in the summer of 1985, congratulated the nation on its great economic successes and attributed them to its racial homogeneity. Other officials, but most conspicuously Nakasone, have indicated that there is good reason to be grateful for the fact that they have not had to accommodate representatives of other races on their soil. In September 1986 Nakasone caused consternation in the United States and elsewhere when he said that the USA was a less 'intelligent' society than Japan because of its black and Hispanic minorities.[60] This was not misunderstood or quoted out of context, as the Ministry of Foreign Affairs claimed in the face of disturbed US reactions. His words were contained in a speech intended solely for Japanese ears, in the context of his long-term campaign to stimulate ethnic pride among the public. Only two of some fifty Japanese journalists who heard him speak found it worth reporting,

since Nakasone had made similar statements before and many Japanese
share such views.

In a 1980 government report to the Human Rights Commission of the
United Nations, Japan denied the existence of minorities in its society.
Such official denial is of great symbolic significance, since the idea of
Japanese homogeneity is vitally important to Japan's administrators.
When foreign nationals become naturalised, they are strongly encouraged
to adopt a Yamato (ethnic-majority) name for their official registration,
despite the absence of any such legal requirement. Officials from the
Ministry of Justice oppose the use of non-Yamato names written in the
Japanese syllabary on the grounds that such names 'do not match the
single-race Japanese society'.[61]

Another manifestation of the homogeneity myth is the image of Japan
as a classless society, with only slight differences between rich and poor.
Every year since 1958 the government has surveyed the Japanese to find
out what they think of their own social status, and since the mid-1960s an
increasing majority – which has climbed to 90 per cent in the 1980s – has
described itself as 'middle class'. The result of this poll is almost invariably
an occasion for the newspapers once again to congratulate their readers on
the fact that they all belong to a homogeneous nation of which they can be
proud. The reports are based on a subjective evaluation; no standard for
the concept 'middle class' is provided, and there is no hint concerning
differences in income.

If incomes are measured against the domestic buying power of the yen, a
considerable number of Japanese must be considered relatively poor.
Several government officials have conceded that real unemployment
rates are roughly double the official figure, and by some calculations they
must be about triple. On the other hand, Japan learned in 1987 to its
great surprise that it had twenty-two billionaires, one more than the
USA (which has double Japan's population). One of them was worth
$21 billion.[62] Exchange rates and horrendously inflationary land prices no
doubt helped boost the statistic, but the people listed must have had
considerable wealth to begin with. In short, it is not reasonable to describe
Japanese society as 'one-class' or 'classless'.

The notions of homogeneity and of a special Japanese purity of
character are often linked together. This is rarely spelled out in so many
words, but it is conveyed in films and television serials in their treatment of
the encounter between Japanese culture and the ways of foreigners.

The idea of a 'pure' *yamato gokoro* or *yamato damashii* (the soul or spirit
of the Yamato people, the true Japanese, a mystical core untainted by
Chinese or Western cultural influence) has made quite a dramatic come-
back, after several decades, following the defeat of 1945, in which it was
kept out of sight. But even if the *yamato gokoro* is not explicitly
mentioned, in the 1980s the idea of homogeneity has begun to be
accompanied by an increased use in the media of the term *minzoku* to
denote the Japanese people or 'race', implying an organismal, familial

solidarity, in some contexts comparable to the Nazi usage of the German *Volk*. Prime Minister Nakasone seemed, judging by some of his speeches, to prefer *minzoku* to *kokumin* or *minshu*, terms for 'people' without the racial overtones, and it is also frequently used in official publications and explanations given by bureaucrats of Japanese attitudes and behaviour. In government reports one finds traces of the assertions once recorded in the *Kokutai no Hongi*, a tract published in 1937 by the Ministry of Education and listing the essential points of the 'national essence'. These supposedly ancient qualities are said to have made Japan the sole industrial power that has created a prosperous society of great harmony, without hostile classes tearing the fabric of national unity.

Serious Western observers of Japan also tend to endorse the reasoning that racial and social homogeneity explain the social cohesion and the 'consensus' and co-operation in politics, frequently pointing out that the mixing of the races took place more than a millennium ago in Japan. Such logic is attractive, especially for observers brought up in a melting-pot country such as the United States or with first-hand experience of recent adjustment problems caused by the influx of migrant workers and former colonial subjects in some European countries. But Japan's 'homogeneity' cannot explain what it sets out to explain, and is very misleading in that it makes one ignore the problematic Japanese minorities that do exist, and an unacknowledged but very significant measure of social tension.

It is true that open disagreement makes many Japanese feel distinctly uncomfortable. The centuries-old approach of blaming both parties to a conflict still continues today. It has been a very effective mechanism for making Japanese subjects put on a continuous show of getting on famously with each other. But Japanese do not love their neighbours more than other people do. Appearances of like-mindedness and uniformity of behaviour effectively camouflage the latent problems of cohesion. Their society abounds in conflict that must be concealed by the myth of homogeneity. The myth covers up the interminable conflict among members of the governing élite, who can be counted on to agree absolutely on only one thing: a continuation of present power arrangements. It also conceals chronic, albeit largely ritualised, political conflict between, on the one hand, the administrators of the System and, on the other, the Japanese left and some other circles and individuals who disagree with what the System stands for.

Lifelong indoctrination

Nihonjinron is basically *kokutai* ideology minus the military factor. By means of the homogeneity myth, Japanese are once again telling themselves and outsiders that they are all part of what is essentially one big happy family.

What holds for the nation as a whole holds even more for some of the smaller units of which it is composed, in particular the large firms that make the salaryman believe he is working not only for his wife and children at home, but also for another large, benevolent family at his place of work. As we saw in Chapter 6 the analogy between corporation and family was propagated in the early decades of this century to counter labour unrest and an incipient union movement.[63] And the structure of the *ie* – a household defined not in terms of its blood-ties but by its economic or political task – served in Tokugawa times as a major device for social control.[64] In a major recent *nihonjinron* work, this pre-modern political construct is presented as the fundamental organising principle of post-war Japan.[65] The theory proceeds on the assumption that group life, with the moral subordination of the Japanese individual to the collectivity, is inescapable. In this it endorses, probably unwittingly, the permanent political tutelage of the Japanese adult.

Western admirers of the incorporation of 'the total man'[66] into Japanese administrative and production structures seem unaware of the fact that this is generally at the cost of ordinary Japanese family life. A cursory appraisal of the married lives of no more than a dozen salarymen should be enough to convince one of this. Nor must it be supposed that through the familistic companies the salaryman gains in genuine intimacy with his fellow workers. On the contrary, the forced nature of these relationships at work often precludes the spontaneity indispensable for intimate bonds.

The family metaphor disguises the power exercised by managers. As one specialist on Japanese industrial working conditions reminds us:

> the various dimensions of the Japanese work ethic rest ultimately on a fundamental power relationship that brooks no misunderstanding . . . there is no doubt that it is the Japanese managers, above all, who maintain most of their traditional managerial prerogatives and hold firm to the reins of power. Worker participation, worker commitment, company training, and so on, must all be understood in this context. For those committed to democratising the firm this hardly represents an ideal to be emulated.[67]

The familist myth is today enthusiastically propagated by the *zaikai*, appealed to by officials and politicians and endorsed by scholars working within the *nihonjinron* perspectives. But if most Japanese really considered themselves part of a grand national family, would they need all these reminders and so much convincing? Another reason to conclude that we are dealing with ideological deception is that Japanese outside the big cities, and Japanese women, are much less prone to explaining themselves with the phrase *ware ware nihonjin* ('we Japanese'). It appears that the further removed Japanese are from the vital parts of the System, the less susceptible they have been to 'big family' indoctrination.

Japanese power is thus disguised on many levels by the ideology of a unique culture. The central aim of this lifelong indoctrination that Japanese undergo is to keep them submissive. And the culture sustained by this political phenomenon reinforces submission in manifold ways. The ideal of accepting the world as it comes is celebrated in popular songs, numerous famous tales and many a television serial. A socially admired attitude of passive acceptance encourages compliance with the demands of, for instance, the education system and the corporations, even when these reach absurd proportions. Resignation in the face of misfortune, whether caused by people or not, is considered a sign of maturity.[68] Making a fuss over being cheated indicates that one is 'immature' – an attitude that invites a great deal of both spontaneous and organised racketeering in Japanese society. Japanese individuals are actively encouraged by many cues in everyday life to 'submerge' their individual selves in the larger social entities of which they are members.[69]

An ideology to dull the mind

The effect of an ideology that dominates intellectual constructs in explaining socio-political reality should be measured not just by its power to seduce intelligent citizens, but also by the extent to which it deprives intelligent citizens of other knowledge. In Japan ideology withholds intellectual stimulation from its citizens by withholding ideas that are fundamentally at variance with it. If the salaryman and the worker at the assembly belt are made to believe that they do what they do, in the way they are made to do it, because of some higher culture that they are all mystically tied to, and if furthermore they are told that this is the source of their happiness, then perhaps they will be less inclined to nurse obstinate thoughts. Even more important, if most commentary that they read in their newspapers corroborates the view that in giving up their individual life to the corporation they are fulfilling a higher destiny, they also become intellectually blunted.

Japanese whose intellectual capacities and personal inclinations might otherwise cause them to wonder at the reason for it all are systematically presented with intellectual garbage. This often drives them to become nihilists or to flee into extreme types of aestheticism.

The success of the modern ideology of Japaneseness is partly due to the general intellectual poverty of post-war Japanese life. In the absence of an intellectual tradition that vigorously analyses the conventional certainties of power relations and the social behaviour these relations have spawned, the accounts of socio-political reality in the sensationalist weekly magazines and the intellectual monthly press tend to be of doubtful quality. They routinely carry *nihonjinron* messages. It is very difficult for serious Japanese commentators to sustain their intellectual vigilance in the face of the overwhelming, overpowering, ubiquitous ideology of Japanese culture. Some intellectuals may be aware of the misuse of the cultural explanation in the area of their own pursuits, yet oblivious to it in other areas. Against the din of reassurances that Japanese love group living, are by nature not litigious, do not need to think logically, *ad infinitum, ad nauseam*, the few voices in the wilderness are heard only by those predisposed to hearing them. One will rarely find them in the newspapers or be exposed to them through television. Such is the power of contemporary Japanese orthodoxy.

The degree of regimentation that the System demands is met with apparent equanimity, simply because it does not occur to most Japanese to question it. As the eminent connoisseur of Japanese life and literature, Edward Seidensticker, puts it: 'The key to understanding Japanese society is to understand that Japanese have not been taught to say No!'[70] Most Japanese middle and high schools, far from encouraging a questioning attitude towards social arrangements, tend to frown on pupils asking questions at all. It is the same with most Japanese parents. The indulged Japanese child may be very recalcitrant, but playing psychological games with the mother is no substitute for learning to view oneself objectively in relation to the social framework. The Japanese do, of course, share in the general human ability to say 'no' to what they themselves have constructed, but young Japanese are not reminded by their upbringing that society is ultimately a product of human design, and not an inevitable consequence of the caprices of nature.

If, against all odds, Japanese individuals nevertheless question their socio-political environment, they are constantly prodded to stop doing so. Japanese clinical treatments for sociogenic psychological disorders, such as Morita and Naikan therapies, suppress the human hankering to establish one's identity as an individual. Patients are led to alter their attitudes towards the outside world, rather than to come to terms with themselves. 'Healing' begins when they empty their minds of personal ways of reasoning and personal emotions.[71]

Japan's institutionalised and 'culturally' sanctioned arrangements of submission and the flexibility permitted the power-holders in their representation of reality create ideal circumstances for the exercise of authoritarian power. In fact, as we have noted, the label 'bureaucratic authoritarianism' probably comes closest to describing the Japanese body politic. The only problem with this is that when one speaks of authoritarianism one expects to be able to point to a source from which the forces controlling society emanate. In the Japanese case these forces appear to be coming from everywhere, as well as being constantly generated from down within society itself. The public authority structure and society – the latter for the salaryman meaning mostly his company – are lumped together in the popular mind and constitute the essentials of 'Japanese culture'. State, society and culture, in one grand amalgam, affect most Japanese as an enveloping natural phenomenon, an inescapable force. The Japanese are made to view this force as virtuous.

11

The System as Religion

Since they consistently employ neither law, nor religion, nor systematic articulate, intellectual inquiry as a means of evaluating their socio-political arrangements, the Japanese have little choice but to measure them in reference to everyday 'truths' based on the demands and dictates of their immediate social environment. There being thus nothing outside the System to overrule or judge it, the System can only judge itself. This means that it is intrinsically virtuous, and that criticism of its essence is impossible; its guardians confirm this when they insist that the order they represent is inherently benevolent. In this way, the System also becomes a substitute for religion.

The religious qualities of the socio-political order that was constructed shortly before the turn of the century, and lasted until the bombs on Hiroshima and Nagasaki, were openly emphasised. State Shinto, established to provide spiritual nourishment for the 'emperor system', functioned as an umbrella organisation incorporating all other religions, which had to abandon any tenets that conflicted with emperor-worship.

State Shinto, together with theories of a 'family state' centring on a divine emperor, is a thing of the past, and for some three decades following defeat in 1945 the Japanese heard much devastating criticism of the 'emperor system'. Yet such criticism has not been based on theories profound and strong enough to serve as an alternative source of final explanations and political beliefs, and no secular system of beliefs, no socialistic, humanistic or liberal world-view, has eradicated the old mythology. Nor has the post-war period produced even a simple determination that Japan should be governed in accordance with its constitution and its laws. Thus the political culture of submission persists, and the System is for all practical purposes an unchallenged surrogate-religious force. The label 'Japanism', often used to describe pre-war behaviour, is still useful in describing practices in the service of the System today. It is of course inextricably bound up with the ideology described in Chapter 10. The fact that the ideology of Japaneseness is nowhere concisely summed up and cannot be found embodied in a neatly bound volume on bookstore shelves is immaterial; it serves its purpose of supporting the System as admirably as would a formal Holy Writ.

Communist ideology has frequently been likened to a religion, has indeed been labelled a 'secular religion'. Its religious characteristics are obvious; it provides a closed philosophical system, capable of 'explaining' everything, which counters critical arguments against it by invoking the principles on which it itself is based. It has spawned a class of exegetes and a pseudo-priesthood. It invests those who use it with the great power of religious fervour expended in the·name of a superior goal. In some ways Japanism is an even more effective surrogate religion than communism, because it is less examined, more taken for granted and more inescapable. And it comes with a number of the peripheral attributes of organised religion, including the risk of fanatical behaviour and the fear of secularisation.

The intensely religious quality of the Japanese power structure is thrown into relief if one examines what has happened to the competition.

Expedient religions

All religions have a social basis, according to a famous sociological theory.[1] Society's order must, at an early developmental stage, be codified and be accorded a sacred quality if it is to be maintained. Political power is most convincingly legitimate if it is believed to be an extension of divine authority, or an expression of divine arrangements. Although the higher religions cannot convincingly be traced to such an elementary origin, religions centred on nature and ancestor-worship are plausibly covered by the socio-political origin theory. Shintoism is one of the most striking examples of religions of this kind that still exist. Native Japanese religious beliefs derive from the idea of *kami* ('divine spirits'), which was originally used to sanctify the group. Communal worship of those divinities mystically affirmed the individual's belonging to that group, and helped legitimise the early Yamato rulers as well as local chieftains. Today, shrine Shinto is basically an ossified system of traditional rites, its purposes by and large forgotten; like 'village' Shinto with its ancestor-worship and the worship of trees, rocks, waterfalls and the like, it offers no spiritual competition to the System. Instead, both still serve to some extent to reinforce veneration of those in power.

As for Buddhism, this was, as we have seen, mixed with Shinto and Confucianism to create a religious hotchpotch that played a major role in sanctioning Japanese power relations well into modern times. Although Buddhism may still serve the individual as a force of consolation in adversity, the political effect of this is to reconcile the individual to the existing social situation. Neither Shintoism nor Buddhism provides the contemporary Japanese with anything approaching political principles, a view of life or even moral standards.

Most Japanese go through a Shinto-style ceremony when they marry, and have Buddhist sutras chanted over them after they die. Shinto shrines provide a centre for communal festivities, while Buddhist temples run the afterlife industries, from wakes, funerals and burials (nearly always after cremation) to periodic services held for the souls of the dead. In the early 1980s tax investigators confirmed the impression that Buddhism is a lucrative business. Its traditional activities had become increasingly mixed with heavy profiting from the tax-exempt status enjoyed by acknowledged religions. Some Buddhist temples make much money by running parking lots, crammer schools and kindergartens, or selling effigies to pray for the souls of aborted babies. Traditional business is profitable too; droning sutras at a funeral nets between a quarter of a million to a million yen, while posthumous names are conferred for similar amounts. Temples that have their own cemeteries – which means that they have many 'parishioners', tied to them by the family graves situated there – can easily make fortunes. One temple in Kyoto, founded by an emperor three hundred years ago and inherited by the daughter of the last abbot, manages blocks of flats, a parking lot, a vegetarian restaurant and a night-club. Buddhist nuns must in theory shave their heads, but abbess Okada Kumien has received special dispensation, since a bald pate would look strange amidst her bar hostesses. Her excuse for this unusual sideline is the need to meet the mounting costs of keeping up an inherited cultural treasure.

There are, of course, a few Buddhist priests who discuss life's problems with their parishioners, but the majority do not consider this a major task. Only the so-called 'new religions' provide their members with any opportunity for deeper involvement.

The 'new religions'

The *shinko shukyo*, or 'newly arisen religions', are products of the past one and a half centuries. One of them, the highly respected Tenrikyo, dating from the late Tokugawa period, dominates an entire city (Tenri city) and has a university, schools, an ethnological museum, a historical library and missionaries and doctors in the Third World. Two other major bodies with a largely rural following, Omotokyo and Konkokyo, date from shortly after the Meiji Restoration.[2] But it was in post-war Japan, after the lifting of all formal suppression, that new religions really began to proliferate. They included such esoteric specimens as Denshinkyo, the 'electricity religion', which worshipped Thomas Edison. In 1951, 720 new religions were registered, but a revision of the law to cope with widespread tax fraud has roughly halved their always fluctuating number.

Some of these religions have become fairly large, rich and powerful. The best-known among them, Soka Gakkai, is of political significance because of its size; it claims 6 million members. It is also the most successful among the *shinko shukyo* that have set up shop abroad. In the 1960s it created a great deal of disquiet in the System with its militant proselytising and active hostility towards other, rival new religions. But it has settled down now and, with its own schools, university, political party and publishing empire, has become a successful, albeit still somewhat controversial, participant in the System.

Another large new group, claiming more than 5 million members, is the Rissho Kosei Kai, which has a colossal wedding-cake-shaped main temple (done in pink, the favourite colour of its foundress, who received the divine call during a nervous breakdown in the 1930s), a famous hospital and the largest concert hall in the country. Like the Soka Gakkai, it is a laymen's organisation descended from Nichiren Buddhism. Co-founder Niwano Nikkyo, who is very much at the centre of the sect, lobbies for the Nobel peace prize and has himself established a 'Niwano peace prize' to improve his chances. The third of the large new post-war sects is PL Kyodan, once known by outsiders as the 'golf religion' because of the hobby of its founder and the roof-top driving ranges on some of its churches.

The most remarkable aspect of the *shinko shukyo*, aside from the enormous wealth that most appear to have no difficulty in amassing, is the utter simplicity of their religious doctrines. One sometimes wonders whether their creeds embody anything substantial that non-members do not already believe in. None of them has developed any intellectually noteworthy doctrines or provided its members much in the way of philosophical, let alone political, guidance. True, Soka Gakkai has spawned the Komeito party. But this new group of parliamentarians – which in the 1970s formally distanced itself from its parent organisation – has not enriched the Japanese political world by providing a new choice based on recognisably alternative political principles. It could just as well be another *habatsu* of the LDP.

The main function of Japan's new religions is social. They provide havens for those who crave intensive group involvement but are not 'members' of a large corporation. Among *shinko shukyo* devotees one finds large numbers of lonely housewives, bar hostesses and workers in marginal occupations.

That the individual could be involved with religion to his inner core is an idea strange to most Japanese. Religion is seen rather as a tool, as something you adopt because it will get you somewhere. A newspaper advice column once told a mother worried about her daughter, who had become 'a different woman' since joining a Christian church, that she should try to find out what personal problems had made her become a convert in the first place.[3] A fair number of intellectuals in the early Meiji period adopted Christianity only to give it up when the immediate results disappointed them.

An exception to the casualness with which people join and quit Japanese religious sects is the Unification Church. This movement originated in Korea, and its followers are known in the West as 'Moonies', after the name of its founder. Japanese Moonies are hardly less fanatical than their Western counterparts. By infiltrating parts of the political and academic worlds – aided by the large funds they have available for buying favours, by their intimidating practices and by their fervent anti-communism – they have become highly influential. The Moonies provide an important backing for those elements in the System that advocate the need for greater Japanese independence through remilitarisation.

The company and society as church

The companies are suspicious of employees who belong, or whose parents belong, to a new religion. The point is often investigated when firms are sifting recruits; religious fervour in Japan is expressed by supreme loyalty to the component one belongs to, and the potential conflict between company loyalty and religious affiliation would be too great. The older Buddhist sects, which take little if any of the adherent's time, pose no threat here. Some companies require their employees to worship at the 'company shrine' on the roof of the office building, which has been known to lead to embarrassment for Christian employees. An explicit reference to the company as a source of religious sustenance was the famous suicide note left behind by an executive of Nissho Iwai, a large trading firm. Before jumping from a building as a result of involvement in a scandal, the manager wrote to all his colleagues that 'the company is eternal, and we should dedicate ourselves to its eternity'.

Beyond the company, the System as a whole provides religious sustenance. It will be remembered that a demonstration of repentance will let most law-breakers off the hook; that the administrators expect the institutions they run to be collectively considered as a fount of benevolence; and that in the extreme cases represented by the heterodox opinions of radical detainees much effort goes into attempts to make them apostatise. While there is great freedom of speech in Japan, any heterodox ideas that become organised and associated with a group appear to activate the System's absorptive or neutralising powers immediately. The moral possibility of individual resistance to the established socio-political arrangements is simply not recognised.

The religious character of Japanese society helps explain the poverty of Japanese intellectual probing of society. Where social concerns are forever paramount, and have religious significance, analysis of society is akin to analysis of the divinity, and such analysis always undermines faith. Just as with the ideology of Japaneseness, embedded in *nihonjinron*, the surrogate religion of Japanism is not recognised for what it is – which makes the System all the more insidiously religious.

Buddhists, Christians, Marxists and fanatics

The fact that a tradition of referring to truths beyond the political order has not taken root in Japan does not of course mean that Japanese are incapable of conceiving and appealing to such beliefs and principles. The Japanese System has not evolved naturally as a substitute for a religion, the product of a people who, for some unexplained reason, were never interested in religious speculation. The human mind inevitably searches for an invisible order governing what the mind's eye perceives. It does so without instruction and often in the face of active obstruction. That people are not merely a product of their upbringing is evidenced by the Japanese experience as much as by any other.

At several junctures in history, Japanese power-holders have eradicated the hints of transcendental values and universal principles that were present in the formal Japanese religions. They have always shown great fear of such potential threats to their presentation of themselves as representing ultimate virtue. We can be sure of this, because some religious groups did not give up without a fight, and had to be actively suppressed.

Buddhist uprisings

Take, for example, Honen (1133–1212), the first of the great Buddhist reformers of the Kamakura period, who preached the possibility of individual salvation. Buddhism had already altered the Shinto view of life after death – which taught a gradual merging with ancestral spirits – by postulating rebirth in a number of different realms. Since around the tenth century, this idea of an individual afterlife had to some extent influenced ethical norms not subject to political control, but it first gained great popularity with the flourishing of the indigenous Japanese Buddhist sects of which Honen was the pioneer. His message was that childlike reliance on Amida Buddha's fatherly love and compassion, rather than on ritual deeds, would lead to rebirth in the Pure Land, a Buddhist paradise. Establishment Buddhism, centred on the monasteries of Mount Hiei near Kyoto, found Honen dangerous enough to take drastic action against him. Its monks burned all the copies of his treatise they could lay their hands on, together with the wooden blocks with which they had been printed. Eventually, Honen's popularity moved the authorities to exile him.

The next great Buddhist theorist, Shinran (1173–1262), also spent most of his life in virtual exile among common people, far from Japan's political and cultural centres. Taking Honen's theory a step further, he preached that simple faith alone would lead to redemption: no chanting of Buddha's name, no ritual, no celibacy – piety alone was the key to salvation. While Buddhism in its imported form had become a tool of the governing élite, Shinran did more than any other Japanese to make the faith accessible to the simplest villagers. The sect he founded, the Jodo Shinshu, is still the largest in the country.

Nichiren (1222–82), the third of the founders of the indigenous

Japanese schools of Buddhism, was the most colourful, the most political and hence the most controversial religious leader in Japanese history. It is significant that more than six centuries later he should be remembered as a singular example of putting individual convictions above the interests of the state.[4] Nichiren taught that belief in the transcendental truth of the Lotus Sutra, accompanied by chanting of its 'sacred name', was necessary to save the souls of individual Japanese and, in turn, the nation as a whole. He predicted that unless there was a general conversion there would be all manner of calamities, including a foreign invasion. Kublai Khan, the Mongol chieftain and ruler of China, did in fact launch invasions against Japan in 1274 and 1281, thereby helping ensure Nichiren's fame in subsequent centuries.

Although Nichiren never called for the overthrow of the ruling class, he did exhort the aristocracy to reform itself and to suppress Jodo Buddhism and the older sects. His attacks on the life-style of the élite in Kamakura and the established Buddhist sects brought him a death sentence (which he miraculously escaped) and exile. After a settlement of uncertain nature with the authorities, he went into retirement in the mountains west of Mount Fuji. There he developed his vision of a single Buddhist church while conducting a voluminous correspondence with followers all over Japan. The universal church of his dreams would be based in Japan, at the foot of Mount Fuji, whence it would spread all over the world.[5] It is no coincidence that Soka Gakkai, the biggest offshoot of the Nichiren sect among the new religions, has its headquarters at that very spot.

While the teachings of the founders of Japan's great indigenous Buddhist sects did not add up to an enduring body of political theory, and while the religious challenges to established authority inherent in their work were never transformed into successful military challenges, they were nevertheless politically significant. Their teachings, though simple, provided for the mass of the people an example of a truth explicitly transcending that represented by temporal authority. It has become clear to historians that a large number of popular rebellions were in part inspired by religion.

The numerous regional peasant uprisings called *ikki* that occurred from at least the early fourteenth century onward, sometimes with the co-operation of discontented warriors, were usually triggered by such causes as heavy village debts, inability to pay taxes or ruined harvests. But transcendental Buddhism had undoubtedly contributed to political consciousness and a sense of unity among villagers. In the century preceding the Tokugawa political settlement, the most formidable *ikki* uprisings were organised by believers of Shinran's sect, Jodo Shinshu, which had blossomed under the great Rennyo (1415–99), chief abbot of the main Honganji temple. Known as the *ikko ikki*, these village-based military actions increased in number along with greater use of naked military power by the warrior leaders, suggesting that there may have been many peasants who understood 'the new exploitative nature of the emerging order'.[6]

Not surprisingly the three generals who, appearing in close succession at the close of the sixteenth century, ended centuries of strife and bloodshed by their gradual unification of Japan, had absolutely no patience with indigenous Buddhism. The first of them, Oda Nobunaga, countered the *ikko ikki* ferociously for some ten years. His view of the Buddhist fighters was demonstrated by the extermination campaigns that frequently followed victorious battles against them. According to one record, some 20,000 sect members were burnt alive in 1574. The same Nobunaga spared defeated enemy barons and regular warriors.[7] The latter were part of the normal order of power, whereas the religiously inspired fighters were not.

Toyotomi Hideyoshi, the second of the great unifiers, used the tactic of putting the Buddhist establishment in his debt. He co-opted popular Buddhism, helping to undermine the *ikki* that had been inspired by it. Once this had been accomplished, the world-view preached by popular Buddhism had to remain suppressed.[8] The theoretical distinction between the laws of the Buddha and the laws of men that had evolved in the preceding centuries was gradually obscured and forgotten. Once again, secular authority became fundamental and obedience to it the paramount duty.[9]

But there are indications that the believers in a 'truth' beyond that of the authorities did not give up that easily, notwithstanding the feats of the third unifier, Tokugawa Ieyasu, who extended his control over Buddhist institutions, regulating their teachings and activities.[10] The Buddhists resisted organised oppression well into the fourth decade of the Tokugawa shogunate that began at the outset of the seventeenth century. An early bestseller, *Kiyomizu Monogatari* (*The Tale of Kiyomizu*), published in 1638, explicitly identified the pockets of ideological recalcitrance in Japan: the *ikko* believers, the followers of Nichiren and the Christians.[11]

The Christian threat

The most striking illustrations of the fear of religious competition in the Tokugawa and Meiji periods, and for several decades into the present century, involved intolerance for Japanese Christians.

In the last decades of the sixteenth century and the first decades of the seventeenth, Portuguese Jesuits and other missionaries made up to one million converts, including some feudal lords. Opinions differ as to what brought this era to an end. According to one theory, the shogun saw the priests as the forerunners of colonisation by the Portuguese or Spaniards. More important, probably, was the Tokugawa shogunate's fear that the less loyal domains might receive military backing from the foreigners. But there was more to it than this. The potential power over the political order of belief in an alien Lord above shogun and emperor, even if this Lord was only in heaven, must have been very frightening to those who ruled. And the relentless persecution of Christians that continued long after the country was virtually cut off from international traffic suggests that the shogunate was indeed afraid of more than political moves by Portugal. As a result of the perceived threat to the established political order, the country was cut off from contact with Westerners except for a handful of Dutch traders, who had managed to convince the shogunate officials that they did not worship the same God as the Portuguese. Following the expulsion of the missionaries, Japanese Christians were tortured, crucified and sent into exile.[12] To prove that they had apostatised, they were made to trample on crosses and swear an oath that began and ended in this curious fashion: 'By the Father, the Son and the Holy Ghost, Santa Maria and all the angels. . . . If I break this oath may I lose the grace of God for ever and fall into the wretched state of Judas Iscariot.'[13] The officials who designed that formula seem to have understood the power of transcendental religion when they saw it.

In 1637, after many Christians had been massacred or forced to recant their religion, supposed apostates were joined by masterless samurai in a rebellion under the Christian banner on the Shimabara peninsula in Kyushu. As many as 37,000 men, women and children marched on and occupied a local castle and held it for four months against shogunate forces. This was to be the last time before the Meiji Restoration, some 230 years later, that a samurai army fought a major battle.

The hankering for something more than the prescribed 'truth' did not disappear entirely with the persecuted Buddhists and Christians. Ando Shoeki, a thinker who lived in the first half of the eighteenth century, was one who saw the shogunate for what it was: arbitrary rule dependent on military power buttressed by ideology.[14] There may have been more like him. Ando's writings were not discovered until 1899, and were introduced to a wider Japanese public only after the Second World War.

Christianity was ruthlessly eradicated. Buddhism was gutted of the transcendental notions it had developed, and several of its sects were outlawed.[15] Under Tokugawa rule the new power relationships were frozen within ideological orthodoxy. All this was crucial in the shaping of Japanese political culture as we know it today. And all of it was the direct result of political decrees.

That the unifying generals understood the political significance of religion is further witnessed by their efforts at religious innovation. Oda Nobunaga, Toyotomi Hideyoshi and Tokugawa Ieyasu were no less upstarts than the ambitious warriors of previous centuries. All three, however, hoped to avoid the political bondage implied in legitimisation by the imperial court, and therefore needed a spiritual basis for their rule. All three, accordingly, tried to solve the legitimacy problem by raising themselves to divine status and launching cults centred on themselves.[16] One of the most famous Japanese architectural complexes, the Toshogu Mausoleum at Nikko, bears testimony to the importance the Tokugawa regime attached to the cult of Ieyasu. In the first century of Tokugawa rule, this shrine vied in popularity with the most important Shinto shrine at Ise, where the emperors worshipped their ancestors.

Dangerous faiths in the twentieth century

In the two and a half centuries of the police state forged by the Tokugawas, no new set of propositions about the relationship of human beings to society or the universe ever had a chance to compete with the regime for the minds of the Japanese. When competition finally arrived in the form of the foreign learning of the Meiji period, the guardians of the power system took a couple of decades to decide on their own doctrines of the individual's relationship to society, then once again took the inevitable protective action.

Again, it started with the Christians. Three decades into the Meiji period, they became the target of official restrictions. In 1899 the Ministry of Education forbade religious instruction in schools. Six years before that, Inoue Tetsujiro, philosophy professor at Tokyo Imperial University, had published his famous *Conflict between Education and Religion* in which he drew 'the logical conclusion . . . that Christianity is absolutely anti-national'.[17] Another nationalist and journalist, Kuga Katsunan, who was famous for his editorials instructing the government on how to preserve Japanese morals, pleaded for an assimilation of Christianity in the way Buddhism had once been absorbed by the political system.[18] The ban on religious education affected Buddhist schools too, to the extent that these had emulated the Christians in trying to become a new ethical force in society. But it was the Christians who 'served the ideologues as metaphorical foreigners in whose alien reflection the silhouette of patriotism emerged that much more clearly'.[19]

The Christians were expected to drop their faith in a supreme God and in individual responsibility so as to fit in with society as sanctioned by the Meiji oligarchy. In other words, Japanese Christianity was to be deprived of precisely those beliefs that made it Christian. Even so, many believers did adjust, albeit at times under protest. Some Christian schools exchanged the Bible for the Imperial Rescript on Education, the catechism of the emperor cult, as their source of moral instruction.

Japan's most famous Christian, Uchimura Kanzo (1861–1930), epitomises the insoluble conflict felt by many Christians who wanted to remain functioning members of the Japanese community – which automatically means accepting that no intellectual or moral command may be considered as overriding the needs of the established socio-political order. Uchimura's training in the United States had, he found, made him unfit for teaching in Japanese schools. In one celebrated episode in 1891 he refused to bow to the emperor's seal affixed to the Rescript on Education, before finally yielding to the pleas of his colleagues. His dilemma is poignantly captured in his famous short piece 'Two J's', dating from 1925:

> I love two J's and no third; one is Jesus, and the other is Japan. I do not know which I love more, Jesus or Japan. . . . For Jesus' sake, I cannot own any other God than His Father . . . and for Japan's sake,

I cannot accept any faith which comes in the name of foreigners . . . my faith is not a circle with one center; it is an ellipse with two centers.

Uchimura sought a Christianity that could be purely Japanese, untainted by Western influence – a tall order if ever there was one. He thought he had found it by keeping the biblical tales and some Christian ethical teachings, but by doing away with the institution of the church.

Among the churches that other Japanese Christians have established, none has given the power-holders much of a headache. In conflict situations, such as when, just before the war, all Japanese were required to worship at the Yasukuni shrine (a state Shinto shrine, home of the souls of fallen soldiers), the authorities had their way. The Vatican told Japanese Catholics that they could consider the gesture a civic duty, and most Protestant churches followed suit. In 1941 several dozen Protestant churches merged to form a government-sponsored United Church of Christ in Japan. The Anglicans and some other groups withdrew from the organisation after the war, but it is still the largest Protestant body in Japan today. Today, only the Jehovah's Witnesses occasionally make news by running into trouble in the schools, when children of believers are asked to do things that conflict with sect rules, and school principals refuse to make exceptions for religious minorities.

Earlier in this century, Japanese Christians were held up as models of how not to be Japanese. It did not help that it was they who had first introduced the political left into Japan. Some of the founders of the Society for the Study of Socialism and its offspring, the Socialist Democratic Party (banned two days after its formation), were Christians, as were the organisers of Japan's first national labour organisation, the Yuaikai.[20]

Both Marxists and Christians were left alone in this century only so long as they accepted social compromises that entailed, as a basic condition, abandonment of the principles essential to their adopted faiths. In the early 1900s a common topic of discussion in high circles was how the government could best suppress 'dangerous thoughts' – meaning, mainly, thoughts derived from the Christian and Marxist interpretations of the world. In 1923 an imperial message was issued in which, without further ado, people were ordered to stop having such thoughts.[21] From the 1930s till the end of the war recalcitrant Marxists were harassed or cajoled into performing *tenko*, the public recanting of their beliefs. Persecution was at its most straightforward in the case of the communists; the Communist Party could easily be portrayed as the agent of a foreign power, since it took its orders from the Comintern.[22] The party was, of course, illegal. It was racked by severe factional wars and further weakened by mass arrests. Its leadership spent most of the war years in prison.

Freedom of expression in post-war Japan has brought no drastic changes in the fortunes of what were once the main sources of 'abnormal foreign thoughts'. Some Christian churches do a roaring business in weddings, but that is because getting married before a Catholic or Protestant clergyman is fashionable. Only 1 per cent of the Japanese population calls itself Christian.

As for Japanese socialists and communists, they have refused to relate their theorising to attainable socio-political goals. The communist organisation is heir to the same habits of Japanist political thought and behaviour as the mainstream components of the System. Until the 1960s the party justified its decisions with reference to the infallibility of the Soviet party, and the myth of collective leadership obscures individual responsibility.[23]

Long-established Marxist stereotypes are influential among a still large but dwindling group of academics and intellectual commentators. Their concept of 'monopoly capitalism' is weighed down with a thick crust of ideological barnacles accrued over three-quarters of a century. They apply it with such unthinking regularity that they convince only each other and perhaps a handful of gullible students.

Nevertheless, this hoary old version of Japanese Marxism is the single firmly established alternative to 'Japanism'. It provides at least some intellectual backing for the only genuine political opposition challenging the System's claim to a monopoly of righteousness. It is no coincidence that the one large political organisation capable of rejecting the 'inescapable embrace' (at least until the mid-1980s) was Nikkyoso, an organisation led by doctrinaire Marxists. And the only consistent opposition to the politicisation of the Japanese judiciary by the judicial bureaucrats, the only energetic attempt to preserve judicial autonomy, has come from Seihokyo, another organisation at least partly under the influence of Marxist ideologues.

Romantic radicalism

The difference between Japanism and genuine religions is that the latter transcend socio-political concerns whereas Japanism by definition cannot, since it is derived from and totally governed by those concerns. The relentless affirmation that the existing arrangements governing daily life are immutable and ultimately meaningful has not satisfied all Japanese all the time. Japanism cannot fully satisfy the human craving for ultimate explanations.

Those cravings are part of the Japanese make-up just as with other people, as has been demonstrated by the historical examples given above. Intermittently, new generations of young Japanese also manifest them. Intelligent students sometimes pass through personal upheavals in which they embrace and abandon belief systems at great speed. The absence of any intellectual anchor makes them peculiarly susceptible to newly encountered ideologies. Since they have not been encouraged to think in terms of universal principles, their sudden discovery of creeds that appear to explain everything often leads to very intense involvement.

When this involvement is a collective one, it is still characterised by much regimentation and discipline. Japanese student activism in the 1960s and early 1970s was quite different from that of Europe and the United States in two respects. The Japanese radicals slavishly mouthed slogans derived from some or other rigidly ideological variant of Marxism. At the same time, they put themselves emotionally into the hands of their leaders, obeying their every command. Battles between riot police and student radicals often created the illusion of having been organised by a choreographer. The radicals, sporting their identical helmets with identical insignia, and identical small towels worn between the helmet straps as masks (intended to protect them against tear-gas), and carrying identical wooden staves, gave an impression as disciplined as that of the riot police in their dark blue uniforms and metal shields, while their running in formation would have put the Bersaglieri, the famous Italian bugle corps, to shame.

The contrast with the student 'revolutionaries' of the West and the subculture associated with them could hardly have been greater. 'Spontaneity' was the imperative of the radical youth culture of the West, its ideal the elimination of all authority restricting the true self – the authority, even, of their own leaders – as well as theories that would channel and thus diminish the 'revolution'.[24] Even so, the fact that the Japanese student movement of that period (as distinct from its more recent radicalised offshoots) ritualised its protest to such an extent that the riot police could easily deal with it does not detract from the strong devotion of many members to notions that scared the System, and their readiness to make a display of that devotion.

Passionate action in the name of some higher cause, action which earned the disapproval or condemnation of the authorities, was not unknown in Japan's more repressive eras. It constitutes, in fact, a venerated tradition that has created many, if not most, of Japan's heroes. To understand the intellectual inspiration of this tradition we must return, once again, to those few inklings of a reality surpassing that of the union of humanity and nature supposedly embodied by the warrior regime. Even though the various movements of officially endorsed Tokugawa learning were wholly domesticated and relentlessly supportive of the regime, they could not be entirely purged of visions that extended beyond the shogunal palace.

The nativist Kokugaku scholars, for one, had such visions when they emphasised Japan's glorious tradition of divinely descended emperors. And the Chinese neo-Confucianist writings that constituted the main portion of what every Tokugawa student memorised must have given the more probing mind occasional glimpses of a universal morality transcending the ideology of the shogunal administrators. More than a glimmering of this was contained in Japanese explications of the philosophy of the Chinese Wang Yangming school. Nakae Toju (1608–48), founder of the Yomeigaku (Yang-ming studies) in Japan, propounded the existence of a principle, pervading the whole universe, called *meitoku* ('true virtue'). When a person finds his or her own *meitoku* he or she automatically becomes virtuous.[25] In pursuing this idea, Nakae conceived of something close to a single personal God, which he referred to as the absolute truth, infinite and the final end of all.[26] His thinking when stretched this far is neither steady nor consistent, but he did at least affirm with certainty the fact of an intuitive understanding of right and wrong.

Yomeigaku came the closest of all Japanese schools of thought to an apprehension of transcendental principle. A masterless samurai, Kumazawa Banzan (1619–91), applied Nakae Toju's teachings to a reform programme in the domain of Okayama, setting the example for socially concerned Japanese after him. The motto of his school was 'Act out of conscience'.[27] Such Yomeigaku notions filtered through to the samurai and gave a vague legitimacy to such passionate action as they felt obliged to resort to under special circumstances.

Early in the nineteenth century, these ideas were transformed into a basis for rebellion. The period's most famous rebel, Oshio Heihachiro (1792–1837), applied Yomeigaku thought to unambiguous political activism.[28] For him the essence of all things, alive or dead, was at once a universal absolute and a creative force; it was an absolute spirit that was also morally right. He concluded from this that action against evil was an immutable command. To treat evil as something outside oneself was in fact to condone its existence in one's own heart. Thus he advocated what he described as continuous 'pure' action, implicitly justifying a permanent state of rebellion. He even went so far as to write that one's actions in society should be 'as if one were mad'.[29] If anything appealed to a universal principle, this was it. But it provided little intellectual basis for sustained political involvement. Oshio translated theory into practice and started a rebellion in 1837, in the course of which a quarter of the city of Osaka burned down. He gave famished farmers swords and sold his library to buy guns and a cannon. The large merchant houses were plundered and burned; Oshio was found by the authorities and committed suicide. His army was tortured and killed to a man.

What happened to Oshio's theory is characteristic of the perversion that heterodox political thought in Japan appears doomed to undergo once it spreads. On the eve of the Meiji Restoration, Oshio was revered by anti-shogunate forces. But his ethical ideals were converted into slogans for 'national survival', meaning expulsion of the foreigners. The idea of saving the poor became transformed into the idea of saving the country.[30] Both the Yomeigaku and Kokugaku movements in their advanced stages had become intellectual weapons with which the power of the Tokugawa bureaucracy could be defied by calling for the restoration of the imperial institution.[31] So intense was the Kokugaku scholars' endorsement of the idea that the emperor sanctified the political order that their message gained an unintended revolutionary potential.

Spread by numerous followers of Motoori Norinaga and Hirata Atsutane among commoners all over the country,[32] the ideas of the mystic value of ancient customs and the imperial blessing helped, in combination with the concept of intuitive moral action exemplified by Oshio, to inspire the young warrior firebrands known as *shishi*, who in the final decades of the shogunate created havoc in the name of re-establishing an imperial Japan. In the end, they contributed to the fall of the Tokugawa regime.[33] The *shishi*, some of them masterless samurai, often lived as vagabonds, but a few became popular heroes. They represented a variety of characters, but the most important among them were xenophobic nationalist zealots who filled the air with their cries of 'Revere the emperor and expel the barbarians!' Their ranks included the terrorists who murdered early European residents in the 1850s and 1860s.

Here we have the beginnings of a romantic tradition of heroes and 'patriotic' scoundrels supposedly inspired by pure Japanist motives in their search for a 'purer' Japan. It is one of the great tragedies in the history of Japanese political thought that ideas which could have served to exert pressure on the established order ended up in the arsenals of those who sought to be more Japanist than the Japanists.

Wartime fanaticism

The romanticised *shishi* tradition provided an acknowledged 'moral' basis for the murders committed by the alleged patriots of the 1930s, mixed-up young men with delusions of grandeur who believed they could 'save' Japan. The purity of spirit extolled by the ideology of Japaneseness examined in Chapter 10 becomes still more enticingly pure when it permits intuitive action to take precedence over disciplined reasoning.[34] Such reasoning, in the view of the Japanists, encourages wrong motives. An important attribute of this radical Japanism is that it often leads to self-destruction. It is expected to do so.

The imagery of a 'pure' spirit made socially respectable by the *kokutai* ideology became a powerful motive force for many Japanese during the war. For Japanist mythology, to go further and contend that the Yamato race was inherently superior and therefore destined to lead in Asia, if not the world, was not such a big step. According to the expanded imagery, Japan enabled all nations it colonised to take their 'proper place' in the world: that is, under the original, purer subjects of the emperor. At the same time, to die for Japan was the most spiritual and most purifying act imaginable. The anger of the psychological cripples who were 'saving Japan' with their assassinations in the 1930s had become a socially acceptable rage that, like all rage, was immune to understanding. The possibility of political dissension was excluded.[35]

We know that many Japanese in this period never stopped using their heads, but the officers who led them into war certainly did. The products of the Army Academy learned to rely on *seishin-shugi*, the victory of spirit over the material, and to ignore logical thought. A large proportion of them had no contact with reality and were pathologically self-confident.[36] Colonel Kobayashi Junichiro, a close friend of War Minister (later Minister of Education) Araki Sadao, warned in a famous pamphlet that excessive reliance on 'material goods' would corrupt the soul of the Japanese Army.[37] Belief in the superiority of Japanese capabilities owing to their 'pure Japanese' character survived the battle of Nomonhan on the Manchuria–Mongolia border in 1939. More than seventeen thousand Kwantung Army soldiers, ordered by their officers to rely on their superior fighting spirit, met death in 'human-wave' clashes with superior Soviet mechanised units and superior tactical skills – an early and terrible defeat that was kept a deep secret from the Japanese public.[38]

The official line even before the Pacific War, propagated by officers who had intimidated their more cautious colleagues into silence, was that Japan's will-power would overcome United States physical might. Admiral Kato Kanji believed that the acknowledged impossibility of victory against vast military superiority could with such will-power be turned into a possibility. At the Imperial Conference that sanctioned a *de facto* decision to go to war, Admiral Nagano Osami, supreme commander of the Imperial Japanese Navy, spoke of the need to fight the USA, because surrender without a struggle would spell 'spiritual as well as physical destruction for the nation'.[39] Defeat occurred, Minister of Education Maeda Tamon explained in a memorandum to school principals following the surrender, 'as a result of insufficient efforts and a lack of true patriotism on our part'.[40]

Another claim that contributed to the general religious mania concerned the boundless energy that had supposedly existed ever since the birth of the country.[41] The *Kokutai no Hongi*, the 1937 propaganda booklet in which the Ministry of Education explained the 'national essence', insisted that the invasion of Manchuria was an 'unavoidable expression of the national vitality'. War flowed naturally from the country's boundless energy, and was needed to maintain its vitality.

Post-war purity

In contemporary Japan, the US-imposed post-war constitution has emasculated the state by renouncing forever Japan's sovereign right to wage war. But while war is no longer considered a noble activity, the idea of an innate Japanese energy, borne out by industrial statistics, is very much alive.

In the same way, the ideal of 'pure' motives and 'pure' acts still creates objects for a pernicious form of sentimental identification. The tradition of breaking through everyday thought into an intensified celebration of Japaneseness, a tradition that starts with the transmogrification of Oshio's fervour into support of a super-Japan and continues via the *shishi* and pre-war supernationalists, is not dead. It provides something ultimate, something replete with meaning, to contrast with the drab materialistic routine of daily life from which it is an escape. It remains today, as it was before the war, a sorry substitute for the individually liberating force of intellectual constructs that transcend Japanism.

The pathetic behaviour of Mishima Yukio, in asking Japan's Self-Defence Forces to rise up and 'restore the emperor', before disembowelling himself 'in the most manly form of Japanese action', fits squarely in this tradition. In 1969 Mishima took students to task in a public debate for having recently given in to police tear-gas and water-cannons and meekly surrendering the Yasuda Hall of Tokyo University (which they had occupied) without a single student making the supreme gesture of jumping to his death. From contemporary commentary it appears that he managed to shame many leftist students.

The belief that radicals have a right to exist if they are prepared to die for their cause could not have been more explicitly stated than in a 1972 editorial in the *Mainichi Shimbun* following a sensational siege by 1,500 policemen of five members of the extremist Red Army. The radicals, who had 'purified' their ranks by torturing eleven comrades to death, subsequently fled into a mountain lodge with a hostage. After ten days of (nationally televised) cautious police action the extremists surrendered, disappointing those who, as the *Mainichi* put it, 'believed that after exhausting their ammunition, they would either take their own lives or die fighting hand-to-hand with the riot police'. The same newspaper continued: 'this belief was utterly betrayed . . . the five youths offered almost no resistance. . . . Such an attitude brings out their "pampered spirit"!'[42] The editor dwelled some more on the pampered way of thinking, contrasting it with the readiness of others to die for their causes. Ian Buruma summed it up:

> The most serious charge against the students was not that they brutally murdered eleven of their friends and a policeman or that their cause was, at best, absurd, but that they failed to die for it. They lacked sincerity, their hearts were not pure. The editor who wrote this piece could hardly be called a sympathiser with the 'Red Army's' goals. But whether he was or was not was beside the point. It was the purity of motive that counted. If only their attitude had been right, they could have been heroes.[43]

The tradition of heroic extremist Japanism remains a potential source of instability. Frustration and tension, both of which can be found in abundance in Japan, could combine with future economic problems and a growing sense that the nation is being deprived of its just goals to ignite emotional and irrational Japanist movements. The structure for them is present among various rightist groups. And they will be able to count on much sympathy as the sense of the need to 'return to true Japanese values' increases along with a sense of being victimised by an anti-Japanese world.

The danger of secularisation

If Japan's strict social norms were to wear off there would not be much underneath, since the political system has prevented the emergence of any religion or ethical belief-system that could be a source of moral principles. Strip Japanese society of its rigid codes of individual submission, and there would be little left to hold it together. Many of the administrators are uncomfortably aware of this.

The reaction against the fanatical wartime version of Japanism, which has been sustained by the Nikkyoso and other leftist groups, has gone much too far in the eyes of these guardians of Japanese morality, who show what to outsiders seems an excessive, unending concern with the moral quality of the emerging generation.

In the early 1960s when I first arrived in Japan, there was much talk about declining customs, disrespectful Japanese youth and the loss of a resolve to work for society. In the late 1980s one hears identical complaints; the national 'spirit' is always seen to be declining. The administrators sometimes seem obsessed with worry that the generation now in school may give it all up: devotion to the companies, housewifely roles, obedience to authorities and toughness for the sake of their country. They share a conviction that something must be done about it.

Bolstering the national spirit

It is against this background that the campaigns in the 1950s and 1980s to 'correct the excesses of the occupation' must be seen, as well as the calls from LDP members and education officials for a new sense of patriotism among young people. There is much open dissatisfaction in many quarters with the absence of moral guidance and the restraints the government faces in seeking to reintroduce it into the schools. The top businessmen-bureaucrats in the economic federations have encouraged the development of an education system that has furthered 'examination hell' excesses, not only because they consider the docile middle-class workforce it engenders good for business, but also because they see its discipline as preventing the break-up of Japanese society. Although the keepers of the Japanese political order would not express it in these terms, what they fear the most is the 'secularisation' of Japanese society. It is significant in this context how casually it is accepted that the government should help nourish 'cultural values', as it did in the Meiji period.

The tensions that exist within Japanese education, caused by contradictions between the Japanese System and beliefs of Western origin, have become more acute in the 1980s. Former prime minister Nakasone hoped to resolve them through an unapologetic reassertion of Japanese mores as interpreted by himself and other staunch Japanists. He has forcefully propagated the need for a thorough and sincere study of what being Japanese is all about as a first requirement for a truly internationalised Japan, contributing to the world's welfare. In answer to a question, put by myself, as to whether Japanese must be taught a morality different from that of other people, Nakasone stated that basic morality may be the same everywhere, but that it has different social bases and comes in different forms, which in the Japanese case necessitates attention from the authorities.[44] Some LDP politicians go considerably beyond this. Education Minister Fujio Masayuki (who had to resign in 1986 after writing that Korea had assented to its own annexation by Japan in 1910) was quite explicit about the need to reintroduce the moral code taught by the Imperial Rescript on Education to restore Japan's traditional moral order. Another education minister, Setoyama Mitsuyo, asserted in 1983 at a press conference that United States occupation officials were indirectly responsible for increased unruliness in Japanese schools. They had been assigned to destroy the customs, morals and history of Japan in order to adjust the Japanese to American living habits. Although resulting in some good, this had not, according to the minister, created a happy people. As a remedy, he suggested that the question of national morality as well as old-fashioned teaching methods should be re-studied; the concepts that he suggested should be instilled in children are all to be found in the Imperial Rescript on Education. Setoyama would no doubt have been forced to resign had he come out with this only six years earlier.

Japanese who think like Nakasone and most of the post-war education ministers, believe that 'individualism', which has allegedly replaced traditional morality since the occupation, has resulted in rampant selfishness and violence. In their 'guidance' concerning teaching about the constitution given in 1987 to the authors of school textbooks, the censors of the Ministry of Education explained the need for a shift of emphasis from guarantees of individual rights to social and national responsibilities. There exists considerable ambivalence about the concept of 'individualism'. It is a code word indicating that the user has the correct ideas about the purpose of education, as set forth in the Fundamental Law of Education adopted in 1947. It is also deemed necessary to provide Japan with more creative thinkers. The important Ad Hoc Council for Educational Reform, established by Nakasone and consisting of academics, intellectuals and businessmen, has wrestled with the notion, and reports produced between 1985 and 1987 left an inescapable impression of believing that more individualism and more creativity would follow from more control. Japanese officials often define their imported terms rather sloppily, thus enabling themselves to take action that is contradictory to stated purposes. Well acquainted with the technique of juggling incompatible realities, Nikkyoso and other critics fear that 'individualism' will be the long-expected Trojan horse smuggling in nationalistic ethics.[45] What the reformers are saying is that in order to stimulate individuality and creativity and bring about meaningful membership in the international community, education must imbue schoolchildren with love for Japan. In their final recommendations for a curriculum of moral education, already in part revived, the educational reform committee members emphasised the teaching of 'respect for Japanese culture', which, in the context in which the phrase is generally used, means respect for existing power relations.

In 1985 the Ministry of Education caused turmoil among educators by issuing instructions to all school heads that they must hoist the national flag and have their charges sing the national anthem at school ceremonies. This first order of its kind was prompted by a report revealing that only 92·5 per cent of primary schools and 86·4 per cent of middle schools hoisted the flag at the ceremony closing the school year, while only 72 per cent of primary schools and 53 per cent of middle schools sang the 'Kimigayo' ('His Majesty's Reign', the unofficial national anthem); not enough, according to the officials concerned, to instil patriotic love in all Japanese children. Nikkyoso, on the other hand, considers both flag and anthem to be remnants of the 'emperor system'. To the ministry's contention that other countries have similar practices, the critics respond that both Germany and Italy changed their national anthems and flags after 1945. Shortly before the Ministry of Education issued its instructions, a publication from the Prime Minister's Office openly stated that some Japanese were allergic to the sight of the flag because of personal war memories, and that for that very reason it was necessary to generate patriotism in a generation with no such memories.

Travelling through Japan, one once again sees, in front of schools, statues of a boy reading a book while carrying firewood on his back. It is Ninomiya Kinjiro, also known as Sontoku, a historical figure born in 1787 who by simultaneous hard work and hard study became a shogunate official and precursor of the movement of agrarian nationalism. The emphasis of his teaching was on the virtues of diligence, thrift, sincerity and mutual co-operation as a token of collective gratitude for blessings received. This would create a 'true society'.[46] The innocent-looking statue, symbolising these Confucianist ethics, was a central prop of moral education in pre-war and wartime schools. And since the number of such statues in primary-school grounds increased rapidly during the years in which the military increased their grip on the country, Ninomiya Kinjiro reminds many Japanese of the 'morals' they thought they had seen the last of when the occupation began to change the Japanese curriculum.

'Forced secularisation' by the outside world

Selfishness and materialism have long been imagined to be Western imports.[47] The virtues of thrift and collective endeavour that Ninomiya

Kinjiro stood for are now being threatened – so many administrators have commented – by foreigners who 'have become work-shy, abandoned production in favour of consumption, and are now losing out to Japanese economic competition'.[48] When in the late 1980s foreign criticism of Japanese economic practices and intransigence on international issues began to be supplemented by more analytical probes into 'nationalistic' Japanese behaviour, a new indignant tone began to creep into the commentary of some of Japan's scholars, editors and other spokesmen. The critical foreigners allegedly aim to weaken the foundations upon which Japanese society is based.

This is explained by some of the more articulate commentators as being the result of the West jettisoning the principle of 'cultural relativism'. As one Kyoto University professor of economics puts it:

> When challenged by cultures and practices outside the Western tradition, increasingly the impulse among Americans and Europeans is to condemn what is non-Western as unethical and unfair. . . . It is against this background of rising anti-cultural relativism among European and American opinion leaders that trade conflicts . . . have gathered momentum. With such philosophical conservatism on the loose, it might be unrealistic for us to expect fair understanding of our culture, and our social structure and customs.[49]

Foreign scrutiny of the Japanese System and the ideology and notions that help sustain it regularly invites vehement Japanese responses, which seems inevitable. It is, after all, tantamount to analysis of an ineffable divinity – which is destructive to any kind of religion. Thus Japan's unofficial but, to all intents and purposes, most prominent mouthpiece in the world, the *Japan Times*, editorialised – apropos of an exchange in an intellectual magazine between a foreign author and a Japanese professor propounding Japanist views – as follows:

> any foreigner who lashes out in an angry and inaccurate fashion at this country's identity, its mythology if you will, encourages Japanese deafness to foreign criticism. The claims to guilt-free national identity are now firmly on the human agenda. But such claims are not the stuff of smooth global relations. Hence the need for patience, for understanding, for tolerance, for good manners.[50]

Without a far-reaching 'secularisation' of Japan, its subjects cannot become true citizens; nor can they gain a clear awareness of where the System's activities, in which many participate with such seemingly religious fervour, are taking them. But since foreigners, especially the representatives of governments and businesses, cannot accommodate Japanese society in its capacity as a substitute religion, since they *do* worry about where Japan is going and since they will always ask questions and suggest answers that cut too close to the bone, they are, indeed, the 'secularising' force the administrators are afraid of. The *Japan Times* and the Kyoto professor, along with numerous other commentators, do not know it, but they are defenders of a faith.

12

The Right to Rule

So long as it is fairly diffuse, the exercise of informal power in Japan causes no acute anguish. If sensed at all by the post-war Japanese, the System's ubiquitous and inescapable power is subtle, vague and rarely locatable. The unofficial methods by which order is kept outside the sanctioning framework of the law are rarely perceived, let alone openly scrutinised, and can therefore never present explicit problems. The exercise of official leadership, on the other hand, causes constant, severe and apparently insoluble tensions.

The Japanese who are formally in charge of the country – the prime minister and his cabinet – are in practice not allowed to exercise the power they should exercise under the constitution. Political leaders who hanker after genuine leadership will always face an elusive yet impenetrable wall of mistrust and unceasing sabotage. No one in Japan is given the unambiguous right to rule. No one person or group of people is ever really accountable for what Japan does. Japanese leadership is thus always incomplete.

The widely remarked weakness of Japan's official leadership is usually explained with reference to a social tradition that discourages 'individualism', and therefore does not produce individualist leaders. But when one considers potentially strong leaders such as Nakasone Yasuhiro, Tanaka Kakuei, Ikeda Hayato, Kishi Nobusuke and numerous 'bosses' of interest groups or gangs, this theory does not hold; Nakasone, for example, was no less 'individualistic' than the foreign counterparts with whom he conferred at the annual summit conferences. The related theory that it is the public which will not accept a strong leader, because it won't have anything to do with individualists, is equally unconvincing. There have always been plenty of popular heroes who behaved quite individualistically, and have been widely admired for that very reason.

To explain this particular issue in culturalist terms ignores the crucial political fact that Japanese who partake in the sharing of power are unremittingly ambivalent about who among them should have the right to rule. This extraordinary – for a modern industrial nation – characteristic is the most fundamental problem of Japanese political life. It is a problem whose repercussions affect, in varying degrees of immediacy, most of the phenomena described in this book. It is essentially and by definition a problem of political legitimacy. I say by definition, because among other things legitimacy always implies a condition where the right to rule has clearly been established.

The legitimacy problem

On the face of it, political legitimacy would appear to be no problem in Japan. Unlike in South Korea or the communist countries of Asia, it is not an issue that draws attention. Admittedly, leftist intellectuals routinely question the legitimacy of a state that is the servant of 'monopoly capitalism'. Affected despair about this binds them together in groups that, as we have seen, actually serve the System by helping to ritualise emotional dissent. But outside this rigid and ritualistic Marxist frame of reference the concept of legitimacy simply does not occur in Japanese political discourse. Nevertheless, the absence of an intellectual frame of reference that might enable Japanese to perceive and discuss the problem does not mean that it is not, potentially, there. The fact that it is never raised may make it all the more insidious.

Self-validation

'Political legitimacy' is a slippery concept. It corresponds to a reality that lends itself even less than most other socio-political phenomena to measurement. It is, moreover, that kind of subtle attribute of a political system that is generally noticed only when it is absent, or when there seems to be not enough of it. Such shortcomings may make themselves felt in acute form on two occasions. The first is at the birth of a new power system, when new habits of obedience are demanded. The other comes 'when the customary ways and limits of power are altered, when subjects are presented with new and disturbing uses of power and are asked to assume new burdens and accept new claims'.[1]

In much contemporary political science, legitimacy is interpreted as something that automatically accompanies or follows from acceptance, acquiescence or consensus.[2] But this cannot be so, because if acceptance, acquiescence or consensus constituted the key to legitimacy, widespread protests against some government action could be mistaken for an indication of the illegitimacy of power-holders. The right to rule must not be thought to depend on good or bad policies. It is something that stands above the incumbents themselves, whether or not they follow disastrous policies. On the other hand, there can be a relative lack of political legitimacy without this becoming manifest in riots or other evidence of an end to acquiescence. Failure to recognise that an absence of opposition does not automatically confer legitimacy can lead to a complete misreading of political situations. Certainly in Japan an aggregate of supportive attitudes, based on what is in part a deliberately induced popular supposition that the authorities are benevolent and have the people's welfare at heart, does not add up to legitimacy.[3]

Legitimacy implies more than acquiescence or consensus because it is, by definition, bestowed upon a political arrangement through an external agency such as a system of laws, a sanctioning deity or whatever else transcends the temporal, political world and is, by common consent, perceived as ruling the rulers as well as the ruled. Seen in this light, it is immediately clear why legitimacy should be a problem in Japan. The Japanese System sets out to be self-validating. It is itself the 'divinity', supplying its own closed system of faith and self-justification. And since a political system cannot legitimise itself, the Japanese System can by definition never be legitimate.

I do not mean to make light of 'acceptance' and 'acquiescence' as political factors. On the contrary, public apathy, an important ingredient for the maintenance of an established power pattern in any country, has so far been a particularly potent factor in the preservation of Japanese political arrangements. 'Shikataganai', 'It cannot be helped', is one of the daily interjections of Japanese life. It acknowledges a fact of nature, like saying 'It's hot!' or 'It's freezing!' Obedience to the dictates of those in power is largely a matter of 'shikataganai', helped by the fact that no clear division is seen between the social order and the political system. But this kind of obedience rests on latent social threats of coercion and therefore, once again, has nothing to do with legitimacy.[4]

Those who are obliged constantly to resign themselves with a sigh of 'shikataganai' to the political status quo are not likely to be excited by the question of who has the right to rule. But passive acceptance is a product of circumstances. Political belief does not enter into it. If the System is all around you and unbeatable, if it is supposed to contain the ultimate meaning of your life and if you do not know where else to look for such ultimate meaning, then there is little else to do but sit back and enjoy it or, alternatively, grin and bear it. From what we have seen of the vagueness of the boundary, in the Japanese imagination, between the private individual and the socio-political realm, and of the religious role of the System, it should be clear that to question the legitimacy of the System would be for most ordinary Japanese like questioning the legitimacy of one's mother.

A problem for the ruling class

In contrast to the average person, the individuals and groups that form the ruling class are often deeply involved in questions of who among them may demand their obedience and co-operation. Though they do not express it in these terms, bureaucrats, LDP politicians, the administrators at the apexes of the industrial hierarchies and newspaper editors are all alike faced with the problem of the right to rule. The prime ministership of Nakasone Yasuhiro offers a splendid illustration of this.

Nakasone appeared fully aware that Japan's international difficulties were to a large extent due to weak national leadership, and he tried harder than any of his post-war predecessors to bring his office closer to the power that the world generally expects prime ministers to exercise.[5] As we saw in Chapter 5, he formed a new administrative agency with the rank of ministry, tried to improve the ability of the Prime Minister's Office to react quickly to emergency situations and found new ways to gain more leverage over the bureaucrats in breaking through deadlocks. One would think that such measures would be welcomed by bureaucrats, LDP politicians and many editorial writers who, uncomfortably aware of foreign pressure and criticism, routinely confirm the need for major structural adjustments, for effective leadership and for a more responsible global role. And there is no doubt that Japan's administrators and commentators, as well as a large segment of the public, noticed the advantage of having a prime minister who was taken seriously by other heads of government. Nevertheless, the very same voices that conceded that a decisive prime minister benefited the country also objected to the way in which Nakasone tried to be stronger and more decisive than his predecessors. As far as probably the majority of his fellow LDP Diet members were concerned, the attempt to establish a credible Japanese leadership was reason for a hearty dislike of Nakasone. The bureaucrats made barely any move to accommodate the policy adjustments he pleaded for; and a pervasive sense of distrust emanated from editorials commenting on his efforts.

Interestingly enough, the public at large was not at all distressed by Nakasone's trying to be a strong leader. The popularity polls indicated that he stood in higher esteem with the people than any of his post-war colleagues. It was the various élite groups that were upset. True, certain groups among Japan's intelligentsia mistrusted him to begin with. Nakasone was notoriously candid about his nationalistic convictions. He was prepared to go much further than his predecessors in breaking taboos connected with Japan's undigested imperialist past, and he is associated with groups and individuals that purvey the idea of Japan as a mono-ethnic, mono-racial society. But on the whole this programme is in line with the wishes of most administrators – it was only his explicitness that caused a few raised eyebrows. The problem was that those who run the various components of the Japanese System simply did not accept unambiguous central political leadership. If Nakasone's predecessors Fukuda Takeo and Ohira Masayoshi had tried to strengthen the office of prime minister, they too would have been greatly mistrusted.

Early problems

Looking back through Japanese history, one can discern a succession of measures that were introduced to compensate for the failure to establish who has the right to rule. These incomplete solutions deserve attention here because most of them continue to have a decisive influence on the manner in which Japanese power is exercised today.

The simplest method of maintaining political order is the threat of physical force. Residues of naked power, for instance the power the police exercise in the arrest of criminals, can be found in all advanced societies, and are accepted as unavoidable by the vast majority of citizens. But for more general political control, brute force has obvious drawbacks. It is not conducive to the stable situation that all power-holders desire if they are intent on holding on to their power. The exercise of naked power may give a ruler prestige, but will not, unless their subjects are masochists, produce positive emotions. Besides, the armed servants that the ruler must employ to keep the threat of punishment credible may, under the leadership of an ambitious captain, turn against him.

To solve both these problems and make subjects, including soldiers, believe that the ruler has a right to control them, a body of theory, together with rituals and other symbolism, is necessary. Early Japanese chieftains asserted the right to rule by claiming an inherent virtue derived from their original kinship with patron deities, and underlined it with clan temples, burial mounds and chronicles. How they fared in these first Japanese attempts at legitimising political power is unclear. The *Nihon Shoki* (*Chronicles of Japan*), the oldest official history, mentions a test, decreed in the year 415 by the Emperor Ingyo, in which clan chiefs and holders of hereditary titles had to subject their claims to their positions to divine judgement by putting their hands in tubs of boiling water. The chronicle relates that truthful claimants remained unharmed, while liars fled in terror, and that thenceforth no one told lies about his descent.[6]

The attempts by the Yamato court in the sixth and seventh centuries to expand its sway over hitherto independent chieftains required new and more compelling definitions of legitimacy. Hence the stress on the need for harmony in Shotoku Taishi's 'constitution', and the eagerness with which Yamato rulers seized upon Buddhism and Confucianism in order to buttress their claims of legitimacy.

The rise of the warrior houses and the age of civil wars speak for themselves. Unsolved problems of legitimacy, wherever they occur, tend to bring military power to the fore.[7] Hence the fact that Japan – most extraordinarily, considering the nearly total absence of any foreign threat – has experienced one form or another of warrior rule for much more than half of its traceable history.

Japan's rulers could – and often had to – give massive demonstrations of military might to back up their political claims. Hideyoshi brought together more than 150,000 soldiers for the siege of Odawara – about ten thousand more than all the army and garrison troops that Charles V needed to rule most of Europe.[8] The third Tokugawa shogun, Tokugawa Iemitsu, symbolically consolidated his regime by marching 307,000 men through Kyoto. The emperor, incidentally, still lived there; he had, of course, no choice but to consent.[9]

An expression frequently used to describe events in pre-Tokugawa Japan was *gekokujo* ('lower overturning the upper'), a term indicating much scrambling for power positions and a lot of opportunism. During the Muromachi shogunate (1338–1573) 'in most matters force was required to back up the exercise of delegated authority'.[10] So much for political legitimacy up to the great watershed of Tokugawa power. And the situation that followed could hardly be considered an improvement.

Tokugawa warrior rule was imposed upon an unenthusiastic and sometimes demonstrably unwilling populace.[11] Contrary to the general impression that Japan enjoyed two and a half centuries of public peace, there were disturbances throughout the period. Despite the relentless suppression of heterodoxy, and an ideology presenting the body politic as the ultimate good, the peasantry, according to one compilation, rebelled 2,809 times and rioted approximately one thousand times.[12] Fujita Yukoku (1774–1826), one of the major Confucian scholars involved in the compilation of the *History of Great Japan*, had no illusions about the willingness of Japan's commoners to support the power-holders, believing that, given the chance, they would eagerly join the ranks of an enemy. This assessment appears to have been shared by his colleagues.[13]

The 'nomenklatura' solution

When legitimacy is unobtainable and direct suppression by force cannot be sustained, there is still a middle way for retaining control:[14] to make sure that groups of people at crucial locations in society believe that the current arrangements are the best for *them*. Their assent can be won by a system of scaled benefits for the military and civil servants. I have observed such a system, in perhaps its neatest form, among the North Vietnamese cadres. The *nomenklatura*, the upper layer with hereditary privileges, of Soviet society also clearly belongs to this category.

Challenges to an established ruling order are unlikely to come from the lowest and least privileged members of society unless these have the support and leadership of certain élite groups. Spartacus-type movements are rare and in the end they fail. On the other hand, those in key positions have very good reasons to hinder change; for them, change in the midst of economic scarcity – the condition in which this kind of system flourishes – is dangerous. Not to toe the line is out of the question since this would mean losing privileges that have begun to appear essential for a decent life. The more control any individual has, the more he stands to lose in the way of purchasing privileges, medical services, élite schooling, good jobs for his children, and so on.

The system that the Tokugawa regime forged closely resembled this *nomenklatura* solution. Its security depended on forcing all 'vassal' lords to reside in the capital during alternate years, and to leave their families as hostages the rest of the time. It also developed, at least in its later phase, a political system reminiscent of the communist examples I have cited. An upper stratum of samurai with inherited privileges guaranteed political continuity. Beneath it, a layer of educated and disciplined lower samurai existed; these were early 'technocrats' entrusted with the daily management of a fairly rapidly evolving political economy and the channelling of wealth from society, through taxes and other levies, to the parasitic upper layer.[15] The lower samurai became increasingly restive but they also realised that if they rocked the boat they would most likely fall overboard themselves.

The *nomenklatura* class of the Tokugawa period rested on a politically apathetic rural populace, largely unseen by the élite and never won over to an active belief in the goodness of Tokugawa rule. Various sources, including European eyewitness accounts, suggest that this military regime ruled more harshly in its waning days than it had in the seventeenth century.[16] It struck Sir Rutherford Alcock as 'an administration based on the most elaborate system of espionage ever attempted'.[17] Even so, it had in practice lost much of its control over the feudal domains. The sudden United States demand in 1853 that Japan open itself to the world seems to have been no more than the final shove that left the tottering apparatus of warrior power ready to collapse when the samurai of Satsuma and Choshu staged their *coup d'état*. The subsequent attitudes of the vassals demonstrated that there was in fact little love lost between them and the regime.[18]

Institutionalising irresponsibility

The first thing the new rulers did, in an attempt to solve their colossal legitimacy problem, was to move the Meiji emperor from his palace in Kyoto to the shogunal castle in Edo, which was renamed Tokyo. This move, together with new institutions connecting the throne with the political process, was intended to suggest that the decisions of the oligarchy were being made in the emperor's name. In reality, the 'restoration' of the emperor in no way restored his temporal powers. Even while the oligarchs were effecting major political changes, they stuck to one major political tradition. All shogunate governments had theoretically been legitimised by imperial appointment. Since the sovereign was sacred and *lèse-majesté* a serious offence, the powerless emperors had always been ideal instruments in power games, and ideal shields for political manipulation.

Mutsuhito, who came to the throne as a boy of fourteen, never seemed to develop an interest in governing. That was irrelevant, however, because, even though the restoration had been preceded by a 'restoration movement', sanctioned by theories based on historical studies showing that the rightful place of the emperor was at the centre, the oligarchs never had any intention of giving him power. (They did ask, though, that he should appear interested; he was once chided by his political masters for paying so much attention to his horses that it had an adverse effect on public opinion.)[19]

Following the Meiji Restoration, the impression existed that the ruling oligarchy was eventually to be replaced by a parliamentary system which would give Japan a respected place in the ranks of modern nations. In the political debate that followed the introduction of new foreign theories, some advocated a constitutional monarchy roughly similar to those of Europe, with Mutsuhito as a king who legitimised prime ministers and cabinets. Such an arrangement would, however, have meant the gradual removal from power of individual oligarchs, and the Meiji constitution that they finally came up with showed clearly that they had seen no advantage to themselves in a limited monarchy. On paper, all power resided in the emperor, who bestowed the constitution on the nation out of his generosity. In practice, a new political system encompassing the exercise of informal power had begun to crystallise – informal power that kept the oligarchs on top. The Meiji constitution provided for yet another system to succeed that of the Tokugawa shogunate and all the other, earlier, unofficial systems that were legitimised by a theory of imperial rule that in fact had little or no connection with the exercise of real power.

The architects of the new state, who came from the class of restive lower samurai, understood that control through a hierarchy of privileges had to be replaced by control through propaganda, and they embarked on a major campaign to persuade the public of the inevitable rightness of their government. The campaign ran away with itself, resulting in the 'national essence' (kokutai) mystique, which made a politically circumscribed constitutional monarchy unthinkable. On a more immediately practical level, they refrained from writing unequivocal provisions into the constitution for the selection of leadership to be legitimised by the emperor, because that would have directly threatened their own positions. If they had allowed power to be concentrated in the hands of the prime minister or anyone else, the coalition of groups comprising the Meiji oligarchy could not have stayed together.[20]

Throughout the decades between then and the new constitution bestowed on the Japanese people by General MacArthur, it remained unclear who had the right to decide anything essential. Groups of elder statesmen, clustered around the emperor, made the system function; but they had no constitutional or legal position in the state, and thus were not accountable.

Who was, then? The Army? The Privy Council? The Diet? The Naimusho? The Foreign Ministry? Whose legitimacy was to be judged? As Maruyama Masao summed it up in a classic paragraph: 'An uncertain sharing of responsibility was preferred so that no one person could be pointed out as bearing the ultimate responsibility for decisions. It is obvious that the mechanism of the Emperor-system state had inherent within it the danger of developing into a colossal system of irresponsibility.'[21]

Japanese power-holders of the Meiji period and later could be held responsible neither for misdeeds nor for flagrant misgovernment. The grave dangers of this tradition for the nation (and other nations) was amply demonstrated in the first half of the twentieth century. Authority for Japan's conquests in Asia officially resided with an emperor who had no practical say in what Japan did. The anonymous decisions of this period changed the political map of Asia, started a war with the world's largest industrial power, caused the death of roughly three million Japanese and between ten and twenty million non-Japanese and led to the communist take-over of China as well as the hastened departure of the European colonial powers from Asia. And this is to name only the major results.

The 'ignorance' solution

One partial solution to the problem of who has the right to rule, introduced in the Meiji period and still vitally important today, is the cult of the ordained, knowledgeable administrator who, supposedly, has no ambition to wield power.

Traditionally, being in the know is associated in Japan with the right to administrative office, which seems understandable enough. The corollary, however, is that those who do not hold office should, ideally, be kept in ignorance. To simplify somewhat, one might say that in Japanese political practice for at least the past three centuries there have been two categories of people: those men entitled to exercise power, who are automatically 'in the know'; and those on the receiving end, who are not.

Popular ignorance and official secrecy were acknowledged by Tokugawa administrators to be essential to the preservation of order. Aizawa Seishisai (1782–1863), author of a seminal work in the context of later *kokutai* ideology,[22] contended that the people should accept the fact that rules existed and were beneficial to themselves, but should not be told what those rules were. He was also open about the fact that the Tokugawa regime deliberately kept the commoners weak and ignorant.[23] More than a hundred years after his death, frustrated exporters trying to break into the Japanese market frequently discovered that their products were subject to regulations of which the officials could not give them any further particulars.

There are good reasons to assume that the power-holders of the Meiji and Taisho periods did not believe what they made the public swallow about a divine and infinitely benevolent emperor, or about the 'family state' and all that went with it. The closing years of the nineteenth century saw the beginnings of a 'vast gulf which opened up between responsible constitutional scholarship and popular attitudes toward the constitution'.[24] The *kokutai* surrogate religion answered any questions about legitimacy that might arise among a public kept purposely in ignorance.

Ideas embodying political doubts were considered really dangerous only when they reached the ears of the common people. Although in the early decades of the present century the power-holders were obsessed with the threat they posed, they did not attempt to stamp them out completely. Most intellectuals either worked directly for the government or supported it in some way, and it was difficult as well as counter-productive to restrict their intellectual production too severely. Academics whose speculations went against the grain of government-dictated ideology were, at least until the late 1920s, accommodated with a fair measure of tolerance.

Post-war Japanese administrators have dropped the term 'dangerous thoughts'; the Japanese probably have more freedom to express critical or belligerent ideas than any other people in Asia, aside from the Filipinos. But the presumption that much of what the administrators know should be kept hidden from ordinary people has definitely survived.

I have been told a number of times by different government officials that, although they agreed with my conclusions and could find no fault with what I wrote, some of my analyses 'would create the wrong impression'. Japanese journalists tend to criticise bureaucratic restrictions on the 'right to know', which go far beyond what can be excused as being in the 'national interest'.[25] The set phrase from Tokugawa days – 'people must not be informed, but made dependent upon the authority of the government' – is occasionally still used today.[26] Fortunately for the officials, the members of the many reporter clubs attached to the ministries nearly always play along in spite of their criticisms of the restrictions.

Japanese administrators need have no qualms about their secretive habits, since these fit in with the generally accepted Japanese management of reality. Those not 'in the know' need not fear being considered lesser, because dumb citizens. Naïveté and ignorance of political intricacies have long been considered part and parcel of the idealised state of Japanese purity and innocence.

Denial of power

The most ingenious partial solution to the problem of the right to rule that Japanese power-holders have hit upon is a systematic denial that any power is exercised to begin with. To get around the legitimacy question, the administrators pretend that they are not interested in power.

This solution, again, came in with the Tokugawas. Thus the Tokugawa shoguns and their deputies did not aspire to power and were not exercising it; they were simply performing the right ceremonies to sustain the natural order. Memories of how they had arrived in a position to preside over those ceremonies were taboo.[27] The Meiji oligarchy and the bureaucracy it spawned were also presented as bodies not interested in power, motivated by a selfless desire to serve the emperor and thereby the nation, for the benefit of the entire Japanese family. Soldiers and sailors, up to the ranks of general and admiral, did the same; they served the emperor without the slightest thought of self-aggrandisement. Today, it would be very difficult to find a Japanese administrator who openly admitted to a desire to gain or hold on to – much less expand – his power, a desire that is of course his main concern.

The solution that denies the possession of, or appetite for, power puts politicians, however, in a quandary. When talking to their constituents, they cannot avoid boasting that they have it and seek more of it. For if they did not have the clout to talk the ministries into building the bridges, roads and airports to benefit the electorate that sends them to the Diet, why should it vote for them? The problem for Japan's politicians has always been that they cannot hide their real political ambitions, a fact that has earned them much disapprobation.

Venal politicians vs virtuous bureaucrats

When the Western concept of a politician accountable to an electorate was introduced after the Meiji Restoration, it created confusion and ambivalence among Japan's leaders and intellectuals. The oligarchy did not, at first, quite know what it wanted. Among the earliest leaders, Kido Koin advocated constitutional government responsible to the will of the people – this, however, to be attained gradually since the people were not yet ready for it. Okubo Toshimichi did not think the parliamentary form suitable, and favoured an absolute government composed of men of ability. Ito Hirobumi, influenced by Okubo, basically agreed with this.[28]

Still, the introduction of party politics was an inevitable concomitant of the Japanese effort to catch up with the West. That meant that something had to be done to curtail the potential for damage, since 'the samurai-bureaucrats in charge found it exceedingly difficult to accept the idea of a loyal opposition; opposition was regarded as a threat not only to themselves but to the state'.[29] As a solution, the oligarchs made sure in their propaganda that anything associated with politics was made to appear as unpatriotic.[30]

The Meiji press on the whole was only slightly less critical of the politicians than were the oligarchy and officialdom. Japan's early journalists were, or pretended to be, scandalised by bribery and other electoral irregularities, thus setting a pattern that is still followed today. Party politics was portrayed to the public of Meiji Japan as vile and directed by narrow self-interest. The idea was hammered home that loyal subjects of the emperor, such as soldiers and officials, should have nothing to do with politics.[31]

Party government was systematically sabotaged. As a foreign political historian of the day summed it up:

Against all the efforts of the political parties to secure responsible government the Upper House [manned by bureaucrats and aristocrats] has backed up the oligarchy, and has stood ready to block all legislation presented by a government which was too closely allied with any party. Attempts at party government, therefore, have generally given place to government by the oligarchs with the support of the members of the parties, now in one combination, now in another, secured either by bribery or owing to their conviction that opposition was fruitless.[32]

The anti-politician propaganda was successfully passed down to succeeding generations. In the 1920s the parties were seen from the Japanist perspective

as embodiments of an unsightly and immoral competitive urge for personal power. Rather than unifying the people with imperial rule, they were portrayed as intruders who sundered a sacred and mystical bond between the emperor and his subjects – a bond of harmonious beauty which, when manifested in imperial benevolence and the loyal obedience of the subject, elevated Japan to a position of moral paramountcy among the other nations of the world.[33]

The relative positions in the power structure of bureaucrats and politicians, which in essence have lasted until the present, were established just before the turn of the century as a result of institutional manipulations by one of the oligarchs, Yamagata Aritomo. Yamagata has attracted less attention than some other Men of Meiji who left more quotable ideas, but in the end he probably wielded more substantial power for a longer period than any of his fellow oligarchs. He was the major force behind the establishment of a conscripted military, and he shaped the powers of the mighty Naimusho in its formative years. He, more than anyone, deserves to be called the creator of Japan's social control bureaucrats. And he 'clung to the position that a competitive political system multiplied divisions in society and detracted from national unity to which all should be sacrificed'.[34]

Even though Diet members were kept at a distance from any executive power, they became incrementally more important because of the mistake made by the oligarchy in giving the Diet a veto right over the budget – a tool, in other words, whereby political parties could force the government to make do with the previous year's budget. This meant that, eventually, the administrators were obliged to mix with the politicians.[35] Nevertheless, the battle for power between the bureaucrats and politicians was, thanks to rules introduced by Yamagata, effectively decided almost before it had begun. Following the collapse of the very first Japanese cabinet of party politicians, which lasted for four months in 1898, Yamagata became prime minister and moved quickly to control any future 'damage' to the nation. Okuma Shigenobu, who led that first party government, had been besieged by requests that the bureaucrats be replaced by politicians.[36] Moderate politicians were pleading for a system of dual access to executive power: not only graduates of the higher civil service examinations, mostly Todai law department graduates, but also members of the Diet and prefectural assemblies should be considered for high appointment. Okuma did not oblige, but Yamagata, having regained power, spread the lie that he had.

The institutional innovation designed by Yamagata virtually closed the door for ever on the possibility of future party cabinets appointing party members as vice-ministers, bureau chiefs or prefectural governors. This had the effect of insulating the bureaucracy from any effects of political decision-making.[37] To make sure that the amended Appointment Ordinance could never be rescinded, he made the Privy Council[38] the guardian over his edicts. And to guarantee that cabinets would always abide by the council's ruling, he 'chose a rare and subtle solution, one void of legal force but massively binding in practice'.[39] He made the emperor issue an 'imperial message' listing a number of ordinances henceforth to be referred to the Privy Council and including among them all those relating to examinations, appointments, discipline, dismissals and rankings of the bureaucrats.

A personal communication from the emperor – as distinct from a formal Imperial Edict – could never be overruled, and there was no precedent or procedure for asking an emperor to rescind it.[40] There remained a very tiny possibility that a later cabinet would nevertheless have the guts to ask the emperor to change his mind, and Yamagata, with ultimate subtlety, even contrived a defence against that. 'To protect the imperial message, he kept it secret. Few outside the Privy Council and the Imperial Household even knew it existed. . . . Yamagata had found an intricate but ingenious way of circumventing the juridical theory that no law can be irreversible.'[41]

Selecting the virtuous administrators

Once the decision took shape among the oligarchs that Japan was not to be ruled by popular mandate through elected representatives, they were faced with the task of structuring and augmenting a ruling class. The formula they adopted still determines the allocation of power in present-day Japan. The principle of hereditary selection was giving way at the time to meritocratic principles. For many years following the restoration, an important qualification for membership in the oligarchy and its bureaucratic extensions was participation in the movement that had led to the *coup d'état*, or membership of the Satsuma or Choshu samurai class. Subsequently 'Western knowledge', preferably absorbed in Europe or the United States, became increasingly important.[42] But by the turn of the century the surest, and almost the sole, way to get into the class of 'those in the know' that manages the country was to graduate from the law department of the University of Tokyo – a tradition that, as we have seen, determines the character of Japanese schooling to this day.

Todai acquired its pivotal position in conferring legitimacy as a result of the treaties providing for extraterritoriality that Japan had signed with the Western powers. As already mentioned, the foreigners were ready to scrap these deeply hated stipulations only if and when legal trials could be conducted by a competent judiciary. It was the desperate need this created that launched the law department of Todai in its function of ordaining the modern samurai. Its graduates did not, initially, need to pass the civil service exams in order to fill the highest posts, and by 1890 their supply was large enough to fill nearly all administrative vacancies and more than half the judicial vacancies.[43]

More than 50 per cent of Todai graduates in the 1880s achieved high status, and one out of every four attained membership in the upper élite, as against one out of twenty-five graduates from Waseda or Keio (the major private universities). Seventy of the 76 vice-ministers in the eight ministries between 1901 and 1926 were Todai graduates.[44]

So far as intellect and skill are concerned, this now firmly entrenched method of ordaining the ruling élite is fairly arbitrary. What was true then is true today: the special 'knowledge' and thus 'virtue' of the bureaucrat, which helps lend their role a semblance of legitimacy, comes down to membership in a class of people that has managed the art of passing the most abstruse entrance examinations. In Chapter 4 I have touched on the general misconception in the West concerning the selection of Japan's élite. Its ranks have been selected mainly for stamina and dedication. Todai graduates tend to be 'bright', but many Japanese with very capable minds of a different cast are discarded and doomed permanently to operate on the fringes. Much capacity for original thinking is wasted. The Japanese ruling class is far more thoroughly schooled than it is educated: a fact of more than peripheral importance for the attitude and approach of Japan's administrators towards the international world.

Depoliticising politics

Legitimacy in post-war Japan is officially bestowed on the government by popular mandate. And elections and a parliament have, indeed, taken over to some extent from the emperor as institutions legitimising current arrangements. But the concept of the sovereignty of the people is not understood by most Japanese, and is certainly not a living principle among those who share power. The appeals to popular sovereignty in the press are purely rhetorical and never coupled to any coherent analysis of the pervasive exercise of informal power that systematically prevents the realisation of this principle. The Diet and elections are not seen as legitimising the existing political order. They have not replaced older institutions in the popular mind, since both already existed when the emperor was formally the bestower of legitimacy, at which time they were widely castigated as diminishing the purity and moral soundness of the Japanese nation.

Before 1945 it was considered that all laws and directives issued in the name of the emperor were, by definition, for the public good. The bureaucrats were therefore, by definition, impartial and just. Politicians, by contrast, were demonstrably spurred on by political considerations, which in the Japanese context could not be differentiated from selfish motives. There is still today a strong tendency to assume that whatever is politically motivated can never be as good as what is (supposedly) motivated by considerations of the public good. Even though it is manifestly clear that they are guided by their own interests and proceed without consulting the public in any way, the bureaucrats' efforts are somehow made to appear more legitimate than anything done by the politicians, who have never been able completely to shake off their original reputation as loutish, self-seeking opportunists. The post-war press is still permeated with an unacknowledged prejudice against politicians, and routinely feeds the public with a view of politics that, though rarely well articulated, is mostly sceptical and negative. Popular suspicion and distaste are heightened by the ease with which political position can be bought and sold in Japan and the inherent instability that this creates among cliques of LDP politicians.

Nevertheless, Japan cannot do away with the politicians, since in theory they form the link between society and the body politic. Without them, the strongest components of the System would consist only of bureaucrats and industrialists, and bureaucratic authoritarianism would become too blatant. Parliamentary proceedings form a façade behind which the administrators manage affairs, just as the imperial throne once did for the Meiji oligarchy.

To counter the lingering distaste for the archetypal politician with his 'egotistical motives', the LDP likes to make it appear that it is nothing more nor less than a collection of benevolent administrators. Roughly one-third of its Diet members – generally the most powerful ones – have in any case travelled the élite administrator course from the Todai law department or its equivalents and on through one of the ministries. Whereas individual LDP members would not be credible if they denied an interest in power, and would raise doubts about their ability to bring pork-barrel benefits to their constituencies, the LDP as a whole can more easily gloss over its *raison d'être*.

In line with its denial of the exercise of power, the LDP likes to present a depoliticised picture of politics. It is greatly helped here by the ancient notion that those in power are more ethical than those out of power, that they are legitimate by the very fact of wielding power. The LDP – despite many a press campaign in which it is lambasted for its 'money politics', its arrogance and its wrong priorities – has a certain aura of respectability that the other parties lack. For all the routine criticism levelled against it, the government party is still treated as if it belonged in a different category from groups entering the political arena with new political suggestions. The latter are easily denigrated as concerned with the interests of a very limited number of citizens rather than of the Japanese people as a whole.

Their desire for some of the LDP's power for themselves automatically stigmatises them as 'self-seeking politicians'.

In Western constitutionalist democracies the problem of legitimacy does not arise, because citizens have recourse to corrective mechanisms whenever the procedures preceding political decisions diverge consistently from a legally sanctioned course. In Japan, where laws do not control the administrators but are tools for administrative control, there is no such recourse. The concept of democracy in Japan is not a pragmatic concept guiding actual political processes. As one of the foremost specialists on Japanese intellectual history remarks, democracy is in Japan a radical concept, valued in an abstract, normative sense. It furnishes the Japanese with a point of reference, based on rational humanitarianism, outside existing politics and history. 'It provides an ethical identification with which to criticise historical trends and the cultural and political content of the present. As in the 1920s . . . democracy is not an empowering ideology for constitutional politics, but critical and quite often antipolitical.'[45]

Japan can be called a 'democracy' by the criteria that Aristotle used in his famous classification of monarchies, aristocracies and democracies, since 'what Aristotle called a democracy was simply an aristocracy of fairly broad membership'.[46] And Japan's 'democracy' is constitutional, but it is not constitutionalist. The democratic provisions of the constitution are ultimately unenforceable, if only because the Supreme Court is in the hands of the bureaucrats.

The disloyalty of institutionalised opposition

In Western constitutionalist democracies, the preservation of a legal order justifying political arrangements is safeguarded by the opportunity to 'throw the rascals out'. As long as voters can choose to transfer power to a different set of power-holders, they can prevent the political system from becoming a System with its own legally uncontrolled dynamics of the abuse of power. For this purpose, a political system must tolerate an institutionalised loyal opposition. We have already seen that one of the most essential traits of the all-embracing Japanese System is that it tolerates no genuine opposition, as was dramatically illustrated by its response to – and the fate of – Nikkyoso, the teachers' union.

The concept of a loyal opposition – a political organisation allowed effectively to oppose government policy yet considered perfectly legitimate – has been particularly troublesome for all countries where the exercise of power has been justified by traditional Chinese theories of government. The political problems of South Korea are related to it. It hampered the 'democracy' of South Vietnam before it was overrun; and the cases of contemporary China and Taiwan are other good illustrations.[47] President Ngo Dimh Diem of Vietnam had much difficulty in dealing with John Kennedy and Henry Cabot Lodge because his Confucianist way of thinking allowed no tolerance of opposition.[48] In the Confucianist tradition, rulers are by definition virtuous; thus to oppose them automatically means to question their legitimacy.

So it still is, essentially, in contemporary Japan. A genuine opposition with the potential to take over the reins of government, or merely to change the policy agenda, is not acceptable to the administrators in the LDP and the bureaucracy. To say that they would feel discomfort in the face of such an opposition is wildly to understate the problem. A genuine opposition would nullify everything they stand for. Thus even Japan's official political system, that respectable mantle hiding the reality of *jinmyaku* deals, is in effect a one-party system.

The LDP is as one with officialdom in its deep distrust of opposition of any kind.[49] When Prime Minister Nakasone made election campaign speeches in which he repeated over and over again, as he did during the campaign of 1986, that the opposition parties behave like wilful kindergarten children, he echoed a deeply embedded prejudice that these parties are not ready to look after the people, whereas the LDP is a supreme model of responsibility. Voting for the opposition, though a widespread practice, is considered a mild form of deviance that can be controlled. Giving one's vote to a party one knows will never be allowed to share power in the central government is an 'expressive' (as distinct from 'instrumental') act comparable to joining a lunch-hour strike or marching past the Diet building with pseudo-revolutionary banners.

The elected parliament that existed before 1945 was an imported institution that, in its original function, theoretically conflicted with the ideology of the 'national essence'. It presupposed the possibility of political choice and political conflict, whereas *kokutai* implied political arrangements as having been endowed by a benevolent emperor and sustaining a conflict-free society. Today, genuine parliamentary politics, with the possibility of sustained legitimate opposition, remains completely incompatible with the powerful Japanist beliefs that postulate a conflict-free society.

The 'mass inclusionary' illusion

The very bases of pluralism in politics are regarded as morally suspect by the administrators, though they can never concede this while Japan is being presented to the world and to the Japanese as a parliamentary democracy. Certain statements coming from the LDP, however, appear to be groping towards a more satisfactory formulation of the actual state of affairs, one that can be used as a conceptual basis for future plans. A month after the July 1986 elections in which the LDP gained a record number of parliamentary seats, Prime Minister Nakasone explained that this victory marked the beginning of what he dubbed 'the 1986 political order'. The birth of this order would be assisted by a new party strategy, with which the 'flexibly conservative' urban voters would all be won over. (Unlike the rural population and business owners, urban housewives, salarymen and students have not been stable supporters of the LDP.) Such additional support for the LDP, according to Nakasone, would signify the end of the '1955 political order' – which is common shorthand for the uneven rivalry between the LDP and the socialists following the formation of the LDP – and the beginning of the '1986 system'.

This was more than mere rhetoric delivered in the flush of victory. Four years previously, LDP ideologues had published an important article whose theory of Japanese political history led to the conclusion that the LDP is destined to entice the labour unions away from the socialists, and to create a new political organisation that can directly absorb the political energies of city dwellers and consumers.[50] What these LDP theorists, as well as Nakasone, were saying more or less out loud was that soon there would no longer be any need for the JSP, their only 'rival'.

With the gradual demise of Marxist-oriented scholarship, the System is beginning to win scholarly support for what it stands for. A favourite new term for it is Murakami Taisuke's 'new middle mass'.[51] Japanese political analysts have begun to refer routinely to a 'mass inclusionary system', by which they understand bureaucratic control that is not open to checks from the public but is nevertheless supported by a majority.

In the final analysis, the claim of undivided support for a depoliticised, 'mass inclusionary' political system is not credible. To begin with, such support is taken for granted and never measured. Also, the United States occupation 'reformers' were not the only ones who counted on vigorous party competition to establish a healthy Japanese democracy. Many Japanese hoped this would happen. And the apparent gradual decline in the fortunes of the LDP in the 1970s, a decline accompanied by much media speculation about the advent of a 'multi-party' era, was welcomed by liberal-minded Japanese. The number of Japanese journalists and scholars who discuss the relative power of various segments of officialdom, and of ordinary people who themselves have sensed the intimidation of which System components are capable, is great enough to make the denial of power unconvincing.

The other countries in Asia with Confucianist-influenced political cultures hindering acceptance of the idea of a legitimate 'loyal opposition' happen to have strong central leadership. Their problem of who has the right to rule may divide the power-holders from a large segment of the population, as is exemplified by South Korea. The Japanese legitimacy problem does not cause such a political division because the ideology of Japaneseness dampens potential political recalcitrance on a national scale. But that does not solve the problem for the ruling élite. The attempted partial solutions examined earlier, especially the outright denial of the exercise of power, have created further problems.

The idea that one can depoliticise a political system is, of course, an illusion. Pretending that relationships and social processes in which power plays a role are not political means that essential distinctions are not made, so that many areas of life normally kept outside the political realm tend, on the contrary, to become heavily politicised. In one sense the System is so depoliticised that there seems to be progressively less and less of what in the West would be considered politics. But precisely because of this one can say that the whole System, with everything in it, is eminently political. As we have seen, this very pervasive political aspect of Japanese life goes in the guise of 'culture'.

The most serious consequence of an ostensibly depoliticised society that denies the existence of genuine conflict, and must constantly create the illusion of unified consent, is that it does not provide the normal means for conflict resolution to be found in modern constitutionalist states. The effect of this is insufficiently appreciated but far-reaching, not least in the context of Japan's international relations. The absence of official institutions for resolving conflict means that Japanese social relationships are shot through with unmediated power – or, to use another word for this, intimidation.

13

Ritual and Intimidation

Japanese are brought up with a socio-political imagery that portrays the authorities as united in an understanding of what the people want and need, an understanding deriving from Japan's essential 'homogeneity'. This notion of a unique sameness that makes compassionate bureaucratic rule possible is also very important to the bureaucratic self-image. It is made explicit in the instructions used for training bureaucrats:

> The organisational climate that makes possible this kind of groupism peculiar to our country stems from our national traditions, from the fact that our country consists of a homogeneous race, which is rare in the world, and from the fact that we go about our lives while mutually grasping one another's feelings, fearing confrontation, regarding 'harmony as noble', mutually restraining ourselves, and aligning ourselves to the thoughts and actions of people in the group.[1]

Another fundamental element in this paramount imagery, referred to in the above quote and inextricably intertwined with the beliefs in homogeneity and benevolence, is the concept of *wa*, which is generally translated as 'harmony', but is rich in connotations. *Wa* is one of the concepts that is widely believed to be difficult or impossible for foreigners to understand. But the 'harmony' of Japanese *wa* is associated with a variety of universal human virtues or qualities such as conciliation, gentleness, accord, accommodation, mellowness, moderation, mollification, peace, pliancy, amiability, appeasement, conformity, softness, order, unison, compromise, and so on.

Wa is in fact the first political concept that Japanese children are taught in their history lessons – when they learn that Japan's first law-giver, Shotoku Taishi, began his famous 'constitution' with the admonition 'regard *wa* as noble, and non-contrariness as honourable'. Prince Shotoku understood the need for *wa* as well as any subsequent power-holders, for he lived in a time of assassinations and battles for the throne, a time when nativist forces were protesting at the encroachments of a foreign religion – Buddhism – whose rituals were being promoted for political purposes.

A less than perfect harmony

A value system governed, ultimately, by social exigencies means the absence of an urge to fight over ideas. This means in turn that revolutions in the accepted meaning of the term are ruled out. In Japanese history, there were uprisings, peasant rebellions provoked by dire economic conditions and intolerable abuses, but they were not sustained and never amounted to a major revolution.

Until a little over a century ago, the leaders of peasant protest movements were often killed even when their complaints were admitted. They tended to be honoured afterwards; shrines were erected in their memory, at which the lords would worship along with the common people.[2] But even great heroes may not disturb the *wa* of society. In 1937 the Ministry of Education distributed two million copies of *Kokutai no Hongi*, a booklet setting forth the ideology of the 'national essence' and claiming that the spirit of harmony had, throughout history, been the source of Japan's national growth. Suzuki Zenko used every opportunity when he was prime minister (1980–2) to explain that *wa* was the central thought in his political philosophy. Since the late 1970s *wa* has appeared frequently in Japanese writing seeking to explain Japanese culture to the rest of the world. Some Japanese will say that *wa* is for Japan what universal values are for the West, the central 'principle' on which their society operates. It is, not surprisingly, frequently mentioned in the same breath as 'loyalty'.

Where the shoe pinches

Striving for *wa* is advocated at many company meetings, and *wa* is often mentioned in public speeches. Certain things, such as not resorting to legal action in order to right wrongs, are considered essential for the preservation of *wa*.[3] In other words, one has to work at *wa* – it does not come automatically. All the emphasis placed on *wa* is a give-away that this is where the shoe pinches. Japanese are obsessed with the idea of harmony precisely because of a subliminal awareness that it is always a very difficult thing to achieve. *Wa* is not an existing, consummate harmony, but the uninterrupted display of a readiness to sacrifice one's personal interests for the sake of a communal tranquillity.

The possibility that parts of the Japanese System might be lacking in *wa* is a profound embarrassment; it suggests the one dreaded imperfection of the idealised socio-political system that would expose its true nature. To keep it out of view entails a major effort, for Japanese society has no less conflict than other societies. The System is anything but static; it is moved by a tremendous internal dynamism, enhanced by strong competition. This competition, based on the principles of meritocracy that began to replace the hereditary allocation of power in the early part of the nineteenth century, starts with the examination system in schools, continues with the acquisition of as high a position as possible in the salaryman world or bureaucracy and is then sublimated into group competition for market share or factional power. Where possible, competition involving large groups is controlled, but that still leaves much room for shifts of balance and anguish about whether one's interests are properly looked after. The effort to keep up a surface decorum is supported by numerous subtle methods of avoiding and suppressing open conflict.

Japanese conflict and its suppression, and what happens when it finally can no longer be suppressed, are wonderfully portrayed, in an extreme and stylised form, in gangster movies. When tension mounts in these films it is normal for the mobsters to be 'hissing and puffing like pressure cookers'.[4] The protagonist who finally takes it upon himself to avenge the insult to his boss (or whatever else evil rivals have perpetrated) knows he will die at the end of it, just like the leaders of peasant rebellions in the Tokugawa period. In these romanticised movie stories, death is the price for upsetting the social order, even if it is for the most honourable cause.

In everyday life, one may not actually hear the hissing and puffing. But a closer look at a Japanese who is upset often gives the impression that, behind a face struggling for control, this is exactly what is going on. If the tension is relieved in public, which happens only rarely, the effect can be explosive: a sudden, very emotional outburst reducing other Japanese present to deep silence. It is usually gone as quickly as the proverbial thunderclap from a sunny sky, the frustrated party regaining his composure and smiling as if nothing had passed.

One of the most common ways of releasing tension is communal drunkenness. Drinking parties constitute one of several escape-valves attached to the pressure cooker of Japanese society. The noisy but ritualistic demonstrations by the tiny radical labour union splinters that have survived in some companies are another.

It is not likely that one will ever run into hissing and puffing bureaucrats. But over dinner with some sake, and with some prodding, their language tends to take on a distinctly military-strategic quality when they describe the relations of their ministries with other ministries, or intra-agency rivalries. Task forces, formed to deal with a particular administrative problem, are forever carrying out advances, tactical retreats and decoy manoeuvres. When Hatano Akira, a former top police official, was made justice minister in the first Nakasone cabinet, he was described as having parachuted into enemy territory. Ministries are always trying to 'colonise' other government agencies, and powerful LDP politicians do the same with ministries. Bureaucratic wars are a major topic of conversation in informed political circles. Ministry officials seconded to some foreign posting or organisation will speak of their war potential in comparison with that of the Ministry of Foreign Affairs.

'Political analysis' in the Japanese press consists essentially of running commentary and speculation in connection with the unceasing power struggle among the *habatsu* of the LDP. Japan's political crises are momentary intensifications of this power struggle; they can aptly be compared to instalments of the Japanese television serials on samurai history whose themes of loyalty and betrayal they markedly resemble.

Bureaucratic wars

Like bureaucrats everywhere, Japanese bureaucrats have natural enemies, but they find their adversaries in rival ministries, rather than among the politicians or the businessmen. A major task for the officials, especially in the middle reaches of a bureau, is to negotiate deals with other bureaucrats. Regarding control of an oil pipeline, for example, the Ministry of Transport will claim that this falls within the area of transportation, while the Ministry of International Trade and Industry (MITI) will insist that it should be in charge since petroleum is a commercial product.[5] Such squabbling can be found almost anywhere, but among Japanese bureaucrats it often grows into major conflicts that totally paralyse official decision-making. Conflict among ministries is criticised by Japanese commentators as 'sectionalism'. It is taken almost for granted that the interests of the ministry come before those of the country. Highly placed bureaucrats will themselves agree that the malfunctioning caused by *nawabari arasoi* ('territorial conflict') exceeds all reasonable limits.[6]

There is very little *wa* to be found in the relationship between the Ministry of Foreign Affairs and MITI; they consider each other natural enemies. Their conflict over territory goes back to the 1930s when the Foreign Ministry staff resigned *en masse* to protest at a plan to establish a ministry of trade which would have taken away these responsibilities from their ministry,[7] which before the war was considerably more powerful than it is now. Recent international conflict over Japanese commercial practices and the conflict over control of Japan's diplomacy have found the two ministries constantly at loggerheads, resulting in contradictory statements to Japan's trading partners.

One spectacular bureaucratic battle was the so-called VAN war in 1984 between MITI and the Ministry of Post and Telecommunications (MPT), which formed part of a wider conflict concerning control over the new telecommunications industries. The VAN (Value Added Network, i.e. advanced data communication services) war was one in which foreigners, mainly Americans, were prodded to participate. In MITI's eyes the new subsector belonged to the realm of the so-called 'information society', an area of industrial development about which it had for years been writing reports and 'visions of the future'. But MPT saw it as part of the communication services under its jurisdiction. MITI demanded complete and unlimited opportunities for foreigners to compete in this area in the Japanese market, whereas MPT insisted on a licensing system that would virtually exclude foreign participation. The battle was partly fought out in the Policy Affairs Research Council of the LDP, giving politicians an

THE ENIGMA OF JAPANESE POWER

important mediating role.[8] The MPT is exceptionally strong because the postal *zoku* (the 'tribe' of LDP Diet members associated with its area of interest) is a more fanatical supporter of its corresponding ministry than any of the other *zoku*.[9]

There is no administrative method to adjudicate conflict between ministries.[10] Hence the importance of *éminences grises*, shadowy power-brokers. Once an inter-ministry conflict is 'settled' through the offices of an outside agent, such as the LDP, this does not mean that the conflict is solved; there is no peace among rival ministries, only armistice.

A less well known but significant conflict is that between the police and the prosecutors. Despite their mutual support on the surface and their joint role as the enemy of ideologically inspired leftists, their mutual disdain is deep-seated. It goes back to the rivalry between the Naimusho and the Ministry of Justice before the war, when the pre-war police sometimes withheld vital information from prosecutors on the track of people harbouring 'dangerous thoughts'.[11] Under the post-war constitution, the police were freed from their traditional hierarchic inferiority to the public prosecutors, but the Criminal Prosecution Law still stipulates that police comply with the prosecutors' instructions. The prosecutors have scored in their rivalry with the police by taking on more political corruption investigations ever since a number of former police bureaucrats joined the LDP and their former colleagues became more hesitant to touch money scandals.[12]

It is a commonplace that the cohesion of a group is promoted by hostility towards other groups close to it; the strong rivalry among Christian churches is a good example. Factional conflict can take on extreme, highly irrational forms in Japan, where the emphasis on solidarity and the demands on the individual for identification with the group are so strong that groups are apt to go on a war footing against each other when there are no other mobilising issues to hold them together. In view of this tendency, the jurisdictions of government agencies are made to overlap as little as possible, which heightens their discretionary powers but makes conflict, when it does occur, all the more bitter.

This pattern in which the semi-autonomy of the parts undermines the coherence of the whole is repeated at various levels of the System. The various departments of a newspaper, for example, generally seem to operate as if they constituted separate publications. Such sectionalism is also endemic to most ministries; conflict between ministry bureaux is sometimes even greater than that between government agencies, and when one section views an impending decision of its bureau as threatening its interests, it may sabotage the plans of the larger group.

The police, too, are riven by several types of severe factional friction. One is a rivalry between criminal and security police extending from police academy to police boxes,[13] another the friction between the Tokyo Metropolitan Police Agency and the National Police Agency.[14]

Despite the identification of individual bureaucrats with their bureau, private conversations that I have had with high officials suggest that the ultimate unit in conflict with other units is, as everywhere else, the single ambitious bureaucrat in rivalry with his immediate colleagues. The Finance Ministry official does not necessarily care much for the bureau that he defends at the expense of the unity of the whole; it is just that his quality as a loyal official will be judged by the success of his bureau. His further career will depend on it, as will, finally, the place he will land as an *amakudari*.

Institutional paralysis

That the endemic conflict in Japan can be seriously detrimental to the public good was underlined by the aftermath of an air crash in August 1985, in which a record 520 people died. Instead of uniting different authorities in an attempt to minimise the tragedy for all concerned, the disaster served only to heighten mutual hostility.

To begin with, confusion about bureaucratic jurisdiction greatly delayed rescue efforts, and most probably cost a number of lives. It took fourteen hours before the first military rescue team made its way to the wreckage on a mountain-side. Four survivors of the crash report that there were more passengers who survived the initial impact and that children's voices could be heard gradually dying away as time passed.

The Japanese Air Force had witnessed the accident on its own instruments, and two Phantom fighters sent out to investigate found the crash site within four minutes, after which they returned to their base without taking further action. It was two and a half hours later that the agency with first responsibility, the civil aviation bureau of the Ministry of Transport, issued its request to the Ground Forces to begin the search. An emergency air-crash rescue team equipped with helicopters does exist in Japan, but it was never called into action. The Gumma prefectural police, in whose territory the plane had come down, did not have helicopters. No Japanese agency reacted to the offer from two US air bases to help with equipment and personnel experienced in difficult mountain searches at night, and these experts stood by fruitlessly for some thirteen hours. Even though the location was known, the first ground troops sent out went to the wrong mountain. Ten hours after the disaster, the helicopter of a Japanese military rescue team found the wreckage, but it took no action because orders for action had gone to another military unit. Hours before soldiers sent out on instructions from the Transport Ministry finally arrived at the site, local villagers had already reached it.

Questions about the disastrous tardiness and manifest lack of effective inter-agency communication were submerged in the subsequent welter of accusations directed at Japan Airlines (JAL). These were to a large extent the result of an older conflict between the Ministry of Transport and the semi-governmental airline company. The transport minister, Yamashita Tokuo, declared in a newspaper interview that, even though he did not know about technical matters, he was sure that JAL was to blame. As a result the Japanese media developed an elaborate campaign in which JAL was portrayed as the great villain. Not a day passed without the newspapers finding some fault with the national airline.[15]

The International Federation of Airline Pilot Associations found reason to issue a declaration reminding all concerned that investigations into air crashes were not primarily meant to apportion blame, but to find the cause so as to prevent similar accidents. It asked the authorities to stop leaking confusing and contradictory information to the press, and pleaded that experts of the manufacturer as well as the US National Transport Safety Board should be included in their investigations. The latter specialists had at that point waited for two weeks in Tokyo to be called upon, and had only once, as a courtesy gesture, been taken to the crash site.

This seemingly odd behaviour of Japan's military units and Transport Ministry becomes clearer when seen in the context of the absence of central leadership. The soldiers adhere painstakingly to the principle of 'civil responsibility' so as to forestall comparisons to their pre-1945 predecessors. A functioning central military authority does not exist. Neither, however, does a civilian organ that can give and co-ordinate commands in times of emergency. The bureaucrats of the agency of first responsibility were not equipped to deal efficiently with the JAL crash. Even more to the point, these bureaucrats and their minister do not see themselves as representatives of a responsible government answerable to a general public that includes civil aviation personnel. They see themselves as partisan members of their own group with interests to defend against other System elements under all circumstances, including those surrounding an air crash. Prime Minister Nakasone, who was on holiday some twenty minutes' distance by helicopter from the crash site and who was known for his advocacy of decisive leadership, conspicuously refrained from visiting the area to help console next of kin and encourage rescue workers. To do so would have created the unwanted impression that the government had taken symbolic responsibility for the event.

The undigested past

Most conspicuously contradicting the mythology of Japan as one happy family, homogeneous and unified in thought and priorities, are the national disputes provoked by what one might call Japan's undigested pre-1945 past: its attempt to rule Asia and the blatant political suppression at home. In this instance, the conflicts are kept alive by groups that belong only partly or not at all to the System. The most important of these national conflicts revolve around the position of the emperor, National Foundation Day, the Yasukuni shrine, revision of the constitution, the introduction of patriotic ethics courses in schools and the status of the Self-Defence Forces. Whenever one of these issues is rekindled by government action or statements, the few remnants of the Japanese left, together with coteries of intellectuals and certain religious groups, can be counted on to react vehemently.

National Foundation Day, or Kigensetsu, was first instituted in 1872 – in the early stage of development of the *kokutai* ideology – to commemorate the day in 600 BC on which the mythical first emperor, Jimmu, allegedly established his capital in Yamato. Also known as Empire Day, it was celebrated on 11 February until the occupation scrapped it as a dangerous vestige of militarist fanaticism. The holiday was reinstated by law in 1966 under a slightly different name. But not until 1985 did a prime minister, Nakasone Yasuhiro, participate in the official ceremonies. A storm of indignant protest had prevented him from attending in 1983, so that much preparation was required to help make his 1985 appearance half-way acceptable. Nakasone's friend, the president of the Chamber of Commerce and Industry, Goto Noboru, was given the task of arranging for the necessary compromises, and Goto's advertising and public relations firm, Tokyu Agency, worked out the details and the publicity. Instead of the proposed three shouts of 'Tennoheika banzai' (too reminiscent of the cry that charging soldiers and kamikaze pilots used when they threw themselves on the enemy), the ceremony called for three 'banzais' for the founding of Japan, and a mere prayer on behalf of the emperor.

The left and the Christians criticised Nakasone for having brought the country 'a step closer to the old militarism', while the nationalists attacked him for having diminished the significance of the commemoration. Some 22,000 teachers, Christians and other opponents participated in protest rallies all over Japan, but about double that number of Japanese joined local celebrations, suggesting that perhaps the balance has turned in favour of the Kigensetsu advocates. Even so, the mythical Jimmu, instead of being ceremonially worshipped, was only referred to in an official speech, which shows how hard put to it the nationalists are to reintroduce bits and pieces from the past.

One of the best-known symbols of national disunity is the Yasukuni shrine, once one of the two most prominent shrines of state Shinto, the artificial 'religion' that consisted of ceremonies intended to add lustre to the 'national essence' mythology. The souls of 2,464,151 soldiers who have died for Japan since just before the end of the last century are formally enshrined in this sanctuary. Among them are Tojo Hideki and the other generals executed by the Allies as war criminals. It is not a war cemetery, but it contains mortuary tablets with the names of the enshrined soldiers and memorials to such élite corps as the Kempeitai (the military police) and kamikaze pilots. Mementoes from the Burma railway, a kamikaze plane and a one-man suicide submarine are among the exhibits of the shrine.

Around 15 August, when Japan commemorates the end of the war, the Yasukuni shrine is the centre of a controversy that has been reignited almost every year since 1975, when Prime Minister Miki Takeo visited the shrine on the day in question. He established this precedent under pressure from the electorally influential Association of War Bereaved Families, but made it clear that he worshipped as a private individual. His successor, Fukuda Takeo, took the compromise a step further by praying as a private individual but signing the visitors' book as prime minister. The next premier, Ohira Masayoshi, who had Christian sympathies, managed to stay away. Suzuki Zenko, who was next, stuck to his major political principle of 'promoting harmony' and resolved not to tell the waiting army of newspaper and TV reporters how he had signed the visitors' book and how he had prayed. It was once again Nakasone who bluntly broke through every remaining barrier. On 15 August 1985 he not only prayed at the Yasukuni shrine in his capacity as prime minister, but offered flowers paid for with government money and walked straight to the inner sanctum – all major symbolic acts. He was also accompanied by most of his cabinet ministers and a couple of hundred LDP parliamentarians.[16]

The Yasukuni shrine controversy has been the most conspicuous of those connected with the undigested past, since for many Japanese it still symbolises what they consider a dangerous slide back towards militarist values. Since Nakasone's much publicised visit, it has also become a source of diplomatic friction with China, where internal opponents of the regime's open-door policies have used anti-Japanese sentiment to strengthen their position. This, in turn, caused Nakasone to scrap his 1986 and 1987 visits, though practically the entire cabinet and droves of LDP parliamentarians showed up on both occasions.

The emperor

Once the focus of Japan's state religion, the emperor, or rather his position in the post-war order, remains very controversial. After 1945, Emperor Hirohito was made to personify the good conscience of a Japan that was supposedly victimised by the war. Yet some Japanese, even in the 1980s, resented the authority in whose name their fathers, husbands and sons were sacrificed. Pressed on this matter, a minority thinks that Hirohito should have resigned in 1945 in a symbolic gesture indicating awareness of the misery perpetrated by those who invoked his 'will'. A much larger and more vocal group is concerned that his son, Akihito, may once again be used as a political instrument by forces that have not confronted and rejected Japan's militaristic and authoritarian past.

Hirohito occupied the 'chrysanthemum throne' longer than any of his 110 real and 14 mythical predecessors.[17] When on his eighty-fifth birthday in April 1986 he celebrated the sixtieth anniversary of his enthronement, this oldest and longest-reigning monarch in the world had, with an unsurpassable sense of duty, lived a life that for sixty-five years had been in the most rigorous way controlled by others. Yet, ironically, political circumstances granted Hirohito a greater potential to exercise power than either his father or grandfather commanded. He chose not to use this power. The only time when military men, acting on behalf of the 'imperial will', clashed with his personal will was on the occasion of the pivotal *niniroku jiken* (26 February Incident) in 1936, an attempted *coup d'état* that left the emperor enraged over the murder of several political figures. He ordered the rebels evicted from their positions and rejected their offer to commit suicide on his command.

Hirohito's personal role in the Second World War remains largely unknown. He is said to have made, at least formally, the major decision in 1945 to accept the Allied terms for surrender, but the true sequence of events may never become known. He himself, long imprisoned by court officialdom, never made any public statement about his motives in the first half of this century, except for a formal reference in 1981, when he declared that he had not been able to prevent the declaration of war on the United States while adhering to constitutional provisions that did not provide for him to make direct political decisions. No one, except his wife and his closest chamberlains (who remain silent), ever had an informal conversation with him.

The account given by General MacArthur about the statement of the emperor at their first meeting on 27 September 1945, does not match at all what a spokesman for the Naimusho reported four days later, or what their Japanese interpreter, the only other person present, remembered. MacArthur wrote many years after the meeting that Hirohito had said, 'I come to you . . . to offer myself to the judgement of the powers you represent as the one to bear sole responsibility for every political and military decision made and action taken by my people in the conduct of war' – a line that has entered many Western history books. From what the Naimusho and the interpreter have said, one must draw the conclusion that the question of responsibility was not raised other than to leave it to 'future historians'.[18]

In speculating about Hirohito's motives, probably the most significant clue is that at the age of seven he was placed under the supervision of General Nogi Maresuke, who had to substitute for father and friend. Nogi, a war hero, was a pathological nationalist for whom a sense of duty and self-sacrifice had religious meaning. When his mentor and only boyhood friend committed ritual suicide upon the death of Emperor Meiji (Hirohito's grandfather), the eleven-year-old crown prince was, as part of his education, forced to come to terms with this without showing any emotion. Nogi had left a testament in which he bewailed the moral weakness of Japan at the end of the Meiji period and appealed for a restoration of the 'Japanese spirit'. There are indications that this had a traumatic effect on Hirohito.

Hirohito never knew any kind of spontaneous pleasure, with the sole exception of a stay with the British royal family which he has described as the most beautiful time in his life.[19] When he was three months old he was taken away from his seventeen-year-old mother. He was not allowed childhood friends or childhood games. He was a stranger to his brothers. His own children were brought up in separate residences. Empress Nagako was the only companion in his life. Before his illness, he found his direct solace in the three days each week he was allowed to spend in his laboratory, a simple wooden shed housing microscopes and specimens for his marine biology research.

Japanese court life remains extremely regimented, rigid and antiquated. After a brief period during the occupation years when, as part of a US-inspired campaign to make him resemble a European monarch, Hirohito travelled through Japan, visiting factories and talking with ordinary people at work, he has had very little contact with his subjects. Compared with the 1950s and 1960s, during which the mythological aspects of the institution were strongly denied, the imperial family is today once again surrounded by taboos. In a booklet published in 1985 by the Association of Shinto Shrines and aimed at middle-school pupils, the old myth of the emperor as a descendant of the sun goddess is reinstated, and a number of LDP members of parliament have again come out with statements about the uniqueness of the Japanese imperial institution which can never be understood by foreigners. The bureaucrats of the imperial household agency refused to permit gold coins issued by the government to com-memorate the sixtieth enthronement anniversary to carry the emperor's portrait. He has never appeared on any coin or stamp for the openly stated reason that these can be easily defaced.

Despite the famous announcement of the emperor's human status on New Year's day of 1946, rightist activists, some nationalistic intellectuals and bureaucrats, and several LDP groups promote a view of his status and role that is little different from when he was still officially a Shinto divinity. In the weeks when Hirohito was near death in the autumn of 1988, cabinet ministers excused themselves from international meetings, celebrities postponed scheduled weddings, TV stations and weekly magazines reduced their frivolous offerings, numerous corporations and schools cancelled festivities and the press contributed massively to creating a quasi-sacred atmosphere.

Although the opinion was widespread that the emperor's illness ought not deprive schoolchildren of their autumn festivals and athletic competi-tions, school authorities need to be concerned about intimidation from proliferating rightist groups. Publishers and editors are for the same reason very careful about anything that appears under their imprint in connection with the imperial family, even under normal circumstances.

Rightest groups and the nationalists in the LDP are expected to use the impending succession ceremonies to seek to expand their influence. The main rite of enthronement, or *daijosai*, which will probably take place a year after Hirohito's death, provides for the symbolic transformation of the new emperor into a woman, followed by his symbolic impregnation by deities and his rebirth with divine qualities. Constitutional stipulations have placed the throne on an even less exalted plane than where Western constitutional monarchies have positioned it, and refer to the emperor as 'the symbol of the people and the unity of the nation'. But the only practical impediment that they are likely to present to the resurgence of emperor worship is that they give dissenters in parliament a legal basis for opposing the expenditure of government money on the religious ceremonies.

The imperial succession carries the potential for renewed and rather virulent nationwide conflict. For the first time since the war, Shinto religious observances will take centre stage, and the way in which individuals react to these could become the measure of their 'purity' as Japanese in the eyes of their nationalistically inclined compatriots.

Mental twilight zone

Another issue connected with the undigested past that illustrates an underlying national disunity is the government's attempt to reintroduce moral education (see Chapters 4 and 11). Yet another concerns the position of the Self-Defence Forces. Their actual status conflicts with post-war agreements enforced by the occupation authorities. Article 9 of the constitution renounces the sovereign right to wage war and specifically forbids the maintenance of land, sea and air forces, as well as other war potential. This was a condition General MacArthur had to write into the constitution to make the retention of the emperor acceptable to the Allies. The irony of the controversy is that since the 1970s the United States has been pressing for increased Japanese defence efforts.

The Self-Defence Forces, the 'higher task' of education, the precise role of the emperor, state support for national commemoration ceremonies and the Yasukuni shrine issue all belong to a peculiar Japanese mental twilight zone characterised by simplistically formulated taboos and unclearly formulated attacks on these taboos. The Socialist and Communist parties, the Nikkyoso, the dwindling leftist labour movement and (depending on the issue) some intellectuals, Christians and representatives of the new religions, who regard themselves as guardians of the post-war constitution, can be counted on to react with yawn-inducing predictability to all actions and statements tending towards reinstatement of what the US occupation authorities removed.

This anti-rightist opposition consists mostly of ritual slogans shouted at rallies, and only rarely of reasoned arguments. Its protests are highly coloured with the ideological utterances so typical of the Japanese left. They do not attempt to tie the separate issues together within a coherent frame of reference so as to present a convincing, lucidly argued case. For a considerable number of non-activist Japanese the route to follow is still the one mapped out by General MacArthur and his reformers: a route never properly followed, yet still recognisable by such US-lit beacons as the new democratic role of the emperor, the ban on state Shinto and 'democratic' education. The controversial issues connected with the undigested past tend to be associated with an uncomfortable sense that certain groups might again lead Japan astray.

The Japanese press, which generally sits on the fence between the two national camps, exemplifies the intellectual incompetence with which these issues are approached. Press reaction to the effort to reintroduce 'moral education' in the schools has shown considerable unease, but this is never expressed in intellectual terms such as would provide points of reference for an unemotional debate.

Japanese who oppose the retrogressive predilections of their administrators focus their attack mainly on symbols. Thus the political left and many intellectuals are adamant that nothing in the constitution must be amended. Even the smallest change in this document written by non-Japanese will, they believe, open the way to a revival of pre-war practices. Connected with this is the fear of a resurgence of militarism. Although this fear strikes many outsiders as exaggerated, it cannot be rationally put to rest, since the developments that cause it remain so vague and since nothing is ever spelled out clearly – an ambiguity that remains a central attribute of the exercise of power in Japan. While the opposition wastes its energies on symbolic issues, socio-economic developments that mark the consolidation of the depoliticised System slip far beyond its control.

Instead of systematic debate about the issues from the undigested past, there is only a stand-off between rightist-conservative and leftist-liberal forces, and a ritualistic repetition of slogans. Many on the left know that to start discussion would merely deliver them into the inescapable embrace, through the obligations that come from any friendly Japanese contact. Gradually the forces of the System appear to be winning out as the voices protesting at the full reinstatement of some of the elements from the undigested past become weaker.

Order through ritual

This prevalence of ritual – instead of the substantive discussion and appeal to reason that to outsiders would seem to be more beneficial to the protesting parties – is characteristic of Japanese conflict on a smaller scale as well. *Wa* is achieved not by reason and of course not by law, but by mechanisms that, although known elsewhere, have reached their ultimate development in Japan.

The ineffective inner voice

To appreciate fully the importance of ritual in Japanese life, we must again consider what the socio-political world looks like to a conventional Japanese in the absence of a tradition of appealing to universal values. The world through Japanese eyes does not, in most cases, contain the certainties that come with a belief in a moral order based on immutable principles, which means that most Japanese have ultimately no intellectual handrail. They cannot appeal to any principle or ideal with which to justify their behaviour in the eyes of their neighbours, fellow workers or superiors. To understand this moral world one must imagine a situation in which good behaviour is constantly determined by individuals' views of how others expect them to behave; in which they can never think 'To hell with them'; and in which conformity to social expectations is not an unfortunate compromise but the only possible way to live.

Daily life, in practice, provides some pragmatic guides to concrete action, embodied in maxims, proverbs and traditional sayings, but they are not enough to justify going against the grain of social expectation. The ideals of good behaviour that we have looked at earlier – 'purity of spirit', 'loyalty' and 'sincerity' – seek to preserve the social order of the moment; they are certainly not weapons with which the individual can tackle the political system. Resistance to whatever is portrayed as beneficial to the community is, as we have seen, decried as springing from purely 'private' – synonymous with egoistic – motives and not conceived of as a possibly valid personal political opinion.

Japanese are not expected to take their cues from an inner voice that reminds them of moral absolutes they came to embrace while growing up. Moral authority is not thought to reside in them as an internalised guide to life. They have no historical models encouraging them to stand up for their beliefs. They cannot repeat after Socrates, and a multitude of thinkers and political activists since, that to follow one's conscience is better than to follow convention. They could, of course, do all these things. But they would risk disapproval and would rarely be rewarded.

The personal sense of *noblesse oblige* harboured by some Japanese, together with the prevailing comity of manners, has a soothing and reassuring effect on social experiences in Japan. Some Japanese devote themselves out of idealism to moral causes. Yet in none of these cases can the individual appeal to personal ideals of conduct in order to justify acts that go against the grain of communal expectations. The Japanese wishing to function in a purely Japanese context must give up logic, moral values and philosophical or scientific 'truths' as ultimate means of defence or attack. It is tempting to label the Japanese pragmatists, but one would have difficulty finding Japanese so consistent in their pragmatism that it could be considered a principle.

Assurances of order

One could say that, rather than being guided by inner computations on the basis of universally applicable rules and abstractions, the Japanese are radar-guided. It is, especially, the surface of things and people that counts. A serious and astute observer of the Japanese scene speaks of the existence of

a set of extraordinarily sensitive conversational and supra-conversational 'feelers' which work constantly to note others' reactions and make the necessary adjustments. These adjustments, though minute, are in aggregate essentially what supports society: ideas and principles are secondary, not supportive in the primary sense. And the universal concepts of kindness, gentleness, humanity and so on are experienced within this context.[20]

In their language and demeanour, Japanese must always help restrain, to a certain extent, their fellow Japanese. Just as individuals cannot appeal to an invisible sanctioning agent to justify individual action, so they cannot, ultimately, point to such laws to keep others from disturbing their private order. They must be alert and suspicious. With respect to their superiors, their greatest concern will be whether the superiors have the best for them in mind. Because there are no ultimate restraining sanctions from within, the restraining must come from outside, and at higher levels of the System all those with a degree of power are constantly busy with containing the powers of others.

The ritual nature of so much in daily life and communication provides constant reassurance that order prevails; this is necessary because the fear of its possible absence is more acute than in the West. The absence of a tradition of explaining the world in terms of universal and immutable truths makes future events less predictable, gives one less protection – no intellectual protection at all – and exposes one to the caprices of forces not understood. The full implications of this situation, in which the only reassurance lies in a strictly controlled social order, are difficult to imagine for those who, throughout their upbringing, have been imbued with a sense of underlying laws and principles.

In Japan social life must be made as predictable as possible to ensure a degree of day-to-day certainty. Hence, Japanese communication tends to be very stereotyped, and Japanese grow up with a fairly strong awareness of how things ought to be and how people ought to behave. There are both 'soft' and 'hard' aspects to their human environment. These complement each other, but are not made to fit into a continuous logical scheme. On the softer side, there is the flexibility that governs the closer personal relationships; here the world is 'wet', emotional and tolerant of idio-syncrasies. But in the 'harder', less friendly mode, the tendency is to place things in ready-made, rigid, immutable categories. In the workaday world, Japanese judge each other by the schools and universities they attended and the companies or government organs they belong to. At an even further remove, foreigners are judged by the respective stereotypes for the countries they come from. The world in this perspective is a jigsaw puzzle where all is judged on the surface and placed accordingly. It is almost as though the great effort that goes into monitoring the shifts and changes in the soft, wet world of the immediate social environment calls for a greater simplicity in the more impersonal world beyond it.

Japanese can be extremely upset when the world and the people in it do not live up to expectations, and they tend simply to dismiss things that do not fit preconceived notions – a common human trait but, once again, with an overwhelming difference of degree. Foreigners are often struck by the apparent impermeability of the Japanese mind, even that of reasonably well-schooled and intelligent individuals, to things that do not fit expected patterns. The same anxiety about the unpredictable can make for extremely inflexible attitudes and behaviour.

Conflict avoidance via hierarchy

Ritual and hierarchy substitute for an internalised set of abstractions in fostering predictability and reducing the likelihood of open conflict. If everybody has a proper place in the scheme of things and sticks to it, much disturbance and upheaval in society can be avoided, and the acceptance of hierarchical order in Japan appears to be the only alternative to festering conflict. Those conflicts that persist on a national scale, such as that concerning the reintroduction of 'moral education', are insoluble because the parties involved, the administrators and the detractors of the System – in this case the Ministry of Education and the teachers' union – do not accept any hierarchical relationship to one another. Conflicts with the outside world similarly fester, because Japanese groups will not subordinate themselves voluntarily to foreign groups. The Agriculture Ministry and the *nokyo*, for example, cannot accept liberalisation of their market for the sake of the national interest, just because foreign countries want to balance their imports from Japan with exports to Japan. The logical reasoning that foreigners bring to bear can never succeed in convincing. Such conflict with outsiders is insoluble – unless, of course, the other country adopts the means of the Japanese System and forces recognition of its own more powerful position.

In the Japanese socio-political order conflict is shunned, dismissed, disavowed, denied, exorcised by ritual, but rarely solved. With no tradition of appealing to universal principles and using legal procedures to keep order in society, individuals and groups accept their lot only because a stronger power holds them in place (though subtle acts of sabotage are expected and condoned). In intimate interpersonal relations, such as between mother and child, husband and wife, and boss and junior, psychological manipulation is often substituted for reasoning out one's attitudes towards each other. Japanese have raised such psychological 'games' to a fine art, and it is largely through learning to play them well that the weak manage to assert themselves.

Thus mutual containment among the semi-autonomous components of the System, and order on the lower levels, are finally determined not by reason but by power. They require subordination. There can be no *wa* without hierarchy. Throughout their lives Japanese are constantly reminded of where they stand, 'up' or 'down', with regard to their relatives, schoolmates, fellow employees and indeed to practically everybody else with whom they come into contact. They are also expected to demonstrate awareness of the rankings of organisations, of whatever kind, through the way they treat their representatives. Social status is the one sphere where they are not conditioned to be comfortable with vagueness.

Hierarchy begins at home, although except in highly placed families the emphasis on 'younger' and 'older' is much less than it was before the war. But in schools children's ranks can be recognised by the uniforms or tags they wear, and ranking in the classroom is plain and open. Hierarchy is very important in university sports clubs and cheer-leading societies. It persists even in more relaxed school clubs. Whereas one's class year seldom matters in United States student clubs, the backbone of Japanese club ties is the hierarchical relationship between seniors and juniors.[21] Ranking is even clearer in the salaryman world. When listening to a Japanese talking on the telephone, it is almost always immediately apparent whether he is talking to someone higher or lower in rank. The common notion propagated abroad of egalitarianism within Japanese work groups (Japanese corporate directors eating their lunch in the same cafeteria as the humblest workers being the often cited evidence) is nonsense. Japanese employees must not only adjust their speech to the rank of the person addressed, but must know the appropriate degree to bow. The rank of everyone in an office is usually immediately apparent from the position of desks and the quality of chairs. As one participant observer has remarked: 'Bosses issue summonses by bellowing across the office; subordinates do not walk to the beckoning, they run.'[22] When Japanese come out in force to negotiate, one can tell the pecking order at first sight. Rankings are recognised across the borders of the many semi-autonomous groups. Daily life in Japan is rather like a diplomatic cocktail party at which most guests are military attachés.

We have already come across one well-known basic ingredient of Japanese hierarchy: the *oyabun–kobun* (parent-role–child-role) relationship of work gangs in the earlier phase of Japan's industrialisation that survives today among gangsters, politicians, traditional craftsmen and theatre artists. Similarly coupled roles are those of *sempai* and *kohai*, the senior and junior worker whose mutual relationship is closer than the normal one among colleagues.[23] In many corporations and government agencies such *sempai–kohai* relationships may grow naturally, but they may also be assigned by superiors, especially in growing firms with a rapidly expanding workforce.

Japanese bureaucratic hierarchy is more hierarchical than the members of most bureaucracies elsewhere would think possible. A middle-ranking official once told me that he liked to smoke a pipe but could never do so at work, since this would give the impression that he thought himself superior to his cigarette-smoking boss. A former Ministry of Finance bureaucrat remembers how another official was transferred because the latter's child had attained a higher ranking in school than the child of his superior who attended the same class.[24] In apartment blocks for policemen's families, the ranking of the policeman directly determines the ranking of his wife and children in that fairly self-contained world,[25] reminiscent of military housing assignments in other countries.

The well-known 'seniority system' of Japanese companies exists to maintain an unambiguous hierarchy, and a few post-war companies that drew attention by promoting some of their staff in accordance with talent and achievements later had problems with superiors who were 'too young' to maintain the normal hierarchic relations with their subordinates.

Formal hierarchic order must be maintained under all circumstances, even when it is widely understood not to correspond to actual power relations. It frequently happens, for example, that the nominal boss of a group does not have the capacity to produce ideas and must rely on an imaginative subordinate to make the decisions. It is essential for good 'human relations' in such a case that the boss should know how to use the talents of the latter without making it too obvious. It is also crucial in most cases that talented members should not claim credit for their superior contribution. The members of a well-integrated group consider it normal that leadership should be in the hands of one of their theoretical equals. In some cases, and particularly outside the place of work, hardly any effort is made to maintain the pretence as to who makes decisions, and if no third parties are present talented subordinates may sometimes treat their boss with greater roughness than would ever be acceptable in the West. Yet in public the normal ritual deference to the superior is scrupulously adhered to. This approach enables the group to keep the seniority hierarchy intact. Whereas in most Western situations the gifted, with leadership ability, would rise faster, in Japan they stay longer at lower levels, resulting in the frequently noticed phenomenon of the relatively high degree of initiative taken by the rank and file.

Within established Japanese relationships those who rank high need not, as a general rule, give reasons for what they ask from those beneath them. Seniors must, however, demonstrate that they have the best in mind for juniors. Conversely juniors are not inclined to inquire into the whys and wherefores of instructions they receive, or the manner in which they are treated, but they accept commands so long as their superiors have not damaged their belief in the benevolence of the motives behind them.

Hierarchical order pervades every nook and cranny of Japanese society. The Bank of Japan zealously guards the pecking order among the large banks, to help maintain an easily controllable lending system.[26] We saw in Chapter 5 that the ranking of LDP parliamentarians, mainly measured by the number of times they have been elected, determines which positions they can hold in committees and when they can be appointed minister, regardless of their talents and skills.

A sense of superiority or inferiority is also usually evident in Japanese attitudes towards other nations. Towards 'models', first China and later the West, the Japanese have always displayed emotional ambivalence. The notion of a strongly hierarchical world order has exacerbated such feelings. While feeling inferior to their models, the Japanese nevertheless have asserted the basic superiority of their own nation by postulating the familiar mythical notions of a 'Japanese spirit'.

The done thing

The obsession with social order has, at least since Tokugawa times, been accompanied by the understanding that much ceremony is needed to ensure its survival. 'In the great chain of being that theoretically connects the Emperor to the humblest laborers via the Shogun, lords and myriad ranks of samurai, farmers, artisans, and merchants, all must perform ceremony so that order may be maintained throughout.'[27]

Hierarchy and ritual are, of course, related, and ritual too is essential to wa. Infringements of the rules of etiquette or failure to sustain the prescribed rituals constitute grave sins. If there is one important way in which the Japanese are clearly different from other people, from Westerners as well as their Asian neighbours, it is in the extent of their ritualistic behaviour. Japanese wrap themselves in rituals. The ceremonial Japanese behaviour noticed abroad gives but a slight impression of what a Japanese must go through at home. A rigid web of formulas covers areas of life and activities, such as sporting events, parties and honeymoons, for which spontaneity would be considered an essential ingredient in other societies.

Japanese do not necessarily love ritual more than other people, but they feel lost without it. The rituals need not at all be old and venerable. A good example of a new ritual, dating from some time in the 1960s but one that has conquered the entire nation, is the Japanese wedding party. Commercial interests, those of large hotels and wedding parlours, have shaped the 'customs' that the majority of marrying Japanese are nowadays subjected to. These wedding parties are extremely rigid, boring and expensive.[28] They are highly predictable, with their identical cake-cutting, flower-offering and candle-lighting ceremonies, the three or four costume changes by the bride (bridal dress, kimono, evening dress and optional honeymoon uniform) and the long speeches by senior employees in the companies of bride and groom in which the jokes at the expense of the couple are almost totally interchangeable from one wedding to the next. The rituals are full of (newly designed) symbolism suggesting that the bride and groom (almost invariably in their early and late twenties, respectively) are only now leaving their childhood.[29] Lacking any kind of festive spirit or spontaneity, these wedding parties are disliked by most people who have to go to them, judging by their common comment, but the entire population puts up with them as the 'done thing'.

Japanese are conditioned from childhood to believe in the done thing, which extends to all areas of life, including leisure pursuits. A conspicuous product of this conditioning is the highly ritualised golf culture. Japanese golf is not in the first instance a sport or pleasant pastime, but for high business officials a bitter necessity, and for the 30 per cent of all salarymen who practise it an extremely serious business. The obligatory *shain ryoko*, or company outing, has in recent years usually consisted of a golf competition. The golf culture offers ideal opportunities to display hierarchic status. Memberships in newly opened courses cost an average ten million yen in the mid-1980s – roughly $77,000.[30] Courses with prestige charge 25 to 50 million yen. Such memberships are traded like stocks and bonds, and are considered excellent investments. But the main function of the extraordinarily costly golf culture is to provide business-men, bureaucrats and politicians of roughly the same hierarchic level with an opportunity to make contacts in a relatively relaxed atmosphere, and thus to expand their *jinmyaku*.

Even among scholars, to do the done thing is more important than any commitment to the quest for truth. Thus the self-respecting Japanese scholar will not touch certain subjects of recent political history or current affairs, leaving these to the journalist, which by implication keeps those subjects in the realm of gossip.

In daily situations Japanese must adhere to an etiquette, as complex perhaps as that in old-fashioned royal courts, that renders the world outside the inner circle of work group, family and intimates almost completely free from unsettling social surprises. Japanese are expected to stick to their roles, and to make the roles clear by their dress, speech and behaviour. There is an easily recognisable mother role, housewife role, *sempai* role, boss role and apprentice role, to mention only the most obvious.

Hierarchy and ritual in Japan are marvellous mechanisms whereby the weak can give in to the strong without loss of their sense of dignity. This avoids much cause for conflict. The conciliation procedures offered in lieu of litigation allow all concerned to save face, and the same is true of the mediation that, in less formal contexts, smooths out a multitude of snags in relationships.

Thanks to the tradition of managing reality, social conflict can be defused without any attempt to resolve contradictions. Logical reasoning is seldom allowed to disturb the all-important *wa*. In the West arguments appealing to logic are an accepted (and expected) part of reconciling differences of opinion. In Japan such argument is associated with conflict itself, and, since all conflict is defined as bad, arguing and debating are not usually recognised as healthy ways to settle disputes. There is practically no scholarly debate, and most Japanese scholars would not know how to carry on such a debate. Visiting foreign academics and intellectuals are nearly always praised, rarely argued with. The risks of losing face are thereby minimised.

Expressive political behaviour

One way of categorising political behaviour is into the 'expressive' or the 'instrumental'. Most behaviour is a compound of both, but when the emphasis is clearly on demonstrating to the world where one stands, as opposed to achieving a certain direct benefit, we speak of 'expressive' actions. These clearly dominate where Japanese opposition movements are concerned.

The annual spring rituals of go-slow actions and strikes organised by Sohyo unions in the 1970s, and the May Day rallies of today, are good examples of such completely harmless ritualised protest. The best example, perhaps, is Japan's radical student movement. Though no longer the common sight they were in the 1960s and early 1970s, detachments of student 'demonstrators' are still occasionally seen participating in a bigger rally. With their identical helmets and near-identical clothes, they snake-dance to the rhythm of shrill whistles and a cadence of voices uttering slogans as if in a trance. They move in hermetic close-formation: breast-against-back, shoulder-to-shoulder, with a small gap between the boys and the girls running behind them. They form a long undulating body, and no chorus line or military unit on any parade ground in the world could improve on their act. Yet none of this achieves anything substantial, nor is it meant to. It is demonstration for its own sake.

Ritualism in the guise of democracy is rampant in the Japanese political world. For the 'management of reality' to operate without a hitch, it is necessary for protocol to be meticulously followed and the forms of democracy fastidiously maintained. Hence the ritual of budget hearings in the Diet. Those hearings are all pre-arranged, but no politician or bureaucrat would dare make light of them. The cabinet is formally responsible to the Diet, and no minister would dream of being absent during the almost wholly ritualistic questions on the budget.[31] Diet interpellations, questions and answers are mostly elaborate performances staged by the bureaucrats. Opposition Diet members often rely on the bureaucrats to supply them with questions, which are subsequently answered by the same bureaucrats. Since the Ikeda cabinet there has been much deference to opposition interpellations in the Diet. But attention is paid more to the tone of voice in which the answer is given than to its substance.

Not to observe political custom can lead to a crisis. Thus, the first thing Nakasone did after the LDP's record gains in the election of June 1986 was to demonstrate ceremonial meekness in the face of the opposition. Failure to show concern lest his own party become 'too arrogant' might have provoked a storm of protest from the press and signs of disapproval from the public. A minority may complain that it is being made subject to the tyranny of the majority, so that a façade of benevolence on the part of the stronger party is virtually obligatory.

The bureaucracy lives in a thoroughly ritualistic world. Officials speak in code. When they say 'the matter will be studied', they mean that nothing will be done. If they promise to 'study it with a forward-looking posture' there is more hope; this means that, as far as circumstances allow, there will be some adjustment. As with the politicians, everything in the world of bureaucrats is settled out of sight, prior to the ritual event at which decisions are formally reached. There have been rare instances of directors-general who in negotiations with foreigners greatly upset their subordinates by not always sticking meticulously to the briefing books that had been prepared.

Ritual and an emphatic demonstration of hierarchy are, furthermore, believed by the bureaucrats to be essential as a means of cultivating respect for authority and thereby the foundation of order in society. Lower-level officials carefully demonstrate deference to their superiors, and always pretend to take matters to a higher level for final decisions. The bureaucratic hierarchy in itself is thought to strike the public with awe.[32] In all of this, the illusion of benevolence is vital. Japanese society requires reassurance that the administrators are doing what they are doing, not for themselves but to promote the stability of the people's livelihood; that they are doing it relentlessly, without relaxing their attention; that they are doing it at the expense of time to themselves; and that they are ever vigilant against unexpected accidents.

Where hierarchy and ritual are powerless

In the political imagery inherited from the Tokugawa period and enhanced by the 'national essence' mythology earlier in this century, the benevolent care of the people by selfless administrators produces the best of all possible worlds and represents ultimate truth. The unity of the people is an essential given in this perspective, not something to be achieved. At worst, this natural state of the nation can be only temporarily disrupted by some fluke occurrence.[33]

Wa is immanent in society, even while all Japanese are expected to exert themselves to maintain it, and this means, as we have seen, that the possibility of conflict is formally ignored. Hierarchy and ritual are amazingly effective in maintaining order under these circumstances, but they cannot cover all eventualities. Where conflicts fester in the absence of a formula for agreeing to disagree, there is a total lack of rational communication that may lead to emotional outbursts and sometimes even to physical violence. This can happen in such unlikely places as the assembly hall of the Diet or in company boardrooms. But even then, the gestures accompanying the stand-off tend to become extremely ritualised.

Until the mid-1960s the Diet was frequently the scene of physical violence when communication between the minority parties and the LDP or its predecessors completely broke down. These brawls were serious enough for the Diet's stenographers to demand a pledge in 1954 that parliamentarians would not walk over their table and not touch them or their notes during the fights. The pledge was reaffirmed in 1971 and at least once more after that.

A good example of a complete breakdown in communication is a dispute between the in-patient and out-patient units at the psychiatry department of Tokyo University Hospital. Their conflict goes back decades, but they are unclear about each other's views because they have ceased all communication.

Just how eerie Japanese non-communication in festering conflicts can become is shown by scenes, recorded on film, of the protest by victims of mercury poisoning in the notorious Minamata case. The victims waved their malformed limbs only inches away from the eyes of executives of the polluting company, Chisso Corporation. Mothers held up their children, malformed and shaking with spasms, immediately in front of the officials' faces. But those faces remained totally impassive and silent. At some point an executive would be overcome by it all and faint, a loyal servant of his company to the last.

It is not easy to ascertain how much disharmony and how much potential for social chaos exist in Japanese society. Because the Japanese media believe it is their task to help defuse social conflict rather than reflect it, much remains unreported. When on one occasion in 1987 riot police clashed with protesters against the revision of the alien registration law in front of the Ministry of Justice buildings, protesters were prevented from emerging from a nearby subway station, handled roughly and thrown on the ground. Yet there were no photographs or reports in the next day's newspapers. Japan's television news programmes did not show any of this either.

I saw riots in Shinjuku in the late 1960s that were started by factions of the student movement but were enthusiastically participated in by salarymen, who helped set fire to overturned cars and throw stones at the police. The subsequent news stories depicted these disturbances as the routine activity of ideologically inspired radical students.

Japan received a glimpse of the potential for social disorder in 1974, when irate passengers who had been cooped up in overcrowded commuter trains, purposely stalled as part of go-slow actions by government railway engineers, smashed an office on a platform of one of Tokyo's stations. Shortly after that, passengers went on the rampage at Ageo station in Saitama prefecture, close to Tokyo. This proved contagious, and within days passenger rioting had spread to several stations in Tokyo. I witnessed ticket machines and windows being smashed by ordinary salarymen at Yurakucho station in Tokyo. This behaviour was somewhat comparable in character, though on a much smaller scale, to the rice riots of 1918. Unorganised, spontaneous commuter riots spread all over the country. The outbursts died down quickly, but the authorities took them seriously enough to plead with the go-slow organisers to go on normal strikes (which are illegal for government personnel) henceforth, so that the stations could be kept closed.

Narita Airport

The most notorious permanent threat of physical conflict in recent years has been the protest movement against Tokyo's new Narita Airport. This protest began in 1966 when the farmers of Sanrizuka, the locality where the airport was to be built, discovered that they were being reimbursed with a mere pittance for the loss of their watermelon and peanut fields. A year later they were reinforced by members of Zengakuren, the then still mighty radical student movement. Between 1971 and 1978 the students built forts and towers, tunnels and underground bunkers. A trench war cost the lives of four riot police and two protesters. Many of the students began to work on the land and marry the farmers' daughters. The hamlets in the area were connected by a network of action corps, including a troop of children. The movement split and became radicalised after losing its respected Christian leader in 1976.

The airport was opened seven years behind schedule and five years after the completion of buildings and runways. In March 1978, days before the planned official opening, the radicals managed to penetrate the control tower via the sewage system and destroy equipment, necessitating another postponement. A significant aspect of this event was that many ordinary Japanese admired the radicals for their achievement and privately cheered them on.

Since the opening of the airport there have been several heavy battles between the riot police and the radicals. It is ironic that visitors to the land of *wa* should arrive at what may be considered one gigantic monument to the Japanese inability to resolve conflict. The airport is Japan's most heavily guarded institution, surrounded by several rings of tall electrified fences that continue deep into the ground to discourage tunnelling. All passengers and well-wishers are scrutinised and sometimes searched by the police when entering the airport grounds. Every several hundred yards there are watchtowers equipped with searchlights and manned around the clock. The road leading to the site has steel barricades in several places, and is dotted with the armoured vehicles and water-cannons of the more than 1,500-strong permanent police guard.

Myth of consensus

The country that I have described so far does not resemble the common portrait of Japan as a society in which human relationships are based on consensus. This is because the much vaunted consensus is a myth. Featured prominently in most popular and much serious foreign writing, and with many American commentators habitually referring to Japan's 'consensus-style democracy', it is one of the most successful myths about Japan. Not surprisingly, administrators who deal with the external world have discovered that 'consensus formation' is a useful excuse for inaction.

The term 'consensus' implies positive support for an idea or a course of action. What is mislabelled 'consensus' in Japan, however, is a state of affairs in which no concerned party thinks it worth while to upset the apple-cart. Parties to a Japanese 'consensus' may, in fact, have very negative feelings about what they 'agree' to. Another phenomenon that passes for 'consensus formation' in the interpretations of many Westerners is complex calculations concerning the interpersonal obligations that are part and parcel of the *jinmyaku* system of each individual involved.

The Japanese term for the process used to arrive at 'consensus' is *nemawashi* ('taking care of the roots'). *Nemawashi* involves talking with the concerned parties so as to prepare them to 'accept' a plan, as one prepares the ground for planting something. Such spadework does not invite 'democratic' objection (with the option of rejection), as a similar process would in the West. Japanese have adopted the word 'consensus' to describe what in their own society is made to appear to be genuine agreement, but often is not.

The notion that policy in Japan is collectively initiated is inaccurate. Japanese are reassuringly human in that, just like other people, they cannot invent by committee. In the meantime, as a former vice-minister once told me: 'The more "consensus" you get, the less will be done.' The process that leads to Japanese-style consensus has a strictly limiting function, whereby the members of a group are given the formal opportunity to object to a proposal that is generally presented as if it were anonymous, emanating from the group as a whole. Where 'consensus' has been established it means that nobody concerned wants to take the risk or the trouble of resisting what a stronger person or group wants to happen. When a face-saving procedure like *nemawashi* is omitted, or has been too quick, Japanese speak of 'the dictatorship of the majority'. The distinction is significant for an understanding of the exercise of power in Japan. The strong have justice on their side so long as they do not implement their will brutishly.

On a company level, Japanese employees have no more say in matters that affect their working lives than employees in any other industrialised society. But the illusion is maintained that dissenting views they may have had on important matters have been duly noted. To create this illusion in companies or any other Japanese collectivity is generally not too difficult, since subjective individual views rarely if ever conflict with what their holders have perceived to be the objective drift of the situation. Japanese have been conditioned to sense this kind of thing very well and adjust their thinking accordingly.

In my experience Japanese groups generally do not appreciate minority opinion and remind their participants of that fact in subtle ways. Minority opinion is a hindrance to the feelings of solidarity within the group, and threatens the all-important show of unity. The leadership of the group must go through the motions of consulting with and getting permission from everyone, especially with important decisions. This process can be very elaborate, but by and large it consists of mere gestures reassuring all members that they are not unimportant. The actual convincing that takes place, the supposed process of consensus formation, leaves the potentially recalcitrant member little or no choice but to give his support. If his negative feelings are strong and he knows of others who share them, he is more likely to form a new faction than struggle within the main group.

The ringi *system*

A common decision-making method that also creates the illusion of consensus is the so-called *ringi* system. Under this system, plans drawn up by lower officials circulate among other officials at ever higher levels, receiving their seals of approval. The appearance of full participation is served, and those who are not in favour of the plan can sabotage it to a certain extent by allowing dust to gather on the *ringi-sho*, the circulated document, before affixing their seal. Officials can indicate implicitly their degree of dissatisfaction with a plan by adjusting the time they wait before passing the document on to the next person. Hence, *ringi* is also known as the 'piling-up system'.[34]

The *ringi* system is a superb mechanism for diffusing and finally obfuscating all responsibility. Not only the bureau director but the entire chain of lower officials have no more than a slight sense of being 'responsible for the result'. The makers of inappropriate decisions are nowhere to be found. The system tends to hamper leadership from the top. A plan conceived by a middle-echelon official is sometimes best launched through informal discussion with a low-ranking official, who drafts an outline that percolates upwards, taking in the desk of the initiator on the way. Some bureaucrats think this system absurd, but a superior who systematically refuses to adhere to it may risk his position.[35] Another frequent effect is to make clear what the officials concerned should not do rather than what they should do.[36] One of Japan's best-known students of the bureaucracy sees the *ringi* system not as a product of the pseudo-family relations in Japanese administrative institutions, but as a mechanism that compels such relations.[37]

The *shingikai*, the consultation institution described in Chapter 5, helps work up a sense of national consensus concerning bureaucratic decisions that seem likely to cause problems with interest groups. *Shingikai* attempt to bring together representatives of those concerned and make them party to what will be presented as a harmonious mutual adjustment.[38] Occasionally they may evolve a fresh – or a first – approach to a pressing issue, but mostly they are symbolic expressions of 'consensus', a proof that the public has been served by having a variety of the best minds thoroughly mull over a course of action.

Order through intimidation

Institutional reins on power are very weak in Japan. The absence of a set of universal beliefs to which all can appeal, the limited controlling function of the legal system, the unaccountability – often the invisibility – of the actual power-holders makes, politically, for a 'nature red in tooth and claw' situation in which power is unbridled and predatory socio-economic practices prevail.

The balance of power

But the teeth and claws are well hidden. Coercion is kept in check by coercion from other parties who fear a diminution of their own power, and is moderated to some extent by layers of ritual. Open displays of power evoke fear in Japan. In the language of Western constitutionalist democracies, there are few 'checks' in Japan, but very special 'balances'. The manifest presence and often the active intervention of a variety of groups are always necessary to keep the System from going out of kilter. All organisations with some power constantly contain the power of others. The balance among the components that make up the Japanese System is achieved by continual intervention by one or more of them to ensure that none will grow so strong and ambitious as to be capable of dominating the rest. What popular influence and legal restraints cannot accomplish must be achieved by a continual grand balancing act. A clique or an individual whose power grows so fast that it cannot smoothly be accommodated by the existing structure will engender a reaction reminiscent of white blood corpuscles converging on an alien substance in the body. What befell former prime minister Tanaka Kakuei is one of the best examples of this. Hence the suspicion, too, of Nakasone when he tried to strengthen the office of prime minister.

The administrators are extraordinarily sensitive to fluctuations of the power balance in their respective realms. An astonishing example is the prosecutors' office and its attitude towards the left. When leftist activists raised a great outcry against corruption, the prosecutors saw the value of their traditional enemies as a cleansing agent acting on the business world and political circles. Although political corruption is 'structural', and the prosecutors would not dream of trying to eliminate it, the System must be guarded against extremes; and with the gradual decline in importance of leftist forces the prosecutors felt that they had to act as a counterbalance and bring more corruption cases to light.[39]

Exploitable weaknesses

The possibility of countering coercion has left the Japanese political order oddly vulnerable to any non-domesticated group that can bring force to bear on it. In other nations, established ruling élites can refer to universally accepted laws and convincing political theory to justify their dominance. The Japanese power-holders cannot. What the shogun could claim, detractors of the shogun's power could claim as well. Political leadership in the past, therefore, had to deal continuously with troublesome, half-autonomous, smaller powers – to fight them, to rally other lords to help keep them in their place, to bargain with them and to some extent to accommodate them.

Intimidation of the various shogunates and of the Meiji, Taisho and early Showa governments was effective where the intimidator was powerful in his own right. The Meiji rulers exercised control in the name of a restored cosmic order fused in the person of a divine emperor. But this introduced a major threat by making it possible for anyone to invoke the 'imperial will' as justification for changing the political order, and opportunities for intimidation increased tremendously.[40] Intimidation is similarly effective within the System today. One important reason why the Self-Defence Forces remain controversial and a source of fear is the absence of a credible institutional check on their power; if Japan's military grows bigger, it will become a body that is capable of much intimidation.

We have already seen two ways in which the System counteracts this curious vulnerability. One is the permanent campaign it wages to co-opt, absorb or emasculate all social elements and forces that vie with it for the ultimate loyalty of the Japanese people. The second is the use of propaganda on behalf of the political status quo.

The absence or presence of power in any setting is very quickly understood by Japanese, and any perception of a shift tends immediately to be reflected in their behaviour. They tend to admire strength and vigour in whatever context it may occur, and for whatever purpose it may exist.

One of the keenest observers of pre-war Japan, Kurt Singer, summed it up succinctly: 'they are peculiarly sensitive to the smell of decay, however well-screened; and they will strike at an enemy whose core appears to betray a lack of firmness'.[41] This should always be kept in mind by foreigners dealing with Japan. In the 1980s Americans have tended to humble themselves before the Japanese in connection with the relatively poor performance of their own economy. Japanese have immediately sensed the weakness and exploited it.

The ubiquity of intimidation

Intimidation is used within trade associations to maintain their hierarchy. The prominent members have much power over the lesser ones and can even, in extreme cases, organise a bankruptcy through the leverage they have over subcontractors, distribution channels and creditors.

There are various ways at the disposal of bureaucratic components of the System to make firms realise their place in the scheme of things. Upstart companies may be taught a lesson for being too aggressive, or for having irritated dominant firms in the industry. One example is Kyocera, a relatively new, adventurous and very successful firm led by a true entrepreneur. It is not part of the established hierarchy of corporations and is therefore particularly vulnerable to manifestations of official displeasure. In June 1985 it was ordered by the Ministry of Health and Welfare to suspend production for thirty-five days, on the grounds that it had been selling (perfectly good) ceramic joints and bones to hospitals for five years without official permission. In fact, the Japanese bureaucracy confronts industry with such a plethora of regulations and official restrictions that no firm can keep complete track of them. The strictness with which they are enforced depends on *jinmyaku* relations and the firm's power within the industrial hierarchy. Under these circumstances, measures such as those against Kyocera are taken only if a lesson has to be taught. The press helps teach the lesson, and the president of the firm in question is obliged ceremonially to beg society's forgiveness.

Far from being abhorred, intimidation is accepted as an inevitable aspect of social and political life; inevitable because the informal, non-legal relations that characterise the System lead very naturally to dependence on informal coercion (i.e. intimidation) to maintain order and safeguard the power of power-holders. The highly valued conformity in Japan is to a large extent enforced by intimidation; until the recent outcry, teachers in many schools encouraged their pupils in bullying practices. For the administrators, intimidation is preferable to legally enforceable normative values, and is widely used to maintain control.

The freedom and *de facto* support that gangsters enjoy is another example of how intimidation helps to operate the System. The fact that they exist and are strong automatically means that they are accepted. Their intimidation has made them 'acceptable'. They may intimidate ordinary people with impunity; the police and most of the courts remain unsympathetic to the victims' plight. As we have seen in Chapter 4, respectable, highly placed people in the System sometimes use them for intimidation purposes.

That intimidation is a preferred alternative to legal sanctions is illustrated by official toleration of the activities of the Burakumin Liberation League (BLL). The denunciation tactics of this group have made it very powerful when it confronts publishers, authors, journalists, editors and teachers. Any of these who says anything about the *burakumin* minority that contradicts BLL ideology runs the risk of being forced to undergo denunciation sessions. These can become fairly unpleasant, with the victims taken against their will to a meeting place where, in the presence of other 'representatives of society', they are given a dressing down by a succession of denunciators. They may be held until they offer their profound apologies. The result is that most references to *burakumin* in books and magazines are cut by editors. The System has attained a *modus vivendi* with the BLL, and both the System and the BLL are opposed to *burakumin* groups affiliated to the Communist Party, which emphasises court action in instances of open discrimination.

It is understandable that government agencies should prefer this type of intimidation to the litigation that some of the *burakumin* under communist guidance initiate. Intimidation can be held in check far better than the creation of new normative rules. Large-scale litigation and the establishment of legal precedents help consolidate norms that can be appealed to by other disadvantaged people and groups and that circumvent the social-control privileges of the administrators.[42] In the field of labour relations, too, virulent conflicts are settled in ways that do not leave precedents as a standard whereby subsequent conflicts can be resolved, and at the same time narrow the scope of action available to the administrators.[43] This means that in Japan there are fewer standards by which to judge the appropriateness of the use of force in labour disputes.

Intimidation works in Japan, no matter where it originates. It worked when the Chinese government made Japanese newspaper correspondents promise never to write anything critical about Mao Tse-tung, the Cultural Revolution and other controversial subjects. It works when Arab countries ask Japanese companies not to trade with Israel. Japan is the only major country in the Western alliance that religiously observes the Arab economic boycott of Israel. No Japanese or economic delegation has ever visited Israel, while the path to the Arab countries is well trodden.[44] No ship flying the Japanese flag has ever entered an Israeli port. Japanese banks do not extend long-term financing for exports of investment goods to Israel, and Toyota has never sold a car in Israel. When New York Mayor Ed Koch criticised this policy at a press briefing, none of the two hundred Japanese journalists present got one line about this in his newspaper.[45] The controversy in the West over the broadcasting of films that could be construed as critical of Arab social practices is unthinkable in Japan, where such films are taken out of circulation at the slightest sign of Arab displeasure. The bureaucracy applies pressure to corporations to stick to such policies, believing that Japan's national security is at stake.

Any foreign country can participate in the Japanese political tug of war by applying *gaiatsu*, or pressure from the outside. Ministries, in the context of their battles with other ministries, have on several occasions been known to encourage foreigners to use *gaiatsu*.[46]

Bureaucratic intimidation

As we have seen, the laws drafted by the bureaucrats for bureaucratic control are purposely left vague. When law and policy come into conflict, officialdom tends to adjust the law to fit the policy, in what is called 'interpretation of the law'.[47] The threat of applying laws in instances where they are not usually applied gives government agencies great powers of intimidation.

This is one reason for the vehement opposition to the anti-espionage bills that have been introduced, unsuccessfully, on a number of occasions, with vague clauses about national security that could be interpreted in a variety of ways. A member of the editorial staff of the *Asahi Shimbun* sums it up:

> It is not that we would be arrested or sentenced to death for what we write in our paper. What those who promote the bill expect is not to arrest us immediately but to make us restrain ourselves. . . . Many correspondents would choose the clever way not to take risks under [the anti-spy law]. As to articles on diplomacy and defence, only authorised ones or scoops within the safety zone would be printed. In this way, a 'desirable environment' for those in executive positions would be created. . . . And the courageous minority would be suppressed.[48]

As for business corporations, their relationship with the bureaucracy is not normally antagonistic, but in such instances of conflict as do occur – when the two parties differ on the details of policies – the companies normally have no option but to comply with bureaucratic wishes. In fact, the bureaucratic technique of 'administrative guidance' that has drawn so much attention from Western observers is itself a species of coercion by intimidation.

'Administrative guidance' is effective because of the leverage bureaucrats have over businesses. The power to withhold licences is an obvious one. Government officials are responsible for approval of applications for almost every conceivable business activity. If they do not like an applicant, for whatever reason, they can hold off a decision on that person's applications. Although there is no legal obligation for a business to abide by the guidance, all abide by it simply because they want to continue to function. This is one of the keys to Japanese bureaucratic control. Official theory notwithstanding, administrative guidance is compulsory.[49]

The coercion is sometimes more straightforward. A high MITI official told me that, since all companies have done something shady at one time or another, they fear exposure if they do not follow MITI's directions. The collecting of information useful in such blackmail is done at the assistant-section-chief level, and the information comes from direct investigations, competitors, clients, the police, enemies in the business community and disgruntled employees. My informant estimates that more than half of all cases of corporate wrongdoing known to the police and MITI bureaucrats are covered up. The main leverage this gives MITI is the fear, not of legal action against the company, but of 'social punishment'. For it is considered most damaging to a firm if its name is disclosed in connection with any kind of scandal.

For the bureaucrats, it is very important that an illusion of voluntary co-operation be maintained, so officials nearly always prefer to approach a potentially recalcitrant company informally, and offer it freedom from 'red tape' in return for compliance with government wishes, even where there is a law regulating the issue at hand.[50] The parties on the receiving end of administrative guidance consider it more salutary for their prestige to co-operate than to invite (informal) compulsion.[51] And ministries dole out favours such as tax privileges and financial help in return for obedience to administrative guidance.

Of the three main tools that bureaucrats use to get their plans implemented – legislative measures, budgetary measures and administrative guidance – they much prefer the last, because it is effective and readily available for quick action. They could in most cases find a law to suit their purpose, but 'administrative guidance' maintains the fiction of voluntary co-operation. When the Ministry of Finance forces the commercial banks to buy government bonds, it refers to this as 'co-operation'. Administrative guidance also provides much greater scope for specific adjustments in consultation with the recipient than would the application of standardised legal regulations. Also, administrative guidance is more effective than legal action, since the laws are less easily enforceable.

The economic ministries have great power to harass firms and banks that do not toe the line. The trump card used by the bureaucrats is the claim that what they 'suggest' is less what they want than what the industry wanted all along. This approach is often used in tandem with bureaucratic manipulation of the power that associations of firms have to enforce conformity, in a strategy whereby the recalcitrant firm is forced to fall in line by threat of ostracism from the community of its competitors. A famous example of this is the way Sumitomo Metals in Osaka was forced to go along with a production cut ordered by MITI in 1965.

Intimidating the administrators

How the bureaucrats view their own place in the System is highlighted by the way they perceive the very rare lawsuits initiated against them. As one Japanese specialist aptly points out, such lawsuits are considered to represent an unwarranted use of force.[52] Legal entanglements hamper official duties, but the bureaucrats dislike litigation mainly because they feel that to give court-room explanations of official actions conflicts with the highly treasured 'confidentiality of the administration'. Court scrutiny, forcing disclosures from bureaucrats, undermines their dignity and, consequently, the settled benevolent state of affairs of the Japanese nation.

Intimidation can thus work both ways. Although the supposed servants of the people have the advantage, and the possibilities for court action against them are so limited as to be almost non-existent, the very possibility that some group or other may attempt to put bureaucrats in the dock has an intimidating effect. Public officials consider such resistance a 'red light', and modify their attitudes in an attempt to keep things from getting out of hand. There is no doubt that they fear public dissatisfaction once this manifests itself in powerful resistance.[53]

Japanese policy patterns are nearly always inflexible until a catastrophe occurs or until those who consider themselves victimised manage a veritable chorus of protest.[54] A movement of opposition or complaint is at first usually ignored or suppressed. But when the realisation dawns that further suppression will only make the movement stronger, officialdom changes its attitude. Those in charge tend to become more flexible and ready to overlook illegal action. In cases where a problem suddenly threatens to become acute, the metamorphosis of the officials concerned, from a stubborn and uncompromising attitude to an accommodating stance, is generally very dramatic.

The intimidation we find in the Japanese System may be called 'structural intimidation'. Without it, the System as we know it would grind to a halt, since it furnishes the power-holders with power. Ritual and hierarchy help preserve order, but do not guarantee security. Only power provides security in Japan. In the absence of law and universal values, power is indispensable for protection. Guarding one's power is best accomplished by subtly displaying and enlarging it. And because this can be done only through informal means, intimidation is an unavoidable and omnipresent characteristic of Japanese society.

14

A Century of
Consolidating Control

A major hindrance to an accurate assessment of the Japanese System is the still very common view that the jolt of defeat in the Pacific War, and the ministrations of the Supreme Commander of the Allied Powers (SCAP), brought into being a Japan that had made a definitive break with its own immediate past. According to this view, the society that emerged in just a few years after 1945 was committed to different principles of governing itself and led by men themselves committed to these principles. Japan's traditional political culture, though of course an influence still to be considered, was seen as somehow having undergone a major metamorphosis.

Acceptance of this view was made easy for many by an influential school of thought that presented the years between the late 1920s and 1945 as an aberration in Japanese history. Until shortly before the Manchurian Incident,[1] according to this theory, Japan followed a historically determined course of 'modernisation'. All the elements that would have turned it into a respectable modern democratic society, such as a parliament and political parties, were in place when the country was temporarily derailed by nationalist fanatics.[2]

This viewpoint has been greatly undermined by recent scholarship, mainly of American historians, which shows how Japan's efforts at empire building and domestic repression can be seen as a logical development growing out of dominant trends in the Meiji period. Yet only in the 1980s have some scholars begun to point out that 1945 was not the watershed it was supposed to have been, and that authoritarian institutions and techniques dating from the first half of the twentieth century have been crucial in shaping present-day Japan.[3]

With the benefit of hindsight we can go one step further and see the Japanese System of the late 1980s as a product of the consolidation of certain bureaucratic and political forces that have been evolving since before the turn of the century, a consolidation that was accelerated by the war.

The fundamental continuity

There is no gainsaying that post-war Japan is a new Japan in many respects. The idea that military adventurism was a great mistake and that the nation should devote itself to peaceful pursuits has undoubtedly been very strong among the general populace, especially from the 1950s to the 1970s. Standards of living, especially in rural Japan, cannot be compared with the poverty that prevailed before the war. Japanese today enjoy much personal freedom, and need not worry about being arrested for what they say. The Japanese public is looked after in a way it has never been before. Nevertheless, in the context of our theme – how power is exercised in Japan – the continuities appear to be of more consequence than the changes; continuities not only in the motivations of the ruling élite, but also in the institutions it has shaped.

Japan rose phoenix-like from the rubble of its bombed cities to become the second most powerful economy in the world, challenging the older industrial countries. However, the mainsprings of this rebirth are not to be found in the economic and political restructuring measures of US-occupation-inspired *demokurashii*, but in the socio-political world and the disavowed 'feudal' practices of a Japan at war. We will examine the details of the astounding history of the Japanese political economy in Chapter 15. First, I must demonstrate more concretely that it is fair to speak of the System as a consolidation of pre-1945 bureaucratic institutions.

Luckiest survivors of the war

The most momentous decision the occupation authorities made when they set about transforming Japan's political leadership was to leave practically the entire bureaucracy intact.[4] The usual explanation for this is that SCAP had no choice but to work through the existing organs of state. But as a specialist on Japanese politics points out, this overstressing of United States dependence ignores the realities of power.[5] The vast majority of those involved in occupation policies were not even aware that any significant decision had been made. The Americans in charge simply assumed that bureaucrats everywhere behaved as they did in the USA, that is to say, as apolitical technicians. The official in charge of labour affairs in SCAP's grand 'democratisation' programme describes how the nerve-centre of operations to reform defeated Japan's officialdom consisted of a single young lieutenant in the Transportation Corps, Milton J. Esman.

> Esman's desk was an oasis of quiet in a tumult of bustling reform activities, for he was in charge of the civil service under Kades, and it seemed that no one else was interested in the subject. No paragraph in the Joint Chiefs' directive JCS 1380/15 even mentioned the bureaucracy. Esman really had no official mission.[6]

The lieutenant was, in a sense, succeeded in his task of 'defeudalising' the bureaucracy by the Hoover Mission, a group of specialists that came at the request of the Japanese government to teach modern administrative methods. But the mission failed even to perceive the significance of the fact that practically all higher civil servants were Tokyo University graduates. Whatever it may have accomplished, it had nothing to do with overhauling the bureaucracy.[7]

The occupation purge eliminated the defeated military organisations, removed fifteen hundred highly placed businessmen,[8] barred a few party politicians from holding public office and dissolved ultra-nationalist organisations. It did not go beyond this to tackle the mainspring of Japan's governing system. The aims of the purge, to some extent contradictory, were neither clearly outlined nor attainable under the circumstances.[9] Moreover the strong incentive to preserve, for political reasons, the 'tranquillity' of the occupation led the US reformers to keep to a minimum interference in areas outside the military and ultra-nationalist organisations.[10] Thus the purge of the bureaucracy was, in its details, left to the bureaucrats themselves, who soon realised that they were free to use a large variety of loopholes; they often simply ignored SCAP instructions.

By 1950, when the return to public life of depurged bureaucrats coincided with the 'Red Purge' (in which more than one thousand government officials and almost eleven thousand company employees suspected of communism or 'communistic-type' thinking lost their jobs), the effects of the occupation purge on Japan's officialdom had been reduced to almost nil. The first major post-war prime minister, Yoshida Shigeru, summed it up: 'The occupation, with all the power and authority behind its operation, was hampered by its lack of knowledge of the people it had come to govern, and even more so, perhaps, by its generally happy ignorance of the amount of requisite knowledge it lacked.'[11]

Reform bureaucrats and the 'new order'

SCAP's ignorance of the true power of Japanese bureaucrats gave the latter the opportunity to develop and integrate further economic institutions they had experimented with, in the context of the wartime industrial effort, from the early 1930s until 1945. This post-war effort was better organised; the bureaucrats had learned from experience and, more important, had been given powers by SCAP that they never had before.

Many of the most prominent figures associated with post-war industrial policy had been known in pre-war and wartime Japan as 'reform bureaucrats', strongly influenced by the ideas of Hitler's Germany and by Mussolini's corporatism. This does not mean that they were converts to Nazism, but that they sponsored the application of German methods to problems of the economy and social control in Japan.[12] Nazi and fascist theory are not generally associated in the Western mind with the Japanese 'economic miracle', but it is doubtful whether this could have occurred without the inspiration of these theories supporting totalitarian state control. In fact, the reform bureaucrats and their apprentices dominated the post-war leadership of the economic ministries, the central bank and the large business federations.

Given their post-war importance, the reform bureaucrats deserve a closer look. The way had been paved for them by earlier reformers, the so-called 'new bureaucrats' who made their appearance after the Manchurian Incident of 1931. These were considered 'new' because they helped reorganise domestic politics and gained prominence through a shift in power-sharing, accompanied by the gradual smothering of the Minseito and Seiyukai parties. Instead of working through these two major (largely bureaucratic) parties, they helped undermine and eliminate party-political influence and revitalised their own alliance with the military. Based mainly in the Naimusho, the bastion of the social-control bureaucrats, they introduced new institutions and established stricter control over local governments and the population via the neighbourhood associations of towns and villages. The actual reform bureaucrats, also known as 'new new bureaucrats', began to draw attention after the fateful coup attempt of 26 February 1936 and the outbreak of full-scale hostilities in China a year later.[13] They had become aware of the crucial role played by economic processes in the social order, and were eager to introduce economic controls.

The reform bureaucrats responded emotionally as well as intellectually to the social confusion and dissatisfaction created by economic uncertainty and rising expectations among the public. Searching for total solutions to these social problems, they were, in their early idealistic phase, influenced by a mishmash of European notions that had emerged in response to tensions and problems of governability. A number of reform bureaucrats had started out as Marxists, or had socialist convictions. Some, in fact, had retained a 'red' tinge, which caused a major scandal and arrests among top officials in early 1941. In their later phase, however, the reform bureaucrats were bound together by Nazi notions, Italian fascism, vigorous Japanism, a thorough aversion to liberal party politics and a belief in strong state control. At crucial junctures in their careers the prominent reform bureaucrats all served in the puppet state of Manchukuo, which had been set up by Japan's Kwantung Army. Indeed, the standard advice of senior bureaucrats to their juniors was 'If you want to call yourself a reformist, you must train yourself in Manchuria'.[14] In Manchuria they learned how to work with military bosses, and how to exploit the economic possibilities of a regimentation far more rigid than anything the home islands had been amenable to. Military planners, partly inspired by the Five-Year Plan in the Soviet Union, had long dreamed of co-ordinating plans for military and civilian economic mobilisation. Pre-eminent among them, General Nagata Tetsuzan first articulated the idea of a 'national defence state', which had a powerful effect on the bureaucrats' imagination.[15]

The notions of the reform bureaucrats found their most articulate expression among the members – bureaucrats, intellectuals and journalists – of a 'research society' called the Showa Kenkyukai. It was founded by a close friend of Konoe Fumimaro, the most important civilian government leader in the years leading up to the Pacific War.[16] Known as Konoe's 'brains trust', the Showa Kenkyukai was a source of inspiration for the New National Structure Movement (also known as the New Order Movement, or Shin Taisei Undo), which aimed to overhaul the political system, to purge Japan of conflicting interests and to promote a totalitarian national unity. The Imperial Rule Assistance Association (IRAA or Taisei Yokusankai), intended as the controlling organisation of the 'new order', was launched in October 1940 in the hope of liberating Japan once and for all from the perennial 'sectionalism' that deprived the empire of its full potential. This effort failed, but the 'economic new order' part of it helped inspire the post-war programme of unlimited industrial expansion.[17]

The institutional centre of operations for the reform bureaucrats was the Cabinet Planning Board (CPB). This central organ for national mobilisation was created in 1937 through a merger of the Cabinet Research Bureau (established two years previously) and the Resources Bureau, a military-economic planning unit. The Army had pushed for the merger, and in the CPB, later nicknamed the 'economic general staff',[18] the military-bureaucrat economic planners shifted their focus from a five-year plan for Japanese–Manchurian industrial development to general mobilisation programmes.[19] The CPB never succeeded in its intended task of meshing the military and civilian sides of the wartime industrial effort. Only after it was merged in 1943 with the then Ministry of Commerce and Industry (MCI) to form the Ministry of Munitions did it become half-way effective.[20] But the CPB may be considered the predecessor of the highly effective post-war Economic Stabilisation Board,[21] while the major functions of the Munitions Ministry were inherited by MITI. We will come back to the IRAA and its legacy later in this chapter.

The strengthening of the economic bureaucrats

Bureaucratic institutions and personnel fitted smoothly into the new Japan that was being 'defeudalised'. One of the closest associates of Tojo Hideki, reform bureaucrat Kishi Nobusuke, who as the most powerful official in the wartime Ministry of Munitions was the central figure among executors of Japan's wartime industrial policy, became the dominant figure of post-war industrial policy.[22] We have noted how Kishi, after a stint in Sugamo prison as a war criminal suspect (never brought to trial), became first one of Japan's best-known prime ministers, then, until his death in 1987, Japan's most influential éminence grise.

Second only to Kishi as a shaper of post-war industrial policy was Shiina Etsusaburo, a Manchurian reform bureaucrat, who had the timely idea, between the surrender and the arrival of the first United States troops, of re-baptising the Ministry of Munitions so that it became the Ministry of Commerce and Industry once more.[23] He himself became MITI minister after the war, and remained a powerful force behind the scenes at the ministry, as well as one of the most prominent leaders of the LDP, until his death in 1979.

The leader of the Ministry of Finance group in Manchuria was Hoshino Naoki, who was president of the wartime CPB. After the war he became a prominent member of the Keizai Kenkyukai, the study group established to re-examine post-war economic policy, which produced the blueprint for policies of economic high growth in the shape of Prime Minister Ikeda's 'income doubling plan'.[24] He was also chairman of the Tokyu Hotel and Trading Group, and of Diamond Publishing, a firm specialising in business publications.

The main architects of wartime financial controls had originally come from the foreign exchange section, established in 1933, of the Ministry of Finance, and were found in its secretariat and the Finance Bureau, an extraordinary ministerial group with great discretionary powers in design-ing state policy.[25] Pre-eminent among them was the reform bureaucrat Sakomizu Hisatsune, who became head of the Economic Planning Agency and postal minister after the war.

Another prominent Ministry of Finance official associated with this wartime planning, Morinaga Teiichiro, was to become vice-minister of finance in 1957–9 and governor of the Bank of Japan during the second half of the 1970s. A third, Shimomura Osamu, determined the pricing policies of the crucial post-war Economic Stabilisation Board, and was later one of the main brains behind Prime Minister Ikeda's 'income doubling plan'.

Many of the crucial wartime controls over lending were co-ordinated in a bureau whose chief, Ichimanda Hisato, was to become governor of the Bank of Japan in 1946, a position he held for eight and a half crucial years before being appointed finance minister. Under his governorship the central bank was popularly known as 'the Vatican'.

The bureaucrats survived the purges with the added advantage of being freed from their sometimes troublesome military associates. Moreover, the occupation authorities, believing that big business had been 'active exponents of militant nationalism and aggression', ordered the dissolution of the *zaibatsu* conglomerates and disbanded the holding companies, which meant that the bureaucrats no longer faced troublesome rivals for power in the business world. The bureau chiefs of each ministry began to attend cabinet meetings, a practice unknown before the war. They became go-betweens between MacArthur's headquarters and government ministers,'[26] and their utterances gained significantly in weight.

When, after the war, Japanese intellectuals and commentators began to refer to the bureaucrats as 'subcontractors of the occupation', they missed the essential fact that the tail was wagging the dog. As Chalmers Johnson puts it: 'the occupation era, 1945–52, witnessed the highest levels of government control over the economy ever encountered in modern Japan before or since, levels that were decidedly higher than the levels attained during the Pacific War'.[27] Perhaps the biggest present bestowed on the post-war MITI bureaucrats by SCAP was the power to form cartels, an essential instrument of Japanese industrial policy that had earlier been the monopoly of the wartime 'control associations'. These associations, created in 1941 after much friction among the various bureaucratic cliques involved and much business opposition, were meant to co-ordinate activities, production targets and the allocation of materials in the various sectors of wartime industry.[28] But the bureaucrats never gained an effective grip on them, since business had made sure that they were headed by the top executive of the largest firm in each sector, thus putting them under effective control of the *zaibatsu*. In disbanding the *zaibatsu*, SCAP forbade any further private cartelisation. To the economic officials of what was to become MITI it suddenly seemed 'as if they had arrived in the bureaucratic promised land'.[29]

Talkative officials have publicly acknowledged that, whereas, formally, Japan underwent a great transformation after the war, the economic system and especially the institutional base for financial controls were retained in the forms they had taken during the war. Two former Ministry of Finance bureaucrats have contrasted the two 'realities', the formal and the substantial, and asserted that this duality was essential in the shaping of the post-war 'miracle'. As they put it, the ideology of democratic equal opportunity caused an explosion of energy in favour of economic growth, while the high growth itself was actually achieved through the reality of strict financial controls.[30] Writing thirty-two years after the war, they noted that the basic law governing the activities of the central bank was still the same as the original law that had reflected the totalitarian economic purposes of the Nazi Reichsbank.[31] They also argued that the creation of the post-war Japan Development Bank, Export-Import Bank and Long-Term Credit Bank can be viewed as a strengthening of the role the Industrial Bank of Japan (which survived) played during the war.[32]

Control bureaucrats turned 'business representatives'

The post-war economic bureaucrats designed and implemented an industrial policy that vitalised the private sector, steering it to an unprecedented degree in directions of their own choice, and fostered the growth of domestic manufacturers through a strong protectionism. This quickly became Japan's dominating – indeed, sole – major policy. This policy would have been seriously hampered without more effective means than they had during the war of co-ordinating plans with the business world. And the demise of the *zaibatsu* was of significance not least because it made room for the four large industrial federations that were to become post-war control centres. Pervaded by bureaucrats, each of them played a major role in the development of the System and its industrial policy: Keidanren as overall co-ordinator and fund-raiser for what later became the LDP; Nikkeiren as co-ordinator of the anti-labour campaign; the Chamber of Commerce as the ostensible guardian, but also the controller, of smaller industries; and Keizai Doyukai as propagandist and formulator of justifications for the general course that developments were taking.

The first 'prime minister of business', as the chief of Keidanren is popularly known, was also known, prior to the end of the war, as 'the god of the control associations'. This was Ishikawa Ichiro, a leader in the chemical industry control association, one of the government-inspired cartels described above. In the later war years, he rose to high position in the Important Industries Control Association (the umbrella organisation co-ordinating the industrial control associations), took the initiative in dissolving that body before SCAP had a chance to do so and formed a short-lived association that became the main element in Keidanren.[33]

Shortly after the war, Ishikawa brought together young economists who had worked on the CPB in order to make a theoretical study of Japan's economic reconstruction. The result was what amounted to a long-term governmental economic programme. One member of the group was Okita Saburo, later to become successively an important official of the Economic Planning Agency, foreign minister, minister in charge of international economic relations and a major international 'buffer' absorbing and deflecting foreign criticism.

The economic-control bureaucrats and the industrial control association officials had, in the year between Japan's surrender and the birth of Keidanren, formed a variety of committees and subcommittees to map out a course for industry in what was initially a very uncertain future. The most prominent among them had also been among the most prominent of the wartime economic officials. Three of the five industrial subcommittees were led by former control association heads. Matsumoto Kenjiro, the first chairman of the coal industry control group and former chairman of the Important Industries Control Association, headed the main committee.

The vice-chairman of the main committee, later to become the strongest figure in Keidanren, was Uemura Kogoro, a prominent reform bureaucrat who early on had helped establish the important link between the military and the Ministry of Commerce and Industry. He was deputy chief of the CPB before heading the coal control association. Like other leaders in the large business federations, he was known after the war as one of the major voices of the business world, which gave most foreigners (and not a few Japanese) the misleading impression that he was an entrepreneur. It can hardly be reiterated too often that the business federations do not represent true entrepreneurs. The wartime businessmen of the *zaibatsu*, who tended to be more entrepreneurial than their post-war successors, were extremely wary of the 'new economic order' that people like Uemura and Kishi were trying to establish, and showed concern over the great admiration that Uemura, after a study trip to Nazi Germany, expressed for Hitler's economic management.[34]

The second Keidanren chief, Ishizaka Taizo, had a reputation for disliking three things: the bureaucracy, the business support for politicians and the interference with the free market. He could afford to be against those things in his speeches and talks with journalists, since it was during his Keidanren tenure that the close relations among the three main classes of administrators were quietly being consolidated.[35] Ishizaka had also been a bureaucrat, at the Ministry of Communications, before moving to Daiichi Life Insurance, a firm closely tied to the government (he served as its president during the war years). Purged by the occupation, he supervised the reconstruction of what is now Toshiba Corporation before becoming, in 1956, Keidanren chairman. A dozen years later he turned the post over to Uemura. Keidanren vice-chairman from 1968, and chairman between 1980 and 1986, was Inayama Yoshihiro, who had served in the pre-war predecessor of MITI before nationalising and again privatising and merging Japan's largest steel companies. In 1970 he created the world's largest steel firm through a merger that established him as Japan's best-known opponent of anti-trust legislation. Nagano Shigeo, who reinvigorated the Japan Chamber of Commerce and Industry (he was chairman from 1969 to 1984), closely co-operating with Inayama, also played a leading role in the national steel industry. He worked for the wartime government, and served as vice-director of the post-war Economic Stabilisation Board.

SCAP went along with plans for the formation of Keidanren on condition that it would not try to engage in economic control and would stay clear of labour relations. Two years later a way was found around the more easily enforceable second prohibition, when several of the people who had established Keidanren, including Uemura, formed or helped form Nikkeiren, the headquarters of union-busting and, later, control organisation in charge of keeping wage rises significantly below productivity increases.

Most of the prominent Nikkeiren organisers were also at the core of Keizai Doyukai, a club that on the face of it seemed to take a much more moderate stand towards socialists and unions.[36] Goshi Kohei, the key figure in its formation, had been chief secretary of the wartime Important Industries Control Association. He was later closely associated with the Japan Productivity Centre, becoming its chairman in 1972. The original purpose of this institute, established with United States assistance, was to acquaint Japanese businessmen with advanced US production methods, but it has since been used to sponsor methods of increasing 'company loyalty', and to teach the virtues of co-operation to not yet tamed enterprise unions.

Another key figure in the establishment of Keizai Doyukai was Hoashi Kei, who had been secretary-general of the umbrella organisation of the control associations, and had in 1941 written a tract about the 'proper relationship' between government and business in the 'new economic order'. In this revealing document he emphasised the need for the voluntary co-operation of business with the authorities: business should be independent, but there should be no return to a 'free economy based on the principle of private profit-making'. The national goal must have priority.[37] He mentioned economic mobilisation in Germany, Britain and the USA during the First World War as good examples of true co-operation between the government and the private sector.[38] But for him the finest example, and the best model for Japan, was 'economic guidance' in Nazi Germany, which he was at pains to distinguish clearly from mere 'economic planning'.[39] Hoashi never doubted that businessmen should be restrained by rules, prompted by the world-wide economic crisis of 1929, which assumed that national goals must take priority; only when those who profited privately also pursued the 'public interest' would the economic system be healthy.[40]

The need for businessmen to heed 'the public interest' echoed through most of the official statements that Keizai Doyukai made during the first couple of decades after the war. The public interest as Hoashi and Keizai Doyukai conceived of it was of course equivalent to the goals of the administrators. It launched a well-publicised theory aimed at seducing potentially intractable forces in the economy, and formulated a list of priorities that amounted, in the words of one of its founders, Otsuka Banjo, to a proposal for 'reformed capitalism'.[41] In 1956 the Doyukai leadership had further refined its programme into a formal declaration which became known as the ideological pointer for post-war management. It saw the Japanese corporation as a public institution in which suppliers and customers as well as workers and management participated. A major task for management, therefore, was to create a harmony of interest among all these parties. The declaration went on to emphasise the collective responsibility of managements of individual firms for the overall welfare of the national economy. It warned, furthermore, that if individual companies each went its own way and failed to make this conscious communal effort, the government would gradually take over to ensure the viability of the economy. This sounded like a rehash of the ideals of Hoashi and the Manchurian bureaucrats. And it is surely as unequivocal an appeal for sacrifice of the prerogatives of private enterprise as was ever made by any large group of businessmen.[42]

In the late 1950s the Keizai Doyukai began to appoint former career bureaucrats to executive positions.[43] Most of its other top members had risen through the hierarchies of the highly bureaucratised businesses that had been gradually intertwining with government bureaucracy ever since the early 1930s. In 1966 leaders of the Keizai Doyukai established the Sangyo Mondai Kenkyukai (Study Group on Industrial Problems), popularly known as Sanken, in an additional effort at the co-ordination of industry believed to be necessary in the face of impending 'liberalisation'.[44] In 1970 Sanken was joined by Keidanren's Uemura Kogoro and a prominent Nikkeiren figure, after which it exercised direct influence over a variety of industrial associations, and by controlling the business membership of governmental *shingikai* (deliberation councils) played an important role in advising the bureaucracy. All twenty-four members of Sanken personally served on one or more *shingikai*.[45] It gradually ceased to function in the early 1980s.

Among the formal aims of these federations, set forth in many public pronouncements in the early stages of their existence, was the promotion of a vigorous democracy. This is reminiscent of the advocacy of greater 'individualism' by the Ad Hoc Council on Educational Reforms, whose reports, it will be remembered, implied that such an aim is best achieved by greater discipline in the schools and better instruction in what it means to be Japanese. The democracy espoused by the *zaikai* left no room for any movement representing the workers, or for socialism (not to mention communism), or indeed for any kind of political principles that might conflict with stable 'conservative' government.

The federation leaders played a crucial role in keeping this 'stability'. They had their doubts about Kishi Nobusuke, who took political risks that they thought endangered the political situation, and were even less enthusiastic about Hatoyama Ichiro, whose resignation they helped bring about in the autumn of 1956. This latter achievement was part of their greatest feat: the bringing together of all 'conservative' cliques under a stable LDP umbrella.[46] In October 1952, three days after an election in which the ruling Liberal Party did badly while the socialists did well, fifty representatives of the four federations held an emergency meeting and adopted a resolution requesting 'stabilisation' of the political situation. This was followed by many similar 'requests' prompted by ceaseless bickering among the future LDP *habatsu*, whose leaders were as yet more concerned with their own political fortunes than with a stable System. Finally, as we saw in Chapter 5, a new political funding system sponsored by Keidanren resulted in 1955 in the realisation of the federations' wishes. The major role in bringing the segments of the LDP together was played by the same Uemura who, in the 1930s, had brought the civilian and military economic planners together.

It was only when Ikeda Hayato succeeded Kishi as prime minister, however, that the federation leaders really allowed themselves to rejoice. They had influenced the selection of previous prime ministers, but in the case of Ikeda they had more or less chosen and groomed him themselves. The same was true of the next prime minister, Sato Eisaku.

Regaining the means of social control

While very kind to the economic-control bureaucrats, the occupation authorities placed bureaucrats steeped in pre-war and wartime *social-*

control methods in a frightful predicament. 'Democratised' education meant teachers organising under Marxist-inspired leadership, and the loss of a whole arsenal of indoctrination methods. Justice Ministry officials had to cope with idealists who actually believed that the law was situated above everyone, including officials; it took at least a decade and a half before they regained control through the secretariat of the Supreme Court. The Naimusho was broken up, and the police were reorganised. While the devastated economy and dire living conditions warranted much economic planning and thus control, the new start with 'democracy' hardly warranted a 'thought police'.

But, by bestowing a constitution upon Japan, General MacArthur, without realising it, did the social-control bureaucrats at least one great favour. The constitution was not wrested from the power-holders by the people. The latter, therefore, were not encouraged to believe that they had the *right* to wrest anything from the ruling élite; and the theory of ultimate benevolence could be maintained. Also as the occupation period reached its mid-point it was gradually becoming clear that the 'damage' the US reformers were inflicting could be contained. By 1949 a popular movement towards genuine reform of the civil service and its selection methods, originating among lower-echelon bureaucrats, engineering bureaucrats and more liberal elements in the higher bureaucracy, had petered out for lack of SCAP support.[47]

The main hazard to the administrators was the new democratic legislature, which could easily undermine social-control mechanisms. The threat was averted thanks to a massive influx into the Diet of veterans of the disbanded Naimusho – the major social-control ministry – that in 1960 was represented by fifty-four of its former officials.[48] The majority of these had been 'purged'. This 'descent' of retired bureaucrats into the pre-LDP conservative parties had begun shortly after the war,[49] aided by the room made for them by the occupation purge of wartime politicians. Some thirty élite bureaucrats joined the Liberal Party ranks for the 1949 elections, and in subsequent elections their number grew to roughly a quarter of the Diet membership, providing Japan with the crucial Yoshida, Kishi, Ikeda and Sato cabinets – during whose tenure the post-war System was consolidated – as well as a majority of the prime ministers following them.

The administrators concerned with public order also made allies among the occupiers, who never understood the depth of the anti-liberalism of their 'subcontractors'. Among these allies was the chief of the Counter-Intelligence Corps (one of the three major sub-units of SCAP), General Charles Willoughby. As the American in charge of labour questions remembered almost forty years later:

In a country where Marxist terminology was the common coin of intellectual exchange and whose trade unions all professed to be socialist at the very least, Willoughby was out of his depth. To him, socialism was just a station on the way to communism.

Democratic socialists were not allies in the fight against the communists but subverters of the established order. . . . Only Japanese conservatives could be trusted. . . . For him, there was no middle ground between the conservatives and the communists.[50]

Post-war careers of the 'thought police'

In his cell in Sugamo Prison, Hiranuma Kiichiro, the powerful public procurator and model social-control bureaucrat, ruminated in 1952 on the unfortunate fact that many people had come to consider the pre-war and wartime Special Higher Police (Tokko, popularly known as the 'thought police') to have been evil, a development that made him worry seriously about the country's future.[51] His worries were a bit premature. A large number of Tokko officials escaped being purged through reshuffling manoeuvres that eluded SCAP.[52] Half of the fourteen Naimusho bureaucrats appointed as supervisors of all police activity (including the Tokko) between 1935 and 1945 served in the post-war Diet.

To name only those Naimusho bureaucrats who fulfilled major functions with the 'thought police' before or during the war and who served in high posts after the war: Machimura Kingo (who suspended publication of magazines such as Chuo Koron and suppressed religious groups) became minister of home affairs and chairman of the National Public Safety Commission overseeing the post-war police; Niwa Kyoshiro (Tokko section chief in Kyoto) became transport minister; and Okazaki Eijo (Tokko section chief in Aichi and Tokyo) became political vice-minister at the Ministry of Labour, the Administrative Management Agency and MITI, and vice-chairman of the LDP's public security committee. Hara Bumbei (Kagoshima Tokko section chief) became an Upper House member and head of the Tokyo metropolitan police. Another section chief of the Tokko in Kagoshima, Okuno Seisuke, was vice-minister of home affairs, education minister and justice minister, before becoming director-general of the National Land Agency in the Takeshita cabinet formed in 1987. The well-known Naimusho official Furui Yoshimi (Naimusho police bureau chief, Naimusho vice-minister, governor of Ibaragi and Aichi) became welfare minister and justice minister. The reform bureaucrat Odachi Shigeo (Naimusho minister in 1944) was education minister and, as we saw in Chapter 3, imported former Naimusho bureaucrats into the Education Ministry for his battle against the teachers' union, Nikkyoso. Nadao Hirokichi (Naimusho vice-minister and Oita governor) became welfare minister and the greatest enemy of Nikkyoso as education minister in four cabinets. Masuhara Keikichi (Wakayama Tokko section chief) became director-general of the Self-Defence Agency. Otsubo Yasuo (in charge of the police section monitoring publications) became parliamentary vice-minister of education and of justice, and chairman of the judicial affairs committee of the Lower House.

Goto Fumio, a leader of the reform bureaucrats and Naimusho minister, who played a major role organising the pre-war and wartime local youth organisations, served in the Upper House after the war.[53]

The list of former 'thought police' officials who re-emerged as politicians is much longer, but I have chosen only those who made a name for themselves with their post-war positions in the central government. A large number of them also ended up as prefectural governors, as officials in the local public safety commissions (theoretically supervising the police) or in lower regional government positions. As my list shows, the former 'thought police' officials tended to drift to government departments concerned with social control: education, welfare, justice and labour. The labour bureaucrats in the Naimusho – also spared by SCAP – were holding the posts of vice-minister and chiefs of the most important bureaux in the Ministry of Labour as late as 1969.[54] As their American chronicler writes: 'Ironically, the labor bureaucrats achieved their greatest autonomy under the aegis of the American state. Like their colleagues in other ministries, these officials became more powerful during the Occupation than ever before or ever again.'[55]

The occupation period gave the social-control bureaucrats an opportunity to forge institutional weapons with which to fend off the labour union advance that they, under United States orders, had initially helped stimulate. The 'Red Purge' ousted officials with post-war 'dangerous thoughts', and set the stage for the dismissal of Education Ministry officials who had 'co-operated too much' with SCAP's democratisation efforts.[56] Steps to remedy the 'excesses of the occupation' in other areas such as the police and anti-trust legislation completed the consolidation of post-war bureaucratic power.

Not all Japanese welcomed the retention of the wartime control bureaucrats. As one author wrote in one of the most respected of Japan's intellectual monthlies, the Tokyo Trials judged acts perpetrated by war criminals against foreigners, but did not consider those committed against the Japanese people. Men who had sent others to the front, who had deprived them of their freedom and property, who had made cruel laws, continued, he pointed out, to hold high positions in post-war cabinets.[57] Showing how the bureaucrats in question disposed of government assets to supply the politicians of their choice with the funds to gain power, the author reminded his readers that in Germany, unlike in Japan, a general sense of justice had prevailed. The Germans themselves tried war criminals who had been acquitted at the Nuremberg Trials.

The institutional memory

The influential post-war careers of these wartime bureaucrats are only part of the story. No less important is the phenomenal institutional memory of the System's components. Japanese bureaucrats, like their counterparts everywhere, constantly seek to minimise their personal responsibility for anything they do. But they differ from their counterparts in the West or Asia in the extraordinary sense of responsibility they are expected to feel towards their organisation. As we have seen in various contexts, Japanese socio-political circumstances leave members of an organisation little choice but to identify strongly with it, and this is especially true of élite groups. Members of MITI, the prosecutors' office, Nikkeiren and all the institutions that guide and control Japan are continually aware of the experiences of their predecessors and the seriousness of their tasks. Institutional memory and institutional motivation go together, because collective experience gives a keen edge to a collective purpose, as well as to passionate partisanship. In Japanese government agencies they are strong, vivid and sharply etched into the minds of the officials. For comparable instances outside Japan, one could point to the Kremlin specialists who deal with the capitalist world; to, possibly, some intelligence organisations; and to churches and secret societies. These special institutions are like ordinary Japanese administrator institutions in the sense that membership can never be a casual or short-term affair (as it is in many US government agencies). Another similarity is that they operate largely under conditions in which the laws of mainstream society hardly affect them, or even bring their own set of 'laws' to their task.

No ministry of the interior of any Western country could, for example, be compared to the Naimusho in its dictatorial powers over the ordinary public. The occupation officials who disbanded it in December 1947 had no inkling of the breadth and depth of its institutional memory and of the force it would remain after its demise. Besides providing the above-mentioned Diet members and vice-ministers, as well as many of the prefectural vice-governors who were key figures at the regional level in post-war Japan, this Hydra-like institution lives on through its social bureau, which became the post-war Ministry of Labour and Ministry of Health and Welfare; its civil engineering bureau, which was turned into the Ministry of Construction and the National Land Agency; its police bureau, which became the National Police Agency; and its local bureau, which after an interim period as a special agency renewed itself as the Ministry of Home Affairs (Jichisho). The last-mentioned institution is generally considered to be the chief heir of its pre-1947 antecedent,[58] but officials from all the offshoots share, in varying degrees, the 'Naimusho spirit'.

In the 1980s several of the Naimusho's descendants are thought to be increasing their relative power. This is certainly true of the Ministry of Home Affairs, whose former bureaucrats already occupy about one-third of the prefectural governorships,[59] as well as prominent positions in municipal governments, so that it has gradually become the most formidable rival to the Ministry of Finance.[60] Most relevant in the context of social control are special committees set up by the Ministry of Home Affairs in local governments to collect information on inhabitants and their jinmyaku. The ministry has the advantage of not being attractive to politicians who use cabinet portfolios to expand their 'political fund' resources, so it is not much bothered by the LDP.[61]

There are also traces of the Naimusho tradition in less obvious places. For example, Shoriki Matsutaro, the powerful post-war boss of the *Yomiuri Shimbun*, Japan's largest newspaper, was in the Naimusho before becoming the newspaper's president in 1924. He exerted himself on behalf of the bureaucrats in the 1936 merger of the news agencies into one government propaganda organ, Domei Tsushinsha.[62] After a stint in prison as a war criminal suspect, he established Nippon Television and became a Diet member and director-general of the Science and Technology Agency.

After the Second World War the military ceased to be a factor, and the police lost their more drastic means of compelling compliance. The education and justice ministries were obliged to give themselves a 'democratic' appearance, which inevitably had an inhibiting effect on the overbearing attitudes of pre-occupation days. But an essential element in the attitude of administrators in the civil service, the notion that they must always control the people, has remained.

Japan's social-control bureaucrats have always believed that their mission goes far beyond the enforcement of regulations that is the normal task of civil servants in most Western nations. With or without support from their military allies, they have always been interested in social engineering, and have viewed such active and inventive interference in civil society as necessary to prevent instability. The Japanese ruling élite had before the war and still has today an overpowering 'daddy knows best' attitude, while, as we have seen throughout this book, the people have been kept under permanent political tutelage. It is this continuity through the pre-war, wartime and post-war periods, rather than the undoubted modification of élitist demeanour and the gains in personal freedom, that most significantly determines the character of the Japanese political system today.

Consolidation

Throughout this book we have seen the results of socio-economic control methods inherited from institutions and people that were in charge during Japan's imperialist phase. It now seems useful to step back for a broader perspective in which to place the motives of the administrators. They are heirs to an uncommonly great fear. Beneath the concerns of the Tokugawa power-holders, the Meiji oligarchs and the bureaucrats in the 1920s who wrote the 'thought control law', one senses their ultimate horror of the evanescence of the political world. Ruling élites everywhere fear disorder, but that of Japan is obsessed by it.

Justifiable fears

Heterodox political ideas and unconventional behaviour are feared because of a strong sense of the fragility of the prevailing order of power relations. This should come as no surprise; outside these power relations there is nothing to sustain socio-political order – no legal framework consistently adhered to and providing a sense of security, no certainties transcending the here and now of political expediency. Japan's ruling élite has more reason to fear disorder than Western élites do, for anything that cannot be anticipated and forestalled directly threatens its security. Westerners take it so much for granted that society is regulated automatically by laws and universal principles that they almost never fully appreciate the acute Japanese sense of the need for constant vigilance. In so far as the order as represented by the System has ultimate meaning, unchallenged by any religious or secular belief-system, maintenance of order must be an ultimate aim.

Just as the problem has remained, so have formidable vestiges of the neo-Confucianist notions that – by presenting existing socio-political relations as the embodiment of ultimate truth – served the Tokugawa shogunate so well as a supporting ideology. The administrators have also inherited from their Tokugawa predecessors a dominating sense of obligation to control the masses. The Japanist ideology, justifying extra-legal power by referring to homogeneity and harmony, cannot completely subdue the bureaucrats' uneasy awareness that the 'culturalist' excuse that keeps them in place does not convince everyone. They know that, just as in the time of Shotoku Taishi and in the Meiji period, harmony needs to be enforced. Success in keeping the lid on the unacknowledged legitimacy problem depends on success in keeping social order.

The administrators of today may not be especially concerned on an individual level, but as members of administrative institutions it is their duty to worry, just as it is the duty of, say, United States anti-trust enforcers to be troubled by the slightest business collusion as a possible sign of the beginning of the end of the free-market system. They demonstrate their ingrained collective concern with order by, for instance, their common vocabulary. Numerous reports and speeches speak of an 'increasingly complex society';[63] it is one of the most frequently used clichés in the press. Ever since the Meiji Restoration and the reopening of Japan to foreign influence, complexity has horrified Japanese power-holders: the political situation could no longer be sized up at a glance. 'Complexity' is often cited today as a justification for interference, and a reference to something as 'becoming too complex' often indicates that it is about to receive more supervision.

The fear of unruliness and unexpected behaviour and, by implication, the need for better bureaucratic control are also conveyed by such terms as 'excessive competition'. The latter means competition carrying risks – in other words, the kind that is common in free-market countries. Administrators also frequently refer to a 'confused situation', by which they mean an unwanted development eluding the bureaucratic grasp.

Borrowing for order

Histories of Japan commonly remark with regard to cultural borrowing that the country 'took only what it needed' and generally 'imported the form and not the content'. This supports what was said in Chapter 1 about the unusual extent to which Japan's power-holders have for centuries restricted the introduction and development of politically significant ideas and institutions. The social changes that the administrators have guided and monitored have most often been viewed as inevitable adjustments to newly appreciated realities rather than purposeful, radical breaks with old habits.

The bureaucrats serving the Meiji oligarchy, alert to the potential dangers of imported ideas and institutions, engaged in *shiso zendo* ('thought guidance') as a means of forestalling social problems of the kind that existed in Europe.[64] At the same time, the Japanese power-holders have borrowed much that they could use to strengthen their own position, and have discovered various foreign methods of social control. The earliest bureaucrats to do so were concentrated in the Naimusho with, at their centre, Kawaji's police force, whose diverse and extensive social duties were inspired by the example of the highly efficient French police. Six decades later, Nazi Germany was a crucial model. The patriotic industrial associations, the precursors of the post-war enterprise unions, grew out of plans based on Hitler's solution for coping with labour. The labour bill of 1936 was an 'obvious imitation of Nazi Germany's 1934 Law for the Organisation of National Labor'.[65] After the Second World War the business administrators turned to largely discarded American ideas for streamlining capitalism, and produced institutions such as quality control circles aimed at enhancing discipline in factories. More recently, the bureaucrats have been studying the causes of the 'advanced country disease' that allegedly enfeebles the European and United States economies today.

When the Meiji oligarchs introduced military conscription in 1873, they knew that, aside from its ostensible function, it also constituted their best hope of enforcing order. This had been anticipated by Aizawa Seishisai, the pre-Meiji author who said that people should obey the rules but not know about them.[66] For Aizawa, the only alternative to keeping people weak and ignorant was to enlist them in an army. Western governments, according to him, had had no choice but to introduce the military draft, since they had failed to check the emancipation of the masses.[67]

Even though the different cliques among the 'emperor's servants' were engaged in unceasing rivalry, their opinions were mostly unanimous with regard to social control. Between early Meiji and 1945 a military–bureaucratic alliance constituted the chief institutional provision for ensuring such control. The figure largely responsible for the original nature of this alliance was Yamagata Aritomo, who has appeared in Chapter 12 as the political genius who permanently insulated the bureaucracy from the caprices of politicians. With greater influence than any of the other oligarchs over the training of the bureaucracy as well as the military, he established a pattern for military influence over civilian society, and educated a group of protégés who continued to carry out his programmes during the first half of the twentieth century. The retired military men who between 1885 and 1906 headed the Naimusho 'virtually comprise the Who's Who of the Army and Navy'.[68] The Ministry of Education also saw to it that the elementary schools exemplified military ideals. Many school presidents were retired officers. The Army, moreover, gave teachers half a year of intensive military training and indoctrination, with the idea not of sending them to front lines in a future war, but of turning village youth into admirers of soldiers and martial values.[69]

The mass of potentially disloyal rural Japanese were regimented through a campaign taking advantage of the rural hierarchy. The local ruling élite, which initially disdained soldiering, was co-opted (following the instructions of a German adviser) by a system in which the educated sons of landlords and other village bosses served as draftees for only one-third or half the time usual for ordinary villagers, and returned to their homes as lieutenants. After the turn of the century, the Naimusho contributed to this regimentation campaign by launching a 'local improvement movement' aimed at replacing the villagers' loyalty to the old hamlets with loyalty to new administrative villages, which were more controllable from Tokyo.[70]

Yamagata's dream was that the schools and military training should complement each other, forming a gigantic institute for inculcating 'national essence' (kokutai) beliefs and thus ensuring an orderly and unified nation.[71] It was to this end that his most important protégé, General Tanaka Giichi, established the Imperial Military Reserve Association, trail-blazer for the other nationally organised, military-led institutions for indoctrination referred to in Chapter 10.

Tanaka Giichi was to continue the mission he had inherited from Yamagata for many years. In 1928, under his prime ministership, the Peace Preservation Law was toughened to include lifetime imprisonment and the death penalty for those who harboured 'dangerous thoughts'. Under his auspices, Justice Ministry bureaucrats who supported the fanatical *kokutai* advocate Hiranuma Kiichiro moved into the Naimusho and from this new base arrested over 3,400 people.[72]

Fluctuating authoritarianism

The bureaucrats did not intervene in society with unmitigated harshness. They saw their task as one of finding Japanist solutions to social problems, presented with a strong emphasis on 'harmony', 'beautiful ancient customs', and so on. Many of the most important democratising reforms of the 1920s were in fact initiated by activist cliques of labour bureaucrats in the Naimusho.[73] Moved by considerations of national security, these bureaucrats had from before the turn of the century been arguing the necessity of taking care of workers, since crippled children and weakly mothers made for weak and unhealthy soldiers.[74] Even so, the initiatives on behalf of workers that came from the Naimusho were supported by a surviving ideal of benevolence.

In the midst of the bureaucratic–military crusade to rescue and safeguard Japan's hallowed order there was an odd political period, from the second decade of this century until 1932, concerning which historians have rather widely diverging opinions. It is referred to as 'Taisho democracy' because it coincided roughly with the Taisho period, the reign of Hirohito's father that lasted from 1912 to 1926. This period saw developments that suggested a potential for structural change in the governing of Japan. There was a measure of political relaxation in the cities, and the political parties became more significant.

Evolutionistic theories have interpreted this as a 'natural' development towards a Western type of parliamentary democracy. As it happened, the promise was not fulfilled. The right to vote was extended to all adult males in 1925, but in the same year the legal basis for 'thought control' was established with the promulgation of the Peace Preservation Law. And after roughly a decade of relative openness and freedom, the military–bureaucratic reaction that came in the late 1920s was all the more intense.[75]

Containing the public

The administrators of post-war Japan have been able to create a world in which socio-political disorder threatening their security and peace of mind is kept to a minimum. Japan's political culture, shaped by a succession of political arrangements in which the cult of submission has been a major common denominator, helps them to do this. This tradition discourages individual growth and fosters dependency. The Japanese accept a high degree of organisation and restrictions; they tolerate the ways that officials meddle in their lives, and do not question their permanent political tutelage. Very few can conceive of civil disobedience as legitimate political action.

Nevertheless, the administrators must remain vigilant, because the tradition established by their predecessors cannot be trusted to continue on its own. We have seen the results of their vigilance throughout this book. University students, salaryman recruits and young factory workers are often treated as if they were still in elementary school. Even older adults are often admonished or advised as if they were children. Military service no longer helps ensure discipline among Japanese adolescent and young adult males, and the post-war family has lost most of its pre-war legal control of its members – but the enforced conformism of salaryman life is a very effective substitute.

Unconventional behaviour and unexpected changes in the routines of life within the System are frightening and must be contained. The administrators tend to react swiftly when they sense that society is becoming cluttered with groups whose behaviour might become unpredictable. A classic pre-war example of this was their clamping down on new religious sects. The bureaucrats were not worried about their teachings, which did not strike at any vulnerable spots in the body politic. The trouble was that these sects proliferated outside the hierarchy of established religions; they were undesirable simply because they were too different from conventional groups.[76]

The energy with which in the late 1980s the authorities have pursued fingerprint refusers is a post-war example of the government bringing its might to bear on a matter that has not even the remotest potential for state-undermining confusion. Some members of the Korean and Chinese minorities who have resided in Japan for several generations object to the rule that they must be fingerprinted for alien registration purposes; they see this practice, which among Japanese nationals is followed only with criminals, as symbolic of the discrimination they suffer. Some other resident foreigners also refuse to be fingerprinted. There is no convincing reason why this antiquated method of identification should still be in use, and a number of sympathetic local municipal offices help the refusers by not reporting them. Although the fingerprinting issue has become a diplomatic burden for the Ministry of Foreign Affairs, the officials of both the Ministry of Justice and the National Police Agency are adamant about enforcing 'order' (sometimes with devices that help police to take a person's fingerprints forcibly), and set examples by refusing to issue re-entry permits or visa renewals, or by issuing deportation orders.

Such control for its own sake also sets an example for the Japanese people. The System would collapse if they did not take social control for granted. The administrators in the editorial offices of the media, no less than those in police and judiciary circles, take arbitrary control in their stride by appealing to its purportedly lofty purpose of guarding public 'morality'.

Whenever possible, the administrators like to combine their setting of examples with a show of 'benevolence'. Take the case of the three 21-year-old Japanese Olympic swimmers who were caught smoking marijuana in

Los Angeles in 1984. Even though they have no jurisdiction beyond Japanese borders, the Japanese prosecutors made much of their 'lenient' decision not to prosecute for the reason that the young men had tried the forbidden weed only once out of curiosity. The swimmers' university was also 'lenient', suspending them and then readmitting them after a semester during which they professed their contrition in diaries sent to the university authorities in instalments.

Long-range control

Japan's administrators, of course, do not see themselves as hatching questionable schemes, out of questionable motives, to increase their hold over the ordinary citizen. The Japanese bureaucratic tradition has conditioned them to believe that society will be undermined if they relax their guard; the idea of citizens who have the political right to decide for themselves remains alien to them.

While there is no unambiguous evidence that Japan's bureaucrats plan restrictive measures far into the future, they gratefully exploit circumstances in the interests of what can be called long-range control. Japanese women, for instance, have no ready access to pharmaceutical birth-control devices. The official reason for this is the allegedly deleterious side-effects of this 'new' drug. Yet in 1986 alone the health bureaucrats permitted the sale of almost half the four dozen genuinely new drugs introduced world-wide that year, the majority of which were of Japanese origin and had been tested only in Japan. The common explanation for keeping efficient birth control out of reach of Japanese is that it would undermine the very lucrative abortion industry (of between one and two million abortions a year),[77] and it is true that the Japan Medical Association has used its once formidable powers to keep 'the Pill' off the Japanese market (except for the purpose of regulating the menstrual cycle, for which a strong-action variant is used – thus vindicating the allegation of negative side-effects). Whether the bureaucrats of the Ministry of Health and Welfare (a remnant of the Naimusho) actively conspired to bring about this control, or whether they merely welcomed the pressure from the doctors as furthering their own ends, its effectiveness in keeping Japanese women where the administrators want them is the same. Japanese officialdom is aware that emancipated female citizens are likely to disturb the domestic labour system, and the ban on the contraceptive pill has deprived most Japanese women of what in Western societies has been the single most important factor in their social emancipation.

Fulfilment of an old dream

The common argument that the present Japanese political system is more competitive and pluralistic than the pre-war order is not, of course, totally groundless.[78] A greater variety of voices participate in the administrative adjustments that must be made to keep the public peace. The administrators are certainly more worried about 'popular opinion' than they were before 1945; in this respect the Japan of the 1980s is more 'democratic' than that of the 1930s.

Yet the decades before the Manchurian Incident saw a far more dramatic competition for power among the various élite bodies. The fledgling political parties dating from the Meiji period had by then, despite systematic obstruction, come sufficiently into their own to compete for power. They had linked up with big business and together they counterbalanced the military. There has been much argument over how potentially democratic Taisho democracy was before the military–bureaucratic alliance brought it to a halt, but the parties did at least compete for the opportunity to form governments or participate in coalitions, and they did challenge the influence of the military and the bureaucracy.[79] Around the time when prime minister Hara Kei formed his cabinet in 1918, the two major parties, the Minseito and the Seiyukai, were also influencing the bureaucrats they were absorbing, and local officials were often replaced when these parties rotated cabinets.[80]

Also, big business, the partner of the politicians, bore a closer resemblance to Western businesses than it does today, both in the structure of corporate relationships and in motivation. Managers unequivocally belonging to the administrator class and closely linked with the national bureaucratic apparatus had not yet taken over totally from the entrepreneurs.

Taisho democracy thus constituted an embryonic form of pluralist party politics not unlike that of the immediate post-war years. The struggle among the parties and other political forces, though veiled by the kokutai mythology, carried a potential for an alternative course of political development that appears to be no longer present today.

The political order in the first three decades of this century was less stable than that in the 1980s because of the greater degree of open competition within it. It underwent much more vehement disturbances than the System does today. This was a thorn in the flesh of many Japanese in high positions, who were acutely aware of the discrepancy between the real situation and the ideology of family-like national unity under the protection of the emperor. In the 1920s endemic conflict became more and more open and threatened to become accepted as a normal state of affairs, thus totally contradicting the harmonious essence of kokutai. Pluralism within parliamentary processes, together with open competition for power outside them, spelt disorder: anathema to those who saw themselves as guardians of Japan's sacred order.

As a result, the 1930s brought a new interest in programmes to promote solidarity among the élite and arouse public enthusiasm for policies aimed at bringing out the greatness of Japan. The reform bureaucrats and their associates in various areas of Japanese society, regardless of whether they were initially influenced by Marxist, Nazi or Italian fascist theories, believed that these aims 'could be obtained only with the formation of a single, totalitarian mass-based political party, closely linked to the government, just like in the Soviet Union, Germany, and Italy'.[81] After the Konoe Fumimaro cabinet came to power in 1937, the New National Structure (or New Order) Movement described above began to emphasise the Japaneseness and sacredness of such an inclusive political organisation.[82]

The final product of the reformists' proposals, the Imperial Rule Assistance Association (IRAA) that Konoe Fumimaro helped establish in 1940, fell far short of the earlier grandiose plans. The actual IRAA functioned less as a colossal body uniting all Japanese energies in giving its international assertion a common direction than as a massive propaganda apparatus fostering further support for the already widely agreed-upon expansionist aims of the government. Its original intentions were never realised because the various groups of power-holders stopped co-operating the moment they grasped that a stronger centre would mean a relative diminishing of their own powers. The Naimusho, the right wing, several military factions and the judicial bureaucrats under Hiranuma were opposed to a centrally organised state led by Konoe. They feared the rise of a dictatorship that would undermine their own power; and when the Army took the lead in efforts to systematise a 'new order' of truly totalitarian quality, the industrialists and groups of bureaucrats as well as rival military cliques lined up in effective opposition.[83]

As Japan enters what its bureaucrats, *shingikai* reports and the press like to call the 'information age' or the 'post-industrial society', it seems as if the political economy of Japan is gradually coming to resemble very closely the vision reflected in the blueprint for the IRAA. Between 1945 and 1955 the constellation of political party forces resembled the situation in the 1930s.[84] Then came the merger of the 'conservative' parties that Uemura Kogoro and other ex-bureaucrat business federation leaders worked so hard to bring about. While this merger did not bring peace to the ranks of the LDP politicians, it did bring significant order to the political world by depositing formal government permanently in the hands of one single organisation. This arrangement, complete with an ideologically inspired party in innocuous opposition, is commonly referred to, as we saw in Chapter 12, as 'the 1955 system'. It is an arrangement that seems almost to have realised what the reformists of the 1930s advocated.

The one-party system preserves the continuity of an administrator-controlled political system untroubled by such unpredictable political factors as genuine entrepreneurs and genuine politicians. Japan today maintains a socio-political 'order' such as it has not experienced since the Tokugawa period. With the salaryman hierarchy providing the flesh and bones of the System, the corporate administrators, together with the officials, keep the workers and the middle-class office clerks in check. The activities of the agrarian administrators in the *nokyo* and the Ministry of Agriculture, together with incessant construction directed more by political considerations than by necessity, keep rural Japan in check. The teachers have been contained. The doctors are paid off. The gangsters continue to help ensure that crime itself is 'administered'. And now even the remnants of an activist labour movement and ideologically inspired opposition are being welcomed within the folds of the System.

A crucial difference between the 1930s and the 1980s is that in the 1930s the visions embodied in the concept of a 'national defence state' and in the New National Structure Movement that inspired the formation of the IRAA were spelled out, and were intended to reshape an existing constellation of élite circles. Some of the latter naturally felt threatened. By contrast, the structure of the post-war System and its goal of unlimited industrial expansion were never packaged in a master-plan that could be attacked. But the objectives of all the post-war élite groups are attuned to the System's structure and goal. Since the interests of the various administrator groups are accommodated, none is eager for changes in the nature of the System; and thus, unlike their pre-war predecessors, the current administrators appear to have solved the problem of domestic political peace.

The manifest destiny of the LDP

An article in the New Year 1982 issue of the LDP party magazine offers a revealing glimpse of how some of the administrators view their own role in the context of the above discussion.[85] A collective product of the editorial board, the article gives a fascinating account of how LDP ideologues interpret history, and how they predict the future of their organisation against that background.

After establishing the fact that the chances of an opposition coalition government have all but disappeared, the article predicts the end of the 1955 system, just as we saw Nakasone doing earlier. It relates this to what it considers the two main characteristics of the political course of events since the Meiji Restoration: the fact that anti-governmental groups in Japan were never suppressed, but that governments always listened to them; and that since 1866 a major change in the political system has occurred once every thirty years or so. The interesting fact about the thirty-year cycles, so the article explains, is that somewhere in mid-course there always occurs a political movement led by groups without access to the political process, and that the cyclical change occurs as a result of the government's accommodation of these movements.

Conveniently jumping over the Pacific War and the United States occupation, the article lists the last two changes as occurring in 1924 and 1955. The movement that followed the cyclical change of 1924 – that led, in other words, to the cyclical change in 1955 – is none other than the New National Structure Movement of the reform bureaucrats. The LDP ideologues explain this as engendered by popular dissatisfaction with the way two political parties were taking turns in forming governments, 'because this was inviting corruption and business control over politics'. The Imperial Rule Assistance Association was formed to cope with this problem. And under a similar programme – the article continues – business firms formed the industrial patriotic associations (Sangyo Hokokukai) in which labour and management allegedly co-operated in running their enterprises.

The LDP authors are more than a little wide of the mark in presenting the New Order Movement as having emanated from the people. Although it attracted groups seeking a greater say in political decision-making, it was dominated by established political cliques, each of which aimed at strengthening its own position within the élite. The LDP spokesmen ignore the imperialist war and the occupation as if they were unimportant sideshows; but it is interesting to see how they accommodate the wartime political institutions. The Sangyo Hokokukai, according to the article, gave workers a voice in the management of their companies. And the IRAA, 'although negatively evaluated today for its militarism and "haw-kishness" ', also did much to return politics to ordinary people. The striking conclusion of the LDP ideologues is that these aspects were inherited by the 1955 system; just as they had been in the IRAA, the political parties were bundled together in the LDP, while the foundations laid by the Sangyo Hokokukai made possible the emergence of a highly desirable enterprise union system.

In short, the authors proudly concede that two of the major character-istics of the System throughout the three decades of high economic growth after 1955 – an unchallenged ruling party and docile unions – are direct descendants of institutions established with the aim of strengthening a country at war. Though quite correct, it is an odd admission; the LDP has not been in the habit of praising these wartime arrangements for the rest of the world to hear.

What of the future? According to the LDP's unusually articulate spokesmen, the middle of the 1980s saw another transformation occurring between two thirty-year cycles. The crucial movements leading up to the '1985 system' were two: the *kakushin jichitai undo*, a campaign to increase the number of mayors and other municipal authorities from among opposition parties, and the *chiiki jumin undo*, local citizens' movements in the big cities aimed at furthering consumer interests. Both movements have died a quiet death (see Chapter 3) – not, the article assures us, because they were ignored but because their demands were accepted and their wishes realised.

Such developments, the LDP authors conclude, clearly indicate the kind of accommodations the party must make to reality; the LDP must also become a political haven for the urban salarymen and their wives, and must gain the support of the labour unions.

One of the central messages of the article is the impending demise of leftist unionism. The mid-1980s did indeed, as will be remembered, see a major development in this context: the break-up of the Japan National

Railways, whose public-sector unions, once relatively activist, had formed the backbone of the leftist Sohyo. Already in the 1986 elections several labour unions were delivering votes to LDP candidates. In several regions local JSP politicians have established working coalitions with strong LDP parliamentarians for the realisation of development projects.[86] Once the new national labour federation, Zenmin Roren, has settled down into a routine existence, the inescapable embrace will be almost complete.

There has always been room in the hearts of the power-holders for organised labour, as long as it was organised on their own terms; after all, the social bureau of the Naimusho promoted labour laws in the inter-war years, and post-war administrators have consistently welcomed 'realistic', i.e. conformist, trade unions.[87] This consolidation of a process that the LDP ideologues correctly described as beginning with the manager–worker councils of the patriotic industrial associations signifies a historical milestone, considering that Christian- and later Marxist-inspired unions have, from the turn of the century, been the only major social groups in persistent conflict with the System.

The dream of a non-political state

As the System makes another great advance in its campaign to eradicate Japanese leftism, it moves ever closer to fulfilment of the dream of a depoliticised state. In the West, too, this is an old dream. The vision of co-operation in one magnificent joint effort to improve human life, and the rewards for this in the form of loving care, has inspired many social engineers and Utopians before and after Marx.

Part of the dream is that a lost paradise can be regained. This notion received its best-known scholarly endorsement in 1887 with the publication of *Gemeinschaft und Gesellschaft* by Ferdinand Toennies. He postulated a dichotomy in which the world of traditional villages, a *Gemeinschaft*, was one of supposedly intimate human bonds, governed by a sense of solidarity rather than by politics. That world had been replaced for most Westerners by the artificial, unfriendly *Gesellschaft*, where cold rules had replaced warm understanding. Even though nobody has found convincing evidence that a *Gemeinschaft*, free of power struggle, ever existed, this dichotomy has had a tenacious and inspiring hold over several generations of romantic dreamers and commune builders in the West. It parallels the *nihonjinron* contrast between the intimate, organic and warm, traditional Japanese community full of 'human feeling', and the calculating, mechanistic and untrusting world of the West in Japanese imagination.

The other part of the dream is the familiar notion of replacing frivolous and wheeling-dealing politics with rational, unselfish and scientific government, in which the nation enjoys the full and systematic benefit of advanced, modern, technocratic expertise. The removal of messy parliamentary procedures and other constitutional hindrances to the carrying out of a national goal has been contemplated by Western political thinkers often enough. It is summed up in Saint-Simon's famous dictum about the administration of things replacing the government of persons. And it is contained in the Marxist view of the future.

A social life in which rational planning would substitute for self-seeking politics is enticing in that it promises solutions to problems that have plagued humanity throughout history. As Isaiah Berlin put it:

> Where ends are agreed, the only questions left are those of means, and these are not political but technical, that is to say capable of being settled by experts or machines like arguments between doctors or engineers. That is why those who put their faith in some immense, world-transforming phenomenon, like the final triumph of reason or the proletarian revolution, must believe that all political and moral problems can thereby be turned into technological ones.[88]

To turn Berlin's argument around, under the 'administration of things' the only question is what the planning would be for. For the Japanese System the answer to this has been clear since the Meiji period: keeping order and becoming strong. And since 1945 the administrators have, without discussing 'ends', consolidated, adjusted and planned for the priority of unlimited industrial expansion as if this were a self-evident good, which is indeed how they see it.

The consolidation of the System has brought an apparent great stability. The question of whether the stability is more apparent than real becomes urgent only when developments that the administrators cannot cope with cause a crisis. And in 1988 it seemed that no domestic tensions could in the foreseeable future reach crisis proportions. The unacknowledged problem of legitimacy has been dealt with in an effective way, certainly more effective than before 1945. It is unlikely to become acute so long as the components of the System can prevent an authoritarian take-over by one among them. The strong tendency towards conflict is suppressed; conflict, as we have seen, is not recognised as politically acceptable.

Yet a completely depoliticised social system does not and cannot exist. Gemeinschafts in Toennies's sense are an illusion, and the irony of the Japanese System, as we have seen, is that it is entirely politicised. The political motivations and functions of the businesses and business federations that form the System's solid core are conspicuous. The contemporary conglomerates do not simply exercise political influence as they do in the West, but they have become integral and totally indispensable organs of the body politic. This fact, together with the unquestioning priority given by the administrators to unlimited industrial expansion, is an essential factor in the context of Japan's international relations, one that, unlike domestic tensions, could very well lead to crisis.

15

The Japanese Phoenix

There are two main threats to the hallowed Japanese order: from Japanese and from foreigners. Both, over the past century and a half, have at times loomed large enough to frighten the ruling élite. The political events leading up to and following the Meiji Restoration can be seen as a sequence of domestic and foreign threats to established power relations, together with the reactions they provoked. For roughly six decades after that, a newly emerged bureaucracy guarded Japan against domestic disorder of thought or behaviour, using for its purpose the gradually evolving surrogate religion of 'national essence', as well as the military–bureaucratic institutions for social control described in Chapter 14. Since around 1955 the threat of domestic political disorder has been even more effectively dealt with through the awesome control capacities of the post-war System. But beyond the reach of these domestic measures there remained the second threat, the one from outside, a threat that by its very nature constitutes a perennial source of disquiet. The outside world simply does not lend itself to traditional Japanese techniques of social control.

The economics of national security

Since a threat to their own sense of security is automatically seen as a threat to the security of the nation, Japan's power-holders and their articulate spokesmen have long portrayed Japan as a country particularly vulnerable to uncontrollable outside forces. From the Meiji period until at least the 1970s this ever-present anxiety, sometimes merely latent, sometimes acute, supplied much of the energy for the effort to catch up.

'Catching up'

In the half-century following the end of Japan's seclusion, the capacity of foreign powers to upset Japanese socio-political arrangements had to be countered by increasing the country's industrial and military strength. Russia and the Western states had to be made to see Japan as an equal strategic entity. The most famous slogan of the Meiji period was 'fukoku kyohei', 'rich country, strong military', and the response to the real or imaginary external threat was an effort to make Japan invincible. Industrialisation at a furious tempo was taken for granted, for in the perception of the power-holders it meant nothing less than political survival, both Japan's and their own. Catching up with the strongest in the world became an obsession – not just a government priority but the highest aim of all patriotic Japanese. To a degree virtually inconceivable to Westerners, many Japanese – with no religion beyond mere socio-political demands – found the ultimate meaning of life, their existential lodestar, in the survival and welfare of the nation.

Catching up also meant control beyond the waters surrounding Japan. In the Meiji period as well as during the Taisho democracy no Japanese with a political voice would have had it otherwise. The political parties went along with the military and the bureaucrats in their plan to make Japan a dominating power. 'The issue was not domination but *how* that domination was to be achieved and by *whom* – diplomacy and economic penetration managed by the Foreign Ministry, political parties and business leaders or military conquest managed by the military establishment.'[1]

Success with the 'strong military' part of the programme was, of course, more readily demonstrable. And judging by the response of the Meiji press, expansionist goals were highly popular. The newspapers supported the Sino-Japanese and Russo-Japanese wars, as well as the insubordination of the Kwantung Army that led to the war in Manchuria and ultimately to the Pacific War. The notorious Hibiya Riot of 1905 and the ensuing confrontations between police and public in many parts of Tokyo (prompting a declaration of martial law) were protests against the terms of the Treaty of Portsmouth. In the following decades, Japanese imperialist expansion was as much in favour with the articulate public as the idea of universal suffrage.

Even so, for one segment of the élite the 'rich country' part of the national mission provided an even greater inspiration. A number of Meiji period writers and officials, swept along by the vogue for Herbert Spencer and Social Darwinism spoke of a 'peacetime war' among nations, stressing the ultimate necessity of economic development and seeing the military as a tool in the forceful creation of foreign markets and sources of supply.[2]

The primary task of the Naimusho (established in 1873) in its first ten years, before Yamagata Aritomo turned it into the main headquarters of the social-control bureaucrats, was the promotion of domestic industry. Its first minister, Okubo Toshimichi, one of the most powerful among the earliest oligarchs, despaired when he discovered on an investigative mission to Europe that the West was too far ahead for Japan ever to catch up.[3] He objected strongly to the plans for a Korean invasion – plans that led to the first major split in the oligarchy – on the grounds that Japan could not afford any such adventures and should think only of strengthening itself economically. Using 70 per cent of the newly established Naimusho's budget, Okubo helped establish a large cluster of government factories; merged a government marine transport firm with Mitsubishi's shipping company to eliminate United States and British dominance in the area of transport; sent export study missions to the West; built a trading system that bypassed foreign agents; gave financial support to the silk, farming and other industries; and sponsored national exhibitions to propagate the advantages of fast industrialisation.[4]

Japan has had an industrial policy ever since the early Meiji period. Taking over enterprises started by the domains, the oligarchy added to them national railway and communications networks and armaments, mining and shipbuilding industries. As Meiji industrialisation took off, government control over the economy became automatic, since the government either put up the capital itself or encouraged private investors to do so by according them protection. Wasteful parallel investment was thus minimised. In practically all major industries, the Meiji government took the initiative. In the early 1880s it switched from direct control over many factories to indirect protection, by virtually giving away what it had built. In 1881 it established a Ministry of Agriculture and Commerce to help regulate this policy and draft the laws that formalised earlier transactions between the oligarchs and their entrepreneurial friends and money-lenders. An economic oligarchy came into being, consisting of politically privileged financial houses that were beholden to the ruling oligarchy and its bureaucratic élite. The *jinmyaku* networks – built on kinship, marriage, bribes or friendships dating from school – that played such a striking role in the course of Japan's modern economic development were already functioning.

Privatisation as a solution to industrial problems has been a major characteristic of Japanese economic policy. Whenever it has seemed safe to do so, the bureaucrats have divested themselves of the bothersome task of direct management. The custom continues, as the handling of the national railways and telecommunications in the mid-1980s indicates. The officials lose little practical jurisdiction, while the economy gains in efficiency thanks to new incentives, the spreading of risk and a controlled form of competition that promotes 'natural selection'. At the end of the nineteenth century, the Meiji bureaucrats easily retained nearly full control over the strategically important mining, heavy manufacturing and transport sectors.

Fostering dedication

The second large catching-up campaign began in the 1950s, after post-war reconstruction had been completed, and continues today. Evincing the same single-minded dedication, it has enabled Japan to outstrip every country except the United States in economic prowess. Again, it was prompted not only, nor even primarily, by what the West understands by economic motivations. The primary goal of Japan's economic pursuits has not been to expand the choices and comforts of its citizens. On the contrary, economic growth has often taken place at their expense, being directly associated with the notion of national security. And since the 'strong military' part of the national mission has had to be scrapped, the economic effort has this time had to bear the entire burden.

Whereas in the Meiji period hasty industrial development was considered vital for national security, today nothing less than industrial dominance will do. That Japan's officials take this for granted is evident if one reads between the lines of their articles and listens closely to their statements. The world must understand, they seem to imply, that they cannot allow *any* of their industries to fail in the face of foreign competition.[5]

Most foreign observers in this century have attested to the unquestioning dedication with which Japanese devote themselves to their tasks. Two decades after the end of the war, with national reconstruction well behind them, salarymen of the same company, seen in a group together, still exude a sense of missionary zeal. In the 1960s especially, Japanese firms gave the impression of being involved in a permanent contest. Competition was, in fact, controlled, but they were incessantly seeking to raise themselves in the business hierarchy, and top rankings within the various sectors were widely publicised. Even housewives and schoolchildren, who might be expected to care little about such matters, had a pretty good idea of which firm loomed largest in which field. Such publicity, and the unanimous impression given by the media (before the pollution scandals) that all this was wonderful, helped generate a phenomenal propelling force. But to be among the top firms at home was only a beginning; the race with the mighty international corporations was already well under way. In conversations with engineers and executives of the large electronic manufacturers in the mid-1970s one sensed that basically they all lived for one thing only: to catch up with and outstrip IBM. Visiting the offices of Fuji Photo Film Company the day after the announcement of the 'dollar shock' (resulting from Nixon's decision in 1971 to stop the convertibility of the dollar into gold, thus forcing a revaluation of the yen), I found a group of distressed, ashen-faced salarymen who explained that their international sales plans, and hence their prospects of catching up with and overtaking Kodak, had received a set-back from which the company might never recover.

The path to perfection

The catching-up disposition has been such an important aspect of Japan's emergence as a major economic power that it is worth examining its ramifications in an area of Japanese life not directly connected with the political economy. 'Progress' in Japan has frequently and for long periods been more immediately measurable than it has been for Westerners. At the outset of its recorded history, in the sixth century, when it was a primitive tribal society without a writing system, Japan had the momentous experience of coming into contact with T'ang China, the most sophisticated civilisation on earth at the time. The adoption of cultural forms with a thoroughness rarely if ever paralleled in history established an attitude towards self-improvement that has been handed down to this day.

Characteristic of this attitude is the notion that there is a 'perfect' way of doing things. In learning a skill – especially in connection with Japanese music, the traditional theatre arts, or judo, aikido, kendo and karate – the emphasis is on automatic, endless, non-reflective repetition of what the teacher does. Mastery is reached by removal of the obstacles between the self and the perfect model, embodied by the teacher.

The idea that the student might have an inborn potential that is uniquely his or her own has had hardly any influence, even in the non-traditional arts. Foreign conductors and music teachers almost uniformly remark on the great technical skill of Japanese performers, together with their relative lack of capacity for personal expression. This reflects in part a lack of courage in a conformist society, but also the fact that musicians who have never studied abroad have rarely been taught that it is *they* who must interpret the music. The 'perfect' way of doing anything is comparable to the rigid expectations in communal behaviour; the performer must, as it were, live up to the model. According to Japanese learning methods, the skill or art has an authoritative and predetermined existence demanding subservience. There is no room for idiosyncratic variation to suit the practitioner's individual aptitude or taste.

The advantage of this approach is that it can produce great technical mastery in the performing as well as the plastic arts, and a serene beauty resulting from total self-confidence. But it has drawbacks too. Progress in a skill is measured by such narrowly defined standards that achievements not covered by these standards may well pass unnoticed. The self-consciousness that the traditional Japanese learning method generates in the earlier stages also tends to act as a brake. Since the style, the precise manner of presentation, is considered crucially important, uncountable repetitions are needed to eliminate this obstructive awareness of the self. Japanese students of traditional skills – and of modern sports – are not quickly allowed to leave their physical movements to take care of themselves so that they can attend to what lies beyond.

I believe there is political significance in this approach to learning. Exposure to the Chinese model came so early in Japanese political development, and T'ang China represented such vastly greater sophistication, that it provided no opportunity to compare governments, adding up, rather, to a lengthy traumatic experience. The power-holders who imported the outward forms of Chinese government almost in their entirety appear to have been motivated by an awareness of a new reality that they in some way had to live up to. I speculate that this is the origin in Japan both of the notion, especially in the arts and learning methods, that there are 'perfect' ways of doing things, and of the pervading sense of always falling short of these 'perfect' ways.

In the nineteenth century Japan suddenly came face to face with the strength and the technological marvels of the USA and European countries. This time the prevailing slogans preached that it was the material achievements of the foreigners that must be emulated, while keeping the Japanese 'spirit' intact. And emulate the Japanese did, on a scale few or no other people have done before or since.

'Panics', depression and new controls

By 1905 Japan had built up an industrial base sufficient to allow it to defeat Russia in the Russo-Japanese War (1904–5). The success of the Meiji oligarchy in stimulating economic development was followed by a further great boost for Japanese industry deriving from the First World War. This good fortune came to an end in 1920, and a chain of 'panics' caused successive 'recessions' and business dislocation. In fact, the Japanese economy continued to grow fast by international standards,[6] but this did not alter the general impression of uncertainty and disorder. Just when adjustments were having a salutary effect, the great Kanto earthquake of 1923 hit Tokyo and its environs. This was followed by deflation in 1925 and the financial crisis of 1927. Many companies, overextended because of the earlier boom, had to be rescued by government loans. The central bank had lent too much after the earthquake, and the resulting financial panic caused the collapse of thirty-seven banks and the rise to near hegemony of the five zaibatsu banks. All this happened against a background of increased tenant-farmer risings and much other social unrest.

Disorder had, in the view of the custodians of Japan's security, reached unacceptable proportions and called for dramatic administrative action. When this came, it marked the beginning of the end for an economic system that despite its strong bureaucratic element still resembled in many ways the laissez-faire economies of the West. During the 'Taisho Democracy' period entrepreneurism flourished, and new businesses, regardless of whether or not they were connected with the bureaucracy, were able to expand into large firms. Profit-making was accepted as the proper function of business. There was a labour market, and an open capital market, as well as free trade of a kind Japan has not known since, and a free inflow of foreign capital. Following the banking crisis, however, Tanaka Giichi formed a cabinet, in April 1927, that was to introduce a new and more controlled approach to economic management. Tanaka Giichi, as seen in Chapter 14, was Yamagata Aritomo's foremost protégé and similarly obsessed with the need for greater social control – he had numerous leftists arrested, and dissolved all 'suspect' organisations. A month after the formation of the Tanaka cabinet, the minister of commerce and industry set up a commerce and industry deliberation council within his ministry, with the purpose of examining what was ailing the Japanese economy and what the government ought to do about it. Chalmers Johnson, the originator of the term 'capitalist developmental state' (CDS), has pinpointed that development as the beginning of the industrial policy that led to post-war high growth. The economic bureaucrats started to think in terms of 'industrial rationalisation' and have never stopped doing so.[7]

The 'Showa depression' of 1930–5, brought on by the 1929 Depression in the West, followed the many 'panics' of the previous decade and helped bring to positions of power the 'reform bureaucrats' with their theories of socio-economic control based on Nazi and Italian corporatist ideas. Simultaneously, one of Japan's best-known ministers of finance, Takahashi Korekiyo, pursued an inflationary policy that was the first Japanese example of economic management of this kind. It worked, aided by stepped-up arms production. The heavy and chemical industries subsequently towed Japan out of the depression. Takahashi had always pleaded for economic rather than military expansion, insisting that 'military expenditures exceeding the ability of the country to pay would not enhance true defense'.[8] For this attitude he was murdered by the super-'patriots' in the 26 February rebellion of 1936. This pivotal event in Japan's political history also marked the demise of moderating forces on Japan's fiscal policy in the face of military demands for optimum spending on the 'national defence state'.

The state capitalist laboratory

The one place relatively free from the deleterious effects of the incessant infighting among élite groups was Manchuria. Especially after the Japanese Kwantung Army had turned it into the puppet state of Manchukuo, this *de facto* colony was viewed by the military and the 'reformists' in the bureaucracy as the ideal setting for promoting industrial schemes, not for private profit but as an expression of the might of the empire. The Army had long been contemptuous of the large Japanese corporations, because they were interested more in profits than in working for the greater glory of the emperor. It therefore wanted to keep the *zaibatsu* out of Manchuria.

The brains behind the Manchurian Incident and other Kwantung Army operations over which Tokyo had lost all control was Colonel Ishiwara Kanji. Ishiwara, a brilliant strategist, was most closely identified with the concept of the 'national defence state', and had gained attention as lecturer at the War College with his ideas about 'the final war' (i.e. between Japan and the USA). He was the idol of romantic military activists. Reaching his most influential position as military economic planner in 1935, Ishiwara immediately began to draw up plans for the development of Manchuria to provide a base for war against the Soviet Union and for a 'Showa restoration' – a revolution led by the radical nationalists that would cleanse Japan of the élite groups that detracted from the 'national essence'.[9] Neither aim was achieved; but it was

Ishiwara, together with his friend and fellow planner of the Manchurian Incident, Miyazaki Masayoshi (who had lived in Russia during the Revolution and had revisited the country in the late 1920s to study economic planning), who sketched the basic economic plans that the Kwantung Army presented to the reform bureaucrats Kishi Nobusuke and Hoshino Naoki for refinement and implementation.[10]

Initially, the South Manchurian Railway (Mantetsu) ran a gigantic economic empire. It was transferred into Japanese hands as a result of the Russo-Japanese War and had all along formed the vanguard of Japan's industrial and commercial penetration of China. It was also the harbinger of Japan's military–political aspirations in Asia, and as such led to the conflict with China that helped trigger the Manchurian Incident. Besides the railway, Mantetsu ran coal-mines, steel works, warehouses, electrical plants, light metal factories, banks, harbours, water transport and aircraft factories, representing some eighty companies in all. It also exploited Chinese labour on a gigantic scale.

Mantetsu found it difficult, however, to raise enough capital for the firms it wished to establish or expand. Thus in the key year of 1937, when all-out war with China made the full-scale exploitation of Manchuria essential, the military and reform bureaucrat planners drastically reorganised Mantetsu, separating its industrial activities from the railway and grouping them under the Manchukuo Heavy Industries Development Company. Half of the newly needed capital was to be provided by one of the so-called 'new zaibatsu', the Nissan combine.

Nissan (the parent firm of what has today become the Nissan Motor Company and the Hitachi conglomerate) was chosen because its leader, Ayukawa Gisuke,[11] a relative and political associate of Kishi Nobusuke, was not, in the eyes of the Army, driven by motives of mere personal gain. Ayukawa spent the next five years setting up Manchurian companies.[12] Here again we see the importance of jinmyaku. Personal relationships were crucial among the reform bureaucrats, between the bureaucrats and the military and between the military and the official government. Thus it was Kishi who convinced the military that his relative Ayukawa was their best choice, by arguing that he was somehow different from the money-grabbing zaibatsu families. In fact, Ayukawa himself owed his industrial position to family connections with leaders of the main conglomerates. A sister of his was married to the highest executive in the Mitsui empire, while three other sisters and various other marital ties related him to a stunning list of family names, representing the cream of the political and economic aristocracy. We will come back to Ayukawa later because he played an important, if not widely noticed, post-war role.[13]

Three methods of forced industrial development pioneered by the economic-control bureaucrats provided key lessons for Japan's post-war economy: a method of financing and a method of guaranteeing market share, both of which we will look at in a moment; and the principle of economies of scale. The task of Ayukawa's Manchukuo Heavy Industries Development Company was to establish one large manufacturing firm for each industrial sector. All these firms were then expected to develop their production capacity to the limit of their potential and at the cost of profits. They had, of course, no competitors in Manchuria.

Two years into the Pacific War, when Japan's prospects were becoming dim, the relationship between Ayukawa's Nissan combine and the Army–bureaucratic alliance soured, and by 1944 the failures of the Manchurian industrial experiment were more impressive than its successes.[14]

Limits of wartime control

The wartime economic bureaucrats never managed to accomplish what their laws, their CPB, their control associations, their Manchurian industrial arrangements and their numerous directives to the *zaibatsu*-dominated business world envisioned. Government agencies and other power groups got in each other's way and worked at cross-purposes – a perennial Japanese problem – so that there was no efficient central control over Japan's wartime economy. In the words of an American wartime observer:

> By 1940 varying degrees of state control were effective over foreign exchange, import and export trade, capital investment, prices, the labor market, consumption industries and the electric power industry. Yet these measures fell considerably short of applying a thorough scheme of state regimentation to the basic industries and the great business monopolies. For the most part they were devised rather haphazardly, as special emergencies arose. In many cases the business interests succeeded in limiting either the statutory controls themselves or the extent of their application and enforcement.[15]

Some of the bureaucrats associated with the New Order Movement had all along been pessimistic about their attempts at central economic control, and later blamed their military allies for pushing them into adopting unworkable policies.[16] Not until after the battle of Midway in 1942 could a start be made with full industrial mobilisation for war purposes, in the form of the 'enterprise readjustment movement'. It involved the bureaucrats more deeply in the affairs of industrial firms than at any time since the early Meiji period, when the government had owned those firms. And it provided another precedent for post-war industrial planning. For, in the words of a more recent observer: 'the wartime enterprise readjustment movement lies at the beginning of the path that leads to the Industrial Rationalisation Council of the 1950s and to the Industrial Structure Council of the 1960s and 1970s'.[17]

Legacy of a mobilised nation

What worked haphazardly during the war worked very well after the war when, thanks to SCAP, the power of the economic bureaucrats increased considerably. Indeed, the two arrangements that have most powerfully determined the nature of Japan's post-war industrial growth are both inherited from wartime economic legislation: first, the financial relationships around which the keiretsu industrial groups and conglomerates emerged; and, second, the neo-mercantilist trade practices. These are the two great factors that have enabled post-war manufacturers to expand their production capacity virtually without risk, have allowed much control over domestic competition and have shielded Japanese industries from foreign competition.

From war-financing to post-war 'keiretsu'

The foundations of the wartime financial control structure were laid years before the outbreak of the Pacific War. It was the abandonment of the gold standard in 1931 that set the stage for a new monetary approach. First, Japan's trade – hitherto relatively free – was curtailed by the Capital Outflow Prevention Law of 1932 and the Foreign Exchange Control Law of 1933. The bases for control were further consolidated by two pieces of legislation passed in 1937 against the background of an international balance-of-payments crisis and the launching of full-scale warfare by Japan's Kwantung Army in China. One of them, the Temporary Measures Law Relating to Exports, Imports and Other Matters, gave the Ministry of Commerce and Industry the right to slow down or stop the import or export of anything it pleased, as well as control over the use of imported raw materials. The other, the Emergency Fund Adjustment Law, controlled lending for new industrial investment and gave the Ministry of Finance powers to divert money to military industries.[18]

The first of these measures provided the basic model for the post-war Foreign Exchange and Foreign Trade Control Law, passed in 1949 – which has been called MITI's single most powerful instrument for carrying out its industrial policy.[19] The second gave MOF officials the habit, persisted in ever since, of directly 'guiding' the banks.

In the early 1940s the central organ for national mobilisation, the Cabinet Planning Board (CPB), tried to accomplish a more effective co-ordination of energies, resources and institutions as part of the 'new economic order'. It planned therefore to combine the offices of minister of finance and governor of the Bank of Japan into a financial control association that would facilitate purging Japan's financial institutions of the profit motive, which by then was seen as greatly detrimental to the purposes of the nation. Although complete implementation of this policy was hampered by endemic infighting among bureaux in the Ministry of

Finance – as well as by friction between the ministry and the CPB and numerous personal quarrels[20] – a monetary control association established in May 1942 created the precedent for post-war central-bank control over the commercial banks.[21]

Probably the most fateful of all wartime financial arrangements, however, was introduced only about a year and a half before the defeat. This was the so-called 'system of financial institutions authorised to finance munitions companies',[22] which was intended to increase the supplies that the military machine was devouring in much greater quantities than earlier planners had expected. A law was put into effect in December 1943, and in January of 1944 the government picked the first 150 'munitions companies' to be matched with the 'authorised financial institutions' that were to provide them with an immediate, unimpeded supply of funds. By the end of February the system was in place.[23] The authorised institutions, mainly the large *zaibatsu* banks, were backed by groups of smaller banks and other financial institutions as well as the Bank of Japan, so that they never found themselves short of money.[24] By 1945 more than six hundred large companies were being funded in this manner, and received 97 per cent of their borrowings through the designated banks. The latter dominated 70–80 per cent of all lending in Japan.[25] The Ministry of Finance had the overall supervision, while the Ministry of Munitions allocated the funds.[26]

This was the original model for the post-war *keiretsu* financing.[27] The extraordinarily close relations between Japanese firms and their 'main bank' date from the final months of the Second World War. Most large Japanese corporations are, as explained in Chapter 2, grouped together around one or another of the so-called city banks; and throughout most of the post-war period they have been unusually dependent on these banks. Whereas before the war the average rate of borrowed capital hovered around 30 to 40 per cent (which is comparable to post-war rates in Europe and the USA), from the late 1940s to the late 1970s major Japanese firms borrowed 80 per cent or more of their capital from the city banks with which they enjoy a *keiretsu* relationship.

Heavily overloaned as they were for most of the post-war years, the banks pumping funds into the *keiretsu* became increasingly dependent on the central bank. An economist at this institution has pointed out, in a comparison with the major Western industrial powers, that 'Japan is the only country where the central bank is a net lender', meaning that loans from and discounts with the central bank exceed deposits of commercial banks.[28] This phenomenon was common enough until mid-Meiji, but from the late 1910s until the financing of the Pacific War the big banks considered it shameful to be in debt to the central bank.[29] In the post-war period the Bank of Japan has fought heavily with the Ministry of Finance over jurisdiction, but has had to give in on major issues. This means that ultimately MOF bureaucrats have had and (despite reports to the contrary) still have tremendous power over the development of basic industries.

Wartime arrangements were legally reinstated in 1947 with the Temporary Interest Rate Adjustment Law, which gave MOF bureaucrats a free hand to set interest rates on loans as well as on deposits. This 'temporary law' was still on the books in the late 1980s. The right to limit the range of activities of all financial institutions completes the range of instruments with which the MOF helps organise Japanese economic behaviour at home and abroad. Western assessments of government–private sector co-operation in Japan have focused too narrowly on how far the bureaucracy directly subsidises industry, thus asking the wrong question. The bureaucrats at the MOF and BOJ have been regulating the allocation of funds, which is the most effective control one can have over industry.

Inherited social-control supports

Besides the laws and institutions of the economic bureaucrats, the post-war legacy of wartime arrangements includes, as we have seen, various consciously shaped – or at least encouraged – supports within the wider social context that have helped to make industrial policy the grand success it has become. One essential prop is the enterprise unions, direct descendants of the Sangyo Hokokukai, the 'industrial patriotic associations' which ordered labour relations for the sake of the war effort (see Chapter 3). Post-war control has in most areas become very much more sophisticated; not only have its wartime origins been forgotten, but it is generally not even recognised for what it is. The information filter represented by the reporter club is a great deal more respectable than straight government censorship, and accomplishes what is probably a more effective kind of supervised standardisation of news and public awareness. As we have seen in Chapter 6, post-war control over the mass media has been largely privatised, with Dentsu as the primary co-ordinating agency.

The man who made Dentsu great, Yoshida Hideo, could do so because he possessed one of the greatest of post-war *jinmyaku*, linked to former reform bureaucrats and other Manchurian connections. During the war, Yoshida had given the economic bureaucrats the backstage help needed to control the systematisation of advertising fees and to merge 186 advertising agencies into twelve companies.[30] He also worked with Tsukamoto Makoto, a colonel in military intelligence in Shanghai who was involved in secret political manoeuvres and the suppression of an anti-Japanese movement in colonised China. Under the premiership of Tojo Hideki, Tsukamoto was appointed section chief of the military 'thought police',[31] and mediated between the wartime government and journalists. After the war, Yoshida made Tsukamoto a director of Dentsu. He also selected one of the leaders of the government's propaganda outfit in Manchuria, Morisaki Minoru, to be president of Video Research, the company that monopolises TV ratings and is ideally placed to stop programmes on the alleged grounds of insufficient audiences.[32] Purged politicians, businessmen and journalists were brought together by Yoshida in a club that met once a month in the occupation years. His *jinmyaku* thus extended, he received permission to establish the first commercial radio station. Because broadcasters in Japan are at the mercy of the bureaucrats for licences, Yoshida's connections in this area were invaluable. Dentsu's office was nicknamed the Second Mantetsu Building because of the many former Mantetsu (Manchurian Railway) executives Yoshida hired. Manchurian bureaucrats and military officers were also 'rehabilitated' and trained by Yoshida for jobs either with Dentsu or in the new commercial radio and TV broadcasting companies. The famous reform bureaucrat Sakomizu Hisatsune, whom we met in Chapter 14, was given an office in the Dentsu building.[33]

The administrators repaid Yoshida for his wartime and occupation period services by turning Dentsu into one of the great Japanese success stories. It more than doubled its sales between 1946 and 1947, quadrupled them the following year, again doubled the figure the year after and quadrupled them again between 1950 and 1955.[34] Since the early 1970s it has been the largest 'advertising agency' in the world. In 1971 Yoshida set up the Masukomi Kondankai ('mass communication round table'), in which representatives of the business federations and the mass media discuss the danger of 'bias' in the media.[35] As we saw, Dentsu dominates commercial TV programming, and is to a large extent responsible for giving the LDP and the bureaucracy the desired *imeeji* (image).

Ayukawa and the subcontractors

Another product of Japan's wartime economy, indispensable for the post-war 'economic miracle', is the subcontracting system, with its quasi-familial relationships between dependent enterprises and their patrons. The system came into its own after the Manchurian Incident, and spread rapidly during the war. As an emergency measure to increase production, manufacturers of military equipment had shifted from producing everything themselves to subcontracting the making of parts and other work to smaller firms.[36] Inefficient small businesses were reorganised and fitted into the war production system.[37] The 1937 law, mentioned above, giving Ministry of Finance bureaucrats a decisive voice in lending to industry also divided companies into three categories: military priority, essential and non-essential. Manufacturers of 'non-essential' commodities were ordered to switch to producing what the country required.[38] The control associations, some of whose leaders were to form the post-war business federations, were given the task of co-ordinating all this.[39]

Big business, as we saw in Chapter 6, has continued to profit greatly from this hierarchical relationship. A number of associations, some 'democratic' and others fairly authoritarian, competed in representing the interests of the small and medium-sized companies in the early post-war phase, and during an economic downturn following the Korean War they tended to believe that their own cartelisation might ameliorate the negative effects of the tightening of the *keiretsu* and the cartels of large businesses. However, as we saw in Chapter 3, any Japanese organisation of significant size that is not ideologically well protected easily becomes prey to a stronger component of the System. Through 'voluntary' adjustments reflecting the desires of big business and mandated by government agencies, the administrators attained decisive control over the small firms.[40]

The major role in this campaign was played by the same Ayukawa who was chosen to organise Manchurian industry. Immediately after the war, Ayukawa worked on a scheme to re-educate returning soldiers and industrialise farming villages.[41] But the occupation authorities stripped him of all his positions and incarcerated him for two years in Sugamo Prison as a war criminal suspect (like Kishi, he was never brought to trial). Soon after, he became an LDP Upper House member, which he remained until his political career foundered on an electioneering scandal in 1959. It is as organiser of Chusho Kigyo Seiji Remmei (Chuseiren), the main owners' federation of small and medium-sized industries, that the post-war economic bureaucrats are most in his debt.

Ayukawa had decided in prison that small and medium-sized firms would play the key role in post-war economic reconstruction.[42] Purchasing a commercial bank in 1952 to organise loans to small companies, he set to working out, together with Hoshino Naoki, the former group leader of the Finance Ministry reform bureaucrats in Manchuria, and Okada Ichiro of Mantetsu, details of what was to become Chuseiren. The rally to mark its formation was held in 1956, and a platform was announced that included plans for a law aiming to 'create a grand unity of small and medium-sized corporations'.[43] Chuseiren's goal was to sign up ten million members and to support candidates in elections. This provided Ayukawa with a nation-wide *koenkai* (support organisation) with which to get re-elected to the Upper House. More important, it provided his old comrade-in-arms, Kishi, with the skeleton apparatus for top-level control of the subcontractors. If the other early post-war associations of subcontractors had not been undermined, they might have become a disturbing force, because several of them were clearly wary of exploitative relationships and hostile towards big business.

Through extravagant spending of his own money, Ayukawa managed to set up numerous local branches and collected some eight million signatures for the law that he had helped the bureaucrats to think up. This law envisaged stipulations making bargaining decisions binding if half of the small firms joined the subordinate association in their industrial field; if two-thirds joined it wanted the 'right' for the member association to ask for bureaucratic regulation of the activities of non-members; and if more than two-thirds joined it wanted the authorities to order non-members to become members. It also provided for exemption of the federation from anti-monopoly law stipulations. The Sohyo federation of labour unions was against the law, as were the Fair Trade Commission and the house-wives' association, but it passed the Diet in 1957 thanks to the personal mediation of Kishi Nobusuke.[44]

Chuseiren was to play a big role in the realisation of yet another economic-control law. In the early 1960s Ikeda's 'income doubling plan' required adjustments in the size and other characteristics of small and medium-sized firms so as to fit in with the industrial schemes then being worked out. MITI, hoping further to expand its power in this area, designed the Small and Medium-Sized Industry Foundation Law to encourage further development of the *keiretsu* corporate groupings. The Communist Party protested that the law would accelerate the increasing control of the large firms over most business areas. Another association of small and medium-sized firms fought against it, arguing that it was meant to develop only certain industrial sectors chosen by the government, and would strengthen bureaucratic control over the small and medium-sized companies. But Chuseiren campaigned vigorously, and the law, with some revisions, passed the Diet in 1963.[45]

After Ayukawa's death, Chuseiren was formally headed by Kishi Nobusuke. Then, when Kishi died in 1987, the 'governorship' of this major federation of small and medium-sized businesses went to 77-year-old Tanaka Tatsuo, a former Manchurian reform bureaucrat, CPB and Munitions Ministry official, post-war chief cabinet secretary, director-general of the Prime Minister's Office, MITI minister, education minister and chief of the LDP's executive council. He is also the eldest son of Tanaka Giichi, founder of the Imperial Military Reserve Association and the prime minister who in 1927 introduced new methods of social and economic control. Tanaka Tatsuo may not be among the most prominent political figures, but his becoming foremost representative of Japan's exploited smaller industries shows that the administrators know how to keep the bridle in family hands.

The occupation legacy

The opportunity to put into practice the unfulfilled designs for a centralised wartime economy and the lessons learned in Manchuria was, as we have seen, handed to the bureaucrats on a silver platter by SCAP. General MacArthur and his 'reformers' also supplied considerable thrust to early post-war industrial policy. At first the occupation measures against big business quite unintentionally had an opposite effect to the 'democratisation' they were meant to accomplish. And after a communist regime had taken over China there was, as we saw in Chapter 3, a deliberate shift in emphasis from 'democratising' Japan to helping it establish a strong economy capable of withstanding a potential communist onslaught in Asia – a shift generally referred to as the 'reverse course'.[46]

Dissolution and reorganisation of the *zaibatsu* holding companies, removal of *zaibatsu* family control and company reorganisation under an economic deconcentration programme affecting some one hundred companies not only strengthened the economic bureaucrats but also elevated bureaucratic managerial personnel to the highest positions in industry. The *zaibatsu* dissolution also released large quantities of securities that passed into government hands along with the financial and administrative control formerly exercised by the conglomerates. Government officials began to take over responsibilities that once belonged to *zaibatsu* managers. Moreover, the scarcity of private capital immediately after the war meant that companies were almost entirely dependent on the bureaucrats for investment funds, which could be obtained through the Reconstruction Finance Bank and later the Japan Development Bank as well as the Japan Export-Import Bank (originally the Export Bank).[47]

The important political decision to emphasise development of the chemical and heavy industries would probably not have been so easy to carry out without the replacement of the old captains of industry. Before the 1930s, when the Ministry of Commerce and Industry had relatively little power and Japan's business world was still fairly autonomous, the economic bureaucrats had discovered that promotion of just these industries helped expand their sphere of authority. By mediating between this sector and military clients in Manchuria, they had succeeded in making their ministry the main supervisory organ over domestic chemical and heavy industries.[48] The bureaucrats knew what they were doing even if, right after the war, the emphasis on heavy and chemical industry did not seem a logical *economic* choice.

Institutions of forced economic development

Post-war reconstruction turned by imperceptible stages into an established policy of unlimited industrial expansion. Without ever debating the pros and cons of such a policy, the Diet endorsed hundreds of laws and amendments to laws that helped to co-ordinate the institutions used in forced economic development. By the mid-1950s the number of bills submitted to the Diet had increased to between 200 and 250 per year. The same pace continued until the early 1960s, when a dramatic decrease indicated that by then the legal apparatus sustaining high growth had been put in place.[49]

Among the most important legal instruments supporting industrial policy was the law controlling foreign trade, which was based on that of 1937. The chief means chosen by the bureaucrats for protecting domestic industry against foreign competition were foreign currency restrictions rather than tariffs.[50] Another important tool in industrial policy was the Enterprises Rationalisation Promotion Law enacted in March 1952. Together with amendments to the Special Tax Measures Law, it provided for stimulative tax exemptions, especially for exporters, and created reserve funds for developing industries. The tax measures came to be collectively known as the 'capital accumulation tax system', and 'the preferential application of the new policies resulted in strengthening existing privileged positions and in making industrial policy much more rigid'.[51]

The Japan Development Bank was set up in March 1951 and was allowed to issue its own bonds. In July 1952 the Fiscal Investment and Loan Plan was created; this 'second budget', backed by Japan's vast postal savings system, was to be used totally at the bureaucrats' discretion. The Export-Import Bank, the Smaller Business Finance Corporation, the Housing Loan Corporation and the Agriculture, Forestry and Fishery Finance Corporation were also established in the early 1950s to generate a flow of funding for investment.

SCAP's contribution to economic legislation, the Anti-Monopoly Law of 14 April 1947, had been amended under the occupation and again in 1953. It was systematically enfeebled, permitting depression cartels and rationalisation cartels, allowing price-fixing and halting the warnings to firms with excessive economic concentration.[52]

In the first quarter of 1949 SCAP's economic policy underwent a dramatic change with the arrival of Detroit banker Joseph Dodge, who introduced the so-called Dodge Line, a set of austerity policies designed to control runaway inflation in the aftermath of the war. The Dodge phase began at a time of economic crisis and was needed to introduce a deflationary policy that the government most probably could not have implemented by itself. The sobering new idea had to be introduced that the prerequisite for attaining the paramount goal of recovery was economic stability, for which, Dodge believed, a balanced budget was essential.

The Dodge Line was partly sabotaged almost from the beginning when the central bank ordered financial institutions to bail out firms on the verge of bankruptcy. A former bureaucrat who contributed to early post-war economic planning has pointed out that this policy was an early sign of the overloan phenomenon, and that it 'foreshadowed the strengthening of the control over commercial financial institutions by the Bank of Japan'.[53] It conflicted with the ideas of SCAP, which ordered it stopped, and for some two years the Dodge Line slowed down the economic bureaucrats.[54] But then to their satisfaction, in a development of major significance for the first stage of the 'economic miracle', the United States began to procure supplies for the Korean War, and everyone's attention shifted to production. After only one year, 1955, in which the banks were not lending more than their deposits warranted, the policies of high growth were making full use of the overloan methods that were to allow Japanese firms to expand so rapidly.[55]

Advantages of trade 'liberalisation'

Not all formal measures inspired by wartime control were acceptable to the entire body of administrators. MITI lost an important battle in 1963 when its Special Measures Law for the Promotion of Designated Industries, sponsored by the Ikeda cabinet, died in the Diet because of business pressure on the LDP. The Ministry of Finance and the banking community also helped stop it, because they correctly interpreted it as an attempt at territorial expansion by the industrial bureaucrats. Moreover, the law, which aimed to empower MITI to set up formal cartels in industries that needed to be made more competitive internationally, and which would have given 'public–private co-operation' cherished by the bureaucrats a legal basis, would have been too reminiscent of the wartime bureaucratic control apparatus.[56] Former MITI vice-minister Amaya Naohiro reflected twelve years later that the fatal flaw of the law had been 'to make explicit what had long been known as part of MITI's industrial policy'.[57]

The law that MITI failed to get to support its meddling in business was drafted against a background of fear of invasion by US and European competitors. Ever since the 1930s business had been protected against imports by foreign currency restrictions. But the administrators knew that 'trade liberalisation' had become inevitable if Japan wanted to be accepted as a true member of the club of free-market countries, and to continue to participate fully in the international economy. Under foreign pressure, import liberalisation, on paper at least, reached 92 per cent in the summer of 1963, thus enabling Japan to attain full status in the GATT and, by joining the OECD, to become the first Asian member of the club of advanced industrial countries.[58]

This undesired development, like others before it, was exploited with much success. The imagined threat of foreign competition acted as a tremendous spur in the industrial-machinery, chemical and car sectors, leading them to renovate their plants and rush headlong into new projects. The *keiretsu* tightened their internal relations in response to the liberalisation programme by increasing the degree of mutual ownership.[59] The aim of the industrial groupings in consolidating their positions in this way was to enable them to establish new companies in the promising new sectors and ensure that they could beat potential foreign competition.

Liberalisation, when it finally came, turned out to be virtually painless. It improved the Japanese position with regard to raw materials, and the sole important domestic victim was the coal industry. Real changes in written rules were made only in areas where Japanese industry was internationally competitive. In sectors such as cars, computers and heavy machinery where Japan wanted to nurture infant industries, a point was made of 'gradual liberalisation'. And MITI, without a law but with much 'administrative guidance' at its disposal, made the most of 'private–public co-operation'.

Once the 'liberalisation' storm had passed, there was so much of this kind of co-operation that the protectionist structures remained standing after their legal supports had been removed. Although on paper the liberalised areas had become free for international competition, the administrators made sure that no genuine competition from cheaper foreign products would take business away from domestic producers, relying on a variety of the devices later to become known as non-tariff barriers. When, in the face of overwhelming foreign criticism in the late 1970s and early 1980s, a programme was started to lift these non-tariff barriers, the structure that they had helped solidify stood so secure and was so impermeable that the programme had hardly any effect on imports.

Structural protectionism

While market forces do not ultimately dictate Japanese economic developments, the market is an important instrument used by the bureaucrats in the ministries and business federations in pursuing their aims. Japanese economic intervention has recently come to be referred to as 'market conforming', as distinct from the more drastic intervention in Soviet-type economies, whose planners accept no free-enterprise allies. But the market-place remains a source of uncertainty, and thus a potential problem for the administrators. A major institution for reducing such uncertainty is the 'distribution *keiretsu*', a constraining web of relationships tying wholesalers and retailers in with a particular manufacturer. The distribution *keiretsu* together constitute what is routinely referred to by Japanese officials and frustrated would-be exporters to Japan as 'Japan's complicated distribution system'.

This is misleading. The distribution system is not complicated. It is rigged.

Wholesalers and retailers are not independent competitive units. A majority of shops retailing durable consumer goods are, in fact, comparable to the regular subcontractors of Japanese manufacturers. They are provided by the manufacturers with capital and, if necessary, technical know-how. The example for the distribution *keiretsu* came from the West, but the Japanese versions became incomparably stronger and more widespread.[60] The most effective single element for control over the Japanese market, they began to develop during the latter half of the 1950s and continued to establish themselves ever more firmly right up to the late 1980s. They have greatly helped in the consolidation of Japan's oligopolies, and have been indispensable for the ubiquitous price-fixing practices. The many innovations introduced to increase the control of the largest firms include dealer associations whose members are under obligation to limit their stock of competing products. The distribution process has, in fact, become a marketing machine steered by manufacturers.[61] It has greatly helped the development of Japan's consumer electronics industry.

Since tariffs and foreign exchange controls were lifted, the distribution *keiretsu*, together with the trade associations that for the most part exclude non-Japanese members, have remained the major guarantee that Japanese manufacturers need not compete with foreigners in their home market. Consumer products not produced or distributed by members of a *keiretsu* –

and this naturally includes most foreign goods – are effectively barred from the normal Japanese market, because their only route to the consumer is through specialised outlets that charge prices generally double, sometimes even quadruple, the original market value of the product.

When a major new market is at stake, such as telecommunications equipment in the 1980s, Japanese industries are always allowed first to consolidate their oligopolistic positions; only then are some competitive foreign products given token market shares. The pattern for this was set in 1936 when a law, designed by Kishi Nobusuke and pushed behind the scenes by Ayukawa Gisuke, restricted the activities of foreign car manufacturers in Japan. In the late 1920s Ford and General Motors began assembling vehicles in Japan. By the mid-1930s the two US companies supplied roughly two-thirds of the Japanese car market, much to the chagrin of the Army, which realised that Ford vehicles were more reliable at the front in China than anything being made by Japanese car manufacturers with government support. Kishi's method of protecting 'important industries', inspired by a couple of study trips to Germany, made 'authorised companies' out of Toyota and Nissan. Ford was forced to drop its plans to expand its manufacturing capacity. Life was made so difficult for both US companies that almost two years before Pearl Harbor they stopped their Japanese production ventures altogether.[62]

The myth of slipping control

There is a very common misconception that uncontrollable and unstoppable developments must bring about important structural changes. At regular intervals foreign observers draw the conclusion that 'Japan Inc.' is being dismantled, and that the days of government supervision of industry are over. There is a widespread notion that the global economic developments of the 1980s, together with the much increased sophistication of Japanese banks and corporations and the transfer of labour-intensive production processes to cheaper foreign labour markets, are diminishing the ability of the bureaucrats to control the private sector. Japanese officials, weary of foreign criticism about controlled trade, applaud these views and help to spread them.

Yet the loosening of controls that can sometimes be discerned should not be taken to mean that the System is about to crumble. It has too many institutions, habits and needs that prop it up. Given the congruence of the 'private' and 'public' sectors, and the mutual-aid habit among Japan's administrators, to ask whether 'industry' is becoming less dependent on, and less beholden to, the 'bureaucracy' is to ask the wrong question. The idea of Japanese industry wrestling with the bureaucracy in order to escape from its grip is, quite simply, false. Besides, the major economic institutions are related to each other in such a manner that freedom from direct bureaucratic interference does not imply that industrial developments have slipped from the bureaucratic grasp. Whereas in the Western perspective bureaucratic meddling is automatically assumed to be abhorrent to business, élite business organisations in Japan would feel naked without the guarantee that, in the final analysis, someone is watching over them. At the level of the individual businessman, and especially among heads of firms in the lower echelons of their sector, the partnership may be involuntary, but the benefits that come with it are appreciated none the less.

Maverick businessmen are not able to oppose the administrators successfully for long. When in the summer of 1984 an enterprising oil-marketing firm tried to switch to direct imports in order to sell at lower prices – which it had every official right to do, but which went against the wishes of the Ministry of International Trade and Industry as well as the Petroleum Association of Japan – the banks withdrew their credit. The following December a new law was passed, ostensibly to liberalise the import of specific oil products, but in effect restricting trade even further by closing the loophole.

The manipulations of the Ministry of Post and Telecommunications (MPT) in connection with the new and potentially very large information-processing and communications market provide a perfect example showing why the notion that the bureaucrats are 'losing control' constitutes a basic misunderstanding of how things work in Japan. The officials concerned mapped the future of the market at various stages in the 1990s. Believing that sales would only increase from 230 billion yen in 1987 to around 560 billion in 1992, they decreed that there was room for only one new company to compete with the recently privatised Nippon Telephone and Telegraph. When officials gave their explanatory briefing to potential foreign competitors, they characterised their regulations and guidance as inspired by their concern to prevent any company from getting into trouble. From their reactions to potential foreign entrants in the Japanese telecommunications market, it became abundantly clear that they do not want genuine competition.

Making Japan invincible

Japan lost the Pacific War, but one vision common to the nationalists of the New Order Movement appears to have been fairly well realised in postwar Japan. By now, a large segment of Japanese big business is moved by 'worthier' motives than profit-making.

Market shares

In the metamorphosis of corporate leadership whereby the money-grabbing entrepreneur became the bureaucratic manager one can trace a remarkably consistent course of development. Industry today shows the culmination of a process that began long before the war, with the separation of ownership and management that occurred when the *zaibatsu* families hired *banto*, professional managers, to look after the firms belonging to their conglomerates.[63] The post-war apotheosis of the manager has led to the almost complete bureaucratisation of the large enterprises, while the disbandment of the *zaibatsu* by the United States occupation made ownership almost invisible if not totally irrelevant. The few large firms that are still run by strong entrepreneurial leaders are now seen as more or less peripheral to the main power bases of the economy. The industrialist of Meiji and Taisho Japan seems a long-forgotten type. Today, the authentic entrepreneur, driven by the urge to become rich, is to be found only in the small or medium-sized firms or, at most, in a few new large firms that are regularly reminded of their subordinate station in the *zaikai* pecking order.

Although this may superficially resemble developments in Western corporations, the latter are still 'owned' to the extent that they remain answerable to stockholders. Since post-war Japanese firms have been strongly discouraged by a complex of tax and other regulations from raising capital on public markets with stocks and bonds, their dividend payments to stockholders are the lowest in the world. In the 1970s the leading companies listed on the first section of the Tokyo Stock Exchange paid on average about 1.5 per cent. As we have seen, the members of a conglomerate tend to own each other. The banks in particular generally hold large quantities of their clients' stocks; and Japanese banks have entirely different priorities from Western stockholders. Company presidents in Japan, instead of being bothered by major stockholders breathing over their shoulders and forcing them to watch the profit charts, have to worry about expansion schemes they and their bankers have agreed on.

The shift from entrepreneur to manager has been paralleled by a gradual shift in emphasis from profit-making to expansion of the firm's market share. In the Western corporate environment the pursuit of profits and the expansion of market share are both respectable and are, of course, interrelated. What has made the post-war Japanese case special is the apparent possibility, for corporations, of ignoring profit for very long periods while pouring all their resources into expansion. The emphasis on conquering market shares and the ability to do so at the expense of profits are relatively new. During the early phase of industrial development in the Meiji period, entrepreneurs were encouraged by the authorities to use the firms transferred to them, or set up with government assistance, for personal enrichment. Similarly, in the first third of this century, when industries in private hands were more clearly separated from the public sector than they are today, companies were driven by a need to maximise profits.

But as the military–bureaucratic alliance strengthened its grip on Japan and emphasis on the 'national essence' reached new heights, profit-making began to be viewed as an unworthy activity,[64] a view encouraged by the allegation that competition for profit had been the source of the economic problems of the 1920s and 1930s. This fitted in well with traditional ways of thought, for the model samurai had always disdained the quest for financial gain, believing service to his lord to be a much nobler pursuit. Thus the Army deplored the old-style *zaibatsu* precisely because of their appetite for profit. The same attitude survived the war; one of the points made by the founders of Keizai Doyukai was that the *zaibatsu* preoccupation with profit was 'harmful and could not possibly contribute to the building of a strong and viable economy or really serve the national interest'.[65] The federation has continued to portray profit as something that gets in the way of dedication to public (read 'administrator') ideals.[66]

The cartel movement sponsored by the government in the 1930s, together with other arrangements that improved the security of the *zaibatsu*, had stimulated among businessmen, too, an awareness of the exciting possibilities of expansionary business methods. It inspired them with new ideas that, with the help of a seemingly inexhaustible flow of credit, were enthusiastically applied from the 1950s onward.

Several deliberately created post-war factors forced large firms to compete for market shares, especially after the mid-1950s.[67] The economic bureaucrats clearly demonstrate the priorities of their thinking when MITI, in the context of recession cartels, decrees capacity reduction on the basis of existing market share rather than plant efficiency. This means that investing firms know that their drive for a larger market share will be rewarded with a guaranteed market share.[68] This major driving force among Japanese corporations has led to oligopoly in many fields. In most industrial sectors one will find one to three companies controlling roughly 70 per cent of the market. The dominating companies agree with each other on prices, and the pressure to conform in other areas is also very great. This, in turn, facilitates controls promoting 'order' within each industry.

Many Western appraisals of the Japanese economy refer to the 'cut-throat' competition that is supposedly normal among corporations. It is not, but such competition does exist and when referred to by officials is invariably described as 'excessive competition'. The phenomenon is almost exclusively confined to the growth sectors of consumer industries, and entails battles for market share between divisions, usually relatively new, of major companies or between new subsidiary companies. Occasionally a spectacular battle develops, such as the one that occurred in the motor-cycle market between Honda and Yamaha in the early 1980s, producing a proliferation of some ten to fifteen new models a month. This instance of genuine cut-throat competition (which Yamaha lost) was caused by an enormous production overcapacity arising from a sudden saturation of export markets.

The home electronics sector, where new products follow each other in quick succession, is the scene of fairly frequent battles for domestic market share involving medium-sized but fast-growing firms. Such battles are generally followed by a weeding out in which the less successful firms end up under the wing of the *keiretsu* giants; all of this is busily monitored by the bureaucrats. More typically, however, the domestic market is a relatively stable arena that allows the Japanese corporation to concentrate on competition abroad. In the battle for foreign market shares, Japanese managers are aided by 'economies of scale' achieved through reliance on a solid share of the home market and relatively high domestic earnings that often subsidise the exports. Such a situation can be attained only by private understandings among firms, not by relentless competition. Large Japanese firms take very few risks. They are ensconced in a protective environment that not only shields them from foreign competitors but also fosters forms of mutual protection. It is this basis that permits them to move simultaneously into foreign markets with rock-bottom prices.

The unbeatable competitor on foreign markets

The large Japanese corporations with strong ties to industrial conglomerates are formidable competitors on foreign markets because they cannot go bankrupt and need not show any profit for a very long time. When a more or less concerted effort is waged to compete with domestic manufacturers in one particular foreign market, they are basically unbeatable. This was shown by the conquest of the world markets for cameras, motor cycles, and videotape-recorders (VTRs), and by the reduction of the home market share for US machine-tool and semiconductor manufacturers to a fraction of what it was before the Japanese began to focus on it.

The VTR case offers a good illustration of the uses of 'economies of scale'. Investments in production capacity made by Japan's seven VTR manufacturers quadrupled output between 1979 and 1981 to 9.5 million units. Two years later the figure had almost doubled, reaching a peak of 33.8 million units in 1986. The more than 13 million sets produced in 1982 represented 140 per cent of world demand at the time. Such overproduction caused colossal inventories and made possible foreign sales at almost any price; and roughly five-sixths of annual production was exported. RCA and Zenith in the USA had long given up (and were pasting their brand names on Japanese-made VTRs), and Philips and Grundig, with their 700,000 units, could hardly compete seriously with the 4.9 million VTRs sent to Europe in 1982 by Japanese firms.

Foreign market shares are achieved by painstaking adjustment of prices to local supply and demand. That Japanese firms have unparalleled elasticity in this regard has been shown by the way they have hung on to US market shares despite the near doubling of the exchange rate of the yen against the dollar. Since relatively few products make up Japan's export package at any one time, Japanese industry can wage fairly concentrated foreign sales campaigns. Their inroads, of course, are mere pinpricks compared with the overall industrial and trade statistics in the West, but at close quarters the concentrated effect is a razor-sharp sword cleaving into established US and European industries. Japanese officials themselves used to speak of 'laser beam' or 'torrential' exports, and in Silicon Valley, the centre of the US advanced technology industry, the term 'rifle precision' has been used in reference to the Japanese incursion.

The experience with semiconductors and machine-tools has opened some American eyes to Japanese methods of competition. Contrary to what Japanese propaganda and overly self-critical Western commentators have suggested, the US firms in this field worked hard and were alert enough. They simply could not, even remotely, match the financing back-up of the Japanese companies; and, as companies subject to the scrutiny of stockholders and boards of directors, their decisions had to be based ultimately on considerations of profitability. Especially in manufacturing sectors utilising the latest technology, US entrepreneurs, to survive, need to show returns on their investments. Their Japanese competitors tend to be subdivisions of giants whose more profitable subdivisions can pay for the onslaught. US law favours foreign firms, because it stipulates punitive action in cases of dumping only when there is clear harm to US industry. In the years that it takes to litigate a dumping case, the Japanese competitor is able to supplant the US firms.[69]

Competitors with large Japanese firms abroad are frequently at an enormous disadvantage in that the latter's fortunes are much less suscep-tible to economic factors. Their home base has the means to grow at the expense of other human pursuits, and operates in an environment where this is deemed perfectly natural. With respect to the losses they can absorb, Japanese exporters are ultimately limited only by the other firms in their *keiretsu* and, especially, by their major banks. In industries con-sidered 'essential', the lending banks can rely on the ultimate guarantee of Japan's central monetary authorities. That means that the decisions involved in lending to those who want to conquer foreign markets are in the first place not economic but political.

The bubble that does not burst

In the 1980s Japanese economic activities unconnected with production also began to command international attention. In the exchange not of goods but of less tangible assets such as stocks, bonds, land and foreign treasury paper, Japan's firms quickly gained another formidable repu-tation. By the middle of the decade Japan had become the biggest 'creditor' nation in the world, largely by investing in US treasury bonds; and serious economic periodicals and ministry officials were drawing proud com-parisons with England in the nineteenth century, or with the USA after the Second World War. Japan's banks were overtaking the largest US and European banks in terms of assets; its four large security companies became a major international presence; foreign banks were being absorbed; and many firms were heavily investing in overseas real estate.

It was only towards the close of the previous decade that the bureaucrats had made large-scale foreign investments possible. The move came just as Japanese firms were beginning to derive high profits from their strong foreign market positions. Enhanced by the then relatively low exchange value of the yen, these profits, combined with the new freedom to explore foreign capital markets (notably by floating Eurodollar bonds), made the large firms less dependent on the City banks for their capital.

By 1985 an ocean of liquidity had formed, as the banking community and monetary authorities pushed loans and encouraged corporations to increase their assets. Prices on the real-estate and stock markets began to rise sharply. This steeply raised the value of assets in general, which translated into collateral allowing corporations to borrow more heavily. By then a phenomenon called *zaiteku*[70] – whereby manufacturers and trading firms, either directly or through hastily established offshoot companies, borrow money to make more money in ways that have nothing to do with their original activities – had already altered the way many large Japanese corporations were calculating their strategies. Some manufacturers and trading companies had begun to resemble banks in these operations, except for their lack of experience and the bigger risks they took. This could not have happened on the scale that it did without the strong protective powers of the *keiretsu* relationships. And there were convincing indications that, as in the case of the institutional investors, many *zaiteku* enterprises were hiding significant failings in their books.

In a Western setting the speculative activities in which Japanese firms have been engaged would have brought the doom-sayers out in crowds. A few did appear in Japan, predicting 'a bursting of the bubble' or 'the bottom falling out' at some point in the near future. But short- and medium-term pessimists overlook a critical factor: that the absence of a clear division between the public and private sectors in Japan, the co-operation (or collusion as it would normally be termed in this context) among the administrators and the ease with which economic processes can be politically controlled all add up to a situation radically different from that in the other capitalist countries, whence such theories of bursting soap bubbles originally came.

The economy of intangibles thrives as long as the market participants have faith that the pieces of paper they exchange are backed up by actual worth. A crisis of confidence causes a stock-market crash. In the West such confidence hinges on the general performance of private enterprises. In Japan it means faith in the ability of the economic managers in the bureaucracy, the banks and the business federations to keep everyone's trust in the economic apparatus going. The difference may seem subtle, but is in fact enormous.

The much publicised savings rate of the Japanese people conferred an important measure of credibility on Japanese 'overloan' practices in recent decades.[71] And when foreigners today wonder about the soundness of Japanese banks, they are told about the large volume of hidden assets the banks are allowed to hold without revaluing them. But there is a curious aspect to the land and securities held in assets or collateral. According to the Economic Planning Agency (with the rank of ministry), the total market value of Japanese land in fiscal 1987 was 4.1 times greater than that of all land in the United States, which is twenty-five times the size of Japan, and has fifty-seven times more inhabitable space. Some of the land in Tokyo is priced ten or more times higher than land in Manhattan business districts. Land, in fact, has taken on a function comparable to that of gold, except of course that its value is independent of foreign market forces. Japanese specialists jokingly refer to a *tochi honi-sei*, or 'land standard'. As for the securities, average Japanese shares on the Tokyo stock market show a price–earnings ratio – stock price measured against profit – of 55.6 compared with 14.0 in New York and 12.3 in London (in January 1988). A number of explanations have been offered for this, but the simplest one is that the administrators in the banks, the ministries and the corporations have discovered a way of making money with money by agreeing not to spoil the party for each other.

That controls exist to make this possible was revealed in October 1987, following the stock-market crisis in New York that reverberated throughout the industrialised world but left Tokyo – contrary to the predictions of many international observers – relatively undisturbed. Working in conjunction with the Ministry of Finance, the 'big four' security firms, which form a *de facto* cartel,[72] seem likely to keep even worse overseas crashes from doing much damage to the Tokyo stock market. In private conversation Ministry of Finance officials have been known to concede that it is easier to influence the stock market than the foreign exchange market.

The combined figure for increases in land and stock prices in 1986 exceeded the entire Gross National Product of that year by nearly 40 trillion yen.[73] Since then land prices have climbed steeply: by an average of 96.2 per cent for commercial and 89 per cent for residential land in Tokyo, and of 21.7 per cent in Japan as a whole, in the space of one year.[74] All this represents a colossal amount of potential collateral for borrowing to fund further *zaiteku* investments and overseas assets. Before Japan's business could indulge in these new expansionary practices, however, the System had to make a major adjustment.

Exploring the world's financial markets

'Financial liberalisation' has loomed large in economic comment on Japan during the 1980s. The fact that it was in progress was constantly being reaffirmed during the decade by the administrators in international dealings, especially with the United States, and many statements by foreign emissaries acknowledged that it was proceeding on schedule. Here, finally, there seemed to be an area where Japan was gradually meshing in with the international system.

A degree of liberalisation of financial and capital markets did indeed take place, but it was of a kind that fitted Japanese purposes, and did not significantly increase the accessibility of the Japanese market to foreign financial institutions. There is no reason, in the light of past experience, to suppose that Japanese officials have any intention of further opening their market to such competition, at least not beyond the degree necessary to acquire temporarily needed foreign expertise.

The Ministry of Finance bureaucrats' apparent concessions were in fact aimed, first, at bringing regulations in line with the way Japanese financial institutions were already operating, and secondly at encouraging the international emancipation of Japanese banks, security houses and insurance firms, enabling them to compete better on the money markets of the world. Until then Ministry of Finance bureaucrats had enforced a strict division of labour, with fences around the banking, securities and insurance territories, and sluices regulating the direction of the money flow, thus creating an orderly and controllable financial market during the period of high growth. But the eagerness of the established financial institutions to embark on new and lucrative activities was being frustrated by what many other administrators had begun to agree were antiquated regulations.

In the second half of the 1980s many foreign observers, especially those responsible for Washington's policies towards Japan, still believed that market forces would replace regulation in the financial field. But MOF 'guidance' remains as important as it ever was. The bank-centred *keiretsu* remain bank-centred. And while the bureaucrats have not relinquished *de facto* control, partial deregulation has had the intended effect of fostering a new sophistication among Japanese financial institutions, as well as significantly increasing investment possibilities for the wealthy firms, allowing them to expand in new directions.

In the same period during which it was gradually discovered that Japanese speculators need not worry overmuch about a crisis of confidence, new financial powers emerged. The commercial banks were tightening their relations with the security firms by exchanging stock and personnel. And the life insurance industry, which was becoming (thanks to Japan's ballooning pension funds) one of the strongest institutional investors on the international scene, was emerging as a third major financial force, offering what amounted to investment instruments on the domestic market. Besides being hooked up to the manufacturing–banking–trading conglomerates, the big insurers have long operated under the protection of the Ministry of Finance. This sector, too, is dominated by a cartel-like 'big three',[75] through which it is easily monitored and guided.

The elusive master-plan

The proliferation in Japan of collusive activities inimical to free-market principles naturally makes one wonder whether all these activities might not be part of one gigantic conspiracy. The question becomes still more pertinent when one considers how collusion is rife in areas of the System not directly connected with the economy. An intense focusing on goals pursued, oftener than not, without adherence to any rules and unhampered by any referee: all this certainly seems conspiratorial. Is the consolidation of the System in a form reminiscent of the plans for the Imperial Rule Assistance Association the result, then, of a political master-plan? Have the economic administrators been consciously working to create the confluence of circumstances that gives them their current international financing power? Such questions, though obvious, have not been popular, partly because those who would contemplate them are too easily branded as 'Yellow peril' alarmists.

There is no convincing concrete evidence for a master-plan. No conspirators have come forward; no documents have been brought to light that reveal anything of the kind. The consolidation of the System would seem to be less the result of purposeful planning on a grand scale than the logical outcome of two centuries-old characteristics of Japanese political arrangements: the absence of agreement among rival cliques concerning the right to rule; and their shared wish to ensure social order without reference to any legal framework or to universal principles.

Japanese political history, I believe, is witness to the fact that political aims need not be fully conscious to be realised. Just as the omnipresent Japanist propaganda emanates, not from a single strong agency at the centre, but spontaneously from the collective need of separate groups of power-holders, so the efforts of these groups to optimise conditions for themselves, to guarantee their own political survival, have dovetailed together into what merely *seems* like conscious implementation of a social engineering blueprint.

It was inevitable that the post-1945 administrators should exert themselves from the outset to minimise the influence of the left, to subdue trade unionism and to 'reverse the excesses of the occupation' as soon as the Americans had left. It was entirely natural, too, that those who had experimented with establishing a 'new economic order' should attempt to apply what they had learned when, after the war, they were given unprecedented scope for setting up such a new order. A tradition of reality management enabled the administrators without many qualms to present their interference as democratic, so long as elections were held and there was a parliament and a seemingly free press. In view of the administrators' constant dread of disorder, it would not have been realistic to expect them to discard the institutions and habits developed before 1945 for the very purpose of staving off that fear.

As for the 'capitalist developmental state' that they have fostered, this pattern of development has not required adherence to rigid principles, and those who chose it may not have been entirely conscious that they were adopting a particular model of economic development. What they did realise, it seems, was that new potentialities in their economic system could constantly be discovered and exploited. This latter tendency is vividly demonstrated in times of apparent adversity. Should the System be seized with a sense that certain unexpected and undesirable developments are unstoppable, the bureaucrats and the élite of other affected components ride the wave, all the time seeking ways to exploit these new developments. The disturbance of normal routine normally causes excessive confusion at first, accompanied by denials that changes are inevitable; but in the second phase groups of administrators will come to the fore to tackle the new circumstances, using them, like a good chess player responding to a surprise move, to gain ground over their rivals.[76]

In this way the appreciation of the Japanese currency to almost double its original value against the US dollar in only two years has been a boon for those who long advocated rationalisation schemes to raise efficiency and thereby the competitiveness of large firms. It has forced the reorganisation of the subcontractor world. When the domestic outcry against industrial poisoning of the environment finally grew into an unstoppable protest movement, forcing major adjustments, MITI bureaucrats were thereby handed on a platter a whole new range of control mechanisms, in the form of anti-pollution regulations that reinforced their leverage over industry. The United States occupation of Japan – which had hardly been the collective goal of the administrators in the 1930s – gave many of them the chance to carry out their plans, from land reform and labour laws to economic mobilisation. The exploitation of such unexpected and initially undesired opportunities is common enough elsewhere, of course, but Japanese bureaucrats and business leaders, obsessed as they are by their power positions versus their rivals, are exceptionally good at it.

Discoveries of new possibilities to expand industrial and financial power also activate the *jinmyaku* and the System's informal processes for large-scale co-ordination among bureaucrats, business federations and corporate administrators. It is reasonable to view the massive expansion of intangible assets that has given the System greater leverage over the international financial system as having been guided in such a way. But this does not make it part of a master-plan drawn up before the new ways of making money were tried out. Nor does it mean that the System unanimously endorses the policies followed. In the case of *zaiteku*, for example, a significant number of influential administrators believed, at least initially, that it might sap the vitality of the Japanese economy. Before he resigned as head of Keidanren, Inayama Yoshihiro expressed worry at the way businessmen were straying from their original business.

The defect of the phoenix

Although there is no convincing reason to suspect that the administrators have worked out a grand master-plan for industrial domination of the world, what they are doing has the same effect as if there were such a plan. It is not difficult to see why this should be so. The administrators see the entire world in terms of the System. Men who do not appeal to universal rules in protecting their flanks at home are unlikely to believe that internationally accepted rules, treaties, agreements or promises are ultimately reliable. Japan strives for industrial dominance because power is the only guarantee for safety; and military power is for the time being, and probably for a long time to come, not feasible. Hence the continued voracity for foreign market shares and foreign technology.

It is essential to grasp two points with respect to this 'natural' Japanese drive. First, Japan has the potential to go a very long way in achieving dominance in certain strategic industries, and could thereby make the West very dependent on it – this has already nearly happened with semiconductors. Secondly, the uninformed supposition of Western trading partners that Japan's political economy is essentially like their own provides a prime condition for achieving the administrators' international ambitions.

The present wealth of Japanese firms – at least in terms of the collateral they can produce – has considerably strengthened their basis for operations on international markets. They buy foreign financial institutions and real estate, not for the sake of medium-range profits, but so as to pull more weight. And if land in Tokyo can be ten times as 'valuable' as land in Manhattan in 1988, the price could be jacked up to twenty times or more within a few years should the administrators need the collateral to make their overborrowing seem respectable.

All the while, Japan's comparative advantage continues to be enhanced by other, more long-standing factors. Subcontracting, temporary employment, lower-paid female labour and early mandatory retirement still give Japanese industry the benefit of very flexible and relatively low labour costs. Only one-third of the workforce has been permanently employed. After retirement, employees continue to work at much reduced salaries. Thirty-five per cent of the labour force continues to work past the age of sixty-five, compared with some 10 per cent in Europe. Also, a conglomerate entering a new industry has an immediately guaranteed domestic market share of some 10 per cent. The Japanese System, moreover, continues to be structurally protectionist, shielding Japanese manufacturers and banks from the type of competition with which the System's corporations have diminished Western firms. The last-mentioned factor seems certain to keep the trade imbalance between Japan and the world permanent.

It is widely believed that Western firms do not try hard enough to penetrate the Japanese market, and the administrators have been only too happy to help spread the notion of European and US business as tired and inefficient. But closer scrutiny of Japanese firms reveals that they are no less prone to bungling than are Western firms – perhaps even more so, when one takes into consideration the companies that cater to the domestic market only. The argument about not trying hard enough, however, is a red herring; the essential point is that those who have tried extremely hard in Japan have mostly failed as dismally as those who have taken it easy. Japanese spokesmen widely advertise the fact that a number of foreign firms that have 'tried hard enough' have been successful in their market. These firms are well known because they belong to the same small sample always mentioned in this context. A select few foreign firms receive assistance to serve as fresh examples of Japanese openness. [77]

An additional and underrated source of Japanese strength is the intimidatory effect of the System's targeting of new industrial areas. The financing methods used here are such that US or European company presidents who take high risks investing in such sectors would be irresponsible and could never justify them to their shareholders.

The greatest apparent international advantage the Japanese System has enjoyed so far lies in Western misconceptions concerning the nature of the Japanese challenge. The United States has been especially vulnerable to Japan's industrial onslaught in that the US government agencies overseeing its interests in this respect have no institutional memory. Every two years or so, new sets of US officials must learn afresh that the Japanese economy does not operate in the same way as their own. Hence the continued self-imposed handicap of doctrinal adherence to inapplicable free-trade theories. The result has been misguided stopgap policies. Increased congressional pressure on the Reagan administration to cope with the Japan Problem produced a double formula to help straighten the trade imbalance: a more expensive yen, and demands that Japan stimulate its domestic economy. Increased domestic demand does, indeed, make growth of the Japanese economy somewhat less dependent on exports, but there is no good reason to expect that it will lead to greater Japanese purchases of the finished products Western countries want to sell. Nor has the expensive yen had the anticipated effect. It may even have worsened still further the West's competitive position by forcing the administrators to streamline relatively inefficient sectors. The yen–dollar rate will have a significant effect on the Japan–USA trade balance only if the US side is prepared to go far beyond what seems likely, by allowing its currency to lose value and prestige even more dramatically than it had in 1987.

Not only did the measures that helped 'adjust' the dollar–yen exchange rate fail to bring the hoped-for result, but they almost doubled the buying ability of Japanese investors on the US market. On top of the strength derived from Japanese financing methods described in Chapter 15, this led to a sudden great surge of Japanese influence on Wall Street and other financial trading centres. A major new factor was hereby introduced, with the potential of dramatically changing Japan's relationship with the US, and with as yet uncertain, but probably important, repercussions for the West in general.

Seen in a long-term perspective, the lack of effective US and European policies towards Japan is not a true advantage to the administrators. On the contrary, their security is in danger. So far, the US legislature has been held back by the example of the Smoot–Hawley Tariff Act of 1930, which was partly responsible for the uncontrollable protectionist chain-reaction that preceded the Great Depression. But at some stage retaliatory measures that could severely damage Japanese interests seem inevitable – especially if frustrations with Japan's economic activities are aggravated by Japanese actions or statements giving Congress the impression that Tokyo is arrogant or morally deficient. The European countries, which are equally fearful of rampant protectionism but have so far been less affected by the expansion of Japanese power, would most likely follow the US example. The European Community, as a unit, will have more reason for vigilance in the face of Japanese marketing aims when, in 1992, all remaining barriers regulating the flow of goods among member countries are eliminated. With the West clearly unwilling to absorb the effects of any further large increase in Japan's economic might – at least if achieved in the same manner as post-war economic growth – the continued feasibility of the Japanese goal of unlimited industrial expansion has become uncertain. Restructuring is thus a vital necessity.

The phoenix has soared majestically for the entire world to see, and has drawn deserved applause and expressions of awe. But it is burdened with an inherent defect that disorientates it. The defect is, of course, in its steering mechanism: in its inability to adopt alternative methods and aims, because of the absence of an individual or unified group with the power to make political decisions to shift goals. The phoenix appears stuck on a collision course.

16

In the World But Not of It

There is a fairly widespread notion that the Japanese nation in the late 1980s is engaged in a grand debate concerning the new policies required by its international predicament and by foreign expectations.[1] Columnists tell us that major changes are afoot and that by now those concerned are discussing not the desirability of such changes but how to fit them in with customary practices. We read that a debate rages about how to import more, and that the Japanese people are waking up to the need to assume international responsibilities in keeping with their economic power.

The notion that such debates take place is wrong. It is rooted apparently in a belief that the Japanese *ought* to be discussing these things, rather than in any evidence that they are. In fifteen years as a correspondent (an occupation conducive of sensitivity to phenomena such as 'national debates') I have discovered neither the 'grand debate' nor the smaller ones concerning imports and the more responsible role. The notion is no doubt fostered by administrators who must deal with the external world and are often desperate to suggest action in areas where they have promised results. It also accords with the general taste of the media for 'Japan at the crossroads' stories. What is mistaken for national soul-searching, however, amounts to no more than the rhetorical flourishes that top administrators add to their speeches, that newspapers habitually put into their editorials and that lard the comments of English-speaking 'buffers' at numerous international panel discussions and study meetings. But the platitudinous reiteration of the need for certain changes does not imply commitment or the ability to bring them about.

The absence of political choice

The notion of a national debate participated in by the Japanese people or their chosen representatives is harmful because it lulls the serious observer into a false sense that shared problems are being studied and solved on the Japanese side. It also constitutes an intellectual hindrance to grasping how the System operates; it gives the impression that Japanese are given a choice, whereas the ordinary Japanese has no idea what choosing among socio-political alternatives means.

Systematic deprivation of choice

The systematic deprivation of choice in practically all realms of life bearing on the political organisation of Japan is essential for keeping the System on an even keel. The Japanese have no choice with regard to political representation: they are stuck with the LDP. They have almost no choice in education: its major function is as a sorting mechanism for the salaryman employment market, and the only way to the top runs through the law department of the University of Tokyo. Once a middle-class Japanese male has been taken on by a company, he has as good as no alternative but to stay with that company. The Japanese have no choice with respect to Japanese sources of news and information: these come in the monotonous tones of a virtually fettered press, or processed by other reality managers such as Dentsu. The choices the market offers them as consumers do not include what the distribution *keiretsu* do not want to distribute.

The common view of the Japanese political process assumes the possibility of political choice. It sees rulers and ruled as engaged in continuous communication for the sake of an ever evolving 'consensus'. Contributing to this consensus-forming process, it is suggested, are the multitude of interest groups, academic commentators, journalists, politicians and bureaucrats whose approval must be won for whatever is being decided. Japan's power-holders have enthusiastically seized on this perspective, because it can be passed off as 'democratic', and because it fits in nicely with the all-important belief in the benevolence of the System.

Exhortations in the press and in statements by prominent administrators seem to afford constant evidence that the nation is preoccupied with certain issues. But continuous reference to the desirability of something does not constitute a debate. This becomes clear when one looks at it closely: everyone always seems heartily to agree with what is being said. When the evils of the *amakudari* system and 'examination hell' receive their annual airing in the press it is obvious that the routine exhortations have a cathartic function, substituting, as they do, for genuine remedial action. Discussions, such as can be found in European countries and the United States, with intellectuals and political representatives putting forward identifiable and conflicting opinions that result in a give and take, in education of the citizenry and above all in altered policies, are unknown in Japan, where nothing of substance is debated in the proper meaning of the term.

While agreeing that some examples of true consensus can be found in Japan, I am struck by the relative lack of consensus compared with, say, the Netherlands or other Western countries with which I am familiar. Either way, 'consensus' does not enter into power relations between ordinary Japanese and the administrators. Theorists who allege that Japan has a 'new middle mass' that is politically fully in tune with what the System offers, thereby implying that the Japanese public has had the political means to express its preferences, have forgotten that no one ever told the Japanese people that they could set their own priorities. Prime Minister Ikeda Hayato summed up Japan's political relations most succinctly when he said: 'The government is the captain and the *zaikai* is the compass of the ship.'[2] At no time have the chosen representatives of the people tried to bring bureaucrats or business federation leaders into line. On the contrary, it was the politicians themselves who were brought into line. The reform bureaucrat Uemura Kogoro, who played a crucial part in this effort, left no doubt as to how politicians were expected to behave when he explained that the establishment of a strong national economy would be out of the question without the merger of 'conservative forces'.[3]

The industrial expansion that was achieved at the cost of the living environment and of housing and welfare policies and has resulted in the highest land prices in the world – all this without bringing amenities taken for granted in much of Europe and North America – was not the offspring of any kind of agreement on what is good for the people. The fateful political manoeuvring that established it as the overriding national priority was not monitored by the press. The public was not asked to participate in the formulation of policies – was never even aware that a choice existed.

The reverse side of the successful System

It is difficult to argue with success, and Japan's post-war economic success has drawn much admiration from the rest of the world. I do not mean to detract from the admirable accomplishments of the Japanese people and the guarantees these have brought of a relatively safe society that can feed everyone, and has only a few thousand homeless. But this book is about how the Japanese are governed. And in this last chapter I must conclude that the overall picture is rather bleak and fraught with danger.

In the eyes of the world, Japan has established itself as a rich country; yet, ironically, most Japanese think of themselves as relatively poor. The discrepancy in perception was never so strong as in the late 1980s, when currency revaluation had raised the per capita national income above that of any other country, leaving the buying power of Japanese salaries among the lowest in the advanced industrialised nations. As a Japanese professor teaching in New York summed it up:

> behind a robust facade of a growing economy that is fueled by rampant speculation, about 80% of the people are bearing the burden of heavy taxes and exorbitant prices for housing, land, food, clothing and other products and services whose markets are shielded from foreign competition. The average Japanese earns about the

same income as his or her American counterpart. But the Japanese must work almost five times as long to buy half a kilogram of fish, five times as long for half a kilogram of rice, nine times as long to buy half a kilogram of beef, and three times as long for four liters of gasoline.[4]

He could have added, among other things, that the privilege of using congested expressways costs a fortune, that telephone and utility rates are the most expensive in the world, that the exorbitantly priced living quarters are minuscule and that urban infrastructural problems cause as much discomfort as they did in the 1960s. Life for the average Japanese in 1988 was filled with more gadgets and much more 'fashion', but was not in any way more comfortable or rewarding or cheaper than it was in 1968, with the one exception that the expensive yen bought many more Japanese a cheap foreign holiday. In some ways, for instance with regard to the prospect of ever owning a place to live, life looked decidedly less promising. And these are merely the material results of how Japanese power is exercised.

The general character and emphases of Japanese education, together with what amounts to indoctrination via the media and the corporations, hamper the development of liberated citizens. The System stultifies where it should stimulate; it actively prevents the self-realisation of the individual. A 'value-free' judgement from the cultural-relativist perspective would leave undecided whether this is a good or a bad thing. But I don't think that such an approach is helpful to the Japanese, useful for Westerners or even possible in the long run. If a horticulturist succeeded in creating a chemical potion that prevented rosebuds from growing into roses, and his garden were filled with buds that never opened and ended their existence by merely shrivelling away, we would have no hesitation in saying that there was something wrong with that garden.

Thus, while the System undoubtedly provides sustenance and a large measure of security to nearly all Japanese, as a form of government it is not a satisfactory substitute for a modern constitutionalist 'state' with a centre of accountability, and with provisions for the non-intimidatory management of political conflict. The System cannot abide independent citizens with a developed sense of political responsibility,[5] which is a further reason why there are no real debates, with a bearing on political reality, in which the ordinary intelligent and talented Japanese individual can participate. This is ineluctably, if not obviously, a general problem for Japan's administrators as well as representatives of the outside world.

Governmental paralysis

The lack of a national debate has direct consequences for other nations. The theory of a forever evolving consensus suggests that the system is dirigible, that it is capable of producing essential policy changes. Yet the great irony of contemporary Japan is that the administrators, driven by their fear of disorder, have through a myriad successful controls nurtured a political economy that is essentially out of control; the System as a whole is rudderless.

As we saw in Chapter 1, a major fiction impeding international understanding of Japan is that its government is capable of making and implementing the kind of decisions associated with sovereignty and international agreements that are routine in other countries. A number of Japanese administrators are fully aware of the immensity of this problem in the context of Japan's international relations. A significant minority among them are pessimistic about its possible consequences, and a few even have catastrophic visions of what might happen to Japan. Yet no one in Japan is directly responsible, so no one lies awake at night worrying about it.

There have been a number of unsuccessful attempts to steer Japan towards new priorities. The one that attracted most international publicity in the late 1980s was the formation of an advisory committee under the chairmanship of the internationalist former governor of the Bank of Japan, Maekawa Haruo. The then prime minister, Nakasone, ordered the committee to present guidelines for a major restructuring of the Japanese economy that would make it less dependent on exports for its growth. What happened subsequently illustrates my point about the absence of Japanese leadership.

In the course of numerous meetings, the members of the committee, most of whom represented ministerial and other interests, picked the Maekawa Report clean of all its concrete proposals. When Nakasone saw the report produced by the committee, he angrily ordered it rewritten because, in his words, it did not reflect awareness of the dire international situation the Japanese economy had got into. The final version, published in April 1986, was no improvement, but Nakasone was powerless.

If all the recommendations of the Maekawa Report had been carried out, they would still have amounted to no more than a very feeble attempt to shift priorities. But even this was not to be, as many administrators were honest enough to make clear. At almost the very moment that Nakasone was in Washington presenting the report as a token of Japanese good faith, LDP politicians said that they could not accept it. Top bureaucrats leaked their 'concern' that Nakasone was misleading President Reagan. The *Nihon Keizai Shimbun* (comparable to the *Wall Street Journal*) tore the report to pieces, and the *Asahi Shimbun* said in an editorial: 'Every time a political leader says one thing abroad and something else at home, distrust of Japan in the world community grows. It is ironic that Nakasone, who is proud of his diplomatic prowess, now repeats the same mistake.'[6] Finally, the Ministry of Foreign Affairs weighed in with a statement that the report did not represent Japanese policy.

The case of the Maekawa Report also illustrates the confusion of tongues that often accompanies a Japanese action. Even as Nakasone's compatriots were pulling the rug from under him, President Reagan,

Secretary of State George Shultz, the *New York Times* and others were praising the 'breakthrough' in Japanese decision-making. Under-Secretary of State for Economic Affairs Alan Wallis went so far as to call it a watershed in Japanese post-war economic thinking. The US administration, of course, desperately wanted to show the bilateral relationship in a positive light, and to demonstrate that its approach to Japan bore results. But even non-governmental commentators and academicians continued to refer to the Maekawa Report as a major statement of Japanese government intentions. In the meantime Japanese officials such as MITI vice-minister Kuroda Makoto were asserting that almost all the recommendations had already been carried out, while some members of the Maekawa Committee were leaking their feelings of frustration that nothing was being done. Maekawa himself was reported to me as being disgusted with the lack of concrete action.[7] Two years after publication of the report, only a couple of points had been implemented; they were minor, and had in any case been part of earlier bureaucratic plans.

The Maekawa Committee represented one more failure to steer the System. The outside world, however, wanting to believe that Japan had a government after all, and believing that it was high time for a major restructuring, showed enthusiasm. This was seized on by the bureaucrats, who actually launched a 'second Maekawa Report' in May 1987 because the first had made such a good impression abroad! Indeed, the chief success of the Maekawa Report has been the reaction to it abroad; in Japan it got no more than lip-service.[8] In 1988 the notion became widespread that circumstances such as the doubling of the value of the yen had achieved in practice what the Maekawa Report intended. But this view stemmed more from wishful thinking than from any evidence of the structural changes envisioned by the report.

The 'Japan' fallacy

If countries find working with Japan 'impossible' it is because, though government officials throughout the world can get used to many things in dealing with other governments, there is one thing they can never bring themselves to believe: that there is no one to deal with on the other side. How serious a conceptual problem – not to say a practical one – this presents can be appreciated from the fact that perfectly normal, and widely used, terms of reference concerning international relations automatically lead one astray when applied to Japan. Even those political observers, editorial writers and foreign government officials who have realised in theory that there is no centre of responsibility often continue from force of habit to assert that 'Japan' should begin to understand this, that or the other, and that 'Japan' ought to take such-and-such action. The habit of referring to a country in anthropomorphic terms takes major assumptions for granted: that there is a core to its identity; that this core enables it to contemplate its future, arrive at decisions and act accordingly; and that through this core it can be held accountable. The assumption is that all countries have the capacity to operate as individual persons with a sense of responsibility towards themselves at least, if not to outsiders.

The United States government especially has been brought to the realisation, in dealing with a succession of Japanese prime ministers including Nakasone, that in the case of Japan one cannot effectively deal with its formal head of government, or anyone else. And various foreign powers have discovered throughout this century that one cannot effectively deal with Japanese negotiators either. Japanese negotiators cannot, in fact, negotiate, because of the constant potential of opposition at home against anything they might do.[9] This difficulty helped determine, to a large degree, Western attitudes towards Japan before the war. As a specialist on Japanese diplomatic history sums it up:

> Never has a nation been so obsessed with securing international trust and yet been so universally mistrusted as Japan in the prewar period. Although horrified by the thought of negotiating failure, Japanese leaders and negotiators nonetheless adopted positions so close to their minimum and so inflexibly conceived that criticism was almost preordained. . . . In every case, leaders and diplomats consciously tried to escape the errors of the past only to fall into the same pitfalls time and time again.[10]

One of the most telling episodes came in the spring of 1984, when relations between the United States and Japan threatened to sour considerably because of the Agriculture Ministry's intransigence over allowing a few more shiploads a year of beef and oranges into Japan, and Nakasone sent his minister of agriculture to Washington to rescue the stalled negotiations. At first Minister Yamamura did not want to go, feeling he had no choice but to show absolute loyalty to his ministry, which in turn was demonstrating its 'sincerity' as defender of the *nokyo*. Once in Washington, he ignored direct instructions from Nakasone, who finally had to plead with him not to abandon the talks altogether. Nakasone repeatedly told his cabinet that Japan had arrived at the point in its international relations where only tangible measures were meaningful, and that not to take them would affect the destiny of the nation. Yet he was castigated for his 'flamboyant demeanour and rosy promises aimed at enhancing his overseas reputation'. Nakasone's reminders that Japan had international obligations led one typical commentator to the conclusion that 'he has used his international pledges as a weapon to suppress all opposition from his critics at home'.[11]

The impossibility of finding any person or institution to negotiate successfully with has, of course, not passed unnoticed by governments that have tried to make agreements with Japan. Foreigners are frequently asked to remain patient while the alleged grand national debate is in progress, and to wait for the general consensus to emerge. A commonly added assurance is that, although the national debate process moves excruciatingly slowly, it will be splendidly effective once a consensus is reached.

One of the most recent pseudo-debates concerns *kokusaika*, 'internationalisation'. Throughout the 1980s the need for 'internationalisation' has been routinely stressed in thousands of newspaper editorials and tens of thousands of speeches. Numerous committees and study groups have been set up to promote it. But in practice 'internationalisation' tends to serve a resurgent nationalism. Within corporations it is generally interpreted as the need for an improved ability to defend Japanese commercial interests abroad. Verbal commitment to a certain cause, or the assertion of a need for it, is in Japan often mistaken for concrete steps, and thus is assumed to have changed the situation substantially. But while the constant repetition of the term *kokusaika* creates a sense that Japan's administrators are taking action to correct the supposed absence of an internationalist disposition among ordinary Japanese people, the last thing they want to encourage is an awareness that genuine internationalisation presupposes a willingness to consider the arguments and wishes of foreigners.

An uncomfortable dependence

The anomalies in Japan's relationships with other countries tend to be obscured by the unusual nature of one particular relationship. As a result of the way it has divided political power, the System is extraordinarily dependent on the United States. Both parties admit that the relationship is a special one; but how very special is a point insufficiently realised by almost everybody. There is no other instance in history where one large and economically powerful nation has remained so dependent on another nation without losing its separate identity. What was said in Chapter 2, concerning the discovery by Japan's administrators that all those tasks by which a state is internationally recognised could be taken care of by US proxy, is not in any way exaggerated. Japan can afford to stay out of international politics, because of the shield offered by the USA. This shield signifies much more than military security and diplomatic protection. Japan could never have become a neo-mercantilist economic power without US forbearance and protection.

An unproven international political power

One must clearly distinguish between Japanese dependence on the United States and the dependence of the European countries. A state with sovereignty (the most fundamental attribute of the state) has two closely linked powers: to enforce obedience internally and to maintain independence in external relations. Japan, as we have seen, has problems on both counts. There is no central agency with the unequivocal right to rule such as could enforce obedience among the rival components of the System. Legal authority is uncertain and not backed by the strongest power within the country. Maintaining independent foreign relations, too, is a problem, because Japan cannot deliver on the promises its government makes and thus needs the indulgence as well as the protection of the USA.

The West European nations are also dependent on the USA for their protection, but this is an arrangement they have entered into as responsible states. Their internal political arrangements do not prevent the conducting of a foreign policy apart from their alliance with the USA. If, on the other hand, Japan were to lose US indulgence it would be forced to do something in which so far it has failed regularly: conduct a foreign policy in which it can be held to account for the deals it makes.

The international awkwardness of the Japanese System, insulated as it is by the extraordinary relationship with the United States, has not been adequately perceived. But developments in this century certainly inspire pessimism about its ability to manage foreign relations outside that context. The attack on Pearl Harbor was suicidal. In the 1930s, when Japan's military power-holders were seriously contemplating the possibilities of war against the United States *and* the Soviet Union *and* Great Britain, and the diplomats were severing cordial relations left and right, none of the power-holders stood up to declare this an insane policy.

Even when defeat became certain, Japan could not muster the leadership to make sure it would retain some control over the terms of surrender. Theories about Japanese readiness to stop fighting before Hiroshima are not based on convincing evidence and reveal ignorance concerning the Japanese political system of the times. They overlook the fact that in 1945 there was no apparatus in Japan that could have chosen peace and rendered any peace negotiations credible. No person or group had the power to make acceptable to all other components of the political system – headless even in war – any surrender conditions that might have been agreed upon. The diplomatic communications reaching Washington were contradictory and ambiguous. Even after the double shock of the atomic bombs and Soviet entry into the war had informed the power-holders of a *fait accompli*, military units still attempted to sabotage the decision of the emperor and to intercept the recording of his surrender speech as it was being carried to a broadcasting station. They also dropped pamphlets from aircraft with appeals to the people to continue fighting.

Japan's limited efforts at post-war foreign policy are not encouraging either. Allowing itself to be intimidated by the Arab world has not resulted in greater security with regard to oil supplies. For a while in the 1970s it seemed that independent approaches to Peking and Moscow were developing, but these were soon shown to be awaiting US cues. Japan's relations with the Soviet Union have developed so that Moscow has more leverage over Tokyo than the other way round, while the policy shifts initiated by Gorbachev have not been seized on to gain an advantage.[12] Japan has sided with China in the Sino-Soviet dispute, but the Chinese market it hoped to gain has not materialised.

The terms under which relations with the Soviet Union were normalised in 1956, under Prime Minister Hatoyama, were subjected within the LDP to intra-party bickering of the most disruptive and disadvantageous kind, as Donald Hellmann has convincingly shown.[13] Striking similarities were apparent in the process leading up to the 'anti-hegemony' treaty with China, signed in August 1978. Here again, the decisive factor was the perennial wrangling within the LDP. Premier Fukuda Takeo initially had no intention of signing what was in fact an anti-Soviet treaty, but was drawn into it through skilful Chinese manoeuvring that made use of the LDP's internal dynamics.

The behaviour of the press at the time was important in itself, and also exemplified the way in which developments of moment in Japanese foreign policy come about. It did not once debate the issue in terms of the merits of the treaty, or of what signing an undertaking to resist 'hegemony' might mean for Japan's security and its relations with its neighbours. It was exclusively interested in the manner and the extent to which the treaty would improve Fukuda's chances of remaining in office for one more term. The comparison with the behaviour of the press during the normalisation talks with Moscow is interesting: 'The tangled tale of intra-party rivalry mingled with and ultimately dominated discussion of the substantive issues, and the newspaper editorials left undisturbed the resulting muddled picture. In aggregate, press coverage inhibited the effect of not only articulate but general opinion on the foreign policy-making process.'[14] If anything, the situation with the Chinese treaty was worse because neither articulate nor general opinion was anywhere in evidence. Nor was there any sign of intellectual give-and-take among the groups of bureaucrats in the Foreign Ministry who were for or against it, and who could fairly easily be identified with, respectively, the China and the Soviet Union desks.

A more recent example of the way in which intra-LDP politics determines Japan's stance towards a powerful neighbour was the way in which the Nakasone government, eager for at least a symbolic 'achievement' in Japan–Soviet relations, was at one stage almost begging Moscow for a visit by Gorbachev, without offering the Soviets anything that might have induced them to comply. Tokyo has always been passive and reactive in its dealings with the two communist giants, and has allowed itself to be manoeuvred into positions in which it is vulnerable to intimidation.

There has been speculation about a possible Japanese 'Gaullism', but without adequate grounds. It is not that Tokyo has any overriding desire to co-ordinate its foreign policy with that of Washington, but that the bureaucrats in the Foreign Ministry and other Japanese institutions are not in a position to accept the consequences of genuine shifts in policy or to deliver on promises made. Tokyo evades foreign questions concerning Japan's global political and economic intentions because there is no one with the authority to answer them. The Ministry of Foreign Affairs has tried in the 1980s, by mediation efforts in the Iran–Iraq war and in connection with the Vietnamese occupation of Cambodia – in neither case successful – to impress the world with Japan's readiness for greater international political participation. But when foreign parties expect commitments, no active policy is forthcoming; and when conflicting domestic interests intrude, any goodwill efforts already under way come to nothing. The credibility of mediation in the Indo-Chinese conflict is undermined by the anger of the ASEAN community at the way Japan, ignoring agreements, is doing fairly large-scale business with Hanoi.

The web of Japanese power relations is so closely woven that there is no room for consideration of foreign interests, or possibility of realignment in consideration of external needs. Foreign factors are normally ignored even when they have a bearing on the long-range national interest. When Prime Minister Miki Takeo went to the first industrial summit meeting in Rambouillet, France, Japan's administrators were extremely anxious that he might involve Japan in undesirable commitments. Cosmetic concessions in international diplomatic dealings are calibrated extremely carefully. The Japanese political world and the media refused to acknowledge and appreciate the service Nakasone performed at the Tokyo summit of 1986. According to accounts by insiders, he excelled as chairman – contrasting greatly with the mediocre performance in 1979 of Ohira Masayoshi, the first Japanese to host an international summit. But Japanese journalistic interest confined itself to what Nakasone was 'giving away' so as to make a good impression on the foreigners, and the effect the summit would have on wrangling within the LDP.

The only circumstance under which international factors are taken into account is a *fait accompli* created by foreign interests. The System can react with alacrity once a fully shared perception of a new external reality has imbued it with a pervasive sense of crisis. OPEC created such a reality with actions that led to the oil crisis, and Japan responded most effectively.

Effective tactics, poor strategy

The accomplishments of the System have been so much admired and applauded that foreigners and Japanese alike tend to overlook its inherent defects and deficiencies, the major one being that it has no control over itself. The success with which Japanese industry and bureaucracy adjusted to changes wrought by two oil crises helped obscure the failure of the administrators as a body to face up to the necessity for a much more basic restructuring, though many concerned Japanese saw the dire need for it, even prior to the Maekawa Report. The Japanese economy is basically dependent on one market – that of the United States, which absorbs roughly 40 per cent of all Japanese exports. Agriculture, heavily protected, is in worse shape than almost anywhere else among the advanced industrialised economies where this sector still plays an important role. Industries that serve only the domestic economy are highly inefficient.

Japan's relatively low standards of comfort, despite its international economic performance, indicate the presence of major structural distortions that need correcting. All the while, the dispersion of power among a variety of administrator bodies, none holding ultimate responsibility, makes long-range, nationally integrated strategic planning impossible.

Circumstances have made the administrators superb tacticians but poor strategists. To those familiar with Japanese history the parallel with the Imperial Army in China in the 1930s is fairly obvious. The aims, of course, are different, but the situations roughly similar in the absence of a restraining, integrated long-range strategy or any perspective of what is desirable, derived from an appreciation of what is politically possible and in the national interest. The Japanese military, working out of Manchuria, proved themselves to be master tacticians. But it was also clear that their actions were not ultimately guided by an overall strategic plan taking into account the world beyond China and containing credible provisions for dealing with the contingencies of a war with the United States. As tacticians, MITI and Ministry of Finance bureaucrats, the banks, the business federations, the *keiretsu* companies and all the other institutions that have helped ensure social discipline and enhance Japanese productivity and export prowess have far outdone what the Japanese military achieved in China. But the overall result is that the nation faces great uncertainty with regard to its global position and, ultimately, its international economic viability.

The day-to-day tactics and medium-range strategies of the more capable administrators ensure further economic growth, allow accumulation of the latest foreign technology and swell the paper assets propping up the impressive effort to gain control over foreign financial institutions and amass foreign real estate. Dazzling as their results are, however, these tactics are not ultimately part of a grand overall strategy – unless, of course, economic conquest of the whole world is the unspoken aim of Japan's administrators. Such an aim would not, even so, constitute a credible strategy, because it could never succeed.

Mishandling of the US relationship

It is inconceivable that a state with a responsible government sensitive to long-term national interests could have allowed the Japan–US relationship to deteriorate to the extent it has. Banking too heavily on US indulgence, Tokyo has badly mishandled its most important relationship – the one on which the entire edifice of its foreign relations is built. Preoccupied with their special pleading in Washington, the administrators failed to notice, or at least failed to communicate effectively to fellow administrators, the fact that Japanese actions, or inaction, were frittering away most of the considerable and genuine affection that the United States had come to have for Japan.

By the end of the 1970s it was becoming rather clear that, in spite of their importance to one another, the world's two largest economic powers did not know how to cope with each other. Their perspectives on the relationship and its problems are incompatible. In American eyes Japan does not, in any field, play a role in the international community commensurate with its wealth. After four decades of benefits, say US critics, Japan should be willing to return the favour and share in the political costs of maintaining the alliance, if only for the sake of its own future security.

More specifically, the Americans think it grossly unfair that, while the Japanese have had almost completely free access to the US market, the Japanese market has not been hospitable to US competition. To say that the two sides are not speaking the same language is to understate the problem. The USA stresses that Japan itself stands to gain from free trade and open markets, but what it means by this – greater choices for the Japanese consumers – is not at all what the Japanese administrators understand by gain. A truly open market would undermine the domestic order, so how, in their eyes, could this ever be considered a gain for Japan?

From the viewpoint of most administrators, it is the USA that wants to change the relationship which for them is like a common-law marriage: no papers were signed, no firm arrangements established; but force of habit has forged something that is no less established and should not be less reliable than a formal treaty.

Not understanding the nature of the Japanese political economy, the USA cannot accept the way it behaves. The actual mechanism and extraordinary degree of Japan's dependence on the USA are but dimly understood in Washington. They are more clearly felt on the Japanese side, but the psychological burden it entails does not often permit an honest self-appraisal. Occasionally, Japanese bureaucrats and columnists even imply the reverse of the real situation by concluding that the USA 'risks losing Japan's support'. The Japanese side is largely unaware of the threat to itself posed by the USA's unwillingness to accept it for what it is. Never having experienced the powers of the US legislature, it cannot imagine its potential wrath.

To smooth feathers ruffled by trade conflicts, the administrators tend to raise expectations in foreign governments that are not subsequently fulfilled. In the case of the USA, Tokyo's ritual arguments and empty promises convince congressmen, businessmen and other Americans only that they are being deceived. Japanese bureaucrats appear not to realise that the frustration of rising expectations – the classic fuel for domestic revolutions – can also be the most explosive of forces in international relations.

We have seen that during the first two years of the Nakasone government the US government had expectations of effective Japanese measures. These were partly based on the personal rapport between the prime minister and the US president, the 'Ron–Yasu' relationship. It was just beginning to dawn on Washington that Yasu got everything, leaving Ron nothing but a show of unanimity on military-strategic matters (which everybody took for granted anyway), when in the spring of 1985 the Senate passed by 92 votes to zero a non-binding resolution warning the president that, if he took no action with respect to trade with Japan, it would do so instead. This sent shockwaves through Japan. But the result only demonstrated that, vis-à-vis the outside world, the System remains politically as paralysed as ever.

The administrators tend to explain the changes in the US attitude towards Japan in terms of a weakening of the USA's economic and political power and of the supposed frustration this has brought about. Much is made of the USA having become the largest 'debtor' nation and Japan its major 'creditor' – in reference to the large-scale Japanese purchases in the 1980s of the government bonds with which Washington covers its budget deficit. The presentation of the USA as a declining power is psychologically so comforting for a once defeated nation that it tends to be overstated.

The complication of US politics and ignorance

A common Japanese complaint is that the United States is irrational and that it is not clear what, after all that Japan has already done, it really wants. In American eyes this is ridiculous; almost every visiting American interviewed by the press hammers on the need for a more open market and reiterates that only the results really count.

Even so, Japanese confusion is to some extent understandable, for official America has been sending mixed signals for a long time. Although the Japan Problem is already decades old, what must pass for a Japan policy in Washington is totally unrealistic. In 1986 approaches were still based on the assumption that by cultivation of cordial personal ties with Japanese 'leaders' reason could be made to prevail, and that in the end the market would straighten out any distortions. Policy measures towards Japan were largely improvised on the spur of the moment, with no coherence and no consistency. More often than not, a specific action was not followed through. For the Reagan administration just as for its predecessors, trade and the economy were considered secondary to security and strategic interests. The departments of State and Defense appear to believe that therapeutic trade sanctions would endanger the status of US bases in Japan. The possibility that Japan's industrial onslaught might, by undermining US strategic industries, actually compromise security, and that the US dilemma derives from its own false assumptions had, at least in 1987, apparently not yet occurred to the US government. Whatever action was taken tended to be based on the wrong premises. As one of the USA's most thoughtful negotiators with Japan put it:

Nothing in US law or tradition . . . anticipated the possibility of industry and trade being organised as part of an effort to achieve specific national goals rather than on the individualistic Western model. . . . The result was a series of negotiations that never focused on the main issues but dealt with symptoms instead of causes.[15]

Political and diplomatic considerations have done much to confuse the situation. To demonstrate success in negotiations, token concessions by Japan have until the late 1980s been routinely presented by the US government as genuine concessions. The eagerness with which the Reagan administration has, with the help of easily manipulated media, presented the financial 'liberalisation' measures as a fundamental break-through has made it more difficult to dismiss equally irrelevant bureaucratic action taken subsequently. Washington would announce success in sector-specific trade talks in the field of communications equipment, while its negotiator, Clyde Prestowitz, was telling me that he had not yet finished negotiating.

By 1987 there had been seven 'market-opening packages' and an 'action programme' of bureaucratic measures whose effectiveness was in doubt from the moment they were announced. Sometimes concessions extracted from Japanese bureaucrats after much wrangling turn out upon closer scrutiny to be the same concessions obtained with great difficulty two or four years previously. I myself and a number of my colleagues have often experienced a giddy sense of unreality at the jubilation with which such measures are usually greeted by Washington. European spokesmen, too, have been in the habit of diplomatically praising Tokyo for insubstantial measures; but what Europe says carries not a fraction of the weight of American statements.

This process is damaging in the long run, because whenever the USA makes a fresh request for what are essentially the same concessions it is seen by many ordinary Japanese as demanding new ones. To make matters worse, the USA has sometimes asked for measures that Japan was willing to implement but that are almost totally ineffectual, such as domestic reflation through a demand package, lowering of interest rates or financial market 'liberalisation'. Hence in the popular imagination the USA has begun to appear insatiable, demanding ever more from Japan, even though it has received almost nothing. Half-hearted measures and measures that were never followed through have created the impression that Washington is a never satisfied nag and that it has basically no legitimate grievance.

The management of international reality

Probably most detrimental to chances of solving the Japan–US conflict is the fact that the United States has permitted it to be discussed within a largely Japanese frame of reference. The administrators have gladly undertaken the management of reality in this particular realm. And the inability of Japanese bureaucrats to deal with their most important foreign relationship from a long-range perspective contrasts strongly with the tactical skill, always ensuring that they have the advantage, with which for some fifteen years they have negotiated with the Americans.

There exists what can best be described as a 'mutual understanding industry', whose Japanese practitioners take it for granted that the world needs to understand Japan more than Japan needs to understand the world. Innumerable panel discussions, study meetings, lectures and symposia plead without exception what is essentially the cause and position of the administrators. Subtle flattery ('You must teach us how to confront our dire problems!') often mutes what might otherwise become critical voices.

The Western tendency for moral self-flagellation and Western intellectuals' habit of denigrating the institutions of their own country have helped shape a general perspective in which Japan is compared favourably to the West and which has been gratefully exploited by Japanese spokesmen. Panel discussions on trade problems become forums for taking the foreigners present to task for insufficient understanding and for not trying hard enough to break into the Japanese market. Nor should one forget a category of people unparalleled in the context of any other bilateral relationship: the Japan apologists. As one historian who was once closely associated with cultural exchange relations between the two countries sums it up:

> Unlike the flow of ideas between the US and Europe, the Japan–US discourse is determined largely by a small group of Japanese and American experts on each other's countries who have bridged the great linguistic and cultural gap. Ostensibly dedicated to mutual friendship, this narrow channel of scholars, journalists, and diplomats serves increasingly to skew the dialogue in Japan's favor. It does this through cultural excuses and other special pleading; by fending off critical analyses; by glossing over sensitive issues in Japan; by assuming adequate Japanese knowledge of the US; and by failing to protest Japan's restrictions on foreign academics and journalists.[16]

The enormous propaganda potential of the System described in previous chapters has been put to good use here. Despite their predictable display of disagreement, all administrators – most crucially those in editorial offices – ultimately echo the same basic contentions. Anyone known to the Japanese authorities to be involved in thinking or writing about Japan is inundated with glossy magazines and other documentary material carrying ostensibly independent opinion that says more or less the same thing in every case. The administrators can also take advantage of general foreign ignorance, of the quick turnover among US officials dealing with Japan, and of the relative lack on the American and European side of any institutional memory. Red herrings are strewn about with unparalleled skill.

One of the administrators' great successes is seen in the general acceptance of the postulate of 'equivalent duty'. Japanese understanding of the US penchant for 'looking at both sides' of things and US defensiveness when confronted with appeals to 'fairness' have led to agreements whose stipulations include measures that the USA itself must take concurrently with those intended by Japan. Both sides promise to exert themselves on behalf of a more open market. Official Japanese statements, comment by the 'buffers' and innumerable editorials and 'analyses' in the late 1980s urge the need for Japan to open its market further and become more responsible internationally, yet in the same breath mention the need for the USA to eliminate its budget deficit and to save more. Until the meteoric rise of the yen against the dollar, the automatically included 'equivalent duty' clauses directed the USA to lower its interest rates and allow the dollar to become cheaper. This 'equivalent duty' tactic results in the unspoken assumption that Japan does not really need to feel too bad about doing nothing so long as the USA does not do anything either, and that 'both sides are to blame'. Any assessment of Japan that is critical can thus be dismissed as 'overly one-sided'.

A related success is the portrayal of Japanese officials valiantly fighting on the side of the USA's remaining free traders against a rising tide of US protectionism. Practically every formal statement on the bilateral relationship made by the Japanese prime minister refers to a 'mutual resolve' to halt protectionist tendencies in the world. In the eyes of nearly all ordinary Japanese the danger comes from members of the US Congress who harbour feelings of ill will towards Japan, and from European governments that know no other way to placate their jobless; very few are aware that the pervasive structural protectionism of the Japanese System is the major cause of the conflict to begin with.

A third and more recent success is the function that the term 'bashing' has attained in Japanese manipulations of opinion. Originally used by some American commentators who believe that US jealousies, frustration and even racism cause the friction with Japan, the term has been enthusiastically adopted by Japanese commentators. It tends to be automatically applied to any critical assessment of Japan and any serious analysis of Japan's international problems that places responsibility at the feet of the administrators. The result is that many observers who wish to appear totally fair are inhibited from saying anything beyond the platitudes that most Japanese commentators can agree on – such as the need to become more international, to open the market a bit further and to participate more fully in world politics. The label 'Japan-basher' is not easily shed.

The administrators are abetted in their favourite tactic of shifting attention from essential to peripheral issues by a body of foreign theorists.

There are still economists who will hear nothing of a Japanese industrial policy. The possibility is dismissed on purely theoretical grounds, without any examination of the institutions through which such a policy might be implemented. Then there is the peculiar type of econometric sophistry that demonstrates that, even should the Japanese market be opened up completely, it would make hardly a dent in the trade balance. Precise figures can be given by experts, who are usually doing research with Japanese funding but who apparently have little inkling of how the System operates. On a more mundane plane, there are old chestnuts such as the oft-repeated contention that if US car manufacturers would just remember to put the steering wheel on the right side they could sell more cars in Japan.[17]

The administrators are also unwittingly aided by US diplomats in their reality management of the relationship. The State Department and the Embassy in Tokyo have long had a tendency to echo the Japanese interpretation of bilateral problems. This tendency has a curious history. The US occupation saw the emergence of 'a series of cross-national alliances between organisations seeking to maximise or protect their own institutional spheres'.[18] Thus US bureaucrats were easily won over as 'friends' by Japanese bureaucrats within the same area of responsibility, and proceeded to bicker with Japan–US bureaucratic allies in other areas. The relationship between the Japanese Ministry of Foreign Affairs and the State Department has been fairly similar in recent decades. And even while US diplomats may not formally agree with their Japanese counterparts, there are influential figures among them who react negatively to critical analyses that their Japanese counterparts would not like to hear.

Compounding the diplomatic problem is the role of the US ambassador, who is seen less as an ambassador in the traditional sense than as a 'guardian' watching over the relationship. In a tradition pioneered by Edwin O. Reischauer (who did much to consolidate the 'exploitative dependence' relationship), Mike Mansfield, who was ambassador for over a decade, frequently seemed a better spokesman for Japan in Washington than the other way round. In his public statements, he tended to repeat the current Japanese line on what the USA ought to do. In dealing with Japan on a diplomatic level one faces a world of ritual and incantations far beyond what is generally considered diplomatically necessary or even acceptable, and a person such as Mansfield fitted in here very well indeed. He had the air of being concerned, but 'fair' and 'non-partisan', as if he wanted to remain above the quarrelling parties. The Japanese press was used to Mansfield's admonishing both countries. In a representative interview, the ambassador was quoted as saying that the larger share of the responsibility for the trade problem lies with the United States.[19] Even supposing that this were correct, it would seem a perfect example of mixing diplomatic signals. Such US attitudes sustain the bureaucrats of the Japanese Foreign Ministry in their belief that the conflict is essentially a public relations problem.

Victimised and alone

Because the world is no longer satisfied to leave relations with Japan as they are, the administrators are now called upon to act as statesmen; it is a role for which they are not equipped by training and, even more important, for which they cannot muster the necessary domestic support. In other words, despite their supreme skills in nurturing a high-growth economy and in maintaining effective social control, they are – measured by what is required of them in the late 1980s – incompetent. But when the public begins to ask why other countries are so critical of Japan and why foreign demands never end, they can hardly concede such incompetence. An alternative explanation, that foreigners do not understand Japan, is worn out by decades of heavy duty. The single remaining explanation is that the world is actually against Japan. And in the 1980s this notion has begun to emerge more and more clearly from between the lines of statements by the administrators, and often fairly explicitly in media editorial comment and serious articles in the intellectual magazines.

This notion of a hostile world is easily accepted in Japan. It fits in with a long tradition of belief in the nation's vulnerability to unpredictable external forces. It fits in to a large extent with the individual psychology of many Japanese, who are not encouraged by upbringing or environment to fight social obstacles in their lives, but to accept them passively. Japanese has an expression for it: *higaisha ishiki*, 'victim consciousness'.

Japan's war sufferings

It fits in, too, with the common Japanese perspective of socio-political events and developments for which no one is accountable and no one held responsible. 'Fortunately at the end, Japan could escape from war,' the *Asahi Shimbun*'s most widely read column once said, in the context of a commemoration of the events of 1945.[20] War in this perspective is like an earthquake or a typhoon, an 'act of nature' that takes people by surprise. As one of Japan's most articulate intellectuals has written about the war in China: 'Seen from the outside, Japan appeared to be invading China with imperialist intentions. Seen from the inside, however, most political leaders felt that Japan was being dragged into the swamp of war as part of some inevitable process.'[21] Today, the 'militarists' are seen as responsible for great suffering among the Japanese, but the moment one gives them faces and names they become, for perhaps the majority of Japanese, patriots who sacrificed themselves for their country.

The general attitude towards the Pacific War is one of the best illustrations of Japanese 'victim consciousness'. Nearly all the war films of the past fifteen years or so show the wartime sufferings of the Japanese poeple, and many young people are amazed when told that neighbouring nations suffered also, possibly more, at the hands of the Japanese.

Atrocities committed in the occupied Asian countries tend to be ignored, and the idea that Japan was the main victim is gaining ground. The early 1950s saw the issue of anti-war films critical of the Japanese wartime military, largely because many Japanese soldiers died. Subsequently, the soldiers abroad began to be portrayed as carrying love for peace in their hearts, in a way reminiscent of Hollywood's 'good Nazi' cliche. From the end of the 1960s on, there appeared films portraying the US occupation as the most awful experience. Finally, the late 1970s and early 1980s saw the appearance of the first genuinely revisionist war films. Japanese soldiers are friendly, gentle, full of goodwill towards the local population in, say, the Philippines, whereas US soldiers are brutes who play football with human skulls (*Dai Nippon Teikoku* – a film that turns General Tojo into a hero). The Imperial Navy consisted of peaceful family men, trying to make the best of a difficult situation for Japan (*Rengo Kantai*). In the Japanese film version of the fall of Singapore, the murder of five thousand Chinese is presented as motivated by fear of the Chinese guerrillas obstructing Japanese order-keeping among a local population that did not understand the good intentions of the occupiers (*Minami Jujisei*). The end of the last-mentioned film shows, out of all context, a mushroom cloud – to remind us who were the really bad men in the Second World War.

Mushroom clouds, it sometimes seems, have become all but mandatory in the war films made by the established Japanese studios. Here is victimhood in its ultimate guise: the atomic bombing of Hiroshima and Nagasaki. The belief in Japanese uniqueness has received very special support from these events: the Japanese did not just suffer, they suffered uniquely; one might even speak of national martyrdom. It has become common in Japan to consider the dropping of the atom bomb as the worst act of the war. Some even see it as the crime of the century.[22] Older Japanese still have some sense of perspective concerning these events. A few will remember that, before Hiroshima was devastated, the generals had formed a civilian militia of 28 million men and women between fifteen and sixty years of age, who were being trained to stop the US invaders on the beaches using only bamboo spears. But a Japanese intellectual or public figure can no longer suggest with impunity that the bombs probably saved hundreds of thousands of lives. And for a week in August the nation indulges in a media-generated display of self-pity. The 'peace park' and museum in Hiroshima – pilgrimage centre for numerous foreign anti-nuclear activists and pacifist groups – do not give the multitude of Japanese visitors any impression that history began before the bomb.

There are lobbies campaigning for the inclusion of a visit to Hiroshima in the itineraries of highly placed or famous foreign visitors. Once there, the visitor will find a small army of reporters ready to convey his or her regrets, feelings of remorse and expressions of sympathy (and sometimes 'excuses') to the Japanese people. The 'studies of peace' that a number of organisations undertake within this context consist of books of children's drawings, photographs and reminiscences on the theme of Hiroshima's

suffering. The actual circumstances surrounding Japan's decision to surrender, and the relative part played in it by the Soviet invasion of
Manchuria compared to the bomb, receive hardly any attention from
Japanese intellectuals. The majority of Japanese high-school students are
taught history by teachers who themselves have hardly any idea of what
transpired in the first half of this century.

Hiroshima is lifted out of history; it is a shrine to Japanese martyrdom.
The suffering is considered to have been for humanity, in order to convey
to the world the importance of peace. But the world has continued to make
war, so that Japan has been betrayed again. The latter line of argument is
pursued by the major film on the Tokyo Trials (*Tokyo Saiban*). This film,
which drew an uncommon degree of attention, implies that Japan went
along with a guilty verdict against its military leaders for the sake of
teaching the world the importance of peace, but that the world did not
keep its side of the bargain. The same idea of martyrdom to no avail –
double victimhood as it were – has been conveyed in a number of serious
magazine articles.[23]

Sacrifice for foreigners

The imagery of national victimhood purveyed in popular culture as well as
in serious articles provides a perfect frame of reference in which to place
Japan's international problems in the 1980s. There is no shortage of 'proof'
that the international system has always obstructed Japan's national
interests. One has only to remember the Asian immigration exclusion act
passed by the US Congress in 1924 – still a favourite point-maker at
conferences and in articles. It appears to ordinary Japanese that, although
Japan must participate in the world's affairs, this participation will get it
into trouble by placing it at the mercy of uncontrollable external forces.

The sense of victimhood is nurtured by the criticism that Western
trading partners level at Japan in connection with lopsided trade balances,
and is thus considerably stronger in the 1980s than it was in the 1960s. The
view that Japan is misunderstood, and that irate trading partners are either
mistaken in their impressions or acting in bad faith, carries much force
because it is presented everywhere in the newspapers, the magazines and
on television. It is also clear that other countries do not have the best in
mind for Japan; the external world is not benevolent. It is therefore seen as
crucially different from Japanese society, in which benevolence of the
superior towards the subordinate is the essential assumption which keeps
the bureaucrats and other administrators in their positions.

Japanese readily believe that adjusting to the demands of the world
means paying a price. Giving in to United States and European pressure
aimed at reducing Japanese economic controls is thus presented by the
administrators as a sacrifice the Japanese 'people' must make for the sake of
coping with trade friction.[24] The Japanese public has rarely been told by
the newspapers that it would benefit from the greater choice and lower

costs of more imported products. The management of reality has twisted perception to a very drastic extent. Many Japanese do not think the West has a case in calling Japanese trade practices unfair, because they are hardly aware that their System is not compatible with the rules of international commerce. Instead, they are told that it is the Western countries that want to change the rules in the middle of the game. It has almost become an article of faith in Japan that foreigners hold it against the Japanese that they do their best, and begrudge the Japanese the fruits of their post-war efforts. The administrators would make it appear that lazy Americans and Europeans want to force their bad habits on the thrifty, hard-working Japanese.[25] The Japanese press is poorly informed, and instead of trying to explore the issue is stuck in the same cocoon of self-justifying rationalisations as the majority of officials.

Even those who confirm the need for structural adjustments often assist in the successful campaign to portray Japan as the victim of unreasonable demands and in criticism of 'less hard-working' foreigners. Traces of both attitudes can be detected in pronouncements by such a key figure as Gotoda Masaharu who was Nakasone's right-hand man in attempts to bring structural changes about, and who compares the situation in the 1980s with that of 1853, when Commodore Perry and his 'black ships' forced Japan to end its centuries-old isolation. Intellectuals commenting on the subject may take the bureaucrats and politicians to task for their failings, but on balance they too portray their country as the easy victim of an unreasonable, capricious Western world. Others praise Japan and its people for their remarkable patience in the face of 'emotional American behaviour'. Some respected authors see an alleged US racism at the root of the problem. There are echoes, too, of the wartime imagery that contrasted an enfeebled USA with a purposeful, dynamic and hard-working Japan. The USA is chastised for believing that 'its rules' are universal by authors oblivious to European (or indeed Chinese, ASEAN, Pakistani and nearly everyone else's) protests. The USA is even, in all seriousness, taken to task for not appreciating the Japanese contributions to world peace.

The administrators as victims

If the general public has an ahistorical and apolitical view of Japan's place in the international world, so, by and large, do the administrators. This is borne out by, for instance, their apparent refusal to see the conflict with the United States and other trading partners in political terms, as requiring political solutions.

Here we come to an essential aspect of the Japan Problem. After decades of economic impact on many other countries, plus the recent increase in its financial leverage over the international economy, Japan undoubtedly exercises power in the world. The Japanese economic onslaught, apparently unstoppable by economic mechanisms, is *ipso facto* a political problem. Yet the administrators who deny that they exercise power in

Japan also deny, implicitly but systematically, their exercise of power abroad. They insist that their international difficulties can and should be solved by economic measures taken by others, or by the workings of the market. They prefer not to see that Japan's massive export drives, and its undermining of certain industrial sectors in the USA and Europe, have political repercussions, that Europeans are beginning to seek a political solution, that the US Congress is trying to legislate one and that the reason the problem will not go away is Japanese political paralysis.

To accept Japan's international problems as being of a political nature would deposit them squarely in a realm of discourse in which the exercise of power would be addressed unambiguously, in which informal relations and processes would be made explicit and in which rules and regulations, binding on the authorities, would become inevitable: a universe of discourse, in other words, that would horrify the top administrators.

Throughout this book we have seen Japan's power-holders in charge of what is in fact a gigantic control mechanism – the System – for keeping order among ordinary Japanese. But it is clear, especially when the perspective shifts to Japan in the international context, that the administrators are also, in the final analysis, victims. They are products of the environment their predecessors created, and any debate on their situation that deviates from conventional lines is unwelcome; it is they who, tied down by their lack of imagination, are the real servants of the System. They are victims of a self-deceit inherited from their predecessors in the Tokugawa shogunate and the Meiji oligarchy: the pretence that they do not exercise power, together with the concomitant denial of any need for universally accepted rules to regulate that power, and hence the problem they have in accepting unambiguous leadership. The administrators have fostered complex personal ties that thrive on mutual aid, and their major task has been, by preventing laws and the courts from becoming the supreme regulators of society, to keep those relationships and the rules that govern them informal. They protect themselves by means of an elaborate rationale denying the forces that actually govern the System and explaining everything as a natural result of Japanese 'culture'. The Prussian vision of a society of perfect regimentation, and the overpowering fear of social disorder to which it is an antidote, both inherited from earlier administrators, limit their movements. They do not have the advantage, enjoyed by politicians, bureaucrats and intellectuals in most Western countries, of a political system that is to a considerable degree responsive to rational argument, to intellectual warnings and to genuine political debate. Some of them whom I know personally are horrified by the realisation that the System is, in fact, not under control.

Ultimate international incompatibility

The denial of the true mechanisms of Japanese power, the pervasive sense of being victimised, the sense of being at once unique and misunderstood, and the absence of leadership all combine to perpetuate Japanese isolation in the world. This isolation is further aggravated by the seemingly insurmountable difficulty of fitting Japan into a larger, 'legal' international framework.

The international world, especially the post-war trade system established under US auspices and sustained by such institutions as the GATT, the IMF and the OECD, operates on norms essentially different from those that make the Japanese System go round. GATT member countries do not usually arrange their relations with fellow members according to estimates of each other's power. The United States has not been intimidating Japan into an awareness of its proper position in the scheme of things. Governments may lie to each other and to their own populations, but in international dealings among non-communist trading nations there is no gap between substantial reality and formal reality remotely comparable to the institutionalised gap found in Japan. To some extent reality may be managed, but at some point foreign journalists, scholarly commentators or exasperated governments will point out the discrepancies between appearance and reality if they think these have become too great.

The Japanese System and what is left of the international free-trade system are incompatible because the latter requires adherence to rules that the administrators cannot afford to accept lest they override their own informal relations. Generally applicable rules governing the opportunities of foreign participants in Japanese society and its market would undermine and ultimately destroy the System by undermining the complex webs of *jinmyaku* and informal procedures. Deals can be made with the System, but the introduction of universal rules within the System itself is not a possible subject for such deals.

Contamination of foreign ways

The isolation of the System breeds popular attitudes that in turn intensify it and alienate the Japanese people even further from the rest of the world. Many foreign observers have seen persisting psychological insularity as one of the main factors in Japan's international problems, and explain it with reference to cultural predilections. What tends to be overlooked here is that isolation is continuously encouraged by the way in which the Japanese are governed. Isolation follows from the way in which the emergence of a bourgeoisie has been halted; from the way in which the middle class has been incorporated into the hierarchy of business firms; from the way in which the school system, rather than educating citizens for Japan, produces administrators and salarymen for predetermined levels of the System's hierarchies.

All this is most clearly demonstrated by the phenomenon of the so-called 'returning youngsters' (*kikoku shijo*) – Japanese children who have received an important part of their education abroad while their fathers

were serving in overseas offices of their companies. Except for training in
engineering and other technical fields, foreign education is generally a
handicap for functioning in the System. Far from being appreciated for the
scope and freshness of the learning and experience that they bring to
Japanese high schools and universities on their return, the young returnees
are actively discriminated against and are often the object of teasing and
class bullying. They are invariably made to feel they are contaminated.
The problem is so great that special schools have had to be established to
remould them into acceptable Japanese. Their teachers complain that
they ask too many questions. Their obvious dislike of proliferating school
rules brands them as potential threats to Japanese social order. They are
urged to mind their manner of walking and of laughing, since these may
immediately mark them as outcasts in their homeland. Companies are not
happy with job applicants who have lived abroad, worrying that their
behaviour may upset the work community.

   In cases where only a small number of Japanese representatives reside in
a foreign city, they demonstrate that there is nothing insurmountable in
their psychological make-up that prevents them from enjoying normal
social relations with other peoples. It is when the expatriate Japanese
community grows, and when a Japanese school is established, that their
isolation becomes acute and they form exclusive Japanese clubs, or
Japanese enclaves within existing local clubs. Subsequently, they tend,
wherever possible, to move into the same town or locality. The extent to
which this is done, and the extent of Japanese isolation from local society,
is incomparably greater than in communities of Americans or Europeans
abroad. From private conversations with Japanese businessmen in South-
East Asia and Europe I have gathered that many feel that they cannot
afford to awaken concern that they are picking up foreign ways, or
suspicion that they prefer the company of foreigners to that of other
Japanese. Thus the behaviour of Japanese abroad is a consequence of
pressure on them by their companies, not of some vague cultural rule.

Shall the System last for ever?

Finally, the most important question: can the situation change? Theoretically, the answer is yes. As I have tried to demonstrate throughout this
book, the System's character is ultimately determined by political relationships. Nothing that is political is irreversible in the long run,
especially if the political dimension is recognised for what it is. There is no
good theoretical reason why the Japanese should for ever be held under
political tutelage.

   What might one do in an ideal situation? For a start, one would have to
abolish Tokyo University. Other basic changes would have to take place
in the legal and party systems. Law courses would have to be instituted in a
large number of universities, and lawyers trained to give individual
Japanese the means to protect themselves against the arbitrariness of the

administrators. Control over the judiciary and over access to the bar would have to be taken away from the secretariat of the Supreme Court, and the artificial limitation on the number of law practitioners would have to be lifted. The schools and the media would have to work to foster individual political awareness and a sense of individual responsibility while de-emphasizing the importance of membership in companies and other organisations. All this would encourage the substitution of legal regulations for *jinmyaku* relationships, and of legally safeguarded processes for the System's informality. Any essential change for the better would also require the emergence of political parties not dependent on the pork-barrel and intent on truly representing the interests of the middle class and factory workers. This would only be a beginning, but under such conditions Japan could conceivably begin gradually to function as the constitutionalist democracy it is supposed to be. And it would move towards a solution of the problem of who, or which institution, has the right to rule.

The activities and the insights of some Japanese groups, such as the activist groups of the federation of bar associations (Nichibenren) or the alternative education reform committee of ordinary citizens, are proof that what I suggest is not asking too much, since they indicate the ability of the Japanese to be genuine citizens and to see themselves as such. Unfortunately, experience so far gives no reason for optimism. If the System is guided by any overriding, sacrosanct aim, it is its own survival, which means the survival of the present constellation of administrators. This aim is mistakenly identified with the survival of Japan. The absence of political debate about national priorities, of parliamentary checks and balances and of a legal framework for solving conflict increases the ever-present risk of an intensification of Japanism. This, in turn, would be conducive to the re-emergence of extremist sentiments aimed at 'saving the nation', which, as in the past, would most likely lead the nation still deeper into trouble. The possibility must be considered that the Japanese System may yet go through another convulsion caused by an acute sense of confrontation with a hostile world. Such a spasm could conceivably bring a determined group to gather power to itself and plot a new course for the country, with a wholly unpredictable outcome.

The most likely possibility, perhaps, is that the System will muddle on, after having come to some *modus vivendi* with the Western world and the United States in particular. But this will require wise policies in the Western capitals.

The wonderful alternative of turning the System into a genuine modern constitutionalist state, and Japanese subjects into citizens, would require realignments of power akin to those of a genuine revolution.

Notes

1 The Japan Problem

1 The distinction between 'adversarial' and 'competitive' trade was first introduced by Peter Drucker in the *Wall Street Journal*, 1 April 1986.

2 For an attempt to connect these and other recent developments within the perspective of the theories advanced in this book, see Chapter 15.

3 Umesao Tadao, 'Escape from cultural isolation', in Japan Center for International Exchange (eds.), *The Silent Power*, Simul Press, 1976.

4 Naohiro Amaya, 'Japan's Peter Pan syndrome', *Asian Wall Street Journal*, 10 January 1986.

5 Chalmers Johnson of the University of California, Berkeley. See his *MITI and the Japanese Miracle*, Stanford University Press, 1982.

6 Among others, see F. A. Hayek, *Law, Legislation and Liberty*, Routledge & Kegan Paul, 1973.

7 Kim Jae Ik, who was the chief economic adviser of South Korean presidents Park Chung Hee and Chun Do Hwan, told me once that Park Chung Hee had these Japanese experiences in mind when instructing the 'architect' of the South Korean economic miracle, Nam Duck Woo, to design the mechanism for rapid growth. Kim Jae Ik himself played a major role in shaping the South Korean 'economic miracle'. He was murdered in the North Korean massacre of South Korean government leaders in Rangoon on 9 April 1983.

8 Christie Kiefer, 'The *danchi zoku* and the evolution of metropolitan mind', in L. Austin (ed.), *Japan: The Paradox of Progress*, Yale University Press, 1976, p. 281.

9 Exceptions include Kurt Singer (*Mirror, Sword and Jewel*, Croom Helm, 1973), Ruth Benedict, Robert N. Bellah, Arthur Koestler and George De Vos.

10 Kato Tsugio, *Asahi Evening News*, 20 January 1983.

11 The same, except for the financial factor, can be said for China.

12 Lafcadio Hearn, *Japan: An Attempt at Interpretation*, Tuttle, 1959, p. 1.

13 Ruth Benedict, *The Chrysanthemum and the Sword*, Houghton Mifflin, 1946, p. 1.

14 Nakagawa and Ota, *The Japanese-Style Economic System*, Foreign Press Center, 1980.

15 Editorial in *Asian Wall Street Journal*, 10 April 1986.

16 Murakami Yasusuke, Kumon Shumpei and Sato Seizaburo, *Bunmei to shite no ie-shakai* [Ie Society as a Pattern of Civilisation], Chuo Koronsha, 1979;

see also Murakami Yasusuke, '*Ie* society as a pattern of civilisation', *Journal of Japanese Studies*, Summer 1984, pp. 281–363.

17 For these and many other continuous careers of social-control bureaucrats, see Chapter 14.

18 Reinhard Bendix, *Kings or People*, University of California Press, 1978, pp. 463–4.

19 Rollo May, *Power and Innocence*, Norton, 1972, p. 102.

20 'Ought we to redefine it in a clear way, or ought we to banish it altogether? My initial reaction is that it should be banished altogether' – Peter Nettle, 'Power and the intellectuals', in Conor Cruise O'Brien and William Dean Vanech (eds.), *Power and Consciousness*, New York University Press, 1969, p. 16, as quoted in May, *Power and Innocence*, op. cit., (n. 18).

21 Abraham Maslow, among other clinical psychologists, defines individual maturity as the integration of the cognitive, affective and conative aspects of the personality. In other words, the desires, emotions and reasoning of a mentally healthy, mature individual are in accord. Abraham Maslow, *Motivation and Personality*, Harper & Row, 1970.

22 Leszek Kolakowski, 'Beyond empiricism: the need for a metaphysical foundation for freedom', in John A. Howard (ed.), *On Freedom*, Devin-Adair, 1984.

2   The Elusive State

1   The pioneering work on instances of this in post-war Japan is Richard Halloran, *Japan – Images and Reality*, Knopf, 1969.

2   'History of the kingdom of Wei (Wei Chi), c. AD 297', in R. Tsunoda and L. C. Goodrich, *Japan in the Chinese Dynastic Histories*, Perkins Asiatic Monograph No. 2, South Pasadena, Calif.

3   'Knowing the will of the gods' was synonymous with 'governing the country' in the ancient Japanese term that was used. Ryosuke Ishii, *A History of Political Institutions in Japan*, University of Tokyo Press, 1980, pp. 5–7.

4   George B. Sansom, *Japan: A Short Cultural History*, Cresset Press, 1952, p. 300.

5   This is a singular case among the advanced non-communist countries. Sweden and Israel are examples of nations ruled for many decades by the same parties, but these were of the left and cannot be said to be in league with industry. The dominating ruling parties in other countries, such as Canada, Norway and Ireland, have occasionally had to make room for the competition for periods of a couple of years or more.

6   The LDP had 1.4 million members in 1978, 3.1 million in 1979 and 1.4 again in 1980. The sudden rise was to a large extent due to the ambitions of one contender for the prime ministership, Komoto Toshio, who paid the membership fee of close to a million members, hoping they would vote for him in newly introduced 'primary elections'.

7   For a recent account of the relationship between central bureaucrats and local government officials, and the role played by the LDP politicians, see Tahara Soichiro, 'Jichisho 2' [Ministry of Home Affairs, part 2], *Shukan Bunshun*, 12 September 1985, pp. 46–51.

8   Masumi Junnosuke, 'Gikaisei to atsuryoku dantai' [The Diet system and pressure groups], *Chuo Koron*, January 1960, p. 46.

9   For the background of the founders and leaders of these federations, see Chapter 14.

10   Mary Elizabeth Berry, *Hideyoshi*, Harvard University Press, 1982, p. 4.
11   Herman Ooms, *Tokugawa Ideology*, Princeton University Press, 1985, pp. 26–8.
12   The Imperial Decree accompanying the abolition of the domains, as quoted in Delmer Brown, *Nationalism in Japan*, University of California Press, 1955, p. 96.
13   Neither 'Ministry of the Interior' nor 'Home Ministry', which are the common English translations of Naimusho, convey the jurisdiction and might of this at times most powerful component of Japan's pre-war System.
14   The only power that parliament was given was to refuse to pass the budget, thus forcing the government to try to make ends meet with a budget equal in size to that of the previous year.
15   Nezu Masashi, *Dainippon teikoku no hokai: Tenno showaki* [The Collapse of Imperial Japan: Record on the Emperor in Showa], vol. 1, Shiseido, 1961, pp. 128–9. I am indebted to David Titus, *Palace and Politics in Prewar Japan*, Columbia University Press, 1974, for drawing my attention to this case.
16   James B. Crowley, 'Japanese army factionalism in the early 1930s', *Journal of Asian Studies*, May 1962, pp. 309–26.
17   Asada Sadao, 'The Japanese navy and the United States', in Dorothy Borg and Shumpei Okamoto (eds.), *Pearl Harbor as History*, Columbia University Press, 1973, pp. 258–9. See also Fujiwara Akira, 'The role of the Japanese army', ibid., p. 195.
18   Ben-Ami Shillony, *Politics and Culture in Wartime Japan*, Clarendon Press, 1981, p. 29.
19   Ibid., p. 83.
20   Chalmers Johnson, *Japan's Public Policy Companies*, American Enterprise Institute for Public Policy Research, 1978.
21   Okumura Hiroshi, *Shin: Nihon no rokudai kigyo shudan* [Six Big Corporate Groups in Japan], Daiamondosha, 1983, p. 25.
22   Kosai Yutaka, *The Era of High-Speed Growth*, University of Tokyo Press, 1986, pp. 26–7.

3   An Inescapable Embrace

1   Kiyomi Morioka, *Religion in Changing Japanese Society*, University of Tokyo Press, 1975, p. 7.
2   The Philippine Catholic Church played a decisive role in the events leading up to Marcos's flight from his palace. See the various statements of the bishops' conference and of the cardinal made in February 1986.
3   Frederick B. Katz, *The Mind of the Middle Ages*, University of Chicago Press, 1953, chapter 4.
4   Nakayama Committee for the Keizai Chosa Kyogikai (Japan Economic Research Conference), *Chosa hokoku 74-7 jumin undo to shohisha undo: sono gendai ni okeru igi to mondaiten* [Research Report 74-7: Citizen and Consumer Movements, their Meaning and Problems in the Contemporary Age], Nihon Keizai Chosa Kyogikai, March 1975. For an attack on this report by the citizens' movement, see Jishukoza Henshu Iinkai, 'Kan, san, gakkai no jumin undo taisaku o hyosu' [Evaluation of the measures against citizens' movements by the bureaucracy, business and academic world], *Gekkan Jishukoza*, vol. 49, 10 April 1975, pp. 1–7.
5   Taguchi Fukuji and Toshinai Yoshinori, 'Atsuryoku dantai to shite no ishikai' [JMA as a pressure group], *Chuo Koron*, April 1959, p. 263.

6   Non-government estimates of the total number of abortions (of which the clinics register only a fraction for tax reasons) range between one and two million a year. See also Chapter 14.

7   A recent example is the proposed AIDS control law, which places the doctors under no compulsion whatsoever. For an account of the strong influence of the relevant LDP politicians over the ministry, see Inoguchi Takashi and Iwai Tomoaki, *'Zoku giin' no kenkyu* [A Study of 'Zoku Diet Members'], Nihon Keizaishimbun, 1987, pp. 194–8.

8   Tsuji Kiyoaki, 'Atsuryoku dantai' [Pressure groups], in Arisawa Hiromi *et al.* (eds), *Keizai shutaisei koza shakai II*, vol. 4, Chuo Koronsha, 1960, p. 232. See Chapter 15 for an account of the important role this group played for the System.

9   Kimura Kihachiro, '33 nendo yosan o meguru atsuryoku' [Pressure on the budget of fiscal 1958], *Chuo Koron*, May 1958, pp. 124–31.

10 See, for instance, *Asahi Shimbun*, editorial, 16 March 1957.

11 The photographer Eugene Smith, who helped draw the world's attention to Minamata with his photo books, suffered a permanent eye injury at the hands of these gangsters.

12 Jiyuminshu Henshubu, '1985 nen taisei e no tembo' [Perspectives for the 1985 system], *Jiyuminshu*, January 1982, p. 224.

13 *Asahi Shimbun*, 8 April 1988.

14 These are the Nihon Izokukai, the Gun On Ren, the Nihon Shoi Gunjinkai and the Goyu Remmei. They want revision of the 'peace' constitution and formal reinstitution of Yasukuni shrine, a pilgrimage centre of the abolished state Shinto (see Chapter 13). They sponsor monuments to soldiers, including executed war criminals.

15 Ishida Takeshi, 'Pressure groups in Japan', *Journal of Social and Political Ideas in Japan*, December 1964.

16 Ibid., p. 335.

17 Takeshi Ishida, 'The development of interest groups and the pattern of political modernisation in Japan', in R. E. Ward (ed.), *Political Development in Modern Japan*, Princeton University Press, 1968, pp. 333–4.

18 Tsuji, 'Atsuryoku dantai', op. cit. (n. 8), pp. 246–7.

19 'Yosan to atsuryoku' [Budget and pressures], part 12, *Yomiuri Shimbun*, 17 December 1965.

20 *Yomiuri Shimbun*, editorial, 13 August 1986.

21 An abbreviation of *nogyo kyodo kumiai* ('agricultural co-operative union').

22 According to statistics from the Ministry of Agriculture, as of February 1985, the total population in Japan's 4,376,000 farming households was 19,839,000 (9,662,000 males and 10,177,000 females); 6,363,000 out of this total were engaged in part-time or full-time farming.

23 Ishikawa Hideo, 'Taiseinai no atsuryoku dantai: Zenkoku Nokyo Chuokai' [A pressure group in the establishment: Zenchu], *Asahi Jaanaru*, 30 May 1965, p. 39.

24 Matsumoto Seicho, 'Kensetsu kanryoron' [On construction bureaucrats], *Bungei Shunju*, February 1964, p. 136.

25 T. J. Pempel, *Policy and Politics in Japan*, Temple University Press, 1982, p. 30.

26 Ishikawa, 'Taiseinai', op. cit. (n. 23), p. 38.

27 Tahara Soichiro, 'Nokyo gaiko o tenkai suru Fujita Saburo Zenchu kaicho' [Fujita Saburo, Zenchu president who promotes *nokyo*'s diplomacy], *Chuo Koron*, March 1980, p. 284.

28 Ishikawa, 'Taiseinai', op. cit. (n. 23), pp. 36–7.
29 Tachibana Takashi, *Nokyo*, Asahi Shimbunsha, 1984. The following information about Miyazaki prefecture is culled from this book.
30 Ibid., p. 343.
31 With the Maintenance of Public Peace Law of 1900, which denied workers the right to organise.
32 Ikeda Makoto, 'Roshi kyocho seisaku no keisei: Naimusho shakaikyoku setchi no igi ni tsuite' [Formation of policy for co-operation between management and labour: the significance of Naimusho's social bureau], *Nihon rodo kyokai zasshi*, no. 226, 1978, pp. 14–23; and Sheldon M. Garon, 'The imperial bureaucracy and labor policy in postwar Japan', *Journal of Asian Studies*, May 1984.
33 The highest organisation rate was 7.9 per cent in 1931 with a total of 368,975. The largest number of union members in pre-war Japan was reached in 1936 with an organisation rate of 6.9 per cent.
34 Sheldon M. Garon, *The State and Labor in Modern Japan*, University of California Press, 1987, pp. 220 ff.
35 Thomas R. H. Havens, *Valley of Darkness: The Japanese People and World War Two*, Norton, 1978, pp. 43–6.
36 For the most complete account of this reorganisation of the Japanese labour movement along lines inspired by Nazi Germany and Italian fascism, see Garon, *State and Labor*, op. cit. (n. 34), chapter 6.
37 Takafusa Nakamura, *The Postwar Japanese Economy*, University of Tokyo Press, 1981, p. 18.
38 Garon, *State and Labor*, op. cit. (n. 34), p. 213. The proposal was by Minami Iwao, who had studied Hitler's labour policies and the German Labour Front.
39 A revised National Public Service Law took away the right of public service employees to strike and bargain collectively. Workers in government enterprises, to whom a different law applied, could still bargain collectively, but were also deprived of the right to strike.
40 Sumiya Mikio, 'Nihonteki roshi kankeiron no saikochiku' [Reconstruction of the theory on Japanese labour relations], *Nihon rodo kyokai zasshi*, vol. 262, January 1981, p. 2. Sumiya makes the interesting point that labour relations in small and medium-sized companies, and those affecting women, are not being studied.
41 Stephen S. Large, 'The patterns of Taisho democracy', in H. Wray and H. Conroy (eds.), *Japan Examined*, University of Hawaii Press, 1983, p. 177.
42 Rengo started on 20 November 1987 with sixty-two labour organisations, whose membership totalled 5.55 million members. This covered some 70 per cent of the private unions.
43 Chamoto Shigemasa, 'Zenmin Roren no hossoku to Zendentsu' [The organisation of Zenmin Roren and Zendentsu], *Sekai*, December 1987, p. 281.
44 Ibid., pp. 283–4.
45 Ibid., pp. 283–4.
46 See Chapters 12 and 14 for the intricate background of these long-term plans of the LDP.
47 Masumi Junnosuke, 'Gikaisei to atsuryoku dantai' [The Diet system and pressure groups], *Chuo Koron*, January 1960, p. 46.
48 An excellent summary and assessment of the motives of the government, the BLL and the JCP in connection with litigation and denunciation practices

connected with the *burakumin* can be found in Frank K. Upham, *Law and Social Change in Postwar Japan*, Harvard University Press, 1977, chapter 3, esp. pp. 116–17, 123.

49 *Burakumin* are three and a half times more likely than non-*burakumin* Japanese to suffer from a physical disorder, according to calculations by a BLL-affiliated research institute. See Murakoshi Sueo and Miwa Yoshio (eds), *Konnichi no buraku sabetsu* [Buraku Discrimination Today], Buraku Kaiho Kenkyujo, 1986.

50 Benjamin C. Duke, *Japan's Militant Teachers*, University of Hawaii Press, 1973, p. 35.

51 Ibid., pp. 107–8; and Donald R. Thurston, *Teachers and Politics in Japan*, Princeton University Press, 1973, p. 15.

52 Yung Park, 'Big business and education policy in Japan', unpublished paper, Humboldt State University.

53 Totsuka Ichiro and Kiya Toshikazu (eds.), *Mombusho* [The Ministry of Education], Hobunsha, 1956, pp. 98–101; and Duke, *Japan's Militant*, op. cit. (n. 50), pp. 124–5.

54 *Nippon Times*, 27 March and 8 April 1956, as cited in Duke, *Japan's Militant*, op. cit. (n. 50), p. 132.

55 Duke, *Japan's Militant*, op. cit. (n. 50), p. 116.

56 See Yung H. Park, *Bureaucrats and Ministers in Contemporary Japanese Government*, Institute of Asian Studies, University of California, Berkeley, 1986, pp. 24–5.

57 Thurston, *Teachers*, op. cit. (n. 51), p. 193.

58 Duke, *Japan's Militant*, op. cit. (n. 50), pp. 153–4.

59 Thomas Rohlen, *Japan's High Schools*, University of California Press, 1983, p. 222; Duke, *Japan's Militant*, op. cit. (n. 50), p. 202; Thurston, *Teachers*, op. cit. (n. 51), p. 83.

60 The *Grus japanensis*.

61 Thurston, *Teachers*, op. cit. (n. 51), p. 132.

62 See Chapters 6 and 7.

63 See Chapters 9 and 10.

64 Justin Williams, *Japan's Political Revolution under MacArthur*, University of Tokyo Press, 1979, p. 258.

65 See, for example, Michio Muramatsu and Ellis S. Kraus, 'The conservative policy line and the development of patterned pluralism', in K. Yamamura and Y. Yasuba (eds.), *The Political Economy of Japan*, vol. 1, Stanford University Press, 1987, pp. 537 ff.

66 See, for example, Pempel, *Policy and Politics*, op. cit. (n. 25). Pempel is one of the very few scholars who have contributed serious analysis to the study of Japanese politics.

4 Servants of the System

1 See Chapter 10.

2 Thomas Rohlen, *Japan's High Schools*, University of California Press, 1983, p. 209. I consider this one of the best books in recent years on any Japanese subject.

3 See Robert M. Spaulding, *Imperial Japan's Higher Civil Service Examinatons*, Princeton University Press, 1967, p. 125.

4 In 1987 these three high schools were Kaisei, Nada and Lasalle, with a

combined 387 of the 3,747 successful candidates admitted to the University of Tokyo.

5	Rohlen, *High Schools*, op. cit. (n. 2), p. 100.
6	Amaya Naohiro, 'World leadership for Japan?', *Japan Times*, 29 June 1986.
7	Kato Shuichi, personal communication.
8	The importance of entrance exams for one suburb of Tokyo is well described by Ezra Vogel in *Japan's New Middle Class*, University of California Press, 1967.
9	The most elaborate studies of the psychological mechanisms involved are by George De Vos. See, among others, his *Socialisation for Achievement*, University of California Press, 1973.
10	Griffis, 'Education in Japan', *College Courant*, 16 May 1874, as cited in Edward R. Beauchamp, 'Griffis in Japan: the Fukui interlude, 1871', in Edward R. Beauchamp (ed.), *Learning to be Japanese*, Linnet Books, Connecticut, 1978, p. 58.
11	*Keizai hatten ni okeru jinteki noryoku kaihatsu no kadai to taisaku* [Topics and Policies on the Development of Human Ability in Economic Development], Keizai Shingikai, 14 January 1963.
12	*Koki chuto kyoiku ni taisuru yobo* [Prospects for Upper-Middle-Level Education], 5 February 1965.
13	*Koki'chuto kyoiku no kakuju seibi ni tsuite no toshin* [Advice on the Arrangement and Development of Upper-Middle-Level Education], Chukyoshin, 31 October 1966.
14	The ranking helps determine the content of the *naishinsho*, the document of recommendation to a chosen school at the next level. Many teachers command obedience by using the possibility of a negative evaluation in the *naishinsho* as a threat – Nikkyoso teachers, personal communication. See also 'Tensei jingo', *Asahi Shimbun*, 8 April 1988.
15	*Asahi Shimbun*, editorial, 14 December 1984.
16	See Chapter 13 for a detailed account of this phenomenon.
17	In October 1985 Nichibenren held a symposium on 'Children's Human Rights and their School Life' and on the occasion issued a report called *Gakko seikatsu to kodomo no jinken* [School Life and Children's Human Rights].
18	Nagase Akiyuki and Ueji Yoshio, both directors of respectable *juku* schools, say that peace of the public schools is maintained by the *naishinsho* system (whereby teachers issue a letter of recommendation evaluating the behaviour of the pupil to the high school which he or she wishes to enter) and the police – 'Kodomo o dame ni shita no wa gakko to oya da' [School and parents ruined the children], *Gendai*, September 1984, p. 383.
19	Ivan P. Hall, *Mori Arinori*, Harvard University Press, 1973.
20	James L. Huffman, *Politics of the Meiji Press*, University of Hawaii Press, 1980, p. 96.
21	Richard Mitchell, *Censorship in Imperial Japan*, Princeton University Press, 1983, p. 55.
22	Ibid., pp. 42–3.
23	Harry Wildes, *Social Currents in Japan*, University of Chicago Press, 1927, as cited in L. W. Beer, *Freedom of Expression in Japan*, Kodansha International, 1984, p. 63.
24	Gebhard Hielscher, in *No. 1 Shimbun*, Foreign Correspondents' Club of Japan, 15 November 1982, p. 6.

25 John Roberts, 'Zaibatsu no seiji no hishinsei domei' [The Unholy Alliance Between Big Business and Politics], *Chuo Koron*, April 1974, pp. 118–28.
26 Young C. Kim, *Japanese Journalists and their World*, University Press of Virginia, 1981, p. 48.
27 Nihon Keizai Shimbunsha (eds), *Jiminto Seichokai* [LDP's Policy Affairs Research Council], Nihon Keizai Shimbunsha, 1983, pp. 159–62.
28 Yamanouchi Yukio, 'Yamaguchi-gumi komon bengoshi no shuki' [Notes of a Yamaguchi-gumi advisory lawyer], *Bungei Shunju*, November 1984, p. 400.
29 Ian Buruma, *A Japanese Mirror: Heroes and Villains of Japanese Culture*, Cape, 1984, p. 168.
30 Yamanouchi, 'Yamaguchi-gumi', op. cit. (n. 28), p. 408; also David Kaplan and Alec Dubro, *Yakuza*, Addison-Wesley, 1986, p. 116.
31 Kaplan and Dubro, *Yakuza*, op. cit. (n. 30), p. 116.
32 'Taoka-ke onzoshi no kashoku no en ni manekareta hitobito' [Those who were invited to the wedding of Taoka's son], *Shukan Asahi*, 7 June 1974, p. 139.
33 Mugishima Fumio, 'Naze nakunaranu boryokudan?' [Why do gangs still exist?], *Asahi Shimbun*, 25 February 1985.
34 For background details, see Ino Kenji, *Yakuza to Nihonjin* [The *yakuza* and the Japanese], Mikasa Shobo, 1973, pp. 254–7.
35 Walter L. Ames, *Police and Community in Japan*, University of California Press, 1981, p. 107.
36 Yamanouchi, 'Yamaguchi-gumi', op. cit. (n. 28), p. 405.
37 Mugishima, 'Naze', op. cit. (n. 33). Taoka started out by organising long-shoremen and blackmailing entertainers, to build up what is probably the largest crime syndicate in the world. In 1984 Yamaguchi-gumi commanded the loyalty of 593 subordinate gangs with a total of almost 13,000 members in 36 out of Japan's 47 prefectures.
38 *Yamaguchi-gumi Jiho*, vol. 2, October 1971.
39 *Yomiuri Shimbun*, 21 December 1987.
40 The *yakuza* are active in the Philippines, and after building bases in Hawaii in the 1970s they began to move to the US west coast, where they procure pornography and white prostitutes for Japanese tourists.
41 Some of this has economic causes. In 1963, when the *yakuza* community reached a peak of about 184,000 members, there were enough victims for the traditional protection rackets and enough gambling to keep the gangs out of each other's hair. In the 1970s the independent medium-sized and small gangs began to deteriorate. The large syndicates – Yamaguchi-gumi, Inagawa-kai and Sumiyoshi Rengo – flourished as they swallowed these smaller groups. The weakened influence and gradual disappearance of a generation of old-fashioned gang bosses meant that many of these larger gangs have had to contend with more disobedience. A gangster told me in the late 1960s that the youth that were joining his organisation no longer seemed to care about valuable traditions. The problem must have grown worse.

5 The Administrators

1 Manabe Shigeki, Chiba Hitoshi, Nakayama Masaru, Matsuzaki Yasunori and Maruyama Noboru, 'Kokkai giin no shin keibatsu o eguru – sei, zai, kankai o musubu daiketsumyaku' [The great networks which form political,

business and bureaucratic relations, and new cliques of Diet members],
Gendai, October 1980, p. 158.

2   Ibid., p. 160.

3   Ibid., p. 161.

4   These figures are from a survey over the early 1980s.

5   Graduates of Harvard in the US bureaucracy number 11.2 per cent. In
1950, 26.5 per cent of Britain's high officials (higher than assistant deputy
minister) were from Oxford and 20.8 per cent from Cambridge.

6   The important prime minister Ikeda Hayato graduated from Kyoto University, and Ohira Masayoshi from Hitotsubashi, both of which are government schools considered equal to Todai. Both these prime ministers
entered politics after a career in the Finance Ministry. Ishibashi and
Takeshita graduated from Waseda University, and Miki from Meiji University. Takeshita would never have become prime minister if he could not
have used the 'machine' that Tanaka built.

7   *Shukan Sankei*, 14 April 1977.

8   The most famous private universities, Waseda and Keio, were represented
by 131 and 159 presidents respectively. See *Cosmos News*, no. 4, Teikoku
Data Bank, July 1985.

9   Kawamoto Taro, 'Sore demo Todai Hogakubu wa Nippon o ugokasu' [And
yet Todai law department moves Japan], *Bungei Shunju*, September 1972,
p. 169.

10 Ibid., p. 177.

11 Kusayanagi Daizo, 'Kofuna nitodate basha: Kensetsusho' [An old-fashioned
two-horse cart: the Ministry of Construction], *Bungei Shunju*, February
1975, p. 143.

12 For details of Kono's interference in personnel matters, see Matsumoto
Seicho, 'Kensetsu kanryoron' [On construction bureaucrats], *Bungei
Shunju*, February 1964, esp. p. 144.

13 Kusayanagi, 'Kofuna', op. cit. (n. 11), p. 142.

14 Both gained close to a million votes. See 'Senkyo ni deru nara kensetsu
kanryo' [Construction officials have the greatest advantage in elections],
Hyo, June 1960, p. 19.

15 For an example from the 1986 election, see 'Kensetsu kanryo gyokai mem-
boku kake', *Yomiuri Shimbun*, 12 June 1986, pp. 19–22.

16 Op. cit. (n. 14), p. 21.

17 Kanryo Kiko Kenkyukai (eds.), *Kensentsusho zankoku monogatari* [The
inside story of the Ministry of Construction], Eeru Shuppansha, 1978,
p. 119.

18 'Tanaka naikaku no "kensetsu daijin" wa naze . . .' [Why the 'construction
ministers' of the Tanaka cabinet . . .?], *Ushio*, February 1974, p. 120.

19 Ito Hirokazu, *Zankoku kensetsu gyokai* [The inside story of the construction
industry], Eeru Shuppansha, 1987, pp. 10, 20–2, 27.

20 Takeuchi Naokazu, Watanuki Joji, Asano Chiaki and Ninagawa Masao,
'Dokengyo ni nottorareta chihoseiji' [Local politics hijacked by the construction industry], *Asahi Jaanaru*, 21 January 1977, p. 28.

21 Ito, *Zankoku kensetsu*, op. cit. (n. 19), pp. 30–2.

22 Kanryo Kiko Kenkyukai, *Kensetsusho zankoku*, op. cit. (n. 17), p. 75.

23 Nihon Keizai Shimbunsha (eds.), *Jiminto Seichokai* [LDP's Policy Affairs
Research Council], Nihon Keizai Shimbunsha, 1983, pp. 165–8.

24 Takeuchi *et al.*, 'Dokengyo ni nottorareta', op. cit. (n. 20), p. 29.

25 Itagaki Hidenori, *'Zoku' no kenkyu* [Study of Diet Member 'Tribes'],

Keizaikai, 1987, p. 75; and Nihon Keizai Shimbunsha, *Jiminto*, op. cit. (n. 23), pp. 165–8.

26   Itagaki, '*Zoku*', op. cit. (n. 25), p. 140.
27   Ogata Katsuyuki, 'Doken gyokai to oshoku' [The construction industry and bribery], *Asahi Jaanaru*, 21 January 1977, p. 24.
28   Kikuchi Hisashi, *Jiminto habatsu* [LDP Cliques], Piipurusha, 1987, p. 119.
29   For a list, see Jiji Tsushinsha Seijibu (eds.), *Takeshita sori 'zen deeta'* [All the Data on Prime Minister Takeshita], Jiji Tsushinsha, 1987, pp. 142–6.
30   *Asahi Shimbun*, 25 December 1987 (evening edition).
31   Kanryo Kiko Kenkyukai, *Kensetsusho zankoku*, op. cit. (n. 17), pp. 70–3, 82–9.
32   *Mainichi Shimbun*, 10 December 1986.
33   Ito, *Zankoku kensetsu*, op. cit. (n. 19), p. 16.
34   Kanryo Kiko Kenkyukai, *Kensetsusho zankoku*, op. cit. (n. 17), pp. 76–8.
35   Honda Yasuharu, 'Sekkei no dekinai gemba kantoku: Kensetsusho' [The Ministry of Construction: an on-site supervisor who cannot design], *Gendai*, February 1974, p. 198.
36   See the discussion on this in Richard Samuels, *The Politics of Regional Policy in Japan*, Princeton University Press, 1983, esp. p. 234.
37   For a study of the Ministry of Finance, particularly its pivotal role in Japan's budgeting process, see John C. Campbell, *Contemporary Japanese Budget Politics*, University of California Press, 1977.
38   Ibid., p. 19.
39   The average ratio of debt to equity among Japan's major corporations is roughly 4 to 1, compared with 1 to 1 in the USA and 2 to 1 in European countries. The ratio of shareholders' equity to total assets is, at 16 to 18 per cent, the lowest among the major industrialised nations – C. T. Ratcliffe, *Kodansha Encyclopaedia of Japan*, vol. 2, 1983, p. 28.
40   Mikuni Akio, *Occasional Paper No. 2: Mikuni on Banking*, Mikuni & Co., 1987, p. 6.
41   Ibid., p. 6.
42   Jin Ikko, *Okura kanryo:cho-eriito shudan no jinmyaku to yabo* [Ministry of Finance Bureaucrats: Networks and Ambitions of a Super-Elite Group], Kodansha, 1982, p. 139; and Kanryo Kiko Kenkyukai (eds.), *Shin Okurasho zankoku monogatari* [The Inside Story of the Ministry of Finance, Part 2], Eeru Shuppansha, 1980, pp. 39–40.
43   Yamaguchi Jiro, 'Zaisei kochokuka kyanpeen no zasetsu to yosan katei no henyo: tenki to shite no showa 40 nendai zenhanki' [The transformation of the budgetary process: the 'break fiscal rigidification movement' as a turning-point], in Kindai Nihon Kenkyukai (eds.), *Nempo Kindai Nihon Kenkyu*, vol. 8, Yamakawa Shuppansha, 1986, pp. 279–304. For a summing up of the problem and the movement meant to solve it, see Campbell, *Contemporary Budget*, op. cit. (n. 37), pp. 241–50; and Ito Daiichi, *Gendai Nihon kanryosei no bunseki* [Analysis of Japan's Contemporary Bureaucracy], Tokyo Daigaku Shuppankai, 1980, pp. 155–206.
44   Yamaguchi, 'Zaisei kochokuka', op. cit. (n. 43), p. 298.
45   The next failed attempt to expand the discretionary powers of the budget officials was made in 1969 and 1970. This was based on the example of a United States programme, the PPBS (Planning Programming Budgeting System), and was accompanied by numerous translated articles and books, as well as learned studies by instant Japanese experts, and by the dire warnings of ministry officials over the 'irrational' intervention of the LDP

and interest groups. 'Ministry of Finance officials seemed to have in mind a utopia of orderly and efficient planning and policy making, where politicians might play some role in establishing the goals of the nation, but would not get in the way of those responsible for the real work' – Campbell, *Contemporary Budget*, op. cit. (n. 37), pp. 107–9.

46   From 1966 the issue of government bonds first began to be of some minor significance in the management of the post-war economy. But in the 1970s, after the two oil crises, and the slackening of domestic demand caused by the lack of large corporate investments, the budget deficit and interest payments on old bonds necessitated ever larger volumes of government borrowing. Japan's businessmen had become dependent on government stimulation of the economy whenever it slowed down, and such stimulation always came in the shape of a 'demand package' for more public works. By the end of the decade, one-third of the national budget was covered by revenue from government bonds. The problem was, however, much greater because a number of public and semi-public corporations were issuing their own bonds. By 1980 the prime minister, backed up by leaders of the business world, gave priority to reducing the dependency on bonds to manageable proportions. Only in 1987 was this attempt beginning to succeed, thanks to increased tax income from the colossal international profits made by Japan's exporting giants.

47   The most recent misadventure for which the Ministry of Finance has at least been partly blamed, and which has created an impression of incompetence, revolves around an attempt to change the ratio of direct versus indirect taxation (in 1987 three-fourths of all tax revenues came from direct taxes). For this purpose the officials designed a sales tax, comparable to the VAT levied in the European Community. The tax was to be levied on every transaction from manufacturers, wholesalers and retailers, and it involved a complex tax-voucher system to avoid double taxation. Because a large number of categories of goods and services would not be taxed, and numerous groups with LDP protection had to be accommodated with exemptions, the resulting scheme became so tangled and distorted that opposing forces from within the LDP had no difficulty in exploiting the chorus of criticism for getting the proposed law rejected. Much of Japanese domestic politics in the late 1980s is likely to revolve around another attempt to introduce the indirect tax.

48   See Kanryo Kiko Kenkyukai, *Shin Okurasho*, op. cit. (n. 42), p. 106.

49   Ibid., p. 153.

50   Chalmers Johnson, 'MITI and Japanese international economic policy', in R. A. Scalapino (ed.), *The Foreign Policy of Modern Japan*, University of California Press, 1977, pp. 23–45.

51   Chitoshi Yanaga, *Big Business in Japanese Politics*, Yale University Press, 1968, p. 162.

52   Ito, *Gendai Nihon*, op. cit. (n. 43), introduction.

53   This, and other information in this section, is based on interviews and informal conversations with MITI officials conducted over several years.

54   Tawara Kotaro, 'Naze ima "Tanaka" na no ka' [Why 'Tanaka' even now?], *Bungei Shunju*, August 1981, p. 93.

55   This is mentioned in a large body of Japanese literature on the subject. For a summary, see Masumi Junnosuke, *Gendai seiji* [Modern Politics], vol. 1, Tokyo Daigaku Shuppankai, 1985, p. 20.

56   Chalmers Johnson, 'Tanaka Kakuei, structural corruption and the advent

of machine politics in Japan', *Journal of Japanese Studies*, Winter 1986, p. 11.

57 Frank C. Langdon, 'Organised interests in Japan and their influence on political parties', *Pacific Affairs*, vol. 34, no. 3, 1961. See also 'Topikku kaisetsu, seito to toshikin', *Mainichi Shimbun*, 30 November 1955.

58 According to a report of the Ministry of Home Affairs, politicians of all parties had a total registered income of 167.59 billion yen in 1986. This was 15 per cent more than in the previous year. Very little of the income of the opposition comes from business. JCP has the highest (official) income through the subscription of its party paper, *Akahata*, which is predictably Marxist but has a reputation of being more honest than other papers regarding certain issues. The JSP must get its funds from the unions. Only the DSP gets money from business, which is no surprise as it votes with the LDP.

59 'Nosabaru "paatii shoho" oshitsuke ni naku kigyo', *Asahi Shimbun*, 4 September 1984 (evening edition).

60 Walter McLaren, *A Political History of Japan during the Meiji Period*, Allen & Unwin, 1916, pp. 364–70.

61 G. E. Uyehara, *The Political Development of Japan 1867–1909*, Constable, 1910, pp. 266–7.

62 According to several press reports during that time.

63 Johnson, 'Tanaka', op. cit. (n. 56), p. 25.

64 Kikuchi, *Jiminto habatsu*, op. cit. (n. 28), p. 204.

65 Nihon Keizai Shimbunsha, *Jiminto Seichokai*, op. cit. (n. 23), p. 27.

66 'LDP–business negotiations never stop', *Daily Yomiuri*, 29 June 1985.

67 Itagaki, 'Zoku', op. cit. (n. 25). pp. 128–9.

68 Yamaguchi Asao, 'Kishi, Ikeda, Sato shusho no "kinmyaku" rimenshi' [The secret history of the 'money networks' of prime ministers Kishi, Ikeda and Sato], *Hoseki*, April 1976, p. 108.

69 Shimizu Ikko, 'Seizaikai no kage no jitsuryokusha, Kishi Nobusuke no shotai' [The true nature of Kishi Nobusuke, a shadow heavyweight of the political and business world], *Hoseki*, January 1976, esp. pp. 90–8.

70 For an anthology of the most important scandals, see Aritake Shuji, *Seiji to kane to jiken to* [Politics, Money and Scandals], Keizai Oraisha, 1970.

71 Fujiyama Aiichiro was chairman of the Japan Chamber of Commerce and Industry, and served in the Kishi cabinet as foreign minister. He converted his property, even his home, into political funds. But his *habatsu* did not outlast him.

72 For these different methods, and which corporations were the major financial sources for important politicians, see Hatakeyama Takeshi, *Habatsu no uchimaku* [The Inside Story of Political Cliques], Rippu Shobo, 1976, pp. 104–6.

73 In an interview in *Asahi Shimbun*, 20 September 1987.

74 For an account of the origins of the current *habatsu* system, see Masumi, *Gendai seiji*, op. cit. (n. 55), p. 7.

75 Campbell, *Contemporary Budget*, op. cit. (n. 37), p. 257.

76 Hatakeyama, *Habatsu*, op. cit. (n. 72), p. 73.

77 For an account of these different tasks, see Masumi, *Gendai seiji*, op. cit. (n. 55), p. 17.

78 'Seikai ni nadarekomu wakate eriito kanryotachi no dasan to kake' [Calculation and challenge of young élite bureaucrats who rush into the political world], *Shukan Asahi*, 27 June 1986, pp. 23–4. The Ministry of Finance

led with 8 of the candidates, followed by MITI with 5, the Agriculture Ministry with 4 and Construction with 3. Nearly half of these candidates were in their late thirties or early forties and had held no rank higher than section chief or assistant section chief in their former ministries. In the past, only former vice-ministers and directors-general, with few exceptions, would seek an LDP candidacy. This relative youthfulness indicated partly a desire to have enough years left to reach top positions at the current promotion rate in the LDP, and partly disappointment with their careers, especially in the Ministry of Finance.

79   'Tsuyokatta kanryo OB: jimin hireiku meibojun kettei', *Asahi Shimbun*, 18 June 1986.

80   The meeting at which this was decided was held on 4 December 1987.

81   Tanaka himself could ignore the bureaucrats when it suited him, as when the chiefs of the budget and tax bureaux feebly tried to resist his bloated budgets of 1972 and 1973. (In 1972 Tanaka's intervention – shortly after he became prime minister – concerned only the supplementary budget.) But he was often highly solicitous of bureaucratic opinion. See Sakakibara Eisuke, *Nihon o enshutsu suru shin-kanryozo* [A Profile of the New Bureaucrats Who Direct Japan], Yamate Shobo, 1977, p. 105.

82   Fukumoto Kunio, *Kanryo* [Bureaucrats], Kobundo, 1959, pp. 142–3.

83   Mainichi Shimbun Shakaibu, *Kanryo* [Bureaucrats], Mainichi Shimbunsha, 1980, pp. 250–1.

84   'Katadori toben no seifu iin, daijin sasaeru kanryogun', *Yomiuri Shimbun*, 8 October 1986.

85   See Inoguchi Takashi and Iwai Tomoaki, *'Zoku giin' no kenkyu* [A Study of 'Tribe Diet Members'], Nihon Keizai Shimbunsha, 1987, p. 11.

86   Kanryo Kiko Kenkyukai (eds.), *Okurasho zankoku monogatari* [The Inside Story of the Ministry of Finance], Eeru Shuppansha, 1976, pp. 130–1.

87   Tahara Soichiro, *Nihon no kanryo 1980* [Bureaucrats of Japan 1980], Bungei Shunju, 1979, pp. 16–19.

88   The journalist was Gebhard Hielscher, Tokyo correspondent for the *Süd Deutsche Zeitung*.

89   See Chapter 2.

90   Nihon Keizai Shimbunsha, *Jiminto Seichokai*, op. cit. (n. 23), p. 19.

91   Masumi, *Gendai seiji*, op. cit. (n. 55), p. 18.

92   Uchida Genko, 'Taikenteki kanryoron' [A view of the bureaucracy based on personal experience], *Chuo Koron*, May 1970, p. 63.

93   One of the first Japanese studies on the subject even holds that Tanaka should be seen as the beginning of the present *zoku* system. See Inoguchi and Iwai, *'Zoku giin'*, op. cit. (n. 85), p. 20.

94   Membership in a *zoku* also depends on the *habatsu* one has joined. The Tanaka *gundan* is overwhelmingly represented in the largest variety of *zoku* fields with the largest number of *zoku* bosses. It dominates the most popular construction, agriculture and transportation *zoku*. The *habatsu* of Miyazawa, on the other hand, is the least well represented. The *habatsu* of Abe Shintaro is well ensconced in the transportation *zoku*. Nakasone has tried to gain influence in the *zoku* dominated by the Tanaka people. *Kanryoha* members of the LDP naturally gravitate towards the PARC division corresponding to their former ministry, and they are expected to play special mediating roles. They are also expected by their former colleagues to defend their former ministry against unwanted political pressures. Individuals' strength in elections is directly related to their *zoku* position.

Only the very strong can afford to concern themselves with policy matters related to defence and education, since these fields are not lucrative and do not bring in votes (though the defence industry has been known to support certain LDP candidates), with the result that LDP members who influence these fields are those who are rather senior, those who have inherited their constituencies from their fathers or those with strong ideological motivations. Belonging to the defence *zoku* is actually considered to be a liability in elections. Other PARC divisions that are relatively unpopular are those of justice, foreign affairs, labour, science and technology, and environment – Inoguchi and Iwai, '*Zoku giin*', op. cit. (n. 85), pp. 134–47, 150.

95 Ezra N. Suleiman, *Elites in French Society*, Princeton University Press, 1978, p. 4.

96 For an overview of the recent increase in the interpenetration of all realms due to the mobile bureaucrats, see Pierre Birnbaum, *The Heights of Power: An Essay on the Power Elite in France*, University of Chicago Press, 1982, pp. 102–6.

97 Suleiman, *Elites*, op. cit. (n. 95), chapter 6.

98 Birnbaum, *Heights*, op. cit. (n. 96), p. 41.

99 E. N. Suleiman, *Politics, Power, and Bureaucracy in France*, Princeton University Press, 1974, pp. 138–56, 201–32.

6 The Submissive Middle Class

1 See Chapter 11.

2 John C. Campbell, 'Policy conflict and its resolution within the governmental system', in E. S. Krauss, T. P. Rohlen and P. G. Steinhoff (eds.), *Conflict in Japan*, University of Hawaii Press, 1984, p. 316.

3 Rodney Clark, *The Japanese Company*, Yale University Press, 1979, p. 41.

4 Sheldon Garon, *The State and Labor in Modern Japan*, University of California Press, 1987, p. 225.

5 John W. Hall, 'Rule by status in Tokugawa Japan', *Journal of Japanese Studies*, Autumn 1974, pp. 44–5.

6 See Chapter 3.

7 See Harumi Befu, 'Corporate emphasis and patterns of descent in the Japanese family', in R. J. Smith and R. K. Beardsley (eds.), *Japanese Culture*, Aldine, 1962, pp. 34–40.

8 Most Japanese Buddhist priests are not celibate.

9 For an extensive account of the relationship between the authorities and the family, see R. P. Dore, *City Life in Japan*, University of California Press, 1958.

10 Nakane Chie was the first social scientist unambiguously to make this point in her comparisons of the Indian and Japanese social structure, and in her famous study in English, *Japanese Society*, University of California Press, 1970.

11 'Kaisha no chorei de yarukoto' [What the morning meetings in companies are all about], *Shukan Yomiuri*, 3 June 1984, p. 127. According to one compilation, 60 per cent of large companies have company songs.

12 See, for instance, Basil Hall Chamberlain, *Things Japanese*, Tuttle, 1971 (reprint of 1905 edn); or William Griffith, *The Mikado's Empire*, Harper & Brothers, 1876.

13 Chamberlain, *Things Japanese*, op. cit. (n. 12), p. 165.

14 Ishii Ryosuke, *A History of Political Institutions in Japan*, University of Tokyo Press, 1980, p. 42.

15 Kozo Yamamura, *Economic Policy in Postwar Japan*, University of California Press, 1967, p. 163.

16 'Kyugekina endaka de shitauke ijime', *Nihon Keizai Shimbun*, 19 May 1986.

17 Felix Twaalfhoven and Tomohisa Hattori, *The Supporting Role of Small Japanese Enterprises*, Indivers Research, Netherlands, 1982.

18 For the best account of the recent legal history of female employment in Japan, and an excellent summary of the official view of working women, see Frank K. Upham, *Law and Social Change in Postwar Japan*, Harvard University Press, 1987, pp. 124–65.

19 Ibid., pp. 150–1.

20 Nihon Keizai Shimbunsha (eds.), *Jiminto Seichokai* [LDP's Policy Affairs Research Council], Nihon Keizai Shimbunsha, 1983, p. 164.

21 Masukomi Kanren Sangyo Rodo Kumiai Kyoto Kaigi (eds.), *Masukomi 1970*, Rodo Jumposha, 1969, p. 136.

22 The pioneering and, to my knowledge, still the best treatment of this phenomenon is Daniel Boorstin, *The Image*, Atheneum, 1961.

23 Tahara Soichiro, *Dentsu*, Asahi Shimbunsha, 1984, p. 17.

24 For a list of the more spectacular instances, see Oshita Eiji, 'Sogo "joho" shosha Dentsu no tabuu' [The taboos of Dentsu, a general 'information' trading company], *Tsukuru*, December 1977, p. 137; and Tahara, *Dentsu*, op. cit. (n. 23), pp. 40–4.

25 Honda Yasuharu, 'Dentsu no himitsu' [The secret of Dentsu], *Shukan Bunshun*, 28 July 1977, p. 37; and Tahara, *Dentsu*, op. cit. (n. 23), p. 37.

26 Kitazawa Shun, *Zankoku kokoku gyokai senso* [Cruel Advertising Industry War], Eeru Shuppansha, 1987, p. 26.

27 Mikami Hiroshi, 'Genron no jiyu o hitei suru Dentsu' [Dentsu denies freedom of speech], in Ino Kenji (ed.), *Dentsu kogairon*, Nisshin Hodo, 1971, pp. 107–8.

28 Ino Kenji, 'Magarikado ni kita Dentsu teikoku shugi' [The turning point of Dentsu's imperialism], ibid., pp. 50 ff.

29 Masukomi Kanren Sangyo Rodo Kumiai Kyoto Kaigi (eds.), *Masukomi 1971*, Rodo Jumposha, 1971, p. 292; also Ino, 'Magarikado', op. cit. (n. 28), p. 39.

30 The reporter is Sakai Sadao. Cited in Kogai Shuzai-kisha Guruppu (eds.), *Osen hanzai o tsuikyu suru* [Chasing Pollution Crimes], Ijiyakugyo Shimpo, 1971, pp. 242–43. See also Suetsugu Seiji, 'Dentsu ni yoru masukomi sosa: sono haikei to konnichiteki yakuwari' [Dentsu's manoeuvring of mass media: its background and present-day role], *Tsukuru*, November 1973, p. 80.

31 Ino, 'Magarikado', op. cit. (n. 28), p. 59.

32 Known as the *kaikiri* system.

33 Domei Tsushinsha, which collaborated with the Army and the government, was created from a merger between Dentsu (a telegraph and news company as well as an advertising agency for the first third of the century) and a news agency run by the press. For more details of Dentsu's wartime connections, relevant to its post-war success, see Chapter 14.

34 Fujita Haruo, 'Dentsu no beeru o hagu' [Unveiling Dentsu], in Ino, *Dentsu kogairon*, op. cit. (n. 27), p. 133.

35 Op. cit. (n. 21). For Kyodo's dependence on the authorities, see also Ino, 'Magarikado', op. cit. (n. 28), p. 41.

36 Oshita, 'Sogo "joho" ', op. cit. (n. 24), pp. 145–6.
37 Kitazawa, *Zankoku*, op. cit. (n. 26), p. 46.
38 Ibid., p. 54.
39 Ibid., p. 55; and Uji Yoshio, 'Kokoku gyokai wa "kin no tamago" o mitsukerareru ka' [Can the advertising industry find the 'golden egg'?], *Purejidento*, October 1986, p. 202.

7 Nurses of the People

1 Irwin Scheiner, 'Benevolent lords and honorable peasants: rebellion and peasant consciousness in Tokugawa Japan', in Tetsuo Najita and Irwin Scheiner (eds.), *Japanese Thought in the Tokugawa Period*, University of Chicago Press, 1978, p. 46.
2 Richard H. Mitchell, *Censorship in Imperial Japan*, Princeton University Press, 1983, p. 82.
3 Ibid., p. 16.
4 A promise some of the intelligentsia had read into the first article of the 'Charter Oath', proclaimed in name of the emperor by the new government in 1868. See Matsumoto Sannosuke, 'The roots of political disillusionment: public and private in Japan', in J. V. Koschmann (ed.), *Authority and the Individual in Japan*, University of Tokyo Press, 1978.
5 Sheldon M. Garon, 'The imperial bureaucracy and labor policy in postwar Japan', *Journal of Asian Studies*, May 1984, p. 442.
6 Keishicho-shi Hensan Iinkai, *Keishicho-shi: Meiji-hen* [History of the Tokyo Metropolitan Police Agency: Meiji Period], 1959, pp. 50–1.
7 D. Eleanor Westney, 'The emulation of western organisations in Meiji Japan: the case of the Paris prefecture of police and the Keishi-choo', *Journal of Japanese Studies*, Summer 1982, p. 315.
8 Ibid., pp. 316–17.
9 See Chapter 14.
10 Walter L. Ames, *Police and Community in Japan*, University of California Press, 1981, p. 23.
11 Lawrence Ward Beer, *Freedom of Expression in Japan*, Kodansha International, 1984, pp. 66–8.
12 Captain Heinrich Friedrich Wilhelm Hoehn, who served as adviser to the Home Ministry between 1885 and 1891. See Ames, *Police*, op. cit. (n. 10), p. 23.
13 This information is based on personal interviews with policemen and specialists on the subject in the mid-1970s.
14 This explanation is that of an informant acquainted with Japanese police practices.
15 Ames, *Police*, op. cit. (n. 10), p. 135.
16 David H. Bayley, personal communication. See also his *Forces of Order: Police Behavior in Japan and the United States*, University of California Press, 1976.
17 Ibid., pp. 134–40.
18 William Clifford, *Crime Control in Japan*, Lexington Books, 1976.
19 Of the 75,163 people who received prison sentences in 1986, only 32,015 went to prison.
20 Some 42 of every 100,000 of the population, compared with 158 in the USA and between 80 and 90 in Britain. Holland has the least, with roughly 20 per 100,000.

21 The committee's report was published by Seihosha in 1984: Tokyo 3
    Bengoshikai Godo Daiyo-kangoku Chosa Iinkai (eds.), *Nureginu* [Falsely
    Accused]. A detailed interpretive account of the committee's findings and
    the meeting of the victims can be found in Igarashi Futaba, 'Koshite "jihaku"
    saserata: daiyo kangoku to enzai' [How people have been forced to confess
    their crimes: substitute prison and false charges], *Sekai*, February 1984, pp.
    220–32. For a ten-year-older account, see Aochi Shin, 'Ayamatta saiban o
    sabaku' [Criticism of misjudgements by the courts], *Ushio*, April 1973.
22 See also Aochi, *Ayamatta*, op. cit. (n. 22), p. 204.
23 The police may keep a suspect for 48 hours before notifying the prosecutors,
    who are then given 24 hours to ask a judge for authorisation for 20 days'
    detention, before a charge is filed.
24 Beer, *Freedom*, op. cit. (n. 11), p. 159.
25 In this context, see Helen Merrell Lynd, *On Shame and the Search for
    Identity*, Routledge & Kegan Paul, 1958, pp. 65–6.
26 *Mainichi Shimbun*, 17 February 1985; and *Asahi Shimbun*, 26 February 1985.
27 For many examples of outrages committed in substitute prisons, see also Goto
    Shojiro, *Saiban o tatakau* [Fighting the Courts], Mainichi Shimbunsha,
    1984, pp. 17–18.
28 Igarashi, 'Koshite "jihaku" ', op. cit. (n. 22), p. 221.
29 Ibid., p. 223.
30 Nakamura Ryuji, the accused in the 'Tsuchida cigarette-tin bomb' case.
31 See also Tim Pearce, Reuters dispatch, August 1984.
32 Maesaka Toshiyuki, *Enzai to gohan* [False Charges and Misjudgements],
    Tabata Shoten, 1982; Hogaku Seminaa zokan (eds.), *Nihon no enzai* [False
    Charges in Japan], Nihon Hyoronsha, 1983.
33 Matsumoto Hitoshi, *Koban no ura wa yami* [The Darkness behind the Police
    Box], Daisan Shokan, 1987, chapter 7; Ise Akifumi, *Nippon keisatsu zankoku
    monogatari* [The Inside Story of the Japanese Police], Eeru Shuppansha,
    1985, chapter 3.
34 Matsumoto, *Koban*, op. cit. (n. 34), chapter 14; and Ise, *Nippon keisatsu*, op.
    cit. (n. 34), pp. 178–9.
35 Menda Sakae, personal communication.
36 Ibid.
37 Ito Hirobumi, 'Some reminiscences of the grant of the new constitution', in
    Okuma Shigenobu (ed.), *Fifty Years of New Japan*, New York, 1909, vol. 1,
    p. 130, as cited in J. L. Huffman, *The Politics of the Meiji Press*, University of
    Hawaii Press, 1980, p. 199.
38 Nitobe Inazo, *Bushido: The Soul of Japan*, Tuttle, 1969 (reprint of 1905 edn),
    p. 34.
39 George Etsujiro Uyehara, *The Political Development of Japan*, Constable,
    1910, p. 24.
40 Kishio Satomi, *Discovery of Japanese Idealism*, Kegan Paul, Trench, Trubner,
    1924, pp. 64–5.
41 Ruth Benedict, *The Chrysanthemum and the Sword*, Houghton Mifflin,
    1946, chapter 5.
42 Dan Fenno Henderson, ' "Contracts" in Tokugawa villages', *Journal of
    Japanese Studies*, Autumn 1974.
43 In 1984, 1,762 murders were committed in Japan, 18,692 in the USA, 1,613
    in the UK and 2,760 in West Germany – *White Paper of the National Police
    Agency*, 1986.

44 2,188 robberies were committed in Japan in 1984, 485,000 in the USA, 24,890 in the UK and 28,000 in West Germany – ibid.
45 Matsumoto, *Koban*, op. cit. (n. 34), pp. 28–43.
46 Bayley, *Forces*, op. cit. (n. 17), p. 152.
47 Tamaki Naoya, former judge of the Osaka High Court, personal communication.
48 Nomura Jiro, *Saiko Saibansho* [The Supreme Court], Kodansha, 1987, pp. 144–5.
49 Ames, *Police*, op. cit. (n. 10), p. 143.
50 Ibid., p. 144.
51 Ibid., p. 163.
52 Matsumoto, *Koban*, op. cit. (n. 34), pp. 3, 63, 207.
53 Garon, 'Imperial bureaucracy', op. cit. (n. 5), p. 452.
54 Nomura, *Saiko Saibansho*, op. cit. (n. 49), p. 124.
55 Ibid., p. 126.
56 Bayley, *Forces*, op. cit. (n. 17), pp. 73–81.
57 Ames, *Police*, op. cit. (n. 10), p. 145.
58 For a detailed account of the experimentation with precedents in social control during the summit, see also Hosaka Kunio, *Shin: Keisatsu kokka Nippon* [Police State Japan], Shakai Hyoronsha, 1986.
59 Ames, *Police*, op. cit. (n. 10), p. 219. See also Chapter 14.
60 Ibid., p. 220.
61 Matsumoto, *Koban*, op. cit. (n. 34), chapter 5.

8   Keeping the Law under Control

1 Ernst Cassirer, *The Myth of the State*, Yale University Press, 1946, pp. 74–5.
2 John W. Hall, *Government and Local Power in Japan*, Princeton University Press, 1966, pp. 26, 34.
3 Ryosuke Ishii, *A History of Political Institutions in Japan*, University of Tokyo Press, 1980, p. 9.
4 Ibid., p. 10.
5 Kiyomi Morioka, *Religion in Changing Japanese Society*, University of Tokyo Press, 1975, p. 7.
6 George B. Sansom, *Japan: A Short Cultural History*, Cresset Press, 1952, p. 183.
7 This was the Taiho code, soon supplanted by the Yoro code of 718. See Ishii, *Institutions*, op. cit. (n. 3), pp. 22 ff.
8 Ibid., p. 23.
9 And that after already having been significantly 'adjusted' to actual practices. See Chapter 5. See also Yamamura Kozo, *Economic Policy in Postwar Japan*, University of California Press, 1967, chapters 4, 5.
10 John Bowle, *Western Political Thought*, Cape, 1947, p. 189.
11 John Dickinson (trans.), *The Statesman's Book of John of Salisbury*, Russell, 1963 (reprint of 1927 edn), p. 259.
12 The *Gukansho*, written by Jien in 1219; see Delmer Brown and Ichiro Ishida, *The Future and the Past*, University of California Press, 1979, p. 26.
13 Cassirer, *Myth*, op. cit. (n. 1), p. 97.
14 Frederick B. Katz, *The Mind of the Middle Ages*, University of Chicago Press, 1953, chapter 8.

15   Cassirer, *Myth*, op. cit. (n. 1), p. 104.
16   Bowle, *Western Political Thought*, op. cit. (n. 10), p. 180.
17   Hugh Trevor-Roper, *Renaissance Essays*, Secker & Warburg, 1985.
18   Robert M. Spaulding, *Imperial Japan's Higher Civil Service Examinations*, Princeton University Press, 1967, pp. 60–1.
19   Noda Yoshiyuki, *Introduction to Japanese Law*, University of Tokyo Press, 1976, p. 44.
20   Kawashima Takeyoshi, *Nihonjin no ho ishiki* [The Legal Awareness of Japanese People], Iwanami Shoten, 1967, p. 49.
21   Carol Gluck, *Japan's Modern Myths*, Princeton University Press, 1985, p. 119.
22   Kawakami Hajime, in *Kawakami Hajime chosakushu* [Collected Works of Kawakami Hajime], vol. 8, Chikuma Shobo, 1964, p. 190.
23   Yanaihara Tadao, 'Kokka no riso' [Ideals of the state], *Chuo Koron*, September 1937, p. 8, cited in Matsumoto Sannosuke, 'The roots of political disillusionment', in J. Victor Koschmann (ed.), *Authority and the Individual in Japan*, University of Tokyo Press, 1978, p. 44.
24   Watanabe Yozo, *Gendai kokka to gyoseiken* [The Modern State and its Administrative Rights], Tokyo Daigaku Shuppankai, 1972, p. 312; Ito Daiichi, *Gendai Nihon kanryosei no bunseki* [Analysis of Bureaucracy in Contemporary Japan], Tokyo Daigaku Shuppankai, 1980, p. 83.
25   Watanabe Yozo, *Ho to iu mono no kangaekata* [The Way of Thought Called Law], Iwanami Shoten, 1959, p. 178.
26   Ibid., p. 183.
27   Watanabe Yasuo, 'Sengo ha kanryoron' [On post-war bureaucrats], *Chuo Koron*, September 1960, p. 209.
28   Noda, *Introduction*, op. cit. (n. 19), p. 159.
29   Ibid., p. 159.
30   See Chapter 3.
31   For an account of the famous pollution litigation cases, and an excellent analysis of the reaction to it by the bureaucrats and the resulting role of the law, see Frank K. Upham, *Law and Social Change in Postwar Japan*, Harvard University Press, 1987, chapters 2, 6.
32   Tanaka Hideo, *The Japanese Legal System*, University of Tokyo Press, 1976, pp. 255–7.
33   This interpretation is very eloquently made in the influential writing of Kawashima Takeyoshi; see his *Nihonjin no ho ishiki*, op. cit. (n. 20).
34   The attitudes of neighbours have generally made it very difficult for one neighbour to resort to litigation against another.
35   Jeffrey Mass, personal communication. Such judicial practices referred to custom and precedent rather than universally applicable concepts of law.
36   The Justice Ministry received 0.7 per cent and the courts 0.4 per cent of the national budget in 1986. During a one-and-a-half-hour special programme on NHK television on 9 May 1987, a former chief justice of the Supreme Court, a former public prosecutor-general, a former president of the federated bar associations, a professor and a famous reporter all agreed that the difficulty of the LTRI entrance exams has caused the current problem of a shortage of prosecutors. But the panellists admired the Japanese for preferring conciliation to litigation, and concluded in unison that 'sincerity' was the quality most required of members of the judiciary.
37   John O. Haley, 'The myth of the reluctant litigant', *Journal of Japanese Studies*, Summer 1978, p. 386.

38 There were 1,531 judges in 1890, and 2,808 in 1987.
39 As of 26 September 1986. Source: Nichibenren.
40 The Japanese figure is for 1985, the others for 1984.
41 These points were made by an experienced lawyer, a representative of the Seihokyo, an organisation described below, which opposes increased bureaucratic control over the judicial system and its politicisation by LDP interests.
42 'Saibanzata wa iya . . .' [No to Litigation], *Asahi Shimbun*, 2 December 1985.
43 For a history of this, see J. A. A. Stockwin, *Japan: Divided Politics in a Growth Economy*, Weidenfeld & Nicolson, 1982 (2nd edn), pp. 205 ff.
44 Upham, *Law*, op. cit. (n. 31), p. 176.
45 Ito, *Gendai Nihon*, op. cit. (n. 24), pp. 82–3.
46 Tahara Soichiro, *Nihon no kanryo 1980* [Bureaucrats of Japan 1980], Bungei Shunju, 1979, p. 272.
47 Noda, *Introduction*, op. cit. (n. 19), p. 148.
48 Miyamoto Yasuaki, *Kiki ni tatsu shiho* [Justice in Crisis], Chobunsha, 1978, p. 98.
49 Ushiomi Toshitaka, 'Sengo no Nihon shakai to horitsuka, 1, saibankan' [Post-war Japanese society and jurists, part 1, the judge], in Ushiomi Toshitaka (ed.), *Gendai no horitsuka, Iwanami koza gendaiho*, vol. 6, Iwanami Shoten, 1966, p. 67.
50 Nomura Jiro, *Saiko saibansho* [The Supreme Court], Kodansha, 1987, p. 75.
51 Miyamoto, *Kiki*, op. cit. (n. 48), p. 98.
52 Tamaki Naoya, personal communication.
53 Ibid. See also Aoki Eigoro, *Saibankan no senso sekinin* [The War Responsibility of Judges], Nihon Hyoronsha, 1963.
54 Ushiomi, 'Sengo no Nihon', op. cit. (n. 49), p. 65.
55 Yonehara Itaru, Kazahaya Yasoji and Shiota Shobei, *Tokko keisatsu kokusho* [Black Paper on the 'Thought Police'], Shin Nippon Shuppansha, 1977, pp. 227–30.
56 Ushiomi, 'Sengo no Nihon', op. cit. (n. 49), p. 84.
57 For the prevalence of intermarriage in the judicial field, especially in the prosecutors' office, see Kubo Hiroshi, *Nihon no kensatsu* [Public Prosecution in Japan], Kodansha, 1986, p. 189.
58 Nomura, *Saiko saibansho*, op. cit. (n. 50), p. 67.
59 *Asahi Evening News*, 9 November 1987.
60 Nomura, *Saiko saibansho*, op. cit. (n. 50), p. 140.
61 Tamaki Naoya, personal communication.
62 Immediately after the occupation ended, conservative politicians urged revision of the constitution on the basis that it had been imposed and was partly inimical to Japanese customs. A year after its formation, the LDP instituted a commission to study the matter, and until 1964 many proposals for alteration were made. The commission did not recommend any course of action as it was clear that the controversy surrounding serious attempts for revision would be too great for the government to handle. Important politicians (such as the late Kishi Nobosuke) have continued to propagate the need for revision. Former prime minister Nakasone is also known as an advocate for Japan's 'own' constitution, but he was well aware of the impossibility of reintroducing the issue during his relatively long term in office. For a good account of the way in which the constitution was imposed, see Stockwin, *Divided Politics*, op. cit. (n. 43), pp. 197–202.
63 Nomura, *Saiko saibansho*, op. cit. (n. 50), p. 67.

64 Judge Miyamoto Yasuaki; see his *Kiki ni tatsu shiho*, op. cit. (n. 48); and Fukuda Akira, 'Saikosai to Seihokyo wa dochira no iibun ga tadashii ka' [Which is right, the Supreme Court or Seihokyo?], *Gendai*, June 1971, pp. 98–106.

65 Fukuda, 'Saikosai', op. cit. (n. 64), p. 103.

66 Nomura, *Saiko Saibansho*, op. cit. (n. 50), p. 77.

67 Fukuda, 'Saikosai', op. cit. (n. 64), pp. 102–3.

68 Nomura, *Saiko saibansho*, op. cit. (n. 50), p. 78.

69 Ibid., p. 79.

70 Shimizu Makoto, 'Senzen no horitsuka ni tsuite no ich-ikosatsu' [A reflection on pre-war jurists], in Ushiomi, *Gendai no horitsuka*, op. cit. (n. 49), p. 12.

71 Activist lawyer, personal communication.

72 Seihokyo representative, personal communication.

73 Tamaki Naoya, personal communication.

74 Ibid.

75 Kubo, *Nihon no kensatsu*, op. cit. (n. 57), p. 41.

76 Between 1981 and 1985 the prosecutor won in 99.991 to 99.995 per cent of all cases, according to the 1986 white paper on crime.

77 Asahi Shimbun (eds.), *Mujitsu wa muzai ni* [The Innocent Should Be Found Not Guilty], Suzusawa Shoten, 1984, pp. 221–7.

78 Ushiomi Toshitaka, 'Sengo no Nihon shakai to horitsuka, 2, kensatsukan' [Post-war Japanese society and jurists, part 2, the public prosecutor], in Ushiomi, *Gendai no horitsuka*, op. cit. (n. 49), pp. 108–10.

79 Gordon Mark Berger, *Parties out of Power in Japan, 1931–1941*, Princeton University Press, 1977, p. 205.

80 Richard H. Mitchell, *Thought Control in Prewar Japan*, Cornell University Press; Berger, *Parties*, op. cit. (n. 79); and Richard Storry, *The Double Patriots*, Chatto & Windus, 1957.

81 Tahara, *Nihon no kanryo*, op. cit. (n. 46), p. 257.

82 Kubo, *Nihon no kensatsu*, op. cit. (n. 57), p. 145.

83 Noda, *Introduction*, op. cit. (n. 19), p. 149.

84 Kubo, *Nihon no kensatsu*, op. cit. (n. 57), p. 42.

85 The Shiratori decision of the Supreme Court in 1975 can be said to have opened the door for a limited number of retrials, mostly involving false original confessions.

86 Chalmers Johnson, *Conspiracy at Matsukawa*, University of California Press, 1972, p. 149.

87 Ito Takashi, personal communication.

88 Tahara, *Nihon no kanryo*, op. cit. (n. 46), p. 273; Kubo, *Nihon no kensatsu*, op. cit. (n. 57), pp. 137–42; Murofushi Tetsuro, 'Kensatsu to seiji' [The public prosecution and politics], in *Gendai no kensatsu* (*Hogaku Seminaa* special issue), Nihon Hyoronsha, August 1981, p. 270.

89 Murofushi, 'Kensatsu to seiji', op. cit. (n. 88), p. 270.

90 Kubo, *Nihon no kensatsu*, op. cit. (n. 57), p. 70.

91 Tamaki Kazuo, who was involved with the *Toshi Jaanaru* money scandal. He died in January 1987.

92 Tahara, *Nihon no kanryo*, op. cit. (n. 46), pp. 277–82.

93 Kubo, *Nihon no kensatsu*, op. cit. (n. 57), p. 15.

94 Ibid., pp. 99–112.

95 John O. Haley, 'Sheathing the sword of justice in Japan: an essay on law without sanctions', *Journal of Japanese Studies*, Summer 1982, p. 266.

96 Ibid., pp. 267–8.
97 *Asahi Shimbun*, 15 December 1986 (evening edition).

9   The Management of Reality

1 See Chapter 14.
2 Kiyohara Jumpei, *Japan Times*, date unknown.
3 The *honne–tatemae* dichotomy is becoming established in analyses of Japan. Depending on how it is applied, it sometimes differs from what I have called 'formal' and 'substantial' reality.
4 Christie W. Kiefer, 'The *danchi zoku* and the evolution of metropolitan mind', in Lewis Austin (ed.), *Japan: The Paradox of Progress*, Yale University Press, 1976, p. 281.
5 Thomas P. Rohlen, *Japan's High Schools*, University of California Press, 1983, p. 268.
6 Maruyama Masao, 'Japanese thought', reprinted in *Journal of Social and Political Ideas in Japan*, April 1964, p. 42.
7 Rohlen, *High Schools*, op. cit. (n. 5), p. 251.
8 Watsuji Tetsuro, 'Keeberu sensei' [Professor Koeber], *Watsuji Tetsuro zenshu*, vol. 6, Iwanami Shoten, 1962, p. 25.
9 For an extensive account of this debate, see Germaine A. Hoston, *Marxism and the Crisis of Development in Prewar Japan*, Princeton University Press, 1986.
10 Edward Seidensticker, 'The pulverisers', *Encounter*, June 1970, p. 83.
11 Maruyama Masao, *Studies in the Intellectual History of Tokugawa Japan*, Tokyo University Press, 1974, p. 170.
12 Among many others, see Suzuki Takao in *Tozasareta gengo* [The Isolated Language], Shinchosha, 1975. For a most erudite attack on this type of nonsense, see Peter N. Dale, *The Myth of Japanese Uniqueness*, Croom Helm, 1986, esp. p. 89.
13 For an excellent account of the Zen influence on political orthodoxies of the Tokugawa period, see Herman Ooms, *Tokugawa Ideology*, Princeton University Press, 1985, pp. 122–43.
14 See Chapter 1.
15 Derk Bodde, 'Harmony and conflict in Chinese philosophy', in H. G. Creel (ed.), *Studies in Chinese Thought*, University of Chicago Press, 1953.
16 Creel, *Chinese Thought*, University of Chicago Press, 1953, chapter 3.
17 This is from Confucius, *Analects*, 11.23.3. See also 14.17–18.
18 Creel, *Chinese Thought*, op. cit. (n. 16), chapter 3.
19 Ishida Takeshi makes the same point in his work. See, for instance, *Japanese Political Culture*, Transaction Books, 1983, p. 12.
20 Ruth Benedict, *The Chrysanthemum and the Sword*, Houghton Mifflin, 1946, p. 41.
21 Yasuo Wakatsuki, 'Unpleasant, other side to Japanese', *Japan Times*, 25 May 1980.
22 This happened to a cartoon Ranan Lurie made while employed by the Asahi, showing Syria in the form of a Lion who had swallowed the Lebanese leader Gemayel – Ranan Lurie, personal communication.

10   Power in the Guise of Culture

1 See, for example, Zevedei Barbu, *Society, Culture and Personality*, Blackwell, 1971, p. 75.

2   Peter Berger, *The Sacred Canopy*, Doubleday, 1967.
3   Ian Buruma, 'We Japanese', *New York Review of Books*, 12 March 1987.
4   Ibid.
5   Asahi Shimbunsha Chosa Kenkyushitsu, *Nihon no kokusaika e no ichi-kosatsu* [A Study of the Internationalisation of Japan], 1987, p. 7.
6   These were ideals that before the Tokugawa settlement probably were only partly reflected in reality. There are indications that, at least in some regions and some stretches over the nearly five centuries during which warrior society developed, there were fairly independent-minded samurai who sold their services to the highest bidder. After the consolidation of the Tokugawa regime, such samurai mobility was largely out of the question. To facilitate their control, the *bakufu* power-holders designed rules that aimed to fix every person in a permanent station in life. The Laws Governing the Military Houses, promulgated in 1615, forbade outsiders to reside in a particular domain, forbade the construction of new strongholds, ordered the reporting of any innovations or factional activity in neighbouring domains, required the notification of marriages and among many more stipulations listed the type of dress to be worn by people of different rank and prescribed other behaviour deemed proper to their station in life. See R. Tsunoda, W. T. de Bary and D. Keene (eds.), *Sources of Japanese Tradition*, Columbia University Press, 1958, pp. 335–8.
7   Herman Ooms, *Tokugawa Ideology*, Princeton University Press, 1985, chapter 4. I am much indebted to this brilliant study of the various ideological constructs of the early Tokugawa period. It is exceptional in its emphasis on the political significance of this thought, and presents a marvellously clarifying perspective on it. See also George Elison, *Deus Destroyed*, Harvard University Press, 1973, p. 227.
8   Ooms, *Ideology*, op. cit. (n. 7), p. 130.
9   Ibid., p. 130.
10 Elison, *Deus*, op. cit. (n. 7), pp. 226–7.
11 Yamamoto Tsunetomo, *Hagakure*, trans. William Scott Wilson, Kodansha International, 1979, p. 17. Donald Richie has called the *Hagakure* the Emily Post of the samurai age, since it is preoccupied with the minutiae of etiquette.
12 Arthur Koestler, *The Lotus and the Robot*, Hutchinson, 1960, p. 208.
13 Noru Hirano, *Daily Yomiuri*, 2 February 1983.
14 Delmer Brown, *Nationalism in Japan*, University of California Press, 1955, pp. 55–6.
15 Bob Tadashi Wakabayashi, *Anti-Foreignism and Western Learning in Early Modern Japan*, Harvard University Press, 1986, p. 37; and David M. Earl, *Emperor and Nation in Japan*, University of Washington Press, 1964, pp. 74–6.
16 Earl, *Emperor and Nation*, op. cit. (n. 15), p. 78.
17 Robert Frage and Thomas P. Rohlen, 'The future of a tradition: Japanese spirit in the 1980s', in Lewis Austin (ed.), *Japan: The Paradox of Progress*, Yale University Press, 1976, p. 264.
18 Ibid.
19 Ooms, *Ideology*, op. cit. (n. 7), p. 290.
20 Richard H. Mitchell, *Censorship in Imperial Japan*, Princeton University Press, 1983, p. 8.

21 As quoted in Satomi Kishio, *Discovery of Japanese Idealism*, Kegan Paul, Trench, Trubner, 1924, p. 73.

22 Ooms, *Ideology*, op. cit. (n. 7), p. 247.

23 The common interpretation that Hayashi Razan established the neo-Confucian orthodoxy at the behest of the founder of Tokugawa shogunate is based on a Hayashi boast. The orthodoxy only emerged in the later part of the seventeenth century. See Ooms, *Ideology*, op. cit. (n. 7), pp. 72 ff., 287.

24 Ogyu Sorai is an interesting subject of debate among historians of Tokugawa thought. He appeared to condone dishonest manipulation by the ruler as long as this served to achieve the moral purposes of the Confucian Way. Maruyama Masao, Japan's highly respected major post-war political theorist, has likened Sorai to Machiavelli, because of having discovered political theory as distinct from political ethics. But others question whether Ogyu's thought did in fact separate politics from morality and nature. See Maruyama Masao, *Studies in the Intellectual History of Tokugawa Japan*, University of Tokyo Press, 1974, p. 83; and Tetsuo Najita, 'Reconsidering Maruyama Masao's studies', *Japan Interpreter*, Spring 1976, pp. 97–108.

25 Tetsuo Najita, 'Methods and analysis in the conceptual portrayal of Tokugawa intellectual history', in Tetsuo Najita and Irwin Scheiner (eds.), *Japanese Thought in the Tokugawa Period*, University of Chicago Press, 1978, p. 14.

26 See Chapter 11.

27 Earl, *Emperor and Nation*, op. cit. (n. 15), pp. 70–2.

28 Masahide Bito, 'Ogyuu Sorai and the distinguishing features of Japanese Confucianism', in Najita and Scheiner, *Japanese Thought*, op. cit. (n. 25), p. 157.

29 Basil Hall Chamberlain, *Things Japanese*, Tuttle, 1971 (reprint of 1905 edn), p. 1.

30 Reinhard Bendix, *Kings or People*, University of California Press, 1978, p. 440.

31 The so-called *Morrison* Incident of 1837 involving the merchant vessel *Morrison*.

32 Nakajima Hirotari, as quoted in Wakabayashi, *Anti-Foreignism*, op. cit. (n. 15), p. 142.

33 Wakabayashi, *Anti-Foreignism*, op. cit. (n. 15), pp. 143–4. Also David Titus, *Palace and Politics in Prewar Japan*, Columbia University Press, 1974, p. 36.

34 Nishi Amane, 'On religion', part one, in William Reynolds Braisted, Adachi Yasushi and Kikuchi Yuuji (eds.), *Meiroku Zasshi*, University of Tokyo Press, 1976, pp. 50–2, 59–62, 73–5.

35 Brown, *Nationalism*, op. cit. (n. 14), pp. 101–3.

36 Takeshi Ishida, *Japanese Political Culture*, Transaction Books, 1983, p. 69.

37 Hiroshi Wagatsuma, 'Problems of cultural identity in modern Japan', in George De Vos and Lola Romanucci-Ross (eds.), *Ethnic Identity*, Mayfield, 1975, p. 315.

38 Delmer Brown and Ichiroo Ishida, *The Future and the Past*, University of California Press, 1979, pp. 8, 210.

39 Wakabayashi, *Anti-Foreignism*, op. cit. (n. 15), p. 13; and Earl, *Emperor and Nation*, op. cit. (n. 15), pp. 91–6.

40 Mitchell, *Censorship*, op. cit. (n. 20), pp. 36–7.

41 Mikiso Hane, *Peasants, Rebels and Outcasts*, Pantheon, 1982, p. 58.

42 *History of the Empire of Japan*, Dai Nippon Tosho KK, 1893, p. 18. This book was prepared for the World's Columbian Exposition, Chicago, 1893.

43 Carol Gluck, *Japan's Modern Myths*, Princeton University Press, 1985, pp. 36–7.

44 Kosaka Masaaki, *Japanese Thought in the Meiji Era*, Pan-Pacific Press, p. 364.

45 George Etsujiro Uyehara, *The Political Development of Japan*, Constable, 1910, p. 7; subsequent references are from pp. 13, 17, 23, 27, 197.

46 Richard J. Smethurst, *A Social Basis for Prewar Japanese Militarism*, University of California Press, 1974.

47 Cited in Richard Storry, *The Double Patriots*, Chatto & Windus, 1957, p. 5, n. 3.

48 See the excellent account of samurai and *yakuza* imagery in films and other forms of entertainment in Ian Buruma, *A Japanese Mirror: Heroes and Villains of Japanese Culture*, Cape, 1984, chapters 9, 10.

49 The first lengthy and thoroughly considered treatment of this phenomenon can be found in Peter N. Dale, *The Myth of Japanese Uniqueness*, Croom Helm, 1986. Dale also gives an excellent account of the psychological consequences of *nihonjinron* rhetoric.

50 Nakasone Yasuhiro (speech as transcribed by the editors), *Chuo Koron*, November 1986, p. 162.

51 Nakasone has clearly acknowledged his intellectual debt to Watsuji Tetsuro in a speech given on 31 July 1983 at Takasaki High School. See *Hato o koete* [Overcoming the Waves], Seisaku Kagaku Kenkyujo, 1986, p. 262.

52 Watsuji Tetsuro, *Climate and Culture*, trans. Geoffrey Bownas, Hokuseido Press, 1961, esp. pp. 61, 135–56.

53 According to specialists there are some biological differences, such as a different rate of alcohol metabolism. But these are very subtle and of no practical importance in the context of this issue.

54 This notion was spread by wartime propaganda, so as to help reconcile the population with the poor food they were offered. Iwamochi's speech was delivered at the Foreign Correspondents' Club of Japan, 19 May 1982. See also Kumon Shumpei, 'Nationalism of long intestine', *Japan Times*, 15 February 1988.

55 See Tsunoda Tadanobu, 'The left cerebral hemisphere of the brain and the Japanese language', *Japan Foundation Newsletter*, April–May 1978. In Japanese: *Nihonjin no no* [The Japanese Brain], Taishukan Shoten, 1978.

56 For a thorough summing up of the relevant theories of Kindaichi Haruhiko, Suzuki Takao and Watanabe Shoichi, see Roy Andrew Miller, *Japan's Modern Myth*, Weatherhill, 1982. Also Dale, *Myth*, op. cit. (n. 49).

57 Earl, *Emperor and Nation*, op. cit. (n. 15), p. 79.

58 Yamamoto Shichihei, 'Modern Japanese returning to Tokugawa values', *Japan Times*, 20 January 1980. His earlier pseudonymous best-seller was: Isaiah Bendasan, *The Japanese and the Jews*, Weatherhill, 1972.

59 Some examples of this effort: Umesao Tadao, *Bunmei no seitai shikan* [On the Ecological History of Civilisation], Chuo Koronsha, 1967; Murakami Yasusuke, Kumon Shumpei and Sato Seizaburo, *Bumei to shite no ie-shakai* [Ie Society as a Pattern of Civilisation], Chuo Koronsha, 1979. In English, see Obayashi Taryo, '*Uji* society and *ie* society from prehistory to medieval times', *Journal of Japanese Studies*, Winter 1985, pp. 3–27, and the four reactions by American Japan scholars following it: Hamaguchi Esyun, 'A contextual model of the Japanese: toward a methodological innovation in

Japan studies', *Journal of Japanese Studies*, Summer 1985, pp. 289–322; and Murakami Yasusuke, '*Ie* society as a pattern of civilisation', *Journal of Japanese Studies*, Summer 1984, pp. 281–363.

60 William Wetherall, *Far East Economic Review*, 19 February 1987, pp. 86–7, for a detailed account of Nakasone's controversial remarks; and the same author in *Japan Times*, 26 November 1986.

61 *Daily Yomiuri*, 1 August 1983. Some officials have objected not only to *katakana* syllabary forms of non-Yamato, especially European, names, but even to Korean and Chinese names that could be written in standard Sino-Japanese characters. In the past Ainu Japanese were forced to Yamatoise their names, and during the colonial period all Korean and Chinese subjects were required to Yamatoise their names under threat of punishment.

62 See all the major Japanese dailies of 13 and 14 July 1987. It is significant that this calculation was made by *Forbes Magazine* in the United States. No Japanese daily followed it up with further investigations.

63 Rodney Clark, *The Japanese Company*, Yale University Press, 1979, pp. 40–1.

64 See Chapters 3 and 5.

65 Murakami, Kumon and Sato, *Bunmei to shite*, op. cit. (n. 59).

66 Nakane Chie, *Japanese Society*, University of California Press, 1970, p. 15; and Dale, *Myth*, op. cit. (n. 49), p. 107.

67 Robert E. Cole, *Work, Mobility and Participation*, University of California Press, 1979, p. 252. Cole remarks that the industrial paternalism was explored by Americans in the first quarter of this century, and dropped as unsatisfactory in the face of the Great Depression and worker militancy.

68 Minami Hiroshi, *Nihonjin no shinri* [The Psychology of the Japanese], Iwanami Shoten, 1953, p. 127.

69 A large number of Japan scholars and more occasional commentators have made this point, giving different reasons for it. Among many others, see Takie Sugiyama Lebra, *Japanese Patterns of Behavior*, University of Hawaii Press, 1976.

70 Edward Seidensticker, personal communication.

71 For a summing up of the methods used in these therapies, see David K. Reynolds, *The Quiet Therapies*, University of Hawaii Press, 1980.

11   The System as Religion

1 Emile Durkheim, *Elementary Forms of the Religious Life*, Free Press, 1965.

2 There is much literature on these 'old' new religions. I have both relied on my memory and referred to Carmen Blacker, 'Millenarian aspects of the new religions in Japan', in Donald H. Shively (ed.), *Tradition and Modernisation in Japanese Culture*, Princeton University Press, 1971.

3 'Jinsei annai' [Life guide] column, *Yomiuri Shimbun*, date unknown.

4 H. D. Harootunian, 'Between politics and culture', in B. Silberman and H. D. Harootunian (eds.), *Japan in Crisis*, Princeton University Press, 1974, p. 144.

5 Masaharu Anesaki, *History of Japanese Religion*, Kegan Paul, Trench, Trubner, 1930, pp. 201–3.

6 Herman Ooms, *Tokugawa Ideology – Early Constructs, 1570–1680*, Princeton University Press, 1985, p. 30. Much of the following information on the quest for legitimacy by the Tokugawa rulers comes from this masterly study, which is rare in its emphasis on political expediency under-

lying the development of early modern Japanese thought. See also Inoue Toshio, *Ikko ikki no kenkyu* [A Study of Ikko Ikki], Yoshikawa Kobunkan, 1968.

7 Ooms, *Ideology*, op. cit. (n. 6), pp. 30–1.

8 Ibid., p. 48.

9 Ibid., p. 129.

10 Ibid., pp. 171–3.

11 Ibid., p. 155.

12 The number of martyrdoms recognised by Rome for the period 1597–1660 is 3,125. This includes only those executed or who died under torture, and not the many who died as a result of ill treatment and destitution. The Jesuit and Franciscan missionaries counted nearly one million converts by 1614 – G. B. Sansom, *The Western World and Japan*, Knopf, 1962, p. 173.

13 Ibid., p. 176.

14 Maruyama Masao, *Studies in the Intellectual History of Tokugawa Japan*, Tokyo University Press, 1974, pp. 249–58; and Ooms, *Ideology*, op. cit. (n. 6), p. 61.

15 Ooms, *Ideology*, op. cit. (n. 6), chapter 5.

16 Ibid., pp. 35–62, 168–9.

17 As quoted in Delmer Brown, *Nationalism in Japan*, University of California Press, 1955, p. 120; see also ibid., pp. 137–8.

18 Kenneth B. Pyle, *The New Generation in Meiji Japan*, Stanford University Press, 1969, p. 130.

19 Carol Gluck, *Japan's Modern Myths*, Princeton University Press, 1985, p. 135.

20 Abe Isoo, a Christian, was prominently involved with all three organisations. His associate in some of these efforts was Katayama Sen, also a Christian, and leader of several fairly radical worker movements. In 1921 Katayama, by then a confirmed Leninist, accepted a Comintern invitation to come to Moscow, where he died in 1933, while advising the Comintern on propaganda in Asia. He is buried in the Kremlin Wall. A third Christian, Suzuki Bunji, founded the Yuaikai in 1912 and played an important role in the later moderate socialist movement.

21 Richard H. Mitchell, *Thought Control in Prewar Japan*, Cornell University Press, 1976, p. 31 and fn. 43.

22 Paul Langer, *Communism in Japan*, Hoover Institution Press, 1972, pp. 6, 10–15.

23 Tachibana Takashi, *Nihon Kyosanto no kenkyu* [A Study of the Japanese Communist Party], vol. 1, Kodansha, 1978, pp. 185–6.

24 K. G. van Wolferen, *Student Revolutionaries of the Sixties*, Interdoc, The Hague, 1970.

25 R. P. Dore, *Education in Tokugawa Japan*, Routledge & Kegan Paul, 1965, p. 37.

26 R. Tsunoda, W. T. de Bary and D. Keene (eds.), *Sources of Japanese Tradition*, Columbia University Press, 1958, p. 382.

27 Ibid., p. 385. Nakae Toju and Kumazawa Banzan were cult figures throughout the Tokugawa period. Their idea that humans have a spiritual identity separate from social expectations, and their pleas for ethical action based on one's intuition of good and bad, were made respectable by their identification with the needy. Both sought the company of poor villagers, turning their backs on the aristocracy and the scholars, who did not appear to consider them a great threat.

28 Tetsuo Najita, 'Oshio Heihachiro', in A. Craig and D. Shively (eds.), *Personality in Japanese History*, University of California Press, 1970, pp. 160–1.

29 Ibid., p. 163.

30 Tetsuo Najita, *Japan: The Intellectual Foundations of Modern Japanese Politics*, University of Chicago Press, 1974, p. 55.

31 Ibid., pp. 56–9.

32 Fujii Jintaro, *Meiji ishinshi kowa* [Lectures on the History of the Meiji Restoration], Yuzankaku, 1926, p. 42.

33 Najita, *Intellectual Foundations*, op. cit. (n. 30), p. 59; and Thomas M. Huber, ' "Men of high purpose" and the politics of direct action, 1862–1864', in Tetsuo Najita and J. V. Koschmann (eds.), *Conflict in Modern Japanese History*, Princeton University Press, 1982, pp. 124–6.

34 Which is of course the powerful undertone of the teachings by Nakae Toju, Kumazawa Banzan and Oshio Heihachiro.

35 Richard Storry, *The Double Patriots*, Chatto & Windus, 1957, p. 24.

36 Fujiwara Akira, 'The role of the Japanese army', in D. Borg and S. Okamoto (eds.), *Pearl Harbor as History*, Columbia University Press, 1973, p. 192.

37 As quoted in James B. Crowley, 'Japanese army factionalism in the early 1930s', *Journal of Asian Studies*, May 1962, p. 314.

38 For an exhaustive account of this battle and the ideological factors that determined its outcome, see Alvin D. Coox, *Nomonhan: Japan against Russia, 1939*, Stanford University Press, 1985.

39 Asada Sadao, 'The Japanese navy and the United States', in Borg and Okamoto, *Pearl Harbor as History*, op. cit. (n. 36), p. 254. The Imperial Conference was the one on 6 September 1941. For Kato Kanji's beliefs, see ibid., pp. 234, 240.

40 Ben-Ami Shillony, *Politics and Culture in Wartime Japan*, Clarendon Press, 1981, p. 135.

41 See Takeshi Ishida, *Japanese Political Culture*, Transaction Books, 1983, p. 35.

42 *Mainichi Daily News*, 2 March 1972.

43 Ian Buruma, *A Japanese Mirror*, Cape, 1984, p. 160.

44 At a Foreign Correspondents' Club luncheon on 7 October 1985. See *Asahi Shimbun*, 8 October 1985.

45 See Chapter 8.

46 Thomas R. H. Havens, *Farm and Nation in Modern Japan*, Princeton University Press, 1974, pp. 25–6, 42–5.

47 Sheldon Garon, *The State and Labor in Modern Japan*, University of California Press, 1987, p. 201; and Robert M. Spaulding, *Imperial Japan's Higher Civil Service Examinations*, Princeton University Press, 1967, p. 54.

48 Watanabe Takeshi, 'Seiron' column, *Sankei Shimbun*, translated as 'What's wrong with thrift?', *Japan Times*, 27 April 1987.

49 Sawa Takamitsu, 'One Japan boom wanes', *Japan Times*, 14 February 1988.

50 'Intellectuals on the Warpath', *Japan Times*, editorial, 4 December 1987.

12 The Right to Rule

1 John H. Schaar, 'Legitimacy in the modern state', in William Connolly (ed.), *Legitimacy and the State*, Blackwell, 1984, p. 111.

2   For a short but incisive treatment of this confusion, see ibid., pp. 108–11;
    and Carl J. Friedrich, *Man and his Government*, McGraw-Hill, 1963,
    p. 233.

3   The widely taught classifications made by Max Weber, of 'traditional',
    'charismatic' and 'rational' types of power, are not satisfactory in this
    context. All three categories, which are not used consistently by Weber
    himself, could be made to apply to the exercise of power on different levels
    in Japan, or for that matter in Western democracies and twentieth-century
    totalitarian systems, without saying much about legitimacy since they don't
    exclude each other. For a critique on Weber's scheme, see Stanislav
    Andreski, *Max Weber's Insights and Errors*, Routledge & Kegan Paul, 1984,
    pp. 96–8.

4   Anthony de Jasay, *The State*, Blackwell, 1985, p. 71. De Jasay is a recent
    author who makes valid points with regard to the distinctions between
    acquiescence and legitimacy; see pp. 67–78.

5   Tanaka Kakuei is also often mentioned as a prime minister interested in
    expanding his power. But for him strengthening the prime ministerial
    institution was not a primary goal. His empire rested on informal rela-
    tions.

6   Delmer Brown and Ichiro Ishida, *The Future and the Past*, University of
    California Press, 1979, p. 368.

7   Stanislav Andreski, *Military Organisation and Society*, 2nd edn, University
    of California Press, 1968.

8   Herman Ooms, *Tokugawa Ideology*, Princeton University Press, 1985,
    p. 44.

9   Ibid., p. 42.

10 Jeffrey P. Mass, 'Introduction', in J. P. Mass and W. B. Hauser (eds.), *The
    Bakufu in Japanese History*, Stanford University Press, 1985, p. 4.

11 Dan Fenno Henderson, 'The evolution of Tokugawa law', in John W. Hall
    and Marius B. Jansen (eds.), *Studies in the Institutional History of Early
    Modern Japan*, Princeton University Press, 1968, p. 214.

12 Irwin Scheiner, 'Benevolent lords and honorable peasants: rebellion and
    peasant consciousness in Tokugawa Japan', in Tetsuo Najita and Irwin
    Scheiner, *Japanese Thought in the Tokugawa Period*, University of Chicago
    Press, 1978, p. 41.

13 Bob Tadashi Wakabayashi, *Anti-Foreignism and Western Learning in Early
    Modern Japan*, Harvard University Press, 1986, pp. 112–13.

14 For a lucid theoretical treatment of the suppression, consent, legitimacy
    continuum, see de Jasay, *The State*, op. cit. (n. 4), pp. 67 ff.

15 Thomas M. Huber, 'The Choshu activists and 1868', in H. Wray and
    H. Conroy (eds.), *Japan Examined*, University of Hawaii Press, 1983.

16 See John W. Hall, 'Rule by status in Tokugawa Japan', *Journal of Japanese
    Studies*, Autumn 1974, pp. 39–40.

17 Sir Rutherford Alcock, *The Capital of the Tycoon*, London, 1863, vol. 2, as
    cited in Hall, 'Rule by status', op. cit. (n. 16).

18 Harold Bolitho, 'The Meiji restoration', in Wray and Conroy, *Japan
    Examined*, op. cit. (n. 15), p. 63.

19 David Titus, *Palace and Politics in Prewar Japan*, Columbia University Press,
    1974, p. 20.

20 Gordon Berger, personal communication.

21 Maruyama Masao, 'Japanese thought', *Journal of Social and Political Ideas in*

Japan, April 1964, p. 44. Translation of Iwanami Koza, *Gendai Nihon no shiso*, vol. 11, Iwanami Shoten, 1957, pp. 3–46.

22 The *Shinron*, or New Theses, the major work of the Mito school, which became the bible of the 'restore the emperor and expel the barbarian' movement. See also Chapter 10.

23 Wakabayashi, *Anti-Foreignism*, op. cit. (n. 13), p. 113.

24 Richard H. Minear, *Japanese Tradition and Western Law*, Harvard University Press, 1970, p. 72.

25 Jung Bock Lee, *The Political Character of the Japanese Press*, Seoul National University Press, 1985, p. 97.

26 'Tami wa shirashimu bekarazu, yorashimu beshi' – see Lee, ibid., p. 98; and Maruyama Masao, *Studies in the Intellectual History of Tokugawa Japan*, University of Tokyo Press, 1974, p. 330, n. 4.

27 Ooms, *Ideology*, op. cit. (n. 8), p. 107.

28 See George M. Beckmann, *The Making of the Meiji Constitution*, University of Kansas Press, 1957, chapter III.

29 Richard H. Mitchell, *Censorship in Imperial Japan*, Princeton University Press, 1983, p. 16.

30 Carol Gluck, *Japan's Modern Myths*, Princeton University Press, 1985, p. 60.

31 Ibid., pp. 53–6.

32 Walter McLaren, *A Political History of Japan during the Meiji Period*, Allen & Unwin, 1916, pp. 356–7.

33 Gordon Berger, *Parties out of Power in Japan*, Princeton University Press, 1977, p. 28.

34 Roger F. Hackett, 'The Meiji leaders and modernisation: the case of Yamagata Aritomo', in Marius B. Jansen (ed.), *Changing Japanese Attitudes toward Modernisation*, Princeton University Press, 1965, p. 268.

35 An oligarch such as Ito Hirobumi established his own party with followers from the bureaucracy in 1900.

36 Robert M. Spaulding, *Imperial Japan's Higher Civil Service Examinations*, Princeton University Press, 1967, p. 112. This unsurpassed study provides the best historical outline in English of modern Japan's bureaucratic institutions.

37 Hata Ikuhiko, *Kanryo no kenkyu* [On Bureaucrats], Kodansha, 1983, p. 109; and Spaulding, *Examinations*, op. cit. (n. 36), p. 117.

38 Established in 1888 in order to advise the emperor on matters pertaining to the draft constitution and other laws. Later it gained jurisdiction over Imperial Rescripts and Ordinances. Its members were former bureaucrats, peers and other, always conservative figures. It was chaired by Yamagata from 1905 until his death in 1922. It effectively restricted the power of party cabinets.

39 Spaulding, *Examinations*, op. cit. (n. 36), p. 119.

40 Ibid., p. 119.

41 Ibid., p. 119–20.

42 See James L. Huffman, *Politics of the Meiji Press*, University of Hawaii Press, 1980, p. 192.

43 Spaulding, *Examinations*, op. cit. (n. 36), p. 89.

44 Byron K. Marshall, 'Professors and politics: the Meiji academic elite', in *Journal of Japanese Studies*, Winter 1977, pp. 79–80.

45 Tetsuo Najita, *Japan: The Intellectual Foundations of Modern Japanese Politics*, University of Chicago Press, 1974, p. 10.

46 Gaetano Mosca, *The Ruling Class*, McGraw-Hill, 1939, p. 52.
47 The autocracies of Indonesia and the Philippines, before the flight of Marcos (countries that do not share in the Confucianist heritage), represent a different type of power dynamics.
48 Ellen Hammer, *Death in November*, Dutton, 1987.
49 An interesting account demonstrating this fact can be found in the context of the struggle against the authorities concerning the construction of Narita Airport: David E. Apter and Nagayo Sawa, *Against the State*, Harvard University Press, 1984, p. 266.
50 Jiyuminshu Henshubu, '1985 nen taisei e no tembo' [Perspectives for the 1985 system], *Jiyuminshu*, January 1982, p. 228. For more on this seminal article, see Chapter 14.
51 Murakami Yasusuke, 'The age of new middle mass politics: the case of Japan', *Journal of Japanese Studies*, Winter 1982, pp. 29–72.

13   Ritual and Intimidation

1   Chiho Jichi Kenkyu Shiryo Sentaa, *Gendai kanrisharon* [Modern Managers], 1977, p. 22.
2   Irwin Scheiner, 'Benevolent lords and honourable peasants: rebellion and peasant consciousness in Tokugawa Japan', in Tetsuo Najita and Irwin Scheiner, *Japanese Thought in the Tokugawa Period 1600–1868*, University of Chicago Press, 1978, pp. 39–59.
3   Kawashima Takeyoshi, 'Dispute resolution in contemporary Japan', in A. T. von Mehren (ed.), *Law in Japan*, Harvard University Press, pp. 43–5.
4   Ian Buruma, *A Japanese Mirror*, Cape, 1984, chapter 10.
5   Sahasi Shigeru, 'Kanryo shokun ni chokugen suru' [Speaking directly to bureaucrats], *Bungei Shunju*, July 1971, p. 108.
6   Ibid., p. 109.
7   Chitoshi Yanaga, *Japanese People and Politics*, Wiley, 1956, p. 307. See also Chalmers Johnson, *MITI and the Japanese Miracle*, Stanford University Press, 1982, p. 134.
8   See Chapter 5. For a detailed account of the 'telecommunications wars' and the dynamics of both ministries, see Chalmers Johnson, *MITI, MPT, and the Telecom Wars: How Japan Makes Policy for High Technology*, Berkeley Roundtable on the International Economy, University of California, Brie Working Paper No. 21, 1986.
9   The MPT has also waged a major bureaucratic war, with a combination of the agriculture co-operatives and the ministries of agriculture and finance, over a 'people's loan' system, which it managed to establish (in 1973) after mediation by the LDP members concerned. See Yung H. Park, *Bureaucrats and Ministers in Contemporary Japanese Government*, Institute of Asian Studies, University of California, Berkeley, 1986, pp. 137–8.
10 Inoguchi Takashi and Iwai Tomoaki, '*Zoku giin' no kenkyu* [A Study of 'Zoku Diet Members'], Nihon Keizai Shimbun, 1987, p. 22.
11 Richard H. Mitchell, *Thought Control in Prewar Japan*, Cornell University Press, 1976, p. 187.
12 Kubo Hiroshi, *Nihon no kensatsu* [Public Prosecution in Japan], Kodansha, 1986, p. 154.
13 Walter L. Ames, *Police and Community in Japan*, University of California Press, 1981, pp. 147–8.

14 Ise Akifumi, *Nippon keisatsu zankoku monogatari* [The Inside Story of the Japanese Police], Eeru Shuppansha, 1985, pp. 12–16.

15 The US aircraft manufacturer was ultimately found to have been negligent in applying the prescribed number of rivets during repairs of the plane's bulkhead. The focus of the conflict was JAL's president at the time of the crash. Takagi Yasumoto was the first who had risen within the organisation, rather than having been put at its head by the ministry. His appointment had been tolerated by the MOT on a short-term basis while its own designated appointee waited in the wings. But Takagi had proven hard to budge once in office and he had also been proved right in predicting the unfavourable outcome of Transport Ministry bungling in connection with landing-right negotiations with Washington: all cause for sour grapes among the transport bureaucrats.

16 To prepare for this exploit, Nakasone had formed an advisory committee which concluded that worship at the Yasukuni shrine was not unconstitutional 'as long as it did not lead to militarism'. But a minority in this group were said to be unable to reconcile themselves with this position, and the press was critical of the choice of committee members. Thirty-six independent scholars, numbering constitutional experts among them, handed to Nakasone their own report concluding that worship at the controversial shrine did in fact violate the constitution, since religion and state should remain clearly separated.

17 To his own reign must be added the five years that he served as regent for his weak-minded father.

18 See Kojima Noboru, 'Tenno to Amerika to taiheiyo senso', *Bungei Shunju*, November 1975, pp. 94–126; and D. Clayton James, *The Years of Mac-Arthur, Vol. 3: Triumph and Disaster*, Houghton Mifflin, 1985, pp. 320–2.

19 During the famous visit at Buckingham Palace in March 1921, Hirohito saw a newspaper for the first time and also for the first time witnessed spontaneous behaviour. King George V walked into his bedroom in a dressing-gown and patted him on the back at breakfast. It was years before his attendants and the court in Tokyo had mentally digested this, but in memory of this unforgettable freedom Hirohito ever after breakfasted on ham and eggs and never again wore a kimono.

20 John Bester, 'Afterthoughts', *Mainichi Daily News*, 15 April 1985.

21 Thomas Rohlen, *Japan's High Schools*, University of California Press, 1983, p. 191.

22 Michael Korver, 'An outsider takes an inside look at Japan's corporate culture', *Japan Economic Journal*, 3 May 1986, p. 41.

23 Nakane Chie, in *Japanese Society*, University of California Press, 1970, has given one of the most succinct but exhaustive accounts of these vertical bonds in Japanese groups.

24 Imai Kazuo, *Kanryo sono seitai to uchimaku* [Bureaucrats, their World and Hidden Behaviour], Yomiuri Shimbunsha, 1953, p. 61.

25 Ise, *Nippon keisatsu*, op. cit. (n. 14), p. 115.

26 Mikuni Akio, *Mikuni on Banking*, Mikuni & Co., 1987, p. 6.

27 Masao Miyoshi, *As We Saw Them: The First Japanese Embassy in the United States*, University of California Press, 1979, p. 87.

28 For an excellent account of these, see Walter Edwards, 'The commercialised wedding as ritual: a window on social values', *Journal of Japanese Studies*, Winter 1987, pp. 51–78.

29   Ibid.
30   At an exchange rate of 130 yen for the dollar, prevailing at the end of 1987.
31   Chalmers Johnson, 'Omote and ura: translating Japanese political terms', *Journal of Japanese Studies*, Winter 1980, p. 110.
32   Ito Daiichi, *Gendai Nihon kanryosei no bunseki* [Analysis of the Bureaucracy in Contemporary Japan], Tokyo Daigaku Shuppankai, 1980, p. 20.
33   For a different line of argument, but a similar conclusion, see J. Victor Koschmann (ed.), *Authority and the Individual in Japan*, University of Tokyo Press, 1978, p. 14.
34   Tsuji Kiyoaki, 'Nihon ni okeru seisaku kettei katei' [The policy-making process in Japan], in *Shinpan-Nihon kanryosei no kenkyu*, Tokyo Daigaku Shuppankai, 1969, p. 157.
35   Ito, *Gendai Nihon*, op. cit. (n. 32), p. 50.
36   Nihon no Kanryo Kenkyukai (eds.), *Oyakunin sojuho* [How to Manipulate Bureaucrats], Nihon Keizai Shimbunsha, 1971, pp. 148–9.
37   Tsuji, *Nihon kanryoisei*, op. cit. (n. 34), p. 163.
38   See, for example, Frank K. Upham, *Law and Social Change in Postwar Japan*, Harvard University Press, 1987, p. 211.
39   Tahara Soichiro, *Nihon no kanryo 1980* [Bureaucrats in Japan 1980], Bungei Shunju, 1979, p. 262.
40   See Robert J. Smith, *Japanese Society*, Cambridge University Press, 1983, p. 27.
41   Kurt Singer, *Mirror, Sword and Jewel*, Croom Helm, 1973, p. 39.
42   Upham, *Law*, op. cit. (n. 38), pp. 122–3.
43   Hanami Tadashi, *Labor Relations in Japan Today*, Kodansha International, 1979.
44   See Howard Stanislawski, 'Japan's Israel problem', *New Republic*, 9 March 1987.
45   For these and other examples, see Willy Stern, 'Japan's 'free traders'' boycott Israel', *Tokyo Business Today*, November 1987, pp. 26–8.
46   A good example can be found in Clyde Prestowitz, *Trading Places*, Basic Books, 1988, p. 161.
47   Watanabe Yozo, *Gendai kokka to gyoseiken* [The Modern State and its Administrative Rights], Tokyo Daigaku Shuppankai, 1972, p. 312.
48   Ishikawa Masumi, 'Shitatakanari "kokka himitsu-ho" an' [The 'spy bill' keeps on surviving], *Chuo Koron*, February 1986, pp. 141–2.
49   See Ito, *Gendai Nihon*, op. cit. (n. 32), p. 23.
50   Ibid., p. 89.
51   Narita Yoriaki, 'Gyosei shido' [Administrative guidance], in Takayanagi Shinichi *et al.*, (eds.), *Gendai no gyosei*, Iwanami Shoten, 1966, p. 138.
52   Ito, *Gendai Nihon*, op. cit. (n. 32), pp. 83–4.
53   Ibid., p. 86.
54   Ibid., p. 53.

14   A Century of Consolidating Control

1   The war in China began with the so-called Marco Polo Bridge Incident on 7 July 1937. Before then, Japan's Kwantung Army had attacked the Chinese garrison at Mukden in September 1931, in an action that has gone

down in history as the Manchurian Incident. This marked the beginning of intensified involvement that led to the above-mentioned war, and thus it is possible also to speak of Japan's fifteen-year war in Asia.

2 Edwin O. Reischauer, history professor at Harvard and US ambassador to Tokyo in the 1960s, has been one of the most influential proponents of this view. For a recent expression of it in an interview, see 'Nihon no susumubeki michi' [The road that Japan should take], *Bungei Shunju*, January 1988, p. 101.

3 A pioneering study in this context, focusing on the continuities of industrial policy and the careers of the officials who shaped it that spanned the pre-war, wartime and post-war periods, is Chalmers Johnson's *MITI and the Japanese Miracle*, Stanford University Press, 1982. See also Sheldon Garon, *The State and Labor in Modern Japan*, University of California Press, 1987.

4 The most complete study on the purge in English is Hans H. Baerwald, *The Purge of Japanese Leaders under the Occupation*, University of California Press, 1959. Baerwald lists 1.9 per cent purged out of 42,251 who were screened. See also Hata Ikuhiko, *Kanryo no kenkyu* [On Bureaucrats], Kodansha, 1983, p. 27. The total of purged personnel was more than 210,000, mostly military. There is a discrepancy in the statistics as to how many were formally purged. The accepted figure for those listed to be purged is 1,800 bureaucrats. According to another statistic, in the final instance the number of bureaucratic purgees came to only 719. See also Kinoshita Hanji, 'Kyu-shihaiso no kaitai to fukkatsu' [Dissolution and revival of the old ruling class], in *Sengo Nihon no seijikatei: Nempo Seijigaku*, Iwanami Shoten, 1953, pp. 69–85.

5 T. J. Pempel, 'The tar baby target: "reform" of the Japanese bureaucracy', in R. E. Ward and Y. Sakamoto (eds), *Democratising Japan*, University of Hawaii Press, 1987, p. 159. Pempel gives an excellent succinct overview of the relationship between occupiers and the Japanese bureaucracy, in which he draws a parallel with the US treatment of German bureaucrats and contrasts this with the systematic overhaul by the Soviet occupiers of the East German bureaucracy.

6 Theodore Cohen, *Remaking Japan*, Free Press, 1987, p. 379.

7 Ibid., pp. 381–2.

8 The exact final number of people purged under a variety of criteria is 1,535.

9 Baerwald, *The Purge*, op. cit. (n. 4), esp. pp. 2–3.

10 Ibid., p. 69.

11 Yoshida Shigeru, *The Yoshida Memoirs*, Houghton Mifflin, 1962, p. 128.

12 Miles Fletcher, *The Search for a New Order: Intellectuals and Fascism in Prewar Japan*, University of North Carolina Press, 1982. See also Juan J. Linz, 'Some notes toward a comparative study of fascism in sociological historical perspective', in Walter Laqueur (ed.), *Fascism*, University of California Press, 1976, pp. 103–4.

13 Hashikawa Bunzo, 'Kakushin kanryo' [Reformist bureaucrats], in Kamishima Jiro (ed.), *Kenryoku no shiso*, Chikuma Shobo, 1965, p. 252.

14 Hata, *Kanryo no kenkyu*, op. cit. (n. 4), p. 125.

15 Mark R. Peattie, *Ishiwara Kanji and Japan's Confrontation with the West*, Princeton University Press, 1975, pp. 186–9.

16 Goto Ryunosuke founded the Showa Kenkyukai in 1933. For a detailed study of its three major intellectuals and its various ideological strands, see Fletcher, *Search for a New Order*, op. cit. (n. 12).

17 Shibagaki Kazuo, ' "Keizai shintaisei" to toseikai: sono rinen to genjitsu'
    ['The economic new order' and the control associations: their ideal and
    reality], in Tokyo Daigaku Shakai Kagaku Kenkyujo (eds), *Senji Nihon keizai*,
    Tokyo Daigaku Shuppankai, 1979, pp. 301, 307–10, 322.
18 Hashikawa, 'Kakushin kanryo', op. cit. (n. 13), pp. 254–6; Johnson, *MITI*,
    op. cit. (n. 3), pp. 123–5; and Hata, *Kanryo no kenkyu*, op. cit.
    (n. 4), pp. 112–18.
19 Nakajima Makoto, 'Showashi o irodoru kakushin kanryo no jidai' [The age of
    reformist bureaucrats in Showa history], *Gendai no me*, September 1978, p.
    52.
20 T A. Bisson, *Japan's War Economy*, Institute of Pacific Relations, New York,
    1945, p. 10. For the merger and many other details of the Cabinet Planning
    Board, see Johnson, *MITI*, op. cit. (n. 3), pp. 137–43.
21 Ito Daiichi, *Gendai nihon kanryosei no bunseki* [Analysis of the Bureaucracy in
    Contemporary Japan], Tokyo Daigaku Shuppankai, 1980, p. 36.
22 For an account of Kishi's *jinmyaku* politics, see Takada Kyoshi, 'Kishi
    Nobusuke', in *Kuromaku kenkyu*, Shin Kokuminsha, 1977, pp. 15–113.
23 Johnson, *MITI*, op. cit. (n. 3), p. 172.
24 'Zaikai no "Ikeda sanmyaku" ' ['Ikeda's networks' among business circles],
    Shukan Asahi, 30 October 1960, p. 8.
25 Ito Osamu, 'Sengo Nihon kinyu shisutemu no keisei' [The formation of post-
    war Japan's financial system], in Kindai Nihon Kenkyukai (eds), *Nempo
    Kindai Nihon kenkyu*, vol. 8, Yamakawa Shuppansha, 1986,
    pp. 225–6.
26 Hata Ikuhiko, 'Kanryo no ikinobiru michi' [How bureaucrats survive],
    Shokun, April 1977, p. 85.
27 Johnson, *MITI*, op. cit. (n. 3), p. 41.
28 For an overview of the control associations, see Shibagaki Kazuo, ' "Keizai
    shintaisei" ', op. cit. (n. 17), pp. 291–336.
29 Johnson, *MITI*, op. cit. (n. 3), p. 173.
30 Sakakibara Eisuke and Noguchi Yukio, 'Okurasho Nichigin ocho no bun-
    seki' [An analysis of the Ministry of Finance/Bank of Japan kingdom], *Chuo
    Koron*, August 1977, pp. 98, 113–20.
31 Ibid., p. 99. The Bank of Japan Law dating from 1942 was amended in1947,
    but left the bank's essential wartime functions intact.
32 Ibid., pp. 99, 117.
33 Akimoto Hideo, *Keidanren*, Sekkasha, 1968, pp. 116–17. The Juyo Sangyo
    Tosei Dantai Kyogikai (Important Industries Control Association) from
    1941 was dissolved in February 1946, replaced by the Nihon Sangyo
    Kyogikai (Japan Industrial Association) in August 1946 and combined with
    the Kinyu Dantai Kyogikai (Financial Corporations Association, formed in
    April 1946) one week later to become the Keidanren.
34 Otani Ken, 'Uemura Kogoro', in *Sengo zaikaijin retsuden*, Sangyo Noritsu
    Daigaku Shuppanbu, 1979, p. 168.
35 Ishizaka's reputation of being against the bureaucracy was partly due to his
    opposition to MITI's proposed Law on Special Measures for Specific
    Depressed Industries, which was never passed. See Chapter 15.
36 Among these leaders of both organisations were Moroi Kanichi, Sakurada
    Takeshi, Imazato Koki and Shikanai Nobutaka. For a comparison of the two
    organisations, see Noguchi Yuichiro, 'Yottsu no keieisha dantai' [Four
    management groups], *Chuo Koron*, October 1960, pp. 161–3.
37 Hoashi Kei, *Toseikai no riron to jissai* [Theory and Reality of the Control

Associations], Shin Keizaisha, 1941, p. 4. Shibagaki Kazuo gives an extensive account of Hoashi's theory, and how essential aspects of it have been realised in the post-war economy, in ' "Keizai shintaisei" ', op. cit. (n. 17), pp. 291–336.

38   Hoashi, *Toseikai no riron*, op. cit. (n. 37), p. 2.
39   Ibid., p. 38.
40   Ibid., pp. 15–16.
41   Otsuka Banjo, 'Keizai minshuka to sono gutaisaku' [Democratisation of the economy and its concrete measures], *Keieisha*, March 1947, pp. 2–9; and Otsuka Banjo, 'Keizai minshuka to shusei shihonshugi' [Democratisation of the economy and reformed capitalism], *Keieisha*, December 1947, pp. 1–5. See also Kuribara Kazuo and Matsuyama Jiro, *Nihon zaikai nyumon* [Introduction to Japanese Business Circles], Gakufusha, 1961, pp. 36–7.
42   The Doyukai theoreticians were then still paying lip-service to the ideal of economic freedom as exemplified by the United States, which is why the second half of their declaration decries monopolies and the dual structure with subordinate subcontractors.
43   Watanabe Yasuo, 'Sengoha kanryo ron' [On post-war bureaucrats], *Chuo Koron*, September 1960, p. 206.
44   Oda Keisuke, 'Doyukai', *Jiyu*, November 1970, p. 170.
45   Kimura Takeo, 'Sanken', *Chuo Koron*, July 1971, p. 188.
46   For an extensive account of these business moves preceding the creation of the LDP, see Chitoshi Yanaga, *Big Business in Japanese Politics*, Yale University Press, 1968, pp. 121–40.
47   See Hayashi Shozo, 'Nihon no pawaa eriito: gendai no kanryo' [Power élites in Japan: bureaucrats today], *Chuo Koron*, May 1960, p. 110.
48   Garon *State and Labor*, op. cit. (n. 3), p. 234.
49   Watanabe, 'Sengoha kanryo ron', op. cit. (n. 43).
50   Theodore Cohen, *Remaking Japan*, Free Press, 1987, p. 92.
51   Hiranuma Kiichiro Kaikoroku Hensan Iinkai (ed.), *Hiranuma Kiichiro kaikoroku* [Memoirs of Hiranuma Kiichiro], Gakuyo Shobo, 1955, p. 215.
52   Ogino Fujio, *Tokko keisatsu taisei shi* [History of the 'Thought Police' System], Sekita Shobo, 1984, pp. 429–31, 435–6.
53   This information is culled from Yonehara Itaru, Kazahaya Yasoji and Shiota Shobei, *Tokko keisatsu kokusho* [Black Paper on the 'Thought Police'], Shin Nihon Shuppansha, 1977, pp. 211–21.
54   Garon, *State and Labor*, op. cit. (n. 3), p. 233.
55   Ibid., p. 235.
56   Yung H. Park, *Bureaucrats and Ministers in Contemporary Japanese Government*, Institute of Asian Studies, University of California, Berkeley, 1986, pp. 63–4.
57   Hayashi, 'Pawaa eriito', op. cit. (n. 47), p. 108.
58   It was formed in 1952 as an agency and was made a ministry in 1960.
59   Jin Ikko, *Jichi kanryo* [Home Affairs Ministry Bureaucrats], Kodansha, 1986, p. 14.
60   Ibid., p. 73.
61   Ibid., p. 215.
62   For the role of the reform bureaucrats in establishing this wartime government mouthpiece, see Hashikawa, 'Kakushin kanryo', op. cit. (n. 13), p. 256.
63   Already in the 1870s commentators were speaking of a *fukuzatsu naru*

shakai ('an increasingly complicated society'); see Carol Gluck, *Japan's Modern Myths*, Princeton University Press, 1985, p. 30.

64   Kenneth Pyle, 'Advantages of followership: German economics and Japanese bureaucrats, 1890–1925', *Journal of Japanese Studies*, Autumn 1974, p. 144.

65   Garon, *State and Labor*, op. cit. (n. 3), p. 212. Garon makes the point that, by paying attention to the nativist rhetoric, historians have overlooked the profound impact of Nazi models on Japanese policies of the day, particularly those relating to the suppression of labour unions.

66   See Chapter 12.

67   Bob Tadashi Wakabayashi, *Anti-Foreignism and Western Learning in Early Modern Japan*, Harvard University Press, 1986, p. 112.

68   Yanaga Chitoshi, *Japanese People and Politics*, John Wiley & Son, 1956, p. 306.

69   Richard J. Smethurst, *Social Basis for Prewar Japanese Militarism*, University of California Press, 1974, p. 11.

70   Kenneth Pyle, 'The technology of Japanese nationalism: the local improvement movement, 1900–1918', *Journal of Asian Studies*, November 1973, p. 58.

71   Smethurst, *Social Basis*, op. cit. (n. 69).

72   Okudaira Yasuhiro, 'Tennosei kokka no jinmin shihai' [Control of the people under the emperor system], in Nakamura Masanori *et al.*, *Taikei Nihon kokkashi 5 kindai 2*, Tokyo Daigaku Shuppankai, 1976, p. 321, as quoted in Herbert Bix, 'Kawakami Hajime and the organic law of Japanese fascism', *Japan Interpreter*, Winter 1978, p. 129.

73   Garon, *State and Labor*, op. cit. (n. 3), pp. 73–4.

74   Ibid., p. 28.

75   Kato Shuichi, 'Taisho democracy as the pre-stage for Japanese militarism', in B. Silberman and H. D. Harootunian (eds.), *Japan in Crisis*, Princeton University Press, 1974.

76   Sheldon M. Garon, 'State and religion in imperial Japan, 1912–1945', *Journal of Japanese Studies*, Summer 1986, p. 299.

77   The two million figure is a common estimate among activist women's groups. According to official statistics there were more than a million abortions per year between 1955 and 1961. By 1981 this figure had shrunk to just under 600,000. Doctors believe that this official figure must be more than doubled because many clinics under-report for tax reasons.

78   For one example of this argument, see Park, *Bureaucrats*, op. cit. (n. 56), p. 134. A very knowledgeable and eloquent defender of this position is Muramatsu Michio; see, for example, Muramatsu Michio and Ellis S. Kraus, 'The conservative policy line and the development of patterned pluralism', in K. Yamamura and Y. Yasuba (eds.), *The Political Economy of Japan*, Stanford University Press, 1987, pp. 516–54.

79   Hata, *Kanryo no kenkyu*, op. cit. (n. 4), p. 108.

80   Ibid., pp. 109–10.

81   Gordon Berger, *Parties out of Power in Japan*, Princeton University Press, 1977, p. 75.

82   Delmer M. Brown, *Nationalism in Japan*, University of California Press, 1955, pp. 219–20.

83   Ibid., p. 220.

84   Junichi Kyogoku, *The Political Dynamics of Japan*, University of Tokyo Press, 1987, p. 11.

85 Jiyuminshu Henshubu, '1985 nen taisei e no tembo' [Perspective for a 1985 system], *Jiyuminshu*, January 1982, pp. 224–9.
86 For an example of this in Tanaka Kakuei's stronghold, see Takabatake Michitoshi, 'Etsuzankai no tsuyoki to yowaki' [Strong and weak points of Etsuzankai], *Ushio*, December 1983, p. 96.
87 Garon, *State and Labor*, op. cit. (n. 3).
88 Isaiah Berlin, 'Two concepts of liberty', in *Four Essays on Liberty*, Oxford University Press, 1969, p. 118.

15 The Japanese Phoenix

1   David A. Titus, 'Political parties and nonissues in Taisho democracy', in H. Wray and H. Conroy (eds.), *Japan Examined*, University of Hawaii Press, 1983, p. 185.
2   Akira Iriye, 'The failure of economic expansionism: 1918–1931', in B. Silberman and H. D. Harootunian (eds), *Japan in Crisis*, Princeton University Press, 1974, p. 238.
3   Tsuchiya Takao, 'Keizai seisakuka to shite no Okubo Toshimichi' [Okubo Toshimichi as an economic policy-maker], *Chuo Koron*, April 1935, p 98. The mission was the famous Iwakura Mission to Europe and the United States that lasted eighteen months in 1871–3.
4   Ibid., p. 109.
5   Clyde Prestowitz, *Trading Places*, Basic Books, 1988, chapter 4.
6   The authority on this subject, Nakamura Takafusa, makes this point, contradicting the widespread view of overall recession. Nakamura Takafusa, *Economic Growth in Prewar Japan*, Yale University Press, 1983, p. 156.
7   Chalmers Johnson, *MITI and the Japanese Miracle*, Stanford University Press, 1982, pp. 102–3.
8   Nakamura, *Economic Growth*, op. cit. (n. 6), p. 266.
9   Mark R. Peattie, *Ishiwara Kanji and Japan's Confrontation with the West*, Princeton University Press, 1975, chapters 6, 7.
10 Nakamura, *Economic Growth*, op. cit. (n. 6), pp. 268–70.
11 Also known as Aikawa Yoshisuke, he had, of course, graduated from Todai, and was a protégé of Marquis Inoue Kaoru, who held many portfolios in Meiji-period governments and had very close ties with the biggest financiers. He started with a foundry, combined it with the Kuhara Mining Company of his brother-in-law, gave it the name Nissan and added subsidiaries, including the famous Hitachi works, to form a 'new *zaibatsu*'. The conglomerate prospered by producing munitions and armaments before being invited to participate in Manchuria. See Ayukawa's own explanation of the deal made with the Kwantung Army, in his article 'Manshu keizai shihai no kii pointo' [The key points of economic control in Manchuria], *Bessatsu Chisei*, December 1956, pp. 198–200.
12 G. C. Allen, 'Japanese industry: its organisation and development to 1937', in E. B. Schumpeter, *The Industrialisation of Japan and Manchukuo, 1930–1940*, Macmillan, 1940, pp. 643–5. For Kishi's introducing Ayukawa to Manchuria, see also Johnson, *MITI*, op. cit. (n. 7), pp. 131–2.
13 For a part of the web of Ayukawa's family ties with prominent figures, see Natori Giichi, *Seizaikaijin no meiun* [Destiny of People in the World of Politics, Business and Bureaucracy], Hokushindo, 1952, pp. 155–9.
14 Ayukawa explained after the war that he had been misled by bureaucrats

such as Shiina Etsusaburo about conditions in Manchuria. See Ando Yoshio, *Showa seiji keizaishi e no shogen* [Testimony on the Political and Economic History of Showa], vol. 1, Mainichi Shimbunsha, 1972, p. 280.

15 T. A. Bisson, *Japan's War Economy*, Institute of Pacific Relations, New York, 1945, p. 3.

16 See, for instance, the remarks by Kaya Okinori, the most prominent Ministry of Finance official in the late 1930s. A number of Showa Kenkyukai (see Chapter 14) members thought the same. See Kaya Okinori, *Senzen sengo 80 nen* [Eighty Years before and after the War], Keizai Oraisha, 1976, pp. 95–6.

17 Johnson, *MITI*, op. cit. (n. 7), p. 160.

18 Ito Osamu, 'Sengo Nihon kin'yu shisutemu no keisei' [The formation of post-war Japan's financial system], in Kindai Nihon Kenkyukai (eds.), *Nempo Kindai Nihon Kenkyu*, vol. 8, Yamakawa Shuppansha, 1986, p. 219.

19 Johnson, *MITI*, op. cit. (n. 7), p. 136.

20 Ito, 'Sengo Nihon', op. cit. (n. 18), p. 223.

21 Ibid., pp. 224–5.

22 Gunju Yushi Shitei Kinyu Kikan Seido.

23 See Okurasho Showa Zaiseishi Henshushitsu (eds.), *Showa zaiseishi* [History of Public Finance in Showa], vol. 11, *Kin'yu 2* [Finance 2], Toyo Keizai Shimposha, 1957, pp. 343–6. The law was the Gunju Kaisha Ho (Munition Corporation Law).

24 The commercial banks were Teikoku, Mitsubishi, Yasuda, Sumitomo and Sanwa; the Industrial Bank of Japan belonged in the same category. They were backed by fifty-six banks designated as 'banks to absorb funds from private sectors'. Ibid., p. 348.

25 Ibid., pp. 349–52.

26 Okurasho Showa Zaiseishi Henshushitsu (eds.), *Showa zaiseishi*, op. cit. (n. 23), vol. 2, *Zaisei kikan* [Financial Institutions], 1956, pp. 275–8. A law passed in April 1945 further endorsed the system (Gunjo Kinyuto Tokubetsu Sochi Ho, Special Law for Munitions Financing).

27 Nakamura Takafusa, *The Postwar Japanese Economy*, University of Tokyo Press, 1981, pp. 16–17; Miyazaki Yoshikazu, *Sengo nihon no keizai kiko* [Economic Structure of Post-War Japan], Shinhyoron, 1966, pp. 48–9; Ito, 'Sengo Nihon', op. cit. (n. 18); Yamazaki Hiroaki, 'Senjika no sangyokozo to dokusen soshiki' [Wartime industrial structure and monopolistic organisation], in Tokyo Daigaku Shakai Kagaku Kenkyujo (eds.), *Senji Nihon keizai*, Tokyo Daigaku Shuppankai, 1979, pp. 286–9.

28 Yoshio Suzuki, *Money and Banking in Contemporary Japan*, Yale University Press, 1980, p. 8.

29 Ibid., p. 9.

30 Tahara Soichiro, *Dentsu*, Asahi Shimbunsha, 1984, p. 69.

31 Ibid., p. 61.

32 Suetsugu Seiji, 'Dentsu ni yoru masukomi sosa: sono haikei to konnichiteki yakuwari' [Dentsu's manoeuvring of the mass media: its background and present-day role], *Tsukuru*, November 1973, pp. 76–9.

33 Kusayanagi Daizo, 'Gendai okokuron: Dentsu' [On a modern kingdom: Dentsu], *Bungei Shunju*, February 1967, p. 194.

34 Tahara, *Dentsu*, op. cit. (n. 30), p. 79.

35 Fujii Haruo, 'Dentsu no beeru o hagu' [Unveiling Dentsu], in Ino Kenji (ed.), *Dentsu kogairon*, Nisshin Hodo, 1971, pp. 165–7.

36 Nakamura, *Postwar Japanese Economy*, op. cit. (n. 27), p. 15.

37 See Okurasho Showa Zaiseishi Henshushitsu (eds.), *Showa zaiseishi*, op. cit. (n. 23), vol. 1, *Soron* [General Discussion], 1965, pp. 227–32.

38 See Osawa Tadashi, *Chusho kigyo seisaku shiron* [On the History of Small and Medium-Sized Industry], Minato Shuppansha, 1970, p. 206.

39 Ibid., p. 208.

40 Tatsumi Nobuharu, 'Chusho kigyo ni okeru soshikika no rekishi to mondaiten' [History and problems of the systematisation of small and medium-sized companies], in Takeuchi Masami (ed.), *Korekara no chusho kigyo soshikika no tembo*, Nihon Seisansei Hombu, 1965, p. 72. For a history of early post-war organisation of small and medium-sized industry, see Higuchi Kenji, 'Sengo chusho kigyo undo no tenkai' [Post-war development of small and medium-sized industry movement], *Gendai Chusho kigyo kiso kozo*, vol. 3, Doyukan, 1976, pp. 223–56.

41 Aikawa Yoshisuke, *Watashi no rirekisho: keizaijin* [My Personal History: People in Business], vol. 9, Nikkei Shimbunsha, 1980, p. 77. Originally published by Nihon Keizai Shimbun, 1965.

42 Ibid., p. 80.

43 Higuchi, 'Sengo chusho kigyo', op. cit. (n. 40), p. 246.

44 Ibid., p. 249.

45 Ibid., p. 252.

46 Whether or not a formal or informal 'reverse course' was ever part of the occupation's conscious policies – a subject of some debate – is immaterial. The shift in emphasis was noticed, and in the view of Japanese intellectuals it has been a very real milestone in early post-war history.

47 Yanaga Chitoshi, *Big Business in Japanese Politics*, Yale University Press, 1968, p. 38.

48 Tsuchikawa Nobuo, 'Seito naikaku to shoko kanryo' [The commercial, industrial bureaucracy and party cabinets: the industrial state policy of the Tanaka cabinet], in Kindai Nihon Kenkyukai (eds.), *Nempo Kindai Nihon kenkyu*, vol. 8, Yamakawa Shuppansha, 1986, pp. 188, 199.

49 Iwai Tomoaki, 'Kokkai naikaku' [Diet cabinet], in Nakano Minoru (ed.), *Nihongata seisaku kettei no hen'yo*, Toyo Keizai Shimposha, 1986, p. 17; and Muramatsu Michio, 'Rippo katei to seito, atsuryoku dantai, kanryo no kankei' [Parties, bureaucrats and pressure groups in the Japanese legislative process: pre-Diet and Diet procedure], *Hokudai Hogaku Ronshu*, vol. 34, no. 1, 1983, pp. 149–50.

50 William W. Lockwood, 'Japan's "new capitalism" ', in Lockwood (ed.), *The State and Economic Enterprise in Japan*, Princeton University Press, 1965, p. 487.

51 Uchino Tatsuro, *Japan's Postwar Economy*, Kodansha International, 1983, p. 66.

52 For the farcical hearings on this, see Yamamura Kozo, *Economic Policy in Postwar Japan*, University of California Press, 1967, chapter 5.

53 Uchino, *Postwar Economy*, op. cit. (n. 51), p. 54.

54 The balanced budget was maintained until long after Dodge's other prescriptions were forgotten. The government was forced to drop it in the late 1960s under pressure to stimulate the economy by public works (see Chapter 5), though departure from it scares the Ministry of Finance bureaucrats up to this day.

55 Suzuki, *Money*, op. cit. (n. 28), p. 14.

56 Johnson, *MITI*, op. cit. (n. 7), pp. 255–60; Uchino, *Postwar Economy*, op. cit. (n. 51), pp. 119–20.

57   As observed by Johnson, *MITI*, op. cit. (n. 7), p. 32.

58   Uchino, *Postwar Economy*, op. cit. (n. 51), p. 120.

59   Okumura Hiroshi, *Shin: Nihon no roku dai kigyo shudan* [Six Big Corporate Groups in Japan], Daiamondosha, 1983, p. 118.

60   For an overview and analysis of the system, see Ishida Hideto, 'Anti-competitive practices in the distribution of goods and services in Japan', *Journal of Japanese Studies*, Summer 1983, pp. 319–34.

61   Ibid., p. 325.

62   Furuta Hisateru, 'Foodo o meguru Kishi to Yoshida' [Kishi, Yoshida and Ford Motor Co.], *Chuo Koron*, July 1986, p. 301.

63   For the role of the *banto*, see John G. Roberts, *Mitsui*, Weatherhill, 1973.

64   See, for example, Shibagaki Kazuo, ' "Keizai shintaisei" to toseikai: sono rinen to genjitsu' ['Economic new order' and the control associations: their ideal and reality], in Tokyo Daigaku Shakai Kagaku Kenkyujo (eds.), *Senji Nihon keizai*, op. cit. (n. 27), p. 302.

65   Yanaga, *Big Business*, op. cit. (n. 47), p. 46.

66   Sakaguchi Akira, 'Zaikai "ipponka" koso no shujiku' [Initiator of the 'unification' of the business world], *Zaikai*, 1 February 1965, p. 53.

67   Miyazaki Yoshikazu, *Sengo Nihon no keizai kiko* [Economic Structure of Post-War Japan], Shinhyoron, 1966, p. 55.

68   Prestowitz, *Trading Places*, op. cit. (n. 5), p. 144.

69   For an excellent detailed account of the Japan–US 'semiconductor wars' as well as the machine-tool saga, see ibid., chapter 2 and pp. 217–29.

70   The term derives from *zaimu*, which means financial management, and 'hi-*technology*'.

71   In the 1980s Japanese continued to save roughly one-fifth of their disposable income. The 'bonus' system, whereby salarymen receive between 20 and 35 per cent of their salary in negotiated sums twice a year, helps stimulate savings. The underdeveloped welfare system is another stimulus; 36 per cent of all personal savings is estimated to serve as insurance for illness or accidents, according to a central bank study. A further impetus for saving is the high cost of education and housing.

72   Nomura, Daiwa, Nikko and Yamaichi.

73   According to the Economic Planning Agency. See also the remark by the president of Sohyo, Kurokawa Takeshi, quoted in *Asahi Evening News*, 19 February 1988.

74   Over the calendar year of 1987. National Land Agency figures made public in March 1988.

75   Nippon Life Insurance, Daiichi Mutual Life Insurance and Sumitomo Mutual Life Insurance.

76   The bureaucrats do, of course, make mistakes. One of their greatest post-war failings was the yen-rate defence of 1971. The authorities supported the dollar by buying 6 billion dollars for eleven days, during which only Japan's foreign exchange market did not close.

77   IBM and Coca-Cola are often singled out as the great foreign success stories in the Japanese market. Both began at a very early stage after the war and had, as it were, historical rights. Nevertheless, they were placed under many restrictions, were initially forbidden to take their earnings out of Japan and through licensing stipulations practically had to help nurture the growth of their Japanese competitors.

16   In the World But Not of It

1   A good recent example is George Packard, 'The Coming U.S.–Japan Crisis', in *Foreign Affairs*, Winter 1987–8.
2   *Nihon Keizai Shimbun* [Dealing with the Policies of the New Conservative Party], 25 December 1961.
3   Uemura Kogoro, 'Shin hoshuto no seisaku ni nozomu', *Yomiuri Shimbun*, 4 November 1955.
4   Yoshi Tsurumi, *Los Angeles Times*, 25 January 1988.
5   This is understood by some Japanese intellectuals. See, for example, Kuroda Katsuhiro in *Japan National Press Club Bulletin*, 10 January 1988; translated as 'Don't preach to South Korea', *Japan Times*, 7 February 1988.
6   *Asahi Shimbun*, 21 April 1986.
7   Personal communication from a mutual friend.
8   See also the comments of George Murakami, the veteran weekly commentator on the Japanese economy, *Asahi Evening News*, 27 April 1987.
9   For the difficulties involved and the consequent methods of Japanese bargaining, see Michael Blaker, *Japanese International Negotiating Style*, Columbia University Press, 1977, pp. 14–17.
10   Ibid., p. 224.
11   Kenzo Uchida, *Japan Times*, 19 June 1987.
12   Chalmers Johnson, 'Japanese–Soviet relations in the early Gorbachev era', *Asian Survey*, November 1987, pp. 545–60.
13   Donald C. Hellmann, *Japanese Foreign Policy and Domestic Politics*, University of California Press, 1969; and Donald A. Hellmann, 'Foreign policy à la LDP', in H. Murakami and J. Hirschmeier (eds), *Politics and Economics in Contemporary Japan*, Kodansha International, 1983, pp. 97–8.
14   Hellmann, 'Foreign policy', op. cit. (n. 13), p. 103.
15   Clyde Prestowitz, *Trading Places*, Basic Books, 1988.
16   Ivan P. Hall, 'Stop making excuses for Japan's insularity', *Wall Street Journal*, 6 July 1987.
17   The fact that an imported car has its steering wheel on the wrong side for Japan is part of its snob-appeal value; it marks the car as foreign. Some imported cars like Mercedes have a lower resale value if they have the steering wheel on the right side. BMW experimented with the import of two right-hand-drive models and found that there was little interest in them.
18   T. J. Pempel, 'The tar baby target: "reform" of the Japanese bureaucracy', in R. E. Ward and Y. Sakamoto (eds.), *Democratising Japan*, University of Hawaii Press, 1987, p. 174.
19   *Asahi Shimbun* interview, English version in *Asahi Evening News*, 3 June 1987.
20   'Tensei jingo' column, *Asahi Shimbun*, date unknown.
21   Kato Shuichi, 'Taisho democracy as the pre-stage for Japanese militarism', in B. Silberman and H. D. Harootunian (eds.), *Japan in Crisis*, Princeton University Press, 1974, p. 234.
22   Several months after Tokyo had been informed that a nuclear bomb was being developed, the Imperial Army initiated its own programme for the development of an atomic bomb under the supervision of Dr Nishina Yoshio. According to one documentary prepared by NHK, General Tojo Hideki conveyed his opinion to Colonel Kawashima Toranosuke that the war might be decided with atomic weapons.

23 For an articulate summing up of the sentiments and ideas involved and a warning against using them as justification for Japan's war effort, see Onuma Yasuaki, ' "Bunmei no sabaki" "shosha no sabaki" o koete' [Beyond the logic of 'civilisation justice' and 'victors' justice'], *Chuo Koron*, August 1983, pp. 162–89.

24 For a representative instance of the public being asked to make sacrifices for the sake of better relations with other countries, see Ministry of Foreign Affairs, *Diplomatic Blue Book*, Summer 1985.

25 Among the numerous instances of this kind, see the conclusions of the former Japanese chairman of the trilateral commission: Watanabe Takeshi, Seiron Column, *Sankei Shimbun*, reprinted in *Japan Times*, 27 April 1987.

Glossary of Japanese Words

Amakudari post-retirement employment of bureaucrats in big business.

Burakumin former outcasts.

Dango rigging tenders for construction projects.

Fujinkai women's circles.

Gaiatsu pressure from outside.

Gekokujo 'those below overcoming those above'; used for lower-ranking officials taking charge, for insubordination or mass uprisings.

Gikan technical career officials.

Gundan lit., army corps; used to describe Tanaka Kakuei's group of politicians.

Habatsu political clique.

Honne real intentions or motives, true meaning.

Ie household, House.

Ijime bullying in schools.

Ikki peasant uprisings.

Jiageya land sharks.

Jimukan administrative career officials.

Jinmyaku network of special informal relations.

Juku cramming school.

Kami shinto divinity.

Keibatsu family groupings through marriage.

Keiretsu a group of corporations tied together by interlocking directorates and mutual shareholding.

Kidotai riot police.

Kisha kurabu reporters' club.

Koban police box.

Koenkai support group for a politician, vote-collectors' organisation.

Kogai environmental pollution.

Kokutai 'national essence'.

Kone connections.

Kyoiku mama education mother.

Minzoku people, race.

Mondai problem.

Naimusho the disbanded, once very powerful Home Ministry.

Nihonjinron theory of Japaneseness.

Nokyo agricultural co-operative organisation.

Omiai formal first meeting of the parties to an arranged marriage.

Paipu lit., 'pipe'; the access politicians have to bureaucrats in connection with pork-barrel projects.

Sangyo Hokokukai pre-war and wartime 'patriotic industrial associations' organising workers for the sake of increased production.

Sarakin loan sharks.

Sarariiman salaried worker.

Sempai the senior party, helper, adviser in a hierarchical relationship.

Shafu 'culture' that gives a company its identity.

Shingikai deliberation council.

Shinko shukyo newly formed religion.

Shunto   spring labour offensive.

Sokaiya   stockholders' meeting fixer, extortionist.

Tatemae   pretence, formal explanation, official motives.

Tenko   apostasy.

Wa   harmony, peace.

Yakuza   gangster.

Zaibatsu   pre-war corporate groupings around a holding company.

Zaikai   the world of big business and finance.

Zoku   'tribe', group of politicians specially concerned with a particular policy area.

Index

Abe Shintaro, 144, 149, 150
abortion, 53, 368
Ad Hoc Committee on Administrative
    Reforms, 153
Ad Hoc Council on Educational
    Reforms, 291, 357
'administrative guidance', 344–5
Administrative Management Agency,
    153, 359
administrators see bureaucracy
adoption, 165
adultery, 174
advertising, 176, 177–80, 386–7
Ageo station, 336
agriculture: co-operatives, 30, 41, 50, 60,
    61; inefficiency, 60; nokyo system,
    60–5
Agriculture, Forestry and Fishery Finance
    Corporation, 391
Ainu, 267
Aizawa Seishisai, 260, 303, 364
Akahori Masao, 226
Akao Bin, 197
Akihito, crown prince, 110
Akita, 39
Alcock, Sir Rutherford, 301
All-Japan Anti-Drug Movement, 104
All-Japan Association for Prevention of
    Venereal Diseases, 54
amakudari ('descent from heaven'), 45
    114, 118, 122, 124, 156
Amaya Naohiro, 392
Amida Buddha, 278
Amnesty International, 191
'ampo struggle' (1960), 198
Ando Shoeki, 281
Anglican Church, 283

Anti-Monopoly Law (1947), 125, 205,
    228, 391
Anti-Prostitution Law, 54
Aoki Shuzo, 208
Aoyama Gakuin University, 87
apologists, 12–13, 188–9, 423
Aquinas, St Thomas, 206
Arabs, 243, 342, 416
Araki Sadao, 38–9, 288
Aristotle, 310
Army, 37, 199, 200, 394, 397; control
    of, 39–40; factions, 39; 'Go-Stop
    Incident', 38–9; influence on
    education, 365; Manchukuo, 39, 42;
    Pearl Harbor attack, 39–40; and the
    reform bureaucrats, 351;
    'samuraisation', 262; see also Kwantung
    Army; Self-Defence Forces
Army Academy, 288
arts, 176
Asahi Shimbun, 91, 97, 102, 200, 243,
    267, 344, 412, 426
ASEAN, 418, 429
Ashida Hitoshi, 136, 144
Association of Shinto Shrines, 324
Association of War Bereaved Families,
    322
atomic bombs, 427–8
Australia, 247
Austria, 81, 258
Ayukawa Gisuke, 382–3, 388–9, 394

Baba Yoshitsugu, 222
balance of power, 339–40
Bank of Japan (BOJ), 44–5, 94, 121,
    331, 352, 384, 385, 386, 391
bankruptcy, 47, 112–13, 171

banks, 121, 380, 385, 396, 399–400, 402
Benedict, Ruth, 14, 17, 193, 243
benevolence, 181–3, 191–3, 202, 210, 334, 428
Berlin, 184
Berlin, Isaiah, 373–4
birth control, 368
boeki masatsu (trade friction), 49
Boissonade de Fontarabie, Emile Gustave, 208
bosozoku (motor-cycle gangs), 103
brains, 265
'break fiscal rigidification' movement, 122–3, 154
bribery, 118, 120, 134, 233–4
Britain, 37, 258; bureaucracy, 44; crime, 194; First World War, 356; laws, 208; lawyers, 214
brothels, 54
Buddhism, 10, 18, 51, 240, 241, 242, 277, 299, 314; benevolence in, 192–3; commercialism, 275; and Japanese lack of logic, 236; and Japanese power relations, 274; in Meiji period, 259; peasant uprisings, 278–80; Shotoku Taishi promotes, 203–4; suppression of, 19, 281, 282; under Tokugawa rule, 249, 255, 281
budgets, 115, 122–3
buffers, 11
bullying, in schools, 91–2, 98, 341
burakumin (outcasts), 74–5, 104, 160, 178, 194, 267, 342–3
Burakumin Liberation League (BLL), 74–5, 342
bureaucracy: administrators as victims, 429–30; authoritarianism, 33; bureaucrats in LDP, 141–3; career moves, 114; close links with business, 44–5; connections, 109–11; and the construction industry, 114–20; control of economy, 351–57; control of ministries, 32; during occupation, 348–9, 352–3; fear of disorder, 363–4; in France, 155–6; graduate entrants, 84–5; hierarchies, 330; and industrial federations, 34; institutional memory, 360–2; intimidation, 341, 343–5; and the judiciary, 215, 216; LDP seats in Diet, 114; in the Ministry of Finance,

121–4; in MITI, 124–5; mutual aid, 114; 'new bureaucrats', 350; numbers, 44; and political discussion, 145–6; and pressure groups, 57–8; protection, 112–13; reform bureaucrats, 349–51, 369, 381; relations with industry, 394–5; relations with politicians, 143–5; *ringi* system, 338; rituals, 334; Seichokai, 154–5; *shingikai*, 145; social control, 347–68; Todai graduates, 111–12; wars, 316, 317–19
Buruma, Ian, 289
bushi (warrior class), 205
bushido (way of the warrior), 250, 251

cabinet, 32, 38, 234, 307
Cabinet Planning Board (CPB), 351, 352, 354, 383, 384, 385
Cabinet Research Bureau, 351
Cambodia, 417
cameras, 398
Capital Outflow Prevention Law (1932), 384
capital punishment, 191
capitalist developmental states (CDSs), 6–8
car industry, 394
cartels, 353, 387–8, 392, 397
Catholic church, 51, 283
censorship, 94–8, 178–9, 255, 260
Central Bank for Agriculture and Forestry (Norin Chukin), 62–3
Chamber of Commerce and Industry, 34, 112, 180, 354, 355
Chamberlain, B.H., 169, 258
Charlemagne, Emperor, 206
Chifuren, 52–3
chiiki jumin undo, 372
Chikafusa, Kitabatake, 260
children: discipline, 91–3; examinations, 87–8; *see also* education
China, 28, 35, 386; benevolence, 192; Chinese in Japan, 367; Communist Revolution, 67, 242, 389; Confucianism, 202, 240, 241–2, 255–6; cultural influences on Japan, 18, 19; Cultural Revolution, 242, 243, 342; diplomatic crisis with Japan, 147; households, 51–2, 165, 167; Japanese attitudes towards, 331; Japanese press

China – *contd.*
reporting of, 97, 243, 342; legal
system, 205; and the Manchurian
Incident, 382; opposition groups, 51,
310; philosophical and moral
teachings, 10; present relations with
Japan, 416, 417; Second World War,
427; Sino-Japanese war, 164, 239,
376, 384; T'ang dynasty, 379;
Yasukuni shrine controversy, 322
Chisso Corporation, 336
choice, absence of, 408–10
Choshu, 301, 307
Christianity, 10, 191, 207, 240, 242,
249, 258–9, 264, 276, 280–4, 318
Chu Hsi school, 255
Chukaku-ha, 75
Chun Doo Hwan, 199
Chuo Koron, 359
Chuo University, 84, 85
Church, Frank, 224
church and state, 205–6
Churchill, Sir Winston, 40
Chuseiren (Chusho Kigyo Seiji Remmei),
54, 388–9
Chusingura, 251
chuzaisho (police office), 183, 184
Cicero, 207
cinema, 175–6, 251, 257, 316, 426–7,
428
civil service *see* bureaucracy
class structure, 172
cliques (*habatsu*), 57, 59, 115–16, 134,
139–41, 143–4, 234, 317
co-operatives, agricultural, 30, 41, 50,
60, 61
COCOM law, 113
Committee for Economic Development
see Keizai Doyukai
communism, 7, 10, 30, 66, 67, 68, 72,
75, 79, 103, 239, 274, 283, 284, 350,
389; Japan Communist Party (JCP),
30, 71, 74–5, 94, 199, 283, 284, 325,
343, 389
companies: class structure, 172;
competition, 397, 398–9, 405–6;
consensus, 337–8; extortion, 105–6;
familistic ideology, 163–4, 166–7,
269–70; hierarchies, 329–30;
intimidation, 341, 343–4; lifetime

employment, 164, 170; loyalty to,
161–3, 169–70; market share, 395–8;
ownership, 395–6; police and, 183;
political funding, 133–6; and religion,
277; salarymen, 159–63, 167; *seishin*
training, 253–4; songs, 167–8;
subcontractors, 170–2; *see also* industry
competition, 397, 398–9, 405–6
Conference of the Justices of the
Supreme Court, 216
confessions, 188–90, 222–3
Confucianism, 10, 18, 165, 202, 241–2,
260, 299; attitude to opposition
groups, 310–11; benevolence, 182,
192–3; and education, 76, 292; filial
piety, 51, 169; and Japanese lack of
logic, 236; and Japanese legislation,
174, 203–4; and Japanese power
relations, 274; *see also*
neo-Confucianism
Confucius, 242
conglomerates, 46–7; *see also* companies
connections (*jinmyaku*), 109–11, 120,
121, 122, 125, 127, 129, 225, 332,
337, 377
consensus, 337–9, 409–10, 414–15
constitution: Meiji, 38, 208, 209, 228,
302; post-war, 212, 228, 288, 291,
358; proposed revision, 218, 320, 325;
protection of prisoners, 223; on role of
emperor, 324
construction industry, 114–20
consumer credit, 99–100
consumer movement, 52–3, 174–5
Consumers' Union of Japan, 53
contraception, 53, 368
contradiction, political uses of, 227–9
Control Group (Tosei-ha), 39
corporal punishment, 91–2
corporate groups (*gurupu*), 46–7
corporatism, 80–1
corruption, 31, 132–8, 224, 233–4,
339–40
Counter-Intelligence Corps, 358
courts of law, 213–20, 222–3, 225
Covenant for Civil and Political Rights,
195
creativity, 89–90, 291
credit, consumer, 99–100
crime, 42, 100–8, 187–91, 194, 221

Criminal Prosecution Law, 318
culture, 245–72; political control, 18–20;
   political origins, 17–18; salaryman,
   175–80
currency values, 53, 404

Dai-ichi Kangyo Bank, 46
Daiichi Life Insurance, 355
daimyo, 20, 36, 182, 205
Daishinin *see* Supreme Court
dango system, 118
death penalty, 191
deficit spending, 123
deliberation councils, 145, 152–3, 154,
   338–9, 357
delinquents, 102
democracy, 28–9, 310, 334, 357, 366
Democratic Party, 132
Democratic Socialist Party (DSP), 30,
   70, 71, 73
Denshinkyo, 275
dentists, 135
Dentsu, 176, 177–80, 386–7, 409
Depression, 381
Diet, 26, 29; boycotts, 31; bribery, 134;
   budget hearings, 306, 334; bureaucrats
   in, 114, 358; foreign policy issues, 96;
   legislation, 33, 210–11; Lockheed
   scandal, 229–30, 232–3; networks,
   110; political discussion, 145–6; and
   post-war economic development, 390;
   prohibits political activities in schools,
   77; violence in, 335
digestive systems, 265
discipline, 50, 91–3, 160, 290
distribution *keiretsu*, 393
divorce, 122, 173
Djilas, Milovan, 226
doctors, 54, 135
Dodge, Joseph, 391
Dodge Line, 391
Doi Takako, 73
Domei, 70, 71
Domei Tsushinsha, 178–9, 362
Donne, John, 238
Douglas-Grumman scandal, 224
Drucker, Peter, 2
drugs, 105, 107, 194
drunkenness, 316
dual economy, 171–2

Economic Planning Agency, 123, 148,
   400–1
Economic Reconstruction Round Table,
   133
Economic Stabilisation Board, 351, 352,
   355
economics: budgets, 115, 122–3;
   bureaucratic control, 351–7; 'catching
   up', 377–8; depression, 380–1; dual
   economy, 171–2; during Second World
   War, 383, 384–5; 'financial
   liberalisation', 401–2, 422; 'free-
   market' fiction, 6–8; Maekawa Report,
   412–13; national security, 375–407;
   trade surpluses, 2
Edison, Thomas, 275
Edo, 101, 301
education: aims, 82; attitudes to logic,
   236–7; bullying in schools, 91–2, 98,
   341; creativity, 89–90; discipline, 91–
   3; examinations, 85–9, 90–1; Imperial
   Rescript on Education, 260, 282, 291;
   and individualism, 291; lack of
   intellectual tradition, 237–8, 272;
   learning methods, 378–9; military
   influences, 365; reform proposals, 89–
   90, 291–2; 'returning youngsters', 431–
   2; teachers' opposition to System, 75–
   9; universities, 84–5
Ehime prefecture, 119
Eisenhower, Dwight D., 103
elections, 30, 56–7, 63–5, 117, 146,
   220, 230, 232, 308, 311
electronics industry, 378, 393, 397,
   398–9
elementary schools, 86, 90, 365
Elizabeth II, Queen of England, 199
Emergency Fund Adjustment Law, 384
emperors, 27–8, 38, 192, 203, 259–60,
   301–2, 322–4
Empire Day, 321
employment *see* labour
enterprise unions, 66, 386
Enterprises Rationalisation Promotion
   Law (1952), 390
entertainment, 175–9
entrepreneurs, 45, 47, 396
Equal Employment Opportunity Law, 173
'escalator system', education, 87
Esman, Milton J., 348–9

ethnic minorities, 194, 267–9
etiquette, 160, 331, 332
Etsuzankai, 131
European Economic Community (EEC), 68, 236, 406
examinations, 85–9, 90–1
executions, 191
Export Bank, 122
extortion, 105–6

Fair Trade Commission (FTC), 118, 124–5, 228
familistic ideology, 163–4, 166–7, 262, 269–70
fanaticism, wartime, 287–8
farming *see* agriculture
fascism, 67, 349–50
feudalism, 205, 239
filial piety, 169
Finance Bureau, 352
'financial liberalisation', 22, 401–2, 422
fingerprints, aliens, 367
First World War, 38, 356, 380
Fiscal Investment and Loan Plan, 115
food prices, 53, 60
Ford, 394
Foreign Affairs, 248
Foreign Exchange Control Law (1933), 384
Foreign Exchange and Foreign Trade Control Law (1949), 384
foreign investment, 399–400
foreign policy, 415–25
Foreign Press In Japan, 95
foreigners, mistrust of, 235–6
France, 44, 258, 418; bureaucracy, 155–6; civil code, 208; education, 84; police, 183, 364
Frederick II, King of Prussia, 206
'free-market' fiction, 6–8
Freedom and Popular Rights movement, 182
Fuji, Mount, 233, 279
Fuji Photo Film Company, 378
fujinkai (women's groups), 52
Fujio Masayuki, 291
Fujita Yukoku, 300
Fujiwara family, 27, 28, 36
Fujiyama Aiichiro, 137
Fukuda Takeo, 111, 125, 136, 137, 140–1, 144, 149, 150, 153, 231, 298, 322, 417
Fukudagumi, 119
Fukui prefecture, 198
Fukuyama, 39
Fundamental Law of Education (1947), 291
Furui Yoshimi, 359
Fuyo, 46

gakubatsu (school clique), 217
Gakushuin University, 87, 110
gangsters, 42, 100–8, 163, 175, 225, 316, 341
Gelasius I, Pope, 205
General Agreement on Tariffs and Trade (GATT), 64, 392, 431
General Motors, 394
Germany (pre-war), 67, 208, 349–50, 355, 356, 364, 369, 394; *see also* West Germany
gikan (technical career officials), 116
Ginza, 197
giri (social obligations), 193
giri-ninjo dichotomy, 257
Go-Daigo, Emperor, 27
'Go-Stop Incident' (1933), 38–9
golf, 332–3
Gorbachev, Mikhail, 416, 417
Goshi Kohei, 355
Goto Fumio, 359–60
Goto Noboru, 180, 321
Gotoda Masaharu, 143, 144, 151, 429
government, 5–6
Greater Japan Youth Association, 262
Greece, 238
Griffis, William, 88–9
Grotius, Hugo, 207
Grundig, 398
Gukansho, 259–60
Gumma prefecture, 319
gurupu (corporate groups), 46–7

habatsu (cliques), 57, 59, 115–16, 134, 135, 139–41, 143–4, 234, 317
Hagakure, 251, 252
Hagino Noboru, Dr, 55
Hakuhodo, 179–80
Hara Bumbei, 359
Hara Kei, 369

Hata Tsutomu, 265
Hatano Akira, 112, 316
Hatoyama Ichiro, 136, 357, 417
Hayasaka Shigeo, 129, 137
Hayashi family, 256
Hayek, Friedrich von, 6–7
health insurance, 54, 196
Hearn, Lafcadio, 14, 17
Heian period, 209
Heike family, 27
Hellmann, Donald, 417
Henry IV, King of France, 206
hensachi system, education, 90
heroin, 194
Hibiya Riot (1905), 376
Hideyoshi, Toyotomi, 36, 280, 281, 299
Hiei, Mount, 278
hierarchies, 329–33, 332, 334–5
higaisha ishiki ('victim consciousness'), 426–9
high schools, 85–6, 87, 90, 237, 272
Himiko, 27
Hinduism, 51, 242
Hiranuma Kiichiro, 222, 359, 365, 370
Hirata Atsutane, 253, 266, 287
Hirohito, Emperor, 322–4, 416
Hiroshima, 39, 273, 416, 427–8
Hitachi, 382
Hitachi Shipbuilding and Engineering, 167
Hitler, Adolf, 40, 347, 355, 364
Hitotsubashi University, 111
Hoashi Kei, 355–6
Hojo family, 28
Hokkaido, 218
Holy Roman Empire, 206
homogeneity, 267–9, 314
Honda, 225, 397
Honen, 278
Honganji temple, 279
honne-tatemae dichotomy, 235–6
Hoover Mission, 349
Hoshino Naoki, 352, 382, 388
hospitals, psychiatric, 195–6
Hotel New Japan, 98
households, 51–2, 165–7, 270
housing, 175
Housing Loan Corporation, 391
Hyogo prefecture, 197

IBM, 378
Ichimanda Hisato, 352
Ichiwakai, 107
ideology, 248–9, 254, 269–72
ie (households), 51–2, 165–7, 270
Iemitsu, Tokugawa, 299
Ieyasu, Tokugawa, 36, 280, 281
ijime (bullying), 91–2
Ikeda Hayato, 33, 110, 125, 131, 136, 137, 139, 142, 295, 334, 352, 357, 358, 389, 391, 410
Ikeda Katsu, 217
ikki (peasant uprisings), 279–80
Imperial Agricultural Association (Nogyokai), 61
Imperial Army, 199, 419
Imperial Military Reserve Association, 262, 365
Imperial Navy, 37, 39–40, 200, 427
Imperial Rescript on Education, 260, 282, 291
Imperial Rule Assistance Association (IRAA), 66, 351, 369–70, 371–2, 403
Imperial Way Faction (kodo-ha), 39
Important Industries Control Association, 354, 355
Inayama Yoshihiro, 111, 355, 404
'income doubling plan', 352, 389
incomes, 268, 410–11
India, 18, 28, 51, 202, 240
individualism, 291, 295
Indochina, 418
Indonesia, 28, 51, 136
Industrial Bank of Japan, 353
Industrial Rationalisation Council, 383
Industrial Structure Council, 383
industry: 'catching up' policy, 375–7; close links with bureaucracy, 44–5; company-as-family ideal, 66; control of workers, 65–72; corporate groups, 46–7; Keidanren, 33; liberalisation, 391–2; Manchurian experiment, 381–3; and the occupation, 389–91; pollution, 55–6, 99, 105, 212, 335; post-war economic control, 353–7; post-war planning, 383, 384; protectionism, 390, 391–2, 393–4; relations with bureaucracy, 394–5; subcontractors, 387–9; *zaikai*, 33–4; *see also* companies
informants, 12

Ingyo, Emperor, 299
Inoue Tetsujiro, 282
inscrutability, 13–15
insider trading, 133–4
Institute for Statistical Mathematics, 266
institutional memory, 360–2, 406
insurance, 54, 63, 196
intellectual tradition, 237–41, 271–2
interest groups, 50, 52, 53–8, 145, 246
interest rates, 99–100
International Commission of Jurists, 195
International Federation of Airline Pilot
  Associations, 320
International League of Human Rights,
  195
International Metalworkers' Federation,
  Japan Council, 70
International Monetary Fund (IMF), 431
International Telephone and Telegraph
  Corporation, 98
internationalism (*kokusaika*), 1, 15–16,
  415
intimidation, 340–6
Iran–Iraq war, 417
Ise, 281
Ishida Kazuto, 217
Ishikawa Ichiro, 354
Ishiwara Kanji, Colonel, 381–2
Ishizaka Taizo, 111, 355
Islam, 51, 242
isolation, 430–2
Israel, 343
itai-itai disease, 55
Italy, 67, 292, 369, 381
Ito Hirobumi, 192, 259, 305
Iwamochi Shizuma, 265

Japan Airlines (JAL), 319–20
Japan Communist Party (JCP), 30, 71,
  75, 94, 199, 283, 284, 324, 342, 389
Japan Consumers' Union, 225
Japan Development Bank, 122, 353,
  390, 391
Japan Export-Import Bank, 353, 390,
  391
Japan Federation of Employers'
  Associations (Nikkeiren), 33, 68, 90,
  161, 354, 355, 361
Japan Federation for the Promotion of
  Car Mechanics, 136

Japan Foundation, 265
'Japan Inc.', 44, 48, 394
Japan Keizai Koho Centre, 247
Japan Medical Association (JMA), 53–4,
  368
Japan National Railways, 32, 70, 153,
  179, 372
Japan Productivity Centre, 72, 355
Japan Socialist Party (JSP), 30, 65, 70,
  71, 72–4, 197, 312, 324, 372
Japan Teachers' Union (Nikkyoso), 75–
  9, 82, 91, 93, 198, 284, 290, 291,
  292, 310, 324, 359
Japan Times, 293, 294
Japanese Air Force, 319
Japanese Fund for Mental Health and
  Human Rights, 196
'Japaneseness', 245–72, 273, 277, 287,
  288
Japanism, 273–4, 277, 284, 287, 289,
  290, 306
Jehovah's Witnesses, 283
Jesuits, 84, 280
jiageya ('land-sharks'), 106–7, 233
Jichiso (Ministry of Home Affairs), 59,
  133, 183, 361–2
Jiji Press, 179
Jimmu, Emperor, 321
jimukan (administrative career officials),
  116
jinmyaku (connections), 110–11, 120,
  121, 122, 125, 127, 129, 225, 333,
  338, 377
Jodo Shinshu, 278, 279
Johnson, Chalmers, 6, 124, 353, 381
journalists, 93–100
Judaism, 242
judges, 213–20, 221, 222–3, 224, 246
Judgment (television programme), 178
judiciary, 213–26
juku schools, 86, 87, 88, 100

Kabuki theatre, 170, 257
Kagoshima, 359
Kajima Corporation, 117, 119
Kajima Morinosuke, 117
Kaku-Fuku war, 40
Kakumaru-ha, 75
kakushin jichitai undo, 372
Kamakura period, 205, 214, 278, 279

kami, 203, 204
Kamo Mabuchi, 252–3
Kanemaru Shin, 118, 119, 142, 143, 144
kanryoha (bureaucrats), 142, 143
Kansai, 74, 104, 200
Kant, Immanuel, 207
Kanto earthquake (1923), 94, 380
Karuizawa-kai, 110
Katayama, 144
Kato Kanji, Admiral, 288
Kato Mutsuki, 135
Kawaji Toshiyoshi, 183, 186, 364
Kawakami Haajime, 209–10
keibatsu (networks), 110, 217
Keidanren, 33, 111–12, 133, 162, 247,
354–5, 357
Keio University, 84, 87, 308
keiretsu (corporate groups), 46, 60, 121,
134, 174, 384, 385, 393, 400
Keizai Doyukai (Committee for Economic
Development), 33, 354, 355–6, 397
Keizai Kenkyukai, 352
Kempeitai, 38, 321
Kennedy, John, 310
Kido Koin, 305
kidotai (riot police), 198–200
Kigensetsu (National Foundation Day),
320, 321
kikiku shijo ('returning youngsters'),
431–2
Kim Il Sung, 73
kindergartens, 87
kinken seiji ('money politics'), 132–6
kisha (reporter) clubs, 94–5, 200, 386
Kishi Nobusuke, 102, 131, 136, 139,
142, 149–50, 198, 295, 351, 355, 357,
358, 382, 388–9, 394
Kishi Seiichi, 219
Kiyomizu Monogatari, 280
koban (police box), 184
Kobayashi Junichiro, Colonel, 288
Kobe, 74, 104, 107, 198
Koch, Ed, 343
Kodak, 378
Kodama Yoshio, 102, 103, 136
Koeber, Dr Raphael, 239
koenkai (political support groups), 56–7,
100, 117, 131
Koestler, Arthur, 251
kogai mondai (industrial pollution), 99

Kokugaku movement, 252–3, 256, 266,
285, 286
Kokumin Kyokai (People's Association),
133
kokusaika (internationalisation), 1, 15–
16, 415
kokutai ('national essence'), 260, 261,
263, 269, 287, 302, 303, 311, 321,
334, 365, 369, 396
Kokutai genri-ha, 39
Kokutai no Hongi, 269, 288, 315
Kolakowski, Leszek, 24
Komeito Party, 30, 233, 276
Komoto Toshio, 112–13, 134–5, 148
Konaga Keiichi, 125–6
kone (connections), 109–10
Konkokyo, 275
Kono Ichiro, 116–17, 140, 142, 143, 222
Kono Yohei, 59
Konoe Fumimaro, 351, 369, 370
Korea, 203, 291, 376; Koreans in Japan,
73, 94, 104, 175–6, 194, 267, 367; *see
also* South Korea
Korean War, 67, 115, 387, 391
Kublai Khan, 37, 279
Kuga Katsunan, 282
Kumamoto University, 55
Kumazawa Banzan, 286
Kuroda Makoto, 413
Kwantung Army, 39, 130, 288, 350,
376, 381–2, 384
Kyocera, 342
Kyodo Tsushin news agency, 178, 179,
236
kyoiku mama ('education mother'), 87–8
Kyoto, 74, 101, 104, 275, 278, 299–300,
301
Kyoto University, 45, 84, 111, 112, 217
Kyushu, 281

labour: class structure, 172; control of,
65–72; costs, 405; enterprise unions,
386; familistic ideology, 163–4;
lifetime employment, 68, 164, 170;
police and, 183; strikes, 67–8;
'temporary' workers, 68–9; wartime
enterprise unions, 66
land prices, 233, 400–1, 405
land-sharks, 106–7
language, 265–6

laws and legal system, 33, 202–26, 246, 343
lawyers, 213–20, 222, 224, 246
leadership, 295–313
learning methods, 379–80
leftist groups, 196–9, 324–5, 339–40
Legal Training and Research Institute (LTRI), 214, 215, 216, 217
legitimacy, political, 296–313
leisure activities, 332
Leninism, 194
Liberal Democratic Party (LDP), 25; and the budget, 123; and bureaucrats, 114, 141–3; cliques, 139–41; and the construction industry, 115, 117–18, 119; Dentsu and, 179–80, 387; dislike of Nakasone, 152; and the dual economy, 171–2; and education, 76, 77, 78, 90, 92; elections, 30; foreign policy, 417; formation, 34; funding, 132–6; future, 371–3; *habatsu* cliques, 234, 317; hierarchies, 331; Kaku-Fuku war, 140–1; *kisha* clubs, 94; legislation, 210; links with gangsters, 102, 103; and the Lockheed scandal, 224, 229, 231, 232–3; and the Maekawa Report, 412; Miki Takeo's resignation, 231; and the ministries, 143–4; and the Ministry of Finance, 122; and MITI, 126; networks, 110; and the New Liberal Club, 59; 1986 political order, 311–12; and the *nokyo*, 60, 63–4; one-party system, 29–30; opposition parties, 30–1, 73, 311; and political discussion, 145–6; presidents, 138–9; and pressure groups, 54, 56–7, 59; protection of politicians, 113; public image, 309; relations with unions, 71–2; and the *sarakin*, 100; scandals, 136–8; stabilisation of, 357; Tanaka and, 131–2; Todai graduates in, 111; *zoku*, 154–5, 157–8
Liberal Party, 132
life insurance, 402
lifetime employment, 68, 164, 170
literature, *nihonjinron*, 263–7
living standards, 2–3, 410–11
lobbying, 12–13
Locke, John, 207
Lockheed scandal, 59, 102, 128–9, 132, 136, 137, 170, 224–5, 229–30, 231, 232–3
Lodge, Henry Cabot, 310
logic, 236–7, 333
London School of Economics, 192
Long-Term Credit Bank, 353
Los Angeles, 367
loyalty, to companies, 161–3, 169–70

Mabuchi, 256
MacArthur, General Douglas, 40, 67, 80, 150, 250, 302, 323, 325, 352, 358, 389
McDonnell Douglas, 137
Machimura Kingo, 359
machine-tool industry, 398, 399
Maeda Tamon, 288
Maekawa Haruo, 412, 413
Maekawa Report, 412–13, 418
magazines, 177, 178–9, 180, 232
Mainichi Shimbun, 97, 178, 289
makoto (sincerity), 252
Malaysia, 28, 51
Management and Co-ordination Agency, 151, 153
Manchukuo, 39, 42, 350, 381
Manchukuo Heavy Industries Development Company, 382–3
Manchuria, 7, 39, 288, 350, 351–2, 376, 381–3, 390, 419, 428
Manchurian Incident (1931), 347, 350, 381–2, 387
Mansfield, Mike, 425
Mantetsu (South Manchurian Railway), 382, 387
Mao Tse-tung, 97, 243, 343
Marcos, President, 51
marijuana, 194, 367
market freedom, 6–8
market share, 395–8
marriage, 110, 112, 119
Maruyama Masao, 112, 237, 240, 302
Marxism, 7, 10, 66, 67, 72, 76, 79, 103, 239, 283, 284, 350
mass culture, 175–80
Masuhara Keikichi, 359
Masukomi Kondankai, 387
matchmakers, 110
mathematics, 236
Matsumoto Kenjiro, 354

May Day rallies, 334
medicine, 53–4
Meiji, Emperor, 259, 301–2, 323
Meiji Enlightenment, 259
Meiji period, 61, 153, 182, 239, 250;
  'catching up', 376; and Christianity,
  282; constitution, 38, 208, 209, 228,
  302; corruption, 134; decline of Meiji
  state, 37–8; education, 93;
  entrepreneurs, 163; filial piety, 169;
  foreign policy, 40; *ie* organisation, 166;
  industrial policy, 7, 377, 378;
  influence on present-day nationalism,
  19; intimidation, 341; laws, 209, 214;
  and religion, 258–9, 260, 276; right to
  rule, 301–3, 304; social control, 364
Meiji University, 84
meitoku ('true virtue'), 286
memory, institutional, 360–62, 406
Menda Sakae, 188, 226
mental illness, 195–6
mercury pollution, 55–6, 335
Mesopotamia, 240, 241
meta-amphetamine, 107, 194
middle class, 159–80, 268
Middle East, 243, 264
middle schools, 86, 90, 272, 292
Midway, battle of (1942), 383
Miki Takeo, 137, 141, 153, 224, 231,
  321, 418
military: control of, 39–40; fear of
  resurgence of militarism, 325; financial
  planning, 385; *see also* Army; Self-
  Defence Forces
Mill, John Stuart, 259
Minamata, 55, 336
ministers, 32–3, 143–5
ministries, 58, 143–5, 317–18
Ministry of Agriculture, 42, 43, 53, 58,
  59, 62, 120, 144, 153, 329, 370, 377,
  414
Ministry of Commerce and Industry
  (MCI), 351, 352, 354, 384, 390
Ministry of Construction, 114–20, 124,
  125, 135, 144, 183, 361
Ministry of Education, 112, 288; clashes
  with Nikkyoso, 75–8; control of
  curriculum, 90; Greater Japan Youth
  Association, 262; *Kokutai no Hongi*,
  315; in Meiji period, 182; military

influences, 365; and moral education,
  92, 291, 329; patriotism, 292; and
  religious education, 282; school
  textbooks, 147–8, 178, 260–1; and
  violence in schools, 91
Ministry of Finance (MOF), 37, 115,
  125, 136, 137, 144, 148, 153, 187;
  administrative guidance, 345; budget,
  119, 122–3, 146; bureaucrats, 122,
  319; 'financial liberalisation', 22, 402;
  functions, 120; hierarchies, 330;
  hostility towards MPT, 124; industrial
  controls, 44, 384–6, 387; and the
  Ministry of Agriculture, 59, 62;
  networks, 110; recruits, 84, 111; and
  the *sarakin*, 100, 175; stock-market
  stability, 401; wartime planning, 352
Ministry of Foreign Affairs, 37, 43, 113,
  115, 148, 150, 199; bureaucratic wars,
  316, 317; fingerprinting of aliens, 367;
  foreign policy objectives, 417–18; and
  Japanese homogeneity, 267; and the
  Maekawa Report, 412; networks, 110;
  recruits, 111; relations with USA, 425
Ministry of Health and Welfare, 54, 125,
  196, 342, 361, 368
Ministry of Home Affairs (Jichiso), 59,
  133, 183, 361–2
Ministry of International Trade and
  Industry (MITI), 62, 87, 115, 119,
  120, 122, 351, 359, 389, 395;
  administrative guidance, 44;
  bureaucratic wars, 124, 317; creativity
  problem, 89; and the dual economy,
  171–2; and the 'economic miracle',
  124–5; institutional memory, 361;
  intimidation, 344–5; legislation, 384;
  and market share, 396; networks, 110;
  pollution control, 404; protectionism,
  113, 391–2; relations with politicians,
  146; vice-ministers, 145
Ministry of Justice, 91, 112, 184, 187,
  189, 191, 214, 217, 222, 225, 246,
  268, 318, 357–8, 365, 367
Ministry of Labour, 183, 359, 360,
  361
Ministry of Munitions, 351, 352, 385
Ministry of Post and Telecommunications
  (MPT), 124, 127, 135, 144, 317–18,
  395

Ministry of Transport, 111, 124, 125, 136, 144, 233, 317, 319–20
Ministry of Welfare, 183
minority groups, 194–5, 267–9
Minseito party, 132, 350, 369
Mishima Yukio, 251, 289
misogi (purification), 234
missionaries, 191, 280
Mitsubishi, 46, 132, 377
Mitsui, 46, 132, 382
Mitsukuri Rinsho, 208
Miura Shumon, 173
Miyazaki Farmers' Federation, 65
Miyazaki Masayoshi, 382
Miyazaki prefecture, 64
Miyazawa Kiichi, 123, 125, 128, 143
mondai, 98–9
'money politics', 132–6
Mongols, 37, 279
monsoon culture, 264–5
Montesquieu, 207
Moonies, 276–7
morality, 82, 241–2, 260, 290, 291, 292, 326
Morinaga Milk Industry, 178
Morinaga Teiichiro, 352
Morisaki Minoru, 386
Morita Akio, 247
Morita therapy, 272
Motoori Norinaga, 240–1, 253, 256–7, 266, 287
motor-cycle gangs, 102
motor cycles, 398
Mukden, 39
Murakami Kotaro, 123
Murakami Taisuke, 312
Muromachi period, 209, 300
music, 379
Mussolini, Benito, 40, 67, 349
Mutsuhito (Meiji), Emperor, 259, 301–2, 323

Nadao Hirokichi, 77, 198, 359
Nader, Ralph, 178
Nagako, Empress, 323
Nagano Osami, Admiral, 288
Nagano Shigeo, 111–12, 355
Nagasaki, 255, 273, 427
Nagata Tetsuzan, General, 350–1
Nagoya, 39

Naikan therapy, 272
Naimusho, 37, 65, 76, 77, 153, 323; benevolence, 182; 'catching up', 376–7; and the Construction Ministry, 116; control of villages, 61; disbanded, 183, 184, 198, 358, 360; familistic ideology, 66; fascist influences, 67; 'Go-Stop Incident', 38–9; and the Greater Japan Youth Association, 262; institutional memory, 361–2; labour laws, 373; 'new bureaucrats', 350; opposition to Konoe Fumimaro's plans, 370; and the police, 200, 318, 359; and social control, 364, 365, 366; Yamagata Aritomo and, 306
Naito Yosaburo, 112
Nakae Toju, 286
Nakamura Masanao, 259
Nakasone Yasuhiro, 41, 95, 97, 113, 119, 143, 251; anti-intellectualism, 240; committee on restructuring of economy, 412; and the deliberation councils, 152–3, 154; distrust of opposition parties, 312; donations from industry, 133; and educational reform, 90, 92; foreign policy, 151–2, 417; individualism, 295; investigates Japaneseness, 266–7, 291; and the JAL crash, 320; and Japanese homogeneity, 267, 268–9; leadership, 298; National Foundation Day celebrations, 321; *nihonjinron* theories, 264; 1986 political order, 311–12, 371; NLC joins cabinet, 59; political rituals, 334; press reporting of, 232–3; and pressure groups, 58; re-election as LDP president, 134; relations with USA, 420–1; rightist threats against, 102; selection as prime minister, 129; and Tanaka, 229–30; Tokyo summit, 418; and the Tokyu Agency, 180; trade relations with USA, 414; tries to strengthen office of prime minister, 32, 149–52, 340; Yasukuni shrine controversy, 322
Napoleon, Emperor, 155
Narita Airport, 55, 75, 337
'national essence' (*kokutai*), 260, 261, 263, 269, 287, 302, 303, 311, 321, 335, 365, 369, 396

National Federation of Agricultural Co-
operatives, 41
National Foundation Day (Kigensetsu),
180, 320, 321
national identity, 257–63
National Land Agency, 111, 359, 361
'national learning', 252–3
National Police Agency (NPA), 91, 116,
143, 151, 183, 198, 200, 318, 361,
367
National Public Safety Commission, 198,
200, 219, 359
national security, economics of, 375–407
National Tax Agency, 119
nationalism, 75–6
Navy, 37, 39–40, 200, 427
Nazism, 67, 194, 268, 349–50, 353, 355,
356, 364, 381
nemawashi, 338
neo-Confucianism, 207, 255–7, 285, 363
Netherlands, 18, 37, 81, 255, 281, 409
networks (*keibatsu*), 109–11, 217
'new bureaucrats', 350
New Liberal Club (NLC), 59
New National Structure Movement (New
Order Movement), 351, 369, 370–2,
383, 395
'new religions', 160, 275–7, 367
New York Stock Exchange, 401
New York Times, 413
newspapers, 93–100, 177, 178, 180, 200,
231–4, 325, 335, 417
Ngo Dimh Diem, 310
NHK, 104, 177
Nichibenren, 92, 190, 215, 433
Nichiren Buddhism, 276, 278–9, 280
Nielsen, 178
nihilism, 238, 271
Nihon Keizai Shimbun, 97, 412
Nihon Seimei, 63
Nihon Shoki (*Chronicles of Japan*), 299
Nihon University, 112
nihonjinron, 263–7, 269, 270, 271, 277,
373
Niigata prefecture, 55, 130, 131, 137
Nikkeiren (Japan Federation of
Employers' Associations), 33, 68, 90,
161, 354, 355, 361
Nikko, 281
Nikkyoso (Japan Teachers' Union), 75–

80, 82, 91, 93, 198, 284, 290, 291,
292, 310, 325, 359
1955 political order, 311–12, 370, 371–2
Ninomiya Kinjiro (Sontoku), 292
Nippon Telephone and Telegraph
(NTT), 71, 123–4 129, 153, 179,
199, 394
Nippon Television, 362
Nishi Amane, 259
Nishida Kitaro, 239
Nissan, 382, 383, 394
Nissan Motor Company, 382
Nissho Iwai, 277
Nitobe Inazo, 192
Nittsu scandal, 224
Niwa Kyoshira, 359
Niwano Nikkyo, 276
Nixon, Richard, 128, 378
Nobel prizes, 89, 102, 236, 276
Nobunaga, Oda, 36, 280, 281
Nogi Maresuke, General, 323
Nogyokai (Imperial Agricultural
Association), 61
nokyo system, agriculture, 61–5, 329, 370
nomenklatura class, 300–1
Nomonhan, battle of (1939), 288
Nomura, 134
Norin Chukin (Central Bank for
Agriculture and Forestry), 62–3
North Vietnam, 300
Nosei Suishin Kyogikai, 59
Nozaka Sanzo, 80
Nuremberg Trials, 360

Obayashi-gumi, 168
occupation, 22, 40–1, 67, 80, 210, 228,
291, 348–9, 352–3, 358, 389–91
Odachi Shigeo, 77, 357
Odawara, 299
OECD, 390, 429
Ogimachi, Emperor, 27
Ogyu Sorai, 256
Ohira Masayoshi, 129, 137, 141, 142,
143, 153, 231, 298, 322, 418
oil crisis (1973), 125, 243, 418
Okada Ichiro, 388
Okada Kumien, 275
Okahara Masao, 225
Okayama, 286
Okayama University, 126

Okazaki Eijo, 359
Okinawans, 267
Okita Saburo, 11, 354
Okubo Toshimichi, 306, 376–7
Okuma Shigenobu, 306
Okuno Seisuke, 359
Olympic Games, 367
omiai (arranged marriages), 112
Omotokyo, 275
on (obligation), 193
one-party system, 28–30
Ono Bamboku, 142
OPEC, 418
opinion polls, 179
opposition groups, 30–1, 50–9, 72–81, 310–11
Ordinance on Labour Management in Essential Industries, 164
Osaka, 38, 74, 104, 171, 198, 233, 286
Oshima Nagisa, 175–6
Oshio Heihachiro, 286, 287, 288
Otsubo Yasuo, 359
Otsuka Banjo, 356
outcasts (*burakumin*), 74–5, 104, 160, 178, 194, 267, 341–2

Pacific War *see* Second World War
Pakistan, 429
Paris, police force, 183, 364
Parliamentarians' League for Revision of the Constitution, 228
patriotic industrial associations *sangyo hokokukai*, 66–7, 371–2, 386
patriotism, 292
Peace Preservation Laws, 184, 198, 210, 365, 366
Pearl Harbor, 39–40, 416
peasant uprisings, 279–80, 300, 315
People's Association (Kokumin Kyokai), 133
People's Political Association, 133
Perry, Commodore Matthew, 37, 429
Persia, 240
Petroleum Association of Japan, 125, 395
Philippines, 28, 51, 136, 211, 304
Philips, 398
philosophy, 237, 240
PL Kyodan, 276
Plato, 24, 203, 207
pluralism, 80–1, 369

police, 42, 100, 103, 105, 107, 183–91, 194, 196–8, 221, 318, 330
Police Law (1954), 198
Policy Affairs Research Council (PARC), 154–5, 317–18
'political ethics', 132, 232
Political Fund Control Law, 132
politics: bribery, 134; concept of state, 26; corruption cases, 224; and culture, 17–20; depoliticisation, 373–4; expressive behaviour, 333–4; funding for political parties, 132–6; future developments, 371–3; *habatsu*, 139–41, 143–4; leftist groups, 196–9; legitimacy, 296–313; links with gangsters, 102; ministers, 31–3; networks, 110–11; one-party system, 28–30; opposition groups, 30–1, 50–9, 72–81; pluralism, 80–1, 369; prejudices against politicians, 308–9; press reporting, 94–7; scandals, 136–8; uses of contradiction, 227–9
pollution, 55–6, 99, 105, 212, 335, 404
Polo, Marco, 14
Portsmouth, Treaty of (1905), 376
Portugal, 19, 255, 280–1
press, 41, 93–100, 178–9, 180, 231–4, 325, 335, 417
Press Ordinance (1875), 94
pressure groups, 50, 52, 53–8, 145, 246
Prestowitz, Clyde, 422
primary schools, 292
prime ministers, 32, 94–5, 111, 115–16, 138–9, 146–53
Prime Minister's Office, 179, 257, 292, 298
prisoners-of-war, 243
prisons, 187–8
privatisation, 71, 377
Privy Council, 37, 38, 307
propaganda, 11–13, 247–8, 249–50, 302
prosecutors, 220–5, 319, 339–40, 361
prostitution, 54, 105
protectionism, 7, 60, 61–2, 353, 390, 391–2, 393–4, 406, 424
Prussia, 208, 261, 430
punishment: capital, 191; corporal, 91–2; prisons, 187–8
Purification Group (Seigun-ha), 39

racketeering, 54, 98, 100, 105–6, 175, 196
railways, 70, 71, 153, 186–7, 335–6
Rambouillet summit, 418
RCA, 398
Reagan, Ronald, 148–9, 152, 406, 412–13, 420–2
reality, 8–9; management of, 227–44
rebellions, peasant, 279–80, 300, 315
Reconstruction Finance Bank, 390
'Red Army', 75, 289
'Red Purge' (1949), 67, 76, 349, 360
Reflections on the PR of the LDP, 179–80
reform bureaucrats, 349–51, 369, 381
Reformation, 207
Reischauer, Edwin O., 424
religion, 9–10, 51, 79, 202, 204, 240–1, 259, 260, 273–87; 'new religions', 160, 275–7, 367; *see also* Buddhism; Christianity; Shintoism
Renaissance, 207
Rengo (Zenmin Roren), 71–2, 372
Rennyo, 279
reporter (*kisha*) clubs, 94–5, 200, 386
research, 89
Resources Bureau, 351
'returning youngsters', 431–2
right to rule, 295–313
rightist groups, 78, 102–3, 197, 219, 289, 324
'rights', 211
Rikkyo University, 84
ringi system, 339
riot police, 198–200, 335, 336
riots, 335–6
Rissho Kosei Kai, 276
ritsu-ryo legal system, 204–5
ritual, 326–39
Roesler, Hermann, 208
Roman Empire, 203, 205, 206
Roosevelt, Franklin D., 40
Rousseau, Jean Jacques, 261
rural areas, 60–5
Russia (pre-1917), 37, 258; *see also* Soviet Union
Russo–Japanese War (1904–5), 37, 65, 376, 380, 382

Saigo Kichinosuke, 219
Saint-Simon, Comte de, 373

Saitama prefecture, 336
Sakomizu Hisatsune, 352, 387
Salaryman Party, 175
salarymen, 159–63, 167, 172, 174–5, 253–4, 269–70, 271
Salisbury, John of, 206
Sambetsu Kaigi, 69
samurai, 20, 93, 101, 166, 182, 209, 250–1, 255, 281, 301, 396–7
'samuraisation', 262
Sanbetsu Kaigi, 67
Sangyo Hokokukai (patriotic industrial associations), 66–7, 370–1, 386
Sangyo Mondai Kenkyukai (Study Group on Industrial Problems), 356–7
Sankei Shimbun, 97, 243
Sanken, 356–7
Sanko Steamship Company, 112–13, 134
Sanrizuka, 337
Sansom, George, 28
Sanwa, 46
sarakin (salary-loan companies), 99–100, 106, 175
sarariiman (salaryman), 159–63, 167, 172, 174–5, 253–4, 269–70, 271
Sasakawa Ryoichi, 102
Sato Eisaku, 102, 125, 131, 136, 139, 140, 142, 146, 153, 357, 358
Satsuma, 301, 307
savings, 45, 99, 115, 124, 174, 400
scandals, 136–8, 178; Lockheed scandal, 59, 102, 128–9, 132, 136, 137, 170, 224–5, 229–30, 231, 232–3
SCAP *see* Supreme Commander of the Allied Powers
schools *see* education
Shultz, George, 413
science, 236
Science and Technology Agency, 362
'second budget', 115
Second World War, 22, 39–40, 75, 236, 251, 288, 323, 347, 376, 383, 384–5, 416, 426
secularisation, 290–3
security police, 199, 318
Seichokai (Policy Affairs Research Council), 154–5, 317–18
Seidensticker, Edward, 240, 272
Seihokyo, 218–19, 224–5, 284
seiji rinri (political ethics), 132

Seijo Gakuen University, 87
seishin training, 253–4
Seiyukai party, 132, 350, 369
Sekigahara, battle of (1600), 36
Sekihotai, 102
Self-Defence Agency, 113, 137, 150, 200, 359
Self-Defence Forces, 78, 161, 200, 218, 251, 289, 320, 325, 341
semiconductors, 398, 399, 405
senbetsu (bribes), 120
Setoyama Mitsuyo, 291
shachokai (presidents' council), 46
Shanghai, 386
share ownership, 46
Shiina Etsusaburo, 141, 231, 351–2
shiken jigoku ('examination hell'), 87–8
Shikoku, 74
Shimane prefecture, 119
Shimbara peninsula, 281
Shimimura Osamu, 352
Shin Taisei Undo, 351
shingikai (deliberation councils), 145, 153, 154, 339, 357
Shinjuku, 336
Shinran, 278, 279
Shinto, 9–10, 167, 203, 204, 234, 236, 240–1, 256, 260, 273–5, 321, 324
shinto shukyo ('new religions'), 160, 275–7, 367
Shinyo Nokyo Rengokai, 62
shipping, 112–13
shishi (warriors), 287
Shoda Michiko, 110
shoguns, 27–8, 36–7
Shoriki Matsutaro, 362
Shotoku Taishi, 203–4, 299, 314, 363
Showa Denko scandal, 136
'Showa depression' (1930–5), 381
Showa Kenkyukai, 351
'Showa restoration', 341, 381
Shufuren, 52
shunto ('spring offensive'), 70
shushin (moral training), 260
sincerity (*makoto*), 252
Singapore, 427
Singer, Kurt, 341
Sino-Japanese War, 164, 239, 376, 384
Small and Medium-Sized Industry Foundation Law, 389

Smaller Business Finance Corporation, 391
Smoot-Hawley Tariff Act (USA, 1930), 406
soap operas, 174, 177
social control, 347–74, 386–7
social Darwinism, 376
social order, 328–32, 335–6
socialism, 72–4
Socialist Democratic Party, 283
Society for the Study of Socialism, 283
Socrates, 203, 327
Sodomei, 66, 67, 70
Sohyo, 69–70, 71, 72, 73, 79, 334, 372, 388
Soka Gakkai, 275–6, 279
sokaiya (gangsters), 105–6
songs, company, 167–8
Sonoda Sunao, 43
Sontoku (Ninomiya Kinjiro), 292
Sony Corporation, 247
Sophia University, 84
Sorimachi Hiroshi, 223
South Korea, 4, 6, 7, 136, 150, 199; opposition groups, 51, 310; political rights, 211; relations with Japan, 73, 147, 152
South Manchurian Railway (Mantetsu), 382, 387
South Vietnam, 310
sovereignty, 26, 51, 308, 415
Soviet Union, 20, 113, 288, 300, 350, 369, 381, 416–17, 428
Spain, 258, 280
Special Higher Police (Tokko), 184, 359–60
Special Measures Law for the Promotion of Designated Industries, 391–2
Special Tax Measures Law, 390
Spencer, Herbert, 376
Spinoza, Baruch, 207
spiritual training, 253–4
Stalin, Joseph, 40, 243
state: concept of, 26, 35–7, 42–3; Meiji Restoration, 37–8; the System, 43–9
stimulant drugs, 107, 194
stock market, 133–4, 396, 401
Stoics, 207
strikes, 67–8, 70, 334, 336

student movement, 75, 175, 196, 219, 285, 289, 333, 335, 336
Study Group on Industrial Problems (Sanken), 356–7
subcontractors, 170–2, 387–9
submission, ethic of, 248, 250, 270–1, 290
sugar, 247
suicide, 88
Sumitomo Metals, 46, 345
summary courts, 225
summit meetings, 148, 151–2, 199–200
Supreme Commander of the Allied Powers (SCAP), 347, 348–9, 353, 354, 355, 358, 359, 360, 384, 389, 391
Supreme Court, 188, 196, 198, 215, 216–18, 219, 220, 225, 310, 358, 433
Suzuki Daisetz, 241
Suzuki Shosan, 250–1
Suzuki Zenko, 43, 129, 141, 147–9, 234, 315, 322
Sweden, 81
Swift, Jonathan, 14

tadashii imeeji (correct image), 234
Tagawa Seiichi, 200
Taiho code, 205
Taisei Yokusankai, 351
'Taisho democracy', 366, 369, 376, 380
Taisho period, 303, 341, 366
Taisyo Pharmaceutical, 178
Taiwan, 4, 6, 7, 136, 310
Takahashi Korekiyo, 381
Takanawa-kai, 110
Takemi Taro, 53, 54
Takenaka Komuten, 119
Takenaka Masahisa, 107
Takeshita Noboru, 111, 113, 118, 119, 125, 129, 139, 141, 144, 152
Takeuchi Noakazu, 53
Tamaki Kazuo, 133
Tanaka Giichi, General, 365, 380, 389
Tanaka Kakuei, 123, 143, 147, 154, 179, 295; background and career, 111, 116, 117, 126–32; election to party presidency, 135; *gundan*, 144; Kaku-Fuku war, 140–2; and Kishi Nobusuke, 149; Lockheed scandal, 224–5, 229–30, 231, 232–3, 340; and Nakasone,

150–1; popularity, 152; scandals, 136–8
Tanaka Kotaro, 217
Tanaka Tatsuo, 389
T'ang China, 379
Taoism, 18
Taoka Kazuo, 104, 107
Taoka Mitsuru, 102
Tashiro Fujiro, 233
tatemae–honne dichotomy, 235–6
Tateyama Toshifumi, 72
taxation, 390
teachers: corporal punishment, 91–2; opposition to System, 75–9; *see also* education
telecommunications, 394, 395
telephone tapping, 199
television, 176–8, 251, 257, 335, 386–7
Temporary Interest Rate Adjustment Law, 385–6
Temporary Measures Law Relating to Exports, Imports and Other Matters, 384
'temporary' workers, 68–9
tenko (apostasy), 184, 197, 198, 283
Tenri city, 275
Tenrikyo, 275
terrorism, 75, 199, 287
Thailand, 28, 51
Thatcher, Margaret, 150
theatre, 175, 257
'thought police', 184, 210, 358, 359–60, 386
Todai *see* Tokyo University
Toei studios, 175
Toennies, Ferdinand, 373, 374
Toho film company, 67
tojinha (grass-roots politicians), 142, 143
Tojo Hideki, 321, 351, 386, 427
Tokaido, 101
Tokko (Special Higher Police), 184, 359–60
Tokugawa shogunate, 38, 164, 202; benevolence, 181–2; control of villages, 61; crime, 101, 104; ethic of submission, 169, 249, 250–1; households, 52, 163, 165–6, 270; Kokugaku movement, 252–3; laws, 208, 209, 213; maintenance of power, 36–7; mathematics, 237; Neo-

Confucianism, 255–7; *nomenklatura* class, 300–1; persecution of Christians, 280–1; right to rule, 304; suppression of individual thought, 254–5

Tokyo, 26, 39, 171, 183, 184, 186, 194, 197, 198, 199, 233, 301, 336, 380, 401

Tokyo Bay, 118

Tokyo Chamber of Commerce, 34

Tokyo High Court, 125

Tokyo Imperial University, 239

Tokyo International Airport, 55

Tokyo Marine Fire Insurance, 63

Tokyo Metropolitan Police Department (MPD), 200, 318

Tokyo Stock Exchange, 396, 401

Tokyo summit (1986), 418

Tokyo Trials, 360

Tokyo University (Todai), 45, 77, 79, 84–5, 111–12, 125, 164, 200, 211, 217, 219, 289, 307–8, 349, 409, 432

Tokyo University Hospital, 336

Tokyu Agency, 180, 322

torture, 188, 190, 208

Toshiba, 67, 113, 355

Toshogu Mausoleum, 281

Totsuka Etsuro, 196

Toyoma prefecture, 55

Toyota, 168, 343, 394

tozama ('outside vassals'), 36

trade: 'free-market' fiction, 6–8; liberalisation, 391–2; protectionism, 7, 60, 61–2, 353, 390, 391–2, 393–4, 406, 424; trade surpluses, 2; *see also* economics

Tsukamoto Makoto, 386

Tsunoda Tadanobu, Dr, 265

26 February Incident (1936), 39, 323, 350, 381

Uchimura Kanzo, 282–3

Uemura Kogoro, 112, 133, 354–5, 356, 357, 370, 410

Ueno park, Tokyo, 186

'understanding', 10–11

unemployment, 268

Unification Church, 276–7

unions, 50, 59, 228; and control of workers, 65–72; demise of leftist unionism, 372–3; enterprise unions,

386; 'temporary' workers, 68–9; wartime enterprise unions, 66

United Church of Christ in Japan, 283

United Nations, 102; Convention on the Elimination of All Forms of Discrimination against Women, 173; Human Rights Commission, 268

United States of America, 236; advertising agencies, 177; attitudes towards Japan, 340; bases in Japan, 78; bureaucracy, 44; crime, 194; ethnic minorities, 267; first contacts with Japan, 37; First World War, 356; and Japanese defences, 325; Japanese dependence on, 415–16, 418; Japanese lobbyists in, 12–13; and Japanese unions, 67–8, 69; lawyers, 214; Lockheed scandal, 136; mutual security treaty with Japan, 78, 103, 149, 198; occupation, 22, 40–1, 68, 80, 210, 228, 291, 348–9, 352–3, 358, 389–91; Pearl Harbor attack, 39; relations with Japan, 41, 412–14, 419–25, 429; relations with Nakasone, 151–2; Second World War, 288; summit meetings with Japan,148, 151–2; television, 177, 178; vulnerability to Japanese industry, 406

universities, 78–9, 84–5, 238

uprisings, peasant, 279–80, 300, 315

US Congress, 406, 424, 428, 430

US–Japan Foundation, 102

US National Transport Safety Board, 320

US Senate, 421

US State Department, 425

Ushiba Nobuhiko, 11

Uyehara, George Etsujiro, 261–2

VAN (Value Added Network) war (1984), 317

Vatican, 283

veterans' organisations, 57

'victim consciousness', 426–9

Victor Company of Japan, 168

Video Research Company, 178, 386

videotape-recorders (VTRs), 398

Vietnam, 136, 300, 310, 418

villages, control of, 60–2

violence, 91–3, 335

wa (harmony), 314, 315, 324, 332, 333, 335
wage bargaining, 70–1
Wallis, Alan, 413
Wang Yangming school, 256, 286
War College, 381
warfare: bureaucratic, 316, 317–19; fanaticism, 287–8; war films, 426–7, 428; *see also* Second World War
warrior class, 205, 250, 255, 299–300
Waseda University, 84, 85, 116, 238, 308
Watanabe Michio, 125, 142, 143
Watsuji Tetsuro, 264–5
wedding parties, 332
Wei, 27
West Germany, 2, 44, 155, 194, 214, 292, 360
Willoughby, General Charles, 358–9
women: attitudes towards, 172–4; birth control, 368; discrimination against in employment, 172–3; education, 87; women's groups, 52
Women's Council for Education, 90
workers *see* labour
World Confederation of Organisations of the Teaching Profession, 77

yakuza (gangsters), 100–5, 106, 107–8, 251
Yamaga Soko, 260
Yamagata Aritomo, 182, 209, 221, 306–7, 365, 376, 380
Yamaguchi-gumi, 101, 102, 104–5, 107–8, 175
Yamaha, 397
Yamamoto Shichihei, 266
Yamamura, 414

Yamashita Tokuo, 320
Yamato, 35, 203, 253, 260, 261, 268, 274, 287, 299, 321
Yamazaki Ansai, 256
Yasukuni shrine, 283, 320, 321–2, 325
yobiko (crammer schools), 86
Yokohama, 98
Yomeigaku, 286
Yomiuri Shimbun, 59, 67, 96, 97, 107, 178, 267, 362
Yoneda Masafumi, 117
Yoritomo, Minamoto no, 27
Yoro code, 205, 208
Yoshida Hideo, 386–7
Yoshida Shigeru, 40, 136, 349, 358
Yoshikawa Koretaru, 256
Yoshimitsu, Ashikaga, 18
Yoshino Sakuzo, 239
Young & Rubicam, 177
Yuaikai, 283
Yurakucho station, 336

zaibatsu, 47, 65, 352, 353–4, 380, 381, 385, 389–90, 395–6, 397
zaikai, 34–5, 132–3, 154, 270, 357
zaiteku, 400, 401, 404
Zen Buddhism, 160–1, 229, 241, 250–1, 253
Zenchu, 62, 265
Zendentsu, 71
Zengakuren, 337
Zenith, 398
Zenkoku Nokyo Chuokai (Zenchu), 62, 265
Zenkyo, 76
Zenmin Rokyo, 71, 72
Zenmin Roren (Rengo), 71–2, 372
zoku, 154–5, 157–8, 318

A NOTE ABOUT THE AUTHOR

Karel van Wolferen left the Netherlands at the age of eighteen and has lived in Japan for most of the past twenty-five years. For some fifteen years he has been East Asia correspondent for the Dutch newspaper *NRC Handelsblad,* covering several countries, from India to Korea. In 1987 he received the highest Dutch award for journalism for his coverage of the Philippine revolution. He writes on Japan aided by a vast amount of personal knowledge, gained through teaching and involvement in business activities before he became a full-time journalist. His great interest in political theory has resulted in articles for scholarly magazines such as *Foreign Affairs,* and a study of student revolutionaries of the sixties. *The Enigma of Japanese Power* was written between September 1986 and March 1988 in a cabin in the mountains of northern Ibaragi, about three hours from Tokyo.